INTERTEXTAL BIBLE COMMENTARY

THE BOOK OF HEBREWS

ITS CHALLENGE FROM ZION

George Wesley Buchanan

Wipf & Stock
PUBLISHERS
Eugene, Oregon

Wipf and Stock Publishers
199 W 8th Ave, Suite 3
Eugene, OR 97401

The Book of Hebrews
Its Challenge From Zion
By Buchanan, George Wesley

ISBN: 1-59752-819-6
Publication date 4/12/2006

TO MY DARLING HARLENE

PREFACE

My serious interest in Hebrews began in Israel where I was engaged in geography and archaeology of the land as well as medieval Jewish literature. I was grateful soon after that for the privilege of writing the commentary for the Anchor Bible Series. Originally that series was conceived by William Foxwell Albright. It was designed to introduce scholarship to lay men and women. Every volume was to be written clearly, and each was to be completed within two years and limited to no more than three hundred pages. I fulfilled those demands; my volume was well received; and more than 30,000 copies were sold; but I was not satisfied with the required haste or the limitations. I have therefore spent the last thirty five years, slowly gaining ever more insights into the many dimensions of this important document—its relationship to earlier scripture, archaeology, law, Jewish customs, classical rhetoric, Greek style and vocabulary, and its relationship to the Promised land. With the permission of Doubleday Publishing Company, I have used, reorganized, modified, and updated portions of the earlier volume and expanded it to nearly twice its size. I have also used material from other articles and books that I have written. These have been acknowledged in footnotes. I am grateful to all the publishers from whom I have benefited by using insights from these works again.

I was one of the very first scholars to recognize the use of midrash (commentary)--not only in post testament Jewish literature and the New Testament, but also in the First Testament itself. I published first in 1965 (*RB* 72) and have since read many papers in academic societies, published several scholarly articles and monographs, and also four Bible commentaries. These have been the first intertextual Bible commentaries ever written that prepared the text of the document in one column together with its earlier scriptural source in a parallel column, so that the reader could easily see in bold face text the relationship between the book and its earlier scriptural sources. This commentary on Hebrews is prepared in the same format as the other commentaries and is the first commentary on Hebrews that ever demonstrated its intertextual character. Because I have spent many happy years as a pastor in close relationship to the church, I have intentionally written this text in an effort to answer the kind of questions lay men and women have asked me.

In the preparation of this volume, I have had many excellent opportunities for research. Most important of these have been the three years I spent in intensive language and literature study at Hebrew Union College in Cincinnati with Horowitz and Scheuer fellowships. I have also received other generous grants and fellowships to spend sabbatical years, summers, and additional trips in Israel, Jordan, Lebanon, and Syria. Additional research was spent at the excellent libraries of the Claremont School of Theology, Cornell University, Indiana University and the governmental university at Göttingen, Germany. My experience in the study and practice of modern civil law has also contributed to my understanding of ancient law and its practice. All of these have added to the background that has prepared me to write this volume on Hebrews. I am grateful for all of these opportunities and support. For nearly fifty years Wesley Theological Seminary has had excellent librarians—Prof. Roland Kircher, Rev. Alan Miller, and Dr. William Faupel. For many years Ms.

Howertine L. Farrell Duncan M.A. M.Div. has been the skillful research librarian who has been an invaluable assistant in my research. One of my former students, Rev. Tom Will Gregory M.Div. has taught me almost everything I know about computer hardware and software, enabling me to prepare such books as this.

I cannot imagine being able to hire any assistant with such superior skills in proof reading and assistance in the preparation of indices as my wife, Harlene. She improves my writing style and catches errors I have made in spelling and typing, not only in English, but also in German, Hebrew, and Greek. In addition to this she is a wonderful wife, for whom I am forever grateful. It is to her that I dedicate this book.

TABLE OF CONTENTS

THE BOOK OF HEBREWS

George Wesley Buchanan

INTRODUCTION

Some people call the Book of Hebrews a midrash and others call it a commentary. Lawyers would call it a legal argument, and religious people would call it a sermon, but regardless of the classification into which it is placed, all readers will recognize that the Book of Hebrews is the finest literature in that class. It is the best commentary on Scripture; it is the best legal argument; it is the best midrash, or the best sermon ever read. The only scriptural legal argument that will compare with Hebrews for excellence of style, logic, or familiarity with legal concepts is the Book of Job. This commentary is designed to help readers understand the meaning and quality of this literature and, at the same time, to appreciate the erudition of the author. No one has to be a scholar to understand Hebrews. If technical terms are used they will also be explained.

The Book of Hebrews is a sermon based on Ps 110. Those readers of this commentary who are acquainted with the commentaries of the church fathers, the early rabbinical literature, or modern court arguments recorded in law journals will find a point of contact with the Book of Hebrews before starting. This commentary is called "intertextual," because the author of the Book of Hebrews based his argument on texts taken from the First Testament (FT). Those who are lawyers will need to think of the first five books of the Bible (the Pentateuch) as if they constituted the American Constitution and the other books of the FT as if they were arguments and interpretations of the law that the author of the Book of Hebrews used as precedents for his argument.

The legal concepts used in antiquity are very similar to those used in court today, and they were all used by the author of the Book of Hebrews—laws, lawyers, judges, principals, legal agents, contracts, liturgies, ceremonies, judgments, plaintiffs, defendants, legal fictions, legal implications, use of accepted texts, methods of exegesis, limitation of data admitted, authority of judges, fines, pardons, penalties, witnesses, bails, and various types of legal arguments. Ancient rhetoricians functioned as modern lawyers and professional public speakers. Legal agents were called apostles and prophets in antiquity, but the roles were very similar. Many of the prophets, psalmists, wisdom writers, rabbis, and church fathers were lawyers, legal counsels, or judges.

Trial techniques practiced today in modern courts were taught by Aristotle and Quintillian hundreds of years ago and have been used by ancient and modern rabbis, lawyers, priests, and preachers ever since. Laws are very stable. Some are changed over the centuries, but when that happens it occurs slowly, cautiously, and often deceptively. When laws become useless or irrelevant, they are still retained on the books. They are simply ignored. For example, the biblical law that requires us to kill anyone who works on the Sabbath is no longer enforced (Exod 35:2). Christians and Jews are permitted by law to purchase slaves from neighboring nations (Lev 25:44), but most of us do not do that anymore. Although we are forbidden to plant two kinds of crops in one field, many people today have gardens with numerous kinds of vegetables (Lev 19:19).

Another way of changing the law is to reinterpret it. For a modern example, the second amendment to the U.S.A constitution guarantees the rights of citizens to bear arms as a protection against possible oppression of the state. Some citizens want to annul this amendment, but they know they would be unsuccessful in any direct action to attack the amendment. Instead they suggest that the amendment be interpreted to mean that only state militia be allowed to represent the citizens and the citizens themselves not be allowed to bear arms. This would nullify the purpose of the law, while still retaining it in the constitution. In fiction the amendment would still exist; in fact it would have no effect and become meaningless.

For another example, the Essenes and other rigorous orthodox Jews who married had to practice the rhythm method of defilement control so that they could be as undefiled as possible and still repopulate the race. Therefore, women were forbidden to marry until they had had at least three menstrual periods to prove that they could bear children. They were considered defiled for two weeks after a menstrual period began, during which time no intercourse was permitted.

After their ritual bath of purification (*meék-vah*, מקוה), they were permitted to have intercourse with their husbands at the time when they were most likely to be fertile. With one intercourse (defilement), the wife could become pregnant and have no further intercourse until the child was born. The purpose of this law was to produce as many children as possible with as little ritual defilement as possible. This rhythm method was rigorously practiced, and sexual intercourse was held to be only for the purpose of producing children.

The law is still enforced. The only method of birth control allowed by the Roman Catholic Church is the rhythm method, but the goal has changed. The church still argues that sexual intercourse is only for the purpose of procreating children, but instead of defilement control it allows the rhythm method for birth control. In fiction the law is the same as it has been for 2,000 years, but it fact it has changed by 180 degrees. Today it is employed to have as much defilement as possible and as few births as possible. This is how laws often change.

Financial accountants will recognize in the Book of Hebrews such terms as treasury, loans, debts, bankruptcy, guarantors, interest, principal, day of accounting, redemption, and forgiveness. These have all been applied theologically to Jewish and Christian ethics and systems of justice.

Those readers who are not familiar with any of these legal, accounting, Jewish, or Christian concepts will learn them as they read. Terms will be defined and interpreted as the need arises to understand different aspects of the Book of Hebrews. For the benefit of scholars, the important words are accompanied by their original Greek, Hebrew, or Syriac equivalents. For those who do not use these languages, the equivalents can be ignored unless the readers want to know how the words should be pronounced. For them a phonetic transliteration is given. The author of the Book of Hebrews was very careful in his choice of words, and he used them repeatedly and effectively so that the reader would not forget his main points.

The introduction to this commentary will not begin with the conclusions of the date, authorship, place, and original readers, except to note that the author was male. In the time when this was written, there were few, if any, feminine religious Jewish or Christian authors. This is especially true of the author of Hebrews, as the content makes obvious. Readers are free to doubt this claim and look for arguments against it as they read.

Readers are also free to reach their own conclusions as they read and compare them with the conclusions of the author of this commentary at the end of the book. Readers are not encouraged to dismiss their own notions and intellect to accept the arguments and conclusions of the author. It is assumed that all readers have good minds that should be fully employed while reading. The introduction will include only a few concepts that readers will need to know before beginning to read the commentary. Some of the concepts and literary forms considered in the commentary are defined below:

MIDRASH

General. A midrash is a commentary. The midrashic method of biblical exegesis, employed by the author of Hebrews, was basic to the Samaritan, Jewish, and Christian understanding of the role of Scripture in religious life. It was also used by Greek and Latin lawyers in Roman courts of law. The Scripture was always closely related to the legal and religious community. It was basic to religious ethics and national justice. Once a certain body of literature was accepted as sacred, later Jews and Christians accepted it and prepared their teachings for their contemporaries on the basis of this sacred text, just as lawyers used the Roman law codes on which to base their arguments for court. For example, the Book of Deuteronomy is basically structured around the ten commandments, recorded in Deut 5. Deut 6 begins with an exhortation to keep these commandments as the central guiding force of Israel's ethics. Parents were admonished to teach these laws to their children and talk of them when they were at home, when they were walking by the way, and when they were going to bed at night or getting up in the morning.

The commandments should be prepared in written form and put in places where they could be seen frequently (Deut 6:4-9). At some later time, the rest of Deuteronomy also became sacred Scripture, and an unknown author of Prov 2-7 prepared a midrashic exegesis based on the exhortatory portion of Deuteronomy (Deut 6:4-9//11:18-22), illustrating the ethical implications involved in lying down, rising up, and walking by the way. The homily in Proverbs, then, is a midrash upon a midrash. Ps 8 was expounded positively by another psalmist (Ps 144:3-4), satirized by Job (Job 7:17-18; 14:1, 4; 15:14; 25:4-6), and used as the basis of a later hymn (1QS 11:15-22). All of these later authors quoted words from Ps 8 and midrashically paraphrased its message for their own needs. In a similar way the beautiful priestly benediction (Num 6:24-26) was paraphrased over and over again in later literature (Pss 4:1, 6; 13:1, 3; 29:11; 31:16, 21-23; 41:2, 4, 10-13; 67:1, 6-7; 80:3, 7, 19; 118:26-27; 119:29, 132, 135; Dan 9:17; 1Enoch 61:7-12; 1QSa 2:1-9; 2Macc 1:2-5; 1QH 9:33-34; PisqRK 13:13).[1]

The word "midrash" comes from the Hebrew root *dah-rásh* (דרש), which means to "examine," "question," or "search." A person preparing a midrash was one who searched the Scripture to find its true meaning, which he then expounded, so the word came to mean to "expound" or "interpret." Another related word is *péh-shehr* (פשר), which means to "interpret." Some of the documents found among the Dead Sea scrolls contain running commentaries on some biblical texts. These texts have brief explanations which begin "Its interpretation (*peh-sheh-róh,* פשרו) is . . ." Because of this characteristic, these are called *pesh-ah-reém* (plural of *peh-sher*).

[1] For a more extensive treatment of this subject see Buchanan, "Midrashim Pre-Tannaites," *RB* 72 (1965):229-39.

Authors of Dead Sea scrolls *pesharim* made almost no attempt to clarify the text itself but only to reinterpret it to suit the situation facing the midrashic author's generation. Other midrashim also did this sometimes, but not always. The *pehsher* is a distinctive type of commentary or "midrash."[1] Two major types of midrash are running commentaries and expositions on special texts. Under these two major headings are many other variations.

Running Commentaries. Among the running commentaries composed in NT times were some of the writings of Philo (*Questions and Answers in Genesis* and *Questions and Answers in Exodus*) and the Tannaitic midrashim: Mekilta (on parts of Exodus), Sifrá (on Leviticus), and Sifré (on parts of Numbers and Deuteronomy). These all disclose the work of rabbis who were well versed in the FT. They were basically organized in consecutive order, with the commentary on one verse following that of the verse just preceding in the Scripture. Sometimes the commentary is brief and sometimes it is elaborate, but the appraisal of any one verse can seldom be completely appreciated by checking that verse alone.

These commentators composed their literary works the way a musical composer might, with many themes woven throughout. As one melody fades into the background, another theme is raised into prominence so as to blend, vary, and move from one score to another. Thus the commentators, while expounding on one verse, sometimes examined one word after another. While studying a certain term or phrase in passage B, for instance, the author may have been reminded of another use of the same expression in passage A on which he had already commented, or in passage C, several verses or chapters further on in the text. In either case, he might choose to explain some detail of another verse (A or C) while interpreting B, even though the commentary might have dealt with it rather briefly or omitted it entirely in direct relationship to the passage A or C. He also frequently supported a point by Scripture passages from other books, which he quoted and on which he sometimes commented briefly in the process. Repetition, collections of similar illustrations, and summary statements were standard literary devices for the composition of midrashim.[2]

Homiletic midrashim. Homiletic (preaching) midrashim are sermons or essays which expound important subjects or texts in the FT. Philo composed some of these (*On the Creation of the World, Allegorical Interpretation, On the Cherubim, The Tower of Babel, Moses, and The Ten Commandments*). Others are included in such collections as *Pesikta de Rav Kahana*, *Tanhuma* and *Pesikta Rabbati*. These exegetes used the same basic methodology of interpretation as that employed by the authors of running commentaries. The main difference is that these are principally based on one text throughout each exposition, even though the authors quoted many other biblical passages as well, as illustrations. These homiletic midrashim would all

---

[1] See A. G. Wright, "The Literary Genre Midrash," *CBQ* 28 (1966):116-17, 418-22.

[2] R. Bloch, "Midrash," in *Dictionnaire de la Bible, Supplement V*, ed. Henri Cazelles (Paris: Letourzey et Ané, 1957), cols. 1265-67, pointed out the following characteristics of rabbinic midrash: (1) it has its point of departure in the Scripture; (2) it is of a homiletical character; (3) it is an attentive study of the text; (4) it is adapted to the present; and (5) it includes *aggadah* and *halakah*. Wright, "Literary Genre," pp. 133-38, has defined the characteristics of midrash too sharply to be applied generally. He is correct in saying that a midrash is a literature about a literature, but the precise form this literature takes varies widely.

qualify as sermons, homilies, or legal arguments. The authors even commented briefly on these other texts when they chose, but all other comments and texts were subordinated to the main text. To this classification belongs Prov 2-7, which is a midrashic exposition (sermon) of Deut 11:18-22//6:4-9, and the main body of "The Book of Hebrews," which is based on Ps 110.

Those scholars who prepared midrashim were not just objective, dispassionate interpreters whose only purpose was to present the text fairly. They were primarily dogmatic theologians, rhetoricians, and exhorters who used the Scripture to prove points they wanted to defend. Like attorneys at law, they defended the case they were employed to prove. Midrashic composers were resourceful apologists with amazing skill in manipulating words, phrases, and passages to suit their own needs in ways that were far removed from the original meaning of the text. The reason such a method was necessary was that the official interpreter had to relate an ancient text that was considered sacred to the needs of a worshiping community in a different period of time and under situations that differed from those that prompted the writing of the Scripture on which they depended. Authors of midrashim were not free to ignore the text, but they also had to present their ideas on the basis of contemporary need and normal logic.

The Scripture gave early preachers their authority to speak. Their use of Scripture represents their skill in presenting their own views on the basis of the sacred text. Rabbis and other Roman lawyers had numerous, well established rules for doing this, and some of them were employed by the author of Hebrews. The midrash on Ps 110 is limited to the first 12 chapters of Hebrews. It is well organized; it includes many passages of Scripture and some poetry which was treated midrashically as if it were Scripture; and it is logically sound, once the author's presuppositions are understood and accepted. This logic will be explained in the commentary, passage by passage, but the following terms will be defined at the outset to prepare the reader to understand the midrashic literature that follows.

Narrative Midrashim. Narrative midrashim are formed by working words or phrases into sentences, assuming that the reader will recognize the quotes or allusions and understand the hidden meaning of the message that comes from the quotations. The best way to introduce anyone to this kind of midrashim is to illustrate it. The following is a beautiful poem written by the Spanish Jew, Judah Halevy (1080-1141 IA). He wrote in Hebrew, but his poem was in Arabic meter, and it rhymed in Hebrew. A translation cannot communicate the poetic beauty of this poem, but the italics, documents, and notes will show the frequency of the subtle allusions Halevy made in this poem which only Jews who were well-versed in their Scripture would recognize.

LONGING FOR ZION[1]

Zion, will you not ask for peace[2] of your captives[3]
who demand[4] your peace
and who are the remnant of your flocks?
From **the West, the East, the North, and the South** (Gen 28:14),
Peace!
far and near, greet **from every side** (1Kings 5:4) of you.
Peace for **the captives of desire** (Zech 9:12),
flowing tears **like dew of Hermon** (Ps 133:3),[5]
longing to let them fall upon your mountains.
To weep for your affliction, I am a jackal;
when I dream of the return of your captivity,
I am a harp for your songs.
My heart will throb loudly for **Bethel**[6] and **Peniel**,[7]
for **Mahannaim**,[8] the meeting places of your pure ones.
There the Shekinah[9] dwells for you,
and your Creator opens your gates[10]
before the gates of heaven,
and the glory[11] of the Lord alone

---

[1] The Hebrew text is taken from Ch. Shirman, *The Hebrew Hymn in Spain and in Provence* (Jerusalem: Bialik, c1960) II, pp. 485-89. The translation is from Buchanan, *Jewish Messianic Movements from AD 70 to AD 1300* (Eugene, Oregon: Wipf and Stock Publishers, 2003), pp. 254-57.

[2] Greet them, "Shalom!" This greeting includes a prayer, "May all your indebtedness to the treasury of merits be cancelled." See Buchanan, T*he Consequences of the Covenant* (Leiden: E.J. Brill, 1970), pp. 234-37.

[3] "Captives" are all Jews in the diaspora who are not free to return to the Promised Land, free from foreign rule, regardless of personal liberty, wealth, social status, or political prestige and influence. See Buchanan, *To the Hebrews* (Garden City: Doubleday, 1972), pp. 69-70.

[4] Not just a greeting, but an insistence that God pardon Zion.

[5] Hermon is the tallest mountain in the Golan Heights, northeast of the Sea of Galilee.

[6] The place where Jacob saw a vision of angels going up and down on a ladder to heaven, reminding him that the place where he was lying, namely the Promised Land, was holy ground. This was during his flight from Esau (Gen 28:12-19).

[7] On his return to confront Esau before entering the Promised Land, Jacob wrestled all night at the Jabbok river and received the name "Israel" (Gen 28:12-19). It was this wrestling match that reminded him of the laws of the Day of Atonement, forced him to repent, and give Esau back his blessing and his birthright in Hebron, while he went north to Shechem and bought land to begin a new family corporation there.

[8] The place where the army of angels met Jacob after his successful separation from the forces of Laban in his return from "captivity" to the Promised Land (Gen 32:1-3, 31). All three locations are centered around Jacob, Esau, the Promised Land, the inheritance, and angelic guidance.

[9] The visible representation of God's real presence on earth. It was seen in the column of smoke that joined earth to heaven and provided a channel through which God could descend to earth. It burned continually in the temple.

[10] Probably the eastern gate into the City of David that provided the entrance to the temple area from the Mount of Olives, the place where the Messiah was expected to appear; or Halevy may have thought of the column of smoke as a gate to heaven, like Jacob's ladder.

[11] The "pillar" of fire by night from the fire on the altar provided lots of light for the surrounding area. It was probably enough to light up the entire 10-12 acre City of David. Without electricity, this light

will be your light (Isa 60:19-20).
There will be no **sun**, moon, and stars [as] your lights (Isa 60:19).
I will choose for my soul to be poured out in the place
where the spirit of God is poured out
over your chosen ones.[1]
You are a royal house;
you are **the throne of the Lord** (1Chron 29:23).
How can slaves[2] sit on the thrones
of your mighty ones?
Who will permit me (Ps 55:8) to wander in the places
where **God was revealed** (Gen 35:7)
to your seers and your messengers?
Who will make me wings so I may wander far off?
I would cast the broken pieces of my heart
among your broken pieces!
I will fall on my face on your land;
I will be greatly pleased with her stones;
I will love your **dust** (Ps 102:15).
Also when I stand at **the graves of my fathers** (Neh 2:3, 5)
I will be amazed at Hebron
over your **renowned grave** (Gen 23:6, 19).[3]
I would go through your forest and your vineyard.
I would stand on your Gilead and be astonished
at your Mount Abarim,
Mount Abarim (Deut 32:49, 50), **Mount Hor** (Deut 32:50),
where there are two **great lights** (Ps 136:6-7),
your luminaries and your teachers.[4]
The life of souls, the air of your land,
and from **the myrrh of freedom** (Exod 30:23),
the grains of your dust (Song S 3:6),
the dripping of honeycomb (Ps 19:11),
your rivers!
It would please my soul **to walk naked and barefoot** (Isa 20:2-3)
over the desolate ruins
where your holiest dwellings were:[5]
in the place of the chest, which was hidden
(Jer 3:16; Yoma 50b; 52b-53b; 70b),
in the place of your cherubim,
who dwelled in your innermost rooms![6]

---

far overpowered the small lamps and torches used elsewhere in Jerusalem. This was known as the glory of God.

[1] The chosen people. The sentence seems to paraphrase Ps 84:10.

[2] Gentiles, destined to be slaves for Jews (Isa 61:5-10), according to Jewish understanding.

[3] The cave of Machpelah, where Sarah was buried.

[4] The "great lights" are the sun and the moon, but here used metaphorically, perhaps, to refer to Moses and Aaron. Aaron was buried on Mount Hor in the Wilderness of Zin (Deut 32:50-51).

[5] Where Jews were forbidden to walk for fear of stepping on the land covering the temple, ark, and other vessels. This is considered sacrilege.

[6] The holy and the holy of holies, where only priests were allowed.

I would cut off and throw away my hair,[1]
and I would curse the time your saints were defiled
in an unclean land.
How can it please me to eat and drink,
when I see **dogs**[2] **dragging** your **young lions**[3] (Jer 15:3; Ezek 38:13)?
Or how can **the light** of day be **sweet to my eyes**
(Eccles 11:7) while still I see in the ravens' beaks[4]
the corpses of your heroes.
--The cup of sorrow,
hold it! Let up a little, for already
my loins are filled (Ps 38:8), and my soul,
from your **bitterness** (Job 9:18).
When I remember **Oholoah**[5] (Ezek 23:4),
I drink your wrath;
then I remember **Oholibah**[6] (Ezek 23:4),
I will find your **old wine** (Ps 75:8).
Zion, perfectly beautiful! **You bind** love and grace
[around your neck] (Prov 6:21) from of old.
With you are bound the souls of your **haberim.**[7]
They rejoice at your tranquility, suffer
at your desolation, and weep over your wounds;
those who, from the pit of captivity, long for you and
pray **each in his place** (Zeph 2:11)
toward your gates.
The flocks of your multitude, who went into exile and
were scattered **from mountain to hill** (Jer 50:6),
and they have not forgotten your fold (Jer 50:5).
Those who hold fast to your skirts
and strengthen themselves
go up and take hold of the branches of your **palm trees** (Song S. 7:9).
Will Shinar and Parthia[8] compare with you in greatness?
Can they compare their vain practices
to your **Thummim and Urim** (Neh 7:65)?
To whom will they compare your messiahs
and to whom, your prophets?
and to whom, your Levites and your princes?
He will change **and sweep away the splendor**
of all idol-worshipping kingdoms (Isa 2:18).

---

[1] His "Nazarite's crown" (Num 6:5-8).
[2] Gentiles.
[3] Princes.
[4] Gentiles thought of as scavengers.
[5] Samaria, which Halevy despised, since it represented the anti-Judaic capital of North Israel.
[6] Jerusalem, which Halevy loved.
[7] *Haberim* were the Jews who tried to keep priestly purity in the diaspora when the temple was not standing, so that there would be a place for the Lord to dwell. They treated their hearths as altars and their homes as the temple in matters of purity.
[8] Shinar symbolized the cultural achievements of Baghdad, the Moslem center, and Parthia symbolized the achievements of Byzantine Christianity.

Your **strength is for the age,**
for generation after generation, your **crown** (Prov 27:24).
Your God **has longed for** you **as a habitation** (Ps 132:13).
Blessed is the man whom he **chooses.**
He will be brought near
and will dwell in **your courts** (Ps 65:5).
Blessed is he who waits, arrives (Dan 12:12),
and sees the rising of your light.
Your dawns will break upon him **to see the prosperity**
of your chosen ones and to exult with joy
(Ps 106:5) in your return
to your past youth.[1]
My heart is in the East, but I am at the end of the West.
How can I taste that which I eat,
and how can it please me?
How can I pay my vows and obligations while still
Zion is in the snare of Edom, and I am [tied] with
an Arabian fetter?
I would gladly abandon all the benefits of Spain,
just as I value highly the privilege of seeing
the dust of the destroyed sanctuary.
Beautiful view! (Ps 48:3) joy of the world!
city of the great king!
My soul longs for (Ps 84:3) you
from the corners of the West.
My deep **affection is kindled** (Gen 43:30)
when I remember times past
your glory which went into exile,
and your dwelling which was destroyed.
Who will permit me on the wings of eagles [to fly]
(Ps 55:7) until **I irrigate with my tears** (Isa 16:9)
your dust and let them mingle?
I have demanded you,
and even if your king is not in you,
and also a scorpion.
I will desire your stones and kiss them.
The taste of your clods will please me more than honey.

Readers who are not sufficiently familiar with Scripture to capture all of the allusions in Judah Halevy's narrative midrash may recognize the allusions in a major song in "The Music Man." One of the key characters was a salesman who was looking for a certain type of woman in the town. He sang,

For no **Diana** will I fall prey.
I hope. I pray
that **Hester** will get just one more **A**.
A sadder but wiser girl is the girl for me.
A sadder but wiser girl for me.

---

[1] Before Jerusalem and the temple had been destroyed.

To get the point of this narrative midrash, the listener has to recognize **Diana** as the goddess of chastity and **Hester** as the main character in Hawthorne's "The Scarlet Letter," who wore the letter **A** on all of her garments to show everyone that she was an adulteress. The A she obtained was not a grade in academic achievement. The salesman did not want a committed virgin but a woman experienced in adultery.

Summary

All three kinds of midrashim occur in the Book of Hebrews. Heb 1-12 constitutes one entire sermon or **homiletic midrash**. Inside this sermon are several small units developed around 1, 2, 3, or more texts. In some of these the words of the FT are woven into the narrative almost inconspicuously. These **are narrative midrashim**. Others begin with a text and then interpret it step by step. They will be made obvious by **bold face type** and comments. Once readers learn to enjoy and recognize the literary skill required to write poetry such as Judah Halevy's and the song in "The Music Man," they will be prepared to understand and appreciate the excellent literary style and vast biblical knowledge exhibited by the author of Hebrews.

Prophecy and the Messiah

R. Yohanan said, "Every prophet prophesied only for the days of the Messiah" (bBer 34b). The author of the Habakkuk Commentary said the prophecy of Habakkuk was for the end of days (1QHab 2:5-6). God had told Habakkuk to write down the things that would happen to the last generation (1QHab 7:1-2). This opinion was widely accepted and rabbis frequently took statements made about FT personages, changed them into future expectations, and applied them to the Messiah. The author of Hebrews did the same. In the first two chapters alone, the author of Hebrews understood Jesus, the Messiah, to be the subject of statements originally made about some unknown Jewish or Israelite king being enthroned, the children of Israel, Solomon, a warrior king, God, and a human being.

Introductions to Scripture.

The author of Hebrews never referred to the FT as something written. Even when he referred to a quotation "in David" (i.e., in the Psalter), he said, **Just as it is prophesied**, rather than saying, "David wrote" or "David said." He understood that all Scripture, even that which he believed had been written by David or Moses, was the word of God, spoken by either God or the Holy Spirit (Heb 3:7). By using the passive voice, he avoided the use of the divine name. The usual introduction is **just as the Holy Spirit says** (Heb 3:7); **just as he said** (Heb 4:3); **just as it also says** (Heb 5:6); **it says** (Heb 1:7, 8); **he says** (Heb 10:5); **he said** (Heb 1:5; 4:3, 4; 8:14); or **saying** (Heb 2:12). In these cases the subject was understood to have been God or the Holy Spirit, although the author never used the expression "God said." Like other Jews and Christians who avoided the use of the divine name, he used such terms as **the one who says to him**, (Heb 7:21), **the one who said** (Heb 5:5; 10:30), or he used passive verbs (Heb 3:15; 7:13; 11:18).

Sometimes introductions conclude with the repetitious word **saying** (Heb 2:6, 12; 6:13; 12:26). These reflect introductions similar to those found numerous times in rabbinic literature. “As it is said” or “just as it is said” (*sheh-neh-eh-már,* שנאמר) occurs frequently. The repetitious “saying” is like the Mishnaic *lay-móhr* (לאמור), as in Yoma 6:2, “As it is written in the law of your servant Moses, saying (*lay-móhr*) . . .”

Florilegia

One of the practices of Jews and Christians of NT times was to gather proof texts on various subjects. These are called *florilegia.* One of the Dead Sea scrolls is called 4QFlorilegium because it contains the following FT passages regarding the Messiah: 2Sam 7:11-14; Exod 15:17-18; Amos 9:11; Ps 1:1; Isa 8:11; Ezek 37:23(?); Ps 2:1; Dan 11:32; 12:10. In the midrash on Psalm 2:9 there is a similar florilegium. Rom 9:15-22 contains a collection of passages from a florilegium on sonship, to which have been added some passages on angels. These are joined by typical midrashic introductions: **has he ever said? . . . and again . . . he said . . . it says . . . to the Son . . . and . . . and . . . has he ever said?** In other places the author of Hebrews listed two or more FT passages together, but they do not seem to represent florilegia of passages on one important topic (see intertexts for Heb 2:12-13; 5:5-6).

Parables

A parable is one kind of analogy. When trying to explain something difficult, usually religious or ethical, Jews and Christians found practical situations that could easily be understood, and they compared the unknown with these for clarification. Rabbis frequently introduced such parables by the formula, “To what can the matter be compared” (*luh-máh hah-dah-váhr dóh-meh,* למה הדבר דומה)? (*Mekilta Pisha* 16:68 and frequently--*et passim*). This is similar to the formula used by Jesus, **To what shall I compare this generation** (*tee-nee duh haw-moi-óh-soh tane geh-neh-áhn tów-tane,* τίνι δὲ ὁμοιώσω τὴν γενεὰν ταύτην)? (Matt 11:16). The author of Hebrews used few analogies; only one of these was a parable, and it lacks the normal introduction. The analogy compares believers to land that receives rain from heaven. If the land produces only thorns and thistles as a result, it is burned off. In the same way, parties to the contract who accept the advantages of the contract and then become apostate can expect severe treatment from God (Heb 6:7-8).

A fortiori

An *a fortiori* argument is a type of analogic reasoning to make a case “for the stronger” reason. It is sometimes called *a minore ad maius,* “from the lesser to the greater.” In Hebrew it is called *kahl wuh-khóh-mehr* (קל וחומר), “light and heavy.” This is an argument which describes a situation related to something small, light, or unimportant (A), and then reasons that the same would be all the more applicable to something great, heavy, or important (B). One FT example was the response of Jacob's sons when Joseph's servants accused them of stealing Joseph’s silver cup.

A. **Look! the money which we found in the mouth of our sacks, we brought back to you from the land of Canaan,**

B. **how then should we steal silver or gold from your masters house**? (Gen 44:8).

Since they were honest in a situation where it was not expected, they should be understood to be all the more honest when dealing in a situation where honesty was required.

In commenting on the manna provided for the rebellious exodus generation, rabbis said:

A. If God thus provided for those who irritated him,
B. how much more (*ahl eh-kháht kuh-máh wuh kuh-máh*, על עחת כמה וכמה)
will he pay a good reward in the future to the righteous? (Mek *Wayassa* 4:43-45).

In a very similar way, Jesus assured his disciples of God's providence:

A. **Consider the lilies of the field, how they grow. They neither toil nor spin, but I tell you not even Solomon in all his glory was clothed like one of these. If the grass of the field which is today and tomorrow is cast into the oven, God thus clothes,**

B. **will he not much more** (*paw-lóh máh-lawn,* πολλῷ μᾶλλον) **clothe you, [O people of] little faith** (Matt 6:28-30; see also 7:9-11; 12:11-12; for examples in Rom, see 5:8-9, 10, 17, 18, 21; 11:12, 15, 24).

There are several *a fortiori* arguments in Hebrews (Heb 2:2-4; 9:13-14; 10:28-29; 12:9; 12:25). The first example is as follows:

A. **For if the word which was spoken through angels became steadfast, and every transgression and disobedience received just recompense;**

B. **how shall we escape, having neglected so great a salvation [as this], which had its beginning when it was spoken through the Lord, was confirmed to us by those who heard, while God supported the testimony with signs, wonders, and various kinds of miracles, and by the distribution of the Holy Spirit according to his will?**

Typology

A typology is a belief that objects, events, persons, and institutions exist and occur in relationship to other corresponding objects, events, persons, and institutions. For earthly things, when considered antitypes, there are prior and corresponding heavenly prototypes or archetypes which were the patterns by which the earthly things were created. For instance, according to Hebrews, there was a heavenly temple not made with hands which was a prototype for the temple made at Jerusalem, which was its inferior antitype. When the typology dealt with earthly things, the pattern was usually referred to as a "type," rather than a "prototype," and its corresponding antitype was also earthly and historical. Typological exegesis was not allegorical. The antitype was not designed to give a hidden meaning to the type or to change the meaning originally intended by it. Rather it anticipated a later event, person, object, or institution which corresponded in some imitative fashion to its earlier type. For instance, the exodus from Egypt was a type of deliverance of which the deliverance from Babylon and the future anticipated deliverance were understood as antitypes.

Frequently the type was expected to be followed by a superior anti-type. Moses was an inferior type to be succeeded by his antitype, the Son (see *Mos* 1:27-158); the levitical priesthood was a type to be succeeded by a superior high priest of the order of Melchizedek; the old contract and Mount Sinai were types for the superior contract and revelation at Mount Zion. Platonic philosophy includes a typology in which all earthly things are but shadows of the heavenly pattern or original. The typology in Hebrews, however, is different. There are heavenly prototypes, to be sure, but they are understood in terms of historical sequence and faith that is foreign to Platonism. Most types were historical and earthly, and they anticipated antitypes that were also historical and earthly.

Anyone who spends hours and years reading exegesis composed by church fathers, rabbis, or other doctrinally oriented exegetes will not be surprised to find some fantastic or trivial points in the arguments. These pious authors were not scientists or analysts but legal dogmatists, writing for other apologists of the same convictions. Rabbis were lawyers and judges, and their methodology is similar to that found in current legal journals. Some of their logic was amazingly creative, even if it would not seem logical to Western minds. Their arguments were accepted, because no one wanted to disagree. They were based on the legal system other legalists accepted as valid. All of these exegetes used typology as one method of interpretation. It was consistent with their belief that time moved in cycles, so that events, institutions, and characters at identical points in earlier and later cycles could be compared typologically, because, to some extent, they were identical, in their judgment. This will be evident after an examination of cyclical time in antiquity.

Time and Cycles

Josephus. After Josephus had described the destruction of Jerusalem in 70 IA, he marveled at the exactness of the cycle of destiny which predestined the temple to burn at the hands of the Romans on the very month and day on which it was burned by the Babylonians, years before the second fall (War 6:268-69). Josephus's easy allusion to cycles was no isolated example, completely removed from normal Hebrew and Jewish thought.

Not only Jews and Christians, but other peoples, like Greeks, Egyptians, Mayas, and Aztecs thought time moved in cycles.[1] It was normal for agricultural peoples to think this way. One day came to an end only to have another begin. The same was true of weeks, years, Sabbath years (seventh years), and Jubilee years (fiftieth years). Seasons moved in a predestined order: like night and day, there was winter and summer every year. Annual feasts were associated with exactly the same seasons every year. People's lives were governed by the reliability of these cycles, so the philosophical members of such societies as these deduced further that in some way longer periods of time, such as ages, also succeeded each other the way day followed night, and they tried to associate these ages so as to be able to predict the events of the one on the basis of its predecessor. Evidence of this way of thinking is not hard to find, and it appears in Hebrews.

---

[1] See further Buchanan, *Jesus: the King and his Kingdom* (Macon: Mercer U. Press, 1984), p. 253, fn.1.

Scripture and Scrolls. In the FT itself, the Koheleth held that the events in time circled like the wind, so that the events that happened currently had already happened before and would happen again (Eccles 1:6, 9). "The Psalm of the Seasons" in the Community Rule took both cycles and seasons for granted and considered them all occasions for praise to God. Just as part of each day was ruled by the day and another part by the night, so the children of light (Jews) ruled part of the time and children of darkness (Gentiles) ruled the rest of the time. These rules were predestined to alternate just as regularly as day and night. (1QS 10:1-9). The Sibyl narrated history in terms of cycles of times, cycles of seasons, and cycles of years (SO 3:289, 627)

Predestined Cycles. One ancient Jewish author reasoned,

> God created all the gentiles which are on the circle of the earth as well as us. He foresaw them and us from the beginning of creation of the circle of the earth until the departure of the age, and nothing has been neglected by him even to minute details, but everything he foresaw, and he moved everything forward as a whole (Assump Mos 12:4).

The same Jewish prophet seemed to think that God predestined Jews and gentiles to relate to each other across the ages of time. 2Bar spelled this out more clearly. He said the time between Adam and the Messiah was divided into 12 periods of alternative good and bad fortune for Israel. These periods were probably considered 24 ages or 12 complete cycles of time (2Bar 53:12; 56:1-69; 4Ezra 14:11-12). On the basis of such predestined cycles of time the NT seer said the four messengers to be released from the Euphrates had been prepared there **for the hour and day and month and year** (Rev 9:15).

A new cycle. Anyone as convinced as these people were that time repeated itself was predisposed to look for signs of objects, people, or events that happened in their own time that matched earlier people, events, or objects and were therefore antitypes of earlier types. One of the more careful biblical typologists was Second Isaiah who recognized some signs in recent history that matched earlier events. 2Isai reasoned that one cycle was over, and a new cycle had begun. The previous cycle had begun with the captivity in Egypt, history continued for the Hebrews with their crossing the sea, going into the wilderness, and there receiving provisions through miracles--water, meat, victory in war, and healing of diseases. Next came the conquest of the Promised Land, establishment of a kingdom, and construction of a temple at Jerusalem. 2Isa's prophecy began in Babylon. He noticed that the captivity in Egypt lasted about 400 years, and the period of Davidic cycle also lasted for about 400 years before the Day of Judgment occurred, Jerusalem was destroyed, and the Babylonian captivity began. From captivity to captivity--the cycle was complete. Jews were starting a new cycle that would require 400 years in captivity again, and that would be followed by a 400 year kingdom period. It would take 40 years for the wilderness experience again, and another 40 years for conquest. The calculated cycle would look like this:

Kingdom	Egypt	wilderness	conquest
50	40	5	5

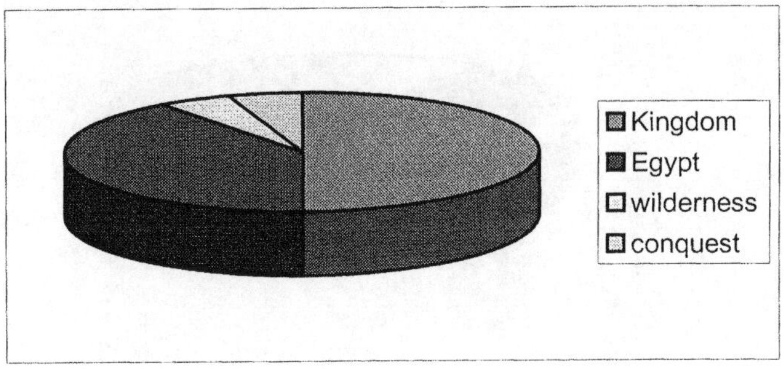

A revised cycle. The good news was that the Jews were able to negotiate a new agreement with Cyrus of Persia. Cyrus had already added Media to his territory, without a war, and he was eager to add Babylon as well. Jews were then in Babylon where they could act as his local spies, helping him to annex Babylon during a feast with a minimum of military action. Jews would assist in this project on the condition that Cyrus would allow them to return to Jerusalem. That would reduce the captivity cycle from 400 years to about 50, and the following kingdom would then be at least 375 years longer, and the wilderness and conquest periods would also be reduced. Second Isaiah then anticipated a cycle that looked like this.

kingdom	Babylon	wilderness	conquest
92.04	5.68	2.27	0

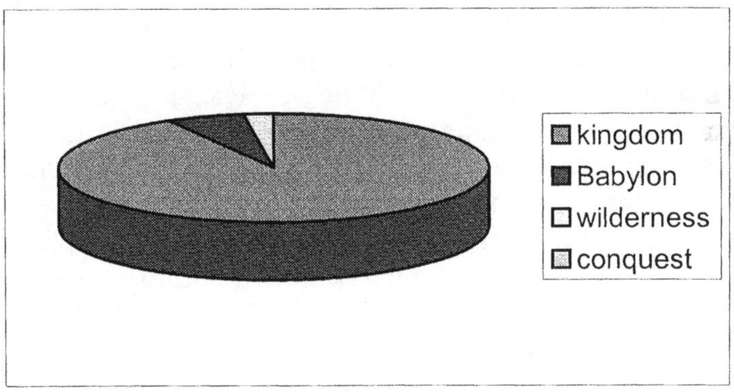

Babylonian Cycle. If Second Isaiah had drawn for himself any such sketches, they have not survived, but that is no disaster. If we could have only one, it is much better for us to have Second Isaiah's poetry than his sketches. We might be able to deduce graphs from poetry, but we could hardly compose Second Isaiah's poetry from graphs. *If,* however, he had diagrammed such a graph as the one above to visualize past history, he might easily have reconstructed another, on that basis, which would project the future graphic cycle--from captivity to captivity.

kingdom	Babylon	wilderness	conquest
75	15	7	3

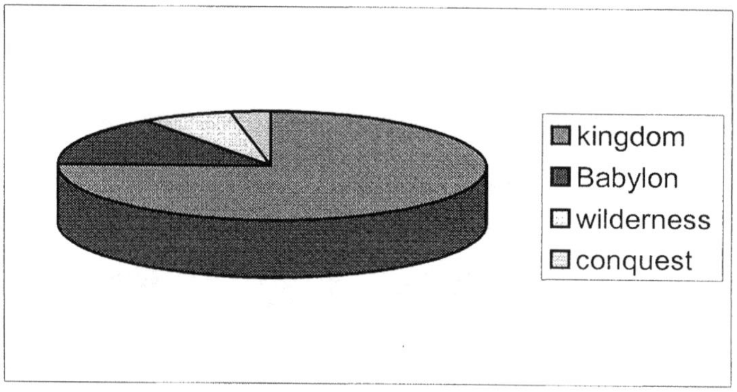

The final judgment. Some of the content of 2Isa's poetry that enables us to deduce his cyclical typology is the following: Just as the Lord's servant, Moses, enabled Hebrews to escape from Egypt, the Lord would again provide a servant to escape from Babylon (Deut 18:18). At that time the wilderness would blossom like a rose (Isa 35:11); the blind would see; the deaf would hear; and the lame would walk (Isa 35:6). This could be expected because Moses had healed Miriam in the wilderness before. As Moses provided water, so there would again be water in the desert (Isa 35:7; 41:17-18; 43:19-20; 44:32-4), and guidance for all those who returned through the wilderness (Isa 35:3-10; 40:10-11; 42:16-20; 50:3). Since they had gone through the sea before, they would go through the waters again (Isa 43:2; 51:11).

Ignored Obstacles. If the prophet had been objective, he would have assumed Jews in Babylon were destined for a 400 year sentence, but he knew that Jews had negotiated with Cyrus to capture Babylon and release Jews to return to Palestine. With this in the offing, he thought everything had been accelerated. Instead of 400 years the captivity would be only about 50. The 40 years' wilderness wandering would be paralleled by a wilderness crossing that would take only a few years to build a new Garden State Parkway from Babylon to Jerusalem. Since there was the political and military backing of Cyrus, he saw no lengthy conquest. Jews would have authority to return in broad daylight, and Cyrus had promised to finance the venture. This was all miraculous, but orderly. It conformed to the first cycle; it was the antitype of the preceding age.

Hasmonean Cycle. When Persia conquered Babylon, and Jewish life was restored in Palestine, it was not nearly as glorious as 2Isa had visualized. Most Jews were not contented, but much later, after the temple had been defiled and cleansed, and Jews were beginning to regain the Promised Land, another cyclical typologist reinterpreted past history so as to make it conform to the previous cycle. By then about 422 years had passed since the beginning of the captivity, rather than 50. This corresponded much better to the Egyptian captivity.

Furthermore, by his time the temple had actually been cleansed and dedicated, so the author of Daniel interpreted the history from the destruction of the temple in 586 BIA to the rededication in 164 BIA--from temple to temple. He forced the facts to make it all come out in sabbaths and cycles, giving a religious interpretation to past history. He was not trying to prophesy future history on the basis of the past. His Sabbath doctrine inconspicuousy changed the captivity period from 422 to 490 years. He concentrated on the first week of years in Babylon and the last week of years in Jerusalem. In between he forced 62 weeks of years, without balancing the totals. True to the dual period of wilderness and conquest, this eschatologist divided the final period into two half weeks of years: l) from the treaty with Antiochus to the defilement of the temple, and 2) from the defilement of the temple to its cleansing. Had this theologian put his interpretation onto a cyclical graph, it might have looked something like this:

Babylon	wilderness	conquest	
98.57	0.71	0.71	0

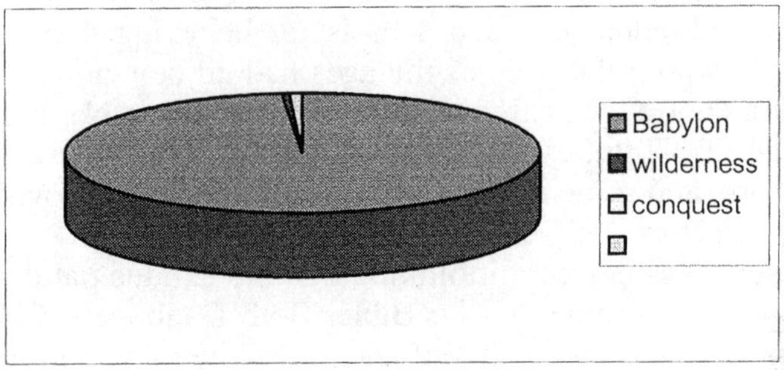

Roman Captivity. By NT times, the new Hasmonean Age, the beginning of which provided high expectations for the author of Daniel and other contemporary Jews who had shared in that famous Hanukkah celebration, had slowly collapsed. Pompey had reentered the temple in 63 BIA; Herod's rule was strong, but very much pro-Roman; Herod's sons could not control the nationalistic rebels, so Rome installed its own governors and tax collectors (6-7 IA).[1] Zealous Jews knew they were no longer free, and they began to reanalyze their past history to find out how long they would have to endure this Roman age before the Jewish age to come would be reinstituted.

They looked for current antitypes of ancient types and current signs of the recurrence of ancient miracles. They were so eager for the new age to come that they forced almost any current event to be a clue to understanding their age. They did not want a sign that would say they were back at the beginning of the Egyptian period just after Joseph. They wanted signs to show that the wilderness period was just about over. This was the tenor of the times into which Jesus and John entered, saying, **The time is up; the Kingdom of Heaven is near**. Jews understood this to mean the time of the Roman control over Palestine was over; and the Jewish kingdom was about to be reestablished at Jerusalem.

[1] International Age is used here as a politically non-discriminating label instead of the Christian abbreviation AD or the discriminating anti-Christian abbreviation CE (Lev 10:10).

Summary. One of the major opponents to the modern revival of typology was Bultmann, who has been upheld by some of his students. Bultmann argued that typology depended upon an ancient oriental cyclical view of time,[1] and, without examining the possibility that Jews and Christians really understood time in terms of cycles, he presumed that such a view was false. He was correct in his analysis that typology and cyclical time concepts belong together, but he was wrong in his assumption that cyclical time was foreign to biblical thought. It was because Jews and Christians thought of time as moving in cycles that they were motivated to study the signs of the times, relate the events of their time to the events of earlier cycles and identify current institutions, people, and events to corresponding institutions, people, and events of earlier times.

The word, "type" was an appropriate term for characters that reappeared, cycle after cycle, and provided a basis for believing they would appear again for Christians to whom the ends of the ages had all coincided. It is clear now that neither typology nor a cyclical view of time are modern NT hypotheses; they are facts that existed in NT times. Hypotheses and conjectures are involved in identifying some of these, and some errors in conjecture undoubtedly will be made, but they can be made on the basis of facts of NT times.

Daube was correct in thinking that the exodus pattern was the most important pattern of deliverance in the Bible. Both Daube and Carmichael were right in discovering typological methodologies in early composition of literature. Literary composers prepared their documents with the invention or identification of new antitypes of Joseph, Phineas, Elijah, or Jesus. They identified their historical period with earlier times in Egypt, the wilderness, the conquest of Canaan, or the dedication of the temple. The end which they anticipated was the antitype of the end of the captivity of Egypt or Babylon, and the kingdom for which they longed was an antitype of the United Kingdom of David or Solomon. They strained their mental resources to make these expectations fit into the cyclical understanding of time that was standard for that period of history in the Greco-Roman world.

Even after the crucifixion, Christian typologists continued to interpret the role of Jesus in relationship to a new exodus and a new entrance into the Promised Land. Some of the complex ways in which these typologcal interpretations were put in writing seem to be reflected in Christian gospels. The next chapter will show how this might have taken place.

Sin and Crime

There is a difference between sin and crime. A sin is some offense against another person. It may be very damaging, but it may be nothing more than an embarrassment or discourtesy. Such an offender would be called a sinner. A criminal, on the other hand, is someone who commits a crime, and a crime is an offense that can be punished by the courts of the state. It is determined by the laws of the state. That which is a criminal offense in one state may not be a criminal offense in another

[1] R. Bultmann, "Ursprung und Sinn der Typologie als hermeneutische Methode," *TLZ* 75 (1950):205-212. One of the scholars who seems to have recognized the inherent relationship between typology and cycles is Prof. M. D. Goulder. See his excellent analysis of the Acts of the Apostles, *Type and History in Acts* (London: S.P.C.K., 1964).

words of the first unit in one sequence and those of the second in reverse order, to form an arrangement such as this:

A		B
	X	
B		A

An example of this is Matt 19:30:

many *first* ones		**will be *last***
	X	
and the *last*		***first*.**

The chiasm in Matt 19:30 is repeated in 20:16, thus forming an inclusion with a chiasm at both ends (see also Matt 10:28; 12:49-50). In addition to words, phrases are sometimes put together chiastically, such as Matt 7:6:

A. **Do not give dogs what is holy,**
B. **and do not throw your pearls before hogs;**
B. **lest they [the hogs]) trample them underfoot**
A. **and they [the dogs] turn to bite you.**

A euphonic chiasm in Hebrews is 4:16b:[1]

hina labomen *eleos* (heé-nah láh-boh-men…éh-lee-ohs)	So that we might receive mercy
X	
kai charin *heuromen* (kai kháhr-een hee-yoór-oh-mehn)	and grace we might find."

"Mercy" and "grace" are synonymous and form a hendiadys here. A hendiadys is taken from the Greek *hehn* (ἕν) which means "one." When two or more words or concepts are said together to refer to one of something, that is a hendiadys. Here "mercy" and "grace" form a hendiadys. Concepts and literary forms that have been discussed in this introduction will be illustrated as occasions arise in the commentary.

---

[1] Fenton, "*Inclusio*," pp. 174-79, and J. M. Moulton, *A Grammar of New Testament Greek* (Edinburgh: T & T Clark, 1963), III, pp. 345-47. Some scholars say the chiasm is first of all a Semitic form, evident in MT Pss 3:8-9; 7:17; 58:7. It is very common in the MT and in Ugaritic literature (see D. N. Freedman, "The Structure of Psalm 137," in *Near Eastern Studies*:188 ( ):203-4, and in Syriac literature.

The Author's Use of the First Testament

This homiletic midrash has been generously interspersed with FT allusions and direct quotations. Although the text on which the entire homily was based is Ps 110, the citation from Jer 31:31-34 is the longest quotation in the entire NT (Heb 8:8-12), but it is not the primary text. According to Westcott, in addition to many allusions, there are 12 direct quotations from the Pentateuch, 11 from the Psalms, 4 from the prophets, and 2 from the writings and the historical books.[1]

For many years scholars have thought the author had access to the LXX (Old Greek) text of the FT alone. Recent studies, however, indicate a far more complex situation. Howard concluded that of 41 possible sources for 35 quotations, 24 are unlike either the MT (Hebrew) or the LXX, 8 are identical to both, 6 are identical to the Masoretic Text (MT), the LXX, and only 2 are identical to the LXX against the MT.[2] The discovery of the Dead Sea scrolls has enabled scholars to understand better the wide variety of textual versions available to biblical scholars in NT times.

Of course, there are still only a few texts that can actually be compared, but there are enough to remind scholars that any study of the texts used by NT authors must consider the possibility that many texts that are no longer extant might have been used then. Among those now available for comparison, Hebrews sometimes agrees with one and sometimes another. In Heb 2:7, 10:5, and 12:6, for instance, the author's argument depends on the LXX. In Heb 1:6 he may have translated the same version as 4QDeut, or he may have had access to a LXX translation of that text. Sometimes the author seems to have used a LXX version different from any extant text, and, for his purposes, inferior both to the LXX and to the MT (Heb 2:16).

In some cases the author used a Greek word that is synonymous to that used in the LXX, such as *daykh-thén-tah* (δειχθέντα) instead of *deh-deeg-mén-awn* (δεδειγμένον), **shown** (Heb 8:5; Exod 25:40); *ah-pang-geh-lóh* (ἀπαγγελῶ) instead of *dee-ay-gáy-saw-mai* (διηγήσομαι) **I will announce** (Heb 2:12; LXX Ps 21:23); *yoo-dáw-kay-sahs* (εὐδόκησας), **you desired,** instead of *áy-tay-sahs* (ἤτησας) or *ay-thél-ay-sahs* (ἠθέλησας), "You requested" or "You looked for" (Heb 10:6; LXX Ps 39:7). These synonyms used by the author of Hebrews might suggest the use of a variant LXX text, but there are other variations that require a different explanation. In his use of LXX Jer 38:31-34, the author used *dee-ah-tháy-saw-mai* (διαθήσομαι) for "I will contract" in Heb 10:16, consistent with the LXX. In Heb 8:8, however, he substituted *soon-tehl-éh-soh* (συντελέσω) for *dee-ah-tháy-saw-mai* (διαθήσομαι). Other differences between these two references are: In Heb 8:10, the author followed the LXX, **with the house of Israel** (*toh oí-koh eés-rah-ehl*, τῷ οἴκῳ Ισραηλ) I; in Heb 10:16, he substituted **to them** (*práws ow-toós* προσαυτούς . In Heb 8:10, he quoted the LXX,

[1] B. F. Westcott, *The Epistle to the Hebrews* (London: Macmilllan and Co., 1889), p. 472.

[2] G. Howard, "Hebrews and the Old Testament Quotations," *NovT* 10 (1968):211. Analysts vary somewhat in their judgment and count. See also F. Schröger, *Der Verfasser des Hebraerbriefes als Schriftsleger* (Regensburg: F. Pustat, 1968), pp. 247-66.

[I will] put my laws	**in their minds**
	X
and on their hearts	**I will write them.**

In Heb 10:16, he altered the quotation to read as follows:

[I will] put my laws	**on their hearts**
	X
and on their minds	**I will write them**."

The important difference between these two quotations in the Greek is the reversal of "minds" and "hearts," forming a chiasm of the statement.[1]

It is very unlikely that the author of Hebrews used one LXX text for the composition of Heb 8 and a different one for Heb 10. It seems rather that he used the same text in both cases and that he paraphrased it as he chose. Since the possibility is great that the author of Hebrews made changes like this in these instances, this provides another variable factor to consider. He may have made all of the changes listed above that might otherwise be attributed to variant texts, but that does not exclude the possibility that he used variant texts. It just raises more doubts and requires careful consideration of the possibilities in each case. These will be treated in the commentary.

Westcott was correct in observing that the author of Hebrews used passages from all parts of the FT as proof texts, considering them all authoritative representations of the word of God, but he did not consider them all "law" as Westcott implies.[2] Paul and John both referred to passages from the prophets or Psalter as "law," but for the author of Hebrews the law was the Pentateuch. This was the code that governed the Levites (Heb 7:5) and must be changed (Heb 7:12). It was fleshly (Heb 7:16); it perfected nothing (Heb 7:19); and it was responsible for establishing as high priests men who are weak (Heb 7:28).

Jesus was different from those priests who offered gifts according to the law (Heb 8:4). The first contract was renewed according to the law of Moses (Heb 9:19) which required blood for cleansing almost everything (Heb 9:22). That law of Moses, however, had only a shadow of the coming good things (Heb 10:1). The sacrifices which the psalmist prohibited were offered according to the law (Heb 10:8). The law of Moses was rated in an inferior position in comparison with the new contract of Christ (Heb 10:28-29). The rest that was promised in Ps 95 together with an oath was superior to the rest promised in the Pentateuch without an oath (Heb 3:7-4:10). The new contract promised by the prophet Jeremiah took precedence over the old contract established in the Pentateuch (Heb 8:8-13). The priesthood of Melchizedek established with an oath in Ps 110 replaced the levitical priesthood established in the Pentateuch (see Heb 7).

---

[1] For a fuller discussion on these texts and others that may have been altered by the author of Hebrews himself, see K. J. Thomas, "The Old Testament Citations in Hebrews," *NTS* 11 (1964-65):303-25.

[2] Westcott, *Hebrews,* p. 473.

Although the author used passages from the Pentateuch for proof texts and supportive texts, he considered the Pentateuch to be the law of Moses, associated with the old contract, the old priesthood, and the temple made with hands, even though it was with God's hands (Exod 15:17). It was an inferior type to be succeeded by something superior, which nevertheless would be of the same general kind. He used Num 18 to explain Ps 110 and Exod 15-17 // Num 14-20 to explain Ps 95, but his defense was built on the Psalter and not on the Pentateuch. Westcott thought it was remarkable that,

> with two exceptions (2Sam 7:14; Isa 8:17 f.), all the primary passages which are quoted to illustrate the true nature of the Person and Work of Christ are taken from the Psalms.[1]

This consistency is remarkable, but it fits in well with the author's general outlook. He considered the Psalms to have been written by David. David and the prophets were all composed after the Pentateuch and therefore reflected a later word of God. Whenever they contradicted the Pentateuch, this meant that the Pentateuch had been superseded.

The author seemed to relate the prophets and the Psalter to the new contract prophesied by Jeremiah and considered that all the prophets prophesied only for the days of the Messiah. Jesus was the Messiah, therefore these prophecies were to be applied directly to the time of the author of Hebrews and the new contract established by Jesus. On the other hand, the Pentateuch was associated with the exodus generation which had been given a fair opportunity to receive the promised rest, but failed because of disobedience. That was the reason why a new opportunity was given later. The author tended to group his concepts into typologies, and this is one of the ramifications of this tendency. The Pentateuch was classed with the old contract, the law of Moses, the disobedient generation, the inferior priesthood, and the temple made with hands. The Psalms and at least some of the prophets were associated with the new contract, the new priesthood, the new law, the days of the Messiah, the temple not made with hands, and the perfect sacrifice. Even the author's use of Scripture reflected these contrasts.

Translations

Contract. Unless otherwise indicated all translations into English quoted here are mine. I have tried to translate ancient texts into modern American, rather than into Shakespearean English. This has been done to remove any unnecessary obscurity. For example, most people in America know what a contract is. It is necessary to sign contracts to obtain employment, buy automobiles, rent houses, purchase land, get married or divorced, or almost any other legal activity. The word "covenant," which was considered good English 400 years ago, is seldom used or understood by average Americans today. Therefore ancient English words and expressions will be replaced here with modern American words as often as possible.

The Hebrew *buh-reét* (ברית), which the translators of the King James version of the Bible rendered "covenant," is here translated either "contract" or "treaty," whichever the context requires. Covenant is not a Hebrew or Greek word. Nor does it have a distinctive meaning in English to distinguish it from contract or

---

[1] Westcott, *Hebrews,* p. 473.

treaty. The Hebrew word for some written type of agreement was *buh-reét*. Hebrews made no distinction of terms between a contract between equals or between unequals. The same is true today. The word "contract" is used for an agreement between an insurance company and a customer, a landlord and a tenant, or two equal partners. The same Hebrew word that means "contract" also means "treaty." The only distinction is that some agreements are made among individuals and others are made among nations. The latter are called "treaties" in American.

Words related to "contract" are terms in Shakespearean English that come out as "ark of the covenant" or "covenanter." The Hebrew word that was translated 400 years ago as "ark" is any box or chest. Noah's "ark" was really a houseboat. The "ark" that held the contract made between the Lord and his people was a chest or trunk, so it will be called here "The chest that holds the contract." Members of the community that had a contract with the Lord and were called "covenanters," will here be called "parties to the contract," "members," "sectarians," "believers," or some such expression.

The great offense in biblical concepts was breaking contracts. This was punishable by the courts of law and is called a "sin" in most Bible translations, but in American legal systems it is called a "crime." To keep before the reader the relationship of contract breaking to offense, and the relationship of offenses to the court system, These offenses will be called "crimes" here.

The divine Name. In the Book of Hebrews the divine name is often avoided in various ways. If, however, the tetragrammaton is ever referred to directly, it is called "the Lord." Because that is so, the translation given is correspondingly "the Lord." Whatever is given in the LXX is likewise translated. If the MT has "the Lord," that is translated, but if the Tetragrammaton is given, that is spelled out so the reader can know what the text really said.

When the MT has the Tetragrammaton, the translation given here is *Yeh-hoh-wah*, because this is the most likely pronunciation used in antiquity. The chances that it was pronounced *Yahweh*, a two syllable word that omits the middle syllable, are almost *nihil*. All of the proper names that include two syllables of the divine name include the middle syllable: Jonathan = *Yah-hóh*-nah-thahn, "*Yah-hoh* has given"; Elijah = Eh-lee-*Yáh-hoh*, "My God is *Yáh-hoh*"; Joshua = *Yáh-hoh*-shoo-ah, "*Yáh-hoh* saves"; Achaziah = Ah-khaz-*Yáh-hoh*, "*Yaho* has taken possession." The first syllable *Yah* sometimes stands alone as an abbreviation or for the necessity of rhythm in a poem, but the manufactured *weh* never exists in a name. When Jews stopped using the divine name they continued to name their children on the basis of the correct pronunciation. Furthermore, when poetry includes the name the poetic meter requires three syllables.

Tenths. The practice of giving one tenth as tax was called "tithing" in sixteenth century English. Since Americans seldom use the word "tithe" in ordinary conversation the Greek word will here be rendered "tenth." That which 16th century English called "tithing" will here be called "taking the tenth." or "assessing the tenth."

Political Points.[1] For centuries Christians and Jews have practiced the fine art of insulting. Jews have insulted other Jews, and Christians have insulted other

[1] Taken from Buchanan, *TheBook of Daniel* (Lewiston: Mellen, c1999), pp. 12-15.

Christians. Jews have also insulted Christians, and Christians have insulted Jews. It is called "defamation," and both groups have done it. There is no benefit to be gained in counting crimes to show who has been the most insulting. At this stage in the game the best thing to do is to see how we can reduce the insults. Some efforts will be made in this commentary to achieve that goal. We will be most successful if instead of trying to prevent others from defaming us, we stop defaming others.

Christians have called the canonical books written before the NT the "Old Testament," implying that it has been transcended and made out of date. This was not done facetiously without scriptural basis. Jeremiah, on the basis of Deut 24:1, said that God had divorced his people, and sent them out of his house. This implied that he had also given them a divorce document (Jer 3:8), thus fulfilling the two requirements for divorce: 1) writ of divorce and 2) sending the bride from the groom's house (mGittin 1-9). On the basis of Jeremiah, then, Christians believed there was no contract between God and his people until Jesus formed a new contract. The initial contract was old and invalid (Heb 8:6-13; 10:16; 12:24).

Second Isaiah, however, disagreed with Jeremiah. He said even though God sent his people away from his temple (house), he did not give them a writ of divorce (*gayt*, גט). Therefore the divorce was not complete, and the initial contract is still valid (Isa 50:1). On this basis, Jews argue that there was no need for a new contract, and the initial contract is not old. Therefore they refuse to call the books related to the contract "the Old Testament." Instead they call it "the Hebrew Scripture" or the *Tah-naak.*

Christians and Jews can disagree on the contracts, but as literature, none of the Scripture is out of date, neither for Jews or Christians. There is a problem, however with calling these books the "Hebrew Scripture." For some this confuses them with only the books written in Hebrew; i.e., the Masoretic text (MT). Others also call the books that have been translated into Greek as "The Christian Bible," because Christians have preserved them, and that translation includes some books not included in the Masoretic text. The canonical books that were composed before the New Testament (NT) are not antiquated—neither the Greek nor the Hebrew canons. This will become especially obvious in this commentary where the pre-NT canonical texts that were used by author of the Hebrews will be given special consideration.

Here the pre-NT canonical books will not be called the "Old Testament," the "Christian Testament," or the "Hebrew Scripture." Instead the collection will be referred to as "The First Testament," (FT) and it will include all of the books of the Roman Catholic canon. FT is a non-doctrinal term. Like the labels IA and BIA, it should not be offensive either to Christians or Jews. It will also avoid staging a conflict between the Greek translations and the MT. It will not characterize these books as Jewish books as over against Greek Christian books. The text of the FT canon comes in Hebrew *and in Greek.* The Greek version is called "Septuagint" (LXX) and the Hebrew text is called the "Masoretic text" (MT).

With the victories of Constantine, Christians believed that this was a confirmation that the new contract God made with Jesus was valid, and that this was the beginning of a new era. They began a new calendar, just as Jews had done during the days of Simon, the Hasmonean, and during the revolt of Bar Cochba. Christians called the beginning of this era *anno domine* (AD)—the year of the Lord, meaning "the year that Jesus became Lord."

Jews have also been offended by the Christian reference to the calendar as BC (before Christ) and AD (the year of the Lord). Since Jesus is not their Messiah, they do not participate in this offense. Instead they refer to this calendar insultingly as BCE and CE—before the common era and the common era. This designation is just as offensive to Christians as BC and AD is to Jews. That which is called **common** by Jews means that which is pagan, profane, idolatrous, gentile. Lev 10:10 commanded Israelites to discriminate between that which was **holy** (*kah-dóhsh*, קדוש) and that which was **common** (*khohl*, חול) (Ezek 22:26). Ezekiel accused the priests of his day of not making these distinctions. He ordered the priests to observe them (Ezek 44:23).

Peter reportedly refused to eat anything that was **common** (*koi-náwn*, κοινόν) or unclean. Following Levitical commandments the author of Rev 21:27 said the new Jerusalem would be **holy**, not containing anything that was **common** (*koi-náwn*). Distinctions between that which is **holy** and that which is **common** have been retained for thousands of years. For instance, one of the prayers Jews recite at the conclusion of each Sabbath is:

> Blessed are you, Lord our God, king of the age, who discriminates between the **holy** (*kah-dóhsh*, קדוש) and the **common** (*khóhl*, חול), between light and darkness, between Israel and the peoples [of the nations], between the Sabbath and the six working days. Blessed are you, Lord, who discriminates between the **holy** and the **common**.[1]

"Common" can be a general term in some contexts, but as it has been used in relationship to the calendar, it is offensive. It does not mean that which is common both to Jews and Christians. It means that the age Christians call the Christian era, Jews call the profane era. The term "holy" is reserved for Jerusalem, Palestine, the Jewish priests, the Jewish festivals, Jewish Sabbaths, and the Jewish people.

Shifting the designation from one insult to the other does nothing to reduce hostility. Christians originally called this the Christian era as a confession of faith. Jews called it common, because it was not under the control of Jews. The Hasmonean age was holy in distinction from the common era when Antiochus Epiphanes was ruling Palestine. It seems unnecessary for these offenses to continue. On the one hand Christians do not rule the world and should give up all aspirations to that effect. We might be willing to call the period marked by the calendar by the politically correct title of "the International Age" (IA). Jews, on the other hand, might also give up any goals they might have for acquiring a holy age and be willing to stop calling Christians "common."

The First Testament will include the books of the apocrypha. Language references will call the Hebrew text the Masoretic text (MT) and the Greek text the Old Greek (LXX). Changing names from "Christian age" (AD and BC) or "common era" (CE and BCE) to "International Age" (IA and BIA) or changing titles like "Old Testament," "Hebrew Scripture," or "Christian Testament" to "First Testament" (FT) will not change any facts of history or literary data, but it might make a small change in the way Christians and Jews treat one another and think of one another. It is an attempt at political correctness and a reduction of hostility.

Conquest theology for both all the sons of Abraham—Christians, Jews, and Muslims--should be relegated to history. We need another calendar designation. Since the era and the literature belong to all of us—or none of us—we need some neutral, inoffensive names. If the ones suggested here are not suitable, someone

---

[1] *The Traditional Prayer Book for Sabbath Festivals*, ed. D. de Sola Pool (New York, 1960), p. 453.

should suggest better ones. The only reason "age" is preferred to "era" is that the abbreviation IE might also be confused for *id est*. The abbreviations for historical periods and scriptural texts suggested here will be used in this commentary on an experimental basis.

Aids in Reading

The documentation in footnotes is regularly abbreviated to save space, but in every chapter, the first use of a every source in that chapter is given in full, so that the reader will not have to go back farther than to the beginning of whatever chapter is being read to find the full documentation.

For the benefit of non-professional readers technical terms are explained and foreign words are both translated and transliterated phonetically.

For the benefit of research scholars Hebrew and Greek texts are given for important words. The use of all of the words in the index is complete. Every word that appears in the index appears there every time that word is used in the text of the book. Geographical names are included in the "Words" index.

CHAPTER ONE

TEXT

Hebrews	First Testament
1:1 In many places and ways God spoke in antiquity to the fathers through the prophets; 2 **in the last of these days** he has spoken to us through a Son, whom he established heir of all, through whom he also made the ages; 3 who, being a reflection of the glory and stamp of his nature, / bearing everything by the word of his	Dan 2:28 God in heaven reveals mysteries, and he has made known to King Nebuchadnezzar what will happen **in the last of the days**. Ezek 38:16 **In the last days**, I will bring you [Gog], over my land, so that the nations may know me, when I am glorified through you before the eyes of the nations.
power, / when he had made a	Ps 110:2 Yehowah will send your **power**ful scepter from Zion, subduing your enemies with a sword.
purification	Lev 16:19 He **shall purify** it and sanctify it [the altar] from the defilement of the children of Israel
for [his] crimes, /	Exod 29:36 You shall make an offering **for crimes** on the Day of Atonement.
he sat down at the right hand of the Majesty in exaltation. / 4 being so much greater than the angels that he inherited a name more excellent than theirs.	Ps 110:1 Yehowah said, **Sit at my right hand** until I make your enemies a footstool for your feet.

COMMENTARY

In many places and ways. The opening verse of Hebrews prepares the reader for all the substance of the document from 1:1-12:29. The first two verses are in beautiful literary parallelism, rhythmically composed:

1: He has spoken	to the fathers	through the prophets
2: He has spoken	to us	through the Son.

The Greek words rendered "many places and ways" are adverbs for which there are not good English equivalents. The force intended is that God's speaking in the past has been diverse both in geographic location and in method of disclosure. He appeared in visions, dreams, symbols, a system of "drawing straws," called the *urim* and *thumnim*, angels, natural events, ecstasy, the column of smoke or fire, and occasionally face to face. These revelations occurred to different people at different periods of history--in Ur of the Chaldees, Haran, Canaan, the Wilderness, Egypt, and Babylon.

God spoke in antiquity to the fathers through the prophets. It is apparent here that God communicated to his people through the **speaking** of his intermediaries. When they **spoke**, it was his voice that the people heard. Moses wrote the commandments of the contract, but God **spoke**. The **fathers** were probably not only Abraham, Isaac, and Jacob, who preceded **the prophets**, but rather all of the religious ancestors listed in 11:4-38, which list the author noted as being incomplete. The intended readers depended on all these **fathers** for their tradition.

Through the prophets renders the Greek *ehn tois pro-pháy-tais* (ἐν τοῖς προφήταις), literally "in" the prophets, but this is a Hebrew idiom, *dee-báyr buh* (דבר בה), translated as in **the Spirit of the Lord speaks through me** (2Sam 23:2 *et passim*). The *buh* in Hebrew in this usage has the force of "through" or "by" rather than "in." **Through the prophets** means by the agency of **the prophets**. God was the principal who had appointed **the prophets** as his legal agents to **speak** his words. A legal agent is legally identical to the principal who commissioned him or her. When the agent **speaks** it is legally the same as if the principal **speaks**. When the **Spirit of the Lord** speaks, that means that the Lord speaks legally. The word **spirit** is a legal term. Legally, the principal **speaks** through the agent, just as a flute player plays through the flute. Both the flute and the agent are means through which a principal plays, **speaks**, or acts. Therefore the translation given is **through.** This verse includes the beautifully alliterative Greek words, *paw-loo-meh-róhs, paw-loo-tráw-paws, páw-lay, paw-tráw-seen,* and *praw-pháy-tais* (πολυμερῶς, πολυτρόπως, πάλαι, πατράσιν, προφήταις). Cosby correctly said of this passage,

> And since many of the rhetorical techniques are not observable in English translation, there is a dimension of persuasiveness available only to the ears of one listening to the Greek text.[1]

They are transliterated here and throughout the commentary so that those who do not read Greek can appreciate the sound of these terms spoken orally, as they may have been. Cosby accurately described this text as one designed for the ear of one *listening* to the text, as if it were being delivered orally. Kennedy said, "Even when reading to himself, a Greek read aloud,"[2] but there are other clues throughout the document to indicate a listening audience and a speaker. The Koran has a confession something like this.

> We have revealed to thee as We revealed
> to Noah and the Prophets after him,
> and We revealed to Abraham, Ishmael,
> Isaac, Jacob, and the Tribes,
> Jesus and Job, Jonah, and Aaron

[1] M. R. Cosby, "The Rhetorical Composition of Hebrews 11," *JBL* 107 (1988):258.

[2] G. Kennedy, *The Art of Persuasion* (Princeton: Princeton U. Press, 1963), p. 4.

> and Solomon, and We gave to David Psalms,
> and Messengers We have already told thee of
> before, and Messengers We have not told thee of;
> and unto Moses God spoke directly--
> Messengers bearing good tidings, and warning,
> so that mankind might have no argument
> against God, after the Messengers; God is
> All-mighty, All-wise.
> But God bears witness to that He has sent down
> to thee; He has sent it down with His knowledge;
> and the angels also bear witness; and God suffices
> for a witness (Koran 4:162-63).[1]

[2] *In the last of these days*. **In the last of these days** is a very literal translation of the Greek *ehp ehs-khá-too tóhn hay-meh-róhn toó-tohn* (ἐπ' ἐσχάτου τῶν ἡμερῶν τούτων). It might also be literally rendered "in these last days." Both translations have the same meaning and are appropriate for the context. A few texts read *ehs-khá-tohn* (ἐσχάτων) probably because of scribal memory of the idiom as it occurs frequently in Scripture.[2]

The idiom **in the last of these days** reflects a Semitic attitude toward time. Semitic words for past are words meaning "before" or "in front of" (*kah-dáhm,* קדם*, kahd-moh-nee-óht* קדמוניות, or *luh-fah-neém*, לפנים) as if the Semite were looking toward his ancestral origins when he talked of the past. The past had happened; it was known and could be faced. The future, on the other hand, could not be seen, so it was considered "behind" or "in back of" the person who stood in the present, because people do not have eyes on the backs of their heads. Words for "tomorrow," "later," "future," and "last" were words like *mah-kháhr* (מחר), *ah-kháhr* (אחר), *ah-khah-reét* (אחרית), or *ah-khah-róhn* (אחרון)--all of which refer to something behind.

This fact provides no data for determining whether Semites viewed time as either a circular or a horizontal phenomenon, but it means that they were realists. They understood the world as it appeared to them. They could not see the future. On the basis of this concept, the author of Hebrews spoke of the future hope as **things not seen** (Heb 11:1). Noah prepared for the future **not yet seen** (Heb 11:7). Christians could look to Jesus whose activity took place in the past (Heb 12:2). This does not mean Semites were not interested in the future, but that their only basis for understanding what the future might be was the past, from which they deduced the future in terms of typologies or patterns of historical events.

Typology is a belief that objects, events, persons, and institutions exist and occur in relationship to other corresponding objects, events, persons, and institutions. For earthly things, when considered antitypes, there are prior and corresponding heavenly prototypes or archetypes which were the patterns by which the earthly things were created. For instance, according to Hebrews, there was a heavenly temple not made with hands which was a prototype for the anticipated temple not made with hands at Jerusalem. Currently the temple built by the Romans was not designed in heaven. It was a pagan temple, a temple made with hands. When the typology dealt with earthly things, the pattern was usually referred to as a "type,"

---

[1] So A. J. Arberry, *Revelation and Reason in Islam* (London: Allen & Unwin, c1957), pp. 13-14.

[2] Gen 49:1; Deut 4:30; Jer 37[30]:24, Ezek 38:16; Dan 2:28; Hos 3:5; Mic 4:1; and 2Pet 3:3.

rather than a "prototype," and its corresponding antitype was also earthly and historical.

Ancients looked for events that were similar to past events to learn where they were in the cycle of time. When they discovered an antitype in their current events, they studied the past to find the corresponding type. When they found the type then they studied all they could learn about that type —what things preceded it and what things followed. They believed that the same things that happened after that type were predestined to happen again in their future. This is why their eschatological beliefs were inseparably tied to history.

Eschatology is derived from the Greek term *és-cha-taws* (ἔσχατος), which means "end." It can mean the end of a stick or the end of a certain period of time, such as the end of a day, a week, an administration, an era. Eschatology is a study applied to ends of *periods* of time—not the end of time itself. The author of Heb 1-12 looked forward to the end of the time when the Romans would rule Palestine, followed by the coronation of their own Messiah, and the establishment of Israel's own kingdom on the Promised Land.

Semites thought of the future as the "behind" aspect of time. One of the idioms that expresses this is *buh ah-khah-reét hah-yah-meém* (באחרית הימים) "in the afterness of days," in the days that are after or behind the present **In the last of these days** refers to the last days of this undesirable age which would be followed by a better future. The author had no thought of the last days of the world, of time, or of the cosmos—only the last days of the contemporary political era.

An eisegete is a person who brings something in from the outside that is not a normal part of a text. Like many other eisegetes since the days of Gunkel and Johannes Weiss, Schenck had assumed that all references to the future area anticipated a future in heaven. **The end of the days** meant the end of the days on earth. The age to come means the future in heaven, and an age meant eternity, according to his interpretation.[1] That was a notion he imported, that does not belong to the meaning of the text itself.

Schenk's importation distorts the basic meaning of Hebrews. Although early Jews and Christians believed that God lived in heaven, somewhere above the clouds, near their temples, the chosen people lived on earth, managed an earthly government, fought battles, ate, slept, and worked on earth. Their religion was closely related to their history on earth. God's commandments were to be fulfilled on earth. The promises of the contract were expected to be fulfilled on earth. The prayers for the kingdom were that they would be fulfilled on earth.

He has spoken to us through a Son. The **Son through** which God **spoke** was his own legal **Son.** The title, "**Son** of God," was a title given to a king. The king was not believed to be the **son** of God, physically or ontologically, but legally. David's physical **son,** Solomon, was called God's **son** (1Sam 7:14), legally. One of the Dead Sea Scrolls spoke of a man who would be called "**Son** of God" and "**Son** of the Most High" (4Q246 2:1). That man would be the king.

Any person who has changed an identification is legally born again and becomes a new creature. This can happen by adoption, naturalization, marriage, or change of religion. A person who is legally born does not change in age, appearance, or health by this new birth, but he or she is legally a new person. In that way a king,

---

[1] K. L. Schenck, "A Celebration of the Enthroned Son: The Catena of Hebrews 1," *JBL* 120 (2001):469-85.

born of human parents, is legally a person born of God. He was physically born when he left his mother's womb as an infant. He was legally born when he was anointed king.

As God's **Son,** the king was God's legal agent. This means that God was the principal, and both Solomon and Jesus were his agents. An agent is the human being through whom a principal acts and speaks. In the Gospel of John Jesus is reported as having declared that he did not do his own will but the will of the Father who sent him. That means he was God's legal agent. Agents are indispensable people for government or business. Nearly all of the world's business, today, is conducted by agents. Agents were at least as important in antiquity, when there was no other way of communicating with someone else at a distance, as there is today. There were no cell telephones, e-mail, fax machines, TV, telegraphs, or radios. If someone wanted to get a message to someone else at a distance and was unable to go, himself or herself, it was necessary to send a messenger. So, if God, from heaven, wanted to communicate with his people, on earth, he would have to send a legal agent, and one of his agents was believed to be the king.

The agent speaks and acts in the name of the principal, in behalf of the principal, and at the responsibility of the principal. Legally, the agent is the principal. The agent does not act in his or her own interests, but in the interests of the principal. The principal, therefore, acts and speaks through the agent. This is the importance of the claim that God has spoken through a **Son**. The **Son** was God's legal agent and was authorized by God to **speak** and act in God's name, and that which the agent said was, legally, God's word **spoken *through* the Son,** in the same way that the president of the U.S.A speaks through the secretary of state to conduct foreign business. The secretary of state speaks the words of the president. In ancient law legal authority was established mostly through ceremonies. In those days, liturgies were just as valid in court as written contracts. Maine said,

> In ancient law [required formalities are] to be transferred to the words and gestures of the accompanying performance. No pledge is enforced if a single form be omitted or misplaced, but, on the other hand, if the forms can be shown to have been accurately proceeded with, it is of no avail to plead that the promise was made under duress or deception.[1]

Jesus was legally born as God's Son and legal agent at the River Jordan when he was anointed by John the Baptist. At that time he received the spirit and spoke with authority. None of the gospels says that Jesus was anointed, but that is implied. When the various judges, Gideon, Jephthah, and Samson, received the spirit they became tribal leaders. When Samuel anointed Saul, Saul received the spirit and became king. Later David was anointed, received the spirit, and became king. When Jesus received the spirit and spoke with authority, his anointing was implied. That which the ancients spoke of as spiritual power, today we would call legal authority. When Moses gave legal authority to certain national leaders to become judges, the text says he shared his spirit with them. When Elijah's staff of assistants saw that Elijah's spirit was on Elisha, they recognized him as the new, legally authorized prophet of Israel, and they followed him.

---

[1] Henry Sumner Maine, *Ancient Law* (USA: Dorset Press, 1861[1986]), p. 260.

When John the Baptist anointed Jesus, Jesus was an adult. He had been born physically as an infant with Mary and Joseph from the line of David as his parents. He was legally born as an adult to became the Son of God, God's legal agent, and the Messiah. He was born again through the legal ceremony of anointing. As God's legal agent, Jesus acted in God's name, in his behalf, and at his responsibility. Legally Jesus was God, although he continued to be the son of David, physically. Paul said of Jesus,

> Concerning his son, who was from the seed of David, according to the flesh, established Son of God in [legal] power, according to the spirit (Rom 1:3-4).

Whom he established heir of all. The Son here is also an **heir,** as might be expected. The word **heir** in other contexts is also associated with "lord." The word *klay-raw--naw-mos* (κληρονόμος), rendered "heir," is derived from the Greek word *klay-ros* (κλῆρος), meaning "lot." In a situation in which lots were drawn to divide property or select a winner, the one who drew the lot was the **heir**. This word came to be used for dividing the property that a father left to his children when he died. Hebrew traditions were probably identical to the Assyrian customs in which lots were drawn to determine which son received which portion of property. When there was only one son, of course, there would also normally be only one **heir.** Where there were more sons than one, however, the property was divided into one share more than there were sons. For example, if there were six sons there would be seven lots. The oldest son would choose and take the first portion, after which he and the other sons would draw lots to determine which share of the property fell to which son. This gave the firstborn the advantage of receiving both the choice share and a normal share of the property.[1]

A king's dynastic succession, however, was normally given to only one son. The heir to the throne was usually the oldest son, but the king might choose a different son to succeed him, as David did (1Kings 1:1-40). Many times sons fought over this position, as some of David's sons did (2Sam 13:23-29; 15:1-18:18; 1Kings 1:5-2:25). Paul observed that an **heir**, while a minor, was no different in position from a slave, even though he was the lord of all (Gal 4:1). It was after he became an adult and had received his heritage that his status changed radically. The authority of the son and **heir** in comparison to other messengers or servants was shown in the attitude of the farmers in one of Jesus' parables, who, after they had killed the son and **heir,** hoped to be able to take over the father's property for themselves (Matt 21:33-41). Had Abraham's servant not succeeded in finding a wife for Isaac, Abraham's seed would have discontinued, and Abraham's property would probably have fallen to the family of the servant (Gen 24).

It was as a king coming into his inheritance that one like a son of man appeared before the Ancient of Days and **was given dominion and glory and a kingdom** (Dan 7:13-14). It was in similar terms of royalty that Jesus said, **All things have been delivered to me by my Father** (Matt 11:27; cf. Luke 10:22). The angel who spoke to Mary said of Jesus,

[1] G. R. Driver and J. C. Miles, *The Assyrian Laws* (Oxford: Clarendon, 1935), pp. 295-97.

> **He will be great, and will be called the Son of the Most High; and the Lord God will give him the throne of his father David . . . and of his kingdom there shall be no end** (Luke 1:32-33).

The angel did not say that Jesus as an infant would **be called the Son of the Most High.** That would not happen until God gave him the throne of his father David. Like Solomon he would become God's son when he was anointed. Jesus' status as **Son** and heir is evident in the NT (John 3:35; 5:22; 13:3; 17:2), and Christians, who are also sons, are by that token **joint heirs with Christ** (Rom 8:17). The younger brother, Jacob, partly out of courtesy and deference, referred to his older brother, Esau, as **lord** (*ah-doh-nai,* אדני), and himself as "servant" (*éh-vehd,* עבד) (Gen 32:4, 18; 33: 13-14). The relationship of David to the Lord was that of a first born, a chosen one, even though, physically, he was Jesse's youngest son. God was the Father who contracted to give his first born the throne (Ps 89). Paul said the heir was **lord of all** (Gal 4:1), and the author of Acts described Jesus, the Messiah, as **Lord of all** (Acts 10:36). Hebrews is consistent, describing Jesus, the Son, as **heir of all**.

The son through whom God spoke was Jesus, the Son of God. Prior to the discovery of the Dead Sea Scrolls, scholars like Kümmel argued that there was no sure proof that the title "Son of God" occurred in pre-Christian or pre-Tannaitic Judaism.[1] In pre-Christian Dead Sea Scrolls, however, a king was called "Son of God" (*bah-ráh dee áyl,* ברה די אל) and "Son of the Most High" (4Q246.2:1). In another fragment a prayer was offered to God for

1) the king,
2) the congregation of God's people Israel, and
3) God's kingdom (*mahm-láhch-tuh-kah,* ממלכתך) (4Q448.B:8).

The king was named. He was King Jonathan (*yóh-nah-than,* יונתן), which would have applied to the king, named in Greek, Alexander Janneus (4Q448.B:2; C:8), who ruled Palestine from 103 to 76 BIA.[2] Alexander Janneus was the king who ruled over God's kingdom when Alexander himself was king of Israel. Just as the titles, Son of God, Son of man, and Son of the Most High are political titles for the Messiah, so also the title, Kingdom of God or the Kingdom of Heaven, is a political and religious title for liberated Palestine.

Alexander was a very cruel king who had 800 leaders in Judah crucified while their families were killed before their eyes. During part of his reign he led mercenary troops against citizens of Judah. Nonetheless, he was the Son of God by virtue of his office, and Judah during his rule was called God's Kingdom. This is the logical conclusion reached by "the correlation of various epithets and titles" that Collins advocates.[3]

Through whom he also made the ages. The subject of this clause is God. God was the principal; Jesus was the agent **through whom** he acted. It was not assumed that

---

[1] W. G. Kümmel, "Das Gleichnis von den bösen Weingartner (Mk 12, 1-9), in der Heilgeschichte und Geschichte," *MThSt* 3 (1965):215-216.

[2] E. Eshel, H. Eshel, Ada Yardeni, "A Qumran Composition Containing Part of Ps. 154 and a Prayer for the Welfare of King Jonathan and his Kingdom," *IEJ* 42 (1992):199-229. The Hebrew text involved is on p. 201.

[3] J. J. Collins, *The Scepter and the Star* (New York: Doubleday, 1995), p. 60.

God made anything with his own hands. He had innumerable messengers who could do the actual work. He had such great authority that he had only to speak and it was done (Gen 1:1-31). The authority of the king was dramatized in the musical play, "Camelot." In the opening song, someone sang:

> It's true! It's true! The king has made it clear.
> The weather must be perfect all the year.

God was similarly pictured as a great king in the poem of creation. He said, "**Let there be light!" and there was light** (Gen 1:3). No details were given, telling how it would be done. All God had to do is give the orders. Others would fulfill them.

Lane followed the RSV in rendering *ai-óh-nahs* (αἰῶνας) "the world," and Attridge[1] translated it "universe," even though it is plural. Schenck called the term "worlds," thinking this was a material creation.[2] None of the three gave reasons for dismissing the normal rendering of this Greek term as **ages**.

Nevertheless, there is some basis for translating it "worlds," because some rabbis and early Christians believed that there were more worlds than one of which the lord was in charge (Mid Ps 18:15; Recog 2:68, 70). Furthermore, the **all** over which Jesus was made **heir** appears to be the same as *toos ai-óh-nahs*, which the RSV has rendered "the world." Another reason is the parallel between Heb 1:2 and Heb 11:3. In Heb 11:3 the claim is made that *toos ai-óh-nahs* **have been put in order by [the] word of God**. This might refer to the creation, coming first in order of events listed in Genesis, followed by the Cain and Abel story (Heb 11:4), 1Enoch (Heb 11:5-6), Noah (Heb 11:7), and others.

Against the RSV translation, many scholars think the temporal force of *ai-óh-nahs* governs here,[3] for the following reasons:

1) It is true that the Greek *ai-óhn* (αἰῶν) and the corresponding Hebrew *oh-láhm* (עולם) can be rendered "world," but such usage is very, very seldom. The sense of "age" is more frequent in both.
2) Thus "the age to come" (*hah oh-láhm hah-báh*, העולם הבא) refers to the period on this one earth when the Messiah will rule.

Barnabas referred to the age as "holy." Just as Jews believed that God created the world, so also they believed that he established the ages, the days of the week, the holiday seasons, Sabbaths, and Jubilees. Jews have had many quarrels over calendars, because they have believed it was very important to celebrate the right feasts on the right days. Some thought that all periods were decreed, established

---

[1] H. Attridge, *The Epistle to the Hebrews* (Philadelphia, Fortress Press, 1989), p. 35.

[2] Schenck, "Enthroned Son," p. 477.

[3] K. F. Keil, *Commentar über den Brief an die Hebräer* (Leipzig: Dreffling und Franke, 1885), pp. 28-29; R. C. H. Lenski, *The Interpretation of the Epistle to the Hebrews and of the Epistle of James* (Columbus: Lutheran Book Concern, 1938), pp. 29-36; S. H. Turner, *The Epistle to the Hebrews in Greek and English* (New York: Stanford and Soards, 1852), p. 19; C. J. Vaughan, *The Epistle to the Hebrews* (London: Macmillan, 1890), p. 5; B. F. Westcott, *The Epistle to the Hebrews* (London: Macmillan and Co., 1892), pp. 8-9.

once-for-all, and finalized so that life consisted only in living out the foreordained periods which God established. Ezra said,

> With a measure he has measured the times (*tempora*);
> by number he numbered the times;
> he will neither move nor stir
> until the predicted measure is fulfilled (4Ezra 4:37).

The post-FT psalmist said,

> He has established the lights in their courses
> for determining the seasons from day to day,
> and they do not deviate from the path which he
> commanded for them.
> In the fear of God their path [is taken] each day,
> from the day in which God created them until the
> age [to come] (*heh-ohs ai-óh-nahs*, ἕως αἰῶνας),
> and they have not deviated since the day he created them,
> from generations of old they have not left their courses
> if God did not command them through his servants (PssSol 18:10-12).

It is probably with this concept of time and creation in mind that the author wrote both Heb 1:2 and 11:3. He was clearly referring to the creation of **all** over which **the Son** was established **heir**, but **all** included not only substance and material; the first of God's creation was light, which was separated from darkness to begin units of time. The author here chose to emphasize the temporal sequence, the periods or **ages** ranging from Adam until Christ. It was **through a Son** that he **made the ages**, putting them **in order** (Heb 11:3). **The Son** was the Father's legal agent **through whom** the Father **made the ages**. The author knew the difference between a world and an **age.** When he spoke of **the foundation of the world** he did not use the term *aye-óhn*. He used the Greek word *káws-maws* (κόσμος) (Heb 4:3). This is the term he would have used if he had meant "world" in Heb 1:2. Weiss also noticed the problem with the translation "worlds." Weiss said,

> The plural *aionen* would in this sense then certainly not include so much a stack of world substances piled up on top of one another, but rather the course of time.[1]

[3]*Who, being a reflection of the glory.* The subject of this clause changed from the earlier clause. There, God was the subject, and Jesus was the object. Here Jesus (the Son) was the subject of the clause. It was after God had made Jesus the **heir** that he became **the reflection of the glory**. **The glory** refers to the legal presence of the Lord, usually identified either with the chest which held the contract,[2] with the column of fire or smoke over the altar, or the altar itself. After the tragedy of Israel's

---

[1] H. F. Weiss, *Der Brief an die Hebräer* (Göttingen: Vandenhoeck & Ruprecht, 1991), p 143.

[2] This has usually been called the "ark of the covenant," using sixteenth century words. In twentieth century American, an "ark" is a chest or a box, and a "covenant" is either a treaty or a contract. Therefore this chest which held the written contract between the Lord and his people is called the chest which held the contract.

defeat by the Philistines, one of Eli's daughters-in-law named her newly born son **The glory has departed**, because **The glory has departed from Israel, for the chest of God has been captured** (1Sam 4:21-22).[1] In Ezekiel's vision the comment was made of the area over the altar, **Such was the appearance of the likeness of the glory of the Lord** (Ezek 1:28). In a vision, Ezekiel saw **the glory** of God move from the temple eastward, presumably toward Babylon where the people were (Ezek 11:23). **The glory** of God was seen in the smoke pouring out from the tent of meeting where the Lord dwelt as he tented in the midst of his people. There the Israelites saw his **glory** (*dóx-ah*, δόξα), which was compared to **the glory** of [**the**] **only one from** [**the**] **Father** (John 1:14). God's presence is here identified with his legal agent, the Son, who was therefore **the glory.**

And a stamp of his nature. This phrase is the second part of the couplet. The author wanted to express the same truth by saying **stamp of his nature** as he had said by **reflection of his glory.** Here it is **the Son** who, as God's legal agent, is **a stamp of** God's **nature**. Those who saw **the Son,** therefore, legally saw the Father (John 14:9). Hebrews also considered Jesus a **reflection of the glory** which meant the same as being a **stamp of his nature**. Both of these things happened because God had made Jesus the **heir**, God's **Son,** and legal agent. In these few verses the author referred to Jesus as

> **the Son,**
> **the heir,**
> **the reflection of the glory**, and
> **the stamp of his nature.**

These were all appellations for Jesus as God's legal agent. This is one of the main points of the author's argument.

The Greek word for **stamp** comes from the verb *khah-ráh-sayn* (χαράσσειν), "to mark, engrave, or **stamp**." The **stamp**, accordingly, refers to the characteristic and distinctive form (2Macc 4:10). It was the equivalent to a signature, and it carried the authority of its owner. Isaac was claimed to have features (*zeév ee-kohn-eév*, זיו איקונין) like those of Abraham (GenR 21:2; 53 #7 [108c]). This does not mean either that Isaac was actually identical to Abraham or that Jesus was identical to God. Both were **reflections** and had both the characteristics and the legal standing of their fathers. Abraham was Isaac's father, physically, and God was Jesus' father, legally, but Isaac was to succeed Abraham as the *pater familias* of the family corporation, and Jesus was the legal agent of God. That which Jesus **stamped**, God **stamped.**

Jesus was the **son, heir,** and **apostle** of God (Heb 3:1). As apostle or agent he was sent with the full authority of the one who sent him. A man's agent is like the man himself, not *physically*, but *legally*. He has the power of attorney for the one who sent him. That which the apostle/agent does is done in behalf of, and has the approval and support of, the one who sent him. The agent has the authority of an ambassador who speaks in behalf of a king in negotiating for his country (mBer 5:5; LamR 1:18-19, #53; CantR 1:2, #3).[2] Jesus said that the one who received his

---

[1] For an examination of the historicity of this event see G. W. Ahlstroem, "The Travels of the Ark: A Religio-Political Composition," *JNES* 43 (1984):141-49.

[2] See K. H. Rengstorf, "Apostolos," *TWZNT* I, :406-48; R. M. Boyer, "God's Agent in the Fourth

apostles whom he had sent received Jesus himself, and not only Jesus, but the one who had sent him (Matt 10:40-42; John 13:20). This is true because legally a man's apostle is like the man himself.

The NT apostles were apostles of Jesus, and Jesus was an apostle of God. Against this background Jesus, in the same context, said, **He who has seen me has seen the Father** (John 14:9) and **the Father is greater than I** (John 14:28). *Legally* Jesus was identical with the Father, but *physically* the Father was greater. He was the principal and as such had greater status. Just as Christians thought of Jesus as an apostle of God, so Jews thought of Moses as the "apostle between Israel and their heavenly Father" (Sifrá b^{e}huqqotai *perek* 8:12; Lev 26:46). As the great apostle (*magnus nuntius*), Moses prayed "every hour, both day and night . . . to him who rules all the world" (Assump Mos 11:17). The law had come through Moses who received it from angels (Acts 7:38-39, 53; Gal 3:19; Jub 1.29; Ant 15.5, 3; PisiktaRab 21 [frequently]).

Samaritans also thought of Moses as their apostle of God: they called him a good apostle, a righteous apostle, an apostle of God, and the apostle of the True One whom God specially chose for apostleship. As apostle, he was also called "Son of the house of God," God's "man," "savior," "prophet," "faithful one," "crown of the righteous of the world," and "light of prophethood."

As an apostle, Moses was entrusted with the mysteries and honored in the things revealed. To Moses was revealed that which preceded creation and also that which follows the day of vengeance. To him was opened the gateway to the unseen. He had drawn near to the holy deep darkness where the Divine One was and had seen the wonders of the unseen (Memar Marqah 2:#12; 3:#6; 4:#4; 5:#3; 6:##3, 11). There are many biblical illustrations of apostolic authority: Jehu was ritually made king when Elisha sent one of the sons of the prophets to anoint him. It was not necessary for Elisha to anoint him himself for the anointing to be authoritative (2Kings 9:1-10). Paul sent a message to the Corinthians, giving them authority to deliver to Satan the man who had been living with his father's wife, because Paul was **with them in spirit**, meaning that his legal authorization was there (1Cor 5:1-5). Delivering him to Satan meant that they were ordered to expel him from the community.

Bearing everything by the word of his power. **Bearing everything by the word of his power** does not picture the Son playing the part of Atlas carrying the world on his shoulder, nor in the sense that God is the "sustainer of the world" or "age" (*soh-bayl oh-lam,* סובל עולם) (ExodR 64c, #36.4). Rather, as ambassador or apostle, the Son has authority over **everything** since he is given legal authority and is supported in everything he does **by the word of [God's] power**. He speaks for the One who sent him,[1] and his authority is as great as God's power. God is obligated by law to fulfill whatever he promises. An early Jewish Christian said that no one could see the **power** either of the Son or even of an angel (Hom 17:16). Both the angels and the Son have delegated **power**. God is the principal.

Gospel" (unpublished Th.M. thesis for Wesley Theological Seminary, 1965), summarized by P. Borgen, "God's Agent in the Fourth Gospel," in *Religions in Antiquity*, ed. J. Neusner (Leiden: E. J. Brill, 1968), pp. 137-48.

[1] *Contra* NEV, "Sustains the Universe." For other interpretations, see R. Williamson, *Philo and the Epistle to the Hebrews* (Leiden: E. J. Brill, 1970), pp. 96-97.

When he had made a purification for [his] crimes. The subject of this clause is still Jesus. It was Jesus, rather than God, who **made** the **purification.** The word here rendered **purification** could also mean "cleansing," but neither the cleansing nor the **purification** was the kind that could be done by washing, laundering, performing ablutions, or any kind of magic. The filth or dirt that had to be removed was crime, and it could be removed only by serving jail sentences, paying fines, being maimed, afflicted, or pardoned. The high priest could make an offering for **crimes,** but it would not be effective unless the criminals had first been reconciled to the people whom they had injured.

There are some textual variants related to the **purification**. Texts DP[46] add "through his" **purification**, and other texts have "through his own" **purification**. These are probably interpretative additions which understood Jesus' crucifixion as an offering for **crimes** intended to **cleanse** the community of its **crime**. The addition of "our" to **crimes** by some of the same texts makes this probability still greater. This is a normal interpretation of the later church that believed Jesus to be completely innocent of **crime** and was therefore defensive about anything that might imply **criminal** activity.

Legally, it did not make any difference whether or not there had ever been any **criminal** activity on Jesus' part. Once he had been cleansed he was innocent, and that was all that was necessary. He began his official task free from crime. The author of Hebrews seemed more interested in portraying Jesus as a king and high priest than in defending his original freedom from defilement, so he felt no difficulty either in composing a small verse of poetry or in using one that described **the Son** as a king who would be purified to be ritually undefiled before he ascended his throne where he could sit at God's "right hand." Once cleared, he was without **crime** (Heb 4:15).

Sat down at the right hand of the Majesty in exaltation. **The Majesty** is a substantive, meaning "**the majesty** of God." To avoid unnecessary possibilities for blasphemy, many Jews and Christians used such words as Heaven (Luke 15:18), **Power** (Matt 26:64), the Throne of **Majesty** (Heb 8:1), The Mighty One (2Bar 85:2, 3), The Place [where God dwells] (GenR 68c; ExodR 64a *et passim*, The Holy One blessed be He (GenR 68c; ExodR 64c), and other adjectives and descriptive expressions instead of the divine name. Most people in NT times did not have chairs on which to sit. Chairs and thrones were reserved only for special people of honor, like judges or kings. Others either **sat** or reclined on the floor or the ground.

In exaltation is not connected with **Majesty** but with the verb **he sat down**. Of course **the Majesty** was also in a position of exaltation, but the point of the statement is that the Son **sat down in exaltation at the right hand of the Majesty**. This is clear from the Psalm the author was interpreting. In the Psalm it was on the king's day of valor that the people volunteered in exultation rather than on Yehowah's day of valor. The reason the word "exultation" was not used at the beginning of the clause was that the author wanted to keep his quotations of Scripture intact. The Psalmist separated these two expressions, so the author of Hebrews did the same.

The enthronement Ps 110 was the primary text for the entire exposition, Heb1:1-12:29. Heb 1:3 set the stage for the rest of the document by this initial quotation. Both in Egypt and in Mesopotamia the king was a **son** of the deity.[1] Solomon was also known as the Son of God (2Sam 7:14). The king in Ps 110 **sat**

[1] S. Mowinckel, *The Psalms in Israel's Worship* (New York: Abingdon Press 1962) 2, p. 54.

down at the right hand of the Lord on the day of his **exaltation**, meaning the day of his anointing, enthronement, and coronation. The author of Hebrews wanted to identify Jesus with the king of Ps 110 so he alluded to that Psalm, using the very words, **sitting down**, **at the right hand**, and **exaltation**. As he did this he affirmed that Jesus, as the Son, was raised to the position of a king when **he sat down at the right hand of the Majesty**.

Greater than the angels. This reference to **angels** at the end of one paragraph is a connection word, introducing the subject of the next unit. There are many connection words in the Book of Hebrews that have been noticed by Vaganay,[1] Vanhoye,[2] and others. It is the first of many instances in which the author compared Jesus favorably to others whom Israelites thought to be **great.** In his judgment, Jesus was not only as **great** as the heavenly **angels,** but even **greater.** The word **greater** appears in the Book of Hebrews 13 times. It occurs only six times in all the rest of the NT. It reflects the many times the author compared Jesus with other important figures. Jesus was not one of the heavenly **angels**, but he was an agent of the Lord as some of them were. **Angels** were messengers, and they might be messengers of any kind,[3] depending on the will of the principal. They might simply carry messages, or they might be legal agents authorized to make judgments in the Lord's behalf. Some would be of one kind and some of another. Therefore Jesus had to be defended against all of the **angels**—even those of the highest rank. Medieval Jews thought that all Jews were greater than the ministering **angels**. One said,

> To tell of the greatness of the King of kings, the holy One blessed be He. Since he loves the Israelites more than the ministering angels, is it necessary to say [that he loves them] more than the Gentiles?[4]

All **angels** were messengers. They were designed to carry messages from one place to another and to fulfill distant assignments. They stood before the Lord, trembling. At the Lord's command they were changed to wind and fire (4Ezra 8:21-22). Some **angels**, however, were also apostles. They were legal agents and were empowered to act with authority. Jesus was an apostle of God (Heb 4:1). That meant he was commissioned to function with the authority of God. This, of course, meant that he had greater authority than **angels** who were not apostles and was even greater than the apostolic **angels** of highest rank.

He inherited a name. **Inherited** is the perfect tense, active voice of *klay-raw-naw-mayn*, which in normal Greek means "to obtain a lot or portion," "to be an heir." In Jewish and Christian thought forms, however, it has a wider meaning. The heirs **inherit** the land, the cities, eternal life, the Kingdom of God, the promises, and salvation. The verb *klay-raw-naw-máyn* (κληρονομεῖν) frequently renders the Hebrew *yah-ráhsh* (ירשׁ), a more active term, which means to take possession, dispossess, succeed. When the Hebrews **inherited** the Promised Land, they

---

[1] L. Vaganay, "Le Plan de l'Epitre aux Hébreux," *Mémorial Lagrange* (Paris, 1940), pp. 269-270.

[2] A. Vanhoye, *La Structure Littéraire de l'Epitre aux Hébreux* (Paris: Desclée de Brouwer, c1963), p. 34.

[3] See A. Bakker, "Was Christ an Angel? A Study of Early Christian Docetism," *ZNW* 32 (1933):255-265.

[4] Buchanan, *Revelation: Its Introduction and Prophecy* (Lewiston: Mellen, 1993), p. 534.

understood that God had allotted it to them, but they also dispossessed the Canaanites and took possession of their **inheritance** by military force. When Antiochus Epiphanes sacked Jerusalem, a Jewish author said of the siege: "They took women and children captive and they **inherited** (*ehk-lay-raw-náw-may-sahn*, ἐκληρονόμησαν) the cattle," which means they took them as plunder (1Macc 1:32; see also LXX 2Sam 7:1, quoted in 4Q Florilegium 1:7). Jesus, as **heir** (κληρονόμος) (Heb 1:2), was made possessor, administrator, or ruler over **all** (Heb 1:2).

A zealous Jew of pre-Christian times urged the Lord to raise up for Israel a king, who would cleanse Jerusalem from Gentiles, which meant driving the criminals out of the **inheritance** (PssSol 17:23-25). For him, as for others, the **inheritance** was the Promised Land which the Messiah was to reconquer and rule. Since his **inheritance** was associated with his sonship, which name he **inherited,** he was evidently made Son, heir, apostle, and high priest (Heb 1:2; 3:1; 5:10) all at once. In this context, the translation "acquired" or "obtained" would be proper for *kehk-lay-raw-náw-may-kehn* (κεκληρονόμηκεν) (Heb 1:4).

Among the Dead Sea scrolls is a collection of messianic passages (4Q Florilegium) which are closely related in subject matter to the first five verses of Hebrews. It contains three references to the expression **in the end of days** (*buh-ah-khah-reét hah-yah-meém*), similar to Heb 1:2. The Massoretic reading of 2Sam 7:1 is, **And the Lord gave him rest** (*hay-neé-akh lo* (הניח לו)) **from all his surrounding enemies**. LXX renders the verb **rest** by the Greek for **inherit. And the Lord made him heir** (*kah-teh-klay-raw-náw-may-sen*) **from all his surrounding enemies**. This adds significance to the words **heir** and **inherit** used by the author of Hebrews (Heb 1:2, 4). In 4Q Florilegium 1:7, the statement is given as a direct address to David from the Lord: "And where he said to David, **And I will give you [rest] from all your enemies."** In the same document is a quotation from 2Sam 7:14, also quoted in Heb 1:5: **I will establish the throne of his kingdom until the age [which follows]. I will be his Father and he will be my Son**. The commentator explained this to mean:

> He is the shoot of David (*tseh-mákh Dah-veéd*, צמח דויד) who stands with the interpreter of the Torah, who [. . .] in Zi[on in] the end of days . . . who will arise to save Israel (4QFlor 1:10-13).

The interpreter of the Torah was the Teacher of Righteousness, the priestly Messiah who was destined to be the high priest at the time the son of David was the royal Messiah.

Summary. This introduction was well written. It introduces a variety of contrasts to be developed throughout Heb 1:1-12:29; it briefly defines the nature of the main character of the exposition; and it supplies a neat transition clause to prepare the reader for the next immediate topic of discussion. The contrasts are between:

1) the ages of antiquity and the age of the author,
2) the fathers and the believers of the author's day, and
3) the prophets and the Son.

Early Jewish and Christian eschatology thought of time as a sequence of days, weeks, generations, or ages, following one another in a circle. When one day or age ended, the next began. There were six common days of labor each week before there was one holy day of **rest.** There were six common years of produce before the holy sabbath year when the land was to receive its year of rest. When one week was over (i.e., reached the end of its cycle) another began. The same was true of a cycle of years, Jubilees, or **ages.** The author of Hebrews thought of deliverance from Roman rule as the age of **rest.**[1] The days of the Messiah were to be those in which Israel gained its freedom, before the period of **rest** during which Israel, rather than Rome, would rule the world. Since Jesus was the Messiah, the author believed himself to be living at the **end** of the sixth **age**, just before the **age of rest**. The expression, **In the last of these days** (Heb 1:2), then, had the same meaning as "at the end of the ages" (Heb 9:26). The **ages** during which the gentiles ruled were the six "common" **ages** before the "holy" **age** of **rest.** The sixth **age** was the **age** or "day" of the Messiah which would come **at the end of the** [common] **ages.** This would be the time after the Messiah had "appeared" (Heb 9:26) and during which the author of Hebrews lived.[2] Rabbis said all the prophets prophesied only for the days of the Messiah (bShab 63a). The author of Hebrews considered Jesus to be the Messiah and the days of the Messiah to be **the last of these days** (Heb 1:2).

Gleason argued that Hebrews was written before the great war of 66-70 IA, when Jews depended heavily on military angels to defend them in war, especially the anticipated war against the Romans (Gal 3:19; Acts 7:38, 53; Ant 15:36; Deut 33:2). Since Jesus was the Messiah, **Son** of God, **Son** of man, and **son** of David, he could be expected to more successful in his militant rule than any of the military angels (Jer 23:5-6:4; Ezra 12:31-3; 13:29-38; Ps Sol 17:4-5, 21-46; 4QpIsa[a] 3:15-25; 4QFlor 17-13; Dan 7:13-14; 1Enoch 46-16; 62:3-11; 69:27-29).[3]

A less happy contrast between the earlier days and the days of the author is evident in the following poem,

> In earlier times and in generations of old
> our fathers had assistants
> --righteous men, prophets, and saints.
> Furthermore, we were in our own land,
> and they assisted us when we committed crimes,
> and they made intercession for us with him who made us,
> because they were confident in their works;
> and the Mighty One heard them
> and acted favorably toward us.
> But now the righteous ones are gathered
> and the prophets have died,
> and consequently we have left our land,

---

[1] The political nature of "rest" will be discussed in greater detail in chapters 3 and 4. C. Spicq, *L'Epitre aux Hebreux* (Paris: J. Gabalda, 1953), in two vols., I, p. 14, is not justified in making a contrast between the entrance into the Promised Land as the hope of the old contract and the entrance into the sabbatical rest (Heb 4:9) as the hope of the new contract. To be sure, the new contract was to be better than the old, but that was principally because it would be effective, whereas the old one was not. Like 2Isa (44:24-28; 49:6-26), the author of Hebrews had dreams of better things, but they were all centered around Jerusalem and Palestine.

[2] For a more detailed account of sabbatical eschatology, see Buchanan, *The Consequences of the Covenant* (Leiden: E. J. Brill, 1970), pp. 9-18.

[3] R. C. Gleason, "Angels and the Eschatology of Heb 1-2," *NTS* 49 (2003):90-107.

and Zion is removed from us.
Now we have nothing at all
but the Mighty One and his law (2Bar 85:1-3).

The tone is different from Hebrews, because 2Bar was written after the war with the Romans had been fought and lost. Michel has correctly called attention to the poetic nature of Heb 1:3 and related it to other poetry in Hebrews (Heb 4:12-13; 7:3).[1] Here the verse was suitably incorporated into the author's description of **the Son** and seems to have been composed originally as a praise to **the Son.** This poem was particularly useful to the author because it contained a quotation from the royal enthronement Ps 110, which provided the author with his primary text. Rabbis applied Ps 110:1 to Abraham, who was called "king" after he had been victorious over all the kings and was then invited to sit at the Lord's right hand (Ps 110). They also said it referred to the Messiah for whom a throne was prepared (Isa 16:5) and for whom the Lord would make war as he did when he made war for Israel against Pharaoh at the Red Sea (Yalqut HaMakiri Ps 110).

The author of Hebrews was interested in the royal enthronement character of Ps 110 because he wanted to present Jesus as a king. Like other kings, he held the position of favor with God **at the right hand** (Heb 1:3). Christians frequently confessed that Jesus held this place of honor and quoted Ps 110 to show it (Mark 12:36; Acts 2:32-36; Rom 8:34; Eph 1:20; Col 3:1; 1Pet 3:22. See also Mark 14:62; 16:19; Acts 7:56; 1Cor 15:25). Jesus, **the Son**, was a true replica of the Father, acted as his agent, and spoke with the authority of the Father. As king he had a special place of honor with the Father that was even greater than that of the angels. This last point was to receive further demonstration.

TEXTUAL DETAILS

The author's repetition begins already in Heb 1. The organization of Heb 1:5-13 follows a pattern similar to that of Heb 1:1-4

Heb 1:1-4	Heb 1:5-13
[1:2] Appointed royal heir	[1:5] Appointed as Son
[1:2] Mediator of the ages	[1:8] His throne is for ages
[1:3] Has complete authority	[1:12] Stable endurance
[1:3] Seated at God's right hand	[1:13] Seated at God's right hand

Heb 1:5-13 is a well structured argument, based on 7 FT texts, contrasting Jesus to **the angels**. This was done by first quoting a text that applied favorably to **the Son** and then another text that applied unfavorably to **the angels.** Over and over the expression, "He" or "it" says. The "He" was God, or the "It" was Scripture. The unit is enclosed as an *inclusio,* beginning with the testimony that God has made Jesus his **Son**, and closing with the invitation for **the Son** to sit at God's **right hand** [on the throne]. Swetnam holds that Heb 1:5-14 follows the pattern of an enthronement ceremony that involves exaltation, presentation, and enthronement.[2]

An *inclusio* is a literary form in which the beginning and ending have many of the same words, making the end sort of a summary. In between the beginning and

---

[1] O. Michel, *Der Brief an die Hebräer* (Göttingen: Vandenhoeck und Ruprecht, 1957), pp. 114-16.
[2] J. Swetnam, "Hebrews 1, 5-14: A New Look," *Melita Theologica* 51 (2000):51-68.

end is included the message, like the meat or cheese in a sandwich. This literary form shows the reader the extent of the unit.

TEXT

Hebrews	First Testament
[5]For to which of the angels has	[Ps 2:5-8]Then [Yehowah] will address them in his anger, / and frighten them with his wrath, / saying, "I have set my king on Zion, my holy hill. / I will tell the decree of
he ever **said**, **You are my son. Today I gave you birth**;	Yehowah [which is as follows]: He **said** to me, **You are my son. Today I gave you birth**. Ask of me, and I will make the nations your heritage, the ends of the earth, your possession."
and again,	[2Sam 7:13-14]He will build a temple to my name, and I will establish the throne of his kingdom until the age [that follows].
I will be his Father, and he will be my son	**I will be his Father, and he will be my son.**

COMMENTARY

To which of the angels? Both quotations in Heb 1:5 are related to kings who are called God's sons. They are parts of a rhetorical question, expecting a negative answer. It was as if it said, "He has never said to any **of the angels** . . ."

You are my Son. Today I gave you birth. The first quotation (Ps 2:7) is from an enthronement Psalm. It pictures the kings of surrounding nations plotting against the Lord and **his anointed one**, meaning his anointed king. While they were doing that, the Lord from heaven laughed and mocked them. In anger he informed them that he had set his king on Zion, his holy hill. It was of that anointed king that he said, **You are my Son, today I have given you birth** (Ps 2:7). The Lord had given **birth** to this adult male when he was already old enough to rule. He became God's son instantly by coronation, without any gestation period. This happened legally by the ceremony of coronation, just as Jesus became God's son instantly by the ceremony of anointing.

The Psalmist spoke of a legal birth that was not the king's infant birth from his mother. It was a legal birth from God. It happened on the very day of the coronation and **anointing.** There was no gestation period or feminine figure involved. This birth was strictly a legal, ceremonial one. The Lord promised his **anointed one** (*meh-sheé-ahkh-oh*, משיחו) (Ps 2:2) that he would make the nations his **heritage.** This **anointed** king would break those nations with a rod of iron, dash them into pieces like a pottery vessel (Ps 2:8-9). Then he would rule them all.

If the kings of the earth were wise, they would submit immediately and serve the Lord with trembling, which means they should surrender unconditionally at once to the new ruler whom the Lord appointed king over Zion. It is such a powerful king as this who is called God's **Son** and his **anointed one**. It is as a mighty king that he was enthroned to sit at God's **right hand.** As such a king he was called **Son**, which is a **greater** name than any of the **angels** had acquired. The rabbis listed together Ps 2:7-8, Ps 110:1, and Dan 7:13-14. The first two references are enthronement Psalms, and the third pictures one like a **Son** of man receiving the dominion, glory, and a kingdom while other nations were made subject to him. Rabbi Yudan said these were all promises which the Lord would fulfill for the Messiah (Mid Ps 2 #9). This means that the rabbis considered the Messiah to be a king, **Son** of God, and **Son** of man. In Matt 16:17, 20, 27, Jesus was identified with the Messiah, **Son** of the living God, and **Son** of man (see also Matt 26:63).[1]

The words rendered **his** and **my** are literally "to him" and "to me," as the RSV renders. The Greek is a literal rendering of the Hebrew *loh luh-ahv . . . lee luh-ben* (לו לאב . . . לי לבן). The *luh* in each case might be rendered "as" or "for." In this case, God would act as a father in relationship to a son. The relationship of Jesus to God was certainly not understood by the author of Hebrews to be a physical relationship, whatever translation be accepted. For other examples of this kind of Semitism see Matt 19:5; Mark 10:8; Luke 3:5; 1Cor 6:16; 2Cor 6:18; Eph 5:31; Heb 8:10; James 5:3.

The second quotation (2Sam 7:14) also refers to Solomon in anticipation of his position as king over the united monarchy of Israel. Through Nathan, God promised David that God would establish Solomon on the throne, and he, as king over Israel, would be God's **Son** and God would be his father (see also 1Chron 17:13). Physically he would still be David's son, but legally, he would become God's **Son.** The kingdom over which Solomon would rule would be the kingdom of the Lord (1Chron 28:5). The king was evidently believed to be in close relationship to the Lord. He was called God's **Son;** he ruled over Israel, Yehowah's kingdom, and **sat** on Yehowah's throne (1Chron 29:23). This further illustrates the significance of the name which Jesus inherited when he was called **Son.** As **Son** he was the Messiah who was **anointed** to be king over the kingdom of Yehowah. This has important implications which will receive further attention as Jesus' role is interpreted according to the author of Hebrews.

Legal Transformation. A king was, in the judgment of his citizens, physically born as an infant human being, but, as an adult, he became **anointed**, crowned, or consecrated all in one day, as a legal identity. Yehowah was known as a masculine deity, and in the physical sphere males do not **give birth**, but this was his legal or second **birth.** It was as a legal agent that the king could be free from **criminal** guilt. The legal agent speaks and acts at the responsibility of the principal. Since God was the principal, the legal agent of the deity was innocent of **crime.** He spoke and acted in behalf of the deity and at the deity's responsibility. The agent himself was innocent. As agents, kings had divine rights. When Rothair was king of the Lombards (beginning 636 IA), his code held that the king could do no wrong. If he decreed that someone should receive the death penalty, that person was unquestionably guilty.[2] It was the king's office that was divine. This attitude toward public office is at least as

---

[1] See S. Mowinckel, *He that Cometh*, tr. G. W. Anderson (New York: Abingdon, 1954), pp. 123, 157-59.

[2] K. F. Drew (tr.), *The Lombard Laws* (Philadelphia: University of Pennsylvania Press, 1973), pp. 17, 53.

old as the fifteenth century BIA. At that time an Egyptian vizier told of his ordination:

> My abilities were not as they had been: my yesterday's nature had altered itself, since I had come forth in the accoutrements [of the vizier, having been promoted] to the Prophet Maat.[1]

This was a legal transformation or recreation that came with his office as the highest judge in the land. It was not the vizier's physical health or strength that had suddenly improved. It was his legal authority. English jurists have followed a logic similar to that of the Egyptian vizier when they held that a king had two bodies--one a natural body and the other a legal body. In the time of Henry VI the English said Henry VI was no longer the same person as he had been before the coronation. This ceremony transformed him.

> As the reason thereof is, because the Body natural and the Body politic are consolidated into one, and the Body politic wipes away every Imperfection of the other Body, with which it is consolidated, and makes it to be another Degree than it should be if it were alone by itself.[2]

Using other words, the jurists argued that the king had become a new creature, legally, when he received the crown. He might also have been said to have been born again, legally. Like high priests and Jesus, Henry VI was legally free from Crime. Crime was one of the imperfections that had been wiped away by the legal body politic. As the highest judge in the land he had authority to pardon any offenses that might once have been attributed to him.

Among the Dead Sea Scrolls there is a document giving the protocol for the banquet which included the men of the council, "if [God] **gives birth** to (*yoh-leéd*, יוליד) the Messiah" (1QSa 2:11-12). Of course, Jews of NT times would have believed that God was the creator who created the Messiah as a human being in the first place, but he would not have created him full grown and trained for rulership. This document was referring to the establishment of the Messiah by anointing some qualified Jew who was already an adult of the proper age for messiahship (age 30-50).[3] **Giving birth** meant that this Jew would be **born** again, legally, at that banquet. This **birth** took place during a legal ceremony when a priest poured oil over his head, not as a physical **birth** from his mother's womb.

Like the Egyptian citizen who became a vizier, when this Jew would be **born** legally his nature would change; his abilities would be different; and he would become a new creature, an anointed king of Israel, even though he would be the same as he was before anointing, physically. He would have the same appearance, the same deformities, the same height and weight as he had before he was "**born** again." It was his status and authority that was changed at his re**birth**.[4] At his legal

---

[1] J. A. Wilson, "The Vizier of Egypt," J. Pritchard, *Ancient Near Eastern Texts* (Princeton: Princeton U. Press, 1969), p. 213.

[2] Plowden, *Reports*, 238. Taken from E. H. Kantorowicz, *The King's Two Bodies* (Princeton: Princeton U. Press, 1957), p. 11, fn. 9.

[3] Buchanan, "The Age of Jesus," *NTS* 41 (1995):297.

[4] See further Buchanan, *Biblical and Theological Insights from Ancient and Modern Civil Law*

birth he became a creature above the law. As a monarch he was the highest judge of the land. No one could take him to court and accuse him of any **crime.** Therefore he was free from **crime** or guilt.

According to the Gospel of John, Jesus told the Pharisee, Nicodemus, that he had **to be born again** if he wanted to see **the Kingdom of God.** Both Jesus and Nicodemus knew it was not possible to be **born again** physically, but **the birth** of which Jesus spoke was being **born** of the water and of the Spirit. This required a *legal* ceremony that changed the person's identity, legally. To become a follower of Jesus Nicodemus would have to be baptized (the water) and legally confirmed (the spirit). Legal birth required legal ceremonies. Since Nicodemus had already been circumcised he was not required to fulfill that obligation. Legally it is possible to **be born** when one is old. Physically, Nicodemus was probably **born** into a Pharisaic home, but legally he could become **born again** as a follower of Jesus (John 3:1-5).

Proselytes. Every proselyte into Judaism was **born again** and began life anew as a child **born** that day (Gerim 2:5; bYeb 48b). This second **birth,** of course, was a legal **birth.** At Sinai all Israel was made anew like a child **born** that day. At that time the people made a contract with the Lord, and they became a new nation as parties to that legal contract. As a member of that legal body or corporation, Israel became a new creature (CantR 8:2, 5).

This took place because Israelites entered the legal process of becoming parties to a contract with the Lord by which they agreed to become his people, and he agreed to become their God. In NT times those who joined mysteries or other pagan sects, such as the Pythagoreans,[1] said that they had been **born again.** Also those who joined the Christian Church were said to have been re**born** or to have become new creatures. When the Vizier said that his nature had changed by his legal installation he used the same basic thought forms in relationship to his installation as Christians, Jews, and other Greek, Roman, and Oriental cults and sects employed in relationship to their initiations, which they considered second **birth** and through which they became new creatures. The rhetorical ceremonies by which people were **born again** were widely known and practiced in the ancient Near East and some of them are still practiced today.

Adoptions and Marriages. Physically, children are usually **born** in homes or hospitals, in Western society, but they can be **born again** in court rooms while being **adopted** by new parents. They are all physically born from females, but they can be legally adopted by males. Those installed or ordained into new families or professions become new creatures, legally. They are not the same as before; they have new obligations, rights, identity, and authority. This does not change them physically. They still have the same intellectual capacities, the same ages, and the same physical ailments and appearances. The ceremony or contract that brings about this change is only a legal change, but it is important. Just as legal **birth** can take place in a court room, it may also take place in a church or a synagogue where legal changes occur by people joining new legal bodies or becoming legally adopted into new families.

(Lewiston:Mellen, c1992), pp. 13-17.

[1] Lucian, *Bion Praxis* 2 used the term *anabionai palin* as the idiom used by the Pythagoreans. For the Mysteries see F. Cumont, *After Life in Roman Paganism* (New York: Dover Publications, c1952), pp. 34, 119. Early scribes used the term *inaeternum renatus* to describe the results of initiation into mysteries.

Until recently a wedding, which could occur either in a church or a court setting, involved the legal adoption and rebirth of the bride into a family to which she had not been physically **born.** Still today 83% of all married American women change their names and become born again members of their husband's families. They are called legal or "in law" members of the new families into which they have been legally born. In antiquity wives were legally divorced from the family into which they had been born, and their children were not considered extensions of the wives parental family trees. Before the wedding ceremonies wives were under the control of their fathers. After the ceremonies wives were under the control of their husbands, who were legally their new fathers. The ceremonies involved the women receiving new rings and new names, identifying their legality to new families.

In a coronation, the deity was believed to **adopt** the king as his or her son. When a new king was established, crowned, and enthroned at Jerusalem, he was adopted as God's **Son**, but this was a legal birth rather than a physical birth. Physically, a male deity does not "bear" sons; a female deity, or goddess, would do that, but legally the deity gives the new king second **birth** as one who is "holy from the womb," even though he had lived up to that time without being God's son. That was the day of his valor, the time when the people voluntarily gave him their support.

It is clear that the FT passage from 2Sam refers to David's first successor on the throne, Solomon. It is also evident that the author of 4Q Flor expected a messiah from the son of David to fulfill this promise, and some scholars just assume that the author of Hebrews also expected a Davidic messiah when he used the same FT quotation.[1] There is no direct evidence, however, that the author of Hebrews interpreted Jesus as belonging to the family of David, and there is very little indirect evidence that might even point in that direction. The author of Hebrews never mentioned David in relationship to Jesus or the Messiah. He portrayed a messiah who was a priest-king, which David and his successors certainly were not; but some Hasmoneans were, and the priest-king described in Hebrews resembles that type of messianic expectation much more closely than any messiahs from the families of David or Aaron. Hebrews understood Jesus to be both king and priest not by virtue of his priestly birth, but by virtue of scriptural authority and rhetorical logic.

TEXT

Hebrews	*First Testament and parallels*
6 And again, when he led his **first born** into the age, he said,	Ps 89:28 I will make him my **first born**, the highest of the kings of the earth.
"Now let all the angels **of God prostrate themselves before him**."	LXX Deut 32:42-43 Rejoice with him, Heavens! **and let all the** sons **of God prostrate themselves before him.**
	4QDeut 32 **All gods prostrate themselves before him.**
	Ps 97:7 **All gods prostrate themselves before him**

[1] F. F. Bruce, "'To the Hebrews' or 'To the Essenes'?" *NTS* 9 (1962/63):221.

COMMENTARY

His first born. The psalmist called David God's **first born. David** was not Jesse's **first born.** Instead, he was the youngest of Jesse's family, but legally he became God's **first born** at the time he was anointed. The term **first born** was a title given to the Messiah or the king. The Messiah was not Adam. He was not the **first born**, physically. Many people had been **born** before Jesus, but the **first born** of a family had a unique status, and it was this special status that was given to Jesus. It was given to him when he was anointed. It was not a physical description, but a legal title. An early Christian creed confessed that Jesus was the head of the church, the **first born** from the dead (Col 1:18; Rev 1:5). In a family corporation, the **first born** was the oldest male member. He was the one who would be the chief and *pater familias.* The chief of the nation, then, would also be the **first born**, even though, like David, he was the last one to have been physically **born** of the family of Jesse. Commenting on **Israel, my first born son** (*beh-koh-reé*, בכורי) (Exod 4:22), rabbis said,

> Thus I shall make the king Messiah [the] **first born**, as it is said, **Also I will give him** [the title of] **first born** (Ps 89:27 [28]; ExodR 37b, 13:1, 19-7).

Zechariah promised that a man whose name was **shoot** (*tse-máhk,* צמח) would build the temple of the Lord, bear the royal honor, and rule upon his throne (Zech 6:12-13). Philo, commenting on LXX rendering for **shoot**, which is "rising" (*ah-nah-toh-lay,* Ἀνατολή) (Zech 6:12), said,

> For this man [*Anatolay*] is the oldest son, whom the Father of all raised up (*ah-néh-tay-leh,* ἀνέτειλε), whom he elsewhere called **first born** (*proh-táw-gaw-nawn,* προτόγονον) (*Confusion of Tongues* 14.62-63).

The various titles that could be applied to the Messiah who was expected to rule Israel from Jerusalem seem to have been widely known in Jewish and Christian circles. He was referred to as **the Son, first born, heir, shoot/rising,** and by other titles that appear further on in the Book of Hebrews.

Pseudo-Clement observed that certain countries had their own names for kings:--Arsaces for the Persians, Caesar for the Romans, and Pharaoh for the Egyptians—"So with the Jews a king is called Christ" (Recog 1:45). Some of these messianic titles could be used in public without non-Jews realizing that they referred to an anticipated military leader, promised in the Scriptures. It seems to have been an acceptable practice for Jews to attribute to the Messiah passages that originally had different subjects or objects in mind. The rabbinic rule of rhetoric that allowed this was: "All prophecy is prophesied only for the days of the Messiah."

The age. The Syriac translated *oi-koo-méh-nay* (οἰκουμένη), *ahl-máh* (עלמא), **the age. The age** to come is also rendered *tayn oi-kou-méh-nayn tayn-méh-loo-sahn* (τὴν οἰκουμένην τὴν μέλλουσαν, in Greek.[1] The Syrian rendering is *ahl-*

[1] Weiss, *Hebräerbrief*, p.163, also noticed that the age mentioned here is the same as the age to come,

máh dah-teéd עלמא דעתיד--**The age which is destined [to come]**. The *ahl-máh* in Syriac was the *oh-láhm* (עולם) in Hebrew. It did not refer to a place but a time period. **The age** into which the Messiah was introduced was **the age** to come, the messianic **age, the age** when foreign rule would cease and Jews would be independent on the Promised Land. It referred to a future *time*. It did not refer to a *place* in heaven. The word *oik-oo-méh-nay* (οἰκουμένη) in Greek is used only twice in the entire document of Hebrews (Heb 1:6; 2:5), and in both places the Syriac renders it by **age.** The context requires that the meaning is not the entire civilized world but either the area ruled by the Messiah or the time at which the Messiah rules over Palestine.

The Greek word, *oi-koo-méh-nay,* sometimes refers to the entire civilized world or the inhabited area. In LXX, *oi-koo-méh-nay* is used to describe the world which God created (LXX Pss 23:1; 88:12; 89:2; 92:1; Jer 10:12; 28:15). In a midrash on Lev 26:33 3Isa promised the Jews in Babylon:

Leviticus 26:33	Isaiah 62:4
Your land will become **desolate** (*shah-máh*, שממה); and your cities will become a **desert** (*khahr-báh*, חרבה).	You will no longer be called **deserted** *ah-zoo-váh* (עזובה), and **your land will** not be called **desolate** (*shah-máh*, שממה), but you will be called "my desire is in it," and **your land** [will be called] "inhabited" *(buh-oo-láh*, בעולה, because Yehowah desires you, and your land will be inhabited (*tee-bah-áyl*, תבעל).

Second Isaiah said,

> You will no longer be called **deserted**
> (*kah-tah-leh-lay-méh-nay*, Καταλελειμμένη)
> and **your land will** not be called **a desert** (*éh-ray-mos*, ἔρημος);
> for you shall be called "my will" (*thél-ay-mah eh-mon*, θέλημα ἐμόν),
> and your land, "inhabited" (*oi-koo-méh-nay,* οἰκουμένη) (LXX Isa 62:4).

MT of the last half of this verse says, **For you shall be called, "My desire is in it"** (*khahf-tsy-bah*, חפצי בה), **and your land "inhabited,"** *buh-oo-láh* (בעולה).[1] This last Hebrew word can mean "administer," "marry," "rule," "be a lord," "be a husband," or "be inhabited." MT follows this verse with **For just as a young man marries a virgin, so your sons will marry you** (Isa 62:5), taking *buh-oo-lah* to mean "married." The contract made with God was a marriage contract, so this statement was made to remind the people that God would give them a new contract and again restore them to the land. LXX rendered this term by the Greek *oi-koo-méh-nay*, which can mean "adminstered," "inhabited," or "the civilized world." He obviously took it to mean an inhabited place where people could live, because he translated Isa 62:5 by **For just as a young man lives together with a virgin, so your sons will live with you** (LXX Isa 62:5).

---

mentioned in Heb 2:5.

[1] From this we get the English translation "Beulah land," pointing the text *buh-yoó-lah*.

In Leviticus the land that was prophesied to be left desolate and the cities that were to be abandoned were the land of Palestine and its cities. Both in the LXX and the MT of Isa 62, the same land was involved, but instead of being left desolated it was to be God's will or desire, and it was to be inhabited. The context rebels against rendering the *oi-koo-meh-nay* being considered the entire civilized world, as has often been mistakenly thought.

In the Lev and Isa context, the *oi-koo-méh-nay* appears to mean the Promised Land to which the Jews expected to return when released from "captivity" in Babylon. Its capital city was Jerusalem or Zion (Isa 62:1). Vanhoye said,

> *Kosmos* designates the visible, material world; *oikoumene* evokes a spiritual reality--the world of relationships among persons.[1]

Whenever the Lord ruled over Palestine, Israel had a king and was free from foreign rule.[2] Enthronement Pss were sung when kings were installed,[3] and Yehowah ruled when Israel's king ruled. When in the inhabited place the world situation was **set straight**, from Israel's point of view, the Lord ruled (Ps 96[95]:10) and judged the *oi-koo-méh-nay* (Ps 96[95]:13). In contrast to desolation was the Lord's will, and in contrast to wilderness was the *oi-koo-méh-nay* (Isa 62:4).

When the Lord's salvation shone forth (Isa 62:1), the wilderness became an *oi-koo-méh-nay*. The "world" which early Jews called *oi-koo-méh-nay* seemed to have existed whenever the *kosmos* was under God's rule or administration. At such a time, God's kingdom would have come, and he would establish a king on the throne of Zion. This is just another way of saying he would lead his first born into the *oi-koo-méh-nay*. Such an understanding of *oi-koo-méh-nay* as this would be consistent with the scriptural passages cited earlier in relationship to the Son and also to the text cited in the next verse.

Grässer acknowledged that *oi-koo-méh-nay* normally refers to a place where people live on earth, but he never-the-less related it as a synonym for :

1) the heavenly fatherland,
2) the future city, and
3) heavenly Jerusalem.[4]

Schenck followed the same vein. He admitted that the term meant an "earthly, human civilization," and that it

> Clearly refers to the coming world as an οἰκουμένη, but it ignores the author's frequent use of imagery that points toward the heavenly realm as the true homeland of God's people (Heb 11:13-16; 13:14), the true promised land.[5]

---

[1] A. Vanhoye, "L'oikoumene dans l'epitre aux Hebreux," *Biblica* 45 (1964):248-53. See also G. Johnston, "OIKOUMENH and KOSMOS in the NT," *NTS* 10 (1963/64):253-54.

[2] Buchanan, *Consequences*, pp. 60-62

[3] S. Mowinckel, *Psalms* I, p. 125.

[4] E. Grässer, *An die Hebräer* (Zurich: Benziger Verlag, c1990) 1, pp. 77, 79.

[5] Schenck, "A Celebration," p. 478.

Heb 11:13-16 refers to the homeland the patriarchs traveled to find, which was not heaven, but Palestine. Heb 13:14 describes the situation of Jesus' crucifixion, outside the gate of Jerusalem, which, according the author of that passage, was not the Christian's lasting city. This is in conflict with the conviction of the author of Heb 1-12, who thought of Jerusalem as a "heavenly city." The two references Schenk offered do not constitute the "frequent" use of the heavenly imagery Schenk claimed were present in the text. In fact they do not provide any examples of heavenly imagery at all.

Angels of God. Heb 1:5-6 forms a small, well organized argument. It begins with the angels and concludes with the angels, with the main point placed in the center—the Son. Vanhoye has noted the further concentration of the emphasis on the Son as follows:

Son   a Son
my   my
are   will be
you   he.[1]

TECHNICAL DETAILS

The quotation from Deut is not exactly like any text extant today. There are enough variants, however, to allow the possibility that the author had access to still others. The following editions of Deut 32:43 are available today:[2]

Qumran Cave 4 (4Q)	Masoretic Text (MT)
1 **Praise his people**, *heavens.,*	1 **Praise his people**, *nations*
(and prostrate yourselves before him, all gods;)	
2 **for he avenges the blood of his** *sons*	3 **for he avenges the blood of his** *servants*
4 **and returns vengeance on his adversaries**	**and returns vengeance on his adversaries**
5 (and pays back those who hate him,)	
6. **and he atones for the land of his people.**	6 **and atones for the land of his people.**

The Septuagint

1. Rejoice, *Heavens*, with him (*háh-mah ow-tóh*, ἅμα αὐτῷ)
2. and let all the *sons of God* prostrate themselves before him;
3. rejoice, *nations*, with his people,
4. and let all *the angels of God* strengthen him,
5. because the blood of his *sons* will be avenged

---

[1] A. Vanhoye, *La Structure littéraire de L'Epitre aux Hebreux* (Paris: Desclee de Brouwer, c1963), p. 70. His illustration is in Greek.

[2] See P. W. Skehan, "A Fragment of the 'Song of Moses' (Deut 32) from Qumran," *BASOR* 136 (1954):12-15. For a different conjecture of the relationship of these texts, see F. M. Cross, Jr., *The Ancient Library of Qumran and Modern Biblical Studies* (Garden City: Doubleday, 1958), pp. 135-37.

6. and he will avenge and pay back justice against his enemies.
7. He will pay back those who hate him,
8. and the Lord will cleanse the land of his people (LXX Deut 32:43).

The question is, how did these texts become so variant? Some conjectures are more likely than others. Since this is a poem, it is more likely that lines two and five of the 4Q text belonged to the original poem, providing parallels for the lines preceding. The Proto-Masoretic text may have contained these lines which some scribe omitted because they were redundant. It would be only an arbitrary guess to select whether "heavens" was more or less original than "nations," or "sons" than "servants." It seems likely, however, that the editor of this LXX passage had access to both the 4Q text and the Proto-Masoretic text, and that he quoted lines one and two from the 4Q text and lines three and four of the Proto-MT. In the 4Q text, line one, there are two objects: "Heavens" (*shah-máh-yim,* שמים) and "his people" (*ahm-móh* עמו). If it were not for the parallel with Deut 32:1, one might render this passage either "Praise his people, Heavens" or "Praise Heaven (= God), his people."

LXX understood God as the object of praise and rendered *ahm-óh* (עמו [his people]) as if it were pointed *eém-moh* (אמו [with him]) and awkwardly translated it "with him" (line 1) and "with his people" (line 3). The version of the 4Q text used by LXX apparently read "sons of God" (*beh-náy ay-leém,* בני אלים) rather than "gods" (*ay-leém,* אלים). LXX, line six, is evidently an abbreviation of lines four and five of the 4Q text, and LXX, line seven, is a similar abbreviation of lines four and five of the unabbreviated MT. LXX translator and editor apparently did not want to choose between the two variants, so instead he included both, first lines one and two of 4Q and then the same two lines of Proto-MT. His line five agrees with 4Q, line three, which was so similar to the Masoretic text, line three, that he did not quote the variant. Then, in the same sequence, he abbreviated first 4Q, lines four and five, into his line six and then Proto-Masoretic text, lines four and five, into his line seven. Since there was no variant between 4Q and MT, line six, he quoted the line only once into his line eight, as he had done with 4Q and MT, line three.

The author of Hebrews may either have used only LXX and put the verb of line two into line four, or he may have had access to a variant that is no longer extant in which line two read "angels of God" instead of "gods" (4Q) or "sons of God" (LXX version of 4Q). These terms are sufficiently close in meaning to have been interchangeable. Perhaps one was substituted for the other in the course of transmission. One of these substitutions may have been made by the author of Hebrews. Angels were also called sons of God (Gen 6:4; Pss 29:1; 89:7; Job 1:6; 2:1; 38:7).

In the Hebrew texts of Deut 32:43, the object of adoration was probably intended to be **his people**, with the **Heavens**, **nations**, **gods**, **sons of God** or **angels of God** doing the worshiping. LXX translator understood God to be the object of worship throughout. He was probably dissatisfied with the theology that suggested any object of worship other than God, so he understood *ahm-óh* to be pronounced and pointed *eém-oh*. This could easily have occurred as the result of a pronunciation error in dictation. The author of Hebrews seems to have used either the Hebrew text similar to 4Q or a different LXX translation of that text, because he was able to change the object to **first born.** It is easily understandable for a scribe to have changed **his people** to **his firstborn**, because Israel, God's people, was called the **first born** (Exod 4:22). The next transfer involved understanding the **first born** to mean the Messiah rather than Israel. Since it was understood also that all the prophets prophesied only for the time of the Messiah, this was a normal interpretation. The text followed here is in agreement with that of Cockerill.[1]

TEXT

Hebrews	First Testament
[7]Now [with reference] to the angels, it says,	[Ps 104:3-4][Yehowah is One] who makes clouds his chariot, who walks on the wings of the wind,
Who makes his angels winds, his ministers, flames of fire;	**who makes winds his angels, flames of fire, his ministers**
[8]but [with reference] to the Son, [it says],	
Your throne, God, is for the age of the age and **the staff of justice is the staff of his kingdom**.	[Ps 45:7]**Your throne, God, is for the age and until** [the next age], **the staff of justice is the staff of his kingdom**

COMMENTARY

Now with reference to the angels. The Greek for [**with reference**] **to the angels** is *pros . . . toos ang-géh-loos* (πρὸς . . . τοὺς ἀγγέλους), literally **to . . . the angels**, but this makes no sense. The message was not *to* the angels but *about* them. Therefore the *pros* (πρός) might be understood as a Semitism, representing the *luh* (ל) used to mean "with regard to," **with reference to**, or "in respect to." When Abimelech finally learned that Sarah was Abraham's wife and called Abraham to account, Abraham admitted, **I said to her [Sarah], "This is a kindness you must do with me: at every place where we come, *say about me*** (*eem-reé lee*, אמרי לי), **'He is my brother'"** (Gen 20:13). LXX renders these pertinent words, **tell me** (*áy-pon eh-meh*, εἰπὸν ἐμέ), a literal rendering, which, like **to . . . the angels** (Heb 1:7), makes no sense. The translator missed the significant meaning of this Hebrew preposition.

Of King Solomon it is reported, **Now King Solomon became greater than all the kings of the world *with respect to wealth and wisdom*** (*luh óh-sher oo-luh-kháwkh-mah*, לעשר ולחכמה, 1Kings 10:23). The intention of this sentence was not that King Solomon become greater . . . to wealth and wisdom any more than Abraham ordered Sarah to "tell" him. The preposition here must be understood to mean **in respect to**.[2] These examples show both the force of the Hebraism and the way in which this meaning could be obscured or overlooked. But it is not only in a Semitic type of Greek that *pros* can bear this force. In classical Greek, as well, *pros* can mean "in relation to," "according to" "**with reference to**."[3] Hence there is no difficulty with the translation given here.[4]

---

[1] G. L. Cockerill, "Hebrews 1:6: Source and Significance," *Bulletin for Biblical Research* 9 (1999); 51-64.

[2] See further *Gesenius' Hebrew Grammar*, ed. and enlarged by E. Kautzsch, rev. and tr. A.E. Cowley (Oxford: Clarendon Press, 1910), pp. 381-82, 458.

[3] W. W. Goodwin, *Greek Grammar*, rev. C. B. Gulick (New York: Ginn and Co., 1930), p. 260.

[4] See also RSV, Moffatt, *Hebrews*, p. 11; B. F. Westcott, *The Epistle to the Hebrews* (London:

The subject represented by the supplied pronoun "it" is "the Scripture" which *says* the quotation given. The author used the quotation because it helped him to depreciate the angels, which he was comparing unfavorably to the Son. Had he chosen not to accept different primary and secondary objects, as many scholars do today, the FT passage would have defeated his purpose.

He makes his angels winds. Ps 104 portrayed God in his greatness, forming all creation and using it according to his will. He stretched out the heavens, laid the beams of his chambers on the waters, and made the clouds his chariot (Ps 104:2-3). In this context, it seems most likely that the passage quoted should read:

> **He makes winds his messengers**
> **flames of fire, his ministers** (Ps 104:4).

Since there are two objects in each line,[1] however, it is not certain whether God **makes winds his messengers** or **his messengers, winds**; **flames of fire, his ministers** or **his ministers, flames of fire**. Although most scholars think God used **winds** and **fire** for his **messengers** and **ministers,**[2] there are some who prefer the opposite reading, as the author of Hebrews did. Stuart paraphrased,

> Who maketh his angels that serve him the ministers of his will, as the winds and lightning are?[3]

Turner argued,

> It is undeniable that the . . . view given in the epistle is at least as much if not more in keeping with the general representation.[4]

A modification of the position taken by the author of Hebrews is the targum on the passage, which reads, **Who makes his messengers** swift as **the wind, his ministers** mighty as **flaming fire** (Targ Ps 104.4). In an ancient prayer in Latin text, the Lord is described as One before whom a trained group of angels (*exercitur angelorum)* stand trembling (*cum tremore*), and at whose word they are changed into wind and **fire** (*in ventum et agnem convertuntur*) (4Ezra 8:21-22). R. Helbo claimed that the Holy One, blessed be He, creates a new company of angels every day, who sing for him and then depart (GenR 32:27; 78.1). Baruch said that the power of God's word was so great that he commanded **flames** and they changed into **wind** (2Bar 48:8).

The Greek word for **angels** means "messengers." Any human being who ran an errand was considered an **angel**. **Angels** of the Lord, of course, could be heavenly beings, but those assigned to running errands were never given administrative power. They were responsible for carrying out orders, not for giving them. The Greek word for **ministers** is *lay-toor-goi* (λειτουργοί) from the words *láy-tos*

Macmillan and Co., 1892), p. 24; C. J. Vaughan, *The Epistle to the Hebrews* (London: Macmillan and Co., 1890), p. 15.

[1] As in LXX Deut 32:43 quoted in 1:6.

[2] M. Dahood, *Psalms* III (Garden City: Doubleday, 1970), pp. 31, 35.

[3] M. Stuart, *Commentary on the Epistle to the Hebrews* (Andover: Warren F. Draper, 1828), p. 55.

[4] Turner, *Hebrews*, p. 35. See also C. A. and E. G. Briggs, *A Critical and Exegetical Commentary on the Epistle to the Hebrews* (New York: Scribner's Sons, 1917) II, pp. 329, 332.

(λεῖτος), "of the people" and *éhr-gon* (ἔργον), "work." Therefore a minister of this kind, in secular life, would be a person holding some public office, one who had responsibilities for service to the state.

In biblical terms, however, the word is almost always employed in relationship to the service of the priests in the temple. It is from this priestly office that the word "liturgy" is derived. These liturgists were ministers who fulfilled assigned tasks at specified times on prescribed days. Like the angels, they were not those who made the major decisions.

8 *But [with reference to] the Son.* The introduction to the quotations in this verse is exactly as it is in Heb 1:7. The *práws . . . táwn whee-áwn* (πρὸς τὸν υἱόν) means [**with reference**] **to the Son** and not just **to . . . the Son.** This is important for understanding the author's use of the quotations involved. Some scholars have taken this as a direct address to **the Son** and therefore believed the author of Hebrews thought Jesus was God. An old example of this reasoning is Turner, who said,

> The only correct translation then is, "Thy throne, O God." As this title is never applied to any Hebrew monarch, it must relate to some superhuman time in such a way as presumes a human nature also.[1]

More recently Montefiore said, "He is superior to them, for he has been raised above them when he was anointed as God."[2] This is not a necessary conclusion. As the *pros* in Heb 1:7 means **in reference to**, and it seems most likely that *pros* (Heb 1:8) should be rendered in the same way, so it is *in reference to* **the Son** that the author quoted a Scripture dealing with the continuance of God's throne, *upon which the Son would sit.* **Your throne, God, is for the age of the age**. When Solomon, was God's **Son** (2Sam 7:14) and ruled over the Lord's **kingdom** (1Chron 29:11), namely Israel, he sat on the Lord's throne (*ahl kee-sáy Yah-hoh-wáh* (על כסא יהוה) (1Chron 29:23; see also 1Enoch 51:3; 55:4; 61:8; 62:2-3, 5; 69:26-27, 29). That did not mean that Solomon was God. It means that Solomon ruled over God's kingdom when he ruled over Palestine, and he sat on God's throne when he ruled from Jerusalem. Therefore, it is just as proper to speak of the endurance of God's throne with reference to **the Son** Jesus who was to **sit on** it as it was to speak of God's throne when Solomon, **the son**, sat on it. The point of the author's argument is that, in contrast to **the angels,** who are as temporal as **wind** and **fire, the Son** was destined for a throne which was **for the age and until** [the next age], as the Scripture says.

At the end of the verse "his" has the stronger textual support (P46Bא), although almost all other texts have **Your** (*sou,* σου) in conformity to LXX and MT. The RSV renders Ps 45:6, "Your divine throne"--the most likely rendering when the next line continues "The scepter of *Your* kingdom . . ."[3] and the address is clearly to the king. The same would be true here in Heb 1:8 if the reading **your** were accepted at the end of the verse. It seems more likely that the author of Hebrews spoke only *in reference to* the Son when he addressed God, mentioning the length of time

---

[1] Turner, *Hebrews* p. 37.

[2] H. Montefiore, *A Commentary on the Epistle to the Hebrews* (New York: Harper & Row, 1964), p. 47.

[3] M. Dahood, *Psalms* (Garden City: Doubleday, 1965) I, pp. 269-73, vocalized the Hebrew *kisseaka*, called it a denominative piel, and rendered it, "has enthroned you." This is reasonable for the Hebrew text, but is irrelevant to Hebrews because the author of Hebrews did not understand it that way.

expected for the throne on which **the Son** would sit. He then changed the pronoun from second to third person in the next line to describe *his* (the Son's) kingdom.

Even though it is unnecessary from this text to affirm that Jesus is God, it would be legally proper, since the Messiah was the legal agent of God and legally equal to God within the limits of his agency.

The Greek *ays tawn ai-óh-nah too ai-óh-naws* (ἐις τὸν αἰῶνα τοῦ αἰῶας) is normally translated, "for ever and ever," but that is misleading. The expression is usually *ays tawn ai-óh-nah tohn ai-óh-nohn* (ἐις τὸν αἰῶνα τῶν αἰῶνων), which literally means, **into the age of the ages**, meaning the greatest of all **ages,** just as the term "king of kings" means the king who rules other kings or the greatest of the kings, and emperor. It is a superlative expression. The word **age** both in Hebrew and Greek refers to a long period of time that is characterized by some king's rule, the rule of some nation over another, a period of war, peace, or something like that. The king under consideration in Ps 45 was to hold down his throne **for the age and until**, meaning until the next **age** came around. The author was not ridiculous. He thought the king involved would rule until he was succeeded by some other king. That was a normal and reasonable expectation. The author of the Book of Hebrews changed the concept a little. To be sure, **the Son** would rule for **the age**, but this would be the best of all ages. That was also a reasonable expectation.

The staff of justice is the staff of his kingdom. **The staff** or scepter was the symbol of royal power and authority. As king, the Son was the highest judge in the land, so this staff was also a symbol of his legislative and judicial authority. Since the king was the Lord's legal agent it was believed that the justice he administered was God's justice, even though kings were often unjust and cruel. Citizens did not challenge their decisions, because they were also considered God's decisions. Ps 45 was a poem addressed to a king and only to God as the king's principal. The king, whom God had blessed, was urged to gird on his sword in glory and ride forth victoriously (Ps 45:3-4). His enemies were destined to fall before his sharp arrows (Ps 45:5). In the Psalm the king was also addressed with reference to his throne and his scepter, but the words could be understood as addressed to God. Since the author of Hebrews wanted to use this royal Psalm, he had to deal with this difficulty in some way, just as commentators do today.

He seems to have handled the problem by speaking **in reference to the Son,** just as he had spoken **in reference to the angels** (Heb 1:7) just before. Then, in reference to **the Son** he spoke of God's throne and **the Son's kingdom**. Next, in the following verse, he continued to deal with **the Son** in direct address as indicated by the Psalm quotation. It seems more likely that the author of Hebrews sensed a difficulty here than that he intentionally confused the **Son with God.** Of course he could confuse the two legitimately, since legally the agent is the principal. For the author, the Son was **the first born, the apostle of God**, **the reflection of God's glory**, and **the stamp of his nature** (Heb 1:3, 6), but he was not God *himself*, physically, ontologically. The relationship was legal, one in which God was the principal, and Jesus was the legal agent. Jesus was not physically God, but since he was legally God, it was legitimate to refer to the agent as the principal. It is the principal who is responsible for all of the agent's statements and actions under the assigned mission.

TEXT

Hebrews	First Testament
[9]**You loved justice, and you hated lawlessness; because of this, God, your God, anointed you [with] oil of joy, [ranking you greater] than your colleagues.**	[Ps 45:8]**You loved justice, and you hated wickedness; Therefore, God, your God, anointed you [with] oil of joy, [ranking you greater] than your colleagues.**

COMMENTARY

[9]*You loved justice and hated lawlessness*. **The Son**, referred to in the third person in Heb 1:8 was addressed in the second person in Heb 1:9. The king who had authority over the kingdom and the administration of justice for the land was one who **loved justice and hated lawlessness**. It was for this reason that he was singled out from among his peers and given the high rank of king. David was reported to have been a king who judged the poor righteously and with equity (Isa 9:7; 11:4). The author of Hebrews interpreted the Psalmist's word *rah-sháh* (רשׁע), "wickedness," as being **lawlessness**. This is a fair translation, since *rah-shah* was a court term. The way a person in antiquity was judged wicked was in court on the basis of the law. A *rah-shah* was a male adult who had been tried in court and found guilty or wicked. In other words, he had broken some law, so he was lawless. He had lived as if there were no law.

God anointed you. There were only two classes of people among the Jews and Israelites that were anointed:

1) the high priests, and
2) the kings.

The son mentioned here, then would have been a king. Although the Son's ability became evident to his contemporaries, his **anointing** came from God. This **anointing** was the rite by which he was made king. God **anointed** kings through the agency of authoritative priests, like Samuel, Zadok, Elisha, or John the Baptist. This rite was so significant that kings were called **anointed** ones or messiahs (Recog 1:45). The Greek for messiah is "Christ," which also means an **anointed** one. It would be difficult to deduce which Israelite or Jewish king was first addressed in this Psalm as God's **anointed** one when he was enthroned, but by the time of the author of Hebrews, Ps 45 was sacred Scripture which described the power and authority of a king who had been **anointed**, and **anointed** ones were called messiahs. Thus when the author of Hebrews took the central figure of Psalm 45 to be the Messiah, he expressed a commonly held opinion. He identified the central figure with Jesus, who, as **Son,** was also a king, the **anointed** one and, according to the author, a mighty one who was victorious in battle, who would crush his enemies and ascend to God's throne in his exalted position at God's right hand from which he would rule justly.

None of the gospels described any event in Jesus' life as an experience of **anointing**, but this is implied. Jesus had a very close association with John the

Baptist, who was a priest, and therefore authorized to **anoint** a king. Herod had John killed, and he was suspicious about Jesus. When asked what Jesus had been doing with John, people probably told him that, like many others, Jesus was baptized by John--but he may have been secretly anointed, just as David and Saul had been before him. At the time Jesus was with John the spirit came upon him (Matt 3:16), he was called **God's son,** and he spoke with authority, being different from the scribes who were only attorneys who acted on the authority of someone else.

After Samuel **anointed** Saul in secret **the Spirit of God came upon him** (*titz-lákh ah-láhv roó-akh eh-loh-heém,* תצלח עליו רוח אלהים) (1Sam 10:10). This also happened to David when he was secretly **anointed.** As soon as Samuel poured oil upon David's head, **the Spirit of Yehowah came upon him**. As soon as David was **anointed**, **the Spirit came upon him,** and **the Spirit of Yehowah** left Saul (1Sam 16:13-14). There seems to have been a close relationship between the reception of legal authority and the acquisition of the Spirit. Before Saul's time the **Spirit of the Lord** took possession of Gideon (Judges 6:2), Jephthah (Judges 11:9), and Samson (Judges 14:19; 15:14), and they all became national leaders. When Moses needed help with the administration of the Israelites, he appointed 70 elders, and **the Lord took some of the spirit that was on Moses and placed it** on them so that they might share the burden. With the spirit came the responsibility and authority of leadership (Num 11:17, 25).

Even apart from the biblical record a certain Norman said that at the moment the king was consecrated, the spirit "leaped" into this king and the king became another man (*alias vir*).[1] This was a legal leap and a legal change. When Paul was with the Corinthians in spirit, he gave them legal authority to expel one of their members from the church (1Cor 5:1-5). In Acts those who were baptized and received the Holy Spirit became legal members of the Christian community. When Jesus breathed the Holy Spirit on the 12 disciples they became apostles or legal agents of the Lord (John 20:22-23). The legal transformations that took place were usually accompanied by some kind of legal ritual or ceremony, like **anointing** with oil, laying on of hands, baptism with water, receiving a crown, changing garments, or being consecrated into some office.[2]

This background of relationships between authority and reception of the Spirit, several of which are related to national leadership, suggests that **anointing** is implied when Jesus **received the Spirit** at the same time he was called **God's son**, a normal name for a king (Matt 3:16-17; Mark 1:10; Luke 3:21-22; John 1:32-34). After Jesus' so-called baptism, he was called one who was **full of the Holy Spirit**. This probably meant that he was authorized to be God's legal agent (Luke 4:1). Jesus is reported to have read Isa 61:1-2 in the synagogue at Nazareth. When he quoted, **The Spirit of the Lord is upon me which has anointed me to preach good news . . .** he said, **Today this Scripture is fulfilled in your ears** (Luke 4:17-21). He did not say that he was **anointed** to be the king of the Jews, but by quoting this Scripture he implied that he was. The good news he was **anointed** to preach was the same message 2Isa proclaimed: the kingdom was soon to be restored to the chosen people, and he was **anointed** to be king when that took place. Those who heard his message noted that Jesus spoke with authority and power (Luke 4:36).[3] Of course, those who did not know 2Isa would not have learned much from his coded

---

[1] Kantorowicz, *The King's Two Bodies*, p. 47.

[2] See further Buchanan, *Insights*, pp. 16-17.

[3] Buchanan, *Insights*, p. 131.

message. Peter reportedly said that God had **anointed** Jesus with **the Holy Spirit** and power (Acts 10:38). Neither of these witnesses says that Jesus was **anointed** to be king, but that is implied. The author of Heb 1:9 quoted Ps 45:8 with the same purpose in mind as Luke did when he quoted Isa 61:1-2. He was claiming that Jesus had been **anointed** through the coded message of Scripture.

The angel supposedly told Mary that the son she would bear would be called Son of the Most High and Son of God; he would inherit the throne of David; he would rule over the house of Jacob, which would be his kingdom (Luke 1:32-37). If all of this happened he would have to be **anointed** king over Israel. That is implied.

Paul said that according to the flesh Jesus was **the son of David**, but according to **the Spirit of holiness he was the Son of God** (Rom 1:3-4). Paul made a distinction between being a son physically and being a son legally. A man was born as a physical son of his physical parents, but he could become a legal son through a legal ceremony. This is what happened when kings were crowned and messiahs were **anointed**. At an enthronement ritual when a Jewish citizen was being established as king on the holy hill of Zion, the psalmist claimed that the Lord announced to this adult Jew, **You are my son; today I have given you birth** (Ps 2:6-7). This was obviously a legal birth without any gestation period. No mention was made that he either was **anointed** or **received the Spirit**, but that was probably implied, just as Jesus' **anointing** was probably implied when he received the Spirit and was called God's son. This follows the logic of implication or that which the rabbis called *geh-zah-ráh shah-wáh* (גזרה שוה).

Implication has been recognized as a legitimate argument for centuries. Today in court it is accepted as fact that a product is warranted by implication to do that which it is understood to do. A milk cow is warranted to give milk; a wood saw is warranted to cut wood; a typewriter is warranted to type. These items are warranted by implication even though no contract says that they will do what they are made to do. If several related facts are given, other facts that are also related are implied. Rabbis said that if a male is reported to have been circumcised it is implied that he was also baptized, since these are accompanying ceremonies. Therefore if Jesus received the spirit at the hands of a priest and afterwards had authority, it was not necessary to say that he was also anointed.

The Sermon on the Mount closes with the notice that Jesus **taught them [the crowds] as one having authority, and not as their scribes** (Matt 7:29). When the high priests and the Pharisees asked by what authority Jesus acted, Jesus did not tell them that he was the authorized messiah. Instead he answered them with a question, asking by what authority John the Baptist functioned (Matt 21:23-25; Luke 20:2-4). If John was a valid priest, then his baptisms and his **anointings** would be valid. Jesus' authority depended on the validity of the ritual John performed on him. The Pharisees would have understood that an appeal to the authority of John the Baptist implied that Jesus had been anointed by him and was therefore a legitimate messiah. The Pharisees were also afraid of the Romans and would have been reluctant to disclose these coded insights to them.

John baptized many people, none of which received royal authority. The Pharisees probably knew that Jesus had been **anointed**, even though he was not openly called "king" until his parousia, when he entered Jerusalem as king (Matt 21:5). The Pharisees were alarmed by the effectiveness of Jesus' program. They interrogated about the source of his authority and the people he had gathered as associates. This would not have worried them if they did not think he had a claim to governmental authority. He had a good chance of becoming king, and they were not being given chief seats in his kingdom. He spoke of the first being last and the last, first (Matt 20:16). They then held the chief positions and they did not want to lose them. They evidently thought that his so-called baptism was more than a mere baptism.

Jesus was called the **son of David, the son of God, the Christ** (i.e., Messiah), king, and **son of man**. These are all names given to Jewish kings. The term **Son of God** was well known as a title for a king. It was used by Greeks, Egyptians, and Israelites. According to Nathan, God promised David that God would make David's kingdom secure, establishing David's son as king after him. When that happened God would be the father of David's son and that **David's son** would be **God's son** (2Sam 7:4-17). **God's son**, of course, was Solomon, and these legal sonships were all legal fictions. But legal fictions are very important in court.

Because citizens became kings in Israel and Judah through an **anointing** ceremony Israelite or Jewish kings were also called **the anointed ones** or Messiahs, which in Greek is "the Christ" (1Sam 2:10, 35; 12:3, 5; 16:6; 24:6, 10; 26:9, 11, 23; 2Sam 1:14, 16, 21; 19:21; 22:51, and frequently). 4Ezra called God's son "the Messiah" (4Ezra 7:28). While Jesus was trying to avoid suspicion of the Romans (Matt 16:16-20), he asked his apostles not to call him the Messiah, but he was recognized as the Messiah by his apostles, and after his death he was openly called the anointed one. Paul did not say, "Jesus died for our crimes," he said, **Christ** (i.e., **the anointed** one) **died for our crimes in accordance with the Scriptures** (1Cor 15:3). He also sometimes mentioned Jesus the Messiah (Rom 3:22, 24). 1Pet referred to the one who had suffered as **Christ**--not Jesus (1Pet 2:21). This would not have happened if Jesus had not been known as the **anointed** one before his death. It was not the personality of Jesus that made his sacrifice a valid means of redemption. It was his office as Messiah that made his death significant.

The title **Son of man** was a code name for king. In the victorious visionary trial in Dan 7, the defendant who was called "the horn" was Antiochus Epiphanes, who died in Persia in 164 BIA. The author of Daniel interpreted his death to be the result of a heavenly court case when he was given a death sentence (Dan 7:11). In the same heavenly court trial the plaintiff was called **one like a son of man**, to whom the divine judge awarded the dominion, the glory, and the kingdom (Dan 7:14). Evidence of this heavenly trial was shown by the death of Antiochus during the same year that Judas the Maccabee won the famous battle of Beth-horon and afterward had the temple cleansed. This was the first celebration of Hanukkah, when the tide of the war turned, and Jews began to gain control of **the kingdom** David and Solomon ruled. Dan 7 is apparently a mythical description of the historical period up to and involving Hanukkah. One of the Dead Sea fragments is a midrash on Dan 7. In that midrash the one that Daniel called **Son of man** (Dan 7:13), the Dead Sea author called "**Son of God,**" "**Son of the Most High**," and also "**king**"[1]

---

[1] Another fragment (*4Q448*) offered a prayer to God for 1) the king, 2) the congregation of God's people Israel wherever they lived, and 3) God's kingdom (*mahm-láhkh-teh-khah*, ממלכתך) (*4Q448*.B, 8). There is no way of misunderstanding what God's kingdom was in this case, because the king was named. It was King Jonathan (*hah-méh-lekh yóh-nah-tahn*, המלך יונתן) (*4Q448*.B, 2; C, 8); who in Greek was called Alexander Jannaeus. He ruled Palestine from 103 to 76 BC. Like the titles, Son of God, Son of man, Messiah, Son of the Most High, the Kingdom of God or the Kingdom of Heaven, God's kingdom is a political title, one that was recognized as a religious title for the Promised Land when it was free from foreign rule. This is the logical conclusion reached by "the correlation of various epithets and titles" that Collins advocates (Collins, *The Scepter*, p. 60).

(4Q246 2:1). Rabbis called the Son of Man the Messiah and also the Son of David (bSan 98a).[1]

Because Jesus was called by all of these titles that were associated with **anointed** kings it is reasonable to assume that he had also been **anointed** the way other kings were, and at that time received the Spirit in secret the way David and Saul did. Although there are texts that say he was **anointed**, they did not specifically say that he was **anointed** king. He acted like a leader who had been **anointed**, had the authority of one who had been **anointed**, received the Spirit the way kings who had been **anointed** did, and he was even called the **anointed** one, and after his death was openly called the **anointed** one. The text does not say that he was **anointed** by John at the time he received the Spirit because of the political situation of his day.

Jesus lived and ministered in a land where Rome ruled against the will of the Jewish inhabitants of the country. Four military leaders who wanted to become kings were killed after the death of Herod the Great. Roman troops were widely distributed to suppress all potential insurrection. Jews engaged in liberating Palestine from Rome had to work underground and speak in coded language which only Jews who were acquainted with Scripture and Jewish tradition could understand. Rome knew what a Son of God, king, or messiah meant, politically, so Jesus referred to himself as the Son of man, which sounded innocent enough to those who did not know Daniel and remember the Maccabean Revolt. He also warned his apostles not to call him the Messiah publicly (Matt 16:20). Instead of saying that John **anointed** Jesus to be the new king, they referred to his baptism, when he received the Spirit and was called God's son. The claim that he had been **anointed** was not said openly, but it was clearly implied.[2]

When Hebrews quoted Ps 45 to mention Jesus' **anointing**, he probably did this intentionally, because he knew that Jesus had been **anointed**, and not simply baptized, by John the Baptist.

TEXT

Hebrews	First Testament
10 And	
You, Lord, **in the beginning**	Ps 102:26-28 **Long ago you**
laid the earth's foundation,	**laid the earth's foundation,**
and the heavens are the works	**and the heavens are the works**
of your hands.	**of your hands.**
11 **They perish, but you endure;**	**They perish, but you endure;**
and they all grow old	**and they all wear out**
like a garment;	**like a garment;**
12 **like** a robe **you will roll them up**;	**like** clothes **you will roll them up**;

[1] Translated from the Hebrew text of S. A. Wertheimer (ed.), ספר פרקי היכלות רבתי (Jerusalem, 1890), 32:3 (10a) - 40:2 (12a). English translation in Buchanan, *Jewish Messianic Movements from AD 70 to AD 1300* (Eugene, Oregon: Wipf and Stock Publishers, 2003), pp. 317, 346; 403, 446, 505, 572. A. Jellinek, בת המדרש (Jerusalem: Wahrmann Books, 1967) III, pp. 78-82. Buchanan, *Messianic Movements,* p. 403; J. D. Einstein (ed.), אוצר מדרשים (New York, 1956, 155b-156a. Buchanan, *Messianic Movements,* p. 446.

[2] This suggestion was first made and reported in Buchanan, *The Gospel of Matthew* (Lewiston: Mellen, c1996) 1, pp. 150-54.

(like a garment)	
and they will be changed;	**and they will change;**
but you are the same,	**but you are,**
and your years will not run out.	**and your years will not be completed.**

COMMENTARY

[10]*And you, Lord, in the beginning.* The connective **And** relates Heb 1:10-12 to Heb 1:7-9. **Now, (on the one hand,) [with reference] to the angels, it says** (Heb 1:7) **but [with reference] to the Son, [it says]**, (Heb 1:8) **and** (Heb 1:10). The **Lord** in Ps 102 clearly referred to God. Here it might also mean God, with the implication that since the Son was **heir of all** (Heb 1:2) and since it was through the Son that the **Lord made the ages** (Heb 1:2), any reference to the endurance of God would also be a reference to the endurance of **the Son.** In other places the author of Hebrews quoted Hebrew Scripture passages that mention the name of the Lord, and in every case the author held the same meaning (Heb 7:21; 8:8, 9, 10, 11; 10:16, 30; 12:5, 6). On the other hand, the author did use the name **Lord** when referring to Jesus (Heb 2:3; 7:14).

Like other scholars of his time, the author was also capable of taking a FT passage out of context and attributing it to the Messiah. This is on the rhetorical rule, "All prophecy is prophesied only for the days of the Messiah." This rule was applied to various of the Dead Sea Scrolls, such as 1QHabakkuk. For example in LXX Deut 32:43, in which the object of worship for the sons of God according to the Proto-Masoretic text was Israel, the author of Hebrews applied it to the first born, namely Jesus (Heb 1:6). Since the term "first born" could be applied either to Israel (Exod 4:22) or to the Messiah, the author made the shift. By the same logic, since **the Lord** was a title of respect used both for God and for kings, such as Jesus, he may also have made the shift here to apply to Jesus the durability of God in contrast to the temporal nature of the angels. If this were the case, then Jesus would also have been thought of as a sort of demiurge through whom God created the heaven and earth as well as the ages (Heb 1:2, 10). In either case it does not mean that Jesus was believed to be God, physically, or was addressed as God.

The phrase **in the beginning** is not an exact translation of the Hebrew *leh-phan-eém* (לפנים), which literally means "in front." Semites looked to the past as if it were in front of them, and it does not say how far in front. Hebrews correctly understood from the context that it went back to the creation so he rendered it "in the beginning."

[11]*They perish, but you endure.* The contrast here is between the endurance of God, which is related to the endurance of the Son, and the ephemeral nature of the creation, including even the heavens to which the angels belong.

They all grow old like a garment. MT has **They all wear out like a garment**, which is more apt than the comparison given here by Hebrews. Although clothes get **old,** the idiom **grow old** is more often used of people, and "wearing out," of clothes. The Hebrew *bah-láh* (בלה) however, can take the meaning **grow old** as well as "rot" or "decay," so the Greek translation of this Hebrew is acceptable.

[12]*Like a robe you will roll them up.* The Greek for **roll them up** is *heh-leéx-ays ow-toós* (ἑλίξεις αὐτούς). A variant (in original hands of aleph D and in Latin MSS)

is *ahl-lax-ays* (ἀλλάξεις), which means **You will change** and is paralleled by *ahl-lah-gáy-sawn-tai* (ἀλλαγήσονται)in the following line. The variant agrees with the Masoretic text (*tah-hahl-eé-phaym wuh-yah-khahl-óh-phu*) (תחליפם ויחלפו) (Ps 102:27) and the Old Greek *(ahl-láx-ays ow-toós, kai ahl-lah-gáy-son-tai)* (ἀλλάξεις αὐτούς καὶ ἀλλαγήσονται) (LXX Ps 101:27). The smoother reading has the poorer textual support and agrees with both the Old Greek and the Masoretic text. It is more natural to think of "changing" in relationship to "robes" than **rolling them up**, although garments can be rolled up after they have been removed. Therefore it seems unlikely that a later scribe would have changed the text to make it more awkward, and it is easily understood why he might improve it, especially when he could do so by making it conform to the FT.

Because the contrast was being made between God and his Son, on the one hand, and the heavens where the angels dwelt, on the other, the author may have preferred the idiom more customarily used in relationship to heaven than to a garment. The phrase **like a garment** does not occur in the extant MT, supported by *papayrus* 46 (Π46); Vaticanus (B); Siniaticus (א); Alexandrinus (A); Bezai (Δ); and 1739, and would make more sense if the imagery from Isa 34:4 had been carried out completely in the first line, so that "garment" would need to be mentioned in the second line to make sense with "will be changed." Then it would have read as follows:

> And like a scroll you will roll them up;
> like a garment also (and) they will be changed.

The only problem with this suggestion is that there is absolutely no textual support for the conjectured word, "scroll." The conjunction could be translated "also," after the addition was made, but the problem probably arose in the Psalm text used rather than any changes made by Hebrews. The Masoretic text needs the phrase, "like a garment." Hebrews has preserved it to make a balanced text. It probably existed in the text Hebrews used and got lost sometime in transmission in MT.

The pronoun **them** has as its antecedent, not the singular **robe**, but the plural **the heavens**. In English the entire verse would make better poetry if the plurals were used all the way--heavens, garments, clothes, them--but this would have broken the meter in Hebrew, so the original probably was singular as the texts report.

TEXT

Hebrews	First Testament
13 Now to which of his angels has he ever **said**, **Remain seated down at my right hand until I place your enemies [as] a footstool for your feet.**	Ps 110:1 Yehowah **said** to my Lord, **Remain seated at my right hand until I place your enemies [as] a footstool for your feet** ?

14 They are all ministering spirits, sent for service of those who are about to inherit salvation, are they not?

TECHNICAL DETAILS

Ps 110 is an important text for Hebrews. It is alluded to many times (Heb 1:3; 5:6, 10; 6:20; 7:3, 11, 17, 21; 8:1; 10:12, 13; 12:1). It was also important to other NT documents (Matt 22:41-45 // Mark 14:62 // Luke 20:41-44; Matt 26:64 // Mark 14:62 // Luke 22:69; Acts 2:34-35; Rom 8:34; 1Cor 15:25; Eph 1;20; Col 3:1; 1Pet 3:22).

COMMENTARY

Now to which of the angels has he ever said? This is a repetition in slightly different words of Heb 1:5, employed here to form an inclusion of the material in between. The quotations that follow are different. Heb 1:5 introduces Ps 2, followed by other FT passages that were used to contrast the inferiority of **the angels** to the superiority of **the Son.** Heb 1:13 reintroduces Ps 110, which is the basic text of his message. This ties the two enthronement Psalms together and helps clarify the role of the Messiah, according to the author. He is to be a powerful ruler who overcomes all his enemies in battle and forces them to become a **footstool for his feet** while he is elevated to the throne at Jerusalem, which means he is sitting at the Lord's **right hand**. It thus echoes the "punch line" of the introductory section, assuring the reader that this is the main point of the discussion.

Remain seated. Following LXX the author used the imperfect imperative tense to indicate that the one to which this Psalm applied was already **seated** at the Lord's **right hand**. The imperfect tense shows continued action. Had he used the aorist tense that would have meant, "Be seated." This is an intended echo of Heb 1:3, **He sat down at the right hand. Remain seated** is the concluding part of an inclusion, a literary form that indicates when the form is complete. This literary form (Heb 1:1-1:13) included an entire list of seven different FT quotations on the same subject and is technically known as a *florilegium* or a testimony book.

The king involved was to continue on his throne until the Lord fulfilled the promises given. Whenever a person became king of Israel or Judah Jews and Israelites believed that he was also given a position in the heavenly council as David was when he ruled the united kingdom (Acts 13:36). Not only was the king a member of the heavenly council, but he was positioned at the Lord's right hand. By using the imperfect, the authors both of Ps 110 and Hebrews were testifying to their belief that the king involved had tenure in this position.[1]

The position **at the right hand** was the preferred position in any gathering where people were classed according to status. The one who **sat** at the host's **right hand** at a banquet for instance, was the guest of honor. In the ancient Near East it was customary for people to recline when they ate. The person at the **host's right hand** reclined so that his head was before the host where he and the host could converse most easily. He was reclining at the bosom of his host. This was the kind of setting implied in the statement, **Many will come from the east and the west and recline with Abraham, Isaac, and Jacob in the kingdom of heaven** (Matt 8:11). The importance attached to the position at a banquet is shown in the parable where the one who took the lowest place was invited before all the guests to take a position

---

[1] On this see further, S. Parker, "The Beginning of the Reign of God--Psalm 82 as Myth and Liturgy," *RB* 102/104 (1995):532-59.

nearer to the host (Luke 14:8-11). This was the position of the beloved disciple at the Last Supper (John 13:23). When the author of the Fourth Gospel said Jesus was at the bosom of the Father he meant the same as the author of Hebrews who said Jesus **was seated** at God's **right hand** (John 1:18)

In the parable of Lazarus and the rich man, Lazarus was finally rewarded by being placed at Abraham's bosom (Luke 16:23; see also bKid 72b) and the rich man was punished by being placed at a distance. In earthly protocol there was no person of higher status than the king. He would always be at the head of the gathering, with the princes and closest allies at his right and left, but he was also thought to be the one closest to God. Therefore he was called God's **son** or "chosen one" (see 1Enoch 55:4; 61:8; 62:2-3). Since this was true, it was normal to describe his status in terms of earthly protocol and say that he was stationed at the Lord's **right hand** when he ascended his throne. In contrast to this position were his "enemies" who were to become his "footstool" and the angels who were mere servants, commissioned during their ephemeral existence to carry out the assignments he gave.

The picture of a king posed as a footstool for someone else was not just a figure of speech. When Joshua and the Israelites were driving the Canaanites out of their cities, they found five kings--from Jerusalem, Hebron, Jarmuth, Lachish, and Eglon--hiding in a cave. At Joshua's command the soldiers filled up the mouth of the cave with rocks, put a guard over it, and after the slaughter had been complete, he commanded that those kings be brought out and placed before him. When they were brought, he told the officers to put their feet on the necks of the kings, telling them not to be afraid, **for this is what the Lord will do for you to all the enemies whom you fight** (Josh 10:26).

After this humiliation of the kings, Joshua killed them all and hanged them up on trees until evening. Then they were taken down, thrown into the cave in which they had hidden, and the mouth of the cave was filled up again with rocks (Josh 10:16-27). Putting their feet on the necks of the opposing kings was a liturgy that indicated the kings' subjection to Joshua and his army. Joshua could have killed the kings without this liturgy, but the liturgy itself was held to be effective. It was as if they had signed a peace treaty which required the kings' unconditional surrender. This ritual set the tenor for the entire future invasion and conquest of Palestine.

When the Psalmist promised the king being enthroned that the Lord would make his enemies become the footstool for his feet he visualized something like this happening. The author of Hebrews had the same idea in mind.

[14]*They are all ministering spirits.* The **ministering spirits** were those who ministered at the altar rather than those who waited tables or performed other types of menial labor. Nonetheless, the **service** (*dee-ah-koh-neé-ah*, διακονία) they rendered was the kind usually related to table serving. The author's use of the two terms for ministering probably reflects his own good taste in literary style, preferring to use synonyms rather than being repetitious. The distinction between the serving that took place at the altar (*lay-toor-geé-ah*, λειτουργία) and that which took place at the meal (*dee-ah-koh-neé-ah*) was not very sharp, because those who served at the altar slaughtered and sacrificed livestock.

Sacrificing involved cooking the beast that had been slaughtered, most of which was then eaten. The **ministering spirits** are here pictured as the ones who administered the sacrifice in preparing a feast for God's chosen people who would **inherit** the **salvation** prepared for the children of Abraham. The **ministering spirits** are identical to the angels whom the Lord makes **spirits, winds**, or **flames of fire** when he chooses (Heb 1:7). The status of **the angels** is shown to be lower than that of **the Son** by their position and function. **The angels** minister in whatever task they **are sent**. **The Son** sits at the Lord's **right hand** (Heb 1:13), like a king who sends messengers and gives orders. The one who **sits** on the throne is far superior to all court servants (see Rev 5:6-7).

SUMMARY

The list of quotations in Heb 1:5-13 has often been called a "florilegium," a collection of Scripture passages devoted to one topic. Heb 1:5-13 is similar to that in 1Clem 36:1-6, and some scholars think both Hebrews and First Clement obtained this information from an independent collection, but it is just as possible and reasonable to think that 1Clem acquired his material from the Book of Hebrews.[1]

The passage that began with a rhetorical question also ended with a rhetorical question (Heb 1:5, 14). The author fenced in his message for this chapter by using verses from Ps 110 both at the beginning (Heb 1:1) and at the ending (Heb 1:13). The quotation from Ps 2:7 in Heb 1:5 is almost parallel to the quotation from Ps 110:1 in Heb 13. Ps 110 is one to which allusions are made throughout the Book of Hebrews, and is evidently the basic text on which this sermon was built. The next part of this division is an admonition reminding the readers of their responsibility to the facts presented.

---

[1] G. L. Cockerill, "Heb 1:1-14, 1 Clem 36:1-6 and the High Priest Title," *JBL* 97 (1978):438-439.

CHAPTER TWO

TEXT

2:1 Therefore we must hold fast to the things that were heard, lest we drift away. 2 For if

1) the word which was spoken through angels became firm, and
2) every transgression and disobedience received just recompense,

3 How shall we escape having neglected so great a salvation [as this], which

1) had its beginning when it was spoken through the Lord,
2) was confirmed to us by those who heard,
4 3) while God supported the testimony with signs, wonders, and various kinds of miracles, and
4) by the distribution of the Holy Spirit according to his will?

COMMENTARY

2:1 *The things that were heard.* **Therefore**, literally, "on account of this" (*dee-áh toó-tow*, διὰ τοῦτο), refers to the superiority of Jesus over the angels, shown in Heb 1. **Hold fast** is a nautical term that was used to anchor a boat to the ground to keep it in place. **Drift away** (*pah-rah-roo-óh-men*, παραρυῶμεν), correspondingly means to be unanchored so that the boat can be tossed and thrown by the waves. It literally means to **flow by.** This word is used to describe a river that flows by a place, or flows aside from its normal channel in the sense of flooding or escaping its channel. Metaphorically, it means to drift, wander from the true path, to transgress.

The son in Prov 3:21 was warned, **Son, do not drift away** (*pahr-ahr-roo-áys*, παραρυῇς), which means, "Observe my counsel and intention," or **hold fast to the things that were heard. The things that were heard** refers to the instruction that the readers had been taught and for which they were responsible (Eph 1:13; 4-21; Col 1:6, 23; 2Tim 1:13; 2:2; 1John 2:7, 24). The emphasis here is upon **hearing** rather than reading, just as God's word at the beginning of Heb 1 was upon speaking. The message of this document may originally have been presented orally. The address was given as if the hearers had been students or catechists, all of whom had been taught in the same discipline, so that they knew the material about which the speaker was speaking.

Spoken through angels. The passive voice was used here to avoid blaspheming God's name. It means "God has **spoken through angels**." This probably refers to the contract that was given at Mt Sinai, i.e., the Scripture, which was traditionally thought to have been delivered by angels. From the LXX the report is

Deut 33:2 **The Lord has come from Sinai**
He appeared to us from Seir
He hurried from Mount Paran
with myriads of holy ones at his right side.
Angels were with him.

An **angel** is an Anglicization of the Greek word for messenger (*áhn geh-laws,* ἄγγελος). There were two types of messengers in antiquity, just as there are today:

1) One type of these just carried packages or letters for which they had no responsibility for the content of the message. The messenger's only responsibility was to see that the assigned items were properly delivered to the intended recipients. Those messengers functioned like mail service, UPS, or FedEx today.
2) The other type of messenger is the legal agent. The legal agent is sometimes called an apostle or prophet. It is a person who speaks in the name of the principal, in behalf of the principal, and at the responsibility of the principal. This is a person who is authorized to negotiate terms and make agreements in behalf of someone else.

Attorneys and ambassadors are legal agents. Kings and prophets were understood to have been legal agents of the deity. At least some of the prophets were held to have been legal advisors to the kings. Those who heard messages from any of these believed that they had word from the deity. If people on earth had messages from heaven they would have had to come through messengers. Anything that the principal wrote down and sent by a messenger was understood to be the word of the principal. It was legally binding. If, instead of a written word, the principal sent a human legal agent to act in his behalf, that agent would have been the word of the principal in the flesh or the incarnate word of the principal. The word of the principal was *in* him, legally. He was legally identical with the principal who sent him. His word would have been legally binding on the principal. When the Fourth Gospel reported that God's word had become flesh (John 1:14), it meant that God had sent a human being as a legal agent to speak and act in his behalf, in his interests, and at his responsibility.

Angels were messengers. They had no message of their own. They either delivered the message or package of the sender, or they acted with authority. If they acted with authority of the person who sent them, they were very special **angels**, called "apostles." They functioned with authority, but they still had no message of their own. They spoke the message of the principal who sent them. Apostles were angels on earth who spoke in behalf of God in heaven. Since God was in heaven he had to communicate to people on earth through agents of some kind. Some were earthly human beings, whereas others were heavenly beings.

The author had been depreciating **angels** in comparison to **the Son**. At this point he made the contrast of his *a fortiori* argument greater by calling attention to the accepted belief that **angels** delivered the law at Sinai. That would have been a written law, which **the angels** only delivered. They did not dictate or write. They were not legal agents. The association of the law given at Sinai to **angels**, in this context, makes the law seem relatively less important. But even this word, delivered by beings of no higher status than messengers, was as **firm** as a written contract, enforced to the letter.

The word was the law given to Moses. In the opinion of the author, Moses wrote the commandments of the contract, but God spoke to him either directly or through the speaking of his messengers (Heb 1:1). There was a widely held tradition that God delivered this through the medium of **angels** (Ant 15:136, Gal 3:19; Acts

7:53; TargOnq Deut 33:2). That was a reasonable assumption, according to ancient concepts. Two thousand years ago, when there were none of the modern means of communication—no cell phones, no radios, TVs, automobiles, airplanes--the only way a person might communicate with someone at a distance was either to go to that person or to send a messenger. Consequently, most of the world's business was conducted by messengers. Since this was the case on earth, it was assumed that God at a great distance away from the earth in his heaven, would have to manage his business on earth through messengers. Since God spoke to Moses at Mount Sinai when God was in heaven, he must have employed **angels** for the undertaking.

[2]*Every transgression and disobedience received just recompense.* The expression **transgression and disobedience** may be a *hendiadys.* That means it is two synonyms describing one activity. The Greek, translated **transgression** (*pah-ráh-bah-sees,* παράβασις), literally means "stepping alongside" and refers to walking out of bounds, off the track, or overstepping the prescribed limitations. The Greek for **disobedience** (*pah-rah-kaw-áye,* παρακοή), literally, "hearing alongside [that which was directed]" or "hearing amiss," means not hearing accurately or hearing something contrary to that which was spoken. Those who heard paid attention and obeyed the commandments heard. Those who ignored the commandments disobeyed them, which means they acted in a contrary way or transgressed. The Hebrew word for hearing (*shah-máh,* שמע) also means obeying. If a person obeyed, that meant that he heard. If he did not obey, he misheard. The Samaritan author said,

> Of the Day of Vengeance, [Moses] warned of the things prepared. Those who back-slide will be punished on the Day of Vengeance. Woe to us! Woe to us. All [severe torture] is prepared for us if we do not learn and from instruction become educated. All wrath [of God] will come upon us (Memar Marqah 4 #3).

The repeated theme threatening punishment and no opportunity for repentance and forgiveness is woven throughout the document (Heb 6:6; 10:17).

[3]*Having neglected so great a salvation [as this].* **Escape** refers to the **just recompense** of **every transgression and disobedience** (Heb 2:2). The rhetorical question expects a negative answer and means, "**We** cannot **escape** . . ." The author used the first personal pronoun **we** to identify himself with his audience. He and they belonged to the same denomination, monastery, or Christian group.

Salvation in Jewish thought form is of two kinds:

1) the deliverance of the individual Jew or the community from some external danger or
2) the acceptance of an individual into the community by conversion. The FT refers to the first type, and deals with the following kinds of **salvation:**
    a) deliverance of a nation from the power of the enemy at war,
    b) reception of a pardon or verdict of "not guilty" in a court case, or
    c) rescue from some other kind of danger.

The FT has no instance of a person being converted to Judaism and being **saved** in the process, but the expression **saved** was used by the Greek mystery religions to describe their members. Later Christianity also used the term **saved** to mean a person had become a Christian. This was called the **salvation** of souls.

In Judaism and Christianity a person was born without a soul. If a baby died unbaptized and uncircumcised, it was not a member of the community. Therefore its death did not require mourning. It obtained a soul by being named and admitted legally into the community through baptism. When a member was excommunicated or became an apostate he or she lost his or her soul. A person's soul was **saved** when he or she was restored to the community. The notion that a soul is a legal identity that is provided and removed through legal ceremony is still believed by Jews and Roman Catholics. In NT times Josephus used some form of the Greek word for **salvation** more than 200 times without ever referring to salvation of souls.

For the author of Hebrews the word **salvation** was used in the same way as in the FT; it refers to the deliverance that the Son provides the community when God makes his **enemies a footstool for [his] feet** (Heb 1:13), and the Son utilizes **the staff of justice** (Heb 1:8) to rule over his people. As the document repeatedly reminds the readers, the opportunity for **so great a salvation** was available to them and should not be neglected. They were already **saved** by becoming members of a Christian group. The **salvation the Son** could provide them was the deliverance of the community itself from the same fate as that experienced by the exodus community. The revelation related to the **salvation** was contrasted to that related to the **word spoken through angels.**

Spoken through the Lord. **The Lord** here means Jesus. Jesus, like the kings and prophets, was a legal agent of God. Nothing is spoken **through** God, because God is the principal. His messages are sent **through** various kinds of messengers. Some messengers were **angels,** but one messenger was the Messiah, Jesus, and he was the one to whom the author directed his attention.

One revelation came through the Mosaic law. That revelation was delivered through **angels**. The other was **spoken through Jesus**. Just as the opening verse (Heb 1:1) began with reference to God's speaking and further mention made his way of speaking through **angels,** here it is Jesus **the Lord** who does the speaking in God's behalf. It was not done through writing, but it was the oral word. The significance of the second revelation was made evident in various ways:

1) First, it was initially **spoken through the Lord,** which evidently refers to the sayings of Jesus,[1] rather than a word directly from God himself.
2) This came to the author and his contemporaries from **those who heard**. This probably means they received it from the ear and eye witnesses--those who saw and heard the very words of Jesus. Those from whom they heard would have been the apostles and their contemporaries who further supported the importance of the things Jesus said.

The author of Hebrews was evidently not one of those witnesses himself, but rather was dependent upon **the things that were heard** (Heb 2:1) from reports he had received directly from the apostles themselves or else from the reports that they left. This means that the author was not one of the original twelve apostles. In order to be apostolic, this document would have to have been written by the Apostle Paul, but it clearly was not composed in Pauline style. This was one of the reasons the Book of

---

[1] K. Berger, "Zum Traditionsgeschichtlichen Hintergrund Christologischer Hoheitstitel," *NTS* 17 (1970-71):413-22, compared Moses and Enoch to Jesus and some angels to show that the term "Lord" means apostle or messenger. This is consistent with the apostolic Christology of Hebrews.

Hebrews had so much resistance in being admitted into the canon. It could not have been apostolic, because the author was obviously one who depended on his information from first generation Christians, of which he was not one. Filaster, in the fourth century, said another reason that Hebrews was not accepted immediately was that it did not allow for second repentance[1].

[4]3) *Signs, wonders, and various kinds of miracles.* The good news that was proclaimed by Jesus was accompanied by numerous **signs, wonders, and various kinds of miracles. The signs** were contemporary events that reminded Jews either of earlier **salvation** events, like the manna from heaven, or of painful events that preceded **salvation** events in the past, like the oppressive treatment by the Egyptians or the Syrians that preceded the Exodus or Hanukkah.[2] These were **signs** that Jews were at that time in the exact spot of the cycle of time as had happened earlier. This meant the good events that had followed earlier would be repeated.

Miracles were the kind of surprisingly good things that resembled earlier blessings, like the opening of the sea, the healing of Miriam, the sun standing still for Joshua, or water springing out of a rock. All of these constituted God's way of corroborating the **testimony** of Jesus and his apostles.

4) An additional testimony was provided by **the distribution of the Holy Spirit** (see Rom 12:3; 1Cor 7:17; 2Cor 10:13; Heb 7:2; Eph 4:7 for use of the term **distribute**) which accompanied the preaching and miracles. There were two steps to becoming a Christian:

a) being legally born again at baptism, and
b)receiving the Holy Spirit with the laying on of hands.

When the **Holy Spirit** was **distributed**, new converts were joining the church. This is especially reported in the account of the first Pentecost (Acts 2:1-41). Whereas the revelation given through Moses was spoken only by angels, the revelation associated with Jesus had four strong supports:

1) the authority of Jesus,
2) the testimony, approval, and support of the apostles,
3) God's approval shown in various kinds of miraculous events, and
4) the provision of the Holy Spirit wherever God chose to reveal his presence.

The presence of the Holy Spirit meant the legal presence of God. The principal was legally present whenever his or her apostle was present. Legally, the apostle was the principal. Jesus was God's apostle or legal agent. The revelation of God came through God's legal agent, Jesus, who provided it through his legal agents, the apostles, who acted and spoke in the name of, in behalf of, and at the responsibility of Jesus, who spoke and acted in behalf of God. This revelation was apostolic, all of the way, whereas **the angels** who brought the law to Moses were only messengers, like UPS, FedEx, or mail carriers who had no authority to negotiate or add anything

---

[1] Filaster, *De Haeresibus* 41.
[2] For example, "Look! I and the children whom God has given me. They will be as signs and wonders in the house of Israel from the Lord of armies who lives on Mount Zion" (LXX Isa 8:18).

to the message they carried. They had no authority to speak. This fourfold description of divine evidence is more than was usually claimed.

Usually only **signs and wonders** are given together in Scripture (Matt 24:24; Mark 13:22; John 4:48; Acts 2:19, 43; 4:30; 5:12; 6:8; 7:36; 14:3; 15:12). Sometimes **signs** and miracles (Acts 8:13), **miracles, signs, and wonders** (Rom 15:19), or **signs, wonders, and miracles** are listed (Acts 2:22; 2Cor 12:12; 2Thess 2:9). Acts 2:1-41 is the only other place in the NT where a four-fold description of divine evidence is reported. There **signs, wonders, and miracles** are listed (Acts 2:22), and the distribution of the Holy Spirit is described (Acts 2:1-21, 33).[1] The Holy Spirit was distributed when authority was shared within the community. In the author's judgment, this was enough evidence to show that the revelation made known through Jesus was far superior to that made known in the Mosaic law.

Noting the well-balanced structure of Heb 2:1-4, Vanhoye illustrated this *a fortiori* argument as follow:

	Became steadfast (2:1)
we (2:1)	to us (2:2)
to the things that were heard (2:1	by those who heard (2:3)
through angels (2:2)	through the Lord (2:3)
was spoken (2:3)	was spoken (2:3)
word (2:2)	salvation (2:3)
steadfast (2:2)	
transgression (2:2)	having neglected (2:3)
just recompense (2:2)	escape (2:3)

how shall we (2:3)?[2]

TEXT

[5]For [it was] not to *angels* [that] he subjected the world to come, about which we speak, [6]but somewhere someone has testified saying:

Hebrews	First Testament
What is man that you pay attention to him or the Son of man that you consider him? [7]For a short time, you have made him lower than the angels, [and] crowned him with glory and honor.	LXX Ps 8:5**What is man that you pay attention to him or the Son of man that you consider him? [6]For a short time, you have made him lower than the angels, [and] crowned him with glory and honor.** You have set him over the works of your hands;

---

[1] This is the first time in this chapter that a parallel is evident between Acts and Hebrews. A second is the reference to the "chief of their salvation" (Heb 2:10; Acts 5:29-32).

[2] A. Vanhoye, *La Structure Littéraire de L'Epitre aux Hebreux* (Paris: Desclée de Brouwer, c1963), p. 76.

[8]**You have put all things under his feet.**	[8]**You have put all things under his feet.**

In **putting all things under**, he left nothing that was not made subordinate to him. Now we do not see **all things** made subordinate to him, [9]but [with reference to the passage] **For a short time having been made lower than the angels**, we see Jesus, because of his suffering of death, **crowned with glory and honor**, so that, by the grace of God, he might taste death for everyone.

COMMENTARY

[5]*[It was] not to angels [that] he subjected the age to come.* According to the LXX when the Most High distributed the nations, he established their boundaries according to the number of **the angels of God** (LXX Deut 32:8). That text implies that there was an **angel** authorized to **administer** each nation, and each **angel** was entrusted for **the age to come** of the country to which it was assigned. It was against that supposition that the author of Hebrews said that **angels** were not in charge of **the age to come**

The expression translated **age to come** is the Greek *oi-koo-méh-nayn tayn méh-loo-sahn* (οἰκουμένην τὴν μέλλουσαν) which the Syriac rendered *ahl-máh dah-teéd,* עלמא דעתיד, which, in turn, is the equivalent of the Hebrew *oh-láhm hah-báh* (עלם הבא), "the age to come." Although most scholars interpret the Greek *oi-koo-méh-nay* to mean the whole universe or the entire civilized world, according to its use in classical literature, it literally means "being at home," and it has the force of "habitation," "place of dwelling," or "well-administered place." In some contexts it means the Roman Empire. This was also one of the names given for the Promised Land when it was under the rule of a Jewish king.

The Syriac translator rendered *oi-koo-méh-nay* by "age" both times it was used (Heb 1:6; 2:5). It meant either the place where the Messiah ruled; i.e., Palestine, or the time when he ruled; i.e., **the age to come.** It was either into Palestine or into **the age to come** that God introduced his son (Heb 1:6). These terms were so closely related that both have the same significance. When the Messiah ruled, he introduced **the age to come** and the place where he ruled would have been Palestine. This future age and this Promised Land were not to be **subjected to angels** but to the Messiah. That is the message of this verse. Jesus, as the Messiah, would have been **subjected** only **to God.**

In the story of the Israelites in the wilderness, the report is that they ate manna for 40 years **until they came to the Land of Canaan** (MT Exod 16:35). The LXX renders this text **until they came to the land of the** *oi-koo-méh-nayn* (οἰκουμένην). This is not "the heavenly world to come," or "the heavenly world of reality," as Lane rendered the text,[1] unless it were understood that Palestine or Canaan was the "heavenly world" or the "heavenly world of reality." **The age to come** did not refer to heaven, as other scholars have also thought.[2] Westcott recognized that fact years ago:

---

[1] W. L. Lane, *Hebrews 1-8* (Dallas: Word Books, Publisher, c1991), pp. 45 and 46.

[2] Nor a "transcendent future," as E. Grässer, *Der Glaube im Hebräer* (Marburg: N. G. Elwert, 1965), p.210, holds.

> The phrase is not to be understood simply of "the future life" or, more generally, of "heaven." It describes, in relation to that which we may call its constitution, the state of things which, in relation to its development in time, is called "the age to come" (ὁ μέλλων αἰων), and, in relation to its supreme Ruler and characteristics, "the Kingdom of God," or "the Kingdom of heaven," even the order which corresponds with the completed work of Christ.[1]

To be still more specific **the age to come** was sometimes identified with the messianic age. The messianic age was the period during which the Messiah would appear and overpower the foreign ruling government with military might. More often the messianic **age** was expected to precede **the age to come,** which would be the time when the Romans would be completely subdued, and the Messiah would rule as king from his throne at Jerusalem (see commentary on Heb 1:6-8). An antitype for the messianic **age** was the 3½ year period of warfare between Judas the Maccabee and the Syrian Greeks, after the temple was defiled and before the temple was cleansed (ca. 167 BIA- 164 BIA). **The age to come** was the period after the conflict was over and taxation was removed (ca. 142 BIA).

An **age** was a chronological period, a unit of time that was characterized in some distinctive way, such as an evil **age**, a good **age**, an **age** of prosperity, or an **age** of oppression. It could describe the period of a certain rule, dynasty, or political control.[2] R. Joshua interpreted **generation generation** (*dor dor*, דור דור) as Mekilta quoted it from Ps 72:5; MT has *dor dorim*, דור דורים) to mean "[a succession] from life in this **age**" to "life in **the age to come**" (Mek *Amalek* 2:186-88).

Ages were thought to be in temporal sequence. Whenever one **age** ended, the **age to come** began. Thus **the age** of Esau-Edom-Rome had to end before **the age** of Jacob-Israel could begin (4Ezra 6:7-10). **Ages** were like human beings or fruit. They became "ripe" or "grew old" before they passed away (2Bar 70-3; 4Ezra 14:10; 6:20; 12:25; 2Ba*r* 4:11; 2Cor 5:17).[3] Barnabas said, "The righteous man both walks in this world (*en toó-toh tóh káws-moh,* ἐν τοῦτῷ τῷ κόσμῳ and expects the holy age (*táwn háh-gee-on ai-óh-nah*, τὸν ἅγιον αἰῶνα)" (Barn 10:11). The holy **age** was **the age to come.** When speaking of a future world at all in this context the meaning was for the world as it would exist in **the age to come**—not a world in heaven.

Grässer agreed that the **age to come,** mentioned here is the same as the references to the **age to come** used in other places. He correctly related it to the promised rest (Heb 4:3-11), the city (Heb 11:10, 16; 12:22), the father land (Heb 11:14), and the unshakable kingdom (Heb 12:28).[4] Weiss translated the relevant expression "The future world" (*die zukünftige Welt*), although, like Grässer, he recognized the expression as the *oh-láhm hah-báh* (עולם הבא), which should be rendered **the age to come**. Then he thought further that the word **age** should be thought of as an aeon.[5] This is the way scholars transfer from temporal biblical concepts to Hellenisticphilosophical concepts. The subject under discussion is still **ages.**

---

[1] Westcott, *Hebrews*, p. 42.

[2] See further M. Eliade, *Cosmos and History,* tr. W. R. Trask (New York: Harper, 1959), pp. 80-81, 126-27, 134-35.

[3] Buchanan, *The Consequences of the Covenant* (Leiden: E. J. Brill, 1970), pp. 15-16.

[4] E. Grässer, *An die Hebräer* (Zürich: Benziger Verlag, c1990) 1, p. 114.

[5] H. F. Weiss, *Der Brief an die Hebräer* (Göttingen: Vandenhoeck & Ruprecht, 1991), pp. 192-93.

Ages when Jews or Christians ruled were considered "holy." That which was not holy was "common" (Lev 10:10). This means that for Jews the Davidic-Solomonic **age** and the Hasmonean age were both holy. For Christians, **the age** that began with the holy Roman Empire was holy. For Jews, it continued to be the "common era." Jews still consider it the common, pagan, profane, idolatrous era and use the abbreviations BCE and CE to describe the nature of **the age**.

If Jews, rather than Christians, had negotiated successfully with Constantine, Jews would have probably called it the holy era, and Christians would have continued to call it the common era. The same period of history is evaluated differently from different perspectives. Both Jews and Christians used the terms "this age" at times when they were ruled by foreigners. At such times, "this age" was the unholy, pagan, gentile age, and they looked forward to the **age to come** when the **ages** would change in their favor and become for them the holy **age.** In between these **ages** the Messiah was expected to arrive.

Since the **age to come** was to be a period that was inhabited (*oi-koo-méh-nay*) by God's chosen people, of course, during which the Messiah would reign, it follows that that **age** would be subject to the Messiah or **Son,** not to **the angels.** The task of **the angels** was to minister to those who were about to inherit **salvation** in the **age to come. The Son,** on the contrary, was to rule. In the FT the *oi-koo-méh-nay* to come was sometimes identified with the Land of Canaan and sometimes with **the age to come**. These two were closely related. It was in **the age to come** that Jews expected to live in peace and prosperity in the Land of Canaan.

6 *Somewhere someone has testified.* **Somewhere someone** (*poó tees,* πού τις) seems to be an oral, rhetorical form used to avoid explicit reference. It does not mean the author did not know where to find the source, because he quoted it accurately and generally seemed well-versed in the Psalms.

What is a human being that you pay attention to him. This is a quotation from Ps 8, and refers in that Psalm only to the nature and privilege of the *homo sapiens.* The author used Ps 8 because

1) it referred to the Son of man, and
2) it depreciated the angels.

Or the Son of man that you consider him? "Human being" and **son of man** in Ps 8 have the same meaning and refer to the nature of the species.

Commentators generally have wandered off the track at this point by overlooking the fact that the main point of the author's discussion up to this point in Hebrews has been about the **Son** and that the title **Son of man** was used in the gospels as another name for the Messiah. Therefore, instead of using this passage to understand the meaning of the title **Son of man** scholars have discussed the meaning of the incarnation[1] and its importance to the nature of man. Montefiore[2] insisted,

---

[1] For example, see S. H. Turner, *The Epistle to the Hebrews in Greek and English* (New York: Stanford and Swords, 1852), p. 3, and Westcott, *Hebrews*, pp. 43, 60 and 69.

[2] H. Montefiore, *A Commentary on the Epistle to the Hebrews* (New York: Harper & Row, 1964), p. 57.

> . . . our writer does not here apply "the Son of Man" in Psalm 8:4 to Jesus at all.

In so doing, Montefiore has simply overlooked some important facts:

1) This quotation was listed together with other FT passages that the author used to describe the nature of the Son, who was Jesus.
2) Ps 2 pictured the king as a Son who would dash the nations into pieces so that they would bow before him and kiss his feet.
3) Other collections of messianic passages include both Ps 110:1 and Ps 8:6 as messianic witnesses.

Ps 110 describes a king as a **Son** who would shatter opposing kings. His enemies would become a footstool for his feet. Both of these Psalms about sons who were kings were identified with Jesus. In the same context the author quoted Ps 8 about **the Son of man**, under whose feet God would **put all things** (Ps 8:6). Although he used a Psalm eulogizing the nature of man, *he employed it to describe Jesus, the Son, in royal terms*. For the author, the term **Son of man,** like Son, heir, and firstborn, seems to have been a title for the Messiah. This possibility will be considered more carefully at the end of the chapter.

7*For a short time, you have made him lower than the angels.* **For a short time** renders the Greek *brah-khoó* (βραχύ) in Hebrews, which is the same word as that which occurs in the Old Greek of Ps 8:6 and renders the Hebrew *muh-áht* (מעט). In the Psalm, both the Hebrew and Greek mean "a little bit," referring to the status of man (see 2Sam 16:1). The context of Hebrews, however, is dealing with "little" in terms of time (as in LXX Isa 57:17) rather than status, so the same word as used in LXX must here be translated **for a short time**. **You have made him lower** (*ay-láh-toh-sas*, ἠλάττωσας) means "You have given him a subordinate rank," since the context deals with **the Son's** status in comparison to that of **the angels**. Jesus as Son of God was destined for glory and honor, but before that happened, Jesus gave up all the money he had and joined a monastery, where all members were penniless (2Cor 8:1-9), being **for a short time** reduced in rank from that of a man of wealth to a daily life of personal poverty.

The word **angels,** like the reference to **the Son of man** and **God's putting all things under his feet**, attracted the author's attention to Ps 8. All three of these points were important to his argument. **Angels** (*ahn-géh-lous*, ἀγγέλους) is the reading of LXX and concurs with the Targum (*mah-lah-kháh-yah*, מלאכיא). Dahood was probably correct in rendering the Hebrew *eh-loh-heém* (אלהים), **the gods,**[1] rather than **God**, as the RSV translates it (Ps 8:5). In relationship to Heb 1:6 it is evident from studying the variants of LXX, MT and 4Q texts of Deuteronomy 32:43 that "gods," "sons of God," and "angels of God" were often used interchangeably, so that the variants "gods" and "angels" introduce nothing startling in Ps 8:5.

The variant **gods** would not have been acceptable to the author of Hebrews, even if it had been available to him. He was contrasting **the Son** to **the angels**, and the LXX passage was one he was able to use to support his argument. Since the author of Hebrews was discussing a **Son** who was a king, it was also important that he be one who **was crowned with glory and honor**. This is consistent with his claim that **the Son** was **exalted** (Heb 1:3), **worshiped** (Heb 1:6), **anointed** (Heb

---

[1] M. Dahood, *Psalms I* (Garden City: Doubleday & Co., 1965), pp. 48, 51.

1:9). He held the staff of **the kingdom** (Heb 1:8), and **sat down** at the Lord's **right hand** (Heb 1:3:13).

[8]*You have put all things under his feet.* God's **putting all things under** the Son's **feet** is also consistent with the author's use of Pss 110 and 2 to show that the **Son's** enemies would become his footstool and prostrate themselves before him to kiss his **feet**. Paul and the author of Eph (Eph 1:20-22) also combined Ps 8 with Ps 110 to describe Jesus' activity as **Son.** Paul said that Jesus would finally deliver **the kingdom** to God, after destroying every rule, authority, and power, but

> it is necessary for him to rule until **he puts all** his enemies **under his feet** (Ps 110:1) . . . for [God] has put **all things under his feet** (Ps 8:7; 1Cor 15:25-27).

Paul continued to explain that **all things** did not include God who had put all things under the **Son's feet,** but that when all of this had been accomplished, the **Son** himself would be subject to God (1Cor 15:27-28). This would follow, because God was the principal and Jesus was the legal agent.

The relationship of **the Son** to God is reasonably clear. **The Son** was to be the king who overthrew all his enemies with God's help; then he would rule from his throne while his enemies were suppressed. When he became the victorious king who ruled all other political forces, he would still be subordinate to God. He would **sit** on God's throne at God's **right hand,** but he would not be God himself, physically. The author of Hebrews, in all probability, also excluded God from the **all things**, even though he emphasized that nothing was omitted of the things that were made subordinate to him. In dealing with Ps 8, Philo said God made everything subject to man that was under the moon, which included all mortal beings that moved in the water, air, or on land, but he did not make the heavenly beings subject to human beings (Op 28:84).

The author of Hebrews, like the NT authors generally, was no longer interested in Ps 8 in relationship to the nature of man as such, but interested only in Jesus, **the Son of man**, who was king and messiah, and as such was destined to rule **all things**, since God had **established** him **heir** of all (Heb 1:2; see also Eph 1:22; 1Pet 3:22). Because he was then at the right hand of God in the heavens, even the heavenly beings, like **angels**, were subject to him. The authors of Eph (Eph 1:20-22) and 1Pet (1Pet 3:22) claimed that, with the ascension, Jesus had already been exalted above all powers, but the author of Hebrews, like Paul (1Cor 15:25-28), admitted that there was no evidence to show that at that point **all things** had so far been **made subject** to Jesus.

[9]*We see Jesus, because of the suffering and death, crowned with glory and honor.* With Heb 2:9 it is first clear that the author was speaking of **Jesus the Son,** rather than of human beings in general. It was **Jesus, the Son** of man, who had been temporarily reduced in rank. It does not say specifically that this reduction involved the incarnation, as many scholars assume, but that is possible. The passage here deals only with his **suffering of death**, which in itself was enough depreciation to constitute a reduction in rank. Although he had been anointed to become king of Israel, his crucifixion postponed his enthronement. This may have been the reduction the author had in mind. His **tasting death** was probably understood in atonement theology. That means that his death benefited all parties to the contract

because it canceled many **crimes** that had accumulated in the debit column of the treasury of merits.

Summary. The whole unit, 1:5-2:9, deals with the superiority of **the Son** over **the angels**. The author argued his case with the strong support of an admirable collection of FT passages. He was not the only one to collect such passages. There were many *florilegia* dealing with the Messiah and some of these overlapped, as the following comparisons show:

Hebrews 1:5-2:9	Midrash on Ps 2:9	**4QFlor**	1Cor 15:25-27	Eph 1:22;
2Sam 7:14		2Sam 7:10-14		
Ps 110:1	Ps 110:1		Ps 110:1	Ps 110:1
Ps 2:7	Ps 2:7-8			
Ps 8:4-6			Ps 8:6	Ps 8:6
LXX Deut 32:43	Exod 4:22	Exod 15:17-18		
Ps 104:4	Isa 52:13	Amos 9:11		
Ps 45:6-7	Isa 42:1	Ps 1:1		
Ps 102:25-27	Dan 7:13-14	Isa 8:11		
		Ezek 37:23 (?)		
		Ps 2:1		
		Dan 12:10		
		Dan 11:32		

Some FT texts were evidently very well-known and popular. Of these five collections, for instance, Ps 110:1 occurs four times; 2Sam 7:14 occurs twice; three collections include Ps 8:6, and two lists include Ps 2:7. All of these used Ps 110 as a messianic Psalm. Referring to the collection on Midrash Ps 2.9 R. Yudan said,

> All these comforting [passages] are in the decree of the King, the King of kings, who will perform them for the messianic king (*luh-méh-lehk hah-muh-sheé-ahk*, למלך המשיח) (*Midr* Ps 2:9).

Like the author of Hebrews, R. Yudan understood **the Son** referred in Ps 110 to be the same as **the Son** described in Ps 2 and also **the Son of man,** which Hebrews related to Ps 8 but which R. Yudan related to Dan 7. Both R. Yudan and the author of Hebrews believed that the titles **Son** and "**Son of man**" could be applied to the Messiah. 4QFlor associated 2Sam 7:14 to Ps 2:1 and other passages dealing with David and his **son,** in somewhat the same way as Hebrews did, although 4QFlor stressed the importance of David's **son** as the Messiah, whereas Hebrews, using the same texts, did not mention David's name at all. Paul and the author of Eph, as well as the author of Heb, related both Pss 110:1 and 8:6 to Jesus the Messiah and considered both **Son** and **Son of man** to be messianic titles.

The author of Heb stylistically related Pss 2, 8, and 110 more closely to each other than the other passages he quoted by beginning his discussion with a quotation from Ps 110 followed by another from Ps 2 and concluding it with a requotation from Ps 110, followed by another from Ps 8. The nature of the Messiah related to these Psalms is vividly described by still another zealous Jew's poem based on Ps 2:8-9 (PssSol 17:23-28):

> 23 Observe, Lord, and raise up for them their king, the son of David,
> at the time in which you see, O God,
> that he may rule over Israel your servant.
> 24 Arm him well that he may shatter unrighteous rulers;
> 25 Cleanse Jerusalem from Gentiles
> that trample [her] down to destruction;
> 26 [that he may] expel criminals from [the] inheritance,
> in wisdom [and] in righteousness,
> shatter the pride of the criminal like a potter's vessel.
> With a rod of iron break to pieces all their substance;
> 27 destroy the lawless Gentiles with the word of his mouth.
> [Let] Gentiles flee from his presence, at his rebuke,
> and [let him] chastise criminals for the thoughts of their heart.
> 28 Then he will gather together a holy people,
> whom he will lead in righteousness,
> and he will judge the tribes of the people
> that have been sanctified by the Lord, his God.

The author of Hebrew's choice of Scripture comes mostly from the Psalms. Of the eight quotations in this section, six are from Psalms, with only one each from the Pentateuch and the former prophets. This may reflect his liturgical interest, or it may simply mean that the material the author needed happened to be in the Psalms. In a way that is characteristic of the author. He framed Heb 1:5-14 with an inclusion, but his borders are not perfectly sharp. One section seems to shade over into the other and prepare the readers for the shift in subject matter. For example, his introduction includes his first mention of Ps 110, which is basic to the section that follows. If it were quoted as the first quotation in verse five rather than in verse three, it would form a perfect inclusion with its requotation in verse 13, but the author did not plan it that way. He formed his inclusion with his introductory question **To which of the angels has he ever said** (Heb 1:5, 13). Within the inclusion in Heb 1:5-14, there is also a smaller literary form. A chiasm is formed by the organization of contrasts:

(5) Son,		(6) angels,
	X	
(7) angels,		(8-12) Son.

The theological argument of this section was interrupted by the ethical exhortation (Heb 2:1-4) that was not necessary to the discussion, but it was evidently important to the author to relate his doctrine to the needs of his listeners, because he followed his doctrine with exhortation throughout the document. He obviously knew the needs of his listeners as if he had been their teacher and counselor. He was not just a visiting preacher or lecturer.

In some ways the argument proceeds from Heb 1:5 to 2:9 with an exhortatory intrusion, and in other ways Heb 1:5-14 forms its own literary unit, framed by an inclusion and including the magic number of seven quotations.[1] To this the reference to Ps 8, together with the exhortation, seems like an appendage. Nonetheless, the subject matter (Son, angels, exaltation, and suppression of enemies underfoot) is coherent throughout Heb1:5-2:9, which forms the beginning argument in defense of **the Son.** The nature of the **Son,** presented in this section, and his relationship to the **Son of man** is an important item that has been generally overlooked by commentators. It will be given still further attention at the end of this chapter.

By the grace of God. There is one variant reading for this phrase. Instead of **by the grace of God** (*kháh-ree-tee theh-oó,* χάριτι θεοῦ) it has "without God" (*khóh-rees theh-oó* (χῶρις θεοῦ). Several scholars have tried to make sense of this variant, without success. Because it is the most difficult of the variant readings, it seems unlikely that later scribes would change the most reasonable reading to this text. Nonetheless it seems just too difficult to interpret correctly, even if it happened to be the original text. The earliest Syriac text was probably "For he, in his Grace, God, tastes death on behalf of everyone."[2] In this text, "God" is evidently used as if it were in explanatory apposition to the pronoun "he." The meaning would be, "For God, by his grace, tastes death on behalf of everyone." This might be understood as if Jesus, as God's legal agent, tasted death, but legally, that which Jesus did, God did. That would be very similar in meaning to the thought that Jesus, by the grace of God, tasted death.

THE SON AND THE BELIEVERS

Hebrews	**First Testament**
10For it was fitting for him [God], for whom were **all things** and through whom were **all things,**	Ps 8:7You have put **all things** under his feet.
	Lev 21:10 The priest who is greater than his brothers, oil having been poured on his head and having been **made perfect** . . .
to **make perfect** the chief of their salvation through sufferings,	
leading many **sons**	What is a human being that you remember him; the **son** of man that you visit him . . . you have crowned him with **glory** and honor
to **glory**. 11For both he [Jesus]	
who sanctifies and those who are	Exod 31:13I am Yehowah **who sanctifies** you.

[1] This is the exact number of quotations in the collection in Midrash on Ps 2:9. Heb 7 is also organized into 7 divisions. The author of Hebrews may have used a florilegium of 7 passages on the Son, to which he added the 8th, Ps 8.

[2] S. P. Brock, "Hebrews 2:9B in the Syriac Tradition," *NovTest* 27 (1985):236-244.

sanctified are all from one. Therefore he [Jesus] is not ashamed to call them "**brothers,**"	
12 saying, **I will announce your name to my brothers;** **in the midst of the congregation** **I will praise you** in song.	Ps 22:23-24 **I will announce your name to my brothers;** **in the midst of the congregation** **I will praise you**. You who fear Yehowah, **praise** him! All you children of Jacob, glorify him!
13 And again: **I will be confident in him** and again:	LXX Isa 8:17 I will wait for the God who has turned his face from the house of Jacob, and **I will be confident in him**. LXX2Sam 22:3 God is my protector. **I will be confident in him**
Look! I and the children whom God has given me	LXX Isa 8:18 **Look! I and the children whom God has given me**. They will be as signs and wonders in the house of Israel.

TECHNICAL DETAILS

From the point of view of literary structure, Heb 2:10-13 does not form a separate unit. This is a continuation of the midrash in Ps 8, quoted in Heb 2:6-8. The author took the words **all things**, **sons**, and **glory** from that Psalm. He then continued his sermon by introducing three more passages from the FT whose meaning is not completely clear until they are seen in their context. It is not easy to recognize the subjects of all sentences, because they are pronouns without obvious antecedents. Another difficulty is that the word **leading** is an aorist participle, which would normally be rendered "having lead." It should probably be considered a proleptic aorist, which takes the work of Christ and its consequences as a unity.

COMMENTARY

10 *It was fitting.* Attridge thought it would not have been proper in Greek or Greco-Jewish theology to suggest that propriety was a consequence of God's nature. It, rather, belonged to human nature.[1] Calling attention to other statements in Hebrews about God's passion (Heb 3:11; 4:3; 10:30-31; 12:29), Mitchell held if propriety were offensive then these statements would have been just as offensive to Greek and to Greco-Jewish theology as the expression Attridge criticized.[2] He further showed, however, that the use of propriety was very important to rhetoric and that it increased in importance from Aristotle to Quintilian. Aristotle, for example, said,

---

[1] H. Attridge, *The Epistle to the Hebrews* (Philadelphia: Fortress, 1980), p. 82.

[2] A. C. Mitchell, "The Uses of pre/pein and Rhetorical Propriety in Hebrews 2:10)."

> Style expresses emotion. . . . Appropriate style also makes the fact appear credible. . . . the hearer always sympathizes with one who speaks emotionally, even though he really says nothing (Rhet. 3.7, 2-5).

Style was designed to be appropriate to the hearer and to the speaker. In a document as rhetorically oriented as Hebrews, this attribution to God was not out of place.

10*Make perfect the chief.* **All things** (*páhn-tah,* πάντα) found also in Heb 2:11, 16, and 17, refers to Ps 8:6, quoted in Heb 2:8. These are **all** the **things** that are to be put **under the Son's feet** (Heb 2:8), which are also the **things** of which God established the **Son heir** (Heb 1:2). If he is **heir** of **all things** and **all things** have been put **under** his **feet,** it would be saying very little more to claim that **all things** were for and through him, but that is not what it says. The subject here is God and not **the Son.** God is the one who **perfects the Son** who is the **pioneer of their salvation**.

The word **perfect** (*teh-lay-óh-sai,* τελειῶσαι) was important to the author's vocabulary. In verbal form it occurs in Hebrews 14 times; as an adverb (*teh-láy-ohs*), once; as an adjective (*téh-leh-aws*, τέλεος), twice; and as a noun (*teh-lay-oh-táce* (τελειωτής), *teh-láy-oh-sees* (τελείωσις), or *teh-lay-áw-tays,* τελειότης), three times. Depending on its context, this verb means to perfect, accomplish, fulfill, complete, or become mature. In a religious context, it usually describes a person who was fully cleansed from **crime**, qualified for full membership in a religious order, or one who observed rigorously all the rules required by the group. It does not have the scientific meaning of a hypothetically straight line or a perfect circle.

The priest who is greater than his brothers was to be anointed with oil. At which time he would **fill his hand** and be allowed to wear high priestly garments (Lev 21:10). This probably meant that his hand was filled with the authority needed to fulfill the duties of his office. Based on the contexts, most translators render, "filling the hand" (*mee-láy ehth yah-dóh,* מלא את ידו), "having been consecrated." The LXX rendered this expression, "perfected," (*teh-teh-lay-óh-méh-noo,* τετελειωμένου), thinking that a priest that was consecrated was **perfected.** The author of Hebrews thought Jesus was qualified to be considered greater than all of his brother priests and had therefore been anointed and was made **perfect**

Other terms that are closely allied to the word **perfect** are "sanctified" and "worthy."[1] A sanctified person is one who has been cleansed from all defilement. A person judged worthy of full admission into a sect was considered **perfect**. To make Jesus fully qualified as **the perfect chief of their salvation**, the training required involved passing **through sufferings**. The author assumed that his readers were informed about the nature of these **sufferings**, because he did not describe them in detail. The extent of this **suffering** was also mentioned, but not described in Heb 2:9, the **suffering of death**. The Son was the **perfect chief,** who after his **suffering of death** was **crowned with glory and honor** (Heb 2:9) and was well-qualified to lead **many [other] sons to glory**.

The **many sons** which Jesus might **lead** to glory would have been other sons of Abraham, Jesus' brothers. Grässer said this could happen because of the "general

---

[1] See H. Ch. Peuch, "Gnostic Gospels and Related Documents," *New Testament Apocrypha*, ed. E. Hennecke, re-ed. W. Schneemelcher, tr. R. Mc. Wilson (Philadelphia: Westminster, 1963) I, pp. 263, 328; Acts of Peter 26; Hippolytus *On Daniel* 4:60; *RecLXX.* 2.8; 3.27 *et al.*

heavenly preexistence of **the Son** and the **sons,"**[1] but there is no direct indication in the entire Book of Hebrews that Jesus preexisted in heaven before his human **birth**. Weiss correctly said that this is certainly not the simple application of the Gnostic idea of a relationship between the savior and the saved or a suggestion that this idea is of heavenly origin. This subject deals with suffering and not heavenly ascent.[2]

The chief of their salvation. The word **chief** is chosen to render the Greek *ahr-khay-gós* (ἀρχηγός), because it is one of several of the words that reflects the FT use of the term. The Greek word renders primarily the Hebrew *róhsh* (ראש), which means "head," "leader," "commander," or "chief." It also renders *nah-seé* (נשׂיא) "leader," "prince," or "general." It is a messianic title, given to Bar Cochba. Ezekiel gave this as the title for the Davidic Messiah (Ezek 34:24; 37:25; 44:3). Another use is for the translation of *sahr* (שׂר), which means "general" or **chief**. The **chief** mentioned here is closely related to national leadership. Jesus was called the "head" of the body, the church (Col 1:18). The body of which Jesus was the leader was a legal body, a corporation, also called the church.[3]

As the head of the eternal corporation, the church, Jesus was its founder, its **chief,** its leader, or its prince. Referring to Jesus, the author of Acts said, **God exalted him chief and savior to his right hand so that he might provide for Israel repentance and the forgiveness of crimes** (Acts 5:31).[4] This is another way of saying that Jesus was the **chief** of Israel's **salvation**.

11*He who sanctifies and those who are sanctified are all from one*. This has almost the same meaning as Paul's reminder,

> **Just as in one body we have many members, and not all members have the same function, thus we [who] are many are one body in Christ and each one members of one another** (Rom 12:4-5; 1Cor 12:12-13).

Christians became members of this **body** by being baptized (1Cor 12:13). The body which is often mentioned in the NT is not a physical body, but a legal one. It is a corporation of Christ, the *corpus Christi*, the **body** of Christ. A corporation is a legal **body** that functions in court the same as a physical body. It can be taxed and sued, and it can also sue others, but there is one difference: a corporation is by definition immortal. The realization that the church is a legal corporation is still reaffirmed in the United Methodist Church when new members are received into **the body** of Christ. The minister announces to the congregation the meaning of this ceremony,

> The church is of God, **and will be preserved to the end of time** [emphasis mine] for the conduct of worship, the due administration of God's Word and Sacraments, the maintenance of Christian

---

[1] Grässer, *An die Hebräer* 1, p. 133.
[2] Weiss, *Hebräer*, p. 212.
[3] On the situation at which Jesus formed the church as a corporation, see Buchanan, *The Gospel of Matthew* (Lewiston: Mellen, 1996) II, pp. 964-980.
[4] See further G. Johnston, "Christ as Archegos," *NTS* 27 (1981):381-85.

> fellowship and discipline, the edification of believers, and the conversion of the world.[1]

All members of the corporation can change, but the corporation lives on. Most corporations consist of more members than one, but there is such a phenomenon as a corporation sole. For example a king is a corporation sole. As such he has two **bodies**, a physical body that is born, grows, becomes ill, and dies. The other body is a legal **body** which never dies. In England, when a king dies, the English say, "The king is dead. Long live the king!" The physical king died, but the political king, the legal king, is immortal, so that England is never without a king. Blackstone defined an old English liturgy transferring property or authority, called "livery of seisin" as follows:

> And then the feoffor [seller], if it be of land, doth deliver to the feoffee [buyer], all other persons being out of the ground, a clod or turf, or a twig or bough there growing, with words to this effect: "I deliver these to you in the name of seisin of all the lands and tenements contained in this deed." But if it be of a house, the feoffor [seller] must take the ring or latch of the door, the house being quite empty, and deliver it to the feoffee [buyer] in the same form; and then the feoffee [buyer] must enter alone, and shut-to the door, and then open it, and let in the others.[2]

The English jurists knew that this was a very old liturgy, but they did not know its age or origin. The same liturgy, however, was employed by the man nearest of kin to Naomi, when he gave his sandal to Boaz and with it the authority to buy the land under discussion and also permission to marry Ruth (Ruth 4:7-10). When Jonathan made a contract with David by which he gave David his right to follow his father, Saul, on the throne and become king, he gave him his robe, his coat of armor, his helmet, and his sword as seisins (1Sam 18:3-4)

Jesus probably formed the church as a corporation at the Last Supper. All the members at that supper were Jesus' legal agents, his apostles. Using a legal liturgy called "livery seisen," he gave each of them a piece of unleavened bread and said, **This is my body** (*sóh-mah,* σῶμα, Matt 26:26). He did not say, "This is my flesh" (*sahrx,* σάρξ). When he did this, he formed a corporation of these legal agents, and it was *his* corporation. This was the beginning of the church. It was not until the **body** of Christ was legally formed that Jesus used another seisin, the fruit of the vine, to renew the contract (Matt 26:28). As the Lord's legal agent he was authorized to act in God's behalf to form a new contract, and as soon as there was a legal **body** to be the other party to the contract, he did precisely that.[3]

Later others were introduced into this corporation through another legal ceremony, baptism. They were **baptized into Christ** (Rom 6:3), and became members of **the body** of Christ or became **in Christ**. This corporation was not called the **body** of Jesus, because it was not the personality of Jesus that was legal. It was his office as the Messiah that authorized him to form the legal corporation. The

---

[1] *The United Methodist Hymnal* (Nashville: The United Methodist Publishing House, c1989), p. 45.

[2] W. Blackstone, *Commentarie on the Laws of England* (Chicago: Callaghan and Co., 1884, 3d ed. rev), vol. 2, p. 314.

[3] For further details about this liturgy see Buchanan, *Matthew* II, pp. 965-982

corporation was a legal body of Christ, and the members of this corporation were **in Christ**. They were in the corporation of which the Messiah was the originator, just as Abraham was the originator of the Hebrew family corporation. After that, Jesus and all of his followers became members of a corporation, his **body.** Jesus, the one who formed the corporation, and the apostles who were formed into the corporation were all one body or corporation., **for both he who sanctifies and those who are sanctified are all from one** (Heb 2:11). Jesus was not only the **chief** of this group; he was also the **sanctifier.** Just as the one who formed the corporation was one with those with whom it was formed, so the **sanctifier** and the **sanctified** were **one**.

He who sanctifies, in the Torah was Yehowah (Exod 31:13), but in this context, is **the Son** and **the chief of their salvation** was the one **who sanctifies**. Since the Messiah was a legal agent of Yehowah he was also justified in **sanctifying.** The word **sanctify** (*hag-ee-áhd-zohn,* ἁγιάζων--Hebrew *kee-dáysh,* קדשׁ) means to cleanse, make holy, or separate from defiled things. For example, when David was attracted to Bathsheba, she was bathing to cleanse herself from her menstrual defilement (*mit-kah-déh-sheht mee-toóm-uh-ah-táh,* מתקדשת מטמאתה), or *sanctifying* herself (2Sam 11:2). On the Day of Atonement, there were ten occasions when the high priest was required to **sanctify** his hands and his feet (mYoma 3.2, 4, 6), meaning he washed them. In the same way those who were baptized into the corporation of Christ were **sanctified.** At Mount Sinai, Moses was directed to **sanctify** the people (*kid-dásh-tam,* קדשׁתם) and have them wash their garments (Exod 19:10). When Job's sons attended a drinking party, Job **sanctified** them, meaning he rose up early the next morning and provided the proper offerings necessary to atone for crimes they might have committed (Job 1:5). The people who were cleansed, **sanctified**, or atoned were called saints (*qeh-doh-sheém,* קדשׁים) or *háh-gee-oi* (ἅγιοι).

The term "saint" or **sanctified** one could refer especially to a person who was very carefully observant of all holiness rules, or it could be used quite generally to refer to any party to the contract, either a Jew or a Christian, since all parties to the new contract were baptized. For instance, Paul used the term in a general sense. Whatever the degree of rigidity by which the author of Hebrews understood and used this term, **he who sanctifies** Christians was Jesus, just as Moses was the one who **sanctified** the people of Israel at the foot of Mount Sinai. **Those who are sanctified** were the Christians, the new "holy people." As in Heb 2:10, the **all** used here was an intentional repetition of the **all** quoted in Heb 2:8 from Ps 8:7.

This new group of **sanctified** people were not just people in general. They were also **all** probably Jews. **From one** probably means from one father, namely Abraham, or **from one** family corporation, which has the same meaning.[1] They were **all** sons; Jesus was **the Son of God** or **the Son of man** and also a son of Abraham, whereas his **brothers** were also legal sons of Abraham. Not **all** sons of Abraham were his physical descendants. Some had been adopted into the family corporation through legal liturgies. They had been "born again" legally as sons of Abraham. **All** proselytes into Judaism or Samaritanism were also sons of Abraham. **All** members of Islam consider themselves to be sons of Abraham.

He was not ashamed to call them brothers. It was not enough that Jesus be of the same faith or point of view as **the brothers**. He had **to be made like** them **in every**

[1] O. Michel, *Der Brief an die Hebräer* (Göttingen: Vandenhoeck & Ruprecht, 1957), p. 80, insisted that both the one who sanctifies and the one from which both originate is God. This makes no sense.

way--blood and flesh, family, and heritage—not just human nature, as some scholars suggest. Grässer was correct in saying that those brothers who had fallen in death with Jesus were guaranteed unity with him in **salvation**,[1] but that was not all. Jesus was identified physically and genetically with **the sons** of Abraham. Lane agreed with Bruce that Jesus, like all other Jews and Samaritans, shared the same **flesh and blood**. After they had said that, however, both Lane[2] and Bruce[3] held that Jesus was not the same as all the rest of the Jews. He had existed before his birth and chose to be human—a choice no other Jews had.

The author of Hebrews never said that he was pre-existent. That pre-existence doctrine was imported eisegetically by Lane, Bruce, and many other scholars. So far as Hebrews is concerned, Jesus became a human being, just like other Jews, by being **born.** As a human being for about 30 years, he was for these years **lower than the angels.** He did not choose to be **born** anymore than anyone else. He inherited the **flesh and blood** of his **birth** parents. Had he been given the privilege of choosing whether or not he would become a human being, then he would not have been just like other human beings. When he became an adult, however, he was able to make choices. One of these may have been to join a monastery. If so, he would at that time have been **born again,** legally. He also chose to accept John the Baptist's invitation to become the new Messiah. At that time he chose to be legally **born again**, as John anointed him.

Jews would never have considered an alien as their high priest. They were very careful to see that the high priest belonged to the correct family, preferably Zadok's line. They objected to the Hasmoneans who were only priests but who **assumed** the position reserved for the sons of Zadok (GenR. 97; 99:2).

This seems to imply that the Christians in which the author was interested were Jewish rather than Gentile Christians, since they, like Jesus, were sons of Abraham. Jesus was **the Son** and the **one who sanctifies**, and Christians were the **many sons** and **those who are sanctified**. This constitutes a religious family, **from one** [father]. Since religion and family origin were very closely associated in Israel, when sects developed in Judaism--each one posing as the redeeming remnant of Israel--celibate, communistic brotherhoods also developed. These sects, like the Essenes, were composed of very serious, devout Jews who tried to keep every jot and tittle of the law. In order to do so, they had to avoid all types of defilement. Since menstrual and seminal discharges were defiling, and since women of child bearing age were ritually defiled half of the time, avoidance of all contact with women became necessary; therefore celibate brotherhoods were formed of men of the same convictions and devotion.

Since celibates could not father children to care for them physically and materially in their old age, it was necessary for these men to form unions that would meet these needs by pooling their resources and taking care of one another as was necessary. These rigid parties to the contract isolated themselves from the rest of the world, including their own families, who might be defiled and serve food not completely approved.[4] When the mother and blood brothers of Jesus came to see him, and he was told of their presence, he responded,

---

[1] Grässer, *An die Hebräer* 1, p. 117.
[2] Lane, *Hebrews,* pp. 60-65.
[3] F. F. Bruce, *The Epistle to the Hebrews* (Grand Rapids: Eerdmans Publishing Co., c1964), p. 31.
[4] Buchanan, *The Consequences*, pp. 238-81.

"Who is my mother, and who are my brothers?" Then stretching out his hand to his disciples, he said, "Here are my mother and my brothers" (Matt 12:46-49)!

This new social **brother**hood provided for its members' needs that a family normally supplied. Therefore the members called one another **brother**. The term **brothers** occurs 217 times in the NT outside of Hebrews, when the term refers to other members of the same contract rather than to blood **brothers**. Not all of these **brothers** were celibate, communal members of rigid brotherhoods. Like the term "saints," sometimes the term **brothers** was used quite generally and inclusively, meaning fellow children of Abraham rather than sectarian **brothers;** so it is not certain that the term **brothers** here refers to such a rigid monastic group as some brotherhoods were, but there are other indications in the document that point in that direction. In any event, the **sanctified** ones are the same as the **brothers**.

12*I will announce your name to my brothers.* The proof text the author used to justify **brothers** was legitimate. The **brothers** mentioned in LXX of Ps 21:23 were not **blood brothers** but the legal sons of Jacob or Israel (LXX Ps 21:24). The author of the Psalm, of course, was not Jesus, as the argument suggests, but biblical interpreters in NT times, both Jewish and Christian, frequently applied FT passages to whatever subject they chose, especially the Messiah. Modern lawyers use legal precedents in a similar way. The LXX word for **announce** *is dee-ay-gáy-so-mai* (διηγήσομαι), but the Hebrews variant is *ah-pahng-geh-lóh* (ἀπαγγελῶ). These words being synonymous, the author may have used a text with the variant he accepted. If he had choices, he may have preferred *ah-pahng-geh-loh* to *dee-ay-gáy-saw-mai* because of its proximity in form to *áhn-geh-laws*, which had received a lot of attention up to that point in the discussion.

The midst of the congregation. The word rendered **congregation** here is the same Greek word that is often rendered "church." Because the author refers to the brothers, the sanctified ones, the sons, and the children also as those whose **names are written in heaven** (Heb 12:23) and members of **the church of the first born [people]** (Heb 12:23), Grässer called this **congregation a "heavenly** church."[1] The text does not say "heavenly," and it would only be fair to call it "heavenly," if "heavenly" were used as a tender expression to describe something on earth that was considered divine or holy. A heavenly church on earth would be a church of God. It would not imply that it existed only in heaven.

The **congregation** was the community composed of sons (Heb 2:10), sanctified ones, or **brothers** (Heb 2:11). **The chief of their salvation** would **lead many sons to glory** by proclaiming the good news or **announcing** the Lord's **name** to the **brothers**.

13*I will be confident in him.* These very words appear both in the LXX of Isa 8:17 and LXX 2Sam 22:3. Scholars have disagreed about which one the author of Hebrews quoted. This is not a crucial debate, because the author of Hebrews knew the FT so well that he probably realized he was quoting from two passages at the

---

[1] Grässer, *An die Hebräer* 1, p. 140.

same time. Vaughan and Michel[1] preferred the 2Sam 22:3 passage. Two points in its favor are:

1) 2Sam 22:3 is supposed to be a quotation from David, and according to Hebrews this passage is supposed to have been said by Jesus; and
2) the author seemed to prefer Psalms, and therefore would be more likely to quote from a psalm of **David** than from one of the prophets.

Against these are the fact that the author has made no attempt, direct or indirect, to identify Jesus with the son of David, and therefore would not have been likely here to affirm a Davidic messianism by choosing a passage that was once attributed to David, rather than another that said the same thing. Although the author seemed to prefer Psalms, the fact that the second half of Heb 2:13 is a continuation of the Isaiah passage indicates that the entire quotation came from Isaiah.

The Greek translated **confident of him** (*peh-poi-thóhs ep-aw-tó*, πεποιθὼς ἐπ αὐτῷ) might also be rendered "persuaded" or "convinced in him." The Hebrew of Isa 8:17 is *wuh-kee-wáy-tee-loh* (וקויתי לו): **but I will hope in him**. Isaiah had contrasted himself to the house of Jacob from whom the Lord had turned his face. Even though the Lord rejected the house of Jacob, Isaiah would hope in **him** (Isa 8:17). The subject of the sentence in Isa 8:17 was Isaiah. The author of Hebrews changed the subject to Jesus and left the object the same, a practice that was customary to the author of Hebrews and to other Christian and Jewish interpreters of that day. The one in whom both Isaiah and Jesus had **confidence** was God, whose name was to be **announced** to the **brothers, in the midst of the congregation**. The object, God, was one of the points that related LXX Ps 21:23 to Isa 8:17, but the main attraction of the Isaiah passage to the Psalm was contained in the word **children**, quoted in the next verse, which could be identified with **brothers** of Heb 2:12, as well as the **sons** of Heb 2:10 and the **sanctified** ones of Heb 2:11.

I and the children whom God has given me in its FT context referred to Isaiah himself, and his children, Shearjashub (Isa 7:3) and Mahershalalhashbaz (Isa 8:3), who were given prophetic names to indicate how the Lord would treat Israel. They were both given as signs. In his customary fashion, however, the author of Hebrews took the **I** to mean Jesus and **the children** to be his followers or **brothers**. Since Jesus was celibate, he had no physical children, but as the chief or father of a new legal corporation, established by a new contract, he was the legal father of all the members of that Christian corporation. God had given them to him, legally; they were God's sons (Heb 2:10) and his **children.** They had been **sanctified** (Heb 2:11). Therefore Jesus was **not ashamed to call them brothers** (Heb 2:11).

TEXT

14Since, therefore, the children share blood and flesh, he also himself shared the same equally, so that he might incapacitate the one who controls death, namely, the devil, 15and release all those who, through fear of death, were subject to slavery through every aspect of life.

---

[1] C. J. Vaughan, *The Epistle to the Hebrews* (London: Macmillan, 1890), p. 46; Michel, *Hebräer* p. 81.

Hebrews	First Testament
16 For he certainly does not **prefer** [**take**] angels	Jer 31: 31 When I **took** them by the hand to bring them from the Land of Egypt.
but he **prefers** [**takes**] **the seed of Abraham**.	Isa 41:8-9 8 But you, Israel, my son Jacob, whom I **chose** **[the] seed of Abraham**, whom I loved, 9 whom I **took** from the boundaries of the land.
17 Therefore he was obligated to be made like **the brothers** in every way, so that he might become a merciful and faithful	Ps 22:23 I will announce your name to **my brothers**; in the midst of the congregation, I will praise you.
high priest [regarding] **divine** services, so that the crimes of the people might be expiated.	LXX Exod 4:16 He will be your mouth, and you will be to him the [source of] **divine** things. LXX Exod 18:19 You will be to the people the [source of] **divine** things. LXX Deut 31:27 For while I have been with you you have been bitter against the **divine** things.

18 For because he himself suffered, having been tempted, he is able to help those who are being tempted

COMMENTARY

14 *Incapacitate the one who controls death.* The expression **flesh and blood** is a customary Jewish and Christian idiom meaning human nature, especially as distinct from **divine** nature (Matt 16:17; 1Cor 15:50; Gal 1:16; Eph 6:12; mNazir 9:5; mSot 8:1). Jews who rejected the yoke of Heaven were ruled by a king of **flesh and blood** (tSot 14:4; tBabQ 7:5). This means that if they rejected Judaism, they had no choice but to become gentiles and submit to a foreign, gentile king. The idiom used by the author of Hebrews, however, was **blood and flesh**. Justin said that the lineal descendants of Jacob were **from blood and flesh** (*hái-mah-tos kai sahr-kós,* αἵματος καὶ σαρκός). Also Jesus was born from **flesh and blood,** but the Christ was born by faith and spirit (Dial 135.6). This is another way of saying that Jesus was physically **born;** the Messiah was legally created. That would have happened when Jesus was anointed. Paul also said that Jesus was from the seed of David according to the flesh, but established son of God in power according to the spirit of holiness (Rom 1:3-4).

When Jesus received the spirit, he became the Messiah, but he was also a human being of **blood and flesh**. This was the **blood and flesh** which Jesus shared equally with other children of Abraham, and may not have referred specifically to human nature at all. It was because of this family heritage that he **was not ashamed to call them brothers.** The expression, **blood and flesh**, may have taken human nature for granted, but meant to specify that among the human beings that existed on earth, Jesus was of the same **blood and flesh** as other children of Abraham. They were all fellow Israelites and belonged to the same family tree (see Deut 17:15).

Members of monastic sects, especially, were all **brothers**, legally, and they all belonged to the same legal family. They were legally sons of **the Son** and those who had been sanctified by the sanctifier. They were also **children** who **shared** the same **blood and flesh**, belonging to the same family corporation, with Abraham as their father.

Because the author was probably speaking to a monastic audience, where all the members were recognized as parts of a special family corporation and called "brothers," he emphasized the fact that Jesus was also their brother, and he not been ashamed of that fact. Those who were considering the possibility of leaving the order should be reminded of that. Jesus may even have been a member of the same monastic order.

There was evidently a strong Jewish and Christian belief that the devil was in control of **death.** Resh Laqish said Satan, the evil inclination, and the angel of death are identical (bBabB 16a). According to the Wisdom of Solomon, **God did not make death** (Sol 1:13). Death entered the world by means of the envy of the devil (*phthoh-noh deh dee-ah-bóh-loo,* φθόνῳ δὲ διαβόλου) (Sol 2:24). Paul also said of all the rules, authorities, and powers that God would put under Jesus' feet that **the last enemy incapacitated** (*kah-tahr-gáy-tai,* καταργεῖται) would be **death** (1Cor 15:26). Paul held that the **crime** of Adam caused death, so that **death** ruled from Adam to Moses (Rom 5:12-21). **Crime** and **death** were closely related; it was **crime** that caused **death. Death** and life were terms not always used to mean just physical existence or lack of existence. In some contexts, life meant existence under the contract, whereas **death** was the existence of those outside. According to this logic, then, the devil caused faithful people to become apostates. In so doing the devil caused the **death** of those who left the faith and broke the contract.

A person who committed a **crime** unto **death** was expelled from the community, excommunicated from "life," and turned over to **death.**[1] Since Jesus' sacrifice was considered enough to cancel all of the **crimes** Israel had accumulated, Israel had become reconciled to God through the **death** of God's **Son** (Rom 5:10); this means **the Son incapacitated** "the devil" **who controls death.**[2] At the same time that Jesus **incapacitated death,** he also brought life and immortality to light through the gospel (2Tim 1:10; see also 1Cor 2:6). The religious **death** caused by **crime** was the **death** which Jesus would **incapacitate**. Believers would continue to face physical **death** after that, but since the sting of **death** is **crime,** and the **crime** had been cancelled, Christians could be **confident** that they would later be raised into "life" (1Cor 15:56).

15*Release all those.* Israel reckoned **crimes** that had not been atoned as debts for which God was the creditor. When the account became overdrawn, the situation was analogous to that of an Israelite who was not able to repay a debt that he owed his fellow Israelite. He would have to work it out at half wages until the debt was

[1] Buchanan, *Consequences,* pp. 110-49.

[2] For Paul the true Israel for whom this was effective was composed of those who had faith in Christ.

repaid. This made him a slave to his brother until the Sabbath year when all debts were canceled.[1] Righteousness is immortal (Sol 1:15), but **crime** causes slavery and **death**. Those who were under a heavy burden because of the debt of **crime** which they could not pay back, were constantly in **fear of death** and were under bondage to the devil. The situation seemed hopeless. The Jew who owed money to his brother and could not pay it back in money could only **hope** for someone else to redeem him by paying his debt, or he would have to work it out completely or at least until the Sabbath year.

These were his only means of "release." From the national and religious point of view, Jesus became the redeemer. Because he was the Messiah for all Israel, he was legally the chief of the family corporation. His authority and his power covered every Jew. Therefore his sacrifice paid the fines for all of their **crimes**. By his death, he released all those who were depressed and enslaved in every possible way. Life under such a bondage of **crime** as this is the most bitter existence possible (2Bar 21:13). Since Jesus provided the necessary offering for atonement, the whole picture has changed. He released parties to the contract from their fear of **death** so that they might all be made alive. The **crime** of Adam caused slavery and **death**. The **death** of Jesus provided the necessary **crime** offering to cancel the debt of **crime** (1Cor 15:20-22). Then those who had been enslaved could be set free; those who had been defeated by the devil would now be victorious (1Cor 15:52-57).

16*He prefers [takes] the seed of Abraham.* The word translated **prefer** (*eh-pee-lahm-báh-neh-tai*, ἐπιλαμβάνεται) means to seize, lay hold of, attack, come up to, reach, or obtain. The Lord **took** the Israelites **by the hand** to bring them **out of Egypt.** It is a slight variant from *ahn-tee-lahm-báh-neh-tai* (ἀντιλαμβάνεται), with the same meanings essentially, in the following LXX quotation: **whom I took** (LXX *ahn-teh-lah-báw-mayn*, ἀντελαβόμην; MT *heh-kheh-záhq-ti*, החזקתי) **from the boundaries of the land**. . . (Isa 41:8-9).

The author must have had a LXX text which had some variants. He shows no sign of wanting to vary the meaning from its FT context. As he used the compound word **take**, he meant, as did the LXX translator by his form of the compound, to **take** by choosing, to **take** one thing in **preference** to another. God chose Abraham. That involved taking him from outside the Promised Land and bringing him to Palestine, the land of the promise.

The **angels** have not been mentioned since Heb 2:9, but they continue to be involved in the comparison with **the Son.** Here, however, the claim is made that Jesus was not only greater than the **angels,** but that the Israelites were also given **preference** over **angels**. Paul was also of the same opinion. He claimed that the saints were destined to judge **angels** (1Cor 6:3). In the Isaiah passage, the subject was God who did the choosing, loving, and taking. As before, the author changed the subject to Jesus who **chose** (took) **the seed of Abraham** rather than **angels**, but the object remains the same. It is Israel, Jacob, or the children of **Abraham** who were the **chosen**, the brothers, and the sons of whom **the Son** was not ashamed.

Westcott was in error in denying this. He held that the author meant the "true seed, those who are children of faith, and not of '**the seed of Abraham**.'"[2] Westcott had been influenced by Paul's judgment at this point and transferred Paul's theology to the author of Hebrews without any justification. The author of Hebrews held that

---

[1] See further Buchanan, *Consequences*, pp. 9-18.

[2] Westcott, *Hebrews*, p. 55. So also Michel, *Hebräer,* pp. 86-87.

Jesus and the sons of **Abraham** were **all from one** (Heb 2:11) father, namely **Abraham**. He shared equally with the children of Israel in **blood and flesh**; he belonged to the same basic ancestry. Since Jesus was one of **the seed of Abraham**, and **the seed of Abraham** were superior to the **angels**, this proves further than Jesus was greater than the **angels**. **Abraham** was the chief and father of the entire family corporation, whether the members were **born** into the family or received by legal admission. This strongly suggests that the author of Hebrews and the community for whom he prepared this document were all members of some branch of Jewish Christianity. The word **angels** refers back to Heb 2:5, forming an inclusion with all of the material in between.

Divine services. The translation **[regarding] divine services**, literally **the things pertaining to God** (*tah práws tawn theh-áwn*, τὰ πρὸς τὸν θεόν), is also used to refer to the offering Paul brought to Jerusalem from the nations (Rom 15:17). Aaron was commissioned to be the spokesman for Moses. He was to be a mouth for Moses and Moses was to be for Aaron **the things pertaining to God** (Exod 4:16). Aaron was commissioned to speak and act in the name of Moses, in his behalf, and at his responsibility. Moses, in turn was God's legal agent, who spoke in his behalf, in his name, and at his responsibility. God was the final principal, but Aaron could speak his word only through the agency of Moses, who communicated **the things pertaining to God**.

Moses' father-in-law told Moses that Moses could not bear the duties of judging the people alone; he must delegate authority. Moses should be to the people **the things pertaining to God** and he should carry their words to God (Exod 18:19). Moses complained that the people were rebellious and stubborn. While he was still alive they embittered **the things pertaining to God** (Deut 31:27). **The things pertaining to God** were evidently offerings, oracles, worship services, or other religious or divine objects and services, or they simply constituted a circumlocution for the word "God." That which LXX renders **the things pertaining to God** MT has *lay-loh-heém* (לאלוהים); *im eh-loh-heém* (אם אלוהים); or *ehl eh-loh-heém* (אל אלוהים), "for God," "belonging to God," "with God," "to God," or something like that.

Therefore he was obligated. There seems to have been an early tradition that developed after the crucifixion of Jesus that this was all part of God's predestined plan. It was **fitting** (Heb 2:10); **it was necessary for the Son of man to suffer** (Mark 8:31); **he was obligated** to suffer (Heb 2:17). Some texts even hold that Jesus predicted it, but it is nowhere clearly predicted in the canonical FT as it now exists. One typological basis for its anticipation might be that Jesus or his followers identified him with the last ruling Hasmonean king, Antigonus. Antigonus, like Judas the Maccabee, was a Son of man. He ruled for about 3½ years, after the Parthians had successfully driven Herod and the Romans out of Palestine. Herod later returned with Roman military support, regained control of Palestine, and had Antigonus crucified. Reporting that incident, Dio wrote,

> Anthony entrusted those people [the Jews] to a certain Herod to rule, but Antigonus he whipped after he had tied him to a cross that which no other king had ever suffered by the Romans (Dio, *Roman History* 49:22, 6; Ant 14:481-91).

Antigonus was the last Son of man prior to Jesus, and Jesus may have let himself be known as the new king of Israel through code, by identifying himself with Antigonus. Since Antigonus was destined to be crucified, so was Jesus.

Faithful high priest. These words constitute the connection words that introduce the reader to the subject in the next chapter (Heb 3:1-2).

So that the crimes of the people might be expiated. Jesus had become the faithful high priest, because the function of the Levites and the Zadokites had not been adequate. They had not successfully **expiated the crimes of the people**.

Although Levites were priests in Israel's early history, Ezekiel decreed that they should be given a subordinate rank because of their behavior before the captivity. Nehemiah enforced Ezekiel's command. By the Maccabean period Levites were clearly understood to be subordinate to the sons of Zadok and were not even classed as priests by some parties to the contract (1QS 1:18-21; 2:2, 5, 11, 20-21). John Hyrcanus broke with the Pharisees, because the Pharisees did not think he should hold the office of high priest. They seemed more concerned about the proper requirements for the high priesthood than for the ruler. Pharisees were willing for John Hyrcanus to rule even though he had no basis for tracing his ancestry to David's line at all (Ant 13:288-97). Hasmoneans were of priestly stock, at least, even though not of Zadok's line. They were frequently on the defensive about their ancestral qualifications for the positions they held. The author of Hebrews had a similar problem in dealing with Jesus as a priest.

Christians claimed that Jesus was a descendant of David, and on that basis could qualify as a messiah, but not as a high priest. He was not even a Levite. Since the author wanted to present Jesus as a priest and king, he had to justify his claim by some forced logic, similar to that used by the Hasmoneans to justify their position. It was a legitimate argument based on acceptable legal data. This involved ignoring his Davidic ancestry, using proof texts to show that he had a different biblical basis for being considered a royal priest, and claiming for him every possible messianic attribute that did not specifically say he was a son of David. The author of Hebrews also made all the priestly claims he could for Jesus without saying he was a son of Zadok. To begin with, he was a son of Abraham, a true Jew. Jesus did belong to the general family. Therefore, to that extent, he had the necessary qualifications to offer sacrifice for **the crimes of the people**. Just being of the right family does not guarantee that the high priest would be **merciful and faithful**, but the author was convinced that Jesus was, and that because of his priestly work the **crimes** of Israel **might be expiated**.

18*He himself suffered.* Mek *Bahod* 10:1-87 is a lenghy dissertation on the merits of **sufferings** which were considered **chastenings** (*yees-soh-reén*, יסורין). **Suffering**, more than prosperity, was an indication of forgiveness; it would bring a man into the age to come; it was a means of atonement, even more effective than sacrifices. Therefore **sufferings** were precious. Since any type of **suffering** was effective for releasing Israel from crime, then of course the voluntary **suffering** of the Messiah was the most effective of all. This was why it was important for the author to make a point of showing that Jesus was of the right **blood and flesh**, the seed of Abraham, so that the sacrifice that he had already made would certainly be effective. It would be credited to his own people and not some other nation. Since he had been **tempted** or tested, his sacrifice would be beneficial to others "who [were] being tempted" or made to **suffer** the same fate. This does not mean that he just set a good example, but that his **suffering** canceled Israel's debt of crime.

Summary. Whereas Heb 1:5-2:9 concentrated directly on points where **the Son** could be compared favorably to the angels, for Heb 2:10-18 this was only a background issue. This section directed its attention to the believers or followers of Jesus in relationship to him. The word **all** quoted in Heb 2:8 was repeated here (Heb 2:10, 11, 17) to relate this passage to that preceding. Terms like **sufferings/suffered** and **brothers**, near both the beginning and the end have a literary purpose in forming an inclusion of this paragraph. Some of the connection words used frequently in this section are: **son** (Heb 1:2, 5, 8; 2:6, 10), **all** (1:2, 3, 11, 14; 2:8, 9, 10, 11, 15, 17), **crimes** (Heb 1:3; 2:17), **angels** (Heb 1:5, 6, 7, 13; 2:5, 7, 9, 16), **inherit** (Heb 1:4, 14), **name** (Heb 1:4; 2:12), and **death** (Heb 2:9, 14, 15).

The relationship of **the Son** to the followers of Jesus is well defined: They, like **the Son,** are sons; like him they are exalted to glory; he and they are from one father, **Abraham**; he claims them proudly as **brothers**; they share the same **blood and flesh**; he has **chosen** ("**taken**") the children of Abraham, and he has been made like them in every way. He was the **sanctifier** and they were the **sanctified**--all were ritually cleansed. Since he was closely identified with the children of Israel, his sufferings would certainly be effective in canceling the heavy debt of **crime** recorded against Israel. Israelites would be able to benefit from the merits he accumulated through his sacrifice. This is a strong argument to justify the Jewish Christian position. It makes no gesture to offer deliverance to the Gentiles.

Although the comparison with **angels** was not the major point of this section, the subject was introduced near the end (Heb 2:16) to assure the reader that the comparison of **the Son** to **the angels** was still in force. The return to **angels** at this point might also have been intended to direct the reader back to the beginning of the whole discussion in Heb 1:5, which introduced the comparison of the **Son** with the **angels**. Heb 2:17-18 also helped prepare the reader for the topic that would follow. All this indicates that a major section is completed at the end of the chapter. This section has been directed to an exaltation of the **Son,** primarily in comparison with the **angels,** but in the process it disclosed the author's understanding of Christology in relationship to the **Son**, the **Son of man**, and the first born. This topic will receive special attention because its understanding is basic to a proper comprehension of the rest of the document.

THE SON AS THE SON OF MAN

IN HEBREWS

When the author of Hebrews described the superior attributes of **the Son,** he drew on FT passages that described a mighty king. Such enthronement Psalms as Ps 2, which identified **the son** as a king on Mount Zion who would break the enemy nations into pieces and rule over them with power, and Ps 110, which described **the son** as a king who **sat** at God's **right hand** while God made the Son's enemies his footstool, supported this description. The author also used passages from 2Sam and Ps 45. 2Sam 7:14 originally described Solomon as God's son when he ruled the United Kingdom from Jerusalem. Ps 45 was addressed to an **anointed** king (Ps 45:7) who was urged to gird on his sword in glory and ride forth victoriously (Ps

45:3-4). His enemies were destined to fall before his sharp arrows (Ps 45:6). From his **divine throne** he would rule justly (Ps 45:6). **The Son of God** was to be a king like Solomon for whom God would make his enemies a footstool (Ps 110:1).

The author of Hebrews identified the **Son of God** with the **Son of man** for whom God had put all things under his feet (Ps 8:6).[1] Since the author also identified Jesus with the king referred to in these expressions, it seems that he understood the expressions **Son of God** and **Son of man** to have the same meaning and to describe a messiah or king. This is evident from one of the Dead Sea fragments:

4Q246	Daniel, First Enoch, and Fourth Ezra
Page 1 [1][. . .] settled over him. **He fell down before** the throne	[Dan 2:46]Then King Nebuchadnezzar **fell down** on his face **before** him, and he worshiped Daniel . F [3:10]Everyone who hears . . . **shall fall down** and worship the golden statue.
[2][. . .] **King of the age**. You are trembling and your change(?)	[3:9]**King**, live **for ages** (לעלמין חיי). [5:10]**King**, live **for ages**! Do not let your thoughts frighten you or your color change. [6:7]**King** Darius, live **for ages**! [6:21]Then Daniel said to the king, "**King**, live **for ages.**"
[3] [. . .] your **vision** and everything.	[2:28]Your dream and **the visions** of your head on your bed are these. [4:1]I had a dream, and it frightened me . . . **the visions** of my head alarmed me.
You are until **the age** [4] [. . .] there will be a depression upon the land [5] [. . .] and a great sifting among the cities [6] [. . .]	[Dan 6:27]He is the God of life, and he exists (*kah-yáhm,* קים) **for ages**. **His kingdom** will not pass away, his government [will endure] until the end.
the king of Assyria and of Egypt [7] [. . .] to be great over the land	[7:13]The **king of the south [Egypt]** will become angry, and he will go out and engage in

[1] In a larger context of conditions under which the Messiah, the son of David, or redemption would come, Daniel 7:13 was quoted by the rabbis, identifying the son of man with the Messiah (bSan 98a).

8 [. . .] will make and everyone will serve
9 [. . .] he will be called (*yeét-kah-ráy*, יתקרא),
and in his name he will be designated (*yeét-ah-máyr*).

battle with him, with **the king of the North [Syria]**

Page 2

1 **Son of God** (*bah-ráh dee áyl,* ברה די אל) he will be labeled (*yeet-ah-máyr,* יתאמר);/
Son of the Most High they will call him./ Like comets of vision 2 their kingdom will be./

7:27 Look! With the clouds,
one like a **Son of man** (*kuh-báhr eh-násh,* כבר אנש) is coming.
The people of the saints
of the Most High.

For years they will rule over 3 the land./ They will trample over everything--/ [One] **people** will trample [another] **people**;
[one] **city** will trample [another] **city**/
4 until **the people**

4Ezra 13:31 They will plan to make war against one another--**city** against **city**, place against place, **people** against
people, and kingdom against kingdom.

Isa 19:2 [Egyptians will fight one another], **city** against **city**, kingdom against kingdom.

of God arise,/ and everything
will rest from the sword.

1Enoch 62.13:15 **will** eat, **rest**, and rise with that **Son of man**.

Dan 7:27 The kingdom, the government, and the greatness of the kingdoms under the entire heaven will be given to
the people of the saints
of the Most High.

5 **His kingdom**
will be a kingdom of the age;/

2:44 The elect ones
The God of heaven
will raise up a kingdom of the ages.

7:14 **His government**
is a government of the age.

all of his
ways will be **in truth**./
He will **judge** 6 the land with **justice**,/
and **everything**

4:34 **All of his** deeds
are **true**, and **his ways**
are **just**.

will achieve **peace** (שלם)./ The sword will cease from the land./

6:26 Then King Darius wrote . . . "May your **peace** (שלמכון) be multiplied.

[7]**Every city will worship** (יסגדהן) **him**./ A great God is in these things,/ [8] and he makes war for him./	[7:28]**All the governments will worship** (יפלחהן) **him**."
	[Dan 11:11]He will raise up a great multitude, and the multitude **will be given into his hand**.
Peoples **will be given into his hand** (ינתן בידו);/ all of them [9] will be thrown down before him.	[7:26]The kingdom, the government, and the greatness of the kingdom **will be given** to the people of the saints of the Most High.
	[*1Enoch 62:9*]Kings, governors, and high officials . . . shall fall down on their faces and **worship** and raise their hopes in that Son of man.
His government is a government of the age,/ and all the depths [. . .	[Dan7:27-28]**His kingdom is a kingdom of the age**.
Page 3 [1]**will obey** (*yeesh-muh-oón,* ישמעון) **him**.	[7:27]Every government will worship and **obey** (*wah-yáysh-tah-muh-oóhn*(ישתמעהון) **him** (Dan 7:27).

When these two columns are placed side-by-side and compared, it is apparent that 4Q246 is a midrash based on various words and themes of Daniel. If the lacunae in 4Q246 were all filled in with the original words, all conjectured solutions to this passage could be judged more accurately. From the words and lines that have been preserved, however, it seems obvious that 4Q246 is a poetic piece that has compressed the message of Daniel into a few short lines. The reader was expected to know Daniel and understand all of the themes that the poet summarized. If we are to understand the message in the twentieth century, we must learn from Daniel the message of 4Q246.

As in Daniel, also in 4Q246 there are two opposing political powers and two historical **ages.** During the first **age**, reflected mostly in page one, a foreign king was in power, and Daniel was the interpreter of his dreams. In Daniel, the foreign king was Nebuchadnezzar, Darius, or one of the Seleucids. In 4Q246 the king was either the same or some later typological equivalent. During this age of foreign control, the kings of Egypt and Syria fought and trampled under their feet the people on whose land the battles raged. Page two is mostly dedicated to the following **age**, or **the age** to come after the gentile **age** would be over. During this **age** the chosen people lived in peace under their own national leader, which was probably Judas the Maccabee. For Daniel this was the Hasmonean age. In both of these documents the word **age** or **ages** was important. This unit will concentrate primarily on page two of 4Q246, the Book of Daniel, and the insights they provide for understanding the historical Jesus.

Both documents deal with a **government** or a **kingdom** that belongs to the **age**; these political entities belong both to the people and the king who rules over the land. The citizens whom Daniel called **the people of the saints of the Most High** (Dan 7:18, 27) the author of 4Q246 called "the people of God" (4Q246). 1Macc 14:27 called Simon **the prince of the people of God** (ασαραμελ = *sar* *ahm áyle*=שׂר עם אל). 1Enoch referred to the people of God as "the holy and elect ones" (1Enoch 62:7) or "the righteous and elect ones" (1Enoch 62:13). All of these names are suitable titles for the chosen people who live on the Promised Land. Daniel called the leader of the chosen people **one *like* a Son of man.** He did not call him a king, because Judas the Maccabee was never officially anointed as a king.[1] The character which Daniel called **Son of man** the author of 4Q246 called "Son of God," "Son of the Most High," and also "king." The title **Son of God** is a well-known title for a king.[2] Alexander the Great was called "the son of Zeus," Caesar was called "the son of God," the Egyptian pharaoh was called "the son of Re," Solomon was known as God's son when he sat on Yehowah's[3] throne ruling Yehowah's kingdom from Jerusalem (1Chron 28:5-7; 2Sam 7:14). 4Ezra called God's son "the Messiah" (4Ezra 7:28).

SCHOLARLY REACTION TO HEB 2:6

Commentators generally have done little to draw attention to the term **Son of man** as it appears in Heb 2:6. Some have just ignored it. Others specifically insist that it has no messianic significance. It is simply an accidental term that happened to be in Ps 8 in parallelism with "man." It has no further significance for the author of Hebrews.[4] Some acknowledged it to be a messianic title, or at least identified with Jesus in some way, but they did not make any attempt to say how.[5] Michel erroneously noted that Ps 8 was not used by the rabbis to refer to the Messiah.[6] Laubach held that, for the author, Ps 8 was used to call attention to Jesus as "the man," i. e., the true man, the second from Adam. He noticed, however, that there was a striking resemblance between the subjection element in Ps 8 and that of Ps 110, but he did not indicate what that meant.[7]

Major studies on the **Son of Man** have given no more attention to Heb 2:6 than commentators have. Jeremias did no more than mention its occurrence in Heb 2:6.[8] Higgins noted that

---

[1] For a defense of this identification see Buchanan, *Biblical and Theological Insights from Ancient and Modern Civil Law* (Lewiston: Mellen, c1992), pp. 96-112.

[2] It did not originate in the Jewish-Christian church, as W. Kramer, *Christ, Lord, Son of God* (London: S.C.M. Press, 1963), p. 111, claimed. Kramer also misunderstood the role of a legal agent when he said God was the agent in Gal 4:4-5. God was the principal who sent the apostle or agent; Jesus was the agent who was sent (pp. 112-13).

[3] For a justification of this pronunciation see Buchanan, "Some Unfinished Business with the Dead Sea Scrolls," *RevQ* 49-52 13 (1988) *Mémorial Jean Carmignac*, ed. F. G. Martínez et E. Peuch (Paris: Gabalda, 1988), pp. 411-20.

[4] J. Moffatt, *A Critical and Exegetical Commentary on the Epistle to the Hebrews* (New York: Scribner's Sons, 1964), p. 23; M. Stuart, *Commentary on the Epistle to the Hebrews in Greek and English* (Andover: Warren F. Draper, 1828), p. 69; Westcott, *Hebrews*, pp. 42-43; H. Windisch, *Der Hebräerbrief* (Tübingen: J. C. B. Mohr, 1931), p. 20.

[5] O. Kuss, *Der Brief an die Hebräer* (Regensburg,: Friedrich Pustet, 1966), pp. 40-41; C. Spicq, *L'Epitre aux Hebreux* (Paris: J. Gabalda, 1953), II, p. 31.

[6] Michel, *Hebräer*, 1957), pp. 70-71.

[7] F. Laubach, *Der Brief an die Hebräer* (Wuppertal: R. Brockhaus, 1867), p. 62.

[8] J. Jeremias, *New Testament Theology*, tr. J. Bowden (London: Scribner's Sons, 1971) I, p. 265.

> Son of Man Christology cannot claim to be prominent in Hebrews like that of the Son of God (1:8; 4:14; 6:6; 7:3; 10:29), for it occurs but once, and then only in this quotation from Ps 8.[1]

He understood the author of Hebrews to have used this Psalm to show that "the promise of sovereignty held out to man has been fulfilled in Jesus."[2] Bultmann completely ignored Hebrews 2:6 in his discussion of the Son of Man.[3] Cullmann said, in reference to Heb 2:6,

> Hebrews applies the psalm [Ps 8] to Jesus as the Son of man. The author's interpretation of the citation indicates that he apparently had quite precise information about the Son of Man doctrine.[4]

Cullmann was correct on this point, but he did not pursue the matter. The doctrine of the Son of Man which the author of Hebrews presented was quite different from that which Cullmann set forth. Cullmann made no attempt to tell what this precise information was. Like most scholars,[5] Cullmann made a clear distinction between the political Messiah who would defeat the enemies of Israel in an earthly war and establish a political kingdom and "the supernatural, heavenly 'Son of Man.'"

Cullmann insisted, "He is a heavenly ruler, not an earthly king."[6] In keeping with this sharp distinction made between the Messiah and the Son of Man, Vielhauer separated the titles so completely as to claim that Jesus never used the term "Son of Man," and that the heavenly Son of Man concept was not at all related to the concept of the Kingdom of God.[7] Proudman went so far as to claim that the Son of man in Daniel was an angel.[8] It was only in adverse response to Vielhauer that some scholars have tried to close the gap that they had previously developed between the Messiah and the Son of man. Marshall argued:

> Furthermore, it is wrong to assert that the Son of man was not in some sense a messianic figure; the author of the Similitudes of Enoch made the identification, and it is hard to see why Jesus could not have made the same identification.[9]

His logic was as follows:

---

[1] A. J. B. Higgins, *Jesus and the Son of Man* (Philadelphia: Fortress Press, 1964), p. 146.
[2] Higgins, *Jesus,* p. 146.
[3] Bultmann, *Theology of the New Testament,* tr. K. Grobel (New York: Scribner's Sons, 1951), I, pp. 5, 7, 9, 26-37, 40, 42-44, 47, 49, 51-53, 79-80, 124, 172.
[4] O. Cullmann, *The Christology of the New Testament,* trs. S. C. Guthrie and C. A. M. Hall (Philadelphia: Westminster Press, 1957), p. 188.
[5] Jeremias, *New Testament Theology,* I, p. 274-75; Teeple, "Son of Man Christology," pp. 213-50; Bultmann, *Theology,* I, 49, et al.
[6] Cullmann, *Christology*, p. 142.
[7] P. Vielhauer, "Gottesreich und Menschensohn in der Verkuendigung Jesu," *Aufsaetze zum Neuen Testament. Theologische Buecherei* 31 (München: Ch. Kaiser Verlag, 1965):55-140.
[8] C. L. J. Proudman, "Remarks on the 'Son of man,'" *CJT* 12 (1966):128-31.
[9] I. H. Marshall, "The Synoptic Son of Man Sayings in Recent Discussion," *NTS* 12 (1965-66):347.

> So far as the interpretation of the vision is concerned, the Son of man is the representative or symbol of the saints of the Most High (Dan 7:18, 22, 27). If he is their representative, he is most naturally thought of as their head, in which case we should probably see a "messianic reference" here.[1]

Spelled out more precisely, the "messianic reference" would imply that the Son of man in Daniel was a king, and that the one "like a Son of man" was a person "like" a king, with all the political implications normally associated with the Messiah. Such an understanding of the Son of man as this would be completely consistent with the Son of man described in Heb 2:6. In reaction to a position similar to Vielhauer's, Walker said:

> . . . it would be very difficult to deduce from these passages that Matthew makes any distinction between the Kingdom of the Son of Man and the Kingdom of Heaven.[2]

It has become more and more difficult for scholars to admit that Jesus was called king, Son of God, and messiah--all of which are royal designations--and at the same time claim that his other title, Son of man, was in no way related to any nationalistic, political movement or aspiration. In addition to emphasizing the heavenly aspect of the vision enthroning the **Son of man,** scholars have identified the term, **Son of man**, with "man" in Philip 2:7. This opens up many distracting possibilities. Once removed from the context involving power, glory, and a kingdom, the **Son of man**, meaning a human being, can then be identified with the suffering servant of Isaiah and the new Adam. Once the humbling aspect is raised, the dominion aspect can be dismissed, and the Son of man is safely removed from political anxiety. This is a rhetorical technique that begins with a conclusion in the hypothesis and circles around to reach a conclusion like the one in the hypothesis. A classical example of this is the proof that a cat has ten tails: 1) hypothesis is that no cat has nine tails. 2) simple addition, one cat has one more tail than no cat. 3) Ergo! A cat has ten tails. There is no definite relationship between proof and truth.

Tödt objected to the methodology employed by these scholars. He said,

> Christological doctrine has been developed in Protestantism mainly with regard to the concepts expressed in Philip 2. The synoptic texts were interpreted to conform to this passage. Accordingly, the synoptic statements could not be understood otherwise than in the predetermined way; the one who has preached on earth could only be seen as the transcendent person, the preexistent Son of God, or the heavenly Son of man, and Jesus' acceptance of earthly restrictions could only be understood as humiliation.[3]

---

[1] Marshall, "Sayings," p. 336. See also A. Caquot, "Les Quatre Betes et le 'Fils d'Homme,'" *Semitica* 17 (1967):37-71, and L.-M. Orrieux, "Le Probleme du fils de l'Homme dans la Litterature Apocalyptique," *LumVie* 12, No. 62 (1963):9-31.

[2] W. O. Walker, Jr., "The Kingdom of the Son of Man and the Kingdom of the Father in Matthew," *CBQ* 30 (1968):577. See also E. Bammel, "Erwaegungen zur Eschatologie Jesu," *StEv* III (1964):3-32.

[3] H. E. Tödt, *The Son of Man in the Synoptic Tradition* (Philadelphia: Westminster Press, 1964), p.

Tödt's analysis did not persuade scholars suddenly to stop understanding the **Son of man** in a predetermined way. Formesyn approved of Tödt's thesis,[1] but Black strongly objected to Tödt's minimizing of the Isaianic influences in the passion sayings.[2] Penetrating studies like those of Tödt and Marshall indicate, however, that some scholars are searching for a more adequate interpretation of the data related to the **Son of man.** These may be willing to consider a fresh approach which takes Heb 2:6 into account. With that expectation, the following analysis of relevant literature will compare the **Son of man** in Daniel and 1Enoch to the royal figure in Heb 2:6.

THE SON OF MAN IN DANIEL, ENOCH, AND THE SCROLLS

The term "son of man" seems to have been used in the FT to mean simply "human being." For instance, Ezekiel was frequently addressed by the Lord as son of man: **Son of man, stand upon your feet** (Ezek 2:1) **or Son of man, I am sending you to the children of Israel** (Ezek 2:3). The most likely meaning of "son of man" in these passages seems to be simply "man" or "human being."[3] In Daniel, however, the "son of man" probably has a different significance.[4] *In a vision* Daniel saw one like a **Son of man** come with the clouds of heaven up to the Ancient of Days. To this being who was like a **Son of man** (*bar eh-náhsh* בר אנשׁ) was given dominion, glory, and a kingdom. All peoples, nations, and languages were to serve him. His dominion and kingdom were to continue **for the age [to come]** (Dan 7:13-14). At the same time the saints of the Most High were given the kingdom, dominion, and the greatness of the kingdoms under the whole heaven; their kingdom and dominion would be for the age, and all other dominions would serve them (Dan 7:27).

The saints of the Most High were the people of Israel who inherited Palestine after the Syrian kingdom crumbled. The Book of Daniel, probably written just before the rededication of the temple said the restoration of worship at Jerusalem, was composed in terms of sabbatical release.[5] Jeremiah had promised that the Jews were to be in captivity for 70 years. That time had long since passed, but the author of Daniel took that to mean 70 weeks of years, which could be manipulated so as to coincide perfectly with the Maccabean victory.[6] Seven weeks of years were spent in Babylon; 62 weeks of years elapsed during the time from the return to Jerusalem

---

296.

[1] R. E. C. Formesyn, "Was There a Pronominal Connection for the Self Designation?" *NovT* 8 (1966):1-35.

[2] M. Black, "The 'Son of Man' Passion Sayings in the Gospel Tradition," *ZNTW* 60 (1969):1-8.

[3] Another possibility is that "son of man" was the self-designation of Ezekiel by which he described his office as a messenger-prophet or eschatological prophet. In any event, it is not the same as the meaning in Daniel, which must be judged by its own context. For the possible relationship of Jesus' use of Son of man to Ezekiel's, see E. Schweitzer "The Son of Man Again," *NTS* 10 (1963-64):256-261.

[4] Although even in Dan 8:17 and 10:16 *behn 'ah-dáhm* (בן אדם) and *beh-nay ah-dáhm* (בני אדם) have generic meanings.

[5] See further Buchanan, *Consequences*, pp. 9-18, or "Sabbatical Eschatology," *Christian News from Israel* 18 (1967):49-56.

[6] This conclusion was reached with ordinary rhetorical logic. The conclusion that this was the fulfillment of Jeremiah's prophecy was the point of departure. The steps in between were adjusted to justify the conclusion on sabbatical terms. It involved assigning 62 weeks of years to the period from the return to Jerusalem until a certain treaty was made, with little concern for mathematical accuracy.

until a certain treaty was made. This totals as follows: 62 plus seven equals 69--only one more week of years until there would be 70 weeks of years--time for the tenth Jubilee! One-half week of years later the temple was defiled and sacrifice was discontinued (Dan 9:24-27).

Before the second half-week of years was over, the temple had been cleansed (Dan 7:25; 8:14, 9:27; 12:7). This means that the author of the Book of Daniel interpreted the Maccabean victory in sabbatical terms. The Jubilee of ten weeks of years was the time when the "captivity" was over, "slaves" were set free, and the land was restored to the "original owners," as at Jubilee. This was a nationalistic interpretation of sabbatical justice. In this context, when the Maccabees were recovering the promised land from the Syrians, and Jews received a new national freedom, Daniel saw a vision during which the saints of the Most High received dominion and the kingdom, and a being like a "son of man" also received dominion, glory, and a kingdom. This being seems to have been like a king who ruled over a territory at the same time his people were citizens of the territory. Since the saints of the Most High were evidently the Jews after the temple had been cleansed and worship restored, the being like a "son of man" was probably Judas, the Maccabee, who had received the dominion, glory, and the beginning of a kingdom.[1]

The Book of Daniel is not a prophecy. Each chapter seems to have been written by a different scholar. The assignment of each writer was to create a drama which would explain, religiously, that which Jews had experienced between the time of the Babylonian Captivity and the defeat of the Syrian army at Beth-horon, followed by the first Hanukkah. For example, one author told about the "Fulbright scholar" program in Babylon; another told about the fiery furnace; still a third told about the lions' den. In each of these Daniel or his friends were the heroes. Daniel

---

[1] Although many scholars, such as Manson, hold to an identification of the son of man with the saints of the Most High in Daniel, this has been difficult to defend. J. Jeremias, *New Testament Theology*, p. 274, agreed that the son of man was a "corporate entity," but he explained that this was so in the sense that "for oriental thought the king or the priest represents his people or his community." In other words, Jeremias really claimed that the son of man was a king or priest, who was corporate only in the sense that other kings and priests are. Cullmann, *Christology*, p. 140, also insisted that "the apocalyptic writer [Daniel 7] identifies the son of Man as the "saints of the Most High." In explaining the relationship of the four beasts to the son of man, he said, "... the vision contains a certain inconsistency: the beasts are interpreted as kings, as *representatives* [italics his], of the world empires, but the 'man' is the nation of the saints itself." He was correct in noting that one would have to maintain an inconsistency in the vision not to see the son of man also as a representative. Jeremias did understand the son of man as a representative, and the author of Dan 7 probably did too. Although Cullmann, *Christology*, p. 140, said the son of man was not a representative figure, as the beasts were, on the next page (p. 141) he said, "But we must by no means forget that the idea of the Son of Man at its ultimate source also includes the idea that the figure of *the* Man represents all men." That interpretation would probably have come as a surprise to the author of Daniel. While insisting on understanding the son of man in Daniel as a corporate personality, Cullmann admitted that later Jewish literature, such as Enoch and 4 Ezra, which depended on Daniel, understood the son of man as an individual (p. 140). When dealing with Jesus, Cullmann said, "Of course Jesus thinks primarily of an individual redeeming figure as do 4Ezra and Enoch, but we must not forget that for Jewish thought the individual interpretation does not *exclude* the collective one" (p. 156). Caquot, "Les Quatre Betes et le 'Fils d' Homme," *Semitica* 17 (1967): 37-71, faced the same type of confusion, but others, like Orrieux, "Le Probleme," pp. 9-31, and M. Cambe, "Le Fils de l'Homme dans les Evangiles Synoptiques," *LumVie* 12, No. 62 (1963):32-64, claim the son of man in Daniel is messianic and not collective.

was an antitype of Joseph in Egypt. In each one the Jews were faced with a crisis that tested their faith, but in every case the crisis was over and the Jews prevailed. These may all have been read before the Jewish crowd at the Hanukkah program. Instead of prophecies, these were all celebration themes that reflected tension that was over and victory that appeared in the first Hanukkah celebration.

The central drama was Dan 7. This was a drama of a court scene that reflected the 3½ year war between the Jews and the Syrian Greeks. This drama theologized the heavenly court case that took place in heaven causing these historical facts to take place.[1] Between 167 and 164 BIA there was a fierce war fought between the Syrians and the Jews. Antiochus was the king of the Syrians, and Judas was the leading general of the Jewish army. Near the end of this war, in the same year, Antiochus Epiphanes sent half of his army to Jerusalem to finish off the Jews, once and for all. During this time he took the rest of the army to Persia to conquer a temple there that would have had lots of valuable gold and silver. He needed this to pay for the war. He lost the battle there, got sick and died. During the same year Judas defeated the Syrian troops at Beth-horon.

This meant total victory for Judas and total loss for Antiochus Epiphanes. The dramatist thought this was the result of God's intercession in heaven, so he designed a drama in which God was the judge (Ancient of Days); Antiochus Epiphanes was the defendant, and Judas was the plaintiff. As the judge entered the scene, all the people stood and were silent. In Jewish courts, when there is a chance that the defendant will receive a death sentence, the defense was given the opportunity to speak first. In this case the defendant, the horn, spoke first and at great length, but he did not persuade the judge. He was given a death sentence. On earth that meant Antiochus died in Persia. Then the plaintiff stepped forward. To him was given the kingdom, the power, and the glory of ruling Palestine. This happened when Judas won the victory of Beth-horon on earth. This drama was written in preparation for the victory celebration at Hanukkah. At the same time, the Palestinian Jews, the Saints of the Most High, were also given the kingdom, power, and glory of the kingdom at Palestine. Dan 7 is a complete unit, dramatizing the victory that took place at the first Hanukkah. It was the beginning of the end of the Syrian age. It does not anticipate any kind of millennial future.

In Daniel's vision, the being like a "Son of man" came with the clouds of heaven (Dan 7:13). In Jewish and Christian literature, dreams and visions have been frequently employed as literary devices to communicate messages dramatically. Thus the four beasts included in the same vision (Dan 7:1-8) *symbolized* four nations that controlled the Jews after the Babylonian captivity. It would be a mistake to assume that all four nations came up out of the sea, literally (Dan 7:3), or that all other details be understood literally. The same would be true of the visions of Ezekiel and Zechariah. When the 70 disciples returned joyfully telling of their success, Jesus said, **I saw Satan fall like lightning from heaven** (Luke 10:18)--a dramatic way of saying that they were winning and Satan was losing. In the same way, Daniel's vision dramatized a being like a "Son of man" coming with the clouds of heaven (Dan 7:13). This did not mean that he had wings or was angelic. It meant that the vision attempted to communicate the belief that the being was divinely appointed.[2]

---

[1] For a careful defense of this position see Buchanan, *The Book of Daniel* (Lewiston: Mellen, 1999; republished by Wipf and Stock Publishers, 2005).

[2] Likewise, the four nations coming up out of the sea may have dramatized the author's conviction

The appearance of the Lord in a cloud was nothing new:[1] The Lord appeared in a cloud of glory when Moses was given the ten commandments for Israel (Exod 19:16-25; Deut 5:4, 22-27; see also 1:33). There was always a cloud of smoke over the tabernacle to indicate the Lord's presence and glory (Num 9:18-23). It was from the cloud that the Lord spoke to Peter, James, and John on the Mount of Transfiguration, saying, **This is my beloved Son, with whom I am well pleased** (Matt 17:1-5). The fact that these events took place in relationship to clouds does not mean that Moses, Jesus, Peter, James, and John were heavenly beings, but that the Lord was present when these important events took place, and that he approved them. Daniel, by relating *a vision*, attempted to say something like that. Just as the time sequence was interpreted in such a way as to show that Jeremiah's prophecy was fulfilled and the people received the benefits of the Jubilee when the land was restored and they were delivered from the hand of the oppressing Syrians, so God's approval of the Maccabean victory was shown by a vision of the Ancient of Days giving the dominion, glory, and a kingdom both to one like a "Son of man" and to the people of the saints of the Most High.[2]

The being **like a Son of man** would seem to be the leader in charge of the Jewish saints who recovered control of the temple, cleansed it and renewed sacrifice. The leader at that time was Judas the Maccabee, one who gave the initial impetus to the rebellion that finally succeeded in overthrowing the Syrians and restoring the United Kingdom to Israel free from foreign rule and taxation. Complete national liberty was not achieved until Simon's rule when the taxation was removed and Simon was appointed high priest (Wars 1:53; 1Macc 13:39-42). Aristobulus I was the first Hasmonean to declare himself king (Wars 1:117), but earlier Hasmoneans, among their own people, were exalted higher than their official titles acknowledged. Simon, for instance, was called by the Hebrew name, "the prince of the people of God" (Greek *ah-sahr-ahm-áyl*, ασαραμελ) a transliteration for *sahr ahm áyl* (שׂר עם אל).[3]

Judas, the leader when the temple was cleansed, was never king, officially, and he may never have been high priest, but he was highly respected by contemporary and later Jews. He was one *like* a Son of man. The suggestion that Judas was the leader whom the author of Daniel had in mind when he described him favorably as one like a Son of man implies that the author was favorable to the Maccabees and their movement, as the calculation of the sabbatical chronology would suggest; but that has not been the view most widely accepted among scholars. Many, such as

---

that they owed their origin to the dragon of the great deep, Tiamat.

[1] A Feuillet, "Le Fils de l'Homme de Daniel et la Tradition Biblique," *RB* 60 (1963):187, observed that the cloud frequently accompanies theophanies, but whenever angels are present, the cloud is absent (cf. Dan 8:15; 9:2 1; 10:5-16).

[2] T. W. Manson, "The Son of Man in Daniel, Enoch, and the Gospels," *BJRL* 32 (1950):171-93, assuming that the Son of man in Daniel 7 was a corporate personality signifying the saints of the Most High, or the contract community, concluded that in the NT it also sometimes applies to the new elect, of whom Jesus was the head, rather than just to Jesus alone. Overlooking the Midrash on Ps 2:9, he erroneously said, "There seems to be no evidence that in Rabbinical circles Son of Man was used as a name for the Messiah" (p. 175). Just because both the saints and the Son of man were given the same kingdom does not mean they were identical. This is the normal relationship of a king to his people.

[3] As S. Tedesche and S. Zeitlin, *The First Book of Maccabees* (New York: Harper & Row, 1950), p. 44, correctly suggested in relation to 1Macc 14:27. The initial alpha probably indicates a prosthetic aleph since the definite article *ha* would not have been present in this combination.

Charles[1] and Montgomery,[2] have understood the author of Daniel to have been in support of the Hasidim but depreciative of the Hasmoneans. The chief basis for their conclusion is their identification of the **little help** given to the Jews in their crisis during the Maccabean Revolt (Dan 11:34). Montgomery said,

> The writer is not a Maccabean but an Asidaean, for he looks for help to God alone.[3]

This is not a fair distinction to make between the Maccabean movement and that of the Hasidim. The pro-Hasmoneans also believed that Abraham, Joseph, Phineas, Joshua Caleb, David, Elijah, Hananiah, Azariah, Mishael, and Daniel were glorified and blessed because of their faithfulness, obedience to God, zeal for the law, witness, mercy, and innocence--not because of their military skill (1Macc 2:51-60). The author of 1Macc quoted Judas as saying,

> **Victory in battle does not depend on the size of an army, but rather on the strength that comes from Heaven. . . . He himself will shatter them before us** (1Macc 3:19, 21; see 4:8-10, 30-33; 7:36-38).

In comparable holy war theology, the poet echoed the following confessions (1QM 11:1-12):

> For yours is the battle, and with the strength of your hand . . . (l)
> For yours is the battle, for the Philistines you subdued many times
> through your holy name . . . (2-3);
> Yours is the battle, and from you is the might,
> and it is not ours . . . (4-5)
> For it is in your strength and in the power of your great valor . . . (6)
> For from of old we have confessed the power of your hand
> against the Kittim . . . (12).

The Hasidim were not opposed to war in principle. At the outset they joined forces with the Hasmoneans in their defense of the law (1Macc 2:42-48). They were willing to fight to restore purified worship in the temple and law observance among the people. Once the temple had been cleansed and a candidate from the tribe of Aaron, Alcimus, had been appointed high priest, they were prepared to make peace with the Seleucids and part company with Judas on this point (1Macc 7:4-14). There is no further report in 1Macc of the activities of the Hasidim after Alcimus slew 60 Hasidim in one day (1Macc 7:15-18). 1Enoch 90:6-12, on which Charles drew for support of his position, gives no clearer picture of the Hasidim after Alcimus' slaughter than does 1Macc. The Hasidim are reported as **those whom Judas the Maccabee leads** (*hohn ah-phay-gáy-tai Ioo-dahs haw Mah-kah-bái-aws*, ὧν ἀφηγεῖται Ιουδας ὁ Μακκααβαῖος) (2Macc 14:6).

---

[1] R. H. Charles, *A Critical and Exegetical Commentary on the Book of Daniel* (Oxford: Clarendon Press, 1929), pp. 309-13.

[2] J. A. Montgomery, *A Critical and Exegetical Commentary on the Book of Daniel* (New York: Scribner's Sons, 1927), pp. 458-59.

[3] Montgomery, *Daniel*, pp. 458-59.

There is not nearly as much evidence for the antipathy between the Hasmoneans and the Hasidim as scholars have implied The latter began as part of the Maccabean rebellion; their rift with the Hasmoneans was over Alcimus, and after Alcimus killed sixty of the Hasidim, we hear nothing more about them. For all we can learn, the Hasidim may have returned to support the Hasmoneans after Alcimus' betrayal, but this is also a conjecture. There certainly is not enough evidence to support the opposite conclusion, that the antipathy continued, and that the author of Daniel was one of their party who opposed the Hasmoneans.

LaCocque said it was a mistake to think the Hasidim were pacifists no matter what. They obviously were willing to take up arms when they needed to. Their attitudes were quite flexible, LaCocque argued, and the pacifism of the Book of Daniel has been overstressed by critics.[1]

According to Charles, the Hasmoneans were the ones who offered a little help[2] and were joined by flatterers who followed the Hasmoneans out of fear (Dan 11:34-35).[3] Montgomery said those were "adherents of doubtful character" who joined Judas' group.[4] No doubt Judas had supporters of both descriptions, but that does not mean they were the ones mentioned in Dan 11:34-35.

Following the consensus Collins said,

> Third, a considerable number of authors have remained persuaded that the "one like a human being" is individual but understand him as a heavenly, angelic being rather than the messiah.[5]

> The decisive objection against the messianic interpretation [of the Son of man] is that nowhere in the book do we find either support for or interest in the Davidic monarchy.[6]

Of course not. The Hasmoneans were not pro-Davidic. It is not easy to untangle these puzzles when the allusions are not specific. Once conclusions are reached, however, it is possible to interpret the reports in such a way as to make the conclusions seem reasonable, even if they are wrong. In this realm of conjecture, previous attempts have not been so successful as to rule out other attempts for consideration. The following interpretation will suggest a hypothesis that is not conclusive, but is different from those accepted up to this point. A point in its favor is that it at least takes into account the evidence that the whole Book of Daniel is centered around the Maccabean victory over the Syrians.

---

[1] A. LaCocque, *Daniel in his Time* (Columbia: University of South Carolina Press, c1988), pp. 30, 43, 44, 50.

[2] R. H. Charles, *Commentary*, pp. 309-10.

[3] N. W. Porteus, *Daniel* (London: S.C.M. Press, 1965), p. 168, said the "little help" came, not from the Maccabees, but from the martyrs--as if they could be distinguished from those who died in the Maccabean Revolt.

[4] Montgomery, *Daniel*, p. 459.

[5] J. J. Collins, *A Commentary on the Book of Daniel* (Minneapolis: Fortress Press, c1993, p. 310.

[6] Collins, *A Commentary*, p. 309. Although the Son of man in Dan 7 was not a son of David, H. M. Teeple, "Son of Man Christology," p. 213, was mistaken in saying "In Jewish eschatology the Son of man was distinct from the Son of David." Rabbis often identified the two. For examples see Buchanan, *Jewish Messianic Movements from AD 70 to AD 1300* (Eugene, Oregon: Wipf andd Stock Publishers, 2003), pp. 317, 346, 403, 505, 572.

In dealing with the crucial passage, Dan 11:29-35, scholars are generally agreed that the reference to the ships of "the Kittim" coming against "him," forcing "him" to withdraw (Dan 11:30), refers to the confrontation of the Roman envoy ("the Kittim") under the leadership of Popilius with Antiochus IV Epiphanes ("him") after he had conquered Egypt (Livy 45:12, 1-6).[1] This aroused the anger of Antiochus, which he expressed by taking action against the holy contract, profaning the temple, and removing the continual burnt offering. This is a description of his plundering the temple at Jerusalem (Dan 11:30-31; 1Macc 1:20-53). The abomination that makes desolate which he is reported to have set up (Dan 11:31) is the same as that reported in 1Macc 1:54. His attempts to seduce with flattery those who violate the contract (Dan 11:32) were successful attempts made to persuade Jews to worship idols and profane the Sabbath (1Macc 1:42), withhold offerings, profane festivals, pollute the sanctuary and the saints, sacrifice pork, and leave sons uncircumcised (1Macc 1:45-47).

This was done under threat of death and promise of reward (1Macc 57; 2:15-18). **But the people who know their God shall stand firm and act!** (Dan 11:32). Among this group were the instructors of the people (*mahs-kee-láy ahm,* משׂכילי עם) who instructed and exhorted the many (*lah-rab-beém,* לרבים) to hold fast to their faith even though they should fall by the sword, flame, captivity, and plunder (Dan 11:33). Those who held fast faced precisely these consequences. Those who owned Scriptures were killed. Mothers who circumcised their sons were put to death with their babies hanging around their necks. Some died rather than eat food not approved by their dietary laws (1Macc 2:57-63). Those who held fast had to live in secret places as refugees (1Macc 1:53).

The Hasmoneans were the main leaders in the whole movement for freedom from heathen oppression and maintenance of their laws. If they were not themselves considered some of the instructors (*mahs-kee-leém*, משׂכילים) who stumbled (*yee-káh-sheh-loo*, יכשׁלו) (Dan 11:35) so as to purify and make (the community) white while they were working alongside religious teachers for the same cause.[2] It was not only the teachers who stumbled and fell. Many of the Jewish warriors also fell and gave their lives as a ransom for the community, believing that their deaths would add credits to the treasury of merits.

Although there was some conflict among the ranks, those who were not pro-Seleucids were in basic unity. It was not as if one party was for Judas and the other for God. Some were compromisers with the Seleucids, and others were loyal, rigorous, law-abiding Jews. The whole patriotic group, of which the Hasidim and the Hasmoneans were parts, were amazingly successful in fighting the Seleucids on their own, but they did receive some help. The question is, from whom? Most scholars say, "From the Hasmoneans," but there were very few Jews who would have considered that help **little**, least of all the authors who composed the chapters in the whole book that interpreted the Maccabean Revolt in terms of God's foreordained and scheduled plan.

---

[1] The Kittim were those who were facing east, as the Romans were (Hab 1:9; pHab 3:13-14).

[2] In Hebrew there seems to be a play on words **the instructors stumbled** (*mahs-kee-leém yee-káh-sheh-loo,* משכילים יכשלו*)*, but the LXX read *dee-ah-naw-ay-tháy-sawn-tai* (διανοηθήσονται), apparently rendering *yahs-keé-loo* (ישׂכילו) "will instruct," which also makes sense.

A little help. Judah was a small land bridge between great countries, like Babylonia, Assyria, Media, Parthia on the northeast, and Egypt on the southwest. Great armies fought on this land for the purpose of controlling this territory. Jews and Israelites took advantage of their position and taxed the countries to pass over their land. They also negotiated for power first from one country and then from anther. When Israel and Judah were ruled by the Egyptians, they called on Assyria, Babylon, or Parthia for support. When they were exiled into Babylon they negotiated with Persia. When they were under Persian control they negotiated with the Syrian Greeks for relief. During the Hasmonean rebellion the only country to whom they could obtain help was Rome. Rome was expanding its boundaries eastward and was eager to cooperate with any rebellion against Syria. It was probably from Rome that Judas obtained weapons to surprise the Syrians with unusual strength at the Battles of Beth-horon and Beth-zur.[1]

At a strategic time Judas made an agreement with Rome in which both countries agreed to support one another in international business and war (1Macc 8:1-32). This **little help** was not really minor, either. Without it the Seleucids may never have been repelled, but it was from the outside, and understandably small in comparison to the force of the Jews themselves and their God. Those who joined themselves with flattery to those who provided the **little help** may have been the opportunists who profiteered by dealing with the Romans as they had dealt earlier with the Seleucids. The author of Dan 11 may have been suspicious of the consequences of transferring loyalty from Syria to Rome.

There was in Judaism an ancient tradition that warned against foreign alliances. The anxiety was justified. The Rome which provided a **little help** later controlled the entire nation. This does not prove that the author of Daniel was pro-Hasmonean, but it shows that Daniel can be understood from that point of view at least as reasonably as from the anti-Hasmonean viewpoint. This allows for the possibility that Judas was the one described as being **like a son of man** who was divinely appointed to his role of leadership. To him was given the dominion and glory and a kingdom (Dan 7:14). His was the government that followed the rule of Antiochus IV Epiphanes, the last remnant of the fourth beast, over the saints of the Most High after the temple had been cleansed and sacrifice restored (Dan 7:23-27). This was depicted as "the end of the age." Although he was not officially a king, Judas was **like a son of man**, which may have meant that he was *like* a king. The likelihood that this was so will become greater when the role of the son of man is examined in 1Enoch and the gospels.

In 1Enoch, the Son of man was one who removed kings from their thrones, and upon whom the kingdom was bestowed (1Enoch 46:4-5). He was named before the Lord of Spirits, the Head of Days (1Enoch 48:1-2), and it was in his name that the righteous would be saved (1Enoch 48:7; 50:3). At the time when the son of man was named, the kings and mighty ones who possessed the land would be downcast because they would be given over in anguish to the son of man who was also the elect one and the anointed of the Lord of Spirits (1Enoch 48:8-10; 62:6). The glory of this elect one was to be forever, and he would judge the secret things (1Enoch 49:2-4; 61:9). Like other good kings, he would judge righteously (1Enoch 50:4).

Like other kings, he would sit on his throne of glory (1Enoch 51:3; 55:4; 61:8: 62:2) and be recognized by the kings and mighty ones (1Enoch 62:1-2) who would prostrate themselves before him and plead for mercy; but that Son of man

[1] See further Buchanan, *Daniel*, pp. 354-59.

would punish them with the sword because they had oppressed the Lord's elect. The righteous and elect however, would feast together with that son of man and be clothed in garments of glory (1Enoch 62:1-63:120). These would be the ones who trusted in the Lord of Spirits. Their lot would be one of joy whenever the son of man sat on his glorious throne from which he would pass judgment, and his authority would be strong before the Lord of Spirits (1Enoch 69:24-29). He would have such authority that he could slay criminals by the word of his mouth. Like other kings, he could order someone killed and his decree would be carried out.

The picture in 1Enoch is very much like that in Daniel. The son of man was a king destined to rule from his throne. When he ruled, the saints of the Most High or the ones elected by the Lord of Spirits would also be in a position of favor. The powerful king who exercised political authority and military might over his enemies is very similar to the Son in Hebrews who was also called the Son of man.

THE SON OF MAN IN THE NEW TESTAMENT

Chronis recently discovered correctly that the Son of Man in the Gospel of Mark was another name for the Son of God.[1] He was not the first, however, to gain that insight. This knowledge was published nearly forty years earlier. Freed[2] noticed correctly that in the Fourth Gospel **Son of man** is used synonymously with Jesus, Son of God, Son, and the first personal pronoun spoken by Jesus. Further, he noted that there is no separate son of man Christology in that document. Ford[3] further concluded that the title **Son of man** was used with the same meaning as the title "Son of God" in all four gospels. For example, when Jesus asked who men said the son of man was and followed by asking who Peter thought Jesus was, Peter said, **You are the Messiah, the Son of the living God** (Matt 16:13-16). Here the subject matter was the same: Jesus, the Messiah, the Son of man, and the Son of the living God. In John, Jesus was identified with the Son of God who was to be glorified (John 11:4) and the Son of man who was to be glorified (John 13:31). Ford's explanation in terms of euphemism, however, is not important for this discussion, and her unsupported agreement with Feuillet that "there seems to be a great deal of originality in Jesus' use of the title "Son of man,""[4] contradicts the evidence.

In Dan and 1Enoch, the Son of man was portrayed as a king who would sit on his throne and rule the people of Israel while judging their enemies. The same was true of the son of man in the NT. In Ps 110, it was a king who would sit at God's right hand as God's son. In Stephen's vision, Jesus, as the Son of man, was seen standing at God's right hand (Acts 7:55-56). The Son of man or the one like a Son of man in the NT was one who would wear a gold crown (Rev 14:14) and sit on his glorious throne (Matt 19:28; 25:31) as other kings do. He would come into his kingdom in glory, as other kings come into their kingdoms. When he did, he would reward his friends and punish his enemies just as other kings do (Matt 16:27-28; Mark 8:38; Luke 9:26). Like other kings he had the authority to judge (John 5:27) and pardon (Matt 9:6; Mark 2:10; Luke 5:24). When Jesus, as the Son of man,

---

[1] Harry L. Chronis, "To Reveal and to Conceal: A Literary –Critical Perspective on 'the Son of Man' in Mark *NTS* 51 (2005): 459-481.

[2] E. D. Freed, "The Son of Man in the Fourth Gospel," *JBL* 86 (1967):402-9.

[3] J. M. Ford, "'The Son of Man'--a Euphemism?" *JBL* 87 (1968):257-66.

[4] Ford, "Euphemism," p. 64.

would sit on his glorious throne, as other kings do, he promised that the apostles would also sit on twelve thrones judging the twelve tribes of Israel (Matt 19:28).

There seems very little basis for forcing an allegorical or metaphorical interpretation either on the thrones for the twelve apostles over the twelve tribes, or on the throne of glory on which the **Son of man** would sit as a king over all twelve tribes of Israel. The Son of man described was a king, just as the son of man in Daniel, 1Enoch, and Hebrews. Jesus, as the Son of man, was destined to sit on his glorious throne with all the nations gathered before him just as the son of man in 1Enoch, and as *king* he would judge the nations, just as the son of man in 1Enoch, who was a king, had done (Matt 25:31-33). So closely identified with the being like a "son of man" in Daniel was the Son of man in the gospels that he was described by a quotation from Dan 7:13-14 (Matt 24:30; Mark 13:26; Luke 21:27). The Gospels of John and Matthew both identified the Son of man with Jesus and the Son of God. Nathaniel confessed:

> Rabbi, you are the Son of God;
> you are the king of Israel (John 1:49).

In this couplet, **the Son of God** means the same as **the king of Israel** who elsewhere was called the **Son of man** or the Messiah--all designations suitable for one who would rule over the Kingdom of God or Palestine.[1] When Hughes distinguished Christ as the son of man, rather than the son of God, holding that "as the incarnate Son he identified himself with mankind (Heb 2:11, 14)," he overlooked all of the political significance of both figures **the Son of man** and the **Son of God.**[2]

When the **Son of man** is understood to be a king, the passages referring to the betrayal of one who pretended to be the Son of man make better sense (Matt 20:18; 26:2, 24, 45; Mark 9:31; 10:33; 14:21, 41; Luke 9:44, 22:22), and the irony of a Son of man, destined to rule in glory, becomes evident when Jesus claimed that the Son of man had nowhere to lay his head (Matt 8:20; Luke 9:58).

Many[3] have avoided the political associations of the **Son of man** concept by

---

[1] For the basis for identifying the Kingdom of God with Palestine, see Buchanan, *Consequences*, pp. 42-90. Although that was not his major thesis, Marshall, "Sayings," *NTS* 12 (1965-66):335-36, opposed Vielhauer's claim that the Kingdom of God and the Son of man were mutually irreconcilable concepts. He called attention to such terms as "dominion," "kingdom," "throne," and "crown" used in association with the Son of man. M. Black, "The Son of Man Problem in Recent Research and Debate," *BJRL* 45 (1962-63):310, also opposed Vielhauer on that point. Teeple, "Son of Man Christology," p. 238, who thought the Son of man was a personification of Israel, said, "...the Son of man Messiah is really as nationalistic as the Son of David. The Son of man of the Similitudes will destroy the gentile kings and exalt the Jewish saints even more thoroughly than the Son of David."

[2] P. F. Hughes, *A Commentary on the Epistle to the Hebrews* (Grand Rapids: Eerdmans, c1977), p. 254.

[3] To cite only a few examples, C. K. Barrett, *The Gospel According to St. John* (London: S.P.C.K., 1967), said ". . . in the synoptic gospels 'Son of God' draws attention to Christ's obedience to God and 'Son of man' means a heavenly being." Bultmann, *Theology* I, p. 49, said, "However, the predominant title in the earliest Church, by the teaching of the synoptic tradition, was 'Son of Man,' which comes out of the apocalyptic hope and means a supra-mundane, pre-existent being who at the end of time will come down from heaven to hold judgment and bring salvation." E. Sjoeberg, *Der Menschensohn im Aethiopischen Henochbuch* (Lund: C. W. K. Gleerup, 1946), p. 50, called the son of man "der ganz besondere himmlische Mensch." See also pp. 58-59; 141-43; 193-94. Teeple, "Son

claiming him to be a corporate personality or a heavenly figure, but the Son of man described in Hebrews was a king who ruled over a nation and had such evident might that kings of other nations would be subject to him. In so doing, the author identified the **Son of God** with the **Son of man** and Jesus as the gospels did.[1] The political nature of the Son of man described in Hebrews was in agreement with that of the figure described in Daniel, Enoch, and the gospels. This understanding of the Son is basic to a true comprehension of Hebrews, and Hebrews was faithful to the Near Eastern understanding of the Son of man and the Son of God as a political king over a given kingdom.

This insight does not negate all theological attributes previously associated with the Son of man such as pre-existence, but it means that these concepts must be interpreted in a way that would be fitting for a Near Eastern king of NT times.

---

of Man Christology," p. 219 said "...for the pre-existent, heavenly Son of Man was utterly incompatible with human type of Messiah born on earth." He further noted, "In Daniel the figure is not the Messiah but the nation of Israel personified..." (p. 243). This latter view was in agreement with E. Schweitzer, "The Son of Man Again," *NTS* 10 (1963-64):122. That understanding was made popular by T. W. Manson, *The Teaching of Jesus* (Cambridge: Cambridge U. Press, 1951), pp. 311-36, and "The Son of Man in Daniel, Enoch and the Gospels," *BJRL* 32 (1949-50):171-93. For articles surveying other scholarly views on the Son of man, see Black, *BJRL* 45 (1962-63):305-15, and I. H. Marshall, "Sayings," pp. 327-351.

[1] For the relationship between a king and a son of God, see S. Mowinckel, *The Psalms in Israel's Worship* (New York: Abingdon Press, 1962) I, pp. 48-49, 54, 60, 62-63, 125. Mowinckel also discussed the theology related to kingship in the ancient Near East.

CHAPTER THREE

TEXT

3:1 Therefore, holy brothers, sharers in [the] heavenly calling, direct [your] attention to Jesus, the apostle and high priest of our confession,

Hebrews	First Testament
2 [who] was **faithful to the One who made him,** just as was	Isa 17:7 On that day the man will turn **to the One who made him**.
also **Moses in his house**. 3 For he [the Christ] is worthy of as	Num 12:7 My servant, **Moses. In** all my **house** he is **faithful**. Mouth to mouth I will speak to him.
much more glory than **Moses** as the builder has more glory than the **house** he built.	LXX1Chron 17:14 I will make him **faithful in** my **house** and in his kingdom for the age.
	1Sam 2:35 I will raise up for myself a **faithful** priest. He will act as my mind and as my spirit, and I will build for him a **faithful house,** and he will go before my Messiah all the days.

COMMENTARY

3:1 *Therefore, holy brothers*. **Therefore** (*háw-then*, ὅθεν), literally, "from which," meaning that the following argument could be deduced from the conclusions reached in the previous chapters. This is the connective term that relates the preceding arguments to the discussion which follows. **Holy brothers** is an affectionate address to the recipients (see Heb 2:12, 17).

The **brothers** involved were legal **brothers**. Either they were **brothers** on the basis that they were members of the family corporation that Jesus formed at the Last Supper, just as all of the Israelites are **brothers** and children of Abraham; or they were members of a monastic brotherhood, all of whom had denied their families into which they had been physically born and accepted a new family into which they were reborn legally.

The term **holy** originally was used to describe those who had kept themselves levitically undefiled so that they dared to enter areas where the Lord's presence was expected to dwell. The Lord's presence was his legal presence. The high priest and the king were both there in Jerusalem as the Lord's legal agents. It was through their existence there that the Lord was legally present. Among those who were **holy** were the priest who ministered at the altar and soldiers who kept themselves undefiled, so that the Lord would be present with them in battle and fight for them (1Sam 21:5; 1QM 7). After the temple had been destroyed in 586 BIA, priests no longer had a **holy** place where the Lord would dwell. Laymen, then, had to take upon themselves the purity rules that were previously observed by the priests. So that the Lord would be with them in Babylon, they tried to establish a "priesthood of all believers." This meant isolating believers from unbelievers, both physically and socially, so that the believers would not become defiled by touching unbelievers who did not observe levitical purity.

This led to the formation of isolated groups or sects who had standards of admission, special initiation instruction and practices, and testing procedures for maintaining perfection within the group and its community dwellings. The sects continued even after the temple was rebuilt partly from habit and partly because they questioned the purity practices of the priests in the temple. Because some of these groups were celibate, the community itself replaced the family, and the members cared for each other in cases of illness and old age. In its newly adopted family each member religiously observed all purity rules (see commentary Heb 2:12, 17). Not all groups were equally strict, and some who mingled with gentiles, like Pauline Christians, still referred to members of their group as brothers, holy or "saints." In addition to being members of the same sect as the author, the members were sons of Abraham, as were also the author and Jesus (Heb 2:16-17). Stuart was partially correct in noting that when the ancient prophets called the whole Jewish nation *keh-doh-sheém* (קדושים, ἅγιοι), or *'ahm kah-dóhsh* (עם הקודש, λαός ἅγιος), they did not mean to assert that every individual among them was *spiritually* sanctified.[1]

Jews and Christians of NT times did not make the great distinction between that which was spiritual and that which was liturgical. The term spiritual was closely allied to terms related to law and authority. A person who had gone through the correct rituals was holy, but different groups had different standards of demands for the number and kind of rituals each member was required to take. There were degrees of sanctification, spirituality, and holiness, but those who were spiritual were also sanctified, holy, and brothers. .

The name **holy** was sometimes used quite generally, simply to mean fellow parties to the contract, strict or not, but the author of Hebrews used terms usually associated with narrow, sectarian members in relationship to the recipients to raise the question about the rigidity of the membership. In rigorous sects, brothers were expected to be holy, but the author did not take that for granted. The fact that he used the adjective holy may have been intended to be descriptive of their nature.

Sharers in [the] heavenly calling. **Sharers in [the] heavenly calling** were members of the group. They were also called sharers of Christ (Heb 3:14) and sharers of the Holy Spirit (Heb 6:4). This is another way of saying **brothers**. **The heavenly calling** (*kláy-seh-ohs ehp-oo-rah-neé-oo*, κλήσεως ἐπουρανίου) was not an invitation to go to **heaven**. It was the same as **the calling** from God (*kláy-sees toó theh-oó*, κλῆσις τοῦ θεοῦ (Rom 11:29).[2] The **calling** image is to picture God shouting at someone to get his or her attention. After the person had recognized the call, he or she listened further to learn what God wanted done. One example of this is the **call** of Samuel (1Sam 3:1-14). The same Hebrew word that means "hear" also means "obey," implying that anyone who heard a **call** from God would obey. A man

---

[1] M. Stuart, *Commentary on the Epistle to the Hebrews* (Andover: Warren F. Draper, 1828), p. 87.

[2] Contra H. Montefiore, *A Commentary on the Epistle to the Hebrews* (New York: Harper & Row, 1964), p. 71, who said this was "not primarily in the sense that God calls from heaven, but inasmuch as Christians are called to heaven."

who was **called** to segregate himself from the gentiles and become a party to the contract, a member of God's **holy** people, joined the community. This means that one who had been **called** was also one who had obeyed and had been initiated into the sect and had become a **brother** and **holy.** Therefore Paul could say,

> **Those whom he has previously set apart, these also he called, and those whom he called, these also he justified, and those whom he justified, these also he glorified** (Rom 8:30).

The calling of God, or **the heavenly calling**, was a distinguishing event which involved membership responsibilities. So members were urged to walk worthily of their **calling** (Eph 4:1), to be worthy of their **calling** (2Thess 1:11), to consider their **calling** (1Cor 1:26), or to confirm their **calling** (2Pet 1:10). Recipients of this document were reminded of their **calling** when they were urged to "direct" their "attention to the Christ." It was assumed that a **calling** from God was a special privilege and demanded a responsible response. Those who had been **called** and had responded and become converts were **called** "sons of heaven" and "sons of light" (11QS), although they lived firmly planted on earth. They were also called "brothers," "sanctified," "holy," "sons of Abraham," "children of God," "sharers in blood and flesh," "sharers of Christ," "sharers in the heavenly calling," and other intimate, religious titles. All of these titles tell something about the group. It was a legal corporation of Christ, and its members were called all of these descriptive titles. These were titles that identified them as members of a very select, privileged group that belonged to the holy land whose capital was Zion, the heavenly city of the God of life. They did not consider it blasphemous to relate themselves and their nation closely to the God they worshipped. Other Christians used similar terms: **the upward calling of God** (Phil 1:23); **the holy calling** (2Tim 1:9).

Jesus, the apostle and high priest of our confession. The meaning of the term **apostle** was considered in relationship to Heb 1:2-3. An **apostle** was a legal agent or an ambassador, who, within the limits of his assignment, was legally identical to the one who sent him.[1] In this instance it means **Jesus** was legally, although not physically, the principal. It was his authority as the Messiah that made him an **apostle**, rather than his function as the **high priest**. The principal was God. Therefore, within the limits of his office, **Jesus** had the same authority as the one who sent him. He had the power of attorney. Many of the NT documents describe the office **Jesus** held and his relationship to God in terms of **apostolic** Christology, but this is the only place in the NT where he was directly called an **apostle.** It is also consistent with the other descriptions given about Jesus in Hebrews (Heb 1:2-3; 2:9, 17).[2] Paul, in his letters, usually identified himself as an **apostle** of Christ. The author of this document identified **Jesus**, himself, as an **apostle** of God. The author

---

[1] In Hebrew a *mah-lahk* (מלאך) like *áng-eh-laws* ἄγγελος in Greek means "messenger," without any special designation. God promised that he would send his messenger (מלאך) before the Israelites. The Samaritan Targum (Exod 23:20) renders this messenger, "apostle" (*sheh-leé-akh* שליח), implying that the messenger was Moses. Since the text also says "whose name is in him," meaning that the messenger was a legal agent, the targum was probably correct in holding that the messenger was a legal agent who went before the Israelites, and was therefore Moses.

[2] Rabbi Huna son of R. Joshua said, "These priests are the agents of the Merciful One (sheh-loh-akh-áy duh-rakh-mah-náh, שלוחי דרחמנא)" (bKid 23b; bYoma 19a).

of Hebrews may or may not have been an **apostle** of Jesus Christ. His interest was not in himself and his own authority but rather in the authority of Jesus as an **apostle** of God. The fourth Gospel correctly distinguished between the Principal and the agent: "The apostle is not greater than the one who sent him (the principal)" (John 13:16). Jesus also told Phillip, "He that has seen me has seen the Father" (John 14:9), but he also added, "The Father is greater" (John 14:28). The apostle is legally identical to the principal, but they are not the same physically.

Further on in the document the author defended his basis for calling Jesus a **high priest**, but here, as in Heb 2:17, the label was given only as a preparatory statement intended to condition the reader for the more elaborate attention that would follow. The **confession** was the creed or collection of doctrinal beliefs to which the members subscribed. It was basically the faith **confessed** by all members of the audience, who were also parties to the new contract. They were also **sharers in the heavenly calling**. That does not mean that the promises they expected to be fulfilled were located in heaven. Jesus was the **apostle and high priest** of this corporation.

This creed or **confession** was usually secret and was sometimes called *dah-áht* (דעת), the **mysteries of the Kingdom of God**, **the mysteries of the Kingdom of Heaven**, or **the gnosis**. Nearly every sect of Christianity or Judaism subscribed to some such **confession.** That does not mean that every time the word "gnostic" is used that the same sect is identified, or that the same **confession** is subscribed.

The author of Hebrews was very much concerned that the readers hold fast to an orthodox theology. That was their **confession.** This theology involved a belief that **Jesus** was the Son, firstborn, Son of man, Messiah, **high priest, and apostle** of God, but it did not claim that he was ontologically "very God of very God." He was the legal agent; God alone was the principal. The **confession** of the order for which Jesus was the **high priest and apostle** was probably quite different, for example, from the Hellenistic, philosophical Gnostics of the post NT period.

2 *Who was faithful.* **Faithful** (*pis-táws*, πιστός) is a quotation from Num 12:7 (Hebrew *neh-eh-máhn*, נאמן). It is one of the connection words first mentioned in Heb 2:17, and is important to the following subject. It is also the word that described Samuel, whom the Lord promised to raise up as a **faithful** priest (1Sam 2:35)[1] The Hebrew *neh-eh-máhn* means "trusted," "trustworthy," "worthy," or **faithful.** In later Judaism it was rendered by the Greek *áhx-ee-aws*, (ἄξιος) (worthy, or trustworthy) or *pis-táws* and used as a technical term to describe those who could be trusted to keep the rules and practices necessary for membership in the sect and not reveal them to others. The Essene who was qualified for membership was considered "worthy" (*áhx-ee-aws*). In rabbinic literature the person who was *neh-eh-máhn* (trustworthy) was distinguished from the person less careful about pentateuchal rules (*ahm hah-áh-retz*, עם הארץ), because he could be trusted to fulfill all the dietary, purity, tithing, and heave-offering regulations that his order demanded. According to Matthew, Jesus sent the 12 out without gold, silver, or copper in their belts, no bag, no sandals, and with only one tunic each. They were told:

> Whatever town or village you enter, find out one who is worthy (*áhx-ee-aws*, ἄξιος) in it, and stay with him until you depart. As you enter the house, salute it. And if the house is worthy *(áhx-ee-ah*,

---

[1] H. P. Smith, *A Critical and Exegetical Commentary on the Books of Samuel* (New York: Scribner's Sons, 1909), p. 23.

> ἄξια), let your peace come upon it; but if it is not worthy let your peace return to you (Matt 10:11-13).

These were rules similar to those observed by the full members of the Essene sect in order to be sure that no member might mistakenly eat improper food or defile himself in some other way in a house that was not holy, worthy, or trustworthy.[1] Pseudo-Clement described a proselyte of the Jews as "an altogether worthy person" (Hom 13:7). He would also be considered "perfect," after he had completed his training. The traveling Christians who were sent out worthily (*áhx-ee-ohs*, ἀξίως) of God, took no food from the gentiles (3John 6-7). The author, who has shown other signs of interest in careful law observance, may have understood this kind of faithfulness or trustworthiness in relationship to Moses, and all the more so to Jesus.

To the one who made him. The one who **made him** means God who **made** Jesus. The question is whether this refers to the time God created Jesus at birth or the time he made him his son by the legal action of anointing, when he became both apostle and high priest as well as Messiah. The latter seems more likely. It is consistent with Heb 1:1 and has the support of the RSV, which rendered *poi-áy-sahn-tee* (ποιήσαντι) in Heb 3:2 "appointed,"[2] the same word it used in Heb 1:2 for *éth-ay-kehn*, (ἔθηκεν). God created everyone, so there is nothing unique about that. Jesus was a human being like other people. Jesus was unique in that God not only created him, but he **made him** apostle and high priest, which is another way of saying that after the anointing Jesus was high priest and king.

God did not just **make** him. He **made him** high priest, just as he also **made** Israel a nation. God had **made** Jesus physically when Jesus emerged from his mother's womb, but Jesus' only responsibility at that time was to breathe and take nourishment. After he was fully-grown, however, Jesus accepted the responsibilities related to messiahship. At that time he took the vows that the liturgy required, and John the Baptist anointed him in behalf of God. That was when God **made** Jesus his son and Messiah.[3]

As also Moses in his house. Moses was also a priest, from the tribe of Levi (Exod 2:1-10); he ministered at the altar (Exod 24:6); and he made atonement for the crimes of his people (Exod 32:30). Moses was also an apostle of God. Here Jesus and Moses are both compared as apostles and priests, together with their houses.

After concluding that Jesus was even more **faithful** than **Moses**, the author showed that Jesus was superior to **Moses**. **Moses** was traditionally praised in superlatives in Judaism. Although Philo said that only God was **faithful** (LA 3:72), he acknowledged that **Moses** was faithful in the sense that he trusted God (LA 3:71). Philo probably deduced this from Num 12:7. According to Philo, the laws of **Moses** were so good that they omitted nothing needful. Through all the years of plenty and famine, not even the smallest part of **Moses**' laws had changed, and they would continue as long as heaven and the universe existed (Mos 2:3, 12-16).

---

[1] Buchanan, *The Consequences of the Covenant* (Leiden: E. J. Brill, 1970), pp. 248-49, 274.

[2] Following B. F. Westcott, *The Epistle to the Hebrews* (London: Macmillan, 1889), p. 75, and J. Moffatt, *A Critical and Exegetical Commentary on the Epistle to the Hebrews* (New York: Scribners, 1989), p. 42.

[3] For justification for the claim that John the Baptist anointed Jesus in secret, see Buchanan, *The Gospel of Matthew* (Lewiston: Mellen, c1996) 1, pp. 147-53.

According to Matthew Jesus agreed with Philo that **not an *iota* or a *horn* would pass from the law** until all the promises were fulfilled (Matt 5:18). Samaritans called **Moses** the great prophet (Memar Marqah 2 #10), the good apostle (Memar Marqah 2 #12), the servant of the Lord, deliverer, savior, chosen one, man of God, and righteous one (Memar Marqah 5 ##3-4). According to Pseudo-Clement, Peter refused to believe anything derogatory about **Moses**. He insisted that **Moses** was not a murderer and that he did not learn from an idolatrous priest. Since he had been called a **faithful** steward, these other allegations were false (Hom 2:52).

The text on which the author commented (Num 12:7) in both Hebrew and Greek is, **in all my house he is faithful.** The author changed the pronoun from **my** to **his** to suit his context and probably omitted **all**. The best text p13, Vaticanus [B], Ambrose, and Washingtoniensis [W]) omitted it but several later texts, probably influenced by FT, included it. When Miriam and Aaron criticized **Moses** because he had married a Cushite woman, the Lord defended **Moses** by contrasting him to other prophets. One of the rabbis commenting on **in all my house he is [most] faithful,** said, "Except than the ministering angels." Rabbi Jose said, "Even than the ministering angels" (SNum 12:7; 103. [27b]).

To other prophets, the Lord spoke in dreams and visions, but to his servant **Moses**, the Lord spoke mouth to mouth (Num 12:1-8). The **mouth to mouth** idiom probably is another way of saying that Moses was an apostle of God. His message came directly from God. He did not obtain it from other agents. The author of Hebrews quoted the Scripture to show that Moses was trustworthy or faithful in the Lord's **house** and also to affirm that Jesus was also **faithful** to **the one who made him** high priest and king. **Moses** was introduced to be compared to Jesus, not to be equated with him. Just as he had argued earlier that Jesus was superior to the angels, the author next set out to show that he was also superior to Moses.[1]

The **house** of **Moses** was not a building but a family. It was identical with the **house** of Israel and the family corporation of Abraham. The Damascus contractors called their own sect the "sure **house** of Israel" (CD 3:19). The targumist held that God promised to maintain David faithful **in his** holy **house** and in his kingdom for the age (Targ 1Chron 17:14).

[3]*For he [the Christ] is worthy of as much more glory than Moses*. It became evident in Heb 3:2 that the Hebrew word *neh-eh-máhn* carried both the meanings **worthy** and faithful. Jesus was held to be faithful (Heb 3:2); he was also called **worthy** *(ahx-eé-oh-tai,* ἀξιωται, Heb 3:3). Not only was Jesus worthy in the sense that Moses was, **he** was **worthy of** still **more glory than Moses**.

The word **house** in the FT sometimes referred to the temple, sometimes to a family or dynasty, sometimes to all Israel. Zadok was called a faithful priest (*kóh-hayn neh-eh-máhn*, כוהן נאמן) for whom the Lord would build a faithful house (*báyt neh-eh-máhn*, בית נאמן) (1Sam 2:35). Later sectarians interpreted faithful house to mean "the priests, the Levites, and the sons of Zadok" (CDC 3:21-4:1).[2]

The house to which Moses was related was probably the house of Israel. Moses was part of that house whereas Jesus was identified with its builder. This

---

[1] Although the author of Hebrews was comparing Jesus with only Moses, Samuel was also considered to be a faithful priest appointed over God's house.

[2] Moses was not called a faithful priest, but he was designated as a priest (Ps 99:6) and a Levite (Exod 33:12-34:35; Num 12:7-8). Philo called him a high priest (*The Life of Moses* 2.66-186; *Who is the Heir?* 182).

does not mean that Jesus was God, but that he was God's apostle, and since from the legal standpoint a man's apostle is like the man himself, Jesus should be related to the builder rather than to the house. As the apostle of the builder, of course, he had more glory than Moses, who belonged to the house. This was not a completely fair contrast, because Moses was also considered an apostle.

TEXT

[4](For every house is built by someone, and the one who has built all things is God.)

Hebrews 3	First Testament Intertexts
[5]Now **Moses was faithful in all** his **house** as a **servant** to testify to the things to be spoken later; [6]but Christ on the other hand, [was faithful] over his **house** as a Son, whose **house** we are if we hold fast the confidence and boasting of hope.	[Num 12:7]It is not so with my **servant Moses. In all of** my **house he is faithful.** [1Chron 17:14]I will make him **faithful in** my **house.**

COMMENTARY

[4]*Every house is built by someone.* Heb 3:4 is a parenthetical statement to clarify Heb 3:3. Hanson thought Heb 3:4 was an inauthentic and incorrect parenthetical addition. By deleting it, he held that the one who built the house was the pre-incarnate Jesus.[1] Heb 3:4 certainly is parenthetical in nature, but not necessarily inauthentic or incorrect. It is consistent with the rest of Hebrews, which acknowledges that the one who has **built** all things is God. This was done, however, through Jesus, whom God established heir of all, through whom he also made the ages (Heb 1:2). Jesus was not God, the creator, but he was the apostle of the creator. Paul also insisted that God was the source of everything: "I planted, Apollo watered, but God gave the growth" (1Cor 3:6). Hanson confused *legal* identity with *physical* identity and deleted Heb 3:4 to reach his conclusion.

[5]*Moses is faithful in all his house.* This argument is based on Num 12:7 where God confessed the extraordinary status of **Moses**. He was God's servant, and he was the only one to whom God spoke face to face and dared to see the form of God. The author of Hebrews, however, believed that Jesus was even greater, and he told why. The **house** which **Moses** and Jesus built were not material **houses**, **built** of stone, cement, wood, and glass. These were legal houses that consisted of members of family corporations. The **house in** which **Moses** was **faithful** was probably the **house** of Israel that was created in the wilderness when the contract was confirmed. TargOnq Num 12:7 has *áh-meé* (עמי, my people) for "**my house.**" TargPsJon Num 12:7 has in all the house of Israel, my people. Since Jesus was the high priest, however, and since there are other indications of sectarian interpretations in Hebrews, the author seems also to have intended house to mean "temple."

---

[1] A. T. Hanson, "Christ in the OT according to Hebrews," *StEv* 2 (1964):394-98.

Some sectarians, such as those governed by the Rule of the Community (1QS), considered themselves more than just a group of Israelites. They comprised a "temple in Aaron" (*kóh-desh buh ah-hah-róhn,* קודש באהרון) and "a **house** of truth in Israel" (*báyt hah eh-méht buh yis-rah-áyl,* בית האמת בישראל) (1QS 5:6), or a "holy **house** for Israel and a foundation of a holy of holies for Aaron" (1QS 8:5-6; see also 9:6). Those who belong to this community are "holy men who walk in perfection" (1QS 9:8). The author of 1QpHab 12:3-4 interpreted Lebanon (Hab 2:17) to mean "the council of the community" (*aht-sáht hah-yáh-khahd,* עצת היחד). Rabbis identified Lebanon with the temple in Jerusalem (Mek *Amalek* 2:3-4*; Sifré* Deut 1:7, 66b; LamR 1:5 #31, 14d).[1] This means that the author of that document considered the council of the community to be a pure or **trustworthy house,** a temple.

Paul reminded Christians at Corinth that they constituted a temple of God and that God's Spirit dwelt in their midst, just as the Lord dwelt in the midst of his people in the tent of meeting in the wilderness or in the temple at Jerusalem (1Cor 3: 16-17; 2Cor 6:16; see also Eph 2:18-22). 1Tim 3:15 defined the **house** of God as the church of the God of life. 1Pet 2:5 described a "spiritual **house**" in a context of priests, sacrifices and a cornerstone--all of which reflect the imagery of a temple.[2] A spiritual **house**, on the one hand, does not depend on precious stones, but, on the other hand, it also is not a **house** that is nothing but vapor and imagination. A spiritual **house** has legal status, whether it has a material structure or not. It is legally incorporated. It can exist without a material building of any kind. It is recognized by courts of law. As a legal corporation it is by definition eternal. All of its members may change but the corporation continues to exist.

The author of Hebrews intended some such meaning by his use of **house**, because he later (Heb 3:6) identified the house with himself and the recipients of the document. This implies that he belonged to a group that tried to keep its entire membership free from any type of defilement. *A priori* that group might have been as liberal as the Corinthians and still have called itself a temple or a spiritual **house**.

The author of Hebrews, however, employed many terms that in sectarian contexts had technical meanings, and he was very much concerned for strict law observance. These characteristics suggest that he belonged to a rigorous law-abiding order of Christianity. This will become more evident as the document is examined further. The Greek word for "servant" is *theh-ráh-pohn* (θεράπων) which according to general usage differs from *doó-laws* (δοῦλος) and *oi-kéh-tays* (οἰκέτης), being a more honorable appellation; e.g., the correlate of *doulos* and *oiketes* is "despot," *dehs-páw-tace* (δεσπότης); but *therapon* is related to "father," *páh-tayr* (πάτηρ), "lord," *keé-ree-aws* (κύριος), or *bah-see-loos* "king," (βασιλεύς)

Moses was often called the Lord's servant (*eh-véhd yeh-hoh-wáh,* עבד יהוה) (Num 12:7; Deut 34:5; Josh 1:1, 7, 13, 15; 8:31, 33; 9:24; 11:12, 15; 12:6, 8; 14:7; 18:7; 22:2; 24:4, 5; 24:9; Judges 2:8). Although subservient to a better and more respectable master, a *theh-ráh-pohn* was a servant, nonetheless, and this was precisely the point the author of Hebrews could use to disparage Moses and exalt Jesus. According to John, even sons of Abraham who have committed crimes are slaves of crime and as slaves would not remain in the house for the age [to come] (*ays-tawn-aye-óh-nah,* εἰς τὸν αἰῶνα, John 8:33-35), but the Son would continue for the age [to come]. Paul also contrasted the slaves of the elemental spirit of the universe to the sons who could call God, "Abba! Father," and be heirs of the

---

[1] Hanson, "Christ in the OT," pp. 393-407.

[2] See further G. Vermes, *Scripture and Tradition in Judaism* (Leiden: E. J. Brill, 1961), pp. 28-39.

whole estate (Gal 4:1-7). To follow this analogy, Moses, as a **servant**, could never be heir of the **house**, but Jesus had been established heir over everything (Heb 1:2). Moses, as a **servant**, could be sold whenever his Master chose, but Jesus, as a **Son** and heir, held a controlling, administrative position. Moses, as a **servant**, filled a utilitarian role.

The things to be spoken later. It does not say "**the things** written" or "**the things to be** read" later. The implication here is that the audience was a listening audience to which the author was **speaking**. The things that would **be spoken later** were **the things** for which Moses prepared the law. These **things** were not intended **to be spoken** during Moses' time but during the ministry of Christ.

Not all parties to the contract would have concurred with the author's depreciative appraisal of Moses in comparison to Jesus. Samaritans claimed that no prophet had arisen or would arise who could compare with the prophet Moses (Memar Marqah 4 #1). It was Moses whom the Lord set over all his possessions (Memar Marqah 4 #1). Moses was both the servant of God and the son of the house of God (Memar Marqah 4 #1). Moses was the great prophet whom the Lord chose for his **apostleship** (Memar Marqah 6 #7); he was **the apostle** of the True One, the faithful one of God's house (Memar Marqah 6 #3). Religious people quarrel about things like this.

In his efforts to exalt the Son, the author of Hebrews selected **Moses** and the angels, all of whom had been highly exalted in Samaritan and Jewish circles, and argued that they were inferior in comparison with Jesus.

6*But Christ as a Son over his house.* By NT times, many years of life in the diaspora had taught Jews to get along without the temple. At some point in their tradition, it became the accepted view that ten adult males constituted a quorum or *meén-yahn* (מנין). The earliest hint of such a belief is recorded in the story of Abraham's intercession for Lot. Abraham asked if the Lord would save the city for 50 just men. The Lord consented to the terms. In case 50 could not be found, Abraham reduced the number by fives and tens until he reached the number ten. After that, he stopped trying to find a group that would qualify (Gen 18:23-33). He seemed to know that five were not enough for a congregation. This interpretation of the story, relating it to communal prayer, may have arisen in Babylon after the fall of the temple in 586 BIA.

Whose house we are. Here the preacher reminded his audience of their holy calling. This was the same kind of reminder that Paul gave the Corinthians,

> **We are the temple of the God of life, just as God said, "I will dwell in their midst, and I will walk in their midst, and I will be their God and they will be my people"** (Lev 26:11-12; 2 Cor 6:16).

Those who were parties to the new contract also constituted the **temple of God** and **sharers of the heavenly calling.**

Ordinarily the temple was considered the **house** of God, the place where he made his name dwell (1Kings 8:29). After the temple was destroyed, however, other adjustments had to be made. Prophets assured the Jews that the Lord would be present with them in Babylon without the temple. In trying to create an alternative to the temple, prayers were made in groups. Later, at least, ten or more adult males were necessary to form such a group, and the area as well as the individuals was required to be levitically undefiled. If these conditions were met, Jews believed that the Lord would be present, legally. Since the Lord's presence was there, the community itself was treated like a temple (1Cor 3:16-17; Eph 2:19-21; 1 Pet 2:4-5; 1QS 8:5-9)

It was with such an understanding as this that the author of Hebrews, when speaking of the **house** of God over which Jesus was the Son and heir, said **whose house we are**, but this was not unconditionally so. Jesus was the apostle and high priest, (Heb 3:1) and the members comprised the temple or **house** in which he officiated. But the listeners would be God's **house** only if they held fast the confidence and boasting of hope. This was an exhortation that the author echoed again and again. He was concerned about the confession that the believers accepted as doctrine. He was afraid that they might waver from its teaching or become discouraged. To avoid the extreme of becoming depressed, the author urged them to remain confident and even boast of their assurance.

Grässer correctly said that Moses, Aaron, and Joshua were related to God's house. Also associated with this was the Promised Land and the *earthly* rest, but the NT Joshua [Jesus], he held, led to the *heavenly* rest. This rest would take place in the future world and the *invisible church.*[1] The text in Hebrews does not make any allowance for this distinction. According to Hebrews Jesus had more glory than Moses, and the rest Moses anticipated was expected to be greater and successfully achieved. Jesus had the status of a son rather than a servant, but no indication was given of a cosmic re-location for either rest.

Summary. Heb 3:1-6 is the opening section of a larger unit 3:1-4:16. At the beginning of the inclusion, heavenly, high priest, and confession occurs in the first verse. In Heb 4:14, the words "high priest," "heaven," and "confession" occur again, framing the section in between. Heb 4:15-16 extend beyond the final part of the inclusion, completing the sense of the unit. This is customary for the author's use of inclusions. Heb 3, like Heb 2 begins with an exhortation, but both are also similar in shifting quickly from exhortation to introduction of more doctrinal subjects.

The first two chapters concentrated on the angels in comparison with the Son. These next two chapters contain an equally well-reasoned comparison of the office and work of Moses to the office and work of Christ. They also deal more with the wilderness experience and the children of Israel in comparison with the opportunities available for the followers of Jesus than was evident in the comparison of the two groups in the first two chapters. Heb 3:1-6 shows still further evidence of the author's rigorous concern for the observance of the law and his understanding of the believers as a holy, ritually pure group that should be kept as free from defilement as the priests should keep the temple, or God's house. Just as the community itself was considered to be a temple, so Jesus must be understood as the apostle and high priest in charge of this temple, just as he was known as the sanctifier in relationship to the sanctified (Heb 2:11). His relationship to God is that of an agent or ambassador to communicate and mediate between God and the believers. Believers should be confident of this and not give up hope in God's fulfillment of his promises.

---

[1] Grässer, *An die Hebräer* (Zurich: Benziger Verlag, c1990) I, p. 172.

TEXT

Hebrews

[7]Therefore, just as the Holy Spirit says:
Today, if you hear his voice [8]**do not harden your minds as** in the rebellion, on **the day of testing in the wilderness,** [9]**where your fathers tested [me] severely and they saw my works** [10]**40 years.** Therefore, **I became indignant with that generation, and I said,** "They always **go astray mentally; they** have **not learned my ways." So** I **swore in my anger,** "[May **such and such curses come upon me] if they enter into my rest!"** (Ps 95:7-11).

First Testament

Ps 95:7-11**Today, if you hear his voice, do not harden your minds as** Maribah, as **the day of testing in the wilderness, where your fathers tested me severely, for they saw my works 40 years. I became indignant with the generation, and I said, People go astray in their minds. They do not know my ways, so I swore in my anger, ["May such and such curses come upon me] if they enter into my rest!**"

Deut 5:3Not with our fathers did Yehowah make this contract , but with us, all of us who are here alive **today**

Ps 132:13Yehowah has chosen Zion [the place] he wanted for his dwelling: [14]This is **my resting place**.

Deut 12:9For you have not come until now **to the rest**, to the inheritance, which Yehowah your God is giving you.

Zech 9:1Damascus is his resting place, because the city of Syria belongs to Yehowah and all the tribes of Israel.

Exod 20:6-7Then Moses did this [as the Lord had commanded] before the eyes of the elders of Israel. He called there the place Massah (testing) and Meribah (rebellion), because the Israelites rebelled and tested Yehowah, saying, "Is Yehowah in our midst or not?"

Deut 6:16You shall not **test** Yehowah your God as you tested in Massah (the testing).

Deut 33:8Whom you **tested** at Massah (the

testing) and rebelled against him over
the waters of Meribah (the rebellion).

Deut 9:22 At Massah (the testing) and at
Kibroth-hatta-ávah you made Yehowah
indignant.

COMMENTARY

7*Therefore, just as the Holy Spirit says*: That which the Holy Spirit says is that which is contained in the Scripture. It is legally God's word. This means that the author of Hebrews was beginning to quote from the Scripture. Ps 95 provides a poetic summary of the report in Exod 20 and Deut 6, 9, and 33 of the **testing** and **rebellion** of the Israelites against Moses. Moses responded by bringing forth water from the rock. Therefore (*dee-áw,* διό) seems to be the beginning of the sentence **do not harden your minds** (Heb 3:8) rather than **be careful, brothers**, . . . (3:12), which seems to be its own introduction to the commentary that follows the FT quotation.

Vaughan objected to both possibilities and concluded that therefore began, "*a suppressed* imperative to be supplied mentally from the general sense of the quotation."[1] Vaughan's objection is that the speaker in Heb 3:9-11 is in the first person and is God. But this really creates no problem. Ancient exegetes frequently changed subjects and applied quotations to others than that originally intended, and furthermore the **just as** indicates that the author was speaking to his generation in the same way and in the same words as the **Holy Spirit**. Since both **the Holy Spirit** and God were thought to be the source of all Scripture, there is no difficulty in shifting subjects from **the Holy Spirit** to God and vice versa when discussing Scripture. (See Heb 9:8; 10-15; also Acts 28:25; 1Clem 13:1; 16:2.)

Today, if you hear his voice. To **hear** in Hebraic thought often implied obedience. When Moses read the book of the contract to the people, the Israelites responded, **That which the Lord has spoken, we will do and we will obey** (*nah-ah-sáy wuh-nish-máh*, (נעשׂה ונשׁמע))--literally, **we will do and we will hear** (Exod 24:7). Those who really **heard** were those who paid attention carefully and accepted that which they had **heard.** That much force, however, is not intended here. If the people obeyed, of course they would not harden their minds, so the meaning is **hear**.

8*Do not harden your minds.* If they did not obey, they would **harden their minds**, they would stubbornly refuse to obey, resisting all reason or logic. Many translators render the Hebrew word, *layv* (לב), as "heart," but in Hebrew thought, this word referred to the source of thinking, willing, and deciding. A frequently occurring expression, **hardening minds** (Exod 4:21; 7:3; 9:12; 10:1, 20, 27; 11:10; 14:4, 8; Deut 2:30; 10:16; 2Kings 17:14; 2Chron 30:8; Isa 63:17), meant "becoming stubborn," "refusing to listen," "paying no attention." The words rendered the rebellion (*toh pah-rah-peek-rahs-móh,* τῷ παραπικρασμῷ) and of testing (*too pay-rahs-moó,* τοῦ πειρασμοῦ) were both proper names, Meribah and Massah, in Hebrew. There was an important play on words in Hebrew, however, because Meribah (*méh-ree-bah,* מריבה) (Num 20:13) means "conflict" or "rebellion" and

[1] C. J. Vaughan, *The Epistle to the Hebrews* (London: Macmillan, 1890), p. 63.

Massah (*máhs-sah*, מסה) (Deut 6:16) means "tempting" or "testing." The LXX translator chose to interpret these words rather than transliterate them, and the author of Hebrews simply quoted the LXX.

Me does not occur in the best texts and was added to concur with one text of the Septuagint and because the sense requires it. **Where your fathers tested me . . . 40 years**. LXX Ps 94:9 (MT and English 95:9) reads

> Where your fathers tested [me]
> they put [me] to the test and saw my works.

Heb omitted the **me**. Some Latin and Syriac texts of Heb 3:9 read the same as the LXX; other Syriac as well as the mass of later Greek manuscripts add to this the word **me**.

The Hebrew has the conjunction for (*gahm*, גם) instead of and (*kai*, καί). It does not make very good sense for the Israelites to have tested the Lord *because* they saw his works, but rather *even though* they saw his works, they tested him. Therefore this seems to be a *hysteron proteron* construction--one in which that which is last really belongs first chronologically. First they saw his works and then they still put him to the test. The force seems to be that this kind of testing and seeing the Lord's works both went on for 40 years, and the Lord never seemed able to prove his trustworthiness to them no matter how many miracles he performed.

Severely is the translation given *ehn daw-kee-mah-seé-ah* (ἐν δοκιμασίᾳ), literally "in a testing," or "in Meribah," Instead of "in a testing" (severely), some later texts have "they tested" or "they tested me" in agreement with the LXX. It seems likely that the author of Hebrews used a LXX text, using a genitive absolute "while testing," no longer extant that omitted the **me** but rendered quite literally a Hebrew text with a stronger force than the MT.

10 *I was indignant.* The Psalm reads, I was indignant with that generation for 40 years. The author of Heb changed the sense when he gave 40 years as the length of time that they saw his works. The Hebrew word *ah-koót* (אקוט) means I loathed. The Greek word *pros-óhkh-thee-sah* (προσώχθισα) is a little softer. It means "I was burdened," "laden with grief," "weighed down," "exhausted," or "indignant." R. Eliezer took the verb from the root *nah-qaht* (נקט) (to contract or hold together) rather than from *koót* (קוט) (to loathe) and so he said, The days of the Messiah will last 40 years, as it is said, "For 40 years I will maintain [contract] with that generation" (bSan 99a). The best texts read this (*taú-tay*, ταύτῃ), for that (*eh-káy-neh*, ἐκείνῃ) generation, which is probably the correct reading. Some later scribes probably changed it to conform to the LXX. It has been changed in this English translation for the sake of clarity.

Following the cycle of the ages the author of Hebrews may have calculated the times, as later rabbis did, to try to place his own situation in the same place as some earlier period in the cycle of history. If that could be done exactly, early Jews and Christians thought, then you could know precisely what would happen next. Since after the 40 years in the wilderness the Israelites moved into the Promised Land, the author may have thought in another 40 years after the crucifixion of Jesus the promises would be fulfilled. The author of Hebrews may have thought he lived in the time that was close to the end of that 40 years. Calculators often stretched or shrank historical periods to force them to fit their own. They did not have to be precise to satisfy their doctrines.[1] This type of "hit-and-miss" prediction was approximately as effective as an almanac for predicting weather. Before the satellite weather observation, the almanac was the best available. So was the ancient technique for predicting future events. Prophets kept track only of successes and overlooked their failures, always assuming that the technique itself was infallible.

Bruce noticed other examples of Jews applying the 40 year period to their own history. Forty years elapsed after the death of the Teacher of Righteousness before all the men of war who returned with the man of falsehood were consumed (CD 20:24-25). After 40 years the wicked would no longer exist (4Qpesher Ps 37, frg A, 1). The author of 1QM expected 40 years of warfare. Eliezer ben Hyrcanus said that the days of the Messiah would last 40 years (bSan 99a).[2] That meant that there would be 40 years under the rule of the Messiah in warfare before the age to come arrived, and there would a long age of peace. There was more than 20 years of warfare after Judas the Maccabee won the famous Battle of Beth-horon (164 BIA) before the complete freedom under Simon (142 BIA). These were the days of the Messiah, when the Hasmoneans ruled.

They always go astray mentally. The word rendered **go astray** means to slide off an inclined plane. The picture is that of a raised road or highway in which one might get off the road and slide into a ditch or get lost. Those who had **learned** the Lord's **ways** should, of course, stay on those paths and not wander off the track into unmapped areas. The Lord's patience was exhausted with the wilderness generation because they were **always** going **astray in mind**, or in their thinking. The last phrase was added to distinguish between their wilderness wanderings and their mental or character wanderings. The wandering that went with aimless nomadic life was used here metaphorically to describe those who did not follow the Lord's directions or commandments. That meant they did not think straight. They were unorthodox.

11 *So I swore.* Oaths, vows, curses, and blessings were all very serious expressions, in Hebrew thought. Ancient Israelites, as well as Jews and Christians of NT times, believed that the Lord would fulfill all blessings and curses that had been uttered, if the conditions associated with them took place. Thus, when Isaac blessed Jacob by mistake, he could not take back his blessing and give it instead to Esau (Gen 27:1-37), nor could Balak change the destiny of Israel once Balaam had pronounced a blessing on that nation (Num 23). These were legal liturgies, and if liturgies were taken under proper conditions with the right number of witnesses according to the standard ceremony they were the same as written, legal contracts.

If an **oath** were administered by a third party, the person administering the **oath** listed the **curses** and the conditions under which they would be received. For example, the woman suspected of adultery was brought before the priest, who made her drink the water of bitterness, and as he administered the oath he warned her that if she had been unfaithful to her husband she would suffer a miscarriage, but if she had been faithful, her pregnancy would be undisturbed. The woman answered,

---

[1] Buchanan, *Jewish Messianic Movements from AD 70 to AD 1300* (Eugene, Oregon: Wipf and Stock Publishers, 2003); *New Testament Eschatology* (Lewiston: Mellen, c1993), pp. 58-89.

[2] F. F. Bruce, *The Epistle to the Hebrews* (Grand Rapids: Eerdmans Publishing Co., 1964), p. 65, fn. 57.

"Amen, amen!" meaning that she accepted the conditions under which the curses would apply (Num 5:16-28). If she received the curses that had been pronounced, it was believed that she had been unfaithful. A self-administered oath was one that Ruth took, speaking to Naomi:

> **Thus may the Lord do and thus may he add, if [even] death separates me from you** (Ruth 1:17; see also 1Sam 3:17; 2Sam 3:35; 1Kings 6:31).

The curses here were only summarized rather than specified. Self administered oaths usually were understood to have the following parts:

(1) the holy being or object by which the oath was invoked;
(2) the curses to be received if the following conditions were not fulfilled; and
(3) the conditions under which the curses would be effective.

Ruth swore that she would not leave her mother-in-law, indicating severe unmentioned curses that she would accept if she did. Sometimes oath-takers intentionally omitted a negative or mispronounced the sacred object involved, so fearful were they of the destructive effects of oaths. For example:

(1) *Qonam!* (i.e., Qorban, the gift for the altar)
(2) may my wife [never] be useful to me,
(3) if I have eaten today (mSheb 3:4; see also mNed 3:2-5).

No. 1 indicates the sacred object by which the oath was taken; no. 2, is the adverse situation that will occur to the oathtaker if no. 3 is not the case. The oath-taker wanted to affirm very strongly that he had not eaten that day. If he had eaten he would be willing to be deprived of satisfaction received from his wife. Although he was sure he had not eaten, he protected himself by mispronouncing the name of the sacred object by which the oath was taken and omitted the negative, without which the conditions of the oath make no sense. Frequently oath-takers omitted the entire list of curses and/or the sacred object by which the oath was taken. They said only, ". . . if I do such and such" and the divine name of the sacred object, followed by a list of curses, was understood. Matt 15:5 quotes Jesus scolding the Pharisees:

> **But you say, "Whoever says to his father or mother, 'Gift!' (i.e., Qorban!) [unmentioned curses understood], if from me you receive benefit, he will not honor his father or his mother."**

The Pharisees were so fearful that Israel might receive the curses understood that they permitted the oath-taker to break the commandment to honor his father and mother rather than to allow the oath to be broken and the curses received.[1] In this case the oath was that the oath-taker would neglect his parents in their old age. That was probably an oath taken by a person who was entering a monastery and was taking vows of poverty, chastity, and obedience only to the monastic order. Under

---

[1] Buchanan, "Some Vow and Oath Formulas in the New Testament," *HTR* 58 (1965):319-26.

such a fearful concept of oath-taking as this, the abbreviated oath in Ps 95 was composed.

If they enter into my rest. Ps 95:11 said only, As I swore in my anger, RSV rendered Psalm 95:11 thus: **Therefore I swore in my anger that they should not enter my rest**. This communicated the basic message involved by replacing the oath formula with an indirect quotation. The initial understanding was that the Lord took an oath by listing some unmentioned curses that he agreed to accept if the oath was broken.

The Lord swore that those who rebelled would not enter into the land, meaning the inheritance, the Promised Land (Num 14:23, 29-30; Deut 1:35). The Lord took an oath that they would not enter into his rest (Ps 95:11), which had exactly the same meaning, but Ps 95:11 said, **As I swore,** meaning "as reported in Deut 1 and Num 14." The Israelites were reminded that they had not yet come to the rest and inheritance which the Lord would give them (Deut 29:9), but after they crossed the Jordan and entered the land and the Lord had given them **rest** from their enemies, then they should offer sacrifice to the Lord (Deut 12:10-11; see also Deut 3:20; 25:19; Josh 1:15; 22:4). Later the Lord gave to Israel all the land which he **swore** to give to their fathers (Josh 21:43), and the Lord gave them **rest** on every side . . . not one of all their enemies had withstood them (Josh 21:44). As Hofius observed, Solomon was a man of **rest** and God provided **rest** for him from all his enemies that surrounded [Israel] (1Chron 22:9). The temple was also called a house of **rest** (1Chron 28:2).[1] This special rest (*Meh-noó-khah,* מנוחה *= kah-tah-pów-sees,* κατάπαυσις) was closely related to existence in the Promised Land.

This meant that not one of all the good promises which the Lord made to the house of Israel had failed (Josh 21:45). It was possible to live on the land without rest from the enemies, but it was not possible to have rest without acquiring the land of Canaan. The rabbis understood that this was the case. R. Judah says "If Israelites had been virtuous, in three days they would have entered the land, as it is said, **And the ark of the contract of the Lord goes before them, a journey of three days, to spy out for them a rest** (Num 10:33) and there is no **rest** but the land of Israel, as it is said, **For you have not entered into rest until now, into the inheritance which the Lord your God gives you** (Deut 12:9)" (sDeut 1:2, 65b, #2).

One of the targumists said, [May the following curses come against me] if they go up to **the rest**—to the house of my temple (TargPs 95:11). Early Christians and Jews always "went up" to Palestine, Jerusalem, Zion, or the temple from any place in the world, regardless of the actual altitudes involved. "Going up" did not mean ascending to heaven. After he had examined all of the references to **rest** in rabbinic literature, Hofius said,

> (The rabbinic exegetes speak of the מנוחה connection with the temple, with Jerusalem, and with the Land of Canaan. In the Letter to the Hebrews in references to κατάπαυσις, the true temples are near one another (8:2; 9:11; etc.), the coming city, heavenly Jerusalem (11:10, 16; 12:22; 13:14) with Mount Zion (12:22), and the promised fatherland (11:14ff.).[2]

---

[1] Otfried Hofius, *Katapausis: Die Vorstellung vom Endzeitlichen Ruheort im Hebräerbrief* (Tübingen: J. C. B. Mohr, 1970), p. 49.

[2] Hofius, *Katapausis,* p. 52.

Hofius thought, however, that there were a few references that anticipated the end of time *(endzeitlichen)* when the chosen people would receive their **rest.**[1] These were passages where the rabbis argued about who would be included and who would be rejected in the **age** to come. These were such groups as those killed in the flood, those who died in the wilderness, the Sodomites, etc. Some rabbis argued that these had a portion in the **age** to come, and that they would live there, whereas others denied that they would be a part of that **age** (tSan 13:1-30).

One rabbi who held that all of these groups would have a portion in the **age** to come said they would worship Yehowah in the holy mountain, in Jerusalem (Isa 27:13; tSan 13:30). This was not anticipating the end of the world, but rather the end of the current **age,** which would be followed in the **age** to come—not in heaven, but in the Land of Israel, on the holy mountain of Jerusalem.

The word **rest** belonged to the terminology associated with Sabbath **rest**. Just as there was one day of rest in every seven, so there was also one year of rest in every seven. In the seventh year, Israelites who had allowed themselves to be enslaved by their Israelite brothers to pay back the money they had borrowed were released to "return home," and on Jubilee years, those who had sold their property because of indebtedness had their property returned to them or to their posterity. In this same thought-form, the Lord announced that the Hebrews could return to Palestine. Their period of "servitude" was over; they were allowed to return "home"; and their land was to be restored.[2] This was their Jubilee, but when they tested the Lord in the wilderness, he withheld the fulfillment of his promise. Yehowah swore that he would not let them enter the Promised Land while that generation was alive; they would not enter into the **rest**. In another context, the Lord promised Moses that his presence would go before them and give the people **rest** (Exod 33:7-14). When David had conquered the Promised Land, the Lord gave him **rest** from all his enemies (2Sam 7:1).

Scholars have admitted that the **rest** mentioned in the FT involved possession and settlement in **the land** of Canaan and that the author of Hebrews used the very same terminology, but they have not been willing to acknowledge that he belonged to the same religious environment in which these terms were used with their FT meanings and that he therefore meant the same by them as Jewish writers of the same time meant. Turner, for instance, on the one hand, insisted that the word **rest** in Ps 95 does not speak exclusively of future rest in heaven. . . . But the texts cited above clearly prove that the settlement in the land of the promised inheritance is itself the **rest** discussed.[3] But on the other hand, when it came to Hebrews, for no internal reason, Turner suggested that we "consider the land of Canaan is a *type* [italics mine] of heaven . . ."[4] In his judgment, His *rest*, that is God's **rest** in heaven of which that in the Promised Land was a *type* [italics mine] . . .[5] and the author certainly employs the word *rest* here to denote the heavenly inheritance.[6] Westcott similarly said,

---

[1] Hofius, *Katapausis*, p. 44.

[2] Buchanan, *Consequences*, pp. 9-18.

[3] S. H. Turner, *The Epistle to the Hebrews in Greek and English* (New York: Stanford and Swords, 1852), p. 56.

[4] Turner, *Hebrews*, p. 57.

[5] Turner, *Hebrews*, p. 60.

[6] Turner, *Hebrews*, p. 61.

> The rest was primarily Canaan, (Deut 12:9-10), and then that divine kingdom and order of which the earthly Canaan was an imperfect type.[1]

Attridge[2] dismissed the subject by saying that

> the term "rest" has a different sense from that accorded it in the psalm, where it refers primarily to the resting place of Canaan.

He offered no basis for showing that Hebrews meant something different from the psalmist or the Torah. Without explanation or justification, Koester echoed,

> The association of rest with Canaan is presupposed in Heb 3:18-19 and 4:8, although for Hebrews the promise of rest in Canaan is ultimately fulfilled in God's heavenly kingdom (12 :22-24).[3]

Although Moffatt interpreted the aspirations of Hebrews as being heavenly in other contexts, he made no effort to venture an interpretation different from those of the rabbis he quoted.[4] Michel quoted Käsemann's view that the **rest** of God according to Hebrews, was nothing other than the heavenly *káws-maws* itself. Michel, himself, identified it correctly with the *oi-koo-meh-nay* (οἰκουμένη) and *páw-lees meh-loo-sah* (πόλις μέλλουσα) which he mistakenly understood as the *jenseitgen Ruhe Gottes* (otherworldly **rest** of God). He offered an existential hope, however, by suggesting that we might begin here and now to participate in a share of the promised **rest**.[5] Lane side-stepped the issue by not discussing it. He simply dismissed it with the words "(Hofius, *Katapausis,* 126)."[6]

The FT and rabbinical references with which these scholars were familiar made it difficult--even arbitrary--to suggest that the author of Hebrews had a different meaning in mind when he used the same terms as the others. They were able to offer no arguments or data to support their desired claim. Their affirmations consisted of special pleading, or, as in the case of Lane, avoidance of the subject. The text here is consistent with other affirmations made in Hebrews in showing that the author expected the promised heritage of the land of Canaan under the rule of the Messiah to be fulfilled for Jesus and his followers.

TEXT

[12]Be careful, brothers, lest there be in any of you an evil heart of unbelief [shown] in
turning astray from the living God; [13]but exhort one another every day, while it is
still called today lest any of you become hardened by [the] deceitfulness of crime.

---

[1] Westcott, *Hebrews*, 1889, p. 82.

[2] H. Attridge, *The Epistle to the Hebrews* (Philadelphia: Fortress Press, 1989), p. 115.

[3] C. R. Koester, *Hebrews* (New York: Doubleday & Co., 2001), p. 258.

[4] J. Moffatt, *A Critical and Exegetical Commentary on the Epistle to the Hebrews* (New York: Scribner's Sons, 1964), pp. 45-46.

[5] O. Michel, *Der Brief an die Hebräer* (Wuppertal: R. Brockhaus, 1867), pp. 1-2, 104.

[6] W. L. Lane, *Hebrews 1-8* (Dallas: Word Books, c1991), p. 86.

14 For we have become sharers of Christ, if indeed we hold fast the initial substance[1] until the end 15 while it is said,

Hebrews	First Testament
Today, if you hear his voice, do not harden your minds as in the rebellion. 16 For who [were the ones who], after they had heard, rebelled? But were they not all those who went out from Egypt through [the leadership of] Moses? 17 And against whom did he **become indignant 40 years?** Was it not against those criminals whose	Ps 95:7-10 **Today, if you hear his voice, do not harden your minds as** Meribah, as the day of testing **in the wilderness**, where your fathers tested me severely, for they saw my works **40 years.** I **became indignant** with the generation, and I said, People go astray in their heart. They do not know my ways,
	Num 14:33 Your sons will be shepherds **in the wilderness 40 years**, and they will bear the burden of your faithlessness until their corpses are finalized **in the wilderness.**
	Num 32:13 He made them wander **in the wilderness 40 years**, until all the generation that had done evil in the eyes of Yehowah had died.
limbs fell in the wilderness? 18 And to whom did he swear	Num 14:29 **Your limbs will fall in this wilderness,** all of your number from 20 years and older
that they **would not enter into his rest** except those who disobeyed? 19 And we see that they were not able to enter because of [their] unbelief.	Ps 95:11 So I swore in my anger, **["May such and such curses come upon me] if they enter into my rest!"**

COMMENTARY

12 *Be careful, brothers, lest there be in any of you an evil mind.* The word rendered **Be careful** is literally "See!" It means, "Watch out!" "Keep your eyes open." This is the opening expression of and inclusion that closes with the words, "and we see" (Heb 3:19). The word unbelief also occurs both in Heb 3:12 and 3:19. This shows that Heb 3:12-19 is a separate, unified paragraph.

Like the author of the legalistic sections of Matthew, Hebrews demanded perfection in character of *all* members of the community. The exclusive terms like

[1] The word translated here is *hoo-paw-stáh-sees* (ὑποστάσις), which means "doctrine," "contract," "the agreement," "the faith," or "the religion." It is dealt with extensively in Heb 11.

"holy brothers" (Heb 3:1), which might have been used rather generally and loosely but might also have been intended definitively, and here clearly understood as the latter. References to the brothers in sacred, undefiled terms, comparing them to a temple, were not intended to be broad generalizations.

Of unbelief. This term reoccurs in Heb 3:19, showing that the material in between Heb 3:12 and Heb 3:19 forms a unit that is framed by an inclusion. There must not be **an evil mind of unbelief** in any one of the brothers. The word **unbelief**, like the word **rest,** was used repetitiously in this discussion (Heb 3:12, 19). The author required even more rigorous law observance than Matthew (Matt 5:17-48; 7:13-14). Matthew at least allowed opportunity for repentance before the member was excommunicated (Matt 18:15-17). This was not the case in Hebrews (Heb 6:4-6; 12:16-17) and the work of others of the same conviction (Vis 2:4-8; Mand 4:3:1-3, 7; Dial 44:4; Strom 3:6; 2:2; Irenaeus *Heresies* 4.42:4) who allowed no repentance.

The psalmist warned his readers not to let their minds become hardened as in the rebellion (Ps 95:8; Num 14:22-23). Using the same words, the author of Hebrews warned his audience in relationship to their minds. They should watch that no single one of them had an evil mind of unbelief, which would be exhibited by **turning away from the living God.**

Turning away from the living God. The words **turning away**, literally means "standing apart," (*ah-paw-stáy-nai.* ἀποστῆναι), taking a position that is different from the one prescribed. In the FT the expression, **living God,** is better rendered "The God of life." The life involved is existence within positive relationship to the contract. God is the one who initiated the contract that formed the corporation in which life is found. Hebrews has mistranslated this term of life as living. The Land of **Life** is the Promised Land. While commenting on the word "minds" from Ps 95, the author of Hebrews supplemented the text with references from Num, reminding the readers of those who turned back from following the Lord (Num 14:43). He also alluded to an evil congregation (Num 14:27) and the Lord's oath, "As I live" (Num 14:21, 28).

C. R. Koester was probably correct in holding that God is enthroned in heaven, but there is nothing in his documentation to show that (Heb 12:22).[1] "Heavenly Jerusalem" is obviously "Zion" (Heb 12:22), the place to which the listeners who heard the message of Heb 1-12 had come, just as the text said.

13*Lest any of you become hardened.* The word translated "one another" is *heh-ow-toós* (ἑαυτούς) literally, "yourselves," but in context this means that they should encourage or exhort one another. The rigorousness of the author is again evident. They should exhort every day to be sure that there was no crime among any of the brothers. Such exhortation presumes congregational contact among the believers with opportunities to visit and encourage each other on a daily basis. This was the same kind of advice offered by Matt 18:15-17.

The urgency of the situation was emphasized on the basis of the word "today" quoted from the Psalm. The time was short. They were obliged to act properly while they still had the chance not utilized by their fathers. The words **become hardened**, also from the Psalm, were used by the author of Hebrews to warn the readers against the repetition of the crime of their fathers in the wilderness.

---

[1] C. R. Koester *Hebrews*, p. 259.

If they should **become hardened** by the deceitfulness of crime, that would be the same as having **an evil heart of unbelief and turning away from the living God**. If that happened, they could expect the same fate as the exodus generation.

14*We have become sharers of Christ*. Heb 3:14 is a summarizing sentence that refers the reader to the beginning of the chapter and picks up words from there on. Those who had become **sharers of Christ** were the same holy brothers who were **sharers of [the] heavenly calling** (Heb 3:1) and **sharers of the Holy Spirit** (Heb 6:4). Those encouraged to hold fast the initial doctrine until the end were the same ones who would belong to God's house, if they would hold fast the confidence and boasting of hope (Heb 3:6). They were also the ones warned to **be careful** (Heb 3:12).

We hold fast the initial substance until the end. The word rendered **substance** (*hoo-paw-stáh-sees*, ὑποστάσις) literally means "standing under," and it is contrasted to **turning aside** (Heb 3:12), which literally means "standing away" (*ah-poh-stáy-nai*, ἀποστῆναι). Instead of standing away and becoming apostate, the listeners were urged to stand under, which meant **holding fast the initial substance**. **The substance** is that which settles to the bottom, the basis, the foundation, the confession, or the faith, depending on its context. The faith, defined by the author in Heb 11, was the **substance of things hoped for and the basis for testing things unseen** (Heb 11:1).

Here the context is religious, textual, or doctrinal. It is the faith, creed, or religion of the sect. The word is translated "confidence" by the RSV, which also translated a quite different Greek word (*pah-ray-seé-ah*, παρρησία) by the same English word. The RSV probably identified the two meanings because of their proximity in use in Heb 3:6 and Heb 3:14, but the author used different terms. Whereas *pah-ray-seé-ah* refers to the boldness which characterizes one who is sure of himself in a situation which would usually make one tremble, *hy-poh-stáh-sis* refers to the reality, essence, or nature of something, or the groundwork or basis of hope. Those who **held fast the initial substance** were those who did not give up the creed or confession which they were taught at the beginning of their catechism.

15*Do not harden your hearts as in the rebellion*. **While it is said** refers to Scripture. The quotation given is a repetition of Ps 95:8, quoted before in Heb 3:7-8. It was repeated here because the author intended to comment on it directly.

16*Those who went out from Egypt through [the leadership of] Moses*. Vaughn has offered an attractive translation that is different from the one given here.[1] By only omitting the accent on the Greek word, *teé-nehs* (τίνες), which would then mean "some" rather than "who?," this verse would read, "For some, after they had heard, rebelled; but not all **those who went out from Egypt** [did so]." This would take into account Joshua and Caleb who did not rebel. In further support of this translation is the strong word used for but (*ahl-áh*, ἀλλ'). When interpreted as a question, this "but" is almost unnecessary. The only problem with this translation is that it does not cohere well with the required translation of the next two verses. Each verse contains "whom" (*teé-see*, τίσι), the dative of the same pronoun. It does not seem likely that the author would have used the same ambiguous pronoun in one case indefinitely and in the other interrogatively, but maybe he did.

---

[1] Vaughan, *Hebrews*, p. 71.

If *teé-nehs* is to be understood interrogatively to mean "Who?," rather than "Some," then the "But" (*ahl-láh'*) was used hyperbolically, as in Matt 3:5, 6 and John 3:26. The author correctly identified the word rebellion of Ps 95 with the activity of the Israelites described in Deut 1 and 14. Instead of entering the Promised Land as the Lord had directed, those who went out from Egypt first sent spies to search out the land to see whether or not it was likely that the Lord could fulfill his promise. This was the testing (Heb 3:9) that they did against the Lord, and after they had heard the evil report of the spies, they rebelled (Num 14:9) and made plans to go back to Egypt (Num 14:4).

17 *Was it not against those criminals whose limbs fell in the wilderness.* Again the author correctly identified the ones involved in the exodus from Egypt as those who had made the Lord indignant (mentioned in Ps 95). After they had rebelled and complained against the Lord and against Moses, the spies who brought back the evil report died from a plague (Num 14:37), and the Lord threatened to destroy all those who came out from Egypt and to disinherit them altogether (Num 14:11-12), but after Moses' intercession, he modified his threat by exempting the children and teenagers, under the age of 20 years. The author of Hebrews wove words and phrases from the Numbers passage into his interpretation of Ps 95. Moses asked the Lord to forgive the crime of the people (Num 14:19; see also 14:40-41), so the author called the people **those criminals**. The Lord promised: **Your limbs will fall in this wilderness** (Num 14:29), so the author referred to the exodus generation as **those whose limbs fell in the wilderness**. The author of Hebrews was acquainted with all of the Pentateuchal sources reporting the activity of the Israelites **in the wilderness** after they left Egypt, and he drew on all of them, taking some words from Exodus, Numbers, and Deuteronomy to supplement his main text from Ps 95.

18 *To whom did he swear that they would not enter into his rest.* The oath mentioned in Ps 95 that God would not let these people enter into his rest refers to Num 14:30: "[May these unmentioned curses come upon me] if you enter the land upon which I raised my hand [in oath] that you would dwell in it." That was the oath the Lord took against the exodus generation which the psalmist interpreted as meaning, **they would not enter into his rest**. This clearly refers to life in the Promised Land, but Stuart said,

> But what was the *rest* in question? Is it quiet possession of the Land of Canaan? No, says the apostle. Believers *now* enter the rest (vs. 3), i.e. the same kind of rest as was anciently proffered. Moreover, God calls it *katapausin mou,* My rest, i.e., (adds he) such rest as God enjoyed, after he had completed the creation of the world; consequently spiritual, heavenly rest.[1]

The text does not justify such interpretations as this. The disobedience about which the author spoke came after the Lord had sworn that they would not enter the land. They then confessed their crime and said that they would repent and enter the land. Moses told them not to, because the Lord would not be with them, but they disobeyed and tried to take the hill country, so the Canaanites and Amalekites defeated them (Num 14:39-45). Weiss related the **rest** involved to **the age to come** (Heb 2:5)

---

[1] Stuart, *Hebrews,* p. 104.

which he took to mean "the world **to come," the heavenly city** (Heb 12:22), which he located in heaven, ignoring the context, which calls it **Zion, heavenly Jerusalem, city of the God of life**. This was the place where both the speaker and the audience were located when this sermon was given. It is unlikely that either the speaker or the audience thought they were in heaven at the time. The next term Weiss used was **the fatherland** for which the ancient fathers were searching (Heb 11:14). Weiss called it a "heavenly" **fatherland,** but the author of Hebrews did not.

Weiss also argued the goal of the heroes by saying they confessed to have been "strangers on the earth" (Heb 11:13). These wandering ancients had lived all of their lives on earth, and were not strangers to it, but when they came to the Promised *Land*, they did not have it in their possession, so they were **strangers in the land.** Later they took possession of it and were no longer strangers. Weiss was not the first to mistranslate "age" as "world" and "land" as "earth," but that distorts the entire message.[1]

The age to come, Zion, and the fatherland are all concepts related to the promised rest that came to the chosen people when David conquered his enemies and established secure borders around the land

19 *We see that they were not able to enter because of [their] unbelief.* After the spies brought back the evil report and the people complained and made plans to go back to Egypt, the Lord, in his anger, asked Moses, "How long will they not believe in me?" (Num 14:11), and he threatened to destroy them. It was on this basis that the author of Hebrews concluded that the exodus generation was not able to enter because of [their] unbelief. The mention of **seeing** was intended to lead the reader or listener back to the warning to **see** at the beginning of this exhortation (Heb 3:12).

Summary. After the author compared Jesus as apostle and high priest with Moses (Heb 3:1-6), he then (Heb 3:7-19) dealt with the negative half of the chapter, comparing the punishment applied to the exodus generation with the opportunities still available to the believers of the author's time. He primarily based his argument Ps 95 and the Book of Numbers. The author apparently had both texts before him. The author first quoted Ps 95. Then he interpreted it on the basis of the rebellion of the exodus generation (Deut 1; Num 14). Heb 3:14 summarized all that had been said in Heb 3 up to that point, but it did not mark the end of the section, Heb 3:15-19 was a further development of the same subject, using the same text. Because the topic was discussed at length, the author summarized it briefly at Heb 3:14 and reintroduced his text at Heb 3:15 so that the reader could keep the author's main point in mind. This is typical of the excellent style of the author. The entire chapter was enclosed in an inclusion, using the word unbelief, mentioned at the beginning, quoting Num 12:7, and at the end, referring to Num 14:11.

[1] H. F. Weiss, *Der Brief an die Hebräer* (Göttingen: Vandenhoeck & Ruprecht, 1991), p. 269.

CHAPTER FOUR

TEXT

Hebrews	First Testament
[4:1]The promise of **entering** into his **rest** is left [unfulfilled]. Let us be afraid, therefore, lest any of you **seem to fall behind**; [2]for the gospel has been preached to us as well as to them, but the message of the report did not help them, since it was not united by **faith**, in those who heard. [3]For we who believe **enter into the rest**, just as he said,	[Ps 95:10]I became indignant with the generation, and I said, People **go astray in their mind**. They do not know my ways.
As I swore in my anger, "[May such and such curses come upon me] if they enter into my rest," namely, [from] the **works** [that] took place from the foundation of the world. [4]For somewhere he said the following concerning **the seventh day: And God**	[Ps 95:11]so **I swore in my anger, ["May such and such curses come upon me] if they enter into my rest!**."
rested on the seventh day from all his works, [5]and again in this [passage]: **"[May such and such curses come upon me] if they enter into my rest**."	[Gen 2:2]On **the seventh day God** finished **his work** which he had done, **and he rested on the seventh day from all his works.**

TECHNICAL DETAILS

The Greek text of Gen 2:2 quoted in Heb 4:4 disagrees with the LXX, but it agrees completely with Philo, De Post Caini 64:18.

Midrashic Method. In typical **midrashic** fashion the author continued to develop his commentary on Ps 95. He did this by introductions, quotations, and interpretations, working into his introductions and commentaries special words that come from the text of the psalm. In the development of his argument, he also brought in a proof text from Genesis. This, too, is normal. Ps 95 is itself a midrash on passages from Numbers and Deuteronomy, and the author of Hebrews used all three texts as his sources.

Lane had to admit that the word **rest** was the main theme of this chapter, occurring seven times,[1] but he again evaded the obvious interpretation by calling it "eschatological," involving the "**age** to come at the consummation of redemption."

---

[1] W. L. Lane, *Hebrews 1-8* (Dallas: Word Books, 1991), p. 95.

He claimed this idea "assumes profound significance when **rest** is understood in this eschatological sense."[1] Eschatology is derived from the Greek term *és-cha-taws* (ἔσχατος), which means "end." It can mean the end of a stick or the end of a certain period of time, such as the end of a day, a week, an administration, an era. Eschatology is a study applied to ends of periods of time. Lane failed to acknowledge that the end involved in this eschatology was the end of God's wrath that kept the Israelites from inheriting the Promised Land. The redemption destined at the consummation was the restoration of the Promised Land. This is obvious from the FT texts quoted. That which assumed "profound significance" was Lane's imagination that moved the interpretation away from biblical concepts.

Lane claimed support for his position by referring to various rabbinic passages that declare that certain groups of people, like those who built the tower, those who rebelled in the wilderness, the men of Sodom, etc. were destroyed in this age and would have no portion in the age to come (tSan 13:12). They did not say that the age to come was anything that would happen at the end of the cosmos, time, or the world or at any place but on this earth. They did not say that "the rest in Canaan was only a type or symbol of the complete rest that God intended for his people,"[2] or that it would take place in "the heavenly sanctuary" that was not at Jerusalem on earth.[3] The "heavenly sanctuary" of which Lane spoke was not Jerusalem, but "a transcendent reality." [4]

Lane said that because Jesus had passed through the heavens that his high priestly ministry is "the guarantee that God's people will celebrate the Sabbath in his presence [in heaven]."[5] The author of Hebrews made no assertion that Christians would follow Jesus into heaven. That was an eisegetical interpretation. Eisegetical means that it did not come from the text itself but was imported from some outside opinion, usually that of the author who made the comment. If Lane had meant the heavenly sanctuary at Jerusalem, that would have been valid.

The age to come in rabbinic testimony is consistent. It is the period of history expected in the future after the Messiah had come, overthrown the enemy, and established a condition of peace and independence for Israel. This would be called Israel's **rest. Rest** in biblical terms does not mean sleeping. It refers to the period of time during a Sabbath. That means either the end of a week, the end of a seven week period, or the end of a Jubilee. In political terms it refers to a period when the Promised Land was free from foreign rule, and its borders were secure.

> Rabbi Elazar of Modi'im said, "If you are meritorious enough to keep the Sabbath, the Holy One Blessed be He is destined to give you six good portions: 1) The Land of Israel, 2) the age to come, 3) the new age, 4) the kingdom of the house of David, 5) the priesthood, and 6) the Levites" (Mekilta, *Vayassa* 5:70-73).

The age to come was reflected in Amram's Kaddish when Jews prayed that God's kingdom would rule, his salvation shoot forth, and his Messiah appear. At that time God was expected to raise the dead, establish the city of Jerusalem, complete the

---

[1] Lane, *Hebrews, 1-8,* p. 98.
[2] Lane, *Hebrews*, p. 101.
[3] Lane, *Hebrews,* p. 102.
[4] Lane, *Hebrews 9-13* (Dallas: Word Books, 1991), p. 467.
[5] Lane, *Hebrews*, p. 103, 105.

temple, root out gentile worship from the land, and restore holy worship in its place. They also prayed for peace from Heaven, life, abundance, salvation, comfort, freedom, healing, redemption, forgiveness, atonement, expansion, and victory for Israel. All of these are nationalistic expectations to take place in the age to come when the Messiah would rule from Jerusalem. Among the things hidden from men were

> the kingdom of the house of David—how long until it is restored in its place, and this guilty kingdom—how long until it is uprooted (Mekilta, *Vayassa* 6:61-64).[1]

Rest is obviously the main topic of Heb 4:1-11, but the author of Hebrews was not speaking of a rest for believers that would take place in heaven, as many scholars have assumed. He may also have believed that there was one, but that was not the subject of this chapter. Silence on the subject proves nothing. Here he concentrated on the restoration of the Promised Land, and scholars should acknowledge that.

COMMENTARY

[1]*The promise of entering into his rest was left [unfulfilled]*. The reason why the **promise** was **left [unfulfilled]** was explained in Heb 3. The exodus generation was disobedient, criminal, rebellious, testing, and lacking in faith. Rabbi Judah said,

> If the Israelites had just been meritorious for three days, they would have entered the land, as it is said, **The chest containing the contract of the Lord goes before them for three days to spy out for them a rest** (Num 10:33). There is no rest except the land of Israel, as it is said, **For until now you have not entered the rest and the inheritance which the Lord your God gives you** (Deut 12:9) (sDeut 1:2, 65b).

At this point, for the first time the contemporary believers were brought into the picture. Basic to the doctrine of interpretation used by the commentator is the belief that every **promise** made in God's word had to be fulfilled. God **promised** that the Israelites could enter the **Promised** Land, but they did not. Instead they died in the wilderness, and the **promise** was left unfulfilled. **Promises** made in antiquity to chieftains of family corporations were made also to the entire corporation, and legal corporations were immortal, by definition. All members of a corporation could die and be replaced, but the corporation would continue. Debts and credits were passed on from generation to generation through the corporation. On that basis, **promises** made to chieftains, like Abraham and Moses, were still expected to be fulfilled to later members of the corporation. The obligation did not die.

Another doctrine of exegesis was that all prophecy was prophesied only for the days of the Messiah. This means the **promise** made to the wilderness generation would bypass all other generations awaiting to be **fulfilled** only in the days of the Messiah. Since the author lived in the days of the Messiah, he expected them to be **fulfilled** in his day.

---

[1] For these and other illustrations see Buchanan, *The Consequences of the Covenant* (Leiden: E. J. Brill, 1970), pp. 63-67.

Since this is the case, and the **promise** was still left pending, it was available for the Christians of the author's generation to receive. Therefore listeners were strongly urged to be careful, even fearful, lest any single one of them should **fall behind**. The verb **to fall behind** (*hoos-teh-ray-kéh-nai*, ὑστερηκέναι) pictures someone in a company marching together with others who march faster than he or she can. The company would not wait for him or her to catch up. The person who could not keep up would fall behind. That means he or she would not reach the destination at the same time the others did and so would fail in mission. The expression **falling behind** may have been for the author a synonym for the Psalmist's expression **going astray** (Ps 95:10). Metaphorically speaking, falling behind in religious matters means not being able to fulfill all of the demands or commandments, being negligent, failing to qualify or measure up. Anyone who had an evil heart of unbelief (Heb 3:12) would *fall behind,* which means the same as turning away from the God of life (Heb 3:12). Hence the warning **be careful** (Heb 3:12), "be afraid."

One of the reasons for the existence of doctrines is to put a limit to interrogation. Once it becomes accepted doctrine it becomes hypothesis for further argument based on it without questioning its accuracy. Christians and Jews today still await the fulfillment of prophecy made more than 2,000 years ago, some of which can never be fulfilled. For example, both Isaiah and Jeremiah prophesied that Media would destroy Babylon, but it never did. Now there is no longer either a Babylon or a Media, so it will never happen. Kaufman listed the following additional instances where Jeremiah made prophesies that were never fulfilled:

1) Many kings did not set up thrones at the gates of Jerusalem (Jer 1:5).
2) The people of Anathoth were not completely annihilated (Jer 11:23; cf. Ezra 2:23).
3) Jehoiakim did not receive the burial of a donkey, and he was not thrown outside Jerusalem (Jer 22:18-19; 36:30; cf. 2 Kings 24:6).
4) Zedekiah did not die in peace (Jer 34:5); God did not remember him in Babylon (Jer 32:5).
5) The exiles were not required to worship other gods day and night (Jer 16:13), and
6) Nebuchadnezzar did not destroy or exile Egypt (Jer 46:13-14)[1].

These facts do not prevent the faithful from continuing with their doctrines. Doctrines, like laws, continue on the books long after their usefulness is gone. There are still laws in some towns in U.S.A where horses never are seen that demand drivers of automobiles to stop, whenever they confront a horse drawn vehicle, turn off their motor and wait until the horse-drawn vehicle is out of earshot before continuing. This law was designed to keep the noise of a Model-T Ford from frightening horses. Once laws get written in books, they are seldom removed. Scriptural law suffers the same fate.

Had the author of Hebrews realized that Jeremiah and Isaiah had been mistaken in some of their prophecies, he would still have continued to use their prophecies with the expectation that they were written to be fulfilled in his day. That was

[1] Y. Kaufman, *The Religion of Israel from its Beginnings to the Babylonian Exile*, tr. and abridged M. Greenberg (Chicago: University of Chicago Press, c1960), pp. 313-14, 429.

acceptable logic for NT Christians and Jews. Twenty-first century Jews and Christians should know better.

Secure establishment in the Promised Land was called a Sabbath rest. After David had secured the borders of the Promised Land, it was said that the land had **rest. Rest** was to take place in Eden (another name for the Promised Land) where the saints would rejoice in the new Jerusalem (Tdan 5:12). There paradise would be opened, a city would be constructed, and the faithful would have **rest** (4Ezra 8:52; Rev 14:1, 13).

[2]*The gospel was preached to us as well as to them.* The **gospel** was related to the Sabbath and Jubilee releases. For the Israelite who had not been able to repay his fellow Israelite the money he had borrowed, there were only two options:

(a) If it was a reasonably small loan, he might work it off at half wages.
(b) If it was a sizable loan, he might have to turn over his estate to the creditor.

In either case, he was considered a captive or a slave to his brother, but not forever. Whenever the Sabbath year came around all the Jews or Israelites were set free from their obligations to their brothers who were their creditors, and whenever the Jubilee year occurred all land that had been surrendered for indebtedness was restored to the Jewish or Samaritan family to which it had originally belonged. These rules did not apply to the Canaanite period.

Israel's theological concepts, vocabulary, and logic were generally transferred from ordinary customs and practices in business, law courts, and society. So the concepts related to Sabbath and Jubilee releases were applied to national eschatological hopes. The Jews who were removed from Canaan, their inheritance, into Babylon were called captives (*sheh-voo-yeém*, שְׁבוּיִם) (Isa 52:2; 61:1; 11QMelch 4), because they were taken away from their land; but they were not all slaves in the usual sense because when the opportunity came for them to return, many preferred Babylon. Within 150 years Jews like Nehemiah had worked themselves into top positions in the government, and the Jewish community in Babylon continued to be a very strong and effective branch of Judaism. So long as Jews were not permitted to return to a free country under the rule of a Davidic king, however, Babylonian Jews called themselves **captives**, who were paying double for all their crimes (Isa 40:1; Jer 16:18; cf. Deut 15:18), working off their debt of unpaid fines at half wages.

Hebrews frequently used words like **captives** metaphorically. For instance, after Rehoboam succeeded Solomon, he went to Shechem to be made king and to introduce himself to the northern community. When asked to reduce the "yoke" that had been placed upon them by Solomon, Rehoboam replied, **My father chastened you with whips, but I will chasten you with scorpions** (1Kings 12:11). The "yoke" consisted of heavy taxation and demands for labor and military service. The chastening would involve still more oppressive treatment, but probably not with whips or scorpions, literally. Likewise the **slaves** in Egypt may not all have made bricks with their own hands (Exod 1:8-14). They had enough respect and credit to borrow silver and gold from their neighboring Egyptians (Exod 11:2; 12:35-36), and they left with cattle, flocks, and herds (Exod 12:38).

Moses was an Israelite who had held an influential position with Pharaoh (Exod 11:3). That may have been a distinct exception, but if it had been, it seems strange that uneducated and uncultured slaves would have had the audacity to challenge his authority (Num 12:1-8; 16:1-30), or that 70 of them could qualify to assist him in his administration (Num 11:16-17). Israelites who were called slaves and captives in these situations were certainly not slaves like the African-Americans were in the United States or like prisoners of war in concentration camps. However the oppression was expressed to them, the main point seemed to be that they were away from their inheritance and not allowed to return home.[1]

The gospel was the announcement of the **good news** (The **gospel**) that the term of service was up (see Lev 26:13). The Sabbath or Jubilee year had arrived. The captives were to be set free, and the land was to be restored to the "original owners," the "true heirs." To the exodus community, the **gospel** was that they were free to leave Egypt and return and have **rest** on the **Promised** Land.

The author said that **the gospel** had **been preached to** him and his contemporary Christians just as it had been to the exodus generation. There is no indication that he was comparing two different **gospels** related to different **promises**. It was the one **promise of entering into his rest** that had been **left** unfulfilled, simply because the exodus generation lacked the faith and obedience to claim it. Therefore the same **promise of entering into his rest** was still **left** for the author's generation.[2]

The message of the report (*haw láw-gaws tays ah-kaw-ays,* ὁ λόγος τῆς ἀκοῆς) may have been the **good news** that they could return to the **Promised** Land, but it was more likely the report (*dah-váhr,* דבר; LXX *hráy-mah,* ῥῆμα) that the spies brought back (Num 13:26). They told the congregation that the land flowed with milk and honey and produced fruit like that which they brought to show them, but they also told them how strong and mighty the people were who lived there (Num 13:26-29). As a result Caleb and Joshua said they should go up at once and take it (Num 13:30), but the others said it was impossible. This was the evil report which prevented the exodus generation from **entering into his rest**. **The message of the report did not help them.** The reason the author of Hebrews gave is obvious and based on the FT--the people did not have faith (Heb 3:19). The exact wording of the text is not very clear. There is textual witness for each of the following readings:

(a) *may soon-keh-keh-rahs-méh-naws tay peés-tay tois ah-koó-sah-seen*
(μὴ συνκεκερασμένος τῇ πίστει τοῖς ἀκούσασιν)
(it) "not being united by /with faith to/in those who heard"
(b) *may soon keh-keh-rahs-méh-noos tay peés-tay tois ah-koo-sah-seen*
(μὴ συνκεκερασμένους τῇ πίστει τοῖς ἀκούσασιν)
(they) "not being united in/with faith to those who heard"
(c) *may soon-keh-keh-rahs-méh-noos tay peés-tay tohn ah-koos-ahn-tohn*

---

[1] After the Soviet Union demanded repayment for the money she had invested in the education of professional Jews, before releasing them to move to Israel, many Israeli newspapers referred to this action as twentieth-century slavery and the economically prosperous Jews in Russia as "slaves." For example, see *Yediot Aharonot*, August 23, 1972, p. 25.

[2] H. Attridge, *The Epistle to the Hebrews* (Philadelphia: Fortress Press, 1989), p. 124, spoke of "'**good news'** with its decidedly Christian overtones." Of course there are both Jewish and Christian overtones to the **good news**. It was the announcement that the Hebrews could leave Egypt. It was heralded by 2Isa (Isa 61:1) and echoed in the NT. Overtones are notes that form part of a chord. They occur only when a chord is in perfect harmony. Attridge wanted a note that contradicts the national, political dimensions of the **good news** in the Bible. This would not be an overtone.

(μὴ συνκεκερασμένους τῇ πεέστει τῶν ἀκουσαντων)
(they) "not being united by faith of those who heard"
(d) *may soon-keh-keh-rahs-méh-noos tay peés-tay tois ah-koos-thay-seen*
(μὴ συνκεκερασμένους τῇ πίστει τοῖς ἀκούσθεισιν)
(they) "not being united in faith to the things that were heard."

There is strong textual witness for only the first two readings. The differences in the readings are mainly in the identification of subjects and objects. In (a) the word was not united to the people who heard. In (b) the people who heard were not united in faith to those who had (previously) heard. In (c) the people who heard were not united to the faith of those who heard. In (d) the people who received the report were not united in faith to the things heard. RSV, following reading (a) has a simple translation: "it did not meet with faith in the hearers." A phrase like this gave rise to variants, but fortunately the differences in meaning are not very great.[1]

[3]*For we who believe enter into the rest*. The Greek *hoó-tohs* (οὕτως) **(thus)** is rendered **the following** in Heb 4:4. The author's step-by-step logic is choice. Having shown that the exodus generation did not **enter into** God's **rest,** he deduced that the **promise was left unfulfilled** in his day. Since his generation had received **the gospel** as the exodus generation had, they had just as good an opportunity to enjoy its fulfillment in his day as the Israelites did after they left Egypt. So he concluded that **We who believe** might **enter into the rest**, because God took an oath that they [the exodus generation] would **not enter into his rest**.

Namely is a possible translation for *kai-toi* (καίτοι) and is the sense the context requires.[2] **From the foundation of the world** means from the very beginning. **The works** mentioned are the acts of God involved in creation itself, which took place during the first six days before the Sabbath day of rest.

[4]*God rested.* Up to this point the author had always meant by peaceful and quiet, independent existence on the Promised Land under the rule of her own king, when he used the term **rest**. Here he related the **rest** in the inheritance to **God's rest** from his labors after creation. He thus also related God's **works** in Egypt and the wilderness to those which took place **from the foundation of the world**. This was to confirm the enduring dimension of God's promise. It also provided a basis for understanding national **rest** in sabbatical terms (see Isa 58:13-14).

Israel normally explained things that were traditional in some way that indicated that God was the initiator of the tradition. They had a Sabbath. They had always had a Sabbath. There was a Sabbath program thousands of years before Abraham. God must have also had a Sabbath. The point to be understood may be that, since God's behavior is a prototype for Israel's, Israel can then be confident that it also will receive **rest** after its **work**s (see *Hom* 17:10). The words **the works** came from Gen 2:2 which was anticipated in Heb 4:3 and quoted in full in Heb 4:4.

[5]*And again [the passage]*. Heb 4:5 is only a repetition of the passage quoted in Heb 4:1, forming an inclusion of the unit (Heb 4:1-5). The quotation stands on both sides of the reference to **God's rest**, so that the reader will know that the author wanted to

---

[1] See further B. F. Westcott, *The Epistle to the Hebrews* (London: Macmillan, 1889), p. 110.
[2] For other examples of this meaning for *kai-toi* see M. Stuart, *Commentary on the Epistle to the Hebrews* (Andover: Warren F. Draper, 1828), p. 110.

relate the two **rests** closely together. This relates **God**'s oath concerning his **promised rest** to Israel to his own **rest,** just as **God's rest** on the seventh day was related to Israel's obligation to observe the Sabbath day. Heb 4:6 is a repetitious elaboration on Heb 4:1 and 2.

The rabbis were not of the opinion Grässer learned from Billerbeck that there would be an eschaton of eternal life. The last day would be eternity.[1] Grässer also denied, however, that Sabbath was equivalent to aeon in the sense of the Alexandrian-gnostic, hebdomas speculation.[2] At this point Grässer was denying the work of several scholars who turned away from the obvious biblical, geographical, and historical background of Hebrews and have tried to identify Hebrews' message with Indian, Egyptian, or post-NT Greek mysticism. The result of this distortion was to treat that which is horizontal as if it were perpendicular, and invent for ordinary words conjectured meanings. For them the journey of Abraham from Haran to Jerusalem was to be understood as going from earth to heaven.

Grässer correctly disagreed with this position, although at other instances in his commentary he agreed with it. The word "Gnostic" means knowledgeable, and in this context refers to a special secret knowledge. Perhaps all sects of Judaism and some groups of Greeks and others had special secret catechisms which only members knew. Those who had a different catechism from the group who wrote the texts called other groups "gnostics," because they had a gnosticism different from their own. The same is true of the word "heresy." Heresy in Greek means "sect" or " denomination." All Christian and Jewish groups were sectarian; That is, they were heretical. Each sect considered itself the true sect and referred to others as heresies. "Hebdomas" means "seven" in Greek, which means that the Alexandrian sect was acquainted with the sabbath system, as were many Near Eastern peoples. Aeon is the Greek word for age, and ages succeed one another, chronologically, just as days, weeks, months, and seasons do. They are not stacked perpendicularly between earth and heaven.

Rabbis did not think that an **age** was eternity, so neither the current **age** nor the **age** to come was eternity. Rabbis anticipated six **ages** of a thousand years each, followed by an **age of rest** when Israel would rule the world. They expected the Sabbath **age of rest** to last a thousand years as well, but they were not always certain about the dates. They hoped and prayed that the **age of rest** would be all good and long. They even asked that **the age** to come would have no end or limit at the same time they asked that it would last a long time.[3] Their concepts of the sabbath were designed to fit into a time schedule. An **age** was not an eternity. It was a period of time.

TEXT

Hebrews	First Testament
6 Since, then, it is left for some **to enter into** it, and the earlier ones, having received the gospel, did not **enter**	

[1] E. Grässer, *An die Hebräer* (Zürich: Benziger Verlag, c1990) 1, p. 210, 216.

[2] Grässer, *An die Hebräer*, p. 219.

[3] R. Yitzkhak ben Ariay Yosef Dohv, *Book of Liturgy of Israel* (Jerusalem: Schoken, c1937) (Hebrew), p. 177.

because of [their] disobedience, [7]he again appoints a certain day, **today**, saying through David, after such a long time [had transpired], as was quoted before: **Today if you hear his voice, do not harden your minds**.	Ps 95:7 **Today, if you hear his voice, do not harden your minds as Maribah**, as **the day of testing**
[8]For if **Joshua**	Deut 31:7 Moses called **Joshua** and said to him before the eyes of all the Israelites, "Hold fast and be courageous, because you will bring this people to the land which Yehowah swore to their fathers to **give them**, and you shall **give them rest**."
had **given them rest**, he would not have spoken of another day than this. Therefore there	Josh 22:4 Now Yehowah your God has **given** your brothers **rest**, just as he has told them.
remains a **Sabbath** for the people of **God**, [10]for whoever **enters into his rest** also **rests** from his **work** himself, just as **God** [rested] from his own [works].	Gen 2:2 On the **Sabbath** day **God** finished his **work** which he had done, and he **rested** on the **Sabbath** day.
[11]Then let us strive to **enter into that rest** so that no one may fall because of the same sort of disobedience.	Ps 95:11 I swore in my anger [may the following unexpressed curses come upon me] if they **enter my rest**.

COMMENTARY

[6]*Because of [their] disobedience.* **Disobedience** is a new word, beginning a new paragraph which concludes with the same word in Heb 4:11, forming an inclusion. The word **disobedience** occurs only in Heb 4:6 and 11 in the entire document. The author's criticism of **the earlier ones** for their **disobedience** (Heb 4:6) and for their lack of faith (Heb 4:2) referred to specific acts related to the same basic event reported in Num 14.

[7]*He again appoints a certain day.* Once his logic moved from showing that **the promise was unfulfilled**, and his own generation was one of the ones for whom it might be fulfilled, the author needed a text to show that it would happen in his day and no other. The **certain day** which was crucial to the author was the **Day** of Atonement, which was soon to occur. The text the author needed was conveniently available in Ps 95: **Today** is a word from the Scripture, which the author, in *peh-shehr* logic, interpreted to mean his own **day**. *Pesher* logic means that he just dogmatically declared one word to mean something else, or he took a term from one context and placed it in a different context to give it a different meaning. This is a rhetorical technique.

First, however, the author acknowledged that this **promise** was recorded in the Psalms of David written many years after the exodus, but the author applied this to his readers: **Do not harden your minds**. This did not mean "eternal now," as Jewett suggested, that would apply anytime, anywhere, to anyone who encountered Christ emotionally along his pilgrim journey.[1] The author, 2,000 years ago, had probably not been trained either in Lycus Valley gnosticism or in twentieth century existentialism.

8*If Joshua had given them rest.* **Joshua** in Hebrew is the same as Jesus in Greek. The **Joshua** discussed here was Moses' successor who finally succeeded in leading the second wilderness generation into the **Promised** Land. The author insisted, however, that the first **Joshua** had not **given them [i.e., the first generation] rest.** He probably meant that the **Promised** Land was not under control until the time of David and Solomon who gave the land rest, but he did not say that, so this has opened the door for extensive inventiveness on the part of scholars. If **Joshua's** conquest was not understood as **rest**, they have argued, then the author must have had in mind something non-political, non-material. Windisch said,

> The earthly Canaan had for Hebrews absolutely no meaning . . . [Joshua] is here not a type but a contrast.[2]

Weiss concurred:

> In any case, there is for the author of Hebrews in context of his reflections, the self-evident assumption, that κατάπαυσις, of which the Scripture speaks, had nothing to do with the earthly land inheritance of Canaan.[3]

Stuart said,

> Hence, he [the author of Hebrews] concludes, it is evident since the rest which is spoken of is not of a temporal nature, but of a spiritual enduring nature that there remains a rest for the people of God, i.e. believers.[4]

Grässer joined the crowd:

> The land of the promise does not lie on the same plane as the goal, the heavenly city . . . Canaan can certainly not be the rest, because it is earthly.[5]

The non-temporal conclusions Stuart and Grässer gave were their own. The author made no mention of a spiritual nature as over against a temporal nature in this

---

[1] R. Jewett, *Letter to Pilgrims* (New York: The Pilgrim Press, c1981), p. 67.

[2] H. Windisch, *Brief an die Hebräer* (Tübingen: J. C. B. Mohr, 1931), p. 34, and R Williamson, *Philo and the Epistle to the Hebrews* (Leiden: E. J. Brill, 1970), pp. 395-97.

[3] B. F. Weiss, *Der Brief an die Hebräer* (Göttingen: Vandenhoeck & Ruprecht, 1991), p. 281.

[4] Stuart, *Hebrews*, p. 104.

[5] Grässer, *An die Hebräer*, p. 215.

context. Neither did he specify a **rest** that took place only in heaven. Spicq concluded that Heb 4:4-5 was added

> to prove that the rest is no longer Canaan but heaven, not an object of pure human hope, but a reality of divine experience.[1]

Spicq admitted that the **rest** about which the author of Hebrews spoke in the FT was to take place on the **Promised** Land where the elect would enter, inherit salvation, and have access to the temple,[2] but Spicq insisted that, for Christians, **rest** is the ultimate celestial blessedness in heaven to be enjoyed at the end of the road.[3] Like Stuart, Moffatt transferred his own assumptions to the author of Hebrews:

> He [the author] simply assumes (a) that God's promise of *kah-táh-pau-sees* (κατάπαυσις) is spiritual . . . (b) as a corollary of this, he assumes that it is eschatological.[4]

By "spiritual" Moffatt did not mean "legal," but "non material" or "religious." By "eschatological" he did not mean the end of the current **age.** He meant "the end of the cosmos or of time." Schroeger said the author must not mean Canaan as **rest**. Therefore he must intend a deeper meaning for the term.[5] Grässer noted the FT instances in which **rest** was associated with the Promised Land and admitted that this prompted the notion

> that Hebrews accepted these Old Testament ideas, but his transposition to a heavenly-otherworldly rest places him much closer in relationship to religious-philosophical speculations of clear apocalyptic-gnostic and Alexandrian provenance.[6]

The Greek philosophical thought, which others have also used to explain Hebrews is misleading. Bruce rejected a millennial interpretation as the importation into the epistle of a concept which in fact is alien to it,[7] but he then proceeded to import his own alien concept. Realizing the close relationship the author of Hebrews placed between **rest** and the entrance into Canaan, Bruce defensively said,

> The meaning of "rest" was not *exhausted* [italics mine] by the earthly Canaan as a goal of the people of God today.[8]

---

[1] C.J. Spicq, *L'Epitre aus Hebreux* (Paris: J. Gabalda, 1953), II, p. 82.

[2] Spicq, *Hebreux,* 2, 82.

[3] Spicq, *Hebreux,* 2, 102.

[4] J. Moffatt, *A Critical and Exegetical Commentary on the Epistle to the Hebrews*, (Edinburgh: T. & T. Clark, 1964), p. 53.

[5] F. Schröger, *Der Verfasser des Hebräerbriefs als Schrifstausleger* (Regensberg: F. Postat, 1968), pp. 114-15.

[6] E. Grässer, *Der Glaube im Hebräer* (Marburg: N. G. Elwert, 1965), p. 106.

[7] F. F. Bruce, *The Epistle to the Hebrews* (Grand Rapids: Eerdmans, 1964), p. 75.

[8] Bruce, *Hebrews,* p. 72.

On the basis that **Joshua** had not given the people **rest,** Bruce contrasted the "temporal **rest"** with the "true **rest,**"[1] which he imported as being non-temporal. Although he admitted uncertainty about the real nature of this **rest,** he affirmed:

> one way or another, this blissful rest in unbroken fellowship with God is the goal to which His people are urged to press forward.[2]

C. R. Koester declared authoritatively, without evidence or explanation,

> Jewish tradition there was a tendency to move from focusing on the land to the city of Jerusalem and finally to the sanctuary. "Jerusalem becomes the quintessence of the land, and the Temple the quintessence of Jerusalem" (Isaacs, *Sacred*, 84).

On the contrary, the more interest there was in Jerusalem and the temple, the more eager Jews were to fight for the land. There was the Maccabean Revolt, the Jewish-Roman war of 66-70 IA, and the Bar Cochba Revolt (132-135 IA)—all of which were designed to get control of the Promised Land, and none of them lost interest in Jerusalem or the temple. None of these rebellions would have been settled with only the restoration of the temple. Koester acknowledged that there were occasions when the land had **rest** (Josh 21:43-45; 22:4; 1Kings 8:56; 1Chron 22:9; 2Chron 15:15; 20:30). He said these **rests** were provisional,[3] implying that they were not true **rest** periods, but the Scripture called them **rest.** The Scripture did not claim that they were invalid, just because they did not last forever. There is no indication that the **rest** that was anticipated was any different. It was normal for people to want another **rest**ful condition that they once enjoyed.

Attridge said that the **rest** Hebrews had in mind was not the biblical, Jewish **rest** associated with the Promised Land, but the allegorical, Hellenistic rest found in such works as Philo and Joseph and Aseneth.[4] One of the examples he gave in the latter source pictures Joseph praying to the Lord to make Aseneth a convert to Judaism. This would involve her being reborn [legally], being made alive by the Lord's life, being numbered among the Lord's people, and entering into the Lord's **rest** (Joseph and Aseneth 8:9).

This kind of "allegory" employed idioms that are well known to the FT, the NT, and rabbinic literature. Existence in contract relationship with the Lord was called **life**. People were baptized into **life** who were already physically alive and breathing. Pagans were considered dead. New converts were "born again" and dated their religious lives from the day of their conversion. When Joseph prayed for Aseneth that she become a convert, he wanted her to enter into the Lord's **rest** on the Promised Land, just the way other Jews wished to do.

There are two problems with the use of Philo. 1) Philo used allegory, to be sure, but this never diverted him from believing that there would be a Messiah ruling over the Promised Land in the new kingdom; and 2) the message in Hebrews does not lend itself to allegorical interpretation. Allegory can be forced onto almost any literature, but literature is not fairly interpreted allegorically unless its author

---

[1] Bruce, *Hebrews,* p. 77.

[2] Bruce, *Hebrews,* p. 79.

[3] C. R. Koester, *Hebrews* (New York: Doubleday & Co., 2001), p. 278.

[4] Attridge, *Hebrews*, p. 126.

intended it to be so interpreted. When this is the case there are usually clues in the literature to govern this. Hebrews does not resemble Bunyan's *Pilgrim's Progress*, Spencer's *Fairy Queen*, or Philo's allegory. Hebrews is not an allegory.

If multiple attestation proved accuracy and truth, then it is clear that there have been enough affirmations to make the case. The problem, however, is that the affirmations were not accompanied by fact and logic. They were simply declared and claimed to be obvious and without question. As soon as affirmations are solidified as hypotheses and dogmas so that they cannot be questioned, truth is imprisoned and valid research is curtailed.

These scholars would not have had to be as inventive as they have been to deny that **the rest** to which Hebrews referred was Canaan if that meaning had not been obvious. Although it was obvious, the scholars mentioned above did not like that meaning, so they displaced it with their own wishes. If it had not been so obvious that the author of Hebrew 1-12 was dealing in historical-geographical-temporal concepts these authors would not have had to work so hard to deny the obvious. Historians are not free to change words to have whatever meanings they want them to have. If they wanted only to write fiction, they would not have had to refer to the Book of Hebrews at all.

Hebrews did not make the sharp distinction between spiritual and national-political-material that modern scholars make. When they used the term "spiritual" they almost always meant "legal." They understood God's will and blessings in terms that affected their national, social, economic, and personal lives. They understood religion in very practical terms. That which seemed best in their society seemed God's will. At that time, in their judgment, that which seemed best for them was peace and prosperity in the land of Canaan under the rule of a Davidic king, so this was considered God's will. It was held to be both a spiritual and a material blessing. It was material, political, and legally conceived. Israel needed a Sabbath, so God must need a Sabbath (Gen 2:2), and he **rested** in Zion (Isa 66:1, Ps 132:14), the way Israel hoped to do.

This may seem anthropomorphic to Americans in the twenty-first century, but even we, in our apparent sophistication, have not transcended some anthropomorphic ways of understanding God's will. The only way we have changed is the character we ascribe to God because of our own understanding of what is best for human beings in society. In trying to understand the views of an author of long ago, however, it is important to try to understand the values and thought forms of his day rather than transposing our own twenty-first-century values to him.

This seems like an easy way to dismiss other scholars who have appeared to import a non-national meaning for the **rest** the author said was still awaiting fulfillment, but an easy dismissal is not intended, for there really is a problem here. The author spoke of the **rest** available to his readers as being the same as that offered to the exodus generation. Initially this **rest** was clearly related to settlement and peace in Canaan. It was reported that Joshua led the Israelites into the promised **rest** (Josh 21:43-45). That would seem to have been the fulfillment, but the author of Hebrews denied that **Joshua** had given them **rest**. It is in trying to understand why the **rest** **Joshua** gave did not meet the qualifications that scholars have introduced some thing not related to the land.[1] Some conjectural interpretation is necessary, but care should be taken to stay within the author's concepts in so doing.

1) The author of Hebrews was a good student of the FT. He interpreted Ps 95 in relationship to Gen 2, Num 14, Deut 31, and Josh 22, because he knew that they dealt with the same subject.
2) He assumed that David wrote Ps 95 (Heb 4:7), and David was not even born until many years after Joshua died.
3) *Ergo*: If David could write in his day that they had not entered the promised **rest** then surely the **rest Joshua** had given was not adequate. Furthermore as the author of Hebrews said that **after such a long time [had transpired]** (Heb 4:7) as elapsed between Moses and David, and David was still wishing the people of his day would hear the Lord's voice (Ps 95:7), then obviously there was no **rest** in David's day either.

To reason this way the author had to give more status to the statement in Ps 95 than in the historical report of **Joshua's** success. This is the way attorneys argue, refuting one testimony by a later precedent and testimony. The author of Hebrews was more interested in proving something *legally* or rhetorically true than something factually true. Although **Joshua** seems actually to have given the people **rest,** and the Book of **Joshua** even says he did, Ps 95 can be interpreted to show that he really did not give them **rest**. Once you agree that this is the case, you can then conclude that the promise of giving the people **rest** is about to be fulfilled in your own day. This is exactly what the author of Hebrews did, because the Promised Land was not free from foreign control in his day. He thought, however, that it soon would be.

That does not mean that the author looked for a non-national, nonmaterial **rest** in heaven. It just means that, according to the Scriptures, the **rest** had not been given as late as David's time. The contemporaries of the author of Hebrews were probably expecting a **rest** that was basically of the same nature as Israelites had anticipated all along, yet one that was to be more prosperous, more peaceful, more luxurious, and in a position of higher dignity among the nations than had been known by any Israelite or Jewish kingdom up to the author's time.

In all probability he also expected that when such a **rest** really came, it would last a very long time (Dan 7:14; GenR 65:23; ExodR 15:21, 31; 50:5). That was the promise given to the Son of man in Dan 7. All independent control the Israelites had of the Promised Land had been of short duration. With the rise of Herod the Great, even the most recent Hasmonean dynasty crumbled, and after Archaelaus was deposed in 6\7 IA, Roman governors and foreign taxes were introduced and Jews lost all semblance of self-rule. This did not mean that all Jews stopped hoping and believing that the Romans could be overthrown and their own nation restored. Many believed, lived, fought, and died to bring this about. It was in this milieu that the author wrote. It seems likely that he hoped to see in his own day the complete fulfillment of the promise.

---

[1] Attridge, *Hebrews*, p. 123, for example, said, "That it still remains open long after the settlement in the land of Canaan requires demonstration and the following argument will provide this by indicating what 'rest' really designates." "The rest to which the psalm referred cannot have been the rest that Joshua provided in the Promised Land" (p. 129).

[9]*There remains a Sabbath for the people of God.* The Greek for **Sabbath** is *sah-bah-tees-máws* (σαββατισμός), a word that occurs only here in the entire NT. The technical name for that situation is a *hapax legomenon,* which means "once said." Furthermore, it occurs only once in other classical literature, where it has the meaning of "Sabbath celebration."[1] The term also appears in Epiphanius, *Panar. Haer* , *Martyrium Petri et Pauli,* chapter 1, and *Apostolic Constitutions* 2:36, 2. In all of these references, the word means "Sabbath celebration," and not just "seven" or "the Sabbath day." Hofius has argued correctly that Hebrews used this term with precisely the same meaning as **rest**. It is not at all a quietistic ideal.[2]

Following this line of reasoning, then, the author concluded that **there remains a** precise **Sabbath** observance **for the people of God**. There were probably many Jews and Christians who had given up hope. So many plans and hopes had failed! The promise must have been either withdrawn or fulfilled long ago, they thought. The author of Hebrews denied these possibilities and urged his people to maintain their confidence and hope.

[10]*Rests from his works.* Earlier the author related God's **work** in creation to his **work** in Egypt and in the wilderness experience. It also involved taxes to foreign countries. **Works** further included doubting, tempting, grumbling, disobeying, and rebelling. This was not **rest**. Whenever they received their **rest** all of this should stop, because the one who enters into **rest** also **rests** from the **works** of this nature just as God **rested** from his **works**. Commenting on **A Song of the Sabbath** (Ps 92:1), rabbis said, "For the age when all is Sabbath" (Mek *Shabbata* 1:41). Real **Sabbath rest** would be **rest** for the nation.

[11]*Let us therefore.* This expression echoes Heb 4:1, **Let us therefore.** The readers were to strive. They were to **be afraid** (Heb 4:1). The author took frequent opportunities to exhort his readers to remain confident, keep all the laws, and be careful not to go astray. The exodus generation that doubted and rebelled obviously had no **rest** or confidence. Christians of the author's day were required to prepare themselves for the **rest** by giving up all grumbling, lack of confidence, and have faith, lest they **fall because of the same sort of disobedience**. **To fall because of** (*ehn. . . . péh-say,* ἐν . . . πέσῃ) pictures someone handicapped by being blindfolded or distracted in some way, in this case by disobedience. Since the Christians of the author's day knew how the exodus generation fell, they should avoid the same mistake of being disobedient. The author evidently did not think his entire audience would go astray and be **disobedient**. He wanted to be sure that not one was.

The author of Hebrews was not the only one to compare his own generation with that which came out of Egypt. Paul also told of the fathers, all of whom went under the cloud, through the sea, were all baptized **into Moses**, by which he meant "into the corporation of Moses." They all drank of the same spiritual drink and ate the same spiritual food. It was legally approved (*kah-sháyr*). Nonetheless, God was displeased with most of them (only Caleb and Joshua were excepted), and dispersed them in the wilderness. That should be an example from which Corinthian Christians should learn, said Paul. They must not be idolaters, immoral, or grumblers who test the Lord, because if they were they would receive the same punishment the wilderness generation received (1Cor 10:1-10).

---

[1] Plutarch, *de superstitutione* 3[2, 166a]. So Hofius, *Katapausis*, p. 103.
[2] Hofius, *Katapausin*, pp. 104-110.

Just as the author of Hebrews understood that Ps 95 was written as prophecy to be applied to his own generation, Paul said the account of the wilderness was written down for the instruction of the parties to the contract of his day, **on whom the end of the ages has come** (1Cor 10:11). By this Paul meant that the captivity was over; Jubilee was about to be sounded; believers were about to receive the **promise** made to Abraham and his posterity; the **good news** had been announced; if Christians believed and behaved properly, they would have the opportunity to enter into his **promised rest**. Details of Paul's eschatological expectations are ambiguous, but his dependence upon sabbatical concepts is clear. One of the rabbis said,

> Our fathers sinned and a judgment was decreed against them: **Your bodies will fall in this wilderness** (Num 14:29), but let us not commit crimes, and let us go and enter the Land of Israel (sNum 82 [21b]).

Neither Paul nor the rabbi said, "Let us go up to heaven," and neither did the author of Hebrews.

TEXT

12For the word of God is living and active,
sharper than any two-edged sword,
penetrating until [there is] a division of soul and spirit,
both joints and marrow;
[it is] critical of designs and intentions of the mind;
13there is nothing created [that passes] unnoticed before him,
but all things are naked and laid bare before his eyes
--regarding which our word [applies].

COMMENTARY

12*The word of God is living and active.* The subject of the **activity** is not **God,** but **God's word**. This refers to the Scripture. **Soul** (*psoo-kháy*, ψυχή) and **spirit** (*pnoó-mah*, πνεῦμα) are very closely related. Sometimes they are used almost synonymously, and both are rendered by the Latin *anima*. Both are used in contrast to *sóh-mah* (σῶμα), "body." *Psoo-kháy* comes from the verb *psoo-kháyn* (ψυχεῖν), "to breathe," "make cool or cold," as a breeze does. *Pnoó-mah* also means wind, air, breath. Paul contrasted between the first Adam, who was a **living soul** (*psoo-kháyn zóh-san*, ψυχὴ ζῶσαν) and the last Adam who was a *pnoó-mah zoh-aw-poi-oón* (πνεῦμα ζωοποιοῦν), a **life-giving spirit** (1Cor 15:45). In religious circles, *psoo-kháy*, was sometimes identified with secular life, which a person surrendered for **life** (*zoh-áy*, ζωή) in a communal order under the contract. **Spirit** (*pnoó-mah*) was related more closely to *zoh-áy* (religious life) than to *psoo-kháy* (secular life).

Sharper than any two edged sword. Becker correctly held that this **sword** was no material sword used in war. He also mistakenly said, however, that it also was not a juridical **sword.**[1] It is precisely its juridical character that makes the **word of God**

[1] E.-M. Becker, "'Gottes Wort' und 'Unser Wort,'" *Biblische Zeitschrift* 44 (2000):257.

sharp. Rabbis claim that if it is not in the Scripture it is not in the world. They did not mean by that that nothing exists outside the Scripture, but that Scripture is the only legal authority that can be used in a Jewish court. It is the basis on which the court judges whether the accused person is guilty or innocent. It determines sometimes whether a person lives or dies. It does not do the killing, like a metal sword, but it determines whether or not a metal sword is used to enforce the decision.

The word of God was the decree of the highest judge. By this word lesser judges were free to make death sentences that were always fatal. Although he used the imagery of a sharp two-edged sword, the author was not talking about a military battle or a surgeon's table where flesh was cut. He was talking about the effectiveness of the **word of God** in a court of judgment. The word of God was the law of the nation. It had the last word in the court of justice.

The author of this poem may have wanted to distinguish between the **spirit** (*psoo-kháy*) which constituted physical breath that keeps animate beings alive, and the holy breath or **spirit** (*pnoó-mah*) that provides legal and religious life with its necessary basis. Philo said "**spirit** is the essence of the **soul"** and "he names the **soul** of man, '**spirit.'"** (PDPIS 80-84; see also Wis 15:11). Both are legal concepts. No one was believed to have either a **spirit** or a **soul** who was not a legal member of the chosen family corporation or body.

C. R. Koester noted that according to LXX Gen 2:7, God breathed "spirit" into Adam, and Adam became a living "soul." That meant, Koester thought, that the two words were synonymous.[1] That does not follow. The spirit caused the life to begin, but the soul was the created being. In the same way, in legal concepts, a legal (spiritual) ceremony is performed on a physical human being and his or her legal status is changed. A pagan receives the spirit and becomes a Christian soul, a member of the church. He or she then is religiously and legally alive. When Saul and David were Israelite citizens they were anointed. At the same time, after each received the spirit he became a king. Various judges received the spirit and became leaders. The spirit is the legal force that gives legal authority. The soul is the recipient of the spirit.

The point of the author's affirmation was to show that the **Word of God** could make divisions and distinctions that are impossible for human beings. To separate between **soul and spirit** was as difficult as distinguishing between **designs and intentions of the mind**. **Joints and marrow** can be humanly separated, but the author wanted to show that there was no area out of God's reach, physical, spiritual (in the sense of being alive), and intentional or moral. There is also the difficulty of distinguishing between the physical and the legal body (the community).

Modern jurists hold that there is no crime that can be committed that cannot be punished. Wherever anyone can reach out to offend, the law can reach back to punish. In actual practice, the courts of law are not perfect. The judge or the jury is obligated to make decisions only on the basis of the data presented to the court by the plaintiff and the defendant. Should any member of the jury or the judge know more about the case than either the plaintiff or the defendant, that person is not allowed to bring it into the discussion for judgment. It is the plaintiff's responsibility to bring as much data into judgment as possible. It is the defense who would like to have important items excluded. Ancient juries and judges did not all have the same rules. In some cases the jury was made up of the best witnesses and the other people

---

[1] Koester, *Hebrews*, p. 274.

who knew the most about the cases. Sometimes judges were permitted both to testify and to judge. The best judgment requires a fully informed jury and judge.

The author of this poem, however, considered God to be the judge. God made judgments without the usual limitations, and the Scripture reported God's judgments. No defendant could escape with his or her crime not fully recognized. The **word of God** was the rule of law used in every case. It was held to be the most complete code of law in the world. No other nation had a coded law so invincible and complete, in Israel's judgment. When God gave a judicious order it was always carried out. It would not return to him empty (Isa 55:11). The author of Hebrews approved this eulogy to the Scriptures, which he himself employed with great care.

An early pastoral benediction prayed that God would keep the recipient of the blessing sound in spirit, soul, and body (1Thess 5:23), which involved every aspect of **life**. The poem in Heb 4:12-13 intends the same complete inclusiveness in the terms expressed. A similar eulogy of the Word is:

> For the swiftness of the Word is inexpressible
> and like its expression is its swiftness and its sharpness
> (OdesSol 12:5.)

Pseudo-Phocylides 124 said the word was a tool, "sharper than iron." The Lord's servant's mouth was **like a sharp sword** (Isa 49:2). Clement says, "Let us notice how near he is, and that nothing escapes him of our thoughts or of the devices which we undertake" (1Clem 21:3). "For he is a searcher of designs and intentions" (1Clem 21:9). 2Bar said the Most High would "carefully scrutinize the deep thoughts (*cogitationes*)" (2Bar 83:3). Enoch said, "For you have made all things, and have all authority; before you all things are manifest and uncovered" (1Enoch 9:5) Rabbi Judah said, "Know what is above you: a seeing eye, a hearing ear, and all your deeds are written in a book" (mAboth 2:1).

13*Nothing created [that passes] unnoticed before him.* The word *teh-trah-khay-lees-méh-nah* (τετραχηλισμένα) is rendered **laid bare**. It comes from the noun *tráh-chay-laws* (τράχηλος), "neck," but the image is not perfectly clear. It may intend to show a person who has left his neck unguarded in wrestling so that his opponent was able to get a "full nelson" on him, or it may indicate a person without armor to cover his throat. Some have suggested that it referred to baring the neck of a sacrificial animal for slaughter.[1] Whatever the exact image, the general meaning is clear. It refers to a person who is defenseless and at the mercy of his opponent. The author of this unit expressed vividly, and beautifully, the thoroughness of God's scrutiny. No part of any human being can escape his examination.

Michel has correctly called attention to the poetic nature of Heb 4:12-13.[2] Line two (see translation) supplements line one, showing how **living and active** the **word of God** is, and the successive lines further supplement, expand, and conclude the description of the omniscience of the word. The unknown author of the poem had prepared a composition that was useful for the author of Hebrews to illustrate his strong attempt to urge his recipients to see that no single one of them disobeyed God in any way. They had to be extremely careful because the consequences would be at least as disastrous for them as for the exodus generation. Furthermore they

---

[1] Windisch, *Hebräerbrief*, pp. 36-37.

[2] O. Michel, *Der Brief an die Hebräer* (Göttingen: Vandenhoeck & Ruprecht, 1957), p. 114.

were sure that no crime would go unnoticed. There was no way they could escape deserved punishment.

The most difficult part of these verses to understand and translate is the last part of verse 13, *pros háwn hay-meén haw láw-gaws* (πρὸς ὃν ἡμῖν ὁ λόγος). Michel rendered this as part of the poem, but it seems more likely to be a midrashic commentary on the poem which the author added. The following three examples will show that such additions are typical of the author:

1) Following a discussion which called attention to Moses' position as only a servant "in his house" (Heb 3:1-5), the author of Hebrews pointed to "Christ as a son over his house," and then commented: "whose house we are" (*hoo oi-kaws ehs-men hay-mace,* οὗ οἶκος ἐσμεν ἡμεῖς) (Heb3:6).

2) In contrast to the temple priests of the family of Aaron, the author spoke of Christ, who "was declared by God a high priest according to the order of Melchizedek," and then commented:
--"concerning which (*peh-reé hou,* περὶ οὗ) our message is extensive and difficult to interpret" (Heb 5:10-11).

3) Claiming the superiority of Christ's priesthood over that of the temple priests the author said, ". . . but he [became a priest] with oath-taking, through the one who said to him: 'The Lord has sworn and will not change his mind; you are a priest for the age.'" Then he commented:
--"just so much more (*kah-táh taws-oó-taw,* κατὰ τοσοῦτο) has Jesus become a warranty of an even better contract" (Heb 7:21-22).

In all three instances the connecting word ("whose," "concerning," or "just so much more") refers to a quotation from the FT in just the same way as the phrase in Heb 4:13 refers to the poem just quoted. This suggests that the phrase in Heb 4:13 is also a commentary to the poem and not a part of the poem itself, as Michel considered it; but that does not solve all of the problems of translation.

Translators have regularly had difficulty with this passage and have reached different conclusions: The KJV rendered the passage, ". . , with whom we have to reckon" and the RSV, ". . . with whom we have to do." The differences are slight and Davidson,[1] Moffatt,[2] and Turner[3] have translations agreeing with one or the other. Some variants are: Delitzsch, "to whom we have to give account."[4] Stuart, "before whom, in whose power, or at whose disposal is our account,"[5] and Spicq, "This is the subject of which we speak" (*c'est de ce sujet dont nous parlon*).[6] Moffatt[7] and others deal more with the meaning of the word *law-gaws* than with the meaning of the whole passage or its relationship to the context. Delitzsch[8] was

---

1. Davidson, *The Epistle to the Hebrews* (Edinburgh: T. & T. Clark, n.d.), p. 97.
2. Moffatt, *Hebrews,* p. 54.
3. S. H. Turner, *The Epistle to the Hebrews* (New York: Stanford and Soards 1852), p. 64.
4. F. Delitzsch, *Commentary on the Epistle to the Hebrews*, tr. T. L. Kingsbury (Grand Rapids: Eerdmans, 1952) I, p. 216.
5. Stuart, *Hebrews,* p. 117.
6. Spicq, *Hebreux* II, p. 91.
7. Moffatt, *Hebrews,* pp. 54-55.
8. Delitzsch, *Hebrews* I, p. 216.

correct in saying that the *praws háwn* of Heb 4:13 could bear the same meaning as the *peh-reé hoo* (περὶ οὗ) of Heb 5:11. This is apparently a *praws* used with the meaning of "in reference to" as in Heb 1:7, 8.

The real problem is supplying missing verbs and understanding antecedents for the relative pronoun *hawn*. Except for Heb 4:13, the only other use of *praws* together with *hawn* also follows a poem. This poem differs from that quoted in Heb 4:12-13 in that it is a paraphrase of Scripture as well as being a poem:

> **By faith Abraham offered Isaac, being tested,**
> **(and) the one who received the promises offered [his] only born.**

The Hebrews comment is:

> **[with reference] to whom (*praws hawn*) it was said, "In Isaac your seed shall be called"** (Heb 11:17-18).

The use of *praws hawn* immediately after the quoted poem and referring back to it is exactly like the small comment immediately following the poem in Heb 4:13. That the poem in Heb 11:17 may have been composed by someone other than the author of Hebrews is suggested by one of the quotations of Scripture taken directly from the MT rather than the LXX which Hebrews normally followed. The Hebrew *yuh-kheéd-uh-kah* (יחידך) (Gen 22:2), **your only one** would normally be rendered by the Greek *maw-náw-geh-naws* (μονόγενος) rather than the LXX *ah-gah-pay-táws* (ἀγάπητος), **beloved.**

The use of the *praws* plus the accusative after a verb that indicated saying rather than the usual Greek use of the dative case is typical of the author of Hebrews. Of the 19 usages of *praws* in this document, 10 are used in this very manner. This suggests a Semitism, reflecting the use of a *láh-mehd* (ל) as a dative indicator. Other usages of *praws* in Hebrews point in the same direction, reflecting a *lah-mehd* used to indicate an indirect object, or possession, purpose, or reference.[1] Of the 19 usages, only two carry the meaning, "against" or "toward."[2]

Even if it were clearly ascertained that this difficult passage is a literal translation of some Semitic original, there still remain only uncertain conjectures as to the meaning of the text. There seem to have been some regularity in the way the author used *praws*, which might help in proposing the conjectures. The only other use in Hebrews of the expression *praws hawn* follows a poem, just as in Heb 4:13. This may mean that the expressions were similar in meaning, but it is far from sure.

The clause *práws háwn eh-lah-láy-thay* (πρὸς ὃν ἐλαλήθη) (Heb 11:18) means "[with reference] to whom it was said." The corresponding passage in Heb 4:13 has no verb: *praws hawn hay-meén haw láw-gaws.* If the same verb were supplied to Heb 4:13 that occurs in Heb 11:18, the passage would read: "with reference to which the word [was spoken] for us" or "to us, for whom the word was spoken." In an exhortation to the readers, the author employed a poem (Heb 4:12-13) as a warning and concluded the poem with a brief, approving comment,

---

[1] See E. Kautzsch, *Gesenius' Hebrew Grammar* (Oxford: Clarendon Press, 1910) tr. A. E. Cowley, #114, f-p, 117n; 119c; 121f; 129; 143c.

[2] Heb 12:4; 13:13. One of these occurs in the thirteenth chapter, which is a postscript added later by a different author. See H. Kosmala, *Hebraer-Essener-Christen* (Leiden: E. J. Brill, 1959), p. 408, and Moffat, *Hebrews*, p. 224.

"Which word is for us," "which word [applies] to us," or some such general comment. The Syriac translation is, "With reference to it, the answer is given us" (*duh-láy yuh-hah-vee-náhn khah-náhn peht-gah-máh*, דלה יהבנן חנן פתגמא).

Another possibility is that it should be understood just as a similar comment which reads "concerning which our message is extensive" (*peh-reé hoo paw-lus hay-meén haw law-gaws*) (Heb 5:11). In this case, *hay-meén haw láw-gaws* is the subject. If Heb 4:13 were similarly rendered, the result would be something like this: "with reference to which (*praws hawn*) our message (*hay-meén haw law-gaws*) [applies]." This would mean that the admonition given in Heb 4:1-11 applies to an understanding of God's scrutinizing word. This translation would support Spicq's translation, "*c'est de ce sujet dont nous parlons.*"[1]

The meaning of **which word applies to us** does not differ very much practically from that of **with reference to which our message applies**. Both are intended to relate the message of the author to the poem he quoted and the entire message was intended to be taken seriously by the readers.

Summary. Given the presuppositions that were accepted in Christianity and Judaism in NT times, the author of Hebrews was an excellent logician and artist in the use of Scripture. Although the entire document (Heb 1:1-12:29) was based on Ps 110, it was proper to utilize other Scriptures to support the main point, and, as here, to develop a separate text by itself that would later contribute to the major point. Heb 4:1-13 is a small midrash by itself, based on Ps 95:7-11 and supported by Gen 2, Num 14, Deut 31, Josh 22, and a small poem which the author quoted in Heb 4:12-13a to strengthen his argument. He wanted to show his readers or listeners the opportunities that were available to the exodus generation, their faulty reaction, and the consequences they received as a result. He did this in order to remind his readers that they had even better chances for success than the exodus generation, but just as great chances for failure.

One reason why he used Ps 95 as his principal text rather than Num 14 or Deut 1 and 31 may have been his conviction that the law had been superseded; another may have been the fact that he believed David wrote the Psalm and that this late authorship would dispel all arguments to the effect that the promise had already been received. Had he used only the Hexateuch, this important point might have been overlooked. His step-by-step logic from the premise that the promise is still pending to his exhortation and warning against disobedience was supported by a poem on the thoroughness with which God, who knows everything, examines every case. This reminder of God's inescapable judgment was the kind of message which should be applied to the author and the readers of the document.

Heb 1 and 2 included the introduction and a comparison of the superiority of the Son to the angels and his relationship to his believers. Heb 3 showed how Moses failed to lead the people to receive the promised **rest**. Heb 4 argued cogently that the **rest** was then available to the author's generation. Each of these sections was concluded with a brief introduction to the subject that would follow. At the conclusion of Heb 4 also, the author prepared the reader for the next major doctrinal subject, **Jesus** the great **high priest**. Jesus had earlier been called a faithful **high priest** (Heb 2:17) and **the apostle and high priest of our confession** (Heb 3:1). The conclusion of Heb 4 will prepare the reader still further to read the discussion of Jesus' priestly qualities in the next chapter, where these will be considered more extensively.

---

[1] Spicq, *Hebreux* II, p. 91.

TEXT

Hebrews

[14]Since, then, we have **a great high priest** [who] has gone through the heavens, Jesus the Son of God, let us hold fast the confession. [15]For we do not have **a high priest** [who is] unable to sympathize with our weaknesses, but [one who] has been **tested** in everything, in ways similar [to ours, yet he is] without crime. [16]Then let us approach the throne of grace with boldness, so that we might receive mercy and find grace for timely support.

First Testament

[1Macc 13:42]The people began to write documents and contracts: "The first year of Simon, **the great high priest**, general, and leader of the Jews."

[Ps 95:8]Do not harden your hearts as in the rebellion, in the day of the **testing** in the wilderness.

COMMENTARY

[14]*We have a great high priest.* The highest ranking **priest** in Judaism was normally called the **high priest**, in Hebrew *koh-hehn hah-gah-dóhl* (כוהן הגדול) **the great priest**, usually rendered *ahr-khee-eh-roós* (ἀρχιερεύς), "the ruling **priest**," in Greek. The first of the Hasmoneans to be given an official title was Simon, who was called **the great high priest, general, and ruler of the Jews** (*ahr-khee-eh-roós meh-gáh-loo kai strah-teh-goó kai hay-goo-méh-noo yoo-dái-ohn* (ἀρχιερέως μεγάλου καὶ στρατεγοῦ καὶ ἡγουμένου Ιουδαίων) (1Macc 13:42). The author of Hebrews may have been influenced by this title when he called Jesus **a great high priest**. There are many other indications that the author of Hebrews was influenced by the literature and theological beliefs related to the Maccabean period and that the Hasmonean priestly rulers influenced his Christology.

The affirmation that Jesus had **gone through the heavens** expressed belief in his ascension, but it was couched in terms of sacrifice in the temple. Most people who lived at the time of the author understood the world in which they lived as it appeared to the naked eye. Because they had no modern telescopes and nuclear powered rockets, their knowledge of **heaven** was limited. It seemed to them that **heaven** was just above the treetops and the hills. God was somewhere in the sky and was always covered with a cloud so that human beings could not see him clearly. His presence was made known when clouds came down and settled around mountains.

Smoke and clouds were very similar to the naked eye, so it seemed that the smoke that went up from a bonfire formed a pillar which would both let God come down to earth and let human beings send things, like incense and offerings, up to God. They evidently thought of several **heavens**, something like floors in an apartment building, but they were described more in terms of tent roofs than concrete floors. Like their goat or camel hair tents that could be rolled up, heaven was described as a scroll that God could spread out (Isa 40:12; 45:12; 48:13) or roll up (Isa 34:4). It was also called a *rah-keé-ah* (רקיע)—"something spread out" (Gen 1:6).

Whenever God wanted to create a new **heaven,** all he had to do was roll up the old one and spread out a new one. Since Jesus' crucifixion was interpreted by the author in terms of a sacrifice on the altar, and since animal sacrifices were cooked or burned completely so that their odor could be sent up through the column of smoke to God in the **heavens,** it seemed reasonable to conclude that Jesus, too, ascended into **heaven,** or through the various **heavens,** up to the very throne of God.

Jesus, the Son of God. **Son of God** was a name ordinarily given to kings, but Philo said the **high priest** was not a man but a divine word (*láw-gaws theh-áws,* λόγος θεός), whose father was God (Fuga 108). The author of Hebrews, however, clearly related the attributes of **the Son** in royal terms; thus he here was thinking of Jesus as both priest and king. A **son** of a deity was not **a son** physically. This was a legal term. A royal son became a **son** by being anointed. He was legally born through an enthronement ceremony. Kings became **sons of God** by virtue of their offices. Jesus was legally conceived by the Holy Spirit and physically born of his Jewish mother. He was born at the end of his mother's gestation period, and spiritually conceived at his anointing by John the Baptist. Calling Jesus **the Son of God** acknowledged him as the Messiah, the king of Israel. Solomon and Alexander Janneus were both kings of Israel and both were called **sons of God.** Hebrews scholars have gone to great lengths to claim that Jesus was both God and man—entirely both, two natures, completely human, but still God, without explaining how this could be possible.[1] All of this is reasonable in legal terms.

Let us hold fast to the confession. The words **hold fast** and **confession** were both important words to the author. In court a **confession** made by the defendant was important for determining the judgment made. Defendants whose truth was doubted were sometimes put on the rack and tortured until they made a **confession.** Sometimes a **confession** would motivate the judge to reduce the potential punishment for the offense involved. Jesus was previously called the **high priest of our confession** (Heb 3:1); so it seemed reasonable for the author and readers to **hold fast** to the **confession**. The author also told the readers to **hold fast** to the **initial doctrine** (Heb 3:14; see also Heb 10:23). Both admonitions probably have the same meaning that members should know the entire doctrine of the sect and be disciplined to practice it unfailingly. Bornkamm suggested that the **confession** is that Jesus is the **Son of God**, and that the baptismal **confession** mentioned in Heb 3:1; 4:14; and 10:23 is:[2]

> **Who, being a reflection of the glory and stamp of his nature,**
> **bearing everything by the word of his power,**
> **when he had made a purification for [his] crimes,**
> **sat down at the right hand of the Majesty in exaltation** (Heb 1:3).

This is interesting, but not convincing. Jesus was certainly important to the **confession**, but the limit and entire content of the creed are not known. It was extensive enough, however, to include rules which were difficult to observe.

---

[1] For example, see P. E. Hughes, *A Commentary on the Epistle to the Hebrews* (Grand Rapids; Eerdmans Publishing Co., c1977), p. 170.

[2] G. Bornkamm, *Studien zu Antike und Christentum* (München: Kaiser, 1959) II, pp. 188-203.

[15]*[One who] has been tested in everything [in ways] similar [to ours]*. The word *pay-ráhd-zayn* (πειράζειν), **to test**, can mean to put to trial by torturing, to seduce, attempt, or experiment. In some ancient cultures, including Roman and Jewish, defendants in a trial were sometimes tortured to force a confession. This is one of the main themes in the Book of Job. Job was put on trial by God and Satan and then **tested** by torture to see if he would **confess.** In the FT **testing** usually refers to the **testing** that the Israelites put the Lord through when they doubted him. The **testing in everything** probably referred to hardships Jesus faced, including the crucifixion. They were the same kind of **tests** which later Christians had to face. Just as Jesus had been made **like the brothers in everything** (*kah-táh páhn-tah tois ah-dehl-foís haw-mee-oh-tháy-nai,* κατὰ πάντα τοῖς ἀδελφοῖς ὁμιωθῆναι) (Heb 2:17), so he was also **tested in everything, in ways similar [to ours]** (*kah-táh páhn-tah kahth haw-mee-oh-tay-tah,* κατὰ πάντα καθ' ὁμιωτήτα).

The difference was that he was **without crime**. When the **high priest** functioned on the Day of Atonement, very careful efforts were made to keep him from being defiled in any way, so that he could be free from defilement. He also offered a bull for a **crime** offering for himself and his family so that he could be absolved from every other type of **crime** against God before he ministered in behalf of the people. This meant that he was legally free from **crime** on the Day of Atonement. This was determined according to the cult rather than according to ethics. Philo claimed even more for him. He said that, in his judgment (*toh-noh,* τῷ νῷ), the high priest was the child of incorruptible parents and free from any kind of defilement, since God was his father (Fuga 109-10).

Philo said further that when the high priest entered the holy of holies, he became more than a man, but not yet God, retaining both mortality and immortality, created and uncreated essence. As such he was the mediator between man and God until he returned from the holy of holies and would again become flesh and blood (Som 2.231-32). Philo claimed that this half divine nature made it possible for the **high priest** to be free from **crime** and defilement. If he had not been sound, he would not have been permitted to serve (Spec 1.293). He was really immune to **crime** (*ah-méh-taw-khos hah-mahr-tay-máh-tohn,* ἀμέτοχος ἁμαρτημάτων). If he ever slipped, the **crime** would never be anything that could not be cleansed, and it would be something imposed upon him by the nation (Spec 1:230). Lane overlooked Philo's testimony when he said,

> Nowhere in the FT nor in contemporary Jewish sources was there expressed the expectation of a high priest who was "without sin."[1]

The double negative, **we do not have . . . un-**, is a good example of *litotes*. It means, "we *do* have a high priest who *is* able." This type of speech is frequent in Semitic style. For example, **Do not lead us into temptation**. (Matt 6:12) means "lead us away from temptation" or **deliver us from evil** (Matt 6:13). **Cast me not away from your presence, and take not your Holy Spirit from me** (Ps 51:11) means "Keep me in your presence, and give me your Holy Spirit."

Jesus was not the only leader of antiquity claimed to be **without crime.** Philo said the high priest was free from any kind of defilement, and the author of PssSol 17:41 said of the anticipated son of David, who would crush the gentiles and lead Israel in peace and prosperity,

---

[1] W. L. Lane, *Hebrews: A Call to Commitment* (Peabody: Hendrickson Publishers, c1985), p. 79.

> And he will be clean from crime (*kah-thah-ráws ah-páw hah-mahr-teé-ahs*, καθαρὸς ἀπὸ ἁμαρτίας) so as to rule a great people (PssSol 17:41).

If the **high priest** and the Messiah were both expected to be free from **crime**, then it seems a reasonable claim for the author, who insisted that Jesus was both king and **priest,** to call Jesus one who was **without crime**. When the author of Hebrews held that Jesus was without crime, it does not necessarily mean that he had never committed a moral offense in his life, nor that he had never even been tempted to commit any crime.[1] It means that he was legally innocent. He could not be punished in court for any offense. It was by virtue of his office that a high priest was legally innocent of **crime** as he entered the Holy of Holies, and it was by virtue of his office that a messiah or king was legally innocent. Since the author presented Jesus as a high priest he may have understood his crucifixion as an offering on the Day of Atonement to have cleansed his own **crimes** as well as those of the faithful, all of whom would have been made free from **crime** or perfect (see also Commentary on 1:3; 7:28; 9:14).

Another possible explanation is that Jesus would be judged innocent, because, like the innocent son of David described in PssSol 17:41, he was a monarch, and all monarchs are legally free from **crime**. Every king is also the judge of the highest court in the land. No one else could take the king to court and have him punished for having committed any **crime**. This is the basis by which the pope is infallible. He is only legally infallible, not really without fault or human frailty. Since Hebrews held that Jesus was both high priest and king, he would have been legally innocent because of his royal position, and he would have been cleansed of his ritual defilement as high priest on the Day of Atonement. Although John Hyrcanus was both **high priest** and king, a certain Pharisee, named Eleazar, suggested to him that he was not really qualified to be **high priest**. Eleazar quickly learned that this particular king did not want anyone to suggest that he was anything but innocent of **crime** and ritually flawless (Ant 13:288-95).

The prophet Nathan pointed out to King David that his affair with Bathsheba and Uriah was wrong. He did this by way of a hypothetical parable of a man who had stolen another man's sheep. David decreed that any person who had committed such a **crime** should be forced to pay fourfold and killed—multiple damages and punitive damages. Once it became clear that David himself was the criminal, however, he was able to mitigate the sentence, since he was also the highest judge in the land (2Sam 11).

If Christ had "full participation in humanity," as Lane claimed, and was even tested as other human beings were, it is reasonable to think that the author held that Jesus was legally without **crime.** Lane, however, insisted that Jesus had always been perfectly free from **crime**. This means that he had never, in his entire life, committed an offense serious enough to require pardon, apology, or forgiveness.[2] That does not seem reasonable for one who had full participation in humanity. To have been as virtuous as that he would have had to have been some kind of super human being, but Jesus was held to have been fully human, just as other kings are.

---

[1] Attridge, *Hebrews*, p. 140, fn. 42, argued that Jesus not only was free from crime but that he did not commit crime. That is more than the text claims.

[2] Lane, *Hebrews 1-8*, pp. 114-15.

In the time of Henry VI the English said Henry VI was no longer the same person as he had been before the coronation. This ceremony transformed him.

> As the reason thereof is, because the Body natural and the Body politic are consolidated into one, and the Body politic wipes away every Imperfection of the other Body, with which it is consolidated, and makes it to be another Degree than it should be if it were alone by itself.[1]

Using other words, the jurists argued that the king had become a new creature, legally, when he received the crown. He might also have been said to have been born again, legally, like Henry VI of England was. The liturgy of anointing wiped away every imperfection of the physical body, and also all of his guilt from previous **crimes** committed, if there had been any.

Throughout Heb 1:1-12:28 the author has shown himself to have been a very logical, consistent legalist. The entire document makes sense, legally. It seems unlikely that he would propose a claim that is as unreasonable as Lane has argued.

16 *Let us approach with boldness the throne of grace.* The term **approach** is used in a priestly-temple context, picturing the high priest on the Day of Atonement **approaching** the altar in the holy of holies. Only the high priest could come this close to the altar. Other priests might enter the holy place; undefiled male Jews were admitted into a court just beyond. Farther still from the altar was the women's court. When a gentile male was converted and became a proselyte, he was allowed to come closer to the holy of holies, but each class was expected to stay within its prescribed limits.

There was no "court of the gentiles" as part of the temple area. Just 600 feet north of the temple area was a Roman military camp, now mistakenly called the "temple mount." That was the Tower of Antonia, built by Romans during the reign of Herod the Great. Some of its huge rock walls still exist in the Old City of Jerusalem. At times Romans kept 6,000 soldiers in that camp. That was the "court of the gentiles," which Jews hated. It was 3 times as large as the entire City of David, and it was so tall that from there Romans could look down upon the City of David, including the temple area.

Only the high priest was allowed to **approach** or come near the **throne of grace**. The **throne of grace** was another name for the throne of God, which either was the altar itself or was on the altar of incense. The huge altar for slaughtering animals was probably behind both the holy place and the holy of holies.

In a monastery, however, which was itself a holy of holies where perfect sacrifices were offered, and all members of the community were undefiled priests, there were no women or potentially defiled Jewish males. These males were all celibate. They were daily kept undefiled. Therefore they were all authorized to approach the throne of grace with boldness.

In non-monastic communities, the **high priest** was the representative and mediator for the people. It was through his agency that they were able to approach God (Heb 7:25). The law was never able permanently to fulfill the needs of those who **approach** by means of the same sacrifices every year (Heb 10:1), but because

---

[1] Plowden, *Reports*, p. 238. Taken from E. H. Kantorowicz, *The King's Two Bodies* (Princeton: Princeton U. Press, 1957), p. 11, fn. 9.

of the sacrifice of Jesus, in an undefiled monastery the monks might confidently **approach** the altar (Heb 10:22). Those who **approached** the altar did so with a gift which the priest offered in their behalf. His **approaching the throne of grace** with the believer's offering constituted the believer's **approach**. The priest was the legal agent authorized to represent the people. When Jesus, as **high priest**, entered the holy of holies, he not only was the priest **who approached the throne of grace** with an offering for the believers, but he was himself the offering.

Israelites offered sacrifices at the altar in Jerusalem. For most of these, the right hind leg of the beast was given to the priests, and the rest was eaten by the people. There were also whole burnt offerings. These were entirely burned, so that everything became ashes or smoke. The smoke was believed to go up to heaven as a gift to God who was not present physically at the feast, but would still participate in this way. Since Jesus was by definition the whole burnt offering, it was assumed that he also ascended in the smoke just like other sacrificial beasts. The smoke which carried the fragrance of the offering to God, carried Jesus himself as the offering **through the heavens**. This **crime** offering was sufficient to cancel all of the **crimes** that had kept the children of Israel removed from and unreconciled to God.

So that we might receive mercy and find grace. Since the offering had already **gone through the heavens**, monks were reconciled, no longer kept at a distance, but invited to **approach the throne of grace with boldness**. Those who did so would benefit from the offering themselves, which means they would **receive mercy and find grace**. This would happen on the Day of Atonement. They would have their **crimes** forgiven and might even have some merits on hand **for timely support**. Since this opportunity was available, of course, the author urged his readers to take advantage of all the benefits available to them. The Greek for **timely support** is *yoó-kai-rawn baw-áy-thay-ahn* (εὔκαιρον βοήθειαν), sometimes translated "time of need." It is literally "**timely** help" or "**timely** assistance." In the context of a Day of Atonement gift and the judgment associated with it the author probably thought that all the support a believer could muster was necessary to make his case favorable at that particular time. The Day of Atonement was precisely the correct time for **crimes** to be cancelled so that the nation's **crimes** might be forgiven.

The Greek word rendered **boldness** is *pah-ray-seé-ah* (παρρησία) literally, "saying everything." It refers to the freedom of citizens to speak and sometimes has the force of "outspokenness." In Hebrews it can mean the unquestioned right to approach God (Heb 3:6, 4:16; 10:19) or the openness with which they should **confess** their faith.[1] Delitzsch had noticed the euphonious chiasm in the concluding line:[2]

heé nah láh-boh-mehn éh-leh-os so that we might receive (Ἵνα λάβωμεν ἔλεος)	X	mercy
kai cháh-reen heúr-oh-mehn and grace (καὶ χάριν εὕρωμεν)		we might find

Summary. The words **high priest**, **heavens**, and **confession** form the concluding parts of an inclusion which refers the reader back to Heb 3:1, where their counter-

[1] See W. C. Van Unnik, "The Christian's Freedom of Speech in the NT," *BJRL* 44(1962):466-88.
[2] Delitzsch, *Hebrews,* II, p. 223.

parts occur. Heb 4:15-16 are further elaborations of this conclusion and preparation of the reader for the content of Heb 5. The importance of the priesthood, the temple, and the treasury of merits to the Jewish doctrine of atonement provides the basis for the author's Christology and understanding of the role of Jesus. Jews and Christians of NT times thought of **heaven** in terms of temple surroundings (see further Commentary at the end of chapter 9). Josephus said the holy of holies was like heaven (Ant 3:123).

Just as the high priest passed through the drape into the holy of holies which was like **heaven,** so Jesus as **a great high priest has gone through the heavens**. Since it was **crime** and defilement that kept others from the holy of holies, and since Jesus' sacrifice canceled all of these, believers no longer were required to keep at a distance from holy things, lest some defilement take place. Instead of being afraid of touching something sacred, believers should be afraid of falling behind (Heb 4:1), but they should **approach the throne of grace with boldness**. It was only in this way that they might receive the benefits tabulated to the credit of Israel in the treasury of merits by the sacrifice of Jesus. In Herod's temple only the high priest was allowed to approach the holy of holies, but in the local monastery, where all of the residents were priests and all were as undefiled as the high priest on the Day of Atonement, there was no danger of defilement. All of the monks were authorized to **approach the throne of grace with boldness.**

Terms of Atonement

The text of Heb 3 and 4 was centered around the rules and liturgy associated with the Day of Atonement. This was basic liturgy for the parties to the contract with God to maintain their position within the contract and receive the promises rather than the curses involved. The contract that God had made with Abraham promised that he would provide for the parties to this contract

1) prosperity,
2) posterity, and
3) the land,

but this would happen only if the parties to the contract kept the commandments that were contained in the contract. If they broke the contract, then they would receive the curses of the contract—famine, pestilence, wild beasts, and the sword. To avoid this eventuality, Israelites and Jews set aside a season of the year to take account of their activity to see that every offense was corrected and every fine was paid. This took place on the season between New Year's Day and the Day of Atonement. Both of these observations were couched in legal terms.

New Year's Day was the time when Jews thought the Lord sat in judgment, opened the books, and reviewed his legal briefs presented by plaintiffs and defendants. The Day of Atonement happened ten days later and was also a judgment day, but the event was couched in financial terms. It was sometimes called the day of reckoning, because that was the day when the books were audited, accounts reconciled, and debits were forgiven, cleared, or carried over into the next year.[1]

---

[1] K. Stendahl, *Paul among Jews and Gentiles* (Philadelphia: Fortress Press, 1976), pp. 23-24, was correct when he said that Paul seldom used the term "forgiveness." He usually spoke of "justification." That does not mean, as Stendahl implied that there was an either /or factor here,

Jews probably thought that the entire period between these two dates consisted of a continuous heavenly court session or auditing session which began with New Year's Day and was concluded at the end of the Day of Atonement (Pesikta Rabbati 15:19). If the kingdom happened to come shortly after the Day of Atonement, as it did under the leadership of Judah the Maccabee, that would prove that Israel's crimes had all been reconciled and forgiven (financial) or pardoned (legal).

This is the way the author of Daniel understood the situation. After the Battle of Beth-horon and the cleansing of the temple, Gabriel told this author of Daniel that 70 weeks of years (490 years) was the predestined amount of time required for Jews and Jerusalem to be punished before their transgressions were completely punished or forgiven, their iniquity completely atoned, and their **crimes** annihilated, leaving both Jews and Jerusalem free from all **crime** (Dan 9:24). All of this had been finalized on the Day of Atonement in 164 BIA.

If, however, the kingdom did not come, that meant Israel was still in its **crimes.** Some Jews had not been forgiven; some **crimes** had not been reconciled. Rabbis said that if all Israel would repent for just one day the kingdom would come. That day was the Day of Atonement. On that day those who did proper penance were made new creatures (Pesikta Rabbati 40:169a). The last opportunity for doing this each year was the period between New Year's Day and the Day of Atonement.

All pious Jews longed for the kingdom, and many believed that the only reason it did not come was that there was a huge national debt of **crime** which God held against the nation. Those like the Pharisees who gave only the required tithes and fulfilled only the obligatory commands simply added no more debts to the financial account, but with the huge debt it would require many works of supererogation to reduce this debt. Therefore, Jesus told his disciples that their righteousness must exceed that of the scribes and Pharisees (Matt 5:20).

The righteousness he demanded of apostles was complete poverty, celibacy, and obedience.[1] They gave—not just the required one tenth. They gave ten tenths of all their possessions and earnings to the community order, called the "poor." Jesus said that if a believer came to the altar bringing his atonement offering and there remembered that he had not been completely reconciled to all of his fellow Jews, he should leave his gift there and go, find his fellow citizen, do whatever was required for reconciliation, and then offer his gift (Matt 5:23-24). That was according to the rabbinic prescription. Consistent with the rules of the Day of Atonement, Jesus taught his disciples to pray that their **crimes** might be forgiven, as they also forgave their fellow believers (Matt 6:12) and he further noted that if they did not forgive those who committed **crimes** against them, neither would their Father in heaven forgive their **crimes** (Matt 6:14). He urged them to settle their disputes out of court and become reconciled to one another (Matt 5:25-26).

The Day of Atonement was for believers only. Gentiles were not involved. Tannaitic rabbis said gentiles did not bring **crime** offerings, because the Scripture said, **The soul that commits crimes** (Lev 4:2). Since the word *soul* could apply only to a Jew it was clear that gentiles were excluded (SLev 4:2). The opportunity to have **crimes** cancelled was limited to Israel alone. Other nations would have their

---

"Justification Rather than Forgiveness." From the theological point of view, both were synonyms and metaphors dealing with the same reality. The person who had been forgiven had been justified and vice versa.

[1] For a justification for this statement see Buchanan, *Jesus: The King and his Kingdom* (Macon: Mercer U. Press, c1984), pp. 173-90.

crimes continue to accumulate until God would foreclose on them, punishing them severely (2Macc 6:12-16). This was the other side of the coin. God could bless Israel with the land only if he also punished the foreign nations in whose hands the land was then held.

Rabbis said that the Day of Atonement atoned for the **crimes** that are between God and believers, but it did not atone for the **crimes** that occurred between a believer and his fellow believer, *unless the offender first appeased the believer whom he had offended* (mYoma 8:9). Rabbis said that if a man brought his guilt offering and did not bring the goods he had stolen, the priest would not offer an atonement sacrifice on his behalf until he brought the goods he had stolen. The offering would stay there and deteriorate until it was removed and burned (tBaba Qama 10:18 [368]).

The requirements for atonement on the Day of Atonement are clear and consistent. They are presumed by rabbis, the gospels, the Pauline letters, Hebrews, and the Johannine epistles. There are three:

1) the appropriate crime offering,
2) believers' reconciliation to one another by repenting and forgiving one another, and.
3) God's forgiveness of the criminal.

There is no Atonement Day theology that offers free **grace** without repentance and reconciliation on the part of the believer. It was Martin Luther, and not Paul, who said salvation was by faith *alone.*[1] Death and the Day of Atonement atone only if accompanied by repentance. The Day of Atonement effects atonement for transgressions between human beings and God, but the process is not complete until there is also reconciliation between a Jew and his fellow believer. The Day of Atonement only clears these offenses if believers are first reconciled among themselves (mYoma 8:8-9; 5:9; sLev 16:83a-b; Sifre Zuta Num 6:27 50; mBaba Qama 8:7; bBaba Qama 92a; jRoshHa-Shana 17b; bShevuoth 13a).

Forgiveness in the New Testament

Authors and leaders in the NT presumed the same basic rules for the Day of Atonement as the rabbis did. Therefore, according to Matthew, Jesus said that anyone presenting a **crime** offering on the Day of Atonement who suddenly remembered that there was some other coreligionist whom he had offended or injured in some way and had not been reconciled, he should stop there, leave his gift, and go, make whatever restitution was necessary for reconciliation. Then he could come and offer his gift, and it would be effective (Matt 5:23-24), but Jesus was acquainted with the same Atonement Day rules as the rabbis.

The debt of crime between two believers had to be corrected before the work of the Day of Atonement could be complete. God's forgiveness was contingent upon the repentance and forgiveness necessary for the reconciliation of the parties to the contract. This does not mean either that **crime** against God is greater or more important than **crime** against the believer or vice versa, as Sanders contests.[2] Both

---

[1] Stendahl, *Paul*, p. 26, also noticed this.

[1] E. P. Sanders, *Paul and Palestinian Judaism* (Philadelphia: Fortress Press, 1977), p. 179.

are obstacles to be removed on the Day of Atonement. Because this was true, a person who had committed **crimes** against some other Jews could not be forgiven by God if the other Jew refused to forgive him or her for the **crime** committed.

The unforgiving servant parable was a Day of Atonement illustration. The one who forgave the huge debt of 10,000 talents was God. The Jew who had been forgiven a huge debt but was unwilling to forgive a small debt to his fellow Jew had his debt restored. If he would not forgive he could not be forgiven (Matt 18:23-35). Jesus concluded the parable, **So also my heavenly Father will do to everyone of you who does not forgive your brother in your heart** (Matt 18:35). This story emphasized a previous teaching that a man should forgive his brother **seventy-seven times** (Matt 18:22).

This was also the point of the parable of the tax collector and the Pharisee in the temple on the Day of Atonement. Although the Pharisee had done many good deeds, he had not become reconciled to the tax collector. Therefore on the Day of Atonement he left the temple without being justified (Luke 18:9-14). Jesus reportedly said if your brother commits crimes you are to rebuke him,

> **and if he repents. forgive him; and if he commits crimes against you seven times in a day, and turns to you seven times, and says, "I repent," you must forgive him** (Luke 17:3-4; see also tGad 6:3-7).

Because the community to which a believer belonged had the right to forgive or withhold forgiveness, Peter, who represented the Petrine sect of Christianity, was understood by his community to have been given authority either to bind or forgive **crimes** on earth: members of this sect believed that the Lord would follow suit (Matt 16:19),[1] thus completing the requirements necessary to judge whether there should be atonement or not. Other groups of Christians and Jews, each of which considered itself to be the only true Israel, held similar beliefs.

Paul followed the same rules as Jesus and the rabbis concerning the Day of Atonement. He believed that Christ had paid the national debt. That was the atonement gift that paid off the huge debt necessary for that accomplishment, but he did not think that was the only requirement of the Day of Atonement. He said,

> **God was in Christ, reconciling the world to himself, not counting their trespasses against them, and he has given to us the reckoning of reconciliation**. (2Cor 5:19).

The Colossian Christians were told that by his death Jesus had reconciled them and presented them before him without any guilt (Col 1:22). They had been forgiven of all their **crimes** at baptism and made alive (Col 2:13), but atonement required that they forgive one another just as the Lord had forgiven them.

On the Day of Atonement (mYoma 8:9) **crimes** were cancelled providing that the proper actions were taken. The two requirements for atonement were the same for Paul, Jesus, and the rabbis, but the doctrine itself was not new. The liturgy and the terms for atonement were recognized very early. They are already assumed in the Book of Genesis. For example, when Jacob came to Peniel on his way to

---

[2] See W R. Farmer, "The Patriarch Phineas," *ATR* 34 (1952):26-30 and Buchanan, *Consequences,* pp. 1-41.

Hebron to claim his birthright and blessing, he had to wrestle with an angel all night. That fight was with his own conscience and his knowledge of the terms of the treaty and the Day of Atonement (Gen 32-33).

He had enough wealth to pay God for his offense against God, and he may have had enough military power to overthrow Esau and take over the family property at Hebron. The problem was that he also was reminded that God's promise of the land and prosperity would be cancelled if he did not get his crime atoned. To remain on the land and receive blessings of posterity and prosperity he had to atone for all of his **crimes**. If not, God would annul the treaty and replace blessings with curses—famine, pestilence, wild beasts, and the sword.

He finally realized that he could not receive God's blessings unless he became reconciled to his brother, Esau. This was an essential part of the Day of Atonement activities. So he sent many gifts ahead to Esau, saying to himself, **I** will atone (*ah-kah-puh-ráh,* אכפרה) him with a gift, and maybe he will forgive me (Gen 32:21). When he met Esau he did not confront him arrogantly with military force. Instead he bowed before him humbly and pleaded with Esau to accept both his gifts and his blessing *(béer-kah-tée,* ברכתי) (Gen 33:11), which means he offered both the birthright and the blessing and gave many punitive gifts to pay for his offenses.

The brothers were reconciled; Jacob met the terms of atonement; Esau went back to Hebron to claim his birthright and his blessing; Jacob went a little north and west to Shechem to another area of the Promised Land, where he purchased land from Khamor (Gen 33:14-19). There was room on the land for both brothers, and because of Jacob's experience at Peniel, they were reconciled without warfare.[1]

The author of Hebrews knew the rules involved with the Day of Atonement. He emphasized the importance of the sacrificial gift. He did not directly mention the importance of reconciliation among the brothers, but this was probably implied by the exhortations that the brothers not commit any crime or be unfaithful in any way. He repeatedly warned his audience of the drastic consequences that would come upon that generation if they wandered, became unfaithful, or offended in any way. He constantly blended his warnings with his signs of hope. The good news was that the atonement gift had been made, and it was adequate. The threat was that the believers would not respond enough to make the Day of Atonement successful. Enthusiasm and conviction are clear in chapters 3 and 4 that concentrate on

1) Jesus as the perfect atonement gift and
2) the urgent necessity for the hearers to keep themselves all perfectly free from crime and faithful.

These chapters provide a suitable message to be delivered between New Year's Day and the Day of Atonement. Heb 3:1-4:16 constitute a unified Day of Atonement message, but the themes given here are not exhausted. They are echoed further on in Heb 5 and other later chapters as the author wove his majestic themes alternatingly as a great symphony throughout the message.

[1] See further Buchanan, *The Book of Daniel* (Lewiston: Mellen, c1999) pp. 287-88.

CHAPTER FIVE

TEXT

Hebrews	First Testament
5:1 For every high priest selected from men is appointed [over] divine things in behalf of men, so	Lev 16:11 **Aaron**
that he might **offer** gifts and **sacrifices for crimes** 2 being able to bear gently with the ignorant and wayward [criminals], since he himself is also clothed in weakness,	will **offer** a bull **crime offering which is his** and he will atone
3 and because of it, is obligated to **offer** [sacrifices] **for his own crimes** as well as those of	**for himself** and for his house. He will slaughter his bull **crime offering.**
	Lev 16:15 He will slaughter the goat **crime offering** which is for
the people. 4 No one takes the honor [of high priesthood] for himself but is invited by God, just as **Aaron** also was,	**the people**.
	Lev 16:16 He will atone the holy place [cleansing] it from the defilement of the Israelites, from their transgressions and all their **crimes**.

COMMENTARY

5:1 *Every priest selected from men*. The word translated **selected** is the Greek *lahm-bahn-áw-meh-naws* (λαμβανόμενος), literally "taken." This forms an inclusion with the word **takes** (*lahm-báh-nay*, λαμβάνει) in Heb 5:4, thus forming a small unit. This unit is completely devoted to telling the duties and qualifications of the office of high priest, generally. In early Judaism and Christianity **priests** were always male. The point of this affirmation was that the **priests** all had to be human. There were no exceptions. This affirmation prepared the way for the author to claim that Jesus was a human being, with all of the limitations and strengths of other human beings.

So that he might offer gifts and sacrifices for crimes. The word rendered **offer** (*pros-phéh-ray*, προσφέρῃ) occurs 19 times in Hebrews. It is a term commonly used in the LXX in relationship to various kinds of sacrifices. It literally means to "bring toward," meaning to bring toward the altar. **Divine things** are, literally, **the things related to God** (*ta pros táwn theh-áwn*, τὰ πρὸς τὸν θεόν). They are the sacrifices that are brought to the altar to be given to God as well as the services and the sacred precincts in and around the temple. The **gifts and sacrifices offered for crimes** were the **crime** and guilt **offerings**. These were specified or determined by the priests. If a person of a certain financial ability committed a certain **crime**, he was obligated to offer a specified sacrifice so that the responsibility for the **crime** might be removed. This was the legal way they had of removing guilt just as today people pay fines and spend time in jail to remove their responsibility to the state for speeding, parking illegally, stealing, rape, murder, fraud or any other type of misdemeanor or felony.

[2]*Being able to bear gently with the ignorant and wayward [criminals].* **To bear gently** (*meh-tree-aw-pah-tháyn,* μετριοπαθεῖν) means "to share suffering," "to moderate or mitigate one's feelings," to empathize or sympathize. It is a moderating action between indifference and over indulgence. Josephus used this term to describe the generous and restrained attitude of Titus and Vespasian toward the Jews after the wars with the Jews were over (Ant 12:128). Philo used it and its cognates to describe Abraham's self-controlled grief at the death of Sarah (Abr 44:257) and Jacob's patience when afflicted (Ios 5:26). Not all **crimes** could be removed.

> If a man said, "I will commit crime and repent, and commit crime again and repent," he will be given no chance to repent [if he said], "I will commit crime and the Day of Atonement will effect atonement," then the Day of Atonement effects no atonement. For transgressions between man and God, the Day of Atonement effects atonement, but for the transgressions that are between man and his fellow, the Day of Atonement effects atonement only if he has appeased his fellow (mYoma 8:8-9).

Because the high priest was not authorized to atone for the **crimes** of intent and malice, the author of Hebrews limited his **gentle bearing** to those who commit **crimes** of ignorance and waywardness. These could be pardoned, and the high priest had an understandingly kind attitude toward those who made these mistakes, because **he himself** was **also clothed in weakness** and committed the same kind of misdemeanors. It was his responsibility to help the offender to reach a satisfactory settlement out of court. Since the author was preparing to show that Jesus himself was fully qualified to become a priest, he had no clue that Jesus belonged to a different nature than other human beings. He was fully human, with all of the **weaknesses** which other human beings inherit. He had to study in order to learn. He had to eat, sleep, recover from illnesses, and also make mistakes in judgment and actions that other human beings make. Like other priests he was **clothed in weakness** and could understand the problems and weaknesses of others. If this were not the case he would not have qualified to become either a priest or a king.

[3]*His own crimes as well as those of the people.* Here as elsewhere, the author of Hebrews has shown his familiarity with Jewish customs and FT. Nothing in the Day of Atonement liturgy assumed that the high priest was infallible in judgment, physical strength, or liturgical skills. He was forced into conditions that made it impossible to become defiled. He was taught Scripture and liturgy necessary for the occasion. No one expected him to be free from **criminal** activity (mYoma). The high priest was required on the Day of Atonement to offer a calf as an offering **for his**

own crimes and those of his family before he offered only a goat for **the crimes of** all Israel (Lev 9:7-17; 16:6-19; mYoma 4:2-5:7).

4*No one takes the honor*. Still considering the office of the high priest generally, the author noted that **no one takes the honor** for himself. God calls men to that office, just as he commanded Moses,

> **Then bring near to you Aaron your brother, and his sons with him, from among the people of Israel, to serve me as priest** (Exod 28:l; see also Num 3:10; Ant 3:188-92).

According to the Scripture it was God who said, **You are a priest for the age** (Ps 110:4). Since the Scripture is the word of God, the word of a Psalm tells what God said. God selects the high priest. Hypothetically that was true. Actually, the high priestly office was also a political appointment and was often tainted with human manipulation.

When Jews lived under their own king, kings chose their high priests, following the proper priestly heritage. When Judah was under foreign rule, foreign kings, such as Syrian or Roman emperors selected the high priests. This was such a coveted position that people negotiated with foreign kings and paid them high prices for the privilege of being high priests. This was a political position that could be obtained through political means. While the temple was standing in NT times, many faithful Jews believed Herod's temple was "made with hands," defiled, and functioned under a corrupt priesthood. These Jews refused to worship there. The author of Hebrews was of this opinion.

TEXT

Hebrews	First Testament
5Thus also the Christ did not exalt himself to become high priest, but [was appointed by] the	Ps 2:5-7Then [Yehowah] will speak to them in his anger; he will frighten them with his wrath: "I have set my king on Zion, my holy hill. I will narrate the statute of Yehowah. He said to me,
One who said to him, "**You are my Son. Today I gave you birth**." 6Just as it also says in another [place],	**You are my Son. Today I gave you birth."**
"You are a priest for the age according to the order of Melchizedek,"	Ps 110:4Yehowah has sworn; he will not retract: **You are a priest for the age according to the order of Melchizedek.**
	1Macc 14:41-42The Jews and the priests wanted Simon to be their leader and high **priest for the [current] age**, until a trustworthy prophet should arise.

COMMENTARY

5-6*Was appointed by] the One who said to him.* **The One who said to him** was God, and he said it through Scripture. The Scripture was **the word** that **belonged to God** (John 1:1). It was the agent that communicated God's message to God's people before this **word became flesh and dwelled among us** (John 1:14). The qualifications that applied to any high priest applied just as well to the Christ, and there are two FT passages to prove it. Two witnesses are enough to prove a case in court. The first passage, quoted earlier (Heb 1:5), proved that Jesus was the Son, and as such, the Christ or the Messiah (Ps 2:7); the other passage showed that the Messiah was also a priest, **according to the order of Melchizedek** (Ps 110:4).

These two Psalms were basic to the author for establishing the Sonship of Jesus (Heb 1:5-13). This provided another time for the author of this document to refer again to Ps 110, to remind the reader that Ps 110 was the text of this entire sermon. Its primary purpose was to prove that Jesus was a priest—a notion that has not been noted on any other basis. In addition to Heb 5:6, 10 the Psalm is quoted also in Heb 1:3, 13; 7:11, 17, 21; 8:8; 10:13. If he had not been able to prove that Jesus was a high priest, his argument that he was the effective **crime offering**, necessary to restore the kingdom on the next Day of Atonement would not have been effective.

At least from the time of Saul and Samuel, it had been customary for the high priest and the king to be different people, and some scholars trace the division of the priestly and administrative offices much earlier, even before there was a kingdom. From the time of Absalom's revolt on, the king was expected to be a son of David, and the high priest a descendant from Zadok. There were exceptional instances when the king also offered sacrifice. For instance, Saul offered sacrifice after Samuel delayed in coming to fulfill this function (1Sam 13:2-10). When the chest holding the contract was brought to Jerusalem, David danced before the Lord and offered burnt offerings and peace offerings (2Sam 6:14-18), but this may only mean that David had the priests offer these sacrifices. The same may be true of Solomon, who offered many burnt offerings on the altars of various high places before the temple was built (1Kings 3:3-4). Since David and Solomon were both principals, they were credited for the work done by their priests.

By the time of the Hasmoneans (2d BIA), moreover, the normal expectation was that the nation would be restored with two leaders--a king from the line of David and a priest from the line of Aaron, or preferably Zadok.[1] In actuality, however, the Hasmoneans, who were priests that were descended through Joarib, were neither sons of David nor of Zadok (GenR 97; 99:2). The Hasidim were opposed to the Hasmoneans, because they were not legitimate high priests, although they approved the Maccabean Revolt at first (1Macc 2:42-48). They were willing to fight to restore purified worship in the temple and law observance among the people. Once the temple had been cleansed and a candidate from the tribe of Aaron, Alcimus, had been appointed high priest, they were prepared to make peace with the Seleucids and part company with Judas on this point (1Macc 7:4-14).

---

[1] Zech 6:9-13; *T .Reuben* 6.7-12; *T. Sim* 5.4-6; *T. Levi* 8.1-17; *T. Judah* 21:1-5, 25; *T. Iss* 5:6-8; *T.* Naph 5:3-6; 6:6, TJos 19:11-12; *1QS* 9:11; CDC 14:19. NumR. 4:18:16 interpreted the two sons of oil (Zech 4:14) as Aaron and David. One would receive the priesthood and the other the kingdom.

The Hasmoneans, however, proved themselves capable of winning the war against the Syrians; so they gradually took over the roles both of priests and of kings. Of the first generation of Hasmoneans, only Simon was given an official rank. **The Jews and the priests approved Simon's being leader and high priest for the age** (*ays táwn ai-óh-nah*, ἐὶς τὸν αἰῶνα) [of Hasmonean rule]--**until a trustworthy prophet arose** (1Macc 14:41-42). This means that he had a temporary appointment. **The age** was not forever.

The prophet was expected to announce the true anointed high priest from Zadok's line and the anointed king from David's line. Many Jews continued to think of the Hasmonean dynasty as a temporary measure, and the Hasmoneans had to begin with this understanding, but the pro-Hasmoneans called Simon also **prince of the people of God** (ασαραμελ = *sáhr ahm áyl*, שׂר עם אל) (1Macc 14:27) as well as the anointed high priest. Although never anointed king, Josephus said of Simon's son John Hyrcanus I, "He was the only one to hold three offices [at once], rule of the nation, high priesthood, and prophecy" (War 1:68). Hyrcanus' oldest son, Aristobulus I, was the first to assume the crown and openly claim to be both high priest and king (War 1:70). By that time, many Jews accepted the Hasmonean rule as legitimate, but others still looked for another prophet and two messiahs, one of Zadok's line and one of David's. It was with this in mind that the restriction was placed on Simon's position.

6*You are a priest for the age.*[1] The expression **for the age** referred to **the age** or generation during which Simon lived. *Ays táwn ai-óh-nah* (ἐὶς τὸν αἰῶνα) is usually translated "forever," but in this instance, at least, it did not mean "forever," because a limit was set for the condition of his rule. This is probably a Greek translation of the Hebrew expression in Daniel 12:3: *luh oh-láhm wah-éhd* (לעולם ועד), meaning **for the age and until** . . . Here it is used to mean **for the age and until a trustworthy prophet should arise**. This expression might best be translated with a question mark, as **for the age until?**–[The Lord knows when]. In this case the understanding was that whenever a faithful or trustworthy (*pees-táws*, πιστός) prophet arose, Simon would stop being leader and high priest. That would be the end of **the age**. An **age** was ordinarily considered chronologically to be a period of about 50 years, a Jubilee, or a generation in length, but this was not followed rigidly.

Ages followed each other in temporal sequence; when an administration or time of fortune changed, the age changed, regardless of the length of time that had elapsed. The Hasmonean age lasted as long as someone from this dynasty was ruling the nation. The **age to come** was expected to begin when the current evil **age** ended (see Commentary on Heb 1:2). It was usually identified either with the messianic **age** which would come at "the end of days," when "this **age"** was drawing to a close, or it would be the **age** of peace that would follow the messianic **age**. In this rare instance, when a current **age** was the beginning of a *good* **age**, it might be followed by an evil **age** of gentile rule, but Jews never liked to think about that. The "until" had to be filled in with whatever was expected to follow the **age** involved.

The end of the **age** that was most prominent in their expectations was the end of the *evil* **age**, when Jews were ruled by some gentile power. Rabbis expected that the Messiah would come at the end of the **age** of oppression. He would drive out the oppressors and establish peace on the land. The sabbath **age** of **rest,** the renewal of the world, or the **age** to come would follow (bSan 97a-b). The Messiah

---

[1] W. L. Lane, *Hebrews 1-8* (Dallas: Word Books, c1991), p. 123.

would not come without "birth pangs," hardships, oppression, and wars, such as those the Hasmoneans fought at the end of the Seleucid (Greek) domination.

Simon's rule came during the "birth pangs," and he ruled until there were signs of peace and **rest.** He was anointed high priest and called prince of the people of God. Among his supporters, he was probably considered a messiah who had come at the "end of days" to restore Israel to her independence and permit the Jewish people to enter into their promised **rest.**[1] His grandson was certainly accepted, at least publicly, as the anointed king, and later rabbis referred to the entire Hasmonean government as the Hasmonean kingdom (*mahl-koót hash-moh-neé,* מלכות השמונאי) (bRoshH 18b). Simon was a high priest, as were his son and grandson, but the purists, like those reflected in the Habakkuk Commentary, could never be satisfied with a ruler who was not from David's line and a high priest that was not a son of Zadok. One of the reasons for this was their belief that their current cycle would have to parallel as an exact antitype of the David-Solomonic cycle.

According to the order of Melchizedek. The story of **Melchizedek** is recorded only in Genesis:

> **The king of Sodom went out to meet him [Abram] after he had returned from his attack against Chedorlaomer and the kings who had [cooperated] with him. [The king met Abram] in the Valley of Shaveh, i.e. the Valley of the Kings. Melchizedek, king of Salem, brought out bread and wine. He was priest of God most high. He [Melchizedek] blessed him [Abram], saying,**
> **"Blessed be Abram before God Most High,**
> **Maker of heaven and earth.**
> **Blessed be God Most high**
> **who has delivered your enemies into your hand."**
> **Then [Abram] gave him a tenth of everything** (Gen 14:17-20).

According to Gen 14:18, Melchizedek was called **priest of the Most High God**; according to Ps 110, the enthroned person who would sit at the Lord's right hand was a **priest for the age according to the order of Melchizedek**. There is a firm tradition that the Hasmoneans were to be identified with both of these passages. Rabbis called John Hyrcanus, "John, high priest of the Most High God" (*yóh-khah-nahn kó-hayn gah-dóhl luh-áyl ehl-yóhn,* יוחנן כהן גדול לאל עליון) (bRoshH 18b). Josephus also referred to John Hyrcanus as "high priest of the God Most High" (*ahr-khi-ehr-éh-ohs theh-oó heep-sís-too,* ἀρχιερέως θεοῦ ὑψίστου) (Ant 16:163). Levi, from whom the Hasmoneans descended, was reported to have dreamed that Levi had been ordained (*ordinatus*) priest of the God Most High, he and his sons, continuously for the age (*usque in saecula*) (Jub 32:1).

Simon was called a **priest for the age** (1Macc 14:41) with the apparent intention of identifying him with the hero (*kóh-hayn leh-oh-láhm,* כהן לעולם) in that enthronement Psalm (Ps 110:4). This would be especially applicable since the one described in that Psalm may not have been called "king," but his activity was described as that of a king, and, like Simon, he was called **a priest for the age**. Initially, Dahood's translation of this name as **His legitimate king, my lord**

---

[1] Buchanan, *The Consequences of the Covenant* (Leiden: E. J. Brill, 1970), pp. 9-18.

(Ps 110:4), may have been correct,[1] but the tradition that identified Ps 110 with Gen 14 did not understand it that way. Hasmoneans were identified with both Ps 110 and Gen 14, which would have required Ps 110:4 to be rendered . . . **Melchizedek**. Whether this was understood by the author of First Maccabees is not certain. That pro-Hasmonean author did not quote the pertinent line.

It would have served his purposes to have Simon accepted as the Lord's legitimate king or to have had his priesthood justified on the basis of **Melchizedek.** The author of Hebrews, however, left no uncertainty. The Psalm that he related to Jesus was also attached to Gen 14 (Heb 7). Because the Hasmoneans did not fit the traditional expectation, they had to defend their position continuously. This was accomplished partly through the subtlety of the author of 1Macc. He did not call Simon a king, but he quoted from an enthronement Psalm intended for a king and describing the activity of a king.

An anti-Hasmonean did not feel the same way about the Hasmoneans. He called their leadership "iniquity in the holy of holies" *impietatem ab sancto sancitatis*) (AsMos 6:1; see also Ant 13:372-76). Similar conditions existed during the period when the author of Hebrews lived. Jesus was understood to have been a son of David, a messiah, and a royal pretender, but not a priest. The author wanted to interpret Jesus' role in terms of a priesthood and his death as a priestly sacrifice. This would put him closer in line with the Hasmoneans and further away from the Davidic ancestry. To shift Jesus from one dynasty to another required the work of a rhetorician or lawyer rather than a historian.

There was no way that the facts of Jesus' ancestry could be changed, but there were *legal* ways by which this could be presented. The result of such an argument as this is like the proof that a cat has ten tails. It really does not, and no amount of argument can change that fact, but legally it can be **proved** that a cat does have ten tails. The logic of this proof is as follows:

Premise: No cat has nine tails.
First step: one cat has one more tail than no cats.
Second step: one plus nine equals ten.
Conclusion: one cat has ten tails.

The same logic applied by Hebrews to Jesus is:

Premise 1: All prophecy is prophesied only for the days of the Messiah.
Premise 2: Jesus is the Messiah.
Step 1: These are the days of the Messiah.
Step 2: Gen 14 is a prophecy.
Step 3: Gen 14 applies to Jesus.
Step 4: Gen 14 tells of a priest named Melchizedek.
Step 5: In so doing he was speaking about Jesus.
Conclusion: Jesus was a priest, and his name was **Melchizedek**.

This is the logical proof given that Jesus was a priest named Melchizedek, but all that it shows is that there is no definite relationship between proof and truth. The manipulation invented by the author came because he had to support his position

[1] M. Dahood, *Psalms III* (Garden City: Doubleday, 1970), pp. 112-18.

rather defensively on the basis of Scripture. He used two enthronement Psalms, one which called its hero **messiah** and **son**, and the other that called him a **priest**. On the basis of these, he could offer an interpretation that was not traditional for Jesus, but one that was patterned somewhat according to the leadership of the Hasmoneans, who assumed both priestly and royal functions.[1] The necessity for all of this logic was to prove that Jesus' death functioned as an adequate offering for the Day of Atonement. This is the primary point of the book of Hebrews. The author was only incidentally interested in the Hasmoneans themselves and did not intend to picture Jesus as a Hasmonean. His goal was to show that Jesus was a priest, and the Hasmoneans happened to be priests and were therefore precedents.

Ps 110 and Ps 2 were quoted earlier to show that Jesus was to be a powerful king, since he was God's son (Heb 1:5, 13). Heb 5:6, however, was the first time the author justified Jesus' priesthood on the basis of Melchizedek's order. For this he needed Ps 110, which he used as his main text for Heb 1-12.

TEXT

Hebrews	First Testament
[7]who, in the days of his flesh, offered prayers and supplications	Ps 116:4 I called upon the name of Yehowah.
to the One who was able **to save him from death**,	Ps 116:8 Because you have **delivered** my soul **from death**, my eyes from **tears**, and my feet from stumbling.
with a loud **cry** and **tears**, and	Ps 22:25 He did not turn his face from **him**. When he **cried** to him, he **heard** him.
from his **anxiety**, was **heard.**	Ps 116:3 I had pain and **anxiety**.
[8]Although he was a Son, he learned obedience from the things he suffered; [9]and, having been ordained, he became a	Ps 116:15 Precious in the eyes of Yehowah is the **death** of his saints.
source of **salvation of the ages** for all those who obey him; [10]he	Isa 45:17 Israel is saved by Yehowah, a **salvation of the ages**.

[1] The "Davidic descent" of Jesus was not even "implied," as F. F. Bruce, "The Kerygma of Hebrews," *Interpretation* 23 (1969):5, holds. Just as the Hasmoneans functioned, even though they were not of the prescribed stock, so the author of Hebrews interpreted Jesus' role as if David and Zadok were not legitimate lines. Like the author of 1Macc, who did not even discuss the legitimacy of the sons of Zadok as over against the Hasmoneans, so the author of Hebrews did not even mention a two-messiah doctrine. Bruce, "Kerygma," p. 7, strains to show that, although not a Levite, Jesus fulfilled Israel's expectation as reflected in the Twelve Patriarchs, CDC, 1QS, 4Q Testimonia, Zechariah, and others.

was declared by God **a** high **priest according to the order of Melchizedek**.

Ps 110:4 You are **a priest** for **the age according to the order of Melchizedek.**

COMMENTARY

7 *In the days of his flesh.* This is a further affirmation on the part of the author that Jesus lived as a fully human being who had pains, anxieties, hungers, thirsts, worries and other difficulties that are normal for human beings. He was recognized as God only because, as the anointed king, he was God's legal agent. A legal agent is legally identical to the principal who sent him on his assignment. Modern scholars have problems with these affirmations of any human struggles Jesus might have had,[1] but the author of Hebrews took all of this humanity for granted. His overall emphasis, however, was not on Jesus' human achievements but on his legal status as God's son and his accomplishments in that office. Weiss correctly said, "The source value of Hebrews for the question of the historical Jesus is total zero."[2] Everything found in this document about the historical Jesus can also be found in other places. Weiss said further, however, that it was not just the "that" of the historical Jesus that interested the author of Hebrews. It was rather the "as."[3]

It is not fair to jump to the conclusion that the author had no interest in the historical Jesus. This document constitutes only one sermon. It was not a catechism of the author's entire beliefs. There are many details of the life of Jesus that are not mentioned in this sermon that the author may have known, believed, and taught—but not in this particular teaching. The only part of Jesus' life that was important for this sermon was his willingness to suffer and die and become an Atonement Day sacrifice for his people. It would not be fair to diagnose any one sermon and determine from that all of the preacher's knowledge and beliefs. The same would be true of an attorney's argument for any case. The sermon of Hebrews deserves the same respect.

Offered prayers and supplications. Following Brandenburger[4] *ays-ah-koos-tháys ah-póh tays yoo-lah-báy-ahs* (εἰσακουσθεὶς ἀπὸ τῆς εὐλαβεῖας) is rendered **from his anxiety, was heard.** RSV renders the same Greek "he was heard for his godly fear." Swetnam translated the phrase, **Having been heard because of his reverence**, relating this text to Ps 22:25.[5] Without noting the relationship of this passage to Ps 116 [114] and the balance of **from his anxiety** and **from death**, this would be a reasonable translation; but in NT Greek *ah-póh* (ἀπό) with the genitive

---

[1] J. Swetnam, "The Crux at Hebrews 5,7-8," *Biblica* 81 (2000):347-61.

[2] H. F. Weiss, *Der Brief an die Hebräer* (Göttingen:Vandenhoeck & Ruprecht, 1991), pp. 322-23, tr. from the German..

[3] Weiss, *Hebräer*, p. 324.

[4] E. Brandenburger, "Text und Vorlagen von Hebr. V 7-10," *NovT* 11 (1969):190-224. Earlier arguments relating Heb 5:7 to Ps 116 are F. Bleek, *Der Brief an die Hebräer* (Berlin: 1840), p. 73; B. Weiss, *Kritisch exegetisches Handbuch über den Brief an die Hebraer* (Göttingen: Vandenhoeck und Ruprecht, 1888), 136a; E. Riggenbach, *Der Brief an die Hebräer* (Leipzig: Deichert, 1922), p. 132A, 49; F Schröger, *Der Verfasser des Hebräerbriefs als Schriftausleger* (Regensburg: F. Prustet, 1968), pp. 120-22; and A. Ströbel, "Die Psalmengrundlage der Gethsemane-Parallel Hebr. 5:7 ff.," *ZNTW* 45 (1954):252-66.

[5] Swetnam, "Crux," p. 354.

more frequently means **from** than "because of," and the allusion to the Psalm seems likely. Brandenburger was not the first, but he has presented a cogent argument for interpreting this verse in relationship to the LXX translation of Ps 114 [MT 116], which clarifies an otherwise difficult passage.

The worshiper in Ps 116 was **offering** a prayer to God, and he expected that the Lord would listen attentively to the voice of his prayer (Ps 116:1). He was encompassed by the snares of death (Ps 116:3), the pangs of Sheol; he suffered **distress and anxiety** (Ps 116:3). The Lord responded and **delivered** his soul **from death**, his **eyes from tears**, his feet **from stumbling** (Ps 116:8). Against this background, Jesus was presented as one, who, in the days of his flesh, **offered prayers and supplications** to God. In an original thanksgiving hymn of the community, Heb 5:7 was composed as a praise to God as **the One who was able to save him** (i.e., Jesus) **from death**. God had listened attentively to the **loud cry and tears** of Jesus' **prayers** to God. God, then, **delivered him from death . . . and from his anxiety**, so that the expectation of Ps 114 was fulfilled.

Brandenburger's claim that this was originally composed as a confession to which the author of Hebrews had access is convincing. The confessional nature of this verse is suggested by the beginning attribution, **who offered**, which is similar to Philip 2:6, **Who, being in the form of God, did not consider . . .** and Col 1:15, **Who is an image of the invisible God**. This is one of the few allusions to the life of Jesus in Hebrews (see also Heb 7:14 and 13:12). These few are all used without clarifying historical events, but as bases for theological interpretations of doctrines.[1] The association of Heb 5:7 with Pss 116 and 22 makes even the allusion to Gethsemane less important. The creed might have been written simply on the basis of Jesus' **suffering**, without any familiarity with the Gethsemane story itself, but it seems more likely that this also was a part of the **suffering** intended in the creed.[2]

8-9 *He learned obedience from the things he suffered.* Heb 5:8 and 9 evidently constitute a second confession which associated Jesus with the **suffering** servant of Second Isaiah, as Brandenburger suggested. The liturgy confessed that Jesus **was a son**, i.e., a king, who by his **suffering** had **been made perfect**, and therefore became **a source of salvation of the ages for all those who obeyed him** (Spec 1:252). The author acknowledged that Jesus was fully human. He **suffered;** he **learned;** he was **obedient.** This meant that he had the ability to choose to be **obedient** or not **obedient.**

The **salvation of the ages** mentioned in Isa 45:17 was provided to Israel by her Savior, Yehowah. The Lord promised to do this **for the sake of my servant Jacob, and Israel my chosen** (Isa 45:4). The servant Jacob was a man of sorrows and acquainted with grief (Isa 53:3); **the Lord laid on him the iniquity of all Israel** (Isa 53:6). It was the Lord's **will to bruise him and put him to grief** (Isa 53:10), he bore the crime of Israel, making intercession for the transgressors (Isa 53:12). For the author of Second Isaiah, the servant constituted the generations of Jews that were cut off from Palestine and removed to, or born in, Babylon where the

---

[1] E. Grässer, "Der historische Jesus im Hebräerbrief," *ZNTW* 56 (1965): 63-91.

[2] Among those who put a good deal of emphasis on Gethsemane in the interpretation of Heb 5:7 are T. Lescow, "Jesus in Gethsemane bei Lukas und in Hebräerbrief," *ZNTW* 58 (1967):215-39; Ströbel, "Psalmengrundlage," pp. 252-66; H. Montefiore, *A Commentary on the Epistle to the Hebrews* (New York: Harper & Row, 1964), pp. 97-98; and C. J. Vaughan, *The Epistle to the Hebrews* (London: Macmillan Co., 1890), pp. 94-95.

members **suffered** to perform enough merits to balance the heavenly books so that the rest of Israel, the second and third generations in Babylon, might return to the Promised Land, **the land of life.** The Jews who died in Babylon before the return became the cause of **salvation of the ages** (Isa 45:17) for their posterity.[1] Grässer was correct in thinking that the **salvation of the ages** that which would arrive in **the age to come (**Heb 2:5**), the rest,** and the **unshakable kingdom** (Heb 12:28). That would be when the Land was restored as Israel's promised **inheritance** (Heb 9:15; 11:8). He thought, however, that all of these would take place only in heaven.[2]

Having been made perfect. **Perfect** is a legal or hypothetical term. Scientifically, nothing is ever really **perfect**, but hypothetically there might be a **perfect** circle or a perfectly straight line. It is not possible, however, for a person to be morally or physically **perfect**. The term that is translated **perfect** in English was not just a hypothetically scientific term. It was a legally qualitative term that was applied to human beings as something that had been realized by some.

If, for example, someone had been tried in court for a **crime** and was declared innocent, for that particular offense, the person was held to have been **perfectly** innocent or **perfectly** righteous from a legal point of view, even though he or she really committed the offense involved. As another example, legally, the high priest was called **perfect** or absolutely righteous and free from **crime** after he had offered a bull as a sacrifice to pay for his **crimes**. This liturgy secured his pardon and made him legally **perfect**. In a Christian context it usually refers to the ethics of the monastery.

For the author of Hebrews, however, Jesus, the Son and high **priest** who had **suffered** like the servant in Babylon, **became a source of salvation of the ages for all those who obey him**. Just as Isa 45:4 claimed that the Lord would call the servant Jacob *by name*, so the author of Hebrews said that God had declared Jesus to be **a high priest according to the order of Melchizedek** (Heb 5:10). The name he was called was **Melchizedek**. During the days of his flesh, Jesus was probably called "Jesus" or the Hebrew name "Joshua," but, according to the legal argument of the author, he was called **Melchizedek**. This was so, because the Scripture said so, and that which was in the Scripture was admissible in court, according to the author.

10*Having been declared by God a high priest.* The Messiah was a legal agent for **God.** He acted under orders. He had to be given authority before he was legally allowed to act in behalf of **God**, in the name of **God**, and at the responsibility of **God.** The principal always has to acknowledge the agent before the agent can act in behalf of the principal. Here **God declared** Jesus as **high priest**. That made Jesus' authority valid. The author of Hebrews believed that every word of Scripture was the word of God. Therefore since it said in Ps 110:4, **You are a priest for the age**, that meant that **God declared Jesus to be a priest.** Neither the Psalmist nor the author of Hebrews, however, thought **the age** meant "forever," as some scholars have interpreted. An **age** is a temporal concept, limited by the context.

---

1. The identification of the servant in Isaiah with the Jews who died in Babylon before an opportunity was available to return removes many difficulties prevalent in other theories. It allows for the servant both to be Jacob and to have a ministry for Israel. It is contingent on the identification of Palestine with the "land of life." For the views of other scholars and the defense of the land of life as Palestine, see Buchanan, *Consequences*, pp. 123-31.

2. E. Grässer, *An die Hebräer* (Zürich: Benziger Verlag, 1995) 1, p. 311.

Brandenburger correctly believed that there were two creeds in Heb 5:7-10. The first was Heb 5:7, and the second was Heb 5:8-10. It seems more likely that the second creed included only Heb 5:8 and 9. Heb 5:10 probably is an editorial comment made by the author of Hebrews, who put these two confessions together with the preceding FT quotations, and concluded by using another FT quotation from the main text of his message, Ps 110. He had already quoted this Ps 110 in Heb 1:3, 13, and 5:6, and suitably quoted it again in Heb 5:10, before moving doctrinally into the more specific discussion of this Psalm in Heb 7:10-10:39.

Rabbis were not agreed upon the true meaning of Ps 110:4. R. Simon ben Gamaliel related it to Zech 4:14. The two olive trees, then, were the Messiah and Aaron, and the most beloved was the Messiah, because R. Gamaliel understood that he was **the priest of the age, according to the order of Melchizedek** (Yalqut HaMakiri on Ps 110; see also AbothRN 34). R. Joshua ben Korcha claimed that Ps 110:4 applied both to Abraham and to Moses, since both were kings and priests (Yalqut HaMakiri Ps 110:4). R. Berekiah said in the name of R. Isaac that the four craftsmen of Zech 2:3 were Elijah, the Messiah, Melchizedek, and the military Messiah (CantR 2:13, 4).

The most important pre-Christian identification of **Melchizedek** with the Messiah was found on one of the scrolls of Cave 11 at Qumran. This document revealed the anticipation of a Jubilee at the end of days for the "captives" (*luh-ah-khah]-reét hah-yah-meém ahl she-boo-yeém*, לאחרית הימים על שׁבוים). The so-called "captives" were the sons of light and belonged to the lot of the heritage of Melchizedek (*mee-nah-khah-láht Mahl-kee séh-dehq; g]oh-ráhl Mahl-[kee]-séh-dehq*, מנחלת מלכיסדק; גורל מלכיסדק) Melchizedek was expected to come to proclaim release to those captives (*oo-keh-ráh luh-heh-máh de-róhr*, וקרא להמה דרור) and atonement for their crimes. All of this was expected to happen in the year of the last Jubilee (*buh-sheh-náht hah-yoh-váyl hah-ah-khah-[r]óhn*, בשׁנת היובל האחרון) which was the appointed time of favor for Melchizedek (*sheh-náht hah-raht-zóhn luh-Mahl-kee-séh-dehq*, שׁנת הרצון למלכיסדק).

At that time God would judge his people and chasten those who showed favoritism to the wicked ones that belonged to the lot of Belial. When Melchizedek arose he would punish them on the day of vindication in the last days. This would fulfill the prophecy of 2Isa, who foresaw one proclaiming good news announcing peace to Zion. The herald of good news was not only the figure Melchizedek, but he was also the one who had been anointed by the *spirit (hah meh-bah-sáyr hoo[' muh]sheé-ahkh hah-roó[ahkh],* המבשׂר הוא משׁיח הרוח). Being anointed by the spirit meant that he was the legitimate or legally approved messiah. David and Saul both received the spirit when they were anointed, and Jesus, after his meeting with John the Baptist, received the spirit, secretly like David and Saul, after which he spoke with authority.

The Jewish author of this document identified **Melchizedek** with the Messiah, who was a warrior king destined to vindicate the chosen people against their enemies and free them from "bondage" to foreign powers. This function of **Melchizedek** compares very well with the king described in Ps 110, the Hasmoneans, and also the **Son** and **high priest** described in Hebrews, who was said to belong to **the order of Melchizedek**.

Without calling him a **high priest** or **Melchizedek**, the rabbis said that when the son of David came, people would lay an iron beam on his neck, so heavy that he would bow from its weight. He would weep and cry,

> "Lord of the age, how great is my strength; how strong is my life's spirit; and how strong are my limbs? Am I not flesh and blood?. . . **My strength is as dry as a potsherd"** (Ps 22:16). Then God replied, "Ephraim, my just Messiah, long ago you have taken it upon yourself, since the six days of creation. Now let your pain be as my pain, for since the day, since Nebuchadnezzer the wicked one, came up and destroyed my house and burned my temple and led my children into exile among the nations of the world, I have not returned to my throne" (Pesikta Rabbati 36:162a).

Summary. Heb 5:1-10 is a unit introducing the reader to Jesus, the **high priest**. It is marked by an inclusion using the key word, **high priest** (Heb 5:1, 10). Since this is a preamble or introduction to the main thesis of the document, the author's summarizing sentences use words that are significant to that section. These are **perfect** (Heb 5:9; 7:28), **salvation** (Heb 5:9; 9:28), and **Melchizedek** (Heb 5-10; 7:1). Before beginning that dissertation, however, the author interrupted his argument with further exhortations.

This unit was well organized. It began by listing qualities of **high priests** in general, and it followed with a presentation of the qualifications that shows that Jesus fitted these qualifications very well. The author supported his claims by using two of his basic quotations from the Pss, followed by two small confessions of faith, which were probably well known in Christian circles of that time. He then concluded with a summarizing sentence that related all of this to his major text, Ps 110. At the end of the exhortation, he reintroduced this summary (Heb 5:6-10) before returning to the thesis introduced here.

TEXT

11Concerning which our message is extensive and exegetically difficult to report, since you have become dull of hearing. 12For, because of the time [that has elapsed], you ought to be teachers [yourselves], but [instead] you again need someone to teach you the simple principles of the beginning of God's words; you have become [infants who] need milk--not solid food. 13For everyone who enjoys milk is unskilled in the word of righteousness, for he is an infant, 14but solid food is for the adults--those who, because of their mature state have their perceptions trained to distinguish good and bad.[1]

COMMENTARY

11*Concerning which our message is extensive and exegetically difficult.* **Concerning which** (*peh-reé-hoo*, περὶ οὗ), like the *praws háwn* (πρὸς ὅν) of Heb 4:12, refers to that which was just said. Jesus was declared a **high priest** according to the order of **Melchizedek** (Heb 5:10). Even though the **message is extensive and difficult to interpret,** the author proceeded to interpret it extensively in Heb 7:1-10:8, but first he interrupted his thesis for an exhortation to the readers who seem to

---

[1] This is in agreement with J. A. L. Lee, "Hebrews 5:14 and ECIS: a History of Misunderstanding," *NovTest* 39 (1997):166. Lee found more than 6,000 usages of the word ἕξις which he studied to reach the conclusion he did to translate Heb 5:14 as it is given here (p. 152).

have become dull of hearing. Weiss noted that its being **exegetically difficult** did not mean it was Gnostic or mystical, as Käsemann suggested.[1] The Greek word for **exegetically difficult** (*doos-ehr-máyn-noo-taws*, δυσερμήνευτος) is used only here in the entire Greek translation of the Bible.

12*You ought to be teachers [yourselves]*. For many sects of Judaism and Christianity, there was a certain length of time allowed for moving from one degree of initiation to another. The first step was baptism, which probably required an initial training; then a more extensive and thorough training was required before full admission. There were unbaptized novices, baptized trainees, and full members. Grässer agreed that this educational progress was in the terms of baptism and catechism instruction. Mysteries and Gnostic salvation are not intended.[2]

1John 2:12-17 referred to these degrees as **children** (*tehk-neé-ah*, τεκνία or *pay-deé-ah*, παιδὶα), **young men** (*nee-ah-neés-koi*, νεανίσκοι), and fathers (*pah-téh-rehs*, πατέρες). The **young men** needed the most exhortation, so that they would hold fast to the severe training required to become **fathers**. Paul classified the new initiates as **infants** (*náy-pee-oi,* νήπιοι) (1Cor 3:1) and the advanced members as **perfect** (1Cor 2:6). The Essenes required one year of training before baptism and two more before becoming full members; the Community of the Rule required the same length of time.

An early sect of Christians in Egypt, whose instructions for training and receiving members has been preserved, normally trained prospective members for three years; then the catechumens were baptized and received at once into full membership. If a catechumen (*kah-teh-choo-méh-naws,* καταεχουμένος) was extremely zealous (*spoo-daí-aws*, σπουδαίος), however, he was allowed to advance more rapidly.[3] The Clementine Christians also baptized catechumens and received them into membership at once, but they required only a three-month training period. Hillel admitted members within 60 days. Shammai required 30 days for the first step and a year for the second.[4] Monastic training would have required more time than general membership.

The simple principles. These are the *stoi-kheé-ah* (στοιχεία) in Greek. They were the ABC's of education.[5] No time is indicated for the training required for the listeners of Hebrews, but, in the author's judgment, they were slow learners and had already taken a longer time than was customary. Had they been zealous, they could now have become **teachers**, which was probably the same status as that which First John called **fathers**. The ones Hebrews depreciatively called **infants** probably belonged to the same class as those 1John referred to affectionately as **children**, the difference being that the author of Hebrews addressed those who should no longer have been **infants**. The author used the word **food** metaphorically to refer to teaching or doctrine. Those who continued mulling over elementary subjects were not yet weaned, academically. Teachers were probably those who taught their inferiors in the basic laws of the Pentateuch, especially the Levitical commands.

---

[1] Weiss, *Hebräer*, p. 329.
[2] Grässer, *An die Hebräer* 1, p. 328.
[3] Buchanan, *Consequences,* p. 289
[4] Buchanan, *Consequences*, pp. 285-93.
[5] G. Delling, "στοιχεία," *ThWNT* 7, pp. 670-82.

[13]*Everyone who enjoys milk.* The word rendered **unskilled** (*áh-pay-raws,* ἄπειρος) describes a person who lacks experience, is untried, or ignorant (see LXX Zech 11:15; Wis 13:18). The idiom comes from the feeding process of people from infancy to adulthood. As infants they begin with only their mother's **milk**. The Shepherd of Hermas listed among the most important deeds a Christian should always do, "words of righteousness" (*huh-ráy-mah-tah dee-kai-aw-soó-nays* ῥήματα δικαιοσύνης) (Mand 8:9) Hebrews considered those not weaned who did not even know what **the word of righteousness** (*láw-gaws dik-ai-aw-seé-nays,* λόγος δικαιοσύνης) was. They were unlearned, **unskilled**, in this area. Polycarp told the Philippians,

> Therefore I encourage all of you to obey the word of righteousness and to practice all endurance which you also saw before your eyes, not only the blessed Ignatius, Zosimus, and Rufus, but also in others from your own group, as well as in Paul himself and the rest of the apostles (To the Philippians 9:1).

[14]*Solid food is for the adults.* The term here rendered **adult** is often translated "perfect." It held a wide range of meanings, one of which described a person who was chronologically mature, no longer a minor, an adult,[1] or a married person (*téh-lay-oi hoi geh-gah-meh-káw-tehs,* τέλειοι ὁι γεγαμεκάτης).[2] That same word also described a full member of a sect in good standing. Only those who walked perfectly (*oo-luh-hít-hah-láyk leh-phah-neém tah-meém,* ולהתהלך לפנים תמים) were admitted into the sect of the rule (1QS 1:8). They were the ones who were fully trained. Although Paul spoke simply to the Corinthians, he said that he imparted wisdom to the **perfect** (*téh-lay-ois,* τέλειοις) (1Cor 2:6). Paul compared the knowledge that was partial (*ehk méh-roos,* ἐκ μέρους) with that which was **perfect** (*téh-lay-awn,* τέλειον) in the same way that he compared being an infant with being a grown man (*ah-náyr,* ἀνήρ) (1Cor 13:10-11). He encouraged the Corinthians not to be **children** (*pai-deé-ah,* παιδία) in their thinking but to be **adults** (*téh-lay-oi,* τέλειοι) (1Cor 14:20). Those who had reached the stage of **perfect** manhood (*áhn-drah-téh-lay-awn,* ἀνδρατέλειον), religiously, were not **infants** who could be carried about with every wind of doctrine (Eph 4:13-14).

Paul considered it his task to make the word of God fully known, allowing even the Gentiles to know **the riches of the glory of this mystery**, **teaching every man in all wisdom** so that every man might be **perfect** in Christ (Col 1:25-28). Paul prayed that the Colossians might stand **perfect** and fully assured in all the will of God (Col 4:12). The concept of being grownup in relationship to physical **age** and stature was used metaphorically to describe religious growth. The same was true of the expression "to discern good and bad." In NT times, "knowing good and evil" meant, first of all, having sexual intercourse, which usually came with **adult**hood, marriage, and other mature responsibilities. Thus when Adam and Eve ate of the tree of the knowledge of **good and evil**, Eve became pregnant and Adam worked for a living.[3]

---

[1] Plato *Leges* 929c; Xenophon *Institutio Cyri* I.2.4, 12, 14; *Oxyrhynchus Papyrus* 485.30.

[2] Pausanias *Grammaticus*, Fragment 306.

[3] Buchanan, "The Old Testament Meaning of the Knowledge of Good and Evil," *JBL* 75 (1956):114-120; *Consequences*, pp. 174-76.

When the children of Israel came to Kadesh-barnea, the Lord commanded them to take the land (Deut 1-21). When they balked, the Lord swore, "**Not one of these men of this evil generation shall see the good land which I swore to give to your fathers**, . . ." (Deut 1:34-35). The promise to the next generation was as follows:

> **Moreover your little ones** (*táhp-khehm*, טפכם) who you said would become a prey, and your sons (*béh-nay-khehm*, בניכם) who this day have no knowledge of **good and evil** (*tóhv wuh-ráh*, טוב ורע), shall go in there, and to them I will give it, and they shall possess it (Deut 1:39).

The same men who received the curse that Deuteronomy placed on them as men who knew **good and evil** were also referred to as those who were **from twenty years old and upward** Num 14:29-30 . This is consistent with the description of the young man by the Rule of the Community (1QS 1.10-11): "He is fully twenty years of age when he knows **good and evil**." The **little one** was a child who had not passed his Bar Mitzwa--under 13 years of age; the **son** was a Bar Mitzwa--between 13 and 20 years of age; and the "man who knew **good and evil"** was 20 years of age or more.[1] Like the person who was **perfect**, he was old enough to marry, pay taxes, provide sacrifices for the temple, bear arms, and in other ways assume **adult** responsibilities. Since the one who had had sexual intercourse was expected to be married and an **adult**, the term "knowing good and evil" came to be an expression applied to **adults** or the age of adulthood.

The author of Hebrews was using these terms of human development metaphorically to describe the listeners' development in faith. Knowing **good and evil** meant they were mentally **adults** or having **their perceptions** adequately **trained**.

The Day of Atonement. Heb 3 and 4 were dedicated to preparing the audience for the Day of Atonement. That message was both assuring and demanding. Since atonement requires both a sacrifice to pay for crimes and reconciliation among the parties to the contract, the sacrifice demand was fulfilled through Jesus. The author emphasized the importance of being innocent of any crime and faithful so that all parties to the contract would be reconciled to one another, making the Day of Atonement effective. Heb 5 continued the Day of Atonement theme, elaborating on the qualifications of Jesus as the perfect high priest who had offered the perfect sacrifice. The author also scolded the audience for not being actually free from crime as the Day of Atonement demanded.

---

[1] Buchanan, *Consequences,* pp. 181-82.

CHAPTER SIX

TEXT

6:1 Therefore, leaving the word of the beginning [teachings] of Christ, let us carry on to perfection, not laying again a foundation of repentance from dead works, faith in God, 2 teaching of ablutions, laying on of hands, resurrection of [the] dead ones, and judgment of [the] age 3 --and we will do this if God is willing.

Hebrews	First Testament
4 For after they **have fallen** by the wayside	Num 14:32 Your dead bodies **will fall** in this wilderness.
	Josh 23:14 There **has** not **fallen** one word of all the **good words** which Yehowah your God has spoken about you. All things have come to you.
it is impossible to renew again for repentance those who have once been **enlightened**,	Neh 9:12 You provided a pillar of cloud during the day and a pillar of fire by night to **enlighten** the way in which they would go (also Neh 9:19).
	Neh 9:20 You gave your good **spirit** to **enlighten** them.
tasted the **heavenly** gift,	Neh 9:15 You gave them bread from **heaven**.
	Exod 16:4 Look! I am raining for you bread from **heaven.**
	Ps 78:24 He rained upon them manna to eat and he gave them bread of **heaven**.
become sharers of the **Holy Spirit,** 5 and	Isa 63:11 Where is he who brought up from the sea the shepherd of his flock? Where is he who put in his midst his **holy spirit**?
	Neh 9:20 You gave your good **spirit** to enlighten them.
tasted **the good word of God** and the miracles of the coming age, 6 [thereby] crucifying and making a public example	Josh 21:43 **good word** which **Yehowah** has spoken to the house of Israel, everything has come [to pass].

of the Son of God for themselves.

Jer 29:10 I will visit you, and I will confirm upon you my **good words** to return you to this place.

COMMENTARY

6:1 *Let us carry on to perfection.* Heb 6 is a continuation of Heb 5. The entire discussion here is dealing with growth in instruction. That which is called **perfection** is a knowledge of the entire learning program. Those who are **perfect** are those who have been graduated. They have become **enlightened.** They have finished the course. They have **tasted the heavenly gift,** and become **sharers of the Holy Spirit,** and **tasted the good word of God.** For those who are in some stage of a learning program, this is encouragement to continue and finish the course.

The beginning [teachings] of Christ can be understood either as Christ's initial teachings (subjective genitive), or the beginning teachings *about* Christ (objective genitive). In favor of the subjective genitive is the reference to the salvation which had its beginning when it was spoken through the Lord (Heb 2:3). The things which Christ originally taught were undoubtedly important to early Christians,[1] and they continued to be basic. These were the chreias and parables reported in the gospels. They were first taught to the apostles, and the apostles probably kept them in written lists to share with others as they proclaimed the gospel to others.[2] The context allows for the possibility that the earliest Christian teachings to which catechumens were exposed might be either the teachings of Jesus or **the beginning teachings about Christ.**[3]

Let us carry on (*pheh-róh-meh-tha,* φερώμεθα) literally means, "let us be **carried**" or "let us **carry** ourselves" along. **Dead works** referred to the life Christians had lived before they were baptized into the community. **Dead** is a legal term, as it is used here. It describes those people who were outside of the contract, living as other pagans. They were physically alive, but so far as Christianity is concerned they were legally dead. **Dead works** were those performed by people who were legally dead. If they were legally **dead,** their good **works** were not accredited to them in the treasury of merits. When a person became one of the parties to the contract, he or she passed from death to **life,** repented of the **works** he or she did as a pagan, and was baptized to cleanse him or her from this defilement. Once a party

---

[1] For an impressive defense of "*tou Christou*" understood as a subjective genitive, see J. C. Adams, "Exegesis of Hebrews 6:1 f.," *NTS* 13 (1966-67):378-85.

[2] See further in Buchanan, *Jesus: the King and his Kingdom* (Macon: Mercer U. Press, 1984).

[3] H. Attridge, *The Epistle to the Hebrews* (Philadelphia: Fortress Press, 1989), p. 164, argued that Hebrews "develops and deepens affirmations that they [the addressees] already make." That, according to Attridge was a "high christology." A high christology is one that affirms Jesus is God, whereas a "low Christology" holds that he was human. Once the legal significance of the messianic role is understood these are both unnecessary options. A messiah was one who either was or was pretending to be a king. A king was understood to be God's son and apostle or legal agent. A legal agent is legally identical to the principal who sent him. For a king the principal was understood to be God. Therefore a king is legally God and the affirmation is one of high christology, but the king is also human and he is not physically identical to God. Therefore this reality supports the low christology view. Kings like David and Solomon were messiahs, kings, apostles of God, legally identical to God, and also very human. Jesus fit these same categories, and the addressees probably knew that.

to the contract, the new initiate was alive and presumably performed no more **dead works**. The **foundation of dead works** was the place where Christians began. Then they left that to take the first step of **faith in God.**

After the fall of Jerusalem, Ezra reasoned that Israel's punishment must have come because of Adam's crime which every person who married repeated. Only those who practiced abstinence would shine like the stars. Others had faces blacker than darkness (4Ezra 7:125). "For how does it profit us if we are promised an immortal time (*immortale tempus*) since we really have done **dead works"** (*mortalia opera*).[1] All those who married, like Adam and Eve, were expelled from the contract, which is the same as the garden of Eden, where they could eat of the tree of **life** (4Ezra). Once expelled, they were **dead**, and all **the works** that they did were **dead works**. Terms like **dead** and "alive" were used metaphorically not only by the rigid, monastic orders of Christianity, but by other Christians as well. The frequency with which the author of Hebrews used terms that were common to communal sects tends to relate him in some way to such a group. **Faith in God**, of course, was a basic belief for all Jews and Christians. The author insisted that without faith it is impossible to please God (Heb 11:6).

2 *Teaching ablutions, laying on of hands*. After they had **faith in God** the next step in admission was to learn all of the rules about **ablutions** and **laying on of hands**. First came the teachings and then the acts of **baptism** and the ceremony of having the elders of the church **lay** their **hands on** the baptized candidates to admit them to membership of the church. **Ablutions**, however, involved more than just the one ceremony of **baptism.** Jewish Christians continued to practice all of the **ablutions** that had been customary for Jews (Clementine Homilies 11:33). Most modern commentators, however, have objected to any suggestion that teaching of ablutions (*bap-tis-móhn did-ah-kháys*, βαπτισμῶν διδακῆς) could possibly refer to the levitical **ablutions** practiced by Jews. Stuart asked,

> But what has the apostle to do here with Jewish ceremonial rites, as the first elements of *Christian doctrine?*

His answer is, "Plainly nothing; so that this exegesis cannot be admitted."[2] Turner explained just as defensively,

> I can see no probability that the author intended any union of such merely external washings with fundamental principles of Christianity.[3]

Montefiore also refused to entertain the possibility that this meant FT **ablutions,** but, observing the plural, deduced that "it must refer to second baptisms for those first baptized by John (Acts 19:5-6)."[4] Grässer held that the notion that Christians

---

[1] Buchanan, *The Consequences of the Covenant* (Leiden: E. J. Brill, 1970), pp. 110-149.
[2] M. Stuart, *Commentary on the Epistle to the Hebrews* (Andover: Warren F. Draper, 1828), p. 139.
[3] S. H. Turner, *The Epistle to the Hebrews in Greek and English* (New York: Stanford and Swords, 1852), p. 71.
[4] H. Montefiore, *A Commentary on the Epistle to the Hebrews* (New York: Harper & Row, 1964), p. 106.

continued to practice ablutions after baptism was "the least likely of all explanations."[1]

Michel left the question unanswered,[2] but Moffatt thought that **ablutions** probably continued among some groups of Christians, even though others objected to them.[3] Moffatt was right on this score. Justin's attack on these practices would have been unnecessary if they had not existed (Apol 1:62) Members of the Clementine Christian sect who had already been **baptized**, were still obligated to keep other purity rules, eating with only those who had been **baptized,** eating only food approved by dietary laws, washing after intercourse, refraining from intercourse during a woman's menstrual period, and, for women, observing the law of purification.[4] To be sure, there was only one baptism for admission into the community, but among Jewish Christians, at least, continual observance of levitical laws was basic to their code of ethics (ClemHom 11:33).

Rather than trying to explain why the author meant something different from that which he said, it is more reasonable to admit that the author of Hebrews and his original readers belonged to a Jewish Christian group where **ablutions** were some of the elementary teachings of the church. That is particularly true of a monastery where every monk bathed before entering the dining room. (War 2:129).

Laying on of hands was a practice sometimes associated with the reception of the Holy Spirit for new initiates (Acts 8:17-19). The doctrine of the **resurrection of [the] dead ones** was prominent in Judaism as early as Maccabean times. It seemed a reasonable extension of Deuteronomic justice. Pious Jews, who were willing to fight and die so that the nation might live and so that other Jews would receive the promise to live on the Promised Land, believed that those who died in the faith would be raised, after the land was freed from foreigners, and allowed to receive their reward of living on the same land under the conditions for which they fought and died. This was not a belief that they would never again cease breathing and become corpses, but that they could finish out their life term of 70 years on the only land where **life** was possible--Palestine.

After the death of Christ, early Christians believed that Jesus had himself been raised, taken into heaven, and that he would return to the Promised Land. At that time, the ones who had "died in Christ" (i.e., as Christians) would be raised to be with him on the Promised Land. When he had failed to return after many years, several varying interpretations were given. One of these was reported by Eusebius (HE 10.4,11-12), who understood Constantine's victory and the establishment of Christianity as the religion of the state, as the **resurrection of the dead**. In praise to Jesus, he said,

> The only unique One, the all-good Son of the all-good Father, for whom the Father saved us, when we were not only sick or afflicted by terrible sores and wounds already decayed, but we were also lying among the dead; . . . [this he did when we] were not just half dead (*hay-mee-thnáy-tahs*, ἡμιθῆτας), but even in tombs and graves,

---

[1] E. Grässer, *An die Hebräer* (Zürich: Benziger Verlag, 1990) 1, p. 342.

[2] O. Michel, *Der Brief an die Hebräer* (Göttingen: Vandenhoeck and Ruprecht, 1957), pp. 145-46.

[3] J. Moffatt, *A Critical and Exegetical Commentary on the Epistle to the Hebrews* (Edinburgh: T. & T. Clark, 1924), p. 75.

[4] Hom. 8:28, 30, 32; Recog. 1:19, 54; 2:72; 6:11; 7:29.

> completely loathsome and stinking, raising [us] up (*ah-nah-lah-bóhn*, ἀναλαβών); as of old, so also now.[1]

Judgment of [the] age (*kréem-ah-taws aye-oh-neé-oo*, κρίματος αἰώνίου) is a court term. To **judge** means to divide, separate, or decide. The **judge** separates the good from the evil, the innocent from the guilty; he determines which of the accused deserve release and which deserve punishment. In Jewish sabbatical eschatology, parties to the contract believed that God would hold a court session in which the gentiles and Israel might offer their complaints against each other. At that time, which would be the end of the evil **age** when the gentiles ruled, Israel would be vindicated and released, freed from guilt as at Jubilee. From that time on, Israel would rule. That would be the **age** to come, the new **age** (Hom 2:2).

The judgment of the age was the turning point in Israel's history. It was a time when the evil **age** in which they were then living was to be judged and decided whether or not it would be continued. Israel, of course, hoped that it would not. It would be finished so that the **age** to come would soon come. The division would be made between the innocent believers and the guilty heathen. Early Jews and Christians were able to face oppression and death for their behavior without denying their traditional heritage because they were confident that this **judgment** would take place, and that it would be favorable for God's chosen people.

Jesus promised that, **at the end of the age** (Matt 24:3), the Son of man would enter into his glory, which would be his position as king over the Promised Land. Then all nations would be gathered before him to learn how he would treat them. Those who helped him or any of his supporters to bring him into this position of power would inherit the kingdom, which meant entering into **life of the age** (Matt 25:31-46). Those who resisted him or failed to help him went away into punishment **of the age** (Matt 25:31-46) or were cast into outer darkness (Matt 25:14-30).

Uncooperative cities, like Chorazin and Bethsaida, would receive worse punishment than Tyre and Sidon, the pagan cities, or Sodom, which God destroyed (Matt 11:20-24). Belief in this doctrine was elementary to the Christians to whom the author of Hebrews wrote.

3 *We will do this if God is willing*. That **which we will do if God is willing is to carry on to perfection.** That which we will **not** do is to **lay again a foundation of repentance from dead works.** The fear of resisting God was offset, then as today, by stating what would happen in the future **if God is willing.** The Hebrew *eém yeér-tsay áh-doh-náy* (אם ירצה אדני), the Arabic *eén-sha áhl-lah,* the Latin *deo volente* (d.v.), and the German *Gott willig* are all frequent in Jewish, Moslem, and Christian usage. James cautioned his readers against saying,

> Today or tomorrow we will go into such and such a town and spend a year there and trade and get gain, since no one knows about tomorrow (James 4:13-14).

Instead, James thought, Christians ought to say, **If the Lord wills, we shall live and we shall do this or that** (James 4:15). To do otherwise would be arrogant (James 4:16). Paul told the Corinthians, **For I hope to remain with you some time, if the**

---

[1] Buchanan, *Consequences*, pp. 321-26.

Lord permits (1Cor 16:7). That which they would do seems to be to advance in Christian maturity as suggested in Heb 6:1.

TECHNICAL DETAILS

This unit has two emphases:

1) growth from earliest training to completion of the course, and
2) a comparison of the situation of the listeners to the Israelites in the wilderness.

The author related this exhortation to the wilderness generation by using certain words that occurred in wilderness passages.[1] He thought the **age of Moses** (*oh-láhm móh-sheh,* עולם מושה) was a type for the **age** in which he and his listeners lived.

COMMENTARY

[4]*Those who have once been enlightened.* **Those who had been enlightened** were those who had achieved **perfection.** They had completed their course of instruction. Light was usually related to knowledge and darkness to ignorance (Ps 19:8; 119:130; Sir 45:17; 1QS 4:2; 1QH 4:5-6).

Once (*háh-pahx,* ἅπαξ) was an important word to the author—one that he used more than **once**. The high priest entered the holy of holies **once** a year (Heb 9:7); Jesus offered himself as a sacrifice **once** (Heb 9:26, 28); men die but **once** (Heb 9:27), if worshipers had **once** been cleansed, they would no longer have a consciousness of crime (Heb 10:2). The author quoted the FT promise that the Lord would shake heaven and earth **once** more (Heb 12:26); this "**once** more" indicated to the author the removal of the things that could be shaken so that the things that could not be shaken might remain (Heb 12:27). This was not only true of Hebrews, however. First Peter said Christ died for our crimes **once** (1Pet 3:18), and Jude told his readers about the faith which was **once** delivered to the saints (Jude 3), and he reminded them that they had **once** been informed (Jude 5). The author of Hebrews also used a more emphatic word for **once** (*eh-pháh-pahx,* ἐφάπαξ) several times (Heb 7:27; 9:12; 10:10 see also 1Cor 15:6).

Justin (Apol 1:61, 12-13; Dial 122:5; 123:2) identified **enlightenment** with baptism. **Enlightenment** was probably the name given to all of the training and ceremonies necessary for conversion, including baptism. In this process pagans were "changed from darkness into **light**" (Odes Solomon 11:19), they were called from "darkness into **light**" and from "death into **life**" (JosAS 8:10). They had become **sharers of the Holy Spirit** (Heb 6:4), which means that they had become legal members of the Christian corporation.

Like most legal ceremonies, baptism was intended to provide a legal second birth, imitating in some way the first physical birth. A child is born from a mother's womb, after the water bag has broken, and enters into life together with the water. Then it draws breath and begins its new life. In an emulating pattern a person who

---

[1] So also D. Mathewson, "Reading Heb 6:4-6 in Light of the Old Testament," *Westminister Theological Journal* 61 (1999):209-25.

was once a pagan, removes all of his or her clothing, and with the physical clothing, leaves all of his or her legal clothing on the bank of a river. The legal clothing includes all debts, obligations, values, offices, and human relationships. That person is then submerged into the water and comes up on the other side of the river as a different person, legally, belonging to a different family corporation, to begin a new and different kind of life. Having declared bankruptcy on all that was before that is afterwards legally dead, there is a new breath and a new life. The newly baptized person has legally died to the past. Since the baptism is for the purpose of joining the Christian body, then the legal death is with Christ, and the legal resurrection is with Christ into the corporation of Christ. This is what Paul meant when he said,

> We who have been baptized into Christ Jesus have been baptized into his death, so that just as Christ was raised from the dead through the glory of the Father, so also we might walk in newness of life. For if we have been united in the likeness of his death, also we will be together in the resurrection. We know this that our old being has been crucified with him in order that the body of crime might be annulled (Rom 6:3-6).

The bodies involved here are legal bodies—corporations--and the lives and deaths are legal lives and deaths. All of this was basic to the argument of the author of Hebrews that this could happen only **once.** Since Christ was crucified only **once,** we could be crucified with him only **once**. We could be buried with him only **once** and be raised with him to newness of life only **once**. This could not happen a second time. The emphasis is for the readers who had **once been enlightened**.[1] This normally came together with baptism (Heb 6:4).

Enlightenment is a term frequently used for instruction. Thus the teachers are **those who make shine** (*mahs-kee-leém,* משׂכילים) (Dan 12:3), and the parties to the contract were called "children of light" (*beh-nay óhr*, בני אור) in some of the Dead Sea scrolls (1QM and 1QS). Justin Martyr said baptism is called illumination because those who learn these things are illuminated in their minds (Apol 1:61; see also 1:65 and Dial 122). The author encouraged the readers to remember the earlier days just after they had become **enlightened** (*phoh-tis-théhn-tahs*, φωτισθέντας). Enlightenment probably meant the intelligence that came from catechism required for baptism. Therefore Justin identified the two, and the Syriac text of Heb 6:4 read **those who have once descended for** baptism (*hah-nóhn dákh-dah zeh-báhn luh-mah-moo-deé-tah nee-kháh-too,* הנון דחדא זבן למעמודיתא נחתו) for **those who have once been enlightened**.

The ones who had completed preparation, had been baptized, and had become Christians were the ones who had been **enlightened.** These two items were so closely associated that anyone who had been baptized, by implication, was also **enlightened.** This did not mean that they were generally brilliant, had high IQ's, and many academic degrees. It meant that they had learned the suitable amount of doctrine for membership. Philo referred to doctrinal wisdom as "heavenly food" (*oo-ráhn-ee-awn troh-pháyn*, οὐράνιον τροφήν) (On Creation 56:158). It was not food that would be consumed only in heaven.

Like Philo, the author of Hebrews related dogmatic **enlightenment** to heavenly food, which the wise tasted. This was **the heavenly gift**. The doctrinal

[1] See A. Winter, *APAX EPHAPAX im Hebräerbrief* (Rome, 1960).

heavenly gift that the wise tasted might have been the common meal, sometimes called the holy meal (*sanctus*) (Recog 3:67) to which sectarians were admitted after their final step of initiation.[1] Only those who had been trained adequately were allowed to eat the food at the common table in the monastery. For monks, every meal was holy, eaten only by those who were ritually clean. All holy food served in the monastery was carefully prepared and passed all of the dietary rules. Their dining hall was treated like a temple (War 2:129).

Attridge said the heavenly gift was a "general image for the gracious bestowal of salvation."[2] Hughes said it was "unlikely that anything physical" was meant by **tasting heavenly food.** It would not have referred to anything like the eucharist, he thought. It was rather an expression that meant receiving God's grace.[3] If the heavenly food that was tasted was doctrinal, then the doctrinal teaching was described as the heavenly gift metaphorically, based on food that was considered holy, as were also all of the things associated with the meal or the Eucharist. Attridge also did not think **heavenly Jerusalem** referred to anything geographical. It was the opposite of anything "this worldly."[4] In both cases he overlooked the full significance of the expressions. The expression, **tasting heavenly food,** surely involved receiving God's grace, but this does not remove the food element, just as the expression, **heavenly Jerusalem,** is not free from geographical significance. **Heavenly food** was something Christians could receive while they were on earth. The word **heavenly** was not a term that was limited in space to the sky.

The first step after final initiation was the privilege of participating in the common meal. Early monks bathed and changed clothes before entering into the dining hall where the holy meal was served only to those who were fully initiated, undefiled members. No one else was admitted to the dining hall. It was there that they received God's grace and food. The Eucharist was a continuation of that reception. The elements of unleavened bread and fruit of the vine were the first and last elements of the Passover, and continued to be used as a symbol of the entire meal.

Also associated with membership initiation was the reception of the Holy Spirit, which occurred either at baptism or later, perhaps when new members had the **hands** of full members **laid upon** their heads. At that time they became **sharers of the Holy Spirit**. The **spirit** was closely associated with authority. When David and Saul received the **spirit** they became kings. When the **spirit** came upon various ones of the judges, they became national or tribal leaders. After Apollos had been baptized, Paul **laid** his **hands** upon him and he received the **Holy Spirit** (Acts 19:1-6). This was evidently the final step by which a person was authorized to be called a Christian. After that the new member shared whatever was authorized with membership. This may have been the holy meal, but it may have been more. In some groups, like the Essenes and the sect governed by the Rule of the Community (1QS), members also shared all material possessions with one another (Acts 4:32-37).

---

[1] Buchanan, *Consequences*, pp. 285-92; C. J. Spicq, *L'Epitre aux Hebreux* (Paris: J. Gabalda, 1953) II, p. 150. R. Williamson, *Philo and the Epistle to the Hebrews* (Leiden: E. J. Brill, 1970) summarized the differing views of many scholars on the meaning of "heavenly gift."

[2] H. Attridge, *Hebrews,* p. 170.

[3] P. E. Hughes, *Commentary on the Epistle to the Hebrews* (Grand Rapids: Eerdmans Publishing Co., c1977), p. 209.

[4] Hughes, *Commentary*, 546.

[5]*Tasted the good word of God and the miracles of the coming age.* When dealing with **the heavenly gift** (Heb 6:4), that which was **tasted** was probably the communal meal, but **tasted** is used metaphorically in Heb 6:5 to mean "sampled" or "had been introduced to," as Josephus used the term in reference to those who had once **tasted** (*hah-pax goo-sah-méh-noos,* ἅπαξ γευσμένος) (War 2:158) the Essene philosophy (see also Ps 34:8; 119:103; Job 34:3; 1Pet 2:3; Matt 16:28). **The good word of God** (*kah-láwn . . .theh-oó huh-ráy-mah,* καλὸν . . . θεοῦ ῥῆμα) refers to God's favorable promise, the contract that God had made with his chosen people. There are some indications in this sermon that some of the hearers were not fully trained and perfected in their monastic training. They were those who had **tasted the good word of God**, but they may not have swallowed the entire program. They still had to go on to perfection.

In the FT this sometimes refers to the promise that God would give the Israelites the land of Canaan. After **the Lord had given** the Hebrews **rest on every side**, the claim was made that **not one word fell of all the good words** (*hah-deh-vahr-eém hah-tohv-eém,* הדברים הטובים) **which the Yehowah your God has spoken** (Josh 23:15). **Of every good word which Yehowah has spoken to the house of Israel everything has come** [to pass] (Josh 21:42-43). Jeremiah picked up this terminology from the book of Joshua and the tradition that spoke of God's promises of the land in terms of God's **good word**. Jeremiah said that after the Jews had served their 70-year sentence in Babylon, the Lord would fulfill his **good words** (*deh-vah-reé hah-tóhv,* דברי הטוב) to return them to Judah (Jer 29:10, also 33:14). The expression **good word** seems to have been a synonym for "promise."

The author of Hebrews probably had the same **good word** in mind, which the readers had only **tasted**. They were just on the verge of receiving the promised heritage. If they would only hold out and not make the same mistakes that the exodus generation had made, they might receive it in full. The sacrifice and ascension of Jesus constituted just a foretaste that the promise would soon be fulfilled. Having **tasted the good word of God** (Heb 6:4), they anticipated becoming **heirs of the coming age** (Heb 9:15) who were about to **inherit salvation** (Heb 1:14).

When Second Isaiah announced the **good news** that the Jews in Babylon would be released to return to Zion, he told of **the miracles** that would be performed to enable every faithful Jew to return. These would be the kind of **miracles** performed in the wilderness to sustain the Israelites until they entered their Promised Land (Isa 35:5-10; 43:15-20; 44:3-4; 49:1-13; *et passim*). They were a foretaste of the good things to come. Since **miracles** accompanied the Israelites between Egypt and the entrance into the Promised Land, and since they were promised to the Jews between Babylon and the Promised Land, Jews of NT times assumed that miracles would accompany the new entrance into the Promised Land. **The coming *age*** *(méhl-awn-taws ai-óh-naws,* μέλλοντος αἰῶνος) was the same as **the habitation to come** (Heb 2:5). This was the time when **the good word of God** would be received in full. The **miracles** (*doo-náh-mays,* δυνάμεις) had been performed in the midst of the readers. They had **tasted** them, but like **the good word of God**, the **age** to come had not fully come.

[6]*After they have fallen by the wayside.* Because the author of Hebrews was very demanding and did not tolerate anything that was not exactly right, he frequently used the prefix *para* (παρα) to describe that which was "off the side." Those who did not follow the straight and narrow path **fell off the side** (*pah-rah-pehs-áwn-taws,* παραπεσόντας) of the true path (Heb 6:6). Mathewson was probably correct in

noticing that these verses have as their scriptural background the wilderness experience (Num 13-14; Ps 95; Deut 1).[1] Those who demonstrated in ways that were not publicly approved demonstrated off the path (*pah-rah-dayg-mah-teéd-zahn-tehs,* παραδειγματίζοντες) (Heb 6:6). Those who were improperly bitter were rebels (*pah-rah-peek-raín-awn-tehs*, παραπικραίνοντες) (Heb 3:8, 15). Those who did not follow the main stream flowed alongside (*pah-rah-roón-taws*, παραροῦντος) (Heb 12:12).

Although the proximity of the promise which the author gave was very encouraging, it was conditional. Those who **had fallen by the wayside**, after they had been initiated into the community and received its benefits, were then guilty and could not be pardoned. It was **impossible** (Heb 6:6**) to renew again for repentance.** This is consistent with the author's doctrine of **repentance** and atonement. In addition to "foreclosures" and consequent "releases" on Sabbath and Jubilee years, Israel's doctrine of forgiveness and reconciliation with God was related to the Day of Atonement. On that day an Israelite could be forgiven his crimes against God, but only on the following conditions:

a) that he repent of his crimes:
b) that he be reconciled with his fellow Israelite against whom he had committed crimes; and
c) that he bring the proper crime and guilt offerings to the altar on the Day of Atonement to pay for his crimes against God.

These were the required methods by which cases could be settled out of court. All of these things had to have taken place before the **judgment.** The Day of Atonement was the very last day that was possible on that particular year. Against this doctrine, the instruction of Jesus makes sense:

> So if you are offering your gift at the altar, and there remember that your brother has something against you, leave your gift there before the altar and go; first be reconciled to your brother, and then come and offer your gift (Matt 5:23-24).

The **gift** would have had no atoning effect unless the party to the contract was first **reconciled to his brother.** The sacrifice was required, like most governmental fines, to pay God and the government for the administration of justice, but it was no substitute for satisfying the offended party. That had to happen before the sacrifice. Paul understood that Jesus was the **crime** offering made for Israel's **crimes** on the Day of Atonement. Like Micah, Paul knew that God could not be appeased with **thousands of rams, with ten thousands of rivers of oil** (Micah 6:7). Since Israel could not provide a gift large enough to meet the required conditions, God took the initiative: he it was who through Christ

> reconciled us to himself and gave us the ministry (*dee-ah-kaw-neé-ah*, διακονία) of reconciliation; that is, God was in Christ [i.e. in the body of Christ, the church], reconciling the world to himself, not counting their trespasses against them, and entrusting to us the reckoning (*láw-gaws*, λόγος) of reconciliation (2Cor 5:18-19).

[1] Mathewson, "Reading Heb 6:4-6," pp. 209-225.

The crime offering that God required, according to Paul, was met by the sacrifice of Christ. Christians were still left to meet the other two requirements:

a) repentance and
b) reconciliation with one another.

Therefore, Paul said Christians were given the ministry of reconciliation. It was because the Colossians had been made alive by God's grace, when he forgave their accumulated debt of crime, that Colossians were required to forgive one another and be patient with each other (Col 3:13). This was necessary to make atonement complete.

Paul rejoiced in his own sufferings in behalf of the Colossians by which he filled up that which was lacking of the tribulations of Christ (Col 1:24-25). The author of Hebrews, however, argued that Jesus' **offering** of himself **once for all** (*eh-pháh-pahx,* ἐφάπαξ) (Heb 7:22-28) was adequate. Since this was true, the merits which were added by that **sacrifice** could be used once, but no more. Once a Christian had been forgiven, there were no further **sacrifices** possible to build up the treasury of merits upon which one might draw. Therefore there could be no further backsliding followed by forgiveness. The tense rigidity of the author of Hebrews' demands were based on the belief that the promise, the **good word** of God would be fulfilled very soon. Crimelessness could not be expected to last forever. This was not only a view held by the author of Hebrews. Philo said the blasphemer could not be forgiven (Flight 84). Rabbis said there was no repentance for anyone who leads the congregation into **crime** (mAboth 5:18).

As the Messiah, Jesus was God's legal agent. God was the principal. If a principal wanted to send a message to someone far away, he or she might write a letter, sign it, and send it by some messenger who had no authority with reference to the message contained. The messenger's task was only to witness that he saw the letter written and signed and to deliver the letter. In that case the messenger was not very important; it was the word of the letter that was important. If it had been signed legally and both written and signed in the presence of the witnesses, it committed the principal to the word in the letter. It could stand up in court the way a contract would (mGit 2.1).[1]

The principal, however, might instead send a messenger who was a legal agent, authorized to negotiate, buy, sell, or sign contracts in behalf of the principal. Such an action would be as valid as if the principal had personally performed the function the agent conducted. Legally the agent was the principal, the word of the principal in the flesh. He was the incarnate way the principal chose to deliver his word to the recipient. This means that the legal agent was very important to the principal. The treatment given to the agent was legally the same as if it were given to the principal himself or herself. When God was the principal and Jesus was the Messiah, Jesus was the word of God incarnate. The sacrifice of this agent was legally the very sacrifice of God's word. The incarnate word was the word of God sent by the agent to the people of God. That is the reason that it was so valuable that it could cancel all of Israel's previous crimes and iniquities. God sent Jesus as his incarnate word. It was not God who had become flesh. It was his word that was incarnate. Therefore Jesus' sacrifice had the same value as if God himself had conducted the sacrifice.

---

[1] Like most other rules of antiquity, the rules of hearsay evidence still apply in courts today.

Since the sacrifice of Christ was enough to cover all the crimes committed before belief, no further sacrifice was available for additional criminal activity (Heb 6:1-12).[1] The people of God had no right to expect God to send another agent whose function it was to be sacrificed. Therefore the author made no attempt to suggest that the readers relearn the doctrine, if it had been forgotten. They were not given a chance to start all over again. **After they have fallen by the wayside**, those who had once accepted the responsibility of membership had utilized the benefits of Christ's sacrifice.

Jesus was not the only ambassador in the world to have been tortured. When people of a subject nation were very hostile to the king of the country that overpowered them, they expressed their feelings by torturing and killing the ambassador and publicly displaying his corpse before the people. This was an act that made the king very angry. For example, when David sent ambassadors to the Ammonites, the Ammonites thought they were really spies, so they shaved off half of each ambassador's beard, cut off their garments at their hips, and sent them away, embarrassed. That which the Ammonites had done to David's ambassadors was just as offensive as if they had done it to David, himself, because legally a person's legal agents are the same as the person himself or herself. This public display angered David, so he sent troops to overpower the Ammonites as punishment (2Sam 10:1-18)

The author of Hebrews thought this same offense had been performed against Jesus, and the offense was not just against some foreign king. It was an offense against God, and it could not be taken lightly. Beneficiaries could not again crucify Jesus and make **a public example of the Son of God for themselves**.[2] That which God had done through Christ was a once-for-all event. At the Last Supper, Jesus performed a legal ritual by which he formed the "body of Christ." A legal body is a corporation. It is the members of this corporation who were authorized to benefit from Christ's sacrifice. Those who left the corporation were at once disqualified for all the benefits of the legal body.

The author of Hebrews was not the only sectarian who believed there was a limit to forgiveness. Following the Book of Hebrews, the Shepherd of Hermas held that crimes committed before baptism would be forgiven, but that there would be no second forgiveness (Mand 4:3; see also Vis 2:2 and Sim 6:2). For gentiles the opportunity for repentance and conversion to Christianity would continue until the last day, but for the saints, forgiveness had reached its limit (Vis 2:2; Mand 4:3). Those baptized should always thereafter live in purity (Mand 4:3; 12.3; Sim 5:7). If they erred after baptism, they would be cast out of the society of the righteous and condemned to death of the age to come (Mand 12:3; Sim 6:2; 7; 8:6, 8; 9:13, 14, 17, 18). Being condemned to "death" meant excommunication from the society where alone **life** was possible.

The Johannine sect counseled that if one of the brothers saw another brother commit a crime, he could pray and God would give him "life," which probably meant that his crime would be forgiven, and he could be retained within the community (1John 5:16-17). This would be true, however, only if it was a crime **not to death** (*hah-mahr-teé-awn may praws tháh-nah-tawn*, ἁμαρτίον μὴ πρὸς θάνατον). Crimes that were **to death** (*praws tháh-nah-tawn*, πρὸς θάνατον)

---

[1] Buchanan, *Consequences*, pp. 226-40.

[2] For a defensive attempt to soften and justify the meaning of the author's clear statement, see C. Spicq, *Hebreux* II, pp. 167-78. Also, but with less distortion, F. F. Bruce, *The Epistle to the Hebrews* (Grand Rapids: Eerdmans, 1964), pp. 122-25.

could not be forgiven by intercessory prayer (1John 5:16-17). This probably meant that the unforgiven sectarian was excommunicated from the contract community where **life** was possible. The sect of St. Matthew had special rules by which a criminal was invited to repent of his crime, but if he refused even after he was tried before the church, he was treated as a gentile and a tax collector (Matt 18:15-17). He was excommunicated. He had been forgiven for the last time. Since he would cease being a member of the chosen people, the Day of Atonement would no longer be effective for him.

Many sectarians believed blasphemy against God or sacred rites was a crime for which there was no forgiveness. Those of that persuasion believed that a person who said a word against the Holy Spirit could not be forgiven either in this age or in the age to come (Matt 12:31-32; GosThom 88:26-30). The rule of the later church followed Matthew and decreed:

> Those who blaspheme the spirit of grace and despise the gift from it, *after grace* [italics mine], for them there will be no forgiveness, neither in this age nor in the age to come (Apos Cons 6:18).

The sect of the Rule decreed:

> Whoever swears (*yahz-keér*, יזכיר) by the Name which is honored over every name . . . either for fear of persecution or for any other reason whatever, shall be separated [from the community] and not allowed to return again (1QS 6:27-7:2; see also 7:16-17, 21-24).

The Zadokites ruled as follows:

> [Let him not] swear either by *áh-lehph* (א) and *Láh-mehd* (ל) = *Ehl* (אל), *Eh-loh-heém* (אלהים) or by *áh-lehph* (א) and *dáh-leth* (ד) = *(ah-doh-nái* (אדני), except for oaths of enrollment [which are taken] with the curses of the contract [taken upon admission to the sect]. If he swears by the curses of the contract before the judges and then transgresses, he is guilty; and [even] if he confesses and repents, they will not forgive him (CDC 15:1-4).

Ezra asked how it profits us if we are promised the immortal time but we perform works that are mortal (4Ezra 7:119). Josephus held that Essenes caught in grievous crimes *(ehp' ahx-ee-aw-khreh-ois hah-mahr-táy-mah-seen*, ἐπ' ἀξιοχρέοις ἁμαρτήμασιν) were cast out of the community and usually died horrible deaths, because they were bound by oath to abstain from eating food not prepared under Essene supervision. They were forced to eat grass and famish with hunger until physical death (War 2:143-44). Early sectarians lived in such closely segregated communities that excommunication was called "death" and sometimes really meant physical death as well as religious death. Those who remained within the community had to be forgiven. If no further forgiveness was possible, they had to be extremely careful not to commit crimes.[1]

According to the Sybil, God's wrath would come down from heaven upon his people to exact just retribution. In advance he would send a savior so that the

---

[1] Buchanan, *Consequences*, pp. 229-33.

saints would have a chance to repent. This meant that they could repent up until then, but afterward it would be too late (*kai meh-táh-noi-ahn éh-khayht ah-póh nun, kai may-kéh-tee may-déhn*, καὶ μετάνοιαν ἔχητ' ἀπὸ νῦν, καὶ μηκέτι μηδέν (SibOr 1:168).

For the community addressed in Hebrews the savior had already come, so they were following the same rules as those advocated by the Sybil when they allowed no further forgiveness. Baruch said that after the appointed time, there would be no duration of the hours, change of ways, place for prayer, sending of petitions, receiving knowledge, giving love, place for repentance of the soul, supplication for offenses, intercession of the fathers, prayer of the prophets, or help of the righteous (2Bar 85:12). The author of Hebrews demanded the same kind of rigid ethics of his readers that other sectarians expected.[1] He warned them that they should not have an evil mind of unbelief nor allow themselves to become hardened by the deceitfulness of crime. As a consequence no one of the members would dare to commit a crime (2Bar 3:13; see also mAb 5:18; bYoma 87a; bSan 107b).

Many scholars and earlier Christians have been embarrassed by the rigidness of the author's justice system. He allowed no room for either repentance or forgiveness. Luther said that this doctrine was contrary to that of the gospels or the Apostle Paul.[2] DeSilva attempted to put that harshness in less punitive light. He described the relationship of patrons to the people they patronized. The patron always provided more than was required for the services he received. The person whom he patronized, therefore, was expected to respond by showing very much gratitude and willingness to provide whatever it was possible for him to give, always knowing he would be forever in debt. If, at that point, the one who had been patronized should not respond gratefully, but instead abandon his patron, he could never expect the patron to take him back.[3] The role of the Christian, then, stood before God like the one patronized before his patron. The Christian had received unlimited benefits from God. Furthermore Christ acted as a broker between the Christian and God, helping the Christian understand God's grace and to represent the Christian to God. The author reminded his listeners of their benefits and warned them of the seriousness of any offense against either the broker or the patron.

The monastic community was especially rigid. Monks took vows of 1) poverty, 2) celibacy, 3) obedience. That meant that they surrendered their wealth, their families, and their personal freedom. Their entire life in the monastery was one of trust. Monks trusted the monastery for their material and medical needs, their emotional support, and their direction in life. The monastery trusted the monks to fulfill their vows precisely. Breach of fiduciary trust has been considered a serious offense in courts across the centuries. Today, in most U.S. courts, punitive damages are assigned to offenders who commit this crime. Breach of monastic vows normally requires expulsion with no opportunities for repentance or forgiveness. Reminding them of their benefits, the author asked rhetorically,

---

[1] There is no textual or traditional support for Spicq's (*Hebreux,* I, pp. 57-58) view that the impossibility was only because of the apostate's unwillingness to repent. Like Esau, he could not return even if he wept to show his earnest desires.

[2] So H. F. Weiss, *Der Brief an die Hebräer* (Göttingen: Vandenhoeck & Ruprecht, 1991), p. 349.

[3] D. A. DeSilva, "Exchanging Favor for Wrath: Apostasy in Hebrews and Patron Client Relationships," *JBL* 115 (1996): 91-116.

[Heb 2:3]**How shall we escape having neglected so great a salvation [as this], which**
1) had its beginning when it was spoken through the Lord,
2) was confirmed to us by those who heard,
[4]**3) while God supported the testimony with signs, wonders, and various kinds of miracles, and**
4) by the distribution of the Holy Spirit according to his will?

How shall we escape is a rhetorical question. It means, "**We shall** not **escape**." All of these benefits put us in a position of indebtedness from which **we** can never recover. **We** can only respond by being faithful. This is one of the important themes the author referred to in Heb 2:1; 6:1-6; and 12:17, repeating this theme effectively throughout his document. Christians have tried to explain this clear meaning of the author's doctrine to suit themselves, but no other explanation is valid. This was part of the monastic theology of the author and his legal brothers.

Just think of the kind of assurances given that salvation was made available to the listeners.

1) It was spoken through Jesus, God's legal agent.
2) Those who heard Jesus speak testified to what he said.
3) Jesus' word was supported with all kinds of signs, wonders, and miracles, and
4) the Holy Spirit was active in propagating the word and gaining new members to the church.

TEXT

Hebrews	First Testament
[7]For **land** that **drinks** the **rain** which comes upon it many times and	[Gen 1:2]And the **land**
produces vegetation [that is] useful to those for whom it is also cultivated,	**produced vegetation**, plants **producing**
receives blessings from **God**; [8]but when **it bears**	seeds after and fruit-**bearing** trees whose seed was in its fruit, after their kind, and **God** saw that it was good.
	[Deut 11:11]**The land drinks** water which the heavens **rain**.
thorns and thistles, it is worthless and nearly a **curse**. Its end is burning.	[Gen 3:17-18]**Cursed** be the ground because of you; with toil you shall eat of it all the days of your life. **Thorns and thistles it will produce** for you.

COMMENTARY

This pericope is a small sermon based on two texts of creation in the early chapters of Genesis. The author formed a parable relating the creation of God to the congregation for whom this message was prepared. His analogy was to the person who once accepted the responsibilities of membership in the community and then became apostate. The author of Hebrews compared the good condition of **the land** as God originally created it with the cursed condition under which Adam had to work it after he had committed a crime.

The land, which is blessed abundantly and has received a good deal of **rain,** is expected to produce **vegetation.** This showed, God was pleased, for the result was good. **The land** did not deserve credit for all that it had produced, because it could not have done so if it had not drunk **the rain which comes upon it many times**. But if, after it had received so much **rain** as this, it produced only **thorns and thistles**, then something had happened to **the land.** Between Gen 1:12 and 3:18, God had cursed the ground. **Land** that produces weeds is later burned off to destroy the weeds, so the end of such land is **burning**. In Europe and the Near East farmers still burn their stubble fields after harvest. This is done to destroy weed seeds and insects, although it also destroys the humus that **the land** needs to produce crops.

The analogy Hebrews gives is not perfect, from the point of view of modern twentieth century farming. The fault today is not with **the land** but with the farmer. If the land produces only weeds, this means the farmer did not plant or cultivate crops. The attorney who argued this case, however, was comparing two texts in Genesis rather than the neglect or cultivation of land. In the first text **the land** produced; in the second it did not. In between Adam and Eve ate the forbidden fruit and received the curse. Therefore the curse on **the land** was the cause of its failure to produce good crops.

Analogous to **the land** in the Genesis texts is the member who becomes apostate. He cannot return and repent. He has to remain faithful all of the time if he expects to receive the reward of the faith. Just as Adam was expelled from the garden where "life" was possible, the member was excommunicated from the community where "life" was possible. For neither Adam nor the member of the sect to which the author belonged was there a second chance. **The Lord placed the cherubim with a flaming sword which turned every way, to guard the way to the tree of life** (Gen 3:24). Ben Sirach's analogy is not so harsh:

> He who washes after [contact with] a dead body and touches it again, what did he gain by bathing? So a man [who] fasts for his crimes and does the same again, who will listen to his prayer? (Sir 34[31]:25-26; see also pTaan 1: 63d, 64a).

Throughout this entire discussion of crime and forgiveness, the subjects seem to have been brothers and not sisters. In the first twelve chapters of Hebrews there is no indication that the group to which the author was writing included married people. Even among married Jews of NT times the Day of Atonement was only for the men, because women had limited legal requirements, and therefore limited guilt. Women were given three commandments for which they were responsible:

1) Their own menstrual purity,
2) lighting Sabbath candles, and
3) sacrificing the first fruits before the rest of the food was cooked or eaten.

If a woman died at child birth it was believed that she had neglected one of these duties.

On the Day of Atonement the high priest offered a sacrifice for himself and his house. His house meant his wife (mYoma 1:1). Probably it was assumed that on the Day of Atonement not only the high priest, but all other males who offered sacrifice offered them in behalf of their wives. Therefore the discussion of crime and forgiveness was closely associated with men and not women. The males were trained at about twelve years of age to be responsible for some of the commandments. Up to that time Jewish males were called "children" or "toddlers" (*tah-peém*, טפים). From about twelve years until 20 years of age, males were called "sons."[1] At that time they participated in a liturgy by which they became "sons of the commandment" or *bahr mítz-wahs* (בר מצוה). There is no record of "daughters of the commandment" or *bahth mítz-wahs* (בת מצוה) in antiquity. In Reformed and Conservative Judaism today girls are trained in law and not only become "daughters of the commandment," but even rabbis. These are current practices, but when we study ancient literature it is important to recognize its meaning against its own environment.

TEXT

9 But concerning you, beloved, we are convinced about the better things belonging to salvation, even though we speak thus; 10 for God is not unjust [so as] to forget your work and the love which you have demonstrated for his name, having ministered to the saints as you still do, 11 but we want each of you to show forth the same zeal toward the fulfillment of hope until [the] end, 12 so that you may not become dull, but [rather] imitators of those who inherit the promises through faith and long suffering.

COMMENTARY

9 *We are convinced of the better things.* This is the author's first note of affection for his readers. It is the only time he called them **beloved**. Although he was basically severe and demanding, the author also knew how to mingle his warnings with assurance and encouragement, and on this one occasion he seemed tender. It was because of his affection for them that he warned them. He did not want them to leave the monastery. The **better things** were those related to **salvation** rather than apostasy. There was no second repentance for those who abandoned their faith, but on the other hand, those who did not abandon their faith did not have to worry. For them there would be only good things ahead.

10 *God is not unjust.* **Work and love** do not belong in separate categories, as if one involved activity and the other feeling. In biblical times, when **love** was used in a contractual framework, it referred to responsibility under contract. Therefore sectarians were commanded to **love** all the sons of light and hate all the sons of darkness (1QS 1:9-10). The sons of light were the members who had brought into the community all of their knowledge, ability, and wealth to share in common with other sectarians (1QS 1:11-12). A man should be either **loved** or hated according to his spirit, which meant either accepted or rejected from the community "according to the cleanness of his hands" (1QS 9:15-16). These segregated sectarians were

[1] See further Buchanan, "The Old Testament Meaning of the Knowledge of Good and Evil," *JBL* 75 (1956):114-120.

warned that **love** for the world meant enmity with God (James 4:4). Those who **loved** the world had no **love for the Father** (1John 2:15). People either chose to love darkness and therefore became sons of darkness or they chose light and became sons of light (1John 2:9-11, 19). Those who joined the sect passed from **death** to **life** because they **loved** the brothers (1John 3:14). Those who joined the group accepted the responsibilities of membership which involved **loving** one another. Monastic communities were distinctly apartheid in structure and life.

In communal groups **loving** one another did not mean having fond feelings toward each other; it meant sharing materially and caring for one another in very practical ways, regardless of feelings. Those who continued in **love** provided hospitality for traveling sectarians (Heb 13:2). Because of Philemon's **love,** Paul could impose sanctions on him and demand that he release Onesimus (Philem 9). Members of contract communities could be commanded to **love**. This was not a new custom of NT times. Joshua encouraged the Hebrews to **love** the Lord their God (Josh 23:11). Deuteronomy commanded them to **love** the Lord their God with all their heart, soul, and might (Deut 6:5), and also instructed them to keep the Lord's charge, his statutes, his ordinances, and his commandments always (Deut 11:1), which apparently meant the same as **loving** God (see also Ps 31:24 [23]). Israelites were not to take vengeance against other parties to the contract (Lev 19:18) but they were to **love** even the stranger who sojourned in their land (Lev 19:33-34).

The Lord commanded Hosea to go **love** a woman (Hos 3:1). In response Hosea bought a woman for 15 shekels of silver and a homer and a lethech of barley, and made her dwell with him under his jurisdiction (Hos 3:2-3). No mention was made of any affection in relationship to this act of redemption, and that is part of the point. In the same way Israel could count on the Lord to fulfill his contract to **love** Israel, even though his feelings toward her were sometimes negative. He acted according to his obligation to **love**. After all, he had signed a contract to do that. In the same way Hosea **loved** the woman as he had been commanded, by providing for her needs.

The commandment to **love** the neighbor as oneself summarized other commandments relating to the neighbor. The corner of the field and part of the fruit crop must be left for him or her; the neighbor's property must not be stolen; and he must not be cheated in business or overworked. As an employee, the brother or sister must be paid due wages day by day, and must not be abused or injured. The fellow citizen must be judged fairly. All of this is involved in **loving** the neighbor (Lev 19:9-18).

Christians were reminded that the greatest **love** required giving up one's **life** (*psoo-kháy,* ψυχή) for his friends (John 15:12-13). They were told that they, like Jesus, should lay down their lives (*psoo-kháy,* ψυχή) for their brothers. This probably meant giving up existence in the world, such as job, family, and position, to join the monastic sect where the new member shared all his possessions with other members of the sect, just as Jesus had done before them (see 2Cor 8:9). This meant following Jesus' example *before* the crucifixion.[1] It meant **loving** the neighbor as oneself. By losing his secular existence (*psoo-kháy,* ψυχή) he found his life (*zoh-áy,* ζωή) and became one of the *beloved.*

Because wives had no right to own property or control money, they had no substance to share or with which to be loving. Therefore Paul commanded them to

[1] For an examination of Jesus' relationship to wealth and communal, celibate groups, see Buchanan, "Jesus and the Upper Class," *NovT* 8 (1964):195-209.

be subject to their husbands, who, in turn, were commanded to **love** their wives (Col 3:18-19; Eph 5:25, 28, 33). These admonitions did not apply to the feelings wives and husbands should have toward one another, but rather to the treatment that should be expected of them and their respective legal rights. When the husband took vows to **love** his wife that gave the wife protection under the law. He was obligated to provide for her.

God **loved** the world and gave his Son (John 3:16). He **loved** the Son and gave all things into his hand (John 3:35). God's **love** was poured into the heads of believers through the Holy Spirit which God gave them (Rom 5:5). The Son of God **loved** parties to the contract and gave himself for them (Gal 2:20; Eph 5:2). Numerous other biblical references show that **love** was very closely related to work, serving, giving, being responsible, and providing. Some **lovers** were nations with whom there were treaties guaranteeing support in time of war. Of course it was possible to have fond feelings toward the one **loved,** but the importance of **love** in early Christian communities was its relationship to **work**, which could be "demonstrated for his name"[1] and in relationship to the contract taken.

Ministering to the saints. The specific way in which the readers demonstrated **love** for his name was in **ministering to the saints**. Particularly in celibate communities, this was very important. In the ancient Near East there was no governmental social security program or pension plan to care for people in their old **age.** The main insurance a person had against neglect and starvation in his old **age** was the provision he could expect from his or her children. Therefore children were commanded to honor their parents, which command involved provision for old **age** (Exod 20:12; Mek *Bahod* 8:1-3; *Decal* 23:116-18). Members of a monastic order, deprived of children, would be neglected in their old **age** and during periods of illness if the community had not made other plans to fulfill the needs otherwise met by members of the family. By pooling their funds and agreeing to work to care for each other, members could live to a comfortable and prosperous old **age** (Hyp 11:4-5; Prob 9:86-87; see also Ant 18:20-22; War 2:122; and Philo 9:4, 19). This was part of the "work and **love**" that was called **ministering to the saints**. Another aspect was hospitality shown to visiting **saints**.

According to Philo, no Essene called his house his own in the sense that he was free to exclude other Essenes, but the door was open to visitors from other places who shared his convictions (Prob 9:85) This means that those who could be trusted to keep the same tithing, heave offerings, dietary, and purity regulations could make demands on their hospitality. Josephus said that Essene customs permitted them to travel without taking any provisions except weapons as protection against brigands, but that in every city an appointed person was responsible for providing visiting Essenes with clothing and other necessities (War 2:125). Hippolytus added that the person assigned to care for traveling Essenes did so from a fund provided for that purpose (Philos 9:4, 20).[2]

Early Christians observed some of the same practices. According to Matthew the twelve were sent out without gold, silver, or copper in their belts, no bags, no sandals, and with only one tunic each. They were told:

---

[1] Buchanan, *Consequences*, pp. 293-308.

[2] Buchanan, *Consequences*, pp. 246-48.

> And whatever town or village you enter, find out one who is worthy (*áhx-ee-aws*, ἄξιος) in it, and stay with him until you depart. As you enter the house, salute it, for if the house is `worthy,' let your peace come upon it; but if it is not "worthy" let your peace return to you (Matt 10:11-13).

It was in view of this kind of hospitality program that disciples were assured that they could ask, seek, and knock, and be sure that their needs would be met (Matt 7:7). This meant they could look for the home of a sectarian member, knock on that door, and ask for hospitality and be sure it would be provided. Other sectarians were required to provide it. It was the traveling missionaries who depended upon the hospitality of other sectarians who were taught to pray, **Give us today our daily bread** (Matt 6:11). It was itinerant disciples who were told not to lay up for themselves treasures on earth (Matt 6-19).

Those **saints** who were not itinerant, who kept supplies on hand to provide for the traveling missionaries, had to lay up treasures on earth, however, or the whole program would have broken down. This provision was called **love** or **ministering to the saints**. That kind of **ministry** could not be taken for granted. Diotrephes was scolded because he not only turned away strangers who came asking for hospitality, but he prevented others from receiving them as guests (3John 9-10). This did not mean that the community was required to accept all guests, but the ones Diotrephes turned away were those who had been sent out under approved levitical standards (*áhx-ee-aws too theh-oó*, ἄξιος τοῦ θεοῦ) (3John 5-6). They were so careful in their habits that they refused to eat food offered by gentiles. Therefore sectarians were obligated to provide for them (3John 7-8).[1] If they failed to do this the missionaries were turned away without any hospitality resources.

In addition to caring for the sick and elderly and providing hospitality for traveling sectarians, a third way of ministering to the saints involved providing financial support in Jerusalem for the saints who were dependent upon contributions from the diaspora for their livelihood (Rom 15:25. 2Cor 8:4; 9:l). The readers to whom the author of Hebrews wrote were meritorious in one or more of these respects. Therefore they were assured that the better things of the salvation that was coming would be theirs (Heb 6:9).

11 *Show forth the same zeal . . . until the end.* The Greek term rendered "fulfillment" is *play-raw-phaw-reé-ahn* (πληροφορίαν) which comes from the verb *play-raw--phaw-ráyn*, (πληροφορεῖν) meaning "to bring in full, to fulfill, or to satisfy," but Vaughan was correct in his insistence that there is nothing in the derivation to suggest conviction or assurance, as the RSV translates it.[2] Furthermore "full assurance of hope" (RSV) does not make much sense. People do not become convinced or assured of a hope. If they hope, they have some assurance. But those who **had tasted the heavenly gift, shared in the Holy Spirit, and tasted the miracles of the coming age** (Heb 6:4-5) might be zealous toward the "fulfillment" or satisfaction of the "hope" that the **good word** of God would be completely realized (Heb 6:4-5). The author's reassurance carries with it his more important message of stressing the serious nature of their religious task. The believers were exhorted to "show forth" "zeal" to **the end.**

---

[1] Buchanan, *Consequences,* pp. 275-82.

[2] C. J. Vaughan, *The Epistle to the Hebrews* (London: Macmillan, 1890), p. 112.

[12]*Those who inherit the promises.* Heb 6:12 is a connective sentence, preparing the reader for the next topic, the **promise** given to Abraham and the basis for the hope discussed above. Christians and Jews of NT times who voluntarily **suffered** to pay off the heavy debt of fines accumulated for the crime that was charged against God's chosen people based their ethics on the passivity of Abraham. Abraham was one of two characters in the FT for whom something was reckoned as righteousness in the heavenly treasury. The other was Phineas, who for his zeal in killing both the mingling Israelite and his foreign bride, was reckoned righteous. These two biblical examples provided Jews and Christians of NT times with standards to follow.

Those who followed the ethics of Phineas had also Joshua and the Hasmoneans as their religious heroes. Those who worked and **suffered** to pay the national heavenly debt followed Abraham. Paul, as a righteous Pharisee, employed the active ethics of Phineas. When he became a Christian he followed the ethics of Abraham, believing that in that way he would lead his people to **inherit the promises** God gave to Abraham who believed against all odds and as a result his children received the **promises** of the land of Canaan as a heritage. Christian and Jewish ethics is basically an imitation ethics. Members are expected to learn about the heroes and heroines of the past and imitate their actions.

Summary. The author accused his readers of being **dull** and formed an inclusion by urging that they not let themselves **become dull.** In between were accusations and assurances, all organized into a pattern. The author accused the readers of staying in kindergarten and listed the concepts related to elementary religious development. He compared this with milk for infants who had not been weaned, and urged them to grow up. Like Paul he encouraged them to put away childish things (1Cor 13:11-12). He also compared them to the land that produced weeds and thistles, deserving only to be burned. The entire unit was exhortative. It began with accusation and urgency and concluded with reassurance and urgency. The **promise** was great; the opportunity was endless; it would be foolish to become lackadaisical, as the readers seemed to be doing. The inclusion was followed by a typical statement introducing the reader to the topic to follow which included three catchwords: **promise** (Heb 6:13), **heirs** (Heb 6:17), **hope** (Heb 6:18).

The Promises of God

TEXT

Hebrews	First Testament
[13]For when God made a promise **to Abraham**, since he had no one else greater [by whom] to swear, **he swore by** him**self** [4]**saying,** "[May the following unexpressed curses come upon me] if I do not **surely bless you and multiply** you."	[Gen 22:15-17]The angel of Yehowah called **to Abraham** a second time from heaven and said, **"By** my**self I have sworn**," **says** Yehowah, "because you have done this and you did not spare your only son, I will **surely bless you and multiply** your posterity."

Thus, after he had suffered patiently, [Abraham] received the **promise**. [16]For men **swear by** someone [or something] greater [than themselves], and every argument [is brought to an] end by the confirmation of an oath.

COMMENTARY

[13]*He swore by himself.* **Promises** and **oaths** were standard parts of contracts and treaties. The occasion for this **promise** followed Abraham's willingness to offer his only son, Isaac, to God as a sacrifice. God prevented the execution of his intent, and at that time **swore by himself** (Gen 22:16) that he would bless Abraham and multiply his seed. For a discussion on the oath formula see the Commentary on Heb 3:11. This unit was introduced to call attention to another instance in which God **swore** and also to compare the sacrifice that Abraham was willing to make of his only son with the actual sacrifice God made of his only son, Jesus.

[14-15]*If I do not surely bless you and multiply you.* The quotation differs from both the LXX and the MT of Gen 22:17. Both texts describe the **oaths** in the third person, whereas the text from which Hebrews drew his quotation included the quotation of a minted **oath** that **God swore**. The meaning is no different. This is only a matter of style. The slight verbal differences are that the quotation for Hebrews stops with **multiply**. The author changed the object from "your seed" to **you**.

The **promise** came to Abraham **after he had suffered** patiently *(mahk-raw-theh-may-sahs,* μακροθεμήσας) in his willingness to sacrifice Isaac. The emotional torture which Abraham suffered has been eulogized extensively both in Jewish and in Christian literature. This suffering was considered meritorious enough to have motivated God to offer the **promise** and **oath** on which an important element of Jewish and Christian faith is based. That which Abraham **received** (*ehp-éh-too-khehn,* ἐπέτυχεν), achieved, obtained, or acquired was the **promise**--not its fulfillment, which the author claimed was still pending in his day. The author's effective repetition is evident here. The **suffering** of **Abraham** was compared to the **suffering** of Jesus who was able to bear gently (5:2), learned **obedience through the things he suffered** (5:8), and members of the community who would inherit the promises through faith and long **suffering** (6:12).

[16-17]*Every argument [is brought to an] end by the confirmation of an oath.* The Greek word for **imposed** is *eh-meh-sít-oo-sehn* (ἐμεσίτευσεν), which means to act the part of a mediator. Josephus told of an occasion when the Israelites took an **oath**, invoking God as the mediator (*meh-sít-ayn,* μεσίτην) (Ant 4:133). In this case, however, God acted as his own mediator. It was customary in biblical times to assume that God functioned according to the customs and practices that were common to Near Eastern society. When there was an **argument**, one member of the discussion might take an **oath,** imposing certain curses upon himself if he were not telling the truth (Spec 2:10). After this there could be little question about his veracity, because it was assumed that God would fulfill the curses upon him if he were wrong. So fearful were Near Easterners of the curses that they often left them unexpressed, even though they were understood. Since this was the custom, **When God wanted very much to show the heirs of the promise**, namely Abraham's seed (Gen 22:17),[1] **the unchangeableness of his will, he imposed an oath [on**

---

[1] Dealing with this heritage, Eusebius referred to the heirs as "heirs of the kingdom" *(tois-klay-raw-*

himself]. This was intended to convince "the heirs" that they had no need for anxiety about God's intention. Philo and the author of Hebrews agreed on God's reason for **swearing** by himself.

> For, indeed, concerning the perfect Abraham, he spoke in this manner**; By myself I have sworn**, says the Lord . . . You see that God **swears** by no other, for there is nothing better than he, but [he swears] by himself, who is the best of all (LA 3:203; see also 3:204, 207, cf. Abr. 273).

TEXT

17 So when God wanted very much to show the heirs of the promise the unchange-
ableness of his will, he imposed an oath [on himself], 18 so that through two un-
changeable things in which it would be impossible for God to falsify, we, the
defendants, may have a strong encouragement [in the oath and promise] to seize the
hope set before us, 19 which we have as a secure and steadfast anchor of the soul,

Hebrews	First Testament
	Lev 16:2, 12, 15 Tell your brother Aaron, and
and one that is **entering into the** innermost [area which is behind] **the curtain**, 20 where Jesus entered [as] a forerunner in our behalf, since he is a high	let him not **enter** at all times **into the holy place** inside **the curtain**.
	Ps 110:4 Yehowah has sworn, and he will not recant,
	"You are a
priest for the age according to the order of Melchizedek.	**priest for the age according to the order of Melchizedek**."

COMMENTARY

18-19 *It would be impossible for God to falsify*. Since God's word was the Scripture, this affirmation meant that the words of the Scripture could not be questioned. The **two unchangeable things** are the **promise** and the **oath**. Philo agrees in his understanding of Gen 22:16-17: "It is good that he confirmed the **promise** by an **oath**, and by an **oath** proper for **God"** (LA 3:203). **God's promise** itself would be **unchangeable** without the **oath,** but the two together gave believers confidence.

The word translated **the defendants** is *kah-tah-phoo-gáwn-tehs* (καταφυγόντες), literally, "fleeing ones" or "fugitives." It is the same term used to describe those who were fleeing to the cities of refuge to escape the punishment of their avengers (LXX Deut 4:42; 19:5; Josh 20:9). It is also the technical name for

---

náw-mois tays bah-see-láy-ahs τοῖς κληρονόμοις τῆς βασιλείας) (*Demonstration Evangelica* V.3 [PG 368], showing the close affinity of the kingdom or the land to the promise in early Christian understanding. F. Delitzsch, *Commentary on the Epistle to the Hebrews* (Grand Rapids: Eerdmans, 1952), tr. T. L. Kingsbury II, p. 310, mistakenly assumed that all Christians believed that *hah-áh-retz* (הארץ) (Gen 12:7; 24:7) meant the whole earth.

defendants in an ancient Greek court. The plaintiff was called a pursuer, and the **defendant** was a fugitive. The plaintiff was chasing the **defendant** in order to catch him and make him do that which he did not want to do. Instead, however, of chasing him physically, as the avenger, chasing the person who was fleeing to one of the cities of refuge was doing, the plaintiff was chasing him in court. The **defendant,** for his part, was trying to get away from his grasp, legally. RSV renders it "have fled for refuge," but that misses the court context. The author pictured the audience as **defendants** in an important trial, the New Year's Day judgment and the final verdict on the Day of Atonement. The stakes were tremendous. If they lost they would miss the promises of God. What a relief to learn that God was the *amicus curiae* (friend of the court) on the side of the defense with both a **promise** and an **oath**!

The **oath** was taken so that the parties to the contract could be certain that the trial would be won, the contract would be carried out, and the Christians were the ones who could draw on the **promise** as affirmed with an **oath.** This provides a strong motivation to take advantage of **the hope** that this **promise** would be fulfilled in their days, as the author led them to believe. **The hope** that was **laid before** was laid before in two ways:

1) It was made available. It was set before as food at a table to be eaten, and
2) It was future; it was a **hope** that would not be fulfilled in the present.

Weiss correctly said that this hope was for a heavenly sanctuary, which is the holy of holies (Lev 16:2, 12, 15).[1] This does not necessarily mean it is in heaven. Many heavenly things are on earth, such as Zion, the city of the God of life, heavenly Jerusalem (Heb 12:22).

The innermost [area which is behind] the curtain. The curtain involved is the hanging that separates the holy from the holy of holies in the temple. Davidson correctly noticed that among FT passages related to this entry are Exod 40:1-9; Lev 8:10-12; and Num 7:1 as well as all other entry passages in Hebrews (10:19-20; 9:12, 24) they picture an earthly sanctuary as the background.[2] As Hofius has clearly shown, this is not the separation wall between earth and heaven that Käsemann, Grässer, and others claim.[3] At the end of his argument, Hofius said,

> Our study of Heb 6:19-20 allowed us an interpretation of the texts, in which it was nowhere necessary to draw in the Gnostic position for an explanation of the thought pattern.[4]

The rabbis pictured God in heaven in the holy of holies, separated from most people by a curtain, but he spoke with the prophets face to face, with the curtain drawn (GenR 52:7 [Gen 20:3]; 74:5 [Gen 31:26]; LevR 1:15 [Lev 1:1]). In heaven the Lord lived in Jerusalem, where he spent his time building a new temple, using all precious stones and for mortar he used the Shekinah to hold the pearls and precious stones together. When Moses asked for the special privilege of seeing the Messiah

---

[1] H. F. Weiss, *Der Brief an die Hebräer* (Göttingen: Vandenhoeck & Ruprecht, 1991), p. 367.

[2] R. M. Davidson, "Christ's Entry 'Within the Veil' in Hebrews 6:19-20: The Old Testament Background," *Andrews University Seminary Studies* 39 (2001): 175-190.

[3] O. Hofius, *Der Vorhang vor dem Thron Gottes* (Tübingen: J. C. B. Mohr, c1972), p. 1.

[4] O. Hofius, *Vorhang,* p. 89.

in heaven, Moses asked the Messiah when would the Lord bring Jerusalem with its temple down to the earth. The Lord built the temple with his own hands, but when he finished it was expected to be placed on earth, just west of the spring of Siloam and the Kidron Valley.[1] Rabbis thought the Messiah would come and clear out all the foreigners, the uncircumcised, and defiled Jews from Jerusalem. Afterward the perfected, rebuilt Jerusalem would be brought down from heaven, together with the temple which would already be rebuilt in heaven.[2] There was a Jerusalem and a temple in heaven, but there was no separation wall between earth and heaven that would keep one Jerusalem excluded from the other.

The quotation varies a little from the LXX Lev 16:2. Instead of *ays-paw-roo-éhs-thoh* (ἐισπορευέσθω), "Let him [not] enter," Hebrews has *ays-ehr-khaw-méh-náyn* (ἐιςἐρχομένην), **entering**, using a synonym with the same meaning. The LXX has *taw háh-gee-awn eh-sóh-teh-rawn* (τὸ ἅγιον ἐσώτερον), "The holy **innermost** place." The MT has "the holy place." The author of Hebrews either used a different text or chose to make some variations of his own, but the context requires that the place be understood as the holy of holies. Gane correctly argued that the curtain involved separated the holy place from the holy of holies. The innermost part was the holy of holies.[3]

The LXX passage refers to the conduct of Aaron on the Day of Atonement. The author's reason for quoting this passage was in continuation of his previous discussion. The hope for which other generations had expected fulfillment since the **promise** that was first made to Abraham might be fulfilled for the author's generation. There is very little to prevent its fulfillment. Other generations had been prevented by the criminal nature of the people, but for believers of the author's generation, all of these crimes had been atoned. Not only did these believers have **hope**, but, through Jesus they had **a strong encouragement as a secure and steadfast anchor of the soul**.

The **soul**, which was **anchored** was the legal bond that secured the member's identity to the corporation. It provided tenure. Josephus said Essenes believed that their **souls** were immortal, that is, they were well **anchored** (Wars 2:156). Those who lost their **souls** were excommunicated from the group in which alone legal and religious life was possible. Essenes were so tightly united that no Essene could eat food that was not prepared by other Essenes in accepted rules of purity. If an Essene was expelled from the community, he was still bound by those same rules, so he was not allowed to eat anything accept uncooked vegetation. Josephus said many of these died miserable deaths. They not only lost their **souls,** but they lost their physical lives (Wars. 2:143).

The word corresponding to **entering** was singular in the LXX and left unchanged by the author of Hebrews. It was not the believers who **entered** this holy place. It was Aaron in the FT and Jesus in the author's time (the word is feminine, referring to **hope**, but signifying Jesus), but it is this **entering** to atone for crimes which clears the way for the reception of the promise. Rabbis said God would

---

[1] S. A. Wertheimer, *Pirke Haykalot Rabbti* (Jerusalem, 1890) 6:3-7 [3b-4a]. tr. into English in Buchanan, *Jewish Messianic Movements from AD 70 to AD 1300* (Eugene, Oregon: Wipf and Stock Publishers, 2003), p. 404.

[2] A. Jellinek, *Bait hah méed-rahsh* (Jerusalem, 1967, in 8 vols.), III, 78-82. tr. into English in Buchanan, *Messianic Movements*, p. 404.

[3] R. E. Gane, "Re-Opening *KATAPETASMA* ('vei') in Hebrews 6:19," *Andrews University Seminary Studies* 38 (2000):5-8.

restore the Promised Land if all Israel repented for just one day (CantR 5:5 #2, 2). That day would be the Day of Atonement, when each year Israel had a chance to have its debt to God forgiven. The author of Hebrews wanted his audience to avoid crimes for that one day.

[20]*Where Jesus entered.* Heb 6:19-20 form the tie between the exhortation that began with Heb 5:11 and the doctrinal discussion that was interrupted after Heb 5:10 but picked up again in Heb 7. The atonement made by **entering** into the **innermost** area was made when **Jesus entered [as] a forerunner in our behalf**. When the members of the audience found themselves **defendants** on the judgment day, it was a comfort to receive God's **oath,** and his legal agent Jesus, sent to be their defense attorney in this trial**, a forerunner on** their **behalf**. This is a reminder of the time the Lord sent a legal angel as the defense attorney to support Joshua in his court trial, with Satan as the prosecuting attorney. In that case Joshua was proclaimed innocent and was restored to his official position (Zech 3:1-10). This suggested the way to return to the discussion on **Melchizedek** for a proper understanding of Ps 110 and Jesus, so the author quoted again the text of the entire sermon of Hebrews to remind his readers or hearers that Ps 110 was the major text. The word **Melchizedek** is a connection word relating this paragraph to the next in Heb 7.

Summary. With Heb 5:11, the author of Hebrews interrupted his exegesis to make an exhortation. At that point he promised to deal with that subject more extensively even though it was **difficult to interpret** (Heb 5:11). At the end of his exhortation he was prepared to return to his initial subject, so he summarized his exhortation in a way that tied it very neatly to the subject he had left (Heb 5:10) and would continue (Heb 7:1). In relationship to the exhortation, he referred to the **two unchangeable things** (Heb 6:18) which provided Christians **strong encouragement** (Heb 6:18) and **a secure and steadfast anchor of the soul** (Heb 6:19). In relationship to the doctrinal discussion, he mentioned Jesus' function as **high priest** who would enter **the innermost [area]** and function for the atonement of the believers, under the authority of **the order of Melchizedek** which was **for the age**.

The author's custom of using analogies was apparent again in this unit. He first explained the significance of an **oath** generally and then showed how important this was to God's **oath**. He explained how this brought about the **promise** and the assurance it left for fulfillment for Christians.

CHAPTER SEVEN

INTRODUCTION

Chapter seven is the central chapter of Hebrews. Michel identified seven subheadings in Heb 7 which are related to seven Greek words used in the divisions.[1] Vanhoye accepted these subheadings but, on the basis of inclusions, grouped them also under three general headings.[2] The inclusions are as follows:

(a) **Melchizedek** and **met** (Heb 7:1, 10),
(b) **perfection** (Heb 7:11) and **perfected** (Heb 7:19), and
(c) **oath** (Heb 7:20, 28).

Vanhoye's division will be followed here. This chapter is well organized around the topic of Melchizedek. Like the rest of Heb 1:1-12:29, Heb 7 is based on Ps 110, but it is also centered around a little poem that is non-canonical (Heb 7:3), and it utilizes another non-canonical poem in conclusion (Heb 7:26). The poem in Heb 7:3 seems to have been important to the author. It is echoed in Heb 7:25, and apparently was used as a proof text in Heb 7:6, 8, and 16.

TEXT

Hebrews	First Testament
[7:1]For this **Melchizedek, king of Salem, priest of the Most High God, who met Abraham returning from smiting the kings, and blessed him**; [2]**and to him** Abraham **apportioned a tenth of all**. First **[Melchizedek]** is interpreted "king of righteousness," and then	[Gen 14:17]The **king of Salem** went out to **meet** him **[Abram]** after his **return from striking** the Chaldeans and **the king** who were with him at the Valley of Shaveh, which is the Valley of the Kings. [18]**Melchizedek,**
[second] also **king of Salem**, which is "**king** of peace." [3]Without father, without mother, without genealogy, having neither beginning of days nor end of life,	**king of Salem**, brought out bread and wine. **He is priest of the Most High God**.
but **resembling the son of God**, he remains a **priest** continually. [4]See how great he is! To him the patriarch	[Dan 3:25]I see four men released, walking in the midst of the fire, and they have no injury, and the appearance of the fourth is **like a son of God**.
	[Gen 14:19]And he blessed him**, saying, "**Blessed be Abram **to** God Most High**, creator of heaven and earth,** [20]**and** blessed **be** God Most High **who has**

[1] O Michel, *Der Brief an* die *Hebraeer* (Göttingen: Vandenhoeck & Ruprecht, 1957) pp. 148-83.
[2] A. Vanhoye, La *Structure Litteraire de l'Epitre aux Hebreux* (Paris: J. Gabalda, 1962), pp. 125-36.

Abraham gave a tenth of [his] choice [acquisitions]. 5Now, even the sons of Levi, on the one hand, receiving the **priest**hood, have a commandment

delivered over your enemies into your hand," and he [Abram] gave him a tenth of all [the booty].

according to law to collect [the] **tenth** [from] the people, that is, their brothers, even though [these] have come from the loins of **Abraham**; 6on the other hand, the one who does not have a genealogy from them collected the **tenth** from **Abraham, and blessed** the one who **had the promises.**

Dan 7:13Look! with the clouds of heaven there comes one **like a son of man** to the Ancient of Days.

Gen 18:18-19**Abraham** . . . all the nations of the land will be **blessed** . . . Yahowah will bring [to pass] with respect to **Abraham** that which he **has promised** regarding him.

TECHNICAL DETAILS

Hebrews' use of **Melchizedek** is typological. Goppelt has called attention to the extensive use of typology in the NT,[1] but Bird mentioned the significance of typology in the FT itself. Some of the types and antiypes he listed are:

1) Exodus of Abraham--exodus of Moses—exodus of Second Isaiah;
2) Sodom of Genesis—Sodom of Jeremiah;
3) Eden of Adam—Eden of Ezekiel;
4) Davidic shepherd, Elijah—Malachi's priestly Elijah—the baptizing Elijah;
5) Adam—Noah;
6) Moses—Joshua;
7) Moses—Elijah;
8) Jacob—the nation Israel.[2]

Bird correctly held that the author of Hebrews did not manufacture the typology of Melchizedek. He already had a pattern before him in the FT. The Psalmist had already uncovered Melchizedek who was the only priest-king type in the entire FT, and since he wanted to exalt a priest-king, he chose Melichizedek as the type for the character he knew as an antitype, who was to be anointed as both a priest and a king (Ps 110). Bird attributed Ps 110 to David, but it more realistically fits the anointing of Simon, the first member of the Hasmonean family to rule the liberated Palestine. Goppelt argued that Melchizedek was really not an antitype of Christ, because there was no connection between Jesus and Melchizedek in redemption history.[3] That is true, but the author of Hebrews was not writing history; he was writing rhetoric. Hebrews is a sermon or a legal argument rather than a historical report. His basic

---

[1] L. Goppelt, *Typos: The Typological Interpretation of the Old Testament in the New* (Grand Rapids: Eerdmans, 1982), tr. D. H. Madvig.

[2] C. H. Bird, "Typological Interpretation within the Old Testament: Melchizedekian Typology," *Concordia Journal* (2000):37-46.

[3] Goppelt, *Typological Interpretation*, p. 164.

sources were literary, and both Gen 14 and Ps 110 were legitimate scriptural sources for him.

COMMENTARY

[7:1]*For this Melchizedek*. The topic of **Melchizedek** was first suggested by a connection word in Heb 6:20.[1] Just a glance at this unit will show that the author has first quoted from a text in Genesis and then developed the meaning of that unit by examining individual words and expressions.[2] Albright read the Heb of Gen 14:18 as follows: *oo-máhl-kee-tzséh-dehk méh-lehk sheh-lohm-<óh> hóht-zee léh-khehm wah-yáh-yeen* (ומלכיצדק מלך שלומו הוציא לחם ויין) and translated it: And **Melchizedek, a king allied to him, brought out bread and wine.**[3] This analysis and rendering would eliminate the problematic term (*salem,* שלם) which was traditionally understood as a place name, as the author of Hebrews confirms in Heb 7:2 (see below). Josephus called it "*Saw-loo-máh*" (σολυμά) and claimed that it was the place that was afterwards called Jerusalem (Ant 1:180).[4] Jerome also identified it with the Salem (John 3:23) near Shechem in Samaria. The **bread and wine** brought out were only normal observances of hospitality. Jewett's invention is imaginary:

> He is very likely viewed as an angelic figure who offered atonement by revealing the secrets of the spiritual cult of bread and wine. Those who followed his cultic instructions would be protected by him against the malevolent angelic forces, thus allowing the elect to ascend to their heavenly homeland.[5]

The text offers no basis for that interpretation. There were secret cults in the area, such as the Mysteries of Mithra, but the author of Hebrews never mentioned them.

The FT text was put together from parts of the LXX translation of Gen 14:17-19. **Melchizedek king of Salem** is at the beginning of Gen 14:18, and **priest of the Most High God**, at the end. From Gen 14:17 comes **met**, **returning from smiting** and **the kings**, but **blessed** comes from Gen 14:19. Instead of the aorist articular infinitive *ah-nah-stréhp-sai* (ἀναστρέψαι) of LXX Gen 14:17, Hebrews has the present participle, *hoo-paw-stréh-phawn-tee* (ὑποστρέφοντι), for **returning**, but the meaning is the same. The author exchanged proper nouns for pronouns, and vice versa, but his report of the account in Genesis was basically fair.

---

[1] M. McNamara, "Melchizedek: Gen 14,17-20 in the Targums, in Rabbinic and Early Christian Literature," *Biblica* 81(2000):1-31, has evidently exhausted the usages of the term **Melchizedek** in early Jewish and Christian literature. This character was sometimes called "a priest," "a high priest," and "Shem." The territory of which he was king is located in Jerusalem, according to some texts, and in other texts, in Samaria

[2] W. L. Lane, *Hebrews 1-8* (Dallas: Word Books, c1991), p. 177, accurately corrected J. Fitzmyer, "Now This Melchizedek," *CBQ* 25 (1963):305-306. The dominant text is not Gen 14, but Ps 110:4. Gen. 14 is an important text but it plays no role in the second half of Heb 7.

[3] W. F. Albright, "Abram and Hebrew: A New Archaeological Interpretation," *BASOR* 163 (1961):52.

[4] Josephus also argued that God rewarded Abram for his generosity in returning the booty to the king of Sodom by making with him the contract by which Abram was promised a posterity as extensive as the stars of the sky (Ant 1:181-82.

[5] R. Jewett, *Letter to Pilgrims* (New York: The Pilgrim Press, c1981), p. 116

It was **Abraham** who **was returning** from war, victorious, and **Melchizedek** was the one who went out and **met him** the way people of a town went out to meet heroes who were returning (War 3:459; 4:112-113; 7:70-71, 101-103, 119)

There is some question about the unity of the text of Gen 14, but the author of Hebrews probably did not know that, so he accepted the event as historical. He also overlooked the fact that **Abraham** was still called **Abram** at the time this event was recorded. The story in Gen 14 is basically as follows: After **Chedorlaomer** and his allies overpowered the kings of Sodom and Gomorrah, capturing Lot, who also lived there, **Abraham** followed them to rescue Lot (Gen 14:1-4). When **Abram** overtook them, with 318 men, he conquered all those **kings**, took their possessions as booty, and returned (Gen 14:15-16).

The **smiting** was done with military weapons. These were battles fought openly on the ground. There was nothing mysterious about them. There is no reference about any of the warriors belonging to secret cults. They belonged to a small army. The **kings** mentioned here had to have been **kings** of very small geographical units if Abraham was able to defeat them all with 318 soldiers.

Modern scholars, acquainted with twentieth and twenty-first century nations and wars, will be surprised to learn of this war that Abraham fought with only 318 soldiers, successfully destroying several kings. These kings were obviously rulers of small towns like Sodom. When Joshua entered the Promised Land he conquered and killed five kings who ruled "kingdoms" located in a small area between Hebron and the Sea of Galilee (Josh 10). They were not emperors of great nations. Two people were interested in **Abram's** success:

1) the **king** of the small town of **Sodom**, at the south end of the Dead Sea, who hoped to recover from **Chedorlaomer** and his allies part of the possessions he had lost, and
2) **Melchizedek**, who was entitled to share in the loot.[1]

Melchizedek blessed **Abram** (Gen 14:18-20), after which **Abram** paid a tenth of his booty, perhaps as tariff for crossing his land. After that **Melchizedek** evidently went his way while **Abram** and the **king of Sodom** continued their negotiations. The author of Hebrews was not interested in the **king of Sodom** or his transaction with **Abram**, even though it was the more important of the two settlements **Abram** made that day. To him, **Melchizedek** was of primary importance, because he, like Jesus, in the author's view, was a **priest king** to whom **Abram gave a tenth of all** (Heb 7:2).

In Heb 3, the author used Ps 95 as his basic text to tell how the Hebrews forfeited the promise after the exodus from Egypt, but he elaborated on the account with the support of Num 14. In the same way, in Heb 7, although much attention is given to the Genesis account of **Melchizedek,** the basic text is Ps 110:4: **You are a priest for the age according to the order of Melchizedek**. Hughes mistranslated the expression **priest for the age** as a "priest forever."[2] The word here rendered **age** is a temporal term, meaning a space in time. The **age** mentioned here is the **age** [to come], which is the good age that would follow the coming of the Messiah.

---

[1] See *Fragments of Philo,* ed. J. R. Harris, p. 72, on Gen 14:18.

[2] P. F. Hughes, *A Commentary on the Epistle to the Hebrews* (Grand Rapids: Eerdmans, c1977), p. 264.

There was no mention of an **order of Melchizedek** in Genesis. The author of Hebrews was not the first to benefit from the figure of **Melchizedek.** Ps 110 was written either for the coronation of Hasmoneans, who became leaders without regal lineage, or it was used beneficially by them to justify their positions as priests and kings, who did not belong either to the **order** of David or Zadok. Using the well-known rhetoric rule that all prophecy was prophesied only for the days of the Messiah, the author of Ps 110 applied **Melchizedek** from Gen 14 to the king to be crowned (QDPLS 178; bSan 19b).

This was valid rhetoric because Hasmoneans were also priests as was **Melchizedek**. They identified themselves with the scriptural priest who had no **genealogy**.[1] Since Hasmoneans were not priests of the order of Zadok, they were free to defend their position on the basis of the **order of Melchizedek**. All of this was rhetorically valid according to Scripture. On the same basis the author of Hebrews appropriated **Melchizedek** and applied this figure to Jesus, the Messiah. He also took the same verse to hold that Jesus was a **priest.** This is a typical way for rhetoricians to argue. Rhetoric is not a technique for discovering truth. It is used only to defend positions already accepted by the rhetorician. Schaeffer listed many references in Zechariah, Malachi, Testament of the Twelve Patriarchs, and Dead Sea Scrolls of messiahs that were priests. In some cases the priestly messiah was ranked higher than the royal messiah. Emphasizing the importance of the priest, he also compared the servant in Second Isaiah to the priestly messiah.[2]

[2]*First [Melchizedek] is interpreted "king of righteousness*." The first half of Heb 7:2 concludes the author's presentation of the **Melchizedek** story; the second half begins his exegesis of the text. This starts by etymologizing the name **Melchizedek.** This word means literally "my **king**" (*máhl-khee*, מלכי) [is] **righteousness** or "justice" (*tséh-dehq*, צדק). Dahood followed Albright in rendering it "legitimate king,"[3] which is the same as the etymology of Josephus (*bah-see-loós deék-ai-aws*, βασιλεὺς δίκαιος) (Ant 1:180; War 6:438) and roughly corresponds to the author of Hebrews' interpretation, **king of righteousness**. Philo called Melchizedek both **king** of peace and "righteous king" (LA 3:79).

[Second] also king of Salem, which is king of peace. The second word for the author to etymologize was *Sah-láym* (Σαλήμ), which the MT pointed *shah-lóhm,* "completed," "paid in full," but the author pointed *shah-láym*, **peace.** Therefore the **king of Salem** was the **king of peace**. Dead Sea scrolls, rabbis, and Josephus follow Ps 76:2 in identifying **Salem** with Zion (Ant 1:180; War 6:438; GenApoc 22:13; TargOnq Gen 14:18), which seems to contradict Gen 33:18. The LXX of Gen 33:18

---

[1] D. W. Rooke, "Jesus as Royal Priest: Reflections on the Interpretation of the Melchizedek Tradition in Heb 7," *Biblica* 81 (2000):86, denies the relationship of the Hasmoneans with the Melchizedek tradition. She holds that Ps 110 predates the Maccabees. In her efforts to disassociate the Hasmoneans from either Ps 110 or Hebrews, Rooke argued that the Hasmoneans were considered, first of all kings, and not as high priests. Simon was declared a high priest, and his son was later declared both high priest and king, as were others who followed him. None of the relevant texts refers to the Hasmoneans as Levites or sons of Aaron, contra Rooke, p. 90, although they may have been.

[2] J. R. Schaeffer, "The Relationship between Priestly and Servant Messianism in the Epistle to the Hebrews," *CBQ* 30 (1968):395-85.

[3] M. Dahood, *Psalms III* (Garden City: Doubleday, 1970) III, pp. 117-18. See also Fitzmyer, "Now this Melchizedek. . .," p. 311.

calls **Salem** "the city of Shechem." This is a literal translation of the MT *shah-láym eer sheh-khéhm* (שׁלם עיר שׁכם), however, which means Jacob entered, **safe and sound, the city of Shechem**. By the time Joshua was written, at least, Jerusalem was known by the name it still holds (Josh 10:1).

Salem was a location near Aenon, where John the Baptist was baptizing (John 3:23), but that only locates it near water somewhere. Eusebius reported that Abraham was admitted as a guest into the temple of the city called Mount Gerizim (*áhr-gahr-uh-zeém*, ἀργαρεζίμ), which, being interpreted, is "Mount of the Most High," and received gifts from **Melchizedek,** who was "king and **high priest** of God" (PrepEv 9:17, 491a; also 7:7-8). It is evident that Jews and Samaritans both made the same claim on the city related to **Melchizedek.** The Samaritan version identifies **Salem** with Mount Gerizim as the place where **Melchizedek** ruled and officiated as **priest**. Since Shechem is at the foot of Mount Gerizim, the one who ruled Shechem would officiate on Mount Gerizim, where the temple was. This supports the LXX translation of Gen 33:18. The author of Hebrews was happy to be able to interpret **Melchizedek, king of Salem** as **king of righteousness** and **king of peace**, since the Messiah was expected to rule justly and to establish peace (Isa 9:5-6; 32:17; Jer 23:5-6; 33:15; Dan 9:24; Zech 9:1-10; Mal 4:2). This did not mean that he would never have war, but that he would overcome all of his enemies so that the land would have **rest** from its enemies (Josh 21:44).

Melchizedek was not really a very important personage in the history of Israel. He met **Abram** once, collected his tariff, and went his way, but the author of Hebrews makes much of the silence. On the basis that if it is not in the Scripture, it is not in the world (so QDPIS 178; bSan 107b?), the author reasoned that since nothing was said about **Melchizedek's** origin in the Scripture, from the legal and rhetorical point of view he did not have any. To support this judgment, the author of Hebrews used a familiar poem.

The author of Hebrews was not the only one to attribute messianic significance to **Melchizedek**. Several Jewish scholars of antiquity identified **Melchizedek** with the Hasmoneans (see Commentary on Heb 5:6). The messianic character of **Melchizedek** is especially clear in one of the Dead Sea scrolls (11QMelch*)*. This document disclosed the expectation of a Jubilee that would come at the end of days for the captives, the sons of light, also called the sons of Heaven, who belonged to the heritage of **Melchizedek. Melchizedek** was to proclaim release to the captives and atonement for their crimes. This would be the last Jubilee, the appointed time of favor for **Melchizedek,** when God would judge his people and punish those who favored the lot of Belial. God would punish them on the day of vindication in the last days. This would come as a fulfillment of Isa 52:7, 9; 61:1-2 which promised that one would come proclaiming good news and announcing peace to Zion.[1] All of this interpretation is coherent with normal biblical beliefs about Jubilee and the Day of Atonement. There is no need to conjecture a "the secrets of the spiritual cult," that Jewett proposed.[2]

[3]*Without father, without mother, without genealogy*. The character, **Melchizedek**, provided a wonderful opportunity for eisegesis. There is very little written about **Melchizedek**, but nevertheless he was included in Scripture. Given the thesis that

---

[1] See also *San*. 97b; Buchanan, *The Consequences of the Covenant* (Leiden: E. J. Brill, 1970), pp. 9-15.

[2] Jewett, *Letter*, p. 116.

there is nothing in the world that is not in the Scripture, so far as rhetorical argument goes, that which the Scripture did not report about **Melchizedek** did not happen.

An eisegete is a person who translates a text, using ideas and meanings that belong to the interpreter's opinions, and interprets the text as if his own notions constituted the real meaning of the text. The author of Hebrews was such as eisegete as that. Since there was no mention in the text of **Melchizedek's** father, mother, or genealogy, the author concluded that none ever existed. This conclusion fit in nicely for monks whose only families were their legal families. They denied any physical genealogy they had once had. Jesus denied the parents who gave him birth and held that his only family was his group of apostles (John 2:4; Matt 12:46-50). He taught his disciples to call no man "father," on earth (Matt 23:9). They were required to hate their formerly family relatives (Luke 14:25-26). This monastic attitude of Jesus might be considered a basis for claiming that Jesus had **no genealogy**. It was not necessary, however, for the author of Hebrews. He needed only his rhetorical skills to use the Scripture as he did.

Furthermore, no mention was made of Melchizedek's death, so he evidently never died. Eisegesis in relationship to **Melchizedek** did not end with the author of Hebrews. Later Justin Martyr (Dial 33) and Epiphanius, (Adv. Haer 2:1, 35-40) noticed that there was no mention of **Melchizedek** having been circumcised. Therefore he had not been circumcised and was, instead, a priest for the uncircumcised. Jerome said since the text does not tell of his marriage, he was celibate and therefore an example for the celibate priesthood (*Adversus Jovinianum* 1:23). Modern eisegetes have felt free to benefit from still further omissions. Grässer, for example said, "Melchizedek is not earthly, but of *heavenly* [emphasis his] origin,"[1] probably because the text does not say that Melchizedek was earthly. Following the same rhetoric it could be argued that he was not heavenly, because the text does not say that he was.

The text tells nothing of Melchizedek's origin. This leaves plenty of room for eisegetical fiction, according to the accepted rules of rhetoric. If the necessity arose it could be argued that Melchizedek had no hair, eyes, ears, or feet. The text does not say that he had scales or fins. Therefore he must not have been *kasher* (כשר). The text does not say he was human. Therefore he must have been angelic, divine, or satanic. The value of this rhetoric rule has no relationship to the disclosure of facts. It shows only the skill and imagination of rhetorical eisegetes.

Michel noted the similarity in poetic structure between Heb 1:3 and Heb 7:3, which he took to be from the same source.[2] If so, it must have been an important source because both were given strategic locations and treated as proof texts. Windisch observed that the terms **without father, without mother, without genealogy**, were often applied to deities in Greek literature.[3] One writer described Athene as *ah-may-tawr* (ἀμήτωρ) (Op 33:100) (motherless) and Hephaistos as *ah-páh-tohr* (ἀπάτωρ) (fatherless).[4] On the basis of Gen 20:2, Philo said Sarah was *ah-máy-tohr* (Ebr 61; Heres 62), and reports that other philosophers claim that the virgin Nike was *ah-máy-tohr* (Op 33:100). Philo's argument for Sarah was on the same basis as that of the author of Hebrews. No mention was made in Scripture of the identity of Sarah's mother. Therefore, either her mother was unknown or she did not

---

[1] E. Grässer, *An die Hebräer* (Zurich: Benziger Verlag, c1990) II, p. 28.

[2] Michel, *Hebräer*, p. 114.

[3] H. Windisch, *Der Hebräerbrief* (Tübingen: J. C. B. Mohr, 1931), p. 60.

[4] Pollux, *Onamasticon* 3:26.

have one. Since that which is not in the Scripture is not in the world, for sake of argument, neither Sarah nor Melchizedek had parents.

Neyrey documented a list of the various Greek deities that were immortal, had no genealogy, and were uncreated. He concluded from this that for the author of Hebrews and the readers of this document, Jesus was a true deity. He was not just a hero made into a deity.[1] The text that convinced Neyrey that Jesus was also a true deity was **Without father, without mother, without genealogy, having neither beginning of days nor end of life (Heb 7:3).** The author, however, did not follow this and say Jesus *was* a true deity. Rather the text said he *resembled* the son of God and was a priest that would never lose his office. Legally, messiahs and kings were considered both sons of God and also God (Heb 1:5-8; Ps. 45:6-7; Ps 2:7). Solomon was called God's son (2Sam 7:14). Judges were called gods, but they still died like other human beings (Ps 82:60-7). The author probably knew as much about Jesus as other NT writers, and he probably realized that he had been born; he knew of his sacrificial death.

Since this poem was once independent of the rest of the document, it is difficult to know whether it was originally intended to show any relationship to the FT or not. Some of the following are possibilities: The expression, **without genealogy,** may echo Isa 53:8: **Who shall declare his generation** (*geh-neh-ahn*, γενεάν)? For the author of Hebrews the importance was that there is no report of **Melchizedek's** death. Since the Scripture is the only source for data, for the sake of argument, therefore, he never died.

Resembling the son of God. The expression **resembling the son of God** may reflect the narrative of the fiery furnace. In that story, **one like a son of God** appeared in the furnace (Dan 3:25). In one of the Dead Sea Scrolls the expression **Son of God** is given as an interpretation of the term, **Son of man** in Dan 7:13, indicating that the terms both were expressions describing a king. The author may intentionally have alluded to two passages in Daniel to describe Melchizedek.

The greatest significance of this poem for the author was that it gave him still more support for his conviction that Jesus was both king and priest. The poem said its subject was one **resembling the son of God,** which means king, and that **he remains a priest continually** (*ays taw dee-ay-neh-káys*, εἰς τὸ διηνεκής). The Greek means "continually," "without interruption," or something like that, depending on the context. In referring to a dynasty, this means the family would never fail to have a male heir to rule.[2] This supported the author's main text, which claimed that Jesus was **a priest for the age** [to come] (*ays tawn ai-óh-nah*, εἰς τὸν αἰῶνα) (Ps 110:4).

The age to come is not eternity. It is a certain period of time that can begin and end. The age to come was the age that followed the evil age under the rule of foreign powers. Before the author's time, Simon, the Hasmonean, had been called **leader and high priest for the age** (1Macc 14:41, 47), which meant **the age** of the Hasmonean rule. This **age** lasted from the rule of Simon (140 BIA) to the rule of Herod the Great (ca 20 BIA) or the Roman governors (6/7 IA).

---

[1] J. H. Neyrey, "'Without Beginning of Days or End of Life,' (Hebrews 7:3):Topos for a True Deity," *CBQ* 53 (1991):439-55.

[2] There are some hints that suggest a Hasmonean subject for the original poem. Judas was never a king, but came like a Son of man (Dan 7). Simon was not a king, either. He was priest, however, and called a prince (1Macc 14:27). He was "like a Son of God."

R. Simeon Hasida said the four craftsmen (Zech 2:3) were the Messiah from David's line, the Messiah from Joseph's line, Elijah, and the righteous priest (*bSuk* 52b). The office of **righteous priest** (*kóh-hehn séh-dehq*) was probably the same office as the "legitimate teacher" or "teacher of righteousness" (*móh-ray tséh-dehq,* מורה צדק), who was also a priest.[1] Throughout his message the author was dependent upon Ps 110, from which he gained his theological and biblical basis for his claims about Jesus. Since Melchizedek was mentioned there, it was very important to deal with him in great detail.

4-5*See how great he is.* **See how great he is** is a rather free translation of the author's figurative *theh-oh-ráy-teh deh pay-leé-kaws hoó-taws* (θεωρεῖτε δὲ πηλίκος οὗτος), **observe how large [is] this one!** The word *pay-leé-kaws* occurs only here and in Gal 6:1 in the entire NT. This means, "**Look** in the Scripture in Gen 14 to **see how great** Melchizedek is."

To him the patriarch Abraham gave a tenth. The **patriarch Abraham** was the chief of the entire Israelite family corporation. Whereas the author paraphrased the LXX Gen 14:20 in Heb 7:2, in Heb 7:4 he quoted **Abraham gave a tenth**. **Choice [acquisitions]** (*ahk-raw-thee-neé-ohn,* ἀκροθινίων) refer to the best of a group, the first fruits. Here it deals with the choice parts of the booty he had taken from the kings. **To collect [the] tithe** is the translation given for *ah-paw-deh-kah-toón* (ἀποδεκατοῦν) which can refer either to the person claiming the tithe from another (1Sam 8:15; Neh 10:37) or to the person who pays the tithe (Gen 28:22; Deut 14:21; 26:12; Matt 23:23; Luke 11:12).

The sons of Levi . . . collect [the] tenth. Heb 7:5 is the first half of an *a fortiori* argument, in which **the sons of Levi** are exalted, so that they can be compared unfavorably to **Melchizedek** and thus exalt **Melchizedek** even higher. The Levites were not the sons of Aaron or Zadok who were designated as priests and were distinguished from the Levites. The Levites were subordinate cultic assistants in the judgment of Ezekiel, Nehemiah, and the community governed by Rule of the Community (1QS 2:19-21), but here, as in Deut 17:9, 18; 18:1; 24:8; 27:9, the priests are called the Levitical priests. Because they were given no inheritance in the land, Levites were assigned certain privileges to compensate for this (Deut 18). Since the Levites were sons of Jacob, they were also descendants of Abraham. They were authorized by law to collect tenths from "their brothers." This ranked them above the other Israelites.

The one who does not have a genealogy. The second part of the comparison deals with **Melchizedek** who **does not have a genealogy from them**, i.e., he does not descend from the Levites or from the Zadokites. In fact he does not have **a genealogy** at all, according to the verse quoted in Heb 7:3. The author knew **Melchizedek** had **no genealogy** because no mention was made of it in the Scripture. The same was true for the Hasmoneans. Mattathias was the grandson of Joarib, who is nowhere mentioned in Scripture, so we do not know from what tribe the Hasmoneans descended. Therefore no argument can be based on their genealogy.

---

[1] See further Buchanan, "The Priestly Teacher of Righteousness," *RQum* 6 (1969):553-58.

Rhetorically, they have no genealogy. The same is true of **Melchizedek**. Like the Hasmoneans, from the report of the Scripture, **Melchizedek** had no genealogy.[1]

According to the rabbis, there is nothing in the world that is not in the Scripture. That does not mean that in actuality nothing in the world exists that is not in the Scripture, but that there is nothing in the world **that can be used in a Jewish court case** that is not in the Scripture. Courts normally to determine before the trial which facts can be admitted as evidence into the trial. All that is excluded is treated as if it did not exist, even though all parties to the trial know that it does. So far as that particular trial is concerned "it is not in the world." Hebrews 1-12 is a legal argument or a sermon. Therefore some data can be excluded from consideration. That means that, so far as legal argument can prove, no claim can be made for **Melchizedek's genealogy.** That possibility is outside of the limits of the argument.

Rabbis and early Christian jurists would not admit into an argument anything that could not be substantiated in Scripture. The Scripture was the legal authority against which all argument must be based. These were the rhetorical rules. Therefore, since there is no report in Scripture of **Melchizedek's** parents or genealogy, for the sake of argument, these were non-existent. **Melchizedek,** however, is reported in Scripture, so he might be mentioned, and he was.

Also on a rhetorical basis, Jesus was identified with **Melchizedek**, even though that was not his name. Another rule of rhetoric was that all prophecy was prophesied only for the days of the Messiah. Since Jesus was the Messiah, all Scripture could be applied to him, including the Psalm that mentioned **Melchizedek** and the reference to Melchizedek in Genesis. This is good rhetoric, but it has no factual value. This means that the claim in Hebrews that Jesus was a high priest was based solely on rhetoric—not on fact. That which has been proved by rhetoric is not the same as that which is factual. Rooke correctly said,

> It is not about a priest who is being made king but about a king who is also being *declared* [emphasis added] a priest.[2]

Via said the same thing slightly differently:

> The Son-priest is what God speaks into existence by addressing the Old Testament word to him (Pss 2;7; 45:6-7; 102:25-27; 110:1-4).[3]

It was the *declaration* or the *speaking* that rhetorically brought Jesus into existence as a priest. God spoke only because the author selected certain words of the Scripture to say that he had.

From other NT sources Jesus was recognized as "Messiah," "Son of God," "Son of man," and "king"—all of which are royal rather than priestly titles. His priesthood was not ontological, as Rooke claims. Nor was it "impossible for him not to be a priest."[4] The argument that the author of Hebrews was making needed Jesus to be a priest, so he declared that Jesus was a priest and then justified his declaration

---

[1] Rooke, "Royal Priest," p. 90, fn 30, said that the Hasmoneans were "priests of the Levitical Aaronide line," but she did not indicate the source of her claim.

[2] Rooke, "Royal Priest," p. 86.

[3] D. O. Via, "The Letter to the Hebrews: Word of God and Hermeneutics," *Perspectives in Religious Studies* 26 (1999):223, 225.

[4] Rooke, "Royal Priest," p. 92.

on the basis of rhetorical rules. The possibility open for Jesus to be a priest is only rhetorical—not ontological. During his physical lifetime Jesus never was a priest or a sacral king. Via correctly said,

> Again we see that the words of Scripture define the identity of Jesus, but the author's *presupposition* [emphasis added] about who Jesus is is what enables him to select the Scripture texts that apply to Jesus and to interpret them in his particular way. That is, it is his *pre-understanding* [emphasis added] that leads him to see Psalm 8 as applying only to Jesus rather than to humankind, which the plainer sense of the Old Testament text seems to indicate.[1]

It is very likely that Jesus never was a priest and was only labeled a priest for the rhetorical needs of the author, but there is another conjectured possibility to consider. Monasticism probably had its origin in Babylon when the temple in Jerusalem no longer existed. Monasticism developed to provide a temporary substitute for a house of the Lord, where the Lord could dwell in purity. Monks kept their monasteries as undefiled as the temple in Zion and their dining room as pure as the altar in Zion (War 2:129). Later Roman Catholic monks were all called "priests" even though they were neither from the tribes of Levi or Zadok. Since he was a monk, he may also have been a priest, possibly also from the same sect as the author of Hebrews. As a son of David by physical birth he was a legitimate king. As a legal son of God by legal ceremony, he was also a priest and a monk.

In some countries there were sacral kings, as Rooke argued. In such cases all kings were also priests, *ex officio*, just as all presidents of the United States are all commanders-in-chief of the United States armed forces. That is true even if the president never served one day in the armed forces. That was not true of Judah or Israel, where the offices of priest and king had been separated ever since the time of David and Zadok. Jesus was evidently part of a program in which John the Baptist was the priest with which he was teamed. The only exception from the time of David to the time of Jesus when a king of Judah was also a priest was during the rule of the Hasmoneans.

National leadership began with the rule of Judas the Maccabee, who may or may not have ever been a high priest. Josephus has two conflicting reports of the origin of Hasmonean priesthood.

1) There was a seven year period before Jonathan when Judah did not have a high priest (Ant 20:237). This seems to have been while Judas was leader of the nation.
2) Judas was made high priest about the time he made a treaty with Rome. At the same time Simon was made general of the armed forces (Ant 12:417), and Simon was renewed in that office during the leadership of Jonathan (Ant 13:145-47).

Marcus reasonably questioned the authenticity of the claim that Judas was high priest.

---

[1] Via, "The Letter," p. 225.

1) That claim is not included in First Maccabees, and
2) it is in conflict with Josephus's other statement.

According to both reports, Judas was not made high priest automatically by virtue of his birth as a priest. Even if Hasmoneans had been Levites, as Rooke claims, Levites were subordinate to the Zadokites, who were the high priests by heritage. Judas was never a sacral king, officially. There continued to be orthodox Jews in the country who thought Hasmoneans were illegitimate high priests. They did not belong to the correct priestly family, namely the Zadokites. Only some of the Hasmoneans became both priests and kings, and they held these positions, not because they had been born priests "of the Levitical Aaronide line," but because they obtained these offices through political and military means along with the authority to hold these two offices at the same time. Without this political and military power, none of the Hasmoneans would ever have become the sacral kings of which Rooke has written. They would not have received it by family inheritance alone.

Melchizedek collected the tenth from Abraham which implies that he was as much superior to Abraham as the Levites were to the Israelites. The high priest, however, collected tithes from the Levites (Lev 18:21; Num 18:26-28), and Jesus was a high priest, according to Hebrews. Furthermore, Melchizedek **blessed** Abram, whom the author calls **the one who had the promises** to indicate his importance, referring to the **promises** God made to Abram in Gen 15 and 18.

The Dead Sea scroll that preserved the role of **Melchizedek** in relationship to Jubilee is preserved in a scroll, the fragment of which is now 25 lines in length (11Qmelch). It was found in cave 11, written in Hebrew. In a separate cave, written in Aramaic, were found five small fragments of another document, featuring Melkireshah (4Qamram). These two names were not both included in the same document, but because the name of one means "king of righteousness" justice, or innocence (*mehl-khee-tséh-dehk*, מלכי צדק) and the other "king of wickedness, evil, or guilt," it was normal for scholars to place them into the same class. If they had been called "attorney of justice" and "attorney of guilt," they might be considered a "plaintiff" and a "defendant," but both were called kings, so they seem to have been good and bad rulers, or innocent and guilty rulers. Kobelski studied both characters and texts in relationship to Heb 7.[1] He related these to Iranian dualism, angelology, Dead Sea dualism, and Heb 7. He compared them to the light-darkness dualism, but he found no direct relationship between Heb 7 and the Dead Sea literature. The author of Heb seemed interested in Melchizedek only in relationship to its scriptural setting. There is no indication that he was interested in Melchireshah at all.

TEXT

7Incontestably, the lesser is blessed by the greater, 8and here, on the one hand,
mortal men receive tithes, but there, on the other hand, it is attested, **He lives**. 9One
might even [extend the figure to] say [that] Levi, who receives tenths, was [himself]
assessed the tenth through Abraham, 10for he was still in the loins of his father when
Melchizedek met him.

[1] P. J. Kobelski, *Melchizedek and Melchireshah* (Washington: CBA, c1981).

COMMENTARY

[7]*Incontestably, the lesser is blessed by the greater*. It is not true that **the lesser is** always **blessed by the greater**. There are **blessings** which the inferior gives to the superior, such as the anonymous woman in the crowd who said to Jesus, **Blessed is the womb that bore you, and the breasts that you sucked** (Luke 11:27) and the occasion when Joab blessed David (2Sam 14:22), but the great majority of the **blessings** listed in the Scripture are those given by God, Aaron, a father, or someone else in a superior position. It was this kind of **blessing** about which the author spoke. When **the greater** blesses **the lesser**, he or she not only narrates a **blessing** but sometimes acts in a way that benefits **the lesser.** When Melchizedek, however, **blessed** Abram he recited a **blessing** for Abram. It was Abram who gave Melchizedek tithes. There is an argument about the matter. **The lesser is** not always **blessed by the greater**. The author of Hebrews, however, claimed that it was and argued on that basis. Since it was already shown that Melchizedek **blessed** Abram, the next step was to show that this meant that Melchizedek was superior to Abram as he did so. Two witnesses were required to uphold a case in court. The author of Hebrews strained to provide both of them.

> 1) The first was to claim that the Levites were inferior to Melchizedek on the basis that they were descendants of Abraham and thereby paid tithes to Melchizedek.
> 2) The second was that **the greater** always **blesses the lesser**, even though that is not always the case.

Rabbis did not concur in the author's depreciative evaluation of Abram in comparison to **Melchizedek.** Following the kind of argument used to show that John the Baptist was inferior to Jesus, rabbis said that as soon as **Melchizedek blessed Abraham, Abraham** objected that a servant must never be given precedence over his master. At that point, **Abram** was given the priesthood. Scriptural proof for that comes from Ps 110:4, which the rabbis claim was written to **Abraham: The Lord said to my Lord, "Sit at my right hand, until I make your enemies your footstool**." This is followed by, **The Lord has sworn, and will not recant, "You are a priest for the age after the order of Melchizedek**." **After the order of Melchizedek** means that because of **Melchizedek, Abraham** was made a **priest for the age,** just as Israel was given a **contract for the age** (*buh-reét oh-láhm* (ברית עולם)) (Isa 55:15). Because the rabbis had different goals, they argued for different conclusions, but both argued from the principle that the Scripture is the only source of authority that is valid. Rhetoricians use this kind of logic to make a text prove whatever they need it to prove. Of course, **Abraham** was no more a priest than Jesus was, but legally the rabbis "proved" that he was, using the same rhetoric and the same text the author of Hebrews used.

Rabbis also claimed that the quotation, **He was a priest of the Most High God** (Gen 14:18), meant that **Melchizedek** was a priest, but not his posterity (bNed 32b). That would also follow, because there is no mention of **Melchizedek's** posterity in Scripture. The author of Jubilees used the statement about tenths in Gen 14:20 to justify tithing in general. This, of course, meant tenths to the priests who were sons of Aaron, Zadok, and Levi. In the Jubilee account, there is a lacuna which covers the section mentioning the name **Melchizedek**. There is no way of knowing whether this was an intentional omission or not (Jub 13:25-26).

[8]*Mortal men receive tenths*. The Levites who **receive tenths** were described as **mortal men**. This is just a statement of basic knowledge. Levites, like others, died. There would be no purpose in making such a statement if it could not be contrasted with **Melchizedek**. Of **Melchizedek, it is attested, *He lives***. Whereas Levites die, Melchizedek **lives**. One is far superior to the other. Furthermore the author would not have contrasted the mortality of the Levites to **Melchizedek**, either, if it had not been for the rhetorical possibility of continuing and claiming for Jesus that which he had gained rhetorically for **Melchizedek.** He wanted to show that Jesus had not died but still **lives.**

When the subject is left undetermined in reference to a statement or testimony, the author regularly meant "God," "the Scripture," or "the Holy Spirit" says or testifies, but there is no basis in the Scripture quoted, or in any of the proof texts from Scripture used by the author, which would justify the claim that **Melchizedek lives**.

The only apparent quotation that might justify this claim is in the little poem quoted in Heb 7:3. There the subject, which the author held to be **Melchizedek**, was said to have no end "of life" (*zoh-áys*, ζωῆς), evidently because his death was not reported in the Scripture. That seems to have been used as a proof text to show that **Melchizedek lives** (*zay*, ζῇ), just as **without genealogy** was used to prove **Melchizedek** was not from the genealogy of the Levites (Heb 7:6). If this is the correct analysis of the data, then the author evidently held the poem to have doctrinal status very nearly that of the Scripture. If only we had access to the source from which this poem was taken, many points would be clearer. It is obvious that the author of Hebrews was proof texting here the way attorneys sometimes use laws and precedents to prove cases. The result achieved by this method is legal proof rather than truth.

[9-10]*Levi, who receives tenths*. The Greek for **one might even [extend the figure to] say [that]** is the little idiom, *hohs éh-paws aye-páyn* (ὡς ἔπος εἰπεῖν), which is very common in Greek literature. It softens an expression. It is a mild indirect apology in advance for that which follows. An English equivalent might be, "If I may be allowed the expression."[1] The argument thus introduced was certainly an extended one: Since Abraham paid tithes to Melchizedek, and Levi was one of the descendants of Abraham, therefore Abraham represented Levi in this act, even though Levi had not yet been born! Levi was considered **still in the loins of his father** Abraham **when Melchizedek met** Abraham. This does not make sense physically. The sperm that produced Levi could not have been preserved endlessly in Abraham's loins. This is only possible as a legal argument.

Legally, the entire family corporation belongs together from beginning to end. All members of the corporation can die and be replaced, but the corporation continues as the family. Possessions, obligations, debts, status, and authority pass from one generation to another and are kept within the family corporation. On this basis, Levi, through the agency of Abraham, gave tithes to **Melchizedek.** Therefore the collector of tenths (Levi) was himself required to give the tenth to **Melchizedek,** who was proved by this act to be much greater than Levi. Then the point of the *a fortiori* argument is, "If Levi is great, how much more so **Melchizedek**!"

---

[1] M. Stuart, *Commentary on the Epistle to the Hebrews in Greek and English* (Andover: Warren F. Draper, 1828), p. 167. For numerous examples, see R. Williamson, *Philo and the Epistle to the Hebrews* (Leiden: E. J. Brill, 1970), pp. 103-6.

Summary. Heb 7 introduced by a quotation from Ps 110:4 referring to **Melchizedek** (Heb 6:20). The opening unit of that chapter (Heb 7:1-10) begins with the catchword, **Melchizedek**, which was taken from Gen 14. The scriptural passage (Gen 14:17-20) and the poem quoted in Heb 7:3 provide the textual basis for the rest of the unit. The inclusion is formed by the words **Melchizedek . . . met** (Heb 7:1, 10). The point of this unit was to show that Jesus was superior to the Levites. The author had already argued that he was superior to the angels and Moses. By showing that Jesus was legally **Melchizedek**, and therefore superior to **Abraham**, he concluded that Jesus was superior also to the **Levites**. His reasons for claiming **Melchizedek's** superiority were as follows:

(a) He received **tenths** from **Abraham**, and, by extension, from the **Levites**;
(b) he **blessed** his inferior, **Abraham**, even though all the nations of the land were **blessed** by **Abraham**; and
(c) **he lives**, in contrast to mortal men like the **Levites**.

This is delightful logic for anyone who likes to play mental games, but it was no game for the author. He fully believed that the Lord was under contract to fulfill the prophecies in the FT as he uncovered them.

TEXT

[11]If atonement had been through the levitical priesthood (for the people were governed by it), what need would there still be for another priest to arise according to the order of Melchizedek and not to be declared according to the order of Aaron? [12]For when the priesthood is changed, there is necessarily a change of law as well, [13]for the one about whom these things are said belonged to a different tribe, from which no one ministered at the altar. [14]For it is clear that our Lord arose from Judah, regarding which tribe Moses said nothing about priests, [15]and it is still more abundantly clear [that] if another priest arises according to the likeness of [16][this one] who did not come into existence according to the law of a fleshly commandment but according to the power of an indestructible life [17]for it is attested, **You are a priest for the age according to the order of Melchizedek**. [18]For, on the one hand, a previously functioning commandment is removed because of its weakness and uselessness--[19]for the law perfected nothing--but on the other hand, [there is the] beginning of a better hope through which we come near to God.

TECHNICAL DETAILS

The long, involved sentence that begins with Heb 7:15, concludes with the second half of Heb 7:19--***If* another priest arises . . . *then*** there is the beginning of a better hope. In between are some statements that make the logic seem more reasonable.

COMMENTARY

[11]*If atonement had been through the levitical priesthood*. The word translated **atonement** (*teh-láy-oh-sees*, τελείωσις) occurs in this form only in Luke 1:45 and

here. In Luke 1:45, it clearly means **fulfillment** of Israel's expectations. In the LXX the term is used in relationship to the liturgy by which Aaron and his sons are to qualify as priests. The RSV has translated it by "ordination" (Exod 29:9, 22, 26, 27, 29, 31, 34).

Aaron and his sons were made priests when God ordered Moses to ordain them. This involved calling Aaron and his sons before Moses.

1) This first involved making the proper priestly garments.
2) These garments were then put on Aaron and his sons.
3) These men were then brought into the holy place before the altar.
4) Aaron was anointed with oil.
5) They became priests when the liturgy was completed (*oo-mee-láyt-tah eht yah-dáhm,* ומלאת את ידם). Literally this means "you have filled up their hand" or "and you shall fill up their hand" (Exod 28:41). By filling up their hand Aaron gave them power or authority.
6) the final step of ordination was the sacrifice.

The Hebrew word *yahd* (יד) usually means "hand" or "arm." It is another word for power or authority. Military weapons are still called "arms" today. Occasionally it means "memorial" or "monument" (Isa 56:5) *Mee-láy* usually means "fulfill," "complete," or "finish." This is the word which the LXX translated *teh-láy-oh-sis* and is often rendered **perfect**. RSV takes the whole expression *mee-láy yáhd* to mean "ordained." In the Levitical context it is a necessary process by which a non-priest is filled with power and authority to become a priest. When Moses filled up their hands he filled them with legal authority and power to function as priests. That which had happened to Aaron and his sons also happened to Jesus, according to the author of Hebrews. In the process he became an ordained **high priest,** and the *only* **high priest.** The problem here is that the verb is also used in the active voice. Not only was Jesus completed or fulfilled, but he also made this happen to others who were **sanctified** (Heb 5:8-9).

These others did not become empowered in the process, so this word must have a different significance, and it is related to the **Day of Atonement.** The liturgy which happened to Jesus seems to have been his **atonement** by which he became **perfectly** free of crime, as other **high priests** do on the **Day of Atonement**. After he became atoned, he was then able to **offer sacrifice** for the people. Here it is translated **atoned completely**, to give expression to the force of completing or finishing something. The LXX took the word **yahd** (יד)to mean "hand," probably not familiar with the broader meaning.

This liturgy was **completed on Aaron and his sons** (Exod 29:9). If the verb "fill" is given the past tense, it means that the liturgy was completed, and Aaron was ordained. If this is taken in the future tense then the completion was accomplished by the sacrifices that followed. In which case, the final step of ordination was the sacrifice.

When the author of Hebrews began his discussion of the priesthood, he first went back to the anointing of Aaron to start his argument. The author assumed that Moses wrote the entire Pentateuch and David wrote all of the Psalms. The sons of Aaron were established priests on the basis of the Pentateuch, which preceded the Psalms by as many years as Moses preceded David. This was the logic by which the author understood the testimony in Ps 95 that the Israelites would not enter into the **rest**, to cancel the claim in Joshua that they had done so. Also here, the Psalms take precedence. In the Pentateuch the sons of Aaron and Phineas were promised the priesthood, for the age, but in Ps 110 there is an **oath** which [came] after the law which established Melchizedek a priest **for the age**. This supersedes the previous **promise**, in the judgment of the author. Since David also wrote Ps 2, which the author identified with Jesus as well as he identified the **priest** in Ps 110 with Jesus, the author reasoned that the **oath** in Ps 110 could also apply to the **Son** mentioned in Ps 2:7. This was rhetorically possible on the basis that all prophecy is prophesied only for the days of the Messiah.

To be consistent with Heb 7:27, which seems to mean that Jesus' sacrifice of himself was for a cleansing of his own, as well as the people's, crimes it would also be the sacrifice of Jesus which **made [him] ordained completely for the age**. This is consistent with the claim that he was empowered completely through **suffering** (Heb 2:10). He learned obedience through the things he **suffered**, in the process of which he was ordained (Heb 5:8-9). This is in contrast to the **offerings** of the levitical **priests** which do not atone (Heb 9:9; 10:1). Jesus' **offering** of himself, however, not only ordained him completely, but also atoned those who were sanctified (Heb 10:14). The relationship of ordination to sacrifice makes it likely that the author understood Jesus' offering to be that which made him as the Son atoned. This supports the interpretation of Heb 1:3 to mean that Jesus made an **offering** for his and the other people's crimes before he ascended to sit at the right hand of God. It also seems consistent with the rest of Heb 7 and the author's doctrine of atonement, but it does not support the concept that Jesus was crimeless before his crucifixion.

The fact that **another priest has arisen** means there was a "need." Therefore there was **no perfection through the levitical priesthood**. This argument would only make sense if the **priest to arise according to the order of Melchizedek** came later than the Levites, and therefore later than **Melchizedek** himself.[1] According to Hebrews, this was Jesus. The order of **Melchizedek** was not the posterity of **Melchizedek**. Just as **Melchizedek** had no genealogy, he also had no posterity, as the Levites did. He had an order, such as a monastic order which had succession by membership and not by inheritance.

The Pentateuchal texts that are relevant here are Gen 15, 18; Exod 28-29, and Lev 8. The Genesis texts report the way the **promises** were given to **Abraham**, and the Exodus and Leviticus texts tell of the liturgy by which **Aaron** and his sons become **high priests**. The contract God made with **Abraham promised** three things:

1) the land of Palestine
2) and extensive posterity, and
3) prosperity.

These were the **promises** the author of Hebrews, like most of his contemporaries, expected to be fulfilled. Since the last time the land had been restored was after the **Day of Atonement** in 164 BIA the author of Hebrews thought the **Day of Atonement** was a necessary factor for the restoration in their own day.

The Hasmoneans were priests and the later ones were messiahs and kings. The Scripture does not say whether they were from the tribe of Levi or not. They were only mentioned as sons of Joarib (1Macc 2:1). No extensive family is reported

---

[1] A. T. Hanson, "The Christ in the OT according to Hebrews," *StEv* 2 (1964):398-402, has argued unconvincingly that the author of Hebrews intended Christ to be identified with Melchizedek himself.

for them. The author turned to the Scripture that dealt with the establishment of **priests** and the rules of the Day of Atonement. That is basically the same meaning as is understood here. It refers to the fulfillment of required obligations of the priestly office. The claim is that the priestly ordination was not adequate to qualify them for their duties.

The infinitive **to arise** (*ahn-eés-tahs-thai,* ἀνίστασθαι) means to arise as one arises from sleep or rises to leave. It also refers to resurrection from the dead. For a **priest to arise** might imply that he had arisen for action, appeared on the scene, or assumed his office. On the basis that God does not allow things that are unnecessary, the author reasoned that **another priest** would not have arisen for action if the existing priesthood had been functioning effectively. That which was important for a **high priest** to make happen was to get all of Israel's crimes forgiven on the **Day of Atonement**. There was within historical remembrance an occasion when the **Day of Atonement** really atoned. The people knew it was effective, because the land was restored. This occurred in 164 BIA, at the end of the Seleucid common age and the beginning of the Hasmonean holy age.

In the Fall of 164 Judas won a famous battle of Beth-horon. This was the turning point of the war with the Seleucids. After the battle, the troops returned to Jerusalem; Judas had the temple cleansed and rededicated. This was the first Hanukkah. This happened after the **Day of Atonement,** and it proved to contemporary Jews that the **Day of Atonement** had been effective; their crimes had been forgiven; and the contract God made with **Abraham** was being fulfilled.

12 *When the priesthood is changed.* For the levitical **priesthood** the **law** was either Leviticus or, more likely, the entire Pentateuch, which the author subordinated to the Psalms. The claim that the laws of the Medes and the Persians could not be changed (Dan 6:9, 13) probably meant that they could not be changed during the term of office for the particular king in power, because kings had the power to change laws when they were made kings and to make new ones after they had become kings. On that basis Jesus said he had authority over the Sabbath (Matt 12:1-8).

Evidently priesthoods worked on the same basis. The laws of the Levites were observed so long as the Levites were in office to administer them. They had been made **priests for the age,** that is for the **age** in which Moses' **law** was in effect. With the messianic **age**, however, there would be a new **priesthood**. The author reasoned that a new **priesthood** had arisen; therefore the new **priesthood** would introduce a new **law** making the old **law** invalid. This coheres with the rabbinic teaching about the Messiah. In **the age** to come there would be a ruling messiah and a new Torah.

13 *The one about whom these things were said.* Since all prophecy is prophesied only for the days of the Messiah, and Jesus was the Messiah, then **the one about whom these things are said**, in the author's judgment, was Jesus, who belonged to none of the priestly families--Aaron, Zadok, or Levi. He belonged to one of the 12 tribes, to be sure, and it was from a tribe from which there was no record of anyone ever serving as priest at the altar. He came, instead, from an order or sect to which he belonged. The order from which Jesus came, according to Matthew was the order of the Nazorians (Matt 2:23).

[14]*For it is clear that our Lord came from Judah.* **Our Lord** refers to Jesus, as also in Heb 2:3. It was generally expected that the Messiah would belong to the tribe of Judah (TgPseudJon Gen 49:9-10; 4Q PatBles 1:4), and Matthew and Luke recorded that Jesus was born in Bethlehem (Matt 2.1-6; Luke 1:32; 2:4-7), but John 7:41 said he was from Galilee. It was also widely accepted that Jesus was from the family of David and that the Messiah should also be a son of David, but the author of Hebrews made no mention of that. He admitted the Judaic origin of Jesus, partly because of tradition, partly because of scriptural prophecy (Gen 49:9-10), and partly because of the Jewish tradition that **Melchizedek** was from Jerusalem, but the author of Hebrews never mentioned the son of David as the Messiah nor Jesus as the son of David. He used messianic prophecies that had usually been applied to the son of David and applied them to Jesus, but without calling Jesus a son of David.[1]

The Greek word for **arose** is *ah-nah-téh-tal-kehn* (ἀνατέταλκεν), a different word from that used in Heb 7:11 to describe the priest to arise. The verb *ah-nah-tehl-láyn* (ἀνατελεῖν) describes rising as the sun, moon, and stars arise, and is used in this way 15 times in the FT. It also describes the sprouting or growing of plants, hair, disease, and human bodies 16 times in the FT. It occurs 25 times with a metaphorical usage in the FT, where the imagery reflects the rising or growth of stellar bodies or planets. Babylon (1), wicked ones (2), fortunes (1), ruins (l), new things (2), Israelites (1), judgment (1), vision (1), righteousness (6), faithfulness (1), life (1), light (meaning knowledge or success) (3), and the glory of the Lord (1) were all reported as subjects that would arise or had arisen to prominence or prosperity, and would increase in prominence.

This word was easily applied to a king or expected messiah. So Ezekiel spoke of a **horn** that would **arise** (Ezek 29:21). Balaam foresaw a **star** that would **arise** from Jacob who would overpower Moab and Edom (Num 24:17-18). Zechariah described Zerubbabel as a shoot, branch, or star, who would **arise** and build the temple in Jerusalem (Zech 6:12). Philo said of this man whose name was **Rising**, about whom Zechariah spoke, that he was the oldest son whom the Father **raised** up and was otherwise called his firstborn (CL 14:61-63). The title, firstborn, was not a description of the order of his physical birth in the family or the nation. It was a legal title of honor that could be applied to anyone who was legally qualified as the Messiah.

In none of the FT usages of the verb *ah-nah-the-láyn* was it employed to mean a "descendant" of a certain tribe or family. Instead of going down (descending by family), he went up (**arose**) in honor. The importance of this term to the author of Hebrews was that Jesus **arose** as the Messiah. Even though this meant **arising** from Judah, in no place in his document did the author of Hebrews explicitly identify Jesus with the son of David, nor did he show any interest in David himself. His only mention of David was in a list of various kinds of leaders (Heb 11:32) and in relationship to the Psalms, which he assumed David wrote. The royal-priestly figure, that he exalted here as the **Son, apostle, high priest, firstborn**, and one from **the order of Melchizedek**, had attributes similar to those of the Hasmoneans, who were also royal-priestly figures and some of them anointed **high priests** and kings, even though they descended neither from the line of Zadok nor from that of David. It may have been with the Hasmoneans in mind that the priest Levi was called "son"

---

1. F. F. Bruce, "The Kerygma of Hebrews," *Interpretation* 23 (1969):5, 7, unwittingly assumed Hebrews was dealing with a two-messiah doctrine which involved a son of David messiah. See also E. Grässer, *Der Glaube im Hebräerbrief* (Marburg: N. G. Elwert, 1965), pp. 73-91.

(TLevi 4:2). They were priests who **arose** from Jerusalem, and later Modein, both in the territory of **Judah** (1Macc 2:1).

The author did not go further and say Jesus descended from the Hasmoneans, but he imitated the logic the Hasmoneans used to justify Jesus' right to claim the high priesthood. He did not claim the priesthood on the basis of genealogy. Not all early Christians were willing even to agree that Jesus came from **Judah.** Some held that it was Galilee (John 7:41). The tradition that Jesus was actually born in Bethlehem (Matt 2:1; Luke 2:1-7) may have developed to conform to the normal messianic expectations (John 7:42). Since other Christians developed their own traditions and accounts of the facts dealing with Jesus, there is no certainty that the author of Hebrews did not make a few innovations himself.

Without denying other messianic expectations, the author of Hebrews used only as much historical material about Jesus as he needed to present him as a **high priest** and king like one of the Hasmoneans, though not from a priestly line. Here he used a verb to describe Jesus' appearance that was normally associated with the Messiah and probably alluded to Gen 49:9-10, which was sometimes applied to the Messiah. He said Jesus came from a tribe that was different from that of the Levites, and that made him authorized by **the order of Melchizedek**. He acknowledged that Jesus was from **Judah,** but he did not say he descended from David. Had he done so that would have associated Jesus with a two-messiah expectation, which would not allow Jesus to be a **high priest** since John the Baptist would have been the expected **high priest**.

By using terms just as he did, he could claim as much as he wanted and no more. **Our Lord arose from Judah**; he was the Messiah; he was not from the tribe of Levi but **belonged to a different tribe**; he was a priest according to the order of **Melchizedek. Moses said nothing about priests** from the tribe of **Judah.** None-the-less the Hasmoneans had arisen from **Judah** and had become **high priests**. Moses also said nothing about Joarib, Mattathias, or any of the Hasmoneans as priests.

Jews in the author's time knew about the Hasmoneans, for the Hasmonean family continued to have a great deal of influence in Palestinian politics until the last of the fortresses had been captured in 73 IA, and their memory never ceased. It was probably in conflict with the Hasmonean pretenders of Jesus' day that the author argued his case. Jesus was not just a son of David. He also had the claim to messiahship that the Hasmoneans claimed. He had been made a superior **high priest.**

15 *If another priest arises according to the likeness of Melchizedek.* TLevi 8:14 predicted that a new king would **arise** from **Judah** who would establish a new priesthood. This reference was probably intended to apply to the Hasmoneans, who were also identified with **Melchizedek** (see commentary on Heb 5:6). Without being of the same family, the author claimed that when **another priest arises** he would be **according to the likeness of [i.e., similar to] Melchizedek**. If the author had any subtle reason for changing the usual wording from "order" to **likeness** of **Melchizedek**, it may mean that the **priest** that was Jesus would be *like* the Hasmoneans, but not of the same family. Of course he may have used a different word for no other purpose than to vary his literary style.

16 *According to the power of indestructible life.* The Levites or sons of Aaron acquired their position **according to the law of a fleshly commandment**. They had inherited their positions from family and tribal descent. Moses had been the one

who commanded that Aaron and his sons would become priests. The law involved was probably the Pentateuch, which the author had insisted would change (Heb 7:12). The offices the Levites had held had been passed down from father to son with no discrimination shown to the quality of the person involved. The term "fleshly" (*sahr-keé-nays,* σαρκίνης) here refers to physical heritage, but it is also a derogatory term used in early Christian and Jewish ethical dualism. Paul contrasted the desires of the spirit to the desires of the flesh. This was not a contrast of the physical to the spiritual, but a contrast of evil action to good action.

The **works of the flesh** were just as ethically oriented as the **works of the spirit**, but from a negative point of view. They did not concentrate on material aspects. They were listed as follows:

> **immorality, impurity, licentiousness, idolatry, sorcery, enmity, strife, jealousy, anger, selfishness, dissension, party spirit, envy, drunkenness, carousing, and the like** (Gal 5:19-21). The fruits of the spirit were also not material: **love, joy, peace, patience, kindness, goodness, faithfulness, gentleness, self-control** (Gal 5:22-23).

The levitical priesthood, then, not only was of physical descent, but it belonged to the classification of "fleshly," which included all things ethically bad.

The claim that Jesus **came into existence . . . according to the power of an indestructible life** (*zoh-áys,* ζωῆς) may be based on the little verse in Heb 7:3, which claimed that Jesus, like **Melchizedek,** had neither **beginning of days nor end of life** (ζωῆς). The term **power** (*doó-nah-mees,* δύναμις) also means "miracle" and may have been intended here to describe Jesus' miraculous origin, but that does not mean a virgin birth. The miracle of Jesus, according to the author, was *not* his physical birth or his descent from a special family. He was **without father, without mother, without genealogy** (Heb 7:3). The miracle was not his conception or his birth but the fact that he **arose;** he **came into existence**. His whole existence was a miracle. He could not be explained according to family origin. Since he had **no end of days** (Heb 7:3; 1 Tim 6:16), his **life** was **indestructible**. The crucifixion could not put an end to his life. That would contrast him to the Levites who were mortal (Heb 7:8), and **came into existence according to the law of a fleshly commandment**. They were born, just as all people are. They had parents and family. They grew up and later died.

17*For it is attested.* The testimony that Jesus was **a priest for the age according to the order of Melchizedek** was given here as if this were proof that Jesus' origin and existence were miraculous, but the text came from the poem quoted in Heb 7:3. This may be one more indication that this poem was originally written about the Hasmoneans, who were identified with **Melchizedek,** because the author seems to have expected his readers to know that the poem and **Melchizedek** belong together. This is another reminder by the author that the text for this sermon is Ps 110.

18*A previously functioning commandment is removed.* According to the author, the people of Israel had been governed by the Levitical priesthood (Heb 7:11). It was necessary for the priesthood to be changed (Heb 7:12), so the law which established the priesthood would also have to **be changed,** too (Heb 7:12). This was the **fleshly commandment** (Heb 7:16) which had **functioned previously**. It was removed because it **completed** or **perfected** nothing, **because of its weakness and uselessness**.

In a similar way Paul discredited the law, which he described as being **of crime and death** (Rom 8:2); it was **powerless . . . in that it was weak through the flesh** (Rom 8:3). In contrast to this is the **law of the spirit of life in Christ Jesus** (Rom 8:2). **The law of the spirit of life in Christ Jesus** was based on the new contract. Therefore it was strong, valid, and powerful. It was not **weak through the flesh.**

19 *[There is the] beginning of a better hope.* Whereas Paul contrasted flesh and spirit when referring to the old and new contracts, the author of Hebrews described the fleshly law or commandment in contrast to the **beginning of a better hope through which we come near to God** (see also Heb 3-6; 6:11, 18; 10:23).

Summary. This section is limited by the words **perfection** (Heb 7:11) and **perfected** (Heb 7:19), which form the inclusion. The main point is that the new priesthood makes the old priesthood obsolete and also the law which brought it into existence. Both priesthood and law were im**perfect**. The law was fleshly, weak, and useless. The reader can be sure about this becauset a new priest has arisen according to the likeness of **Melchizedek.** He is not from the same tribe as the Levites. In fact, he has no parents or genealogy. His is a miraculous existence **without beginning of days nor end of life**. Therefore his **life** is **indestructible.** He is the priest who has given us a **beginning of a better hope through which we come near to God**. This new priest is **our Lord** who **arose** from Judah. He **came into existence,** but was not born as the high priest and messiah. He became high priest and messiah legally.

This tenor is similar to that of the rest of the document which shows Jesus superior to the best of the old contract. The term **better** occurs 12 times in the document. The fondness of the author for the perfect tense is evident in Heb 7:13-14 as well as the following additional places: Heb 1:4, 13; 2:14; 3:3, 14; 4:2, 4, 14, 15; 7:3; 8:5, 6; 9:18, 26; 10:14; 11:5, 17, 28; 12:2, 3. The conclusion of this unit also prepares the reader for the next division that will be concentrated on the better hope in the new priest.

TEXT

Hebrews

20 And just as much as it was not without
oath-taking (for they are **priests** [who]
became [such] without **oath**-taking,
21 but he [became a priest] with
oath-taking, through the one who said to
him: **"The Lord has sworn, and will
not retract, 'you are a priest for the
age'"** 22 just so much more has Jesus be-
come a surety of an even better contract.
23 Now those are numerous, since they
became **priests** because [their predeces-
sors] were prevented by death from con-
tinuing [in office], 24 but he [is one]
because he remains **"for the age"** [and
therefore] has **the priesthood** without
change. 25 Therefore he is also able to

First Testament

Ps 110:4 **Yahowah has sworn, and he will not retract, "You are a priest for the age**, according to the order of Melchizedek."

Exod 29:9 **The priesthood** will be theirs, [following] a statute **of the age**, and you

	shall ordain Aaron and his sons.
save those who come **near to** God through him for the entire [age], since he always lives to make intercession in their behalf. 26For it is fitting for such a one	Exod 28:1You shall bring **near to** you Aaron and his sons, from the midst of the people
also to **become** high **priest for** us, holy, innocent, undefiled, separated from criminals, and become higher than the heavens,	of Israel, and to **become priests for** me.
27who does not have the daily necessity, as the high **priests** do,	Exod 29:1This is what you shall do to sanctify them as **priests for** me.
first to offer **sacrifices** for their own crimes, then those of the people, for he did this once for	Exod 29:10You shall **sacrifice** the bull before the tent of meeting.
all, having **offered** himself. 28For the law establishes men [as] high **priests** [who] have weakness, but the word of the **oath** which [came] after the law	Ps 110:3Your people **offered** themselves in the day your troops [gather] in holy splendor.
[establishes] a **Son**, **ordained for the age**.	Exod 29:9The priesthood will be theirs, a rule **of the age**. You shall **ordain** Aaron and his **sons.**

COMMENTARY

20*Not without oath-taking*. The construction **just as much as** (Heb 7:20) . . . **just so much more** (Heb 7:22) (*kahth háw-sawn . . . kahtáh taws-oótaw*, καθ᾽ ὅσον . . . κατὰ τοσοῦτο) is typically rabbinic and also typical for the Greek rhetoricians. It seems to mean about the same as *kuh-ah-sháyr . . . ahl ah-káht kah-máh wuh-kah-máh* (כאשר . . . על כמה כמה). The double negative gives the expression the same meaning as **with oath-taking**. The **oath** was essential to a valid contract, and the author wanted to prove that the new contract that Jesus made was a true contract, sealed with oaths.

This little midrash (Heb 7:20-7) is based on the most important FT text in Hebrews. The author started out with the word **oath-taking**, because the text refers to God's swearing or taking oaths. Then he quoted the text (Ps 110:4) and continued his midrash working into his commentary words from the text, like **priest**, **oath**, and **for the age**. This is normal Jewish homiletical midrash. Then he turned to a text involving the qualification liturgy required for Aaron and his sons. He assumed that the biblical qualifications were valid. A new priesthood would have to fulfill the same procedure.

The sons of Aaron had been given the perpetual priesthood when they were originally designated to be the **priests** (Exod 29:1-9; see further Exod 28-29; Lev 8-9; Sir 45:15). Phineas, the forefather of the Hasmoneans (1Macc 2:54) was also granted the perpetual **priesthood,** but the author of Hebrews did not mention him at this point, because no report was given in Numbers of the **installation** ceremony employed in his case. On the basis of Ps 110, the author of this midrash held that for Jesus there was an additional factor: Jesus was **installed** with an **oath**. On the other hand, there is no mention of the Levites being installed with **oaths.** Therefore silence proves that they **functioned** without having been initiated with **oaths**.

21 *The Lord has sworn and will not retract.* This is a repetitious saying. The point of **swearing** is to assure that there will be no **retraction**. The word translated **retract** is *meta-meh-lay-tháy-seh-tai* (μεταμεληθήσεται). Etymologically it is formed from the preposition "after" and the verb "to care," "be anxious about," "take thought." This word, then, means to have an "after thought" or an "after care," to give the matter a second thought. Since a second thought might reverse the decision, it has come to mean "repent," "retract," "recant," or "change one's mind." The claim of both Ps 110 and the author is that God made a firm decision about this and he would never give it a second thought. It could not come up for reconsideration. It was like the law of the Medes and the Persians (Dan 6:15). The **oath** which God took to establish a position was applied to the **promise** made to Abraham (Gen 22), the rejection of the exodus generation from the **promised rest** (Ps 95), and the **promise** that someone would be **a priest for the age according to the order of Melchizedek**. In each case the author of Hebrews called attention to the significance of the **oath.** It is the **oath** that distinguished the **promise** made to Jesus from the **promises** made to the sons of Aaron or Phineas.

The text in Ps 110:4 does not say, "**You are a priest** forever," as Koester holds.[1] It says, **You are a priest for the age**, meaning that he was currently appointed **priest**, and he would continue throughout the **age**, however long that would be. An **age** is a temporal term. **The age of David** lasted as long as David was king, but David was not king forever, and Hebrews did not claim that much for **Melchizedek** (Heb 7:17). He expected him to **remain into the age without interruption** (Heb 7:23).

22 *A warrant of an even better contract.* A **warrant** (*éng-goo-aws*, ἔγγυος) is a bond, bail, collateral, escrow, or some kind of guarantee that a **promise** will be fulfilled. In this case, God had made the **promise** with an **oath**, and Jesus had become the guarantee that **the promise** would be fulfilled. The word **warrant** was closely associated with other titles given to Jesus. He was the "mediator" (Heb 8:6; 9:15; 12:24), "source" (Heb 5:9), "anchor" (Heb 6:19), "forerunner" (Heb 6:20), and "prime *leader* **and perfector of the faith"** (Heb 12:2).

A **contract** is a formal document that is made between two or more parties defining their agreed-upon behavior in relationship to one another. It can be established either in writing or by ceremony or both. The law and commandment associated with the Levites were weak and useless. Grässer correctly said that

> With it [the word "contract"] Hebrews alone, of all New Testament writings, offers anything like a 'contract theology.' [Contract, *dee-ah-tháy-kay*] διαθήκη is for him as important as [the Kingdom of God, *Bah-see-láy-ah too theh-oó*] βασιλεία τοῦ θεοῦ is for the synoptic gospels or [church, *eh-klay-seé-ah*] ἐκκλησία is for the letters of Paul.[2]

---

[1] C. R. Koester, *Hebrews* (New York: Doubleday & Co., 2001), pp. 360-62.

[2] Grässer, *An die Hebräer* 2, p. 56. tr from the German.

He further held, "That between *nomos* [regulation] and *diatheke* [contract] he [the author of Hebrews] makes hardly any distinction."[1]

Although Moses fulfilled or **perfected** the ceremony by which the Aaronic priests were installed, nevertheless they **perfected,** "completed," or "fulfilled" nothing, but with Jesus as the high **priest for the age** there is assurance that a better **contract** would be established between God and his people. Note the care with which the author used the terms taken from Ps 110 and Exod 28 and 29. He employed them in ways that would qualify Jesus and disqualify the sons of Aaron.

The first **contract** that was made between God and his people was with Moses as God's legal agent. This was a marriage **contract** which provided that the people would follow the terms of the **contract** which were set down in the FT. If they failed to keep **contract** with God, then there were written terms of punishment. If the people became unfaithful, then God would divorce them, following the terms in Deut 24:1. He would give them a divorce document and send them out of his house (temple). If the people were faithful, however, God would bless them with the land, prosperity, long life, and independence.

When the temple at Gerizim and the temple at Jerusalem were both burned, and the people were sent into captivity in Nineveh and Babylon, Jeremiah said that this meant God had divorced his people, sending them out of his house. Never the less, following Hosea, after they had been adequately punished for their crimes, Jeremiah concluded that then God would make with them a new and better **contract**, just as he had done in the wilderness after they broke the **contract** made at Sinai (Exod 34). The **contract** Jeremiah promised is the one of which the author of Hebrews spoke. Jesus was the new legal agent who acted in behalf of God to make a new **contract**, and it was a better **contract** than the one God made through Moses.

The **contract** Jesus made, about which the author of Hebrews spoke, was probably made at the Last Supper Jesus ate with his apostles. He had previously commissioned these disciples to become apostles--legal agents of Jesus. This means they acted and spoke in Jesus' name, in his behalf, and at his responsibility.

In antiquity **contracts** were made both in writing and through liturgy. If a liturgy was followed exactly, before witnesses, and with no part omitted, then it was legally as binding in court as a written document. In old English law the liturgy for transferring property or authority was called "livery seisin." If a person, for example, agreed to sell his land to a buyer, after all the negotiations had been completed, the following liturgy would conclude the action. The buyer would stand outside of the property, and the seller would stand on his property. Then the seller would take some part of the land--a clod of dirt or a twig from a tree--and hand it to the buyer. This symbol was the seisin. It represented the entire property being sold. At that point the seller would step off the land, the buyer and the witnesses would step on it, and the exchange would be completed.

English jurists knew that this was a very old tradition, but they did not know how old. In Judea, however, it was considered an old tradition already in Israel **when dealing with redemption and exchange** (Ruth 4:7) at the time the Book of Ruth was written. This was the liturgy followed by Boaz and Naomi's next of kin when the next of kin took off his sandal, gave it to Boaz, and said before witnesses that with this liturgy went the right to buy Naomi's property and marry Ruth (Ruth 4:7-10). The sandal was the seisin, although that name was not used. When Jonathan recognized that David would succeed Saul by force he made a contract

[1] Grässer, *An die Hebräer* 2, p. 57.

with him that he could be Saul's follower if he would not destroy Jonathan's family when he became king. They agreed, and Jonathan confirmed the agreement by giving David his armor, helmet, robe, and sword as seisins (1Sam 18:3-4).

When Jesus was with his apostles, all of whom were legal agents, he took the ordinary Passover bread, and added a new liturgy to the Passover meal. He gave the bread to each of the apostles and said to them, **This is my body**. He did not say, **This is my flesh**. He meant, "This bread is the seisin of **my body.** With this seisin is established my legal body." This was the formation of the **body of Christ**, the corporation of Christ, the church.

A legal **body** functions just like a human individual in court. It pays taxes; it can sue and be sued. It differs in that it is immortal. Although all of the members change, a corporation endures forever. With a legally formed **body of Christ**, the new people of God, then Jesus formed a new **contract**, using the fruit of the vine as a seisin. He said, **This cup is the new contract in my blood**. This did not mean that the cup was the **contract** itself anymore than the old English seller meant that the twig or the clod of dirt was all that was involved in this negotiation. The twig or clod of dirt was the seisin of the property. **The cup** was the seisin by which the **contract** was formed. It was the symbol that was necessary to form a **contract** through liturgy. It was like the sandal given to Boaz, the sword and armor given to David, or the twig from a tree given to someone who bought land. The author of Hebrews evidently knew about this **contract**. He concluded that this was the new and better contract that Jeremiah promised.[1]

23-24 *[Their predecessors] were prevented by death.* Another contrasting point between Jesus and the Levites is that they were plural and he was singular. Josephus said there were 83 **high priests** from the time of Aaron until the temple was destroyed in 70 IA (Ant 20:227). This concurs with pYoma 11, which says there were between 80 and 85. Some rabbis held that there were more than 300 **high priests** during the period of the second temple alone (bYoma 9a). Because they were mortal (Heb 7:8), the Levitical **priests** needed many replacements. Jesus seemed to suit the author's monastic ideal. Just as a monk was required to separate himself from his family and deny it, so the author denied that Jesus had any parents or genealogy. Legally this was so, because when Jesus took his monastic vows he denied the family into which he was born. His was a miraculous, indestructible existence. Not only did Jesus not have a genealogy, but like other celibates, he had no posterity. This, of course, was a legal fiction. Jesus actually had been born of a human mother, and he had once belonged to a family, but he legally denied all of this when he joined a monastery.[2]

Jesus was legally not part of a whole tribe or dynasty that maintained the office of **high priest** down through the generations, like the Levites. He alone held the office. He alone was the **warranty**. There was no danger of corruption in the future, as Malachi said had happened to the Levites (Mal 2:1-17). This makes his **priesthood** much superior. This **high priest** was not mortal. He continued to minister **for the age**. Therefore there would be no **change** during his **priesthood.**

---

[1] For a further description of this ceremony see Buchanan, *The Gospel of Matthew,* (Lewiston: Mellen, c1996) II, chapter 26.

[2] See further Buchanan, "Jesus and other Monks of New Testament Times," *Religion in Life* 48 (1979):136-42.

[25]*He always lives*. Before his crucifixion, Jesus formed a corporation, the body of Christ, forming a legal ceremony, using the parcels of Passover to establish the legal body of Christ, of which he was the head. In a corporation is all of the members can change, but the corporation itself is eternal. It **always lives.** Since this the the Body of Christ, through this corporation Jesus **always lives**. **Those who approach God through him** were the people whom he represented when he offered sacrifice for atonement of crimes. Because of his ministry, their crimes were forgiven. **The entire [age]** (*ays taw pahn-teh-léhs*, ἐις τὸ παντελες) seems parallel with **for the age** (Heb 7:24). Both apply to Jesus' term as priest. The unbrokenness of this ministry was emphasized by the expression **continually** (*ays taw dee-ay-neh-kéhs,* ἐις τὸ διηνεκές) (Heb 7:3), and **indestructible** (*ah-kah-tah-loó-taws*, ἀκατα-΄λυτος) (Heb 7:16). Thee do not mean "forever." **For the age** probably meant for the messianic age when Jesus, as Son and high priest, would rule and officiate.[1]

[26]*It is fitting for such a one*. Using the same verb, the author said,

> [10]For **it was fitting for** him [God], for whom were **all things** and through whom were **all things**, to **make perfect** the chief of their salvation through sufferings, leading many **sons** to **glory** (Heb 2:10).

Some things were **fitting for** God and other things **are fitting for us**. It was God who acted in both instances. In one case he provided us with a **high priest,** and in the other instance he made perfect the chief of their salvation. In both cases the members of the holy corporation were to be the beneficiaries.

Three of the adjectival words and phrases of this verse are nearly identical in meaning, and they all describe the condition required of a **high priest** when he **functioned** in the temple--**holy, innocent**, and **undefiled.** All **priests** who served in the temple where God's presence was understood to dwell were obligated to keep themselves "holy," which meant "undefiled" by any type of levitical impurity (2Macc 14:36; 15.34; James 1:27; 1Peter 1:4). On the Day of Atonement, the **high priest** bathed five times and washed his hands and feet ten times (mYoma 3:3). To avoid defilement, the **high priest** was. "separated from criminals" for seven days so that he would not be defiled on the Day of Atonement. He was put on short rations the day before the Day of Atonement to prevent a defiling nocturnal discharge (mYoma 1:1-8) or to prevent any need for elimination in the holy place.

On the Day of Atonement, transgressions against God could be atoned, but only on the condition that the believer first appease his neighbor against whom he had committed crimes and become reconciled to him (mYoma 8:9). This is probably the condition described as **innocent**, (*áh-kah-kaws,* ἄκακος), which sometimes means "simple" or "naive," almost to a fault (Prov 14:15). Legally it means **innocent** of any crime. After the **high priest** had sacrificed a bull for himself and his house, he was considered to be legally free from crime and guilt or **innocent**. For a **priest** this would describe the moral condition necessary for atonement. If a **high priest** were not **separated from criminals**, he would become defiled by them and be incapable of interceding for his people. **The priest** and the Levite were not free to help the man on the road from Jerusalem to Jericho who was **half dead**, because of their fear that he might die and defile them by their contact with a corpse (Luke

[1] Buchanan, *Consequences,* pp. 15-18.

10:29-32). The nature of the **priestly** office is reflected in the appointment of Levi to the **priesthood.**

> Therefore, the Most High has heard your prayer so as to separate you from iniquity and that [you] may be to him a son and a servant and minister of his presence (TLevi 4-2; see also Ant 3:258).

The claim that Jesus, as **high priest,** was **higher than the heavens** may have reflected the visual concept of a sacrifice taken up to God in the heavens through the column of smoke that touches heaven (see discussion at the end of Heb 9). It was not a unique claim for one who thought of the heavens as being like a tent roof, just above the treetops and the hills. Enoch's spirit was believed to have ascended into the heavens where he could see the sons of God (1Enoch 70:1-4; 71:1), and Isaiah was thought to have been raised to see all of the seven heavens (AscIsa 7:6-8, 13, 17, 18, 24, 28, 32; 8:1; 9:1). The structure and content of this verse suggest that it is part of the same poem from which the verse in Heb 7:3 was taken.

Grässer followed Josuttis in saying that Jesus was not only possessed of all of the virtues Hebrews attributed to him, but that the kingdom of **Melchizedek** was superIsraelitish, superhistorical, and supergovernmental.[1] That is more than either Genesis or Hebrews claimed for him.

[27]*First to offer sacrifices.* The author's familiarity with liturgical customs is reflected here. The law instructs that the **high priest**, on the Day of Atonement, must **first offer** a bull as a crime offering for himself and his family, and afterward he was to offer a goat as a crime offering for the **crimes of the people** (Lev 16:6-28; mYoma 4:3-6:3). There is a problem, however, in the claim that **high priests** do this "daily" (*kahth hay-méh-rahn,* καθ' ἡμεραν) whereas the atonement offerings the author described took place only on the Day of Atonement, so far as is generally known. Some possible explanations for this situation are these:

(a) The author may have rendered the Aramaic *yoh-mah* (יומא) which literally means "the day," but was used as a technical term for "the Day of Atonement," by *kahth hay-méh-rahn*, meaning "daily" (cf. Heb *yoh-máhm*, יומם, "by day").

This would have been caused by a misunderstanding of the Aramaic of some document and a faulty attempt to give the expression sense in Greek. The document may have been one that compared the action of the **high priest** on the Day of Atonement with that of Jesus.

(b) He may have tried to increase the contrast by confusing the **high priest's** function on the Day of Atonement, which Lev 16 spells out clearly, with the daily sacrifices which were also performed (Lev 6:13, 19-22; Num 28:3-4; mTamid 7:3; Sir 45:14).

(c) The author may have meant by "every day," "every day on which he ministered to atone for the people."

(d) Daily sacrifices may have been understood as atoning sacrifices. High priests actually **functioned** on days other than the Day of Atonement (mTamid 7:3; War 5:231). According to Jub 6:14, Noah's posterity was commanded to supplicate every day both morning and evening with blood, and seek forgiveness, just as Noah

---

[1] Grässer, *An die Hebräer* 2, p. 74.

sacrificed a kid for atonement (Jub 6:2).[1] Philo said the high priest offered prayers and sacrifices every day *kahth heh-kahs-tehn hay-méh-rahn* (καθ' ἕκαστεν ἡμέραν) (Spec 3:131). The solution to this problem is not certain.

Another puzzling question is the meaning of the claim **for this he did once for all**. What did he do? Did he "offer sacrifices for [his] own crimes as well as for those of the people"? *A priori* it would seem that **this** which he did **once for all** was the same as that which the priests did **daily**, which the author understood to include *two* offerings. The one offering of Christ was better than the *two* offerings the **high priest** made every day or every year. This would imply that Jesus' sacrifice also cleansed his **own crimes** as well as the **crimes of the people**. Rabbis believed that the **suffering** associated with death would atone for crimes of the individual himself (AbothRN 39). Furthermore the poem in Heb 1:3, applied to Jesus, said,

> **when he had made a purification for [his] crimes,**
> **sat down at the right hand of the Majesty in exaltation**.

This seems to mean that when Jesus was crucified, and therefore sacrificed, then he was exalted. His sacrifice provided the cleansing or crime offering. If Heb 1:3, 7:3, and 7:26 were all from the same poem originally, the author's interpretation of Heb 7:26 and 7:27 would be expected to be consistent with that of Heb 1:3. This seems to be the most normal interpretation, but it poses some difficulties. The claim in Heb 4:15 is that Jesus was tempted in the way other people are, but still he was without crime. This is usually understood to describe his day-by-day moral conduct. It is in a context, however, that allows a different interpretation. Heb 4:14-15 describes Jesus who had gone through the heavens, meaning he had already been sacrificed. His temptations may have been only those associated with his crucifixion, at which time he did not betray his cause by committing crimes. Without denying this kind of logic, Vaughan said of this interpretation:

> To say so would be to contradict the whole language of the Epistle (as well as the Scripture throughout) as to the crimelessness of Christ. In many places a text may be found which, taken by itself and isolated from all others, might seem to be capable of an Arian or Sociman meaning. But confront it with the *tenor* of Scripture, and all is consistency.[2]

Vaughan, however, did not demonstrate his general claims and show that the entire epistle and Scripture excluded this possibility. In fact, the interpretation Vaughan disparaged is consistent with Heb 1:3 and the expiatory understanding of death according to the rabbis. The only difficulty is with the claim to crimelessness in Heb 4:15, and even that may be understood in reference to the crucifixion alone, and not to Jesus' entire life. It is possible that the deed which Jesus **did once for all** meant only cleansing for the crimes **of the people**, as most scholars assume, but that is not the only possibility. The fact that Jesus **offered himself** as a **sacrifice** was very important to the author's understanding of atonement (Heb 8:3; 9:14, 26; 10:10-12).

---

[1] See further Michel, *Hebräer,* pp. 180-81; S. G. Sowers, *The Hermeneutics of Philo and Hebrews* (Richmond: John Knox Press, 1965), pp. 69-70.

[2] C. J. Vaughan, *The Epistle to the Hebrews* (London: Macmillan, 1890), p. 139.

[28]*After the law [establishes] a Son, ordained for the age*. That which here is rendered, **ordained** is normally translated **perfected.** It is the Greek translation for the Hebrew *mee-láy-tah yahd* (Exod 29:9). Literally this means **you shall fill the hand,** meaning "You shall provide the power and authority." The context for this expression is involving the ordination of Aaron and his sons. At a certain point in the service, God told Moses to **fill the hand**. After this Moses, Aaron, and Aaron's sons put their hands on the head of the beasts and slaughtered them. This was the final step in the ordination service. TargNeofiti renders this passage,

> "You shall pay an offering of the hands (*tuh-shah-láym kahr-báhn yah-dove*, תשלם קרבן ידוי) of Aaron and an offering of the hands of his sons" (TargNeofExod 29:9).

Both Jonathan and Pseudo Jonathan translated this, "You shall sacrifice a sacrifice (*tahk-ráyv kohr-bahn-áh*, תקריב קורבנא)[1] (TargJon; TargPsJon Exod 29:9). The Levitical parallel to this report said, **Then he sacrificed the second ram, the filled ram** (*ayl hah-mee-loo-eém*, איל המלאים), **and Aaron and his sons pressed their hands on the head of the ram** (Lev 8:22). Neofiti and Pseudo Jonathan both also called it "the final ram" or the "completed ram" (*dah-kahr-áh dahsh-lah-moh-táh* (דכרה דאשלמותה) (NeofTarg; PsJohTarg Lev 8:22). That which MT rendered **the filled ram**, LXX translated *kree-áhn tehl-ay-óh-seh-ohs* (κριάν τελειώσεως), **perfect ram** or **completed ram** (LXXLev 8:22).

The Greek term used here is from the same Greek verb the LXX used in Exod 29:9. It is also the same Greek verb the author of Hebrews used *teh-teh-lay-oh-méh-nawn* (τετελειωμένον) (Heb 7:28), which is usually translated **perfected.** The Syriac translated the Greek of Heb 7:28 by *gah-mee-ráh luh-ah-láhm* (גמירה לעלם), which means "finished," "completed," or "accomplished for the age." This is the same force intended by the FT, the LXX, and both targums of Leviticus and Exodus.

This means that the author of Hebrews was not trying to say that Jesus was **perfected** in any twentieth century scientific sense. He had not chosen that word himself at all. He simply took it from the LXX intertext dealing with the ordination of Aaron and his sons. Moses completed the ordination of Aaron and his sons by sacrificing two rams on which Aaron and his sons placed their hands. It was the sacrifice that finished the ceremony and made the sons of Aaron legitimate priests. The same was true of Jesus. He had been anointed and ordained as a **high priest** by oil and sacrifice. Because he completed the legitimizing ceremony, he was a **high priest** even though he was not one of the sons of Aaron. He was superior because his was a superior sacrifice. It was not the blood of rams but his own blood that was sacrificed at this ceremony.

The imperfect **law** which was weak and useless (Heb 7:18-19) was the same **law** which **establishes men [as] priests [who] have weakness**. The **law** involved was probably the whole Pentateuch. The author of Hebrews understood that there was a certain procedure by which priests were established. This procedure was defined in Exodus and Leviticus, and it applied to Jesus.

---

[1] TgPsJon had תקרב rather than, תקריב but both have the same meaning.

Vanhoye correctly noted the importance of the passive voice.[1] Initially Aaron and his sons were made **priests.** Aaron was not born a **priest.** He and his sons became **priests** through a liturgy God provided through directions given to Moses. Aaron's sons had functioned during the reign of David and his sons, but a more recent **priesthood** took over the ministry of the **priesthood** and the rule of the country during the reign of the Hasmoneans. They claimed superiority over the sons of David, because God had evidently chosen the Hasmmoneans in preference to the sons of David. It was this combined priestly-royal function of the Hasmoneans that provided the opposition to the author of Hebrews. He claimed that Jesus surpassed both the sons of Aaron and the Hasmoneans. Neither Aaron nor Jesus was born a **priest**; both were made priests through ceremony. Jesus was made a high priest through a superior sacrifice.

Summary. The concluding section of chapter seven was framed as an inclusion by the word **oath**, which occurs in Heb 7:20 and 28. Oaths were customary parts of contracts in antiquity. Since they normally did not involve anything written, That which made a contract secure was the oath. The author of Hebrews argued that the **oath** made the **promise** given to the **priest** in Ps 110, whom he understood to be Jesus, superior to the **promises** given to the sons of Aaron and Phineas. Also the fact that the Psalms were written after the Pentateuch means that the later **promise** in the Pss supersedes the earlier **promises** made by Moses. The argument that Jesus was without parents or posterity, in contrast to the Levites for whom lineage was important, may support the possibility that the author was not only a very rigid legalist concerned about the ethics of a communal group, but that Jesus represented his monastic ideal of celibacy and denial of family. Heb 7:25-26 seems to be related to the poem quoted in Heb 7:3. Heb 7:26 may even be a verse of the same poem. Complete qualification seems to have been finalized by sacrifice, in the author's judgment. Therefore it was Jesus' self-sacrifice that made him qualified. It also cleansed him from crime (Heb 1:3), since he offered himself for his own crimes as well as for those of the people.

The author's use of Scripture here shows that he gave more credence to the Psalms than to the Pentateuch. This may be because the prophets and Psalmists contained more material suitable for his eschatological purposes, or it may be that he related the Pentateuch typologically with the old contract that had been superseded.

SUMMARY OF CHAPTER SEVEN

Michel holds that Heb 7 is divided into 7 subheadings, based on the following seven terms: 1-3, Melchizedek; 4-10, tithing; 11-14, order; 15-19, law; 20-22, oath-taking; 23-25, "for the age"; and 26-28, high priest.[2] This is an attractive division of the chapter, although it makes very small units. It is not so convincing, however, as Vanhoye's three divisions which are all marked by inclusions. The argument moves in an orderly and progressive fashion from a discussion of the relative merits of Melchizedek and Abraham to a depreciative analysis of the Levites who were Abraham's sons, mortal men, imperfect in their function, on the basis of an

---

[1] A. Vanhoye, "La Teleiosis du Christ: Point Capital de la Christologie Sacerdotal D'Hébreux," *NTS* 42 (1996):331.

[2] Michel, *Hebräer*, pp. 158-83.

imperfect law, to an appreciative evaluation of Jesus as the perfect priest, installed by a promise accompanied with an oath, based on a later testimony.

This **high priest** was without parents or posterity, his once–for-all sacrifice cleansed both him and his believers for **the age.** If the poem in Heb 7:3 which seems to be echoed in Heb 7:25 and used as a proof text in Heb 7:6, 8, and 16 was part of the same poem quoted in Heb 7:26, then the author may have intended the parts of this poem to function as an inclusion for the whole chapter. The final verse acts as a summarizing sentence, picking up terms used throughout the chapter: **For the age** (Heb 7:28) may be intended to refer the reader to Melchizedek in the opening and concluding verses of the first section (Heb 7:1, 10). **Perfect** is the word in Heb 7:28 that recalls the opening and concluding verses of the second section (Heb 7:11, 19). The **oath** mentioned in Heb 7:28 refers the reader to the beginning; of the third section (Heb 7:20).

That which was a part of the old contract also belonged to the new. With Jesus there was a new **contract**, a new priesthood, a new sacrifice. Not only was all of this new, but it was better than the old. Angels continued to function in the new **contract** as they had in the old, but they were clearly subordinate and inferior to the Son. The servant Moses was replaced by the Son Jesus; in place of the levitical **priesthood** was the **priesthood** according to the order of **Melchizedek,** established by a later **promise** and confirmed by an **oath** as a **priesthood for the age**. The Levites were mortal but Jesus' life was indestructible. Levites were not **perfect** and they were established by a law that could not **perfect** anything, but Jesus was a son who was qualified as **high priest for the age** by the word of the **oath**. Not only in Heb 7, but in the previous 6 chapters as well, Jesus was shown to be superior to anything belonging to the old **contract**, and this proof was presented on the basis of Ps 110 around which the whole document (1:1-12:29) was oriented. Furthermore, the new which was better than the old also replaced much that was old so that the old became unnecessary.

CHAPTER EIGHT

TEXT

Hebrews	First Testament
8:1 Most important of the things said [is that] we have such a high **priest** [as this] who	Ps 110:4 Yehowah has sworn, and he will not recant, "You are **a priest** for the age according to the order of Melchizedek."
sat down at the right hand of the throne of Majesty in the heavens,	Ps 110:1 Yehowah said to my Lord, **Sit at my right hand** until I make your enemies a footstool for your feet.
2 a minister of the holy things and of the true **tent which the Lord set up** --not **man**.	LXX Num 24:6-7 As **tents which the Lord set up** and as cedars beside waters. A **man** shall come from his seed and he will rule many nations.
	MT Num 24:6-7 As **tents which Yehowah** planted, and as cedars beside waters. Water will flow out from his buckets; his seed [planted] with much water.

3 For every high **priest** is established for the purpose of offering gifts and sacrifices; therefore it is necessary for this one also to have something that he might offer. 4 If, then, he had been on earth, he would not have been a **priest**, since there [already] are those who offer the gifts according to the law, 5 who minister [as] a copy and shadow of the heavenly things, just as Moses was advised when he was about to finish the **tent**:

Hebrews	First Testament
"**See**," he said, "**[that] you do everything according to the pattern which you saw on the mountain.**"	Exod 25:40 **See that you do [everything] according to the pattern which you saw on the mountain**.

6 But now he has acquired as much a more excellent ministry [than the previous one] as he is also a mediator of a better contract, which has been made into law on the basis of better promises.

COMMENTARY

8:1 *Most important of the things said.* The Greek for **most important** is *keh-pháh-lai-awn* (κεφάλαιον), which means literally, "belonging to the head." It sometimes means "first of all" or "in summary" as well as being a reference to the main point. Here it refers not only to the discussion in Heb 7, but to the very beginning of the book. The author's reintroduction of a passage from Ps 110 reminds the reader that this Psalm is the main text of the entire book. **The throne of Majesty in the heavens** is a euphemism for God, similar to **the Majesty in exaltation** (Heb 1:3), used also in relationship to Ps 110.

The idea of a throne or a temple in heaven was quite common to Jewish thought in NT times. The following message was ostensibly given to Levi:

> And then the angel opened for me the gates of heaven and I saw the holy One, the Most High (*tawn háh-gee-awn heép-sees-tawn,* τὸν ἅγιον ὕψιστον) seated upon the throne, and he said to me, "Levi, I have given you the blessing of the priesthood until I come and dwell in the midst of Israel" (TLevi 5:1-2).

The temple in heaven was closely related to that in Jerusalem:

> You have said [we should] build
> a temple on your holy mountain,
> an altar in the city of your dwelling,
> an imitation (*meé-may-mah,* μίμημα) of the holy tent
> which you prepared from the beginning (Sol 9:8).

According to the rabbis:

> "Dwelling" (*Zeh-boól,* זבול), is that in which Jerusalem and the temple and an altar are built, and **Michael, the great prince** (Dan 12:1), stands and offers a gift on it, as it is said: **I have surely built for you a house of dwelling** (*zeh-boól,* זבול), **a place for you to dwell for ages** (1Kings 8:13). And from where do we conclude that it is called **heaven**? As it is written, **Look down from heaven and see from your holy and glorious dwelling**) (Isa 63:15; bHag 12b).

This also reflects another common custom of believing that God's presence is both in heaven and in the temple. These are the places where he dwells. So close was the heavenly Jerusalem to the earthly Jerusalem that R. Johanan said,

> The Holy One blessed be He said, "I will not come into Jerusalem in heaven (*Yeh-roo-shah-laí-yim shel mah-ah-láh,* ירושלים של מעלה) until I come into Jerusalem which is on earth (*Yeh-roo-shah-laí-yim shel mah-táh,* ירושלים של מטה)." How [can I know] there is a Jerusalem in heaven? Is it not written, **Jerusalem, you are built like a city that is compact together"** (bTa'anith 5a)?

By this he meant that two Jerusalems, one in heaven and one on earth, are compact together. The two Jerusalems were so closely identified that priests who served the temple at Jerusalem were compared to angels of heaven:

> And may the Lord give to you [Levi] and your seed greatness and great mercy, and cause you and your seed, from among all flesh, to draw near to him and serve him in his sanctuary as the angels of the presence and the holy ones (Jub 31-14).

We have such a high priest [as this]. This was not said as a "critique of the Lycus Valley cult," as Jewett held.[1] It is in the context of Jewish and Israelite faith, affirming the kind of priest that was needed at Jerusalem, and the kind of priest their faith intended.

"The throne" in the temple was on the altar, where God's presence dwelt, legally. When Jesus, as the **high priest,** entered the holy of holies in the temple in heaven instead of facing the altar while standing or kneeling, he **sat down at the right hand** of God's throne. This claim echoed that made at the beginning of the sermon (Heb 1:3), and it was echoed again at **important** places (Heb 10:12; 12:2). **The right hand** was the chief seat of honor. He ascended into the heavens where he participated in the heavenly council, being seated at the most important position. Parker has shown that ancient Near Easterners believed that each country had its own god in heaven where they all were members of the same council.[2] Kings on earth were the agents of the deities in heaven. According to Acts David was one of the agents who served in the council of God while he was king of Israel (Acts 13:36). As Messiah, Jesus was authorized to belong to the heavenly council.

2*A minister of the holy things*. Prof. W. F. Albright said that the word *demiourgos* doubtless formerly belonged to the text as the subject of the second line of this couplet:

> A minister of the holy things
> and an intercessor (*demiourgos*) of the true tent.

If a synonym for **minister** did not drop out of the text, the word **minister** was understood to apply both to **the holy things** and to **the true tent**,[3] both of which are designations of the same place of worship. The word used for **minister** is *lay-toor-gáws* (λειτουργός). In religious contexts, it is the office of a **priest** (Heb 1:7; 8:2; 10:11; Num 7:5; Isa 61:6; Jer 33:21; Neh 10:39, LA 3.135; Fuga 93). The **holy things** are the sacred precincts and objects related to the temple or **the true tent**. This verse is based on the LXX version of Num 24:6-7, which is quite different from the MT.

The author of Hebrews took the **man** from LXX Num 24:7 and placed it in contrast to **the Lord**, mentioned in LXX Num 24:6. The temple that had been in

---

[1] R. Jewett, *Letter to Pilgrims* (New York: The Pilgrim Press, c1981), p. 132.

[2] S. Parker, "The Beginning of the Reign of God—Psalm 82 as Myth and Liturgy," *RB* 102/104 (1995/6):532-59.

[3] P. E. Hughes, *A Commentary on the Epistle to the Hebrews* (Grand Rapids: Eerdmans, c1977), pp. 283-87, was justified in rejecting the interpretation of "tent" as "body." Neither the text nor the context requires it.

Jerusalem, served by sons of Aaron and Levi, had been made by human beings. This was in contrast to the **high priest** from **Melchizedek's** order who ministered at **the true tent which the Lord set up**. After the fall of Jerusalem, Jews believed that the temple which God had recorded on the palms of his own hands had been taken from his people, just as Paradise was taken from Adam, because of his crime. The temple had been shown to Adam, Abraham, and Moses before it was built in the land. Then God preserved both the temple and Paradise to be restored later (2Bar 4:1-7), so the temple the Romans destroyed was not the temple God had made. This was made by human beings, or, using another of the author's expressions it was **made with hands** (Heb 9:11).

3*The purpose of offering gifts and sacrifices.* In a pattern similar to Heb 6:16, the author first explored what the custom was for **priests** in general. He then applied it to Jesus in particular. This is a well-known rabbinic argument, called *kuh-láhl oo-fuh-ráht* (כלל ופרט). According to this logical argument, that which is true of the general is true also of the particular parts within the general whole. Since all **high priests** in general were **established for the purpose of offering gifts and sacrifice**, and Jesus was a **high priest**, it follows that he also would be responsible for **offering gifts and sacrifices.** To fulfill this requirement, of course, he must have the necessary gifts to offer.

4*On earth, he would not have been a priest.* **On earth priests** were ordained for their offices because of their family connections. Jesus was not a son of Aaron, so he would never have achieved that status. Just as the author had argued earlier (Heb 7:11) that another **priesthood** would not have arisen if the old one had been adequate, he reasoned here that there were already priests to **offer the gifts according to the law**. Since God creates nothing unnecessarily, it follows that he would not have created a duplicate priesthood. Therefore, Jesus' **function** was not **on earth** as the Levites' ministry was.

There [already] are those who offer the gifts. At the time the author wrote, this was true. The temple at Jerusalem was **functioning**. Therefore, the author obviously wrote before the destruction of the temple in 70 IA.

5*A copy and shadow of the heavenly things.* The temple is that at which the levitical **priests function** only as an imitation **and shadow** of the **heavenly** temple. The **copy** (*hoo-poh-dáyg-mah-tee*, ὑποδειγματι) and s**hadow** (*skee-áh*, σκιᾷ) are terms that have prompted many scholars to interpret the whole Book of Hebrews in terms of Platonic philosophy.[1] In Greek, *skee-áh* was used philosophically and otherwise to describe a silhouette, outline, or reflection, whereas in Hebrew, *tsayl* (צל) figuratively meant "shelter" or "protection." This was the copy given to Moses on the mountain, which God said Israelites were to follow when they built a temple (Exod 25:40). The contrast between the earthly temple in Jerusalem and the *heavenly* pattern reflects Near Eastern concepts inherited from the FT. Platonic

[1] W. F. Howard, *The Fourth Gospel in Recent Criticism and Interpretation* (London: The Epworth Press, 1955), p. 115; T. W. Manson, "The Son of Man in Daniel, Enoch, and the Gospels," *BJRL* 32 (1950):124-26; J. Moffatt, *A Critical and Exegetical Commentary on the Epistle to the Hebrews* (New York: Scribners' Sons, 1964) pp. xxi ff., 107 ff.; V. Taylor, *The Atonement in New Testament Teaching* (London: The Epworth Press, 1941), pp. 101-02.

philosophy is one branch of this outlook, but the point of view in Hebrews does not come from the Platonic branch. This can be shown negatively and positively. Negatively, this is not Platonic because:

(a) Plato's ideal world was not a place, like heaven, where anyone could enter--even Jesus. It could only be reached by the intellect.
(b) The contrast in Hebrews was temporal. Jesus, at a particular *time* entered the true tent--a concept thoroughly Platonic. It did not contrast just an **earthly copy** with its heavenly reality, but also historical time in the past with future time which was to succeed it.[1]

Positively, according to the FT, not only the tabernacle in the wilderness but also Solomon's temple at Jerusalem, was built according to the plan received from God's hand (Exod 25:40; 1Chron 28:19; Sol 9:8; Ps 78:69; Mek *Shirata* 10:29-42). It was constructed by God's own hands (Exod 15:17), and God made his name to dwell there (1Kings 8:29; Ezek 48:35). Since the temple came to earth from God in heaven, it was therefore **heavenly.**

While in captivity, after the temple had been destroyed by the Babylonians, Ezekiel was given a vision of the ideal temple which he described in detail so that the temple in Jerusalem might be built according to that plan when the land was restored (Ezek 40-48). Zion was not the only ancient temple for which a **heavenly** prototype was claimed. The temple built at Lagash was the result of a dream in which the goddess Didaba revealed to the king the plan of that temple.[2] Like Jerusalem (2Bar 4:2-7; Tob 13:16; Isa 60:11-14; Ezek 40), other cities were built according to **heavenly** archetypes. This was true of cities such as Sippar, Nineveh, and Assur.[3] Segiriya, the palace fortress in Ceylon, was patterned after the model of the **heavenly** city Alakamanda.[4]

Plato was not alone in his idea that all **earthly things** were created after a **heavenly** archetype. This concept was quite common in the Near East, and the particular form of this concept given by Plato was not that reflected in Hebrews. The author of Hebrews evidently owed his concept to other Near Eastern influences. Platonism belongs to the same general point of view as that shared by the author of Hebrews, but Hebrews was not directly influenced by the Platonic variety of this outlook.[5] Weiss argued, the typology involved (Heb 2-5)

---

[1] See further R. Williamson, "Platonism and Hebrews," *SJT* 16 (1963): 418-10.

[2] M. Eliade, *Cosmos and History,* tr. W. R. Trask (New York: Harper, 1959), p. 7; E. Burrows, "Some Cosmological Patterns in Babylonian Religion," in *The Labyrinth*, ed. S. H. Hooke (London: S.P.C.K., 1935), pp. 65 ff.; C. T. Fritsch, "TO ANTITYPON," *Studia Biblica et Semitica* dedicated to Th. C. Vriezen (Leiden: E. J. Brill, 1966), pp. 100-107.

[3] Eliade, *Cosmos,* p. 8.

[4] Eliade, *Cosmos,* p. 9.

[5] Eliade, *Cosmos,* pp.6-10. R. Williamson, *Philo and the Epistle to the Hebrews* (Leiden: E. J. Brill, 1970), p. 557, said: ". . .although something like the language of Philonic Platonism may be found in 8:5, there is no trace in the verse, or indeed anywhere else in the epistle, of the fundamental attitudes of conviction which constitutes Platonism either in its original or in its Philonic form. The Writer of Hebrews does not even use his philosophical terminology in anything approaching a rigorously philosophical way."

> is in clear distinction from Philo, again in the "horizontal" typology, [with] the old and new priestly service, temporally following one after the other.[1]

After the temple which had been built according to the pattern given on Mount Sinai was destroyed in 70 IA, Jews looked forward to the time when the **heavenly** city and the **heavenly** temple would appear on earth still more luxurious than before in the position where the archetype formerly stood--Zion (4Ezra 7:26; 8:52; SibO 5:420-29). According to Pseudo-Philo, Joshua called the altar built across the Jordan by the two and a half tribes stationed there an "**altar made with hands**" (*sacrarium manufactum*) (PseudoPh 22:5). That was a pagan altar.

Some of the Dead Sea scroll fragments seem to reflect an anticipation of the destruction of the then existing temple and the establishment of one built with God's hands (4QFlor see also 11QT). Flusser compared this to the report that Jesus planned to destroy the temple and build another not made with hands.[2] The expression **made with hands** (*khay-roh-poí-ay-taws*, χειροποίητος) frequently referred to idolatry in the LXX, rendering *eh-leél* (אליל) or *eh-leé-leem* (אלילים).

Daniel rendered these terms "gods" or "idols made with hands"; Stephen described both the temple and the golden calf as objects "made with hands"; and Paul was quoted in relationship to the gentile temples in Athens as saying that the Lord did not dwell in temples **made with hands** (Acts 7:48; see also Isa 2:18; 19:1; 31:7; LXX Dan 5:4, 23; 6:27[28]; Acts 7:41, 48; 17:24).[3] If that represented an actual report, then the well-trained Jews in the audience would have known he meant that the temples in Athens were all pagan. Gentiles probably understood the expression literally.

It is possible, even probable, that many orthodox Jews and Christians, such as the Essenes, the authors of the Manual of Discipline (1QS), the Habakkuk Commentary (1Qp Hab), and the Damascus Document (CD), as well as the author of Hebrews thought of the temple built by Herod as the particularly pagan temple made with hands, to which they referred, in contrast to the temple that had been built by Solomon in Zion, David's City, and which was rebuilt by the returning Babylonian Jews and the Hasmoneans. The high priest in the Herodian temple was sometimes called "the wicked priest."

1Enoch spoke of the temple, that was like a tent. It had been folded up and carried off. After that, however, the Lord of the sheep provided a new temple (*bet hadis*) which was bigger, but placed where the old one had formerly stood (1Enoch 90:28-29). 4Ezra thought that when the Messiah would be revealed, the city which had previously been hidden would appear (4Ezra 7:27, Arabic text). When the Son is revealed, Zion will become visible to all people, prepared and built without hands (*parata et aedificata . . . sine manibus*) (4Ezra 13:36).[4] Eusebius referred to the

---

[1] H. F. Weiss, *Hebräer*, p. 439.

[2] D. Flusser, "Two Notes on the Midrash on 2 Sam 7," *IEJ* 9 (1959):99-104; see also Y. Yadin, "A Midrash on 2Sam 7 and Ps 1-2 [4Q Florilegium]," *IEJ* 9 (1959):93-98; R. Hummel, *Die Auseinandersetzung zwischen Kirche und Judentum* (München: Chr. Kaiser, 1963), pp. 106-7; Matt 26:61; 27:40; Mark 14:58; 15:29; John 2:9; Acts 6:14.

[3] S. G. Sowers, *The Hermeneutics of Philo and Hebrews* (Richmond: John Knox Press, 1965), p. 110, n. 57.

[4] For this whole discussion, see Buchanan, *The Consequences of the Covenant* (Leiden: E. J. Brill, 1970), pp. 76-80.

Christian church after the liberation by Constantine as the new temple (HE 10:4,1-5,14).

The author of Heb may have expected the **heavenly** Jerusalem to be restored to earth and the real temple to be one ministered on earth by Christ in behalf of his church, the body of Christ. At the time of the writing, however, the only real temple was in **heaven**, and it was from there that Jesus functioned as priest. That does not mean that there was no temple at Jerusalem when this author was writing. It means that Jesus was in **heaven**, so therefore, that is the place where he would **function,** and his **heavenly** temple was the only real one. He was not "on earth" to **offer gifts according to the law** (Heb 8:4), serving only **a pattern and shadow of the heavenly things**. Scholars have found it difficult to think of Jesus **offering sacrifice** in **heaven**. The only **offering** he was thought to have made was the crucifixion, which was understood to be on earth.[1] The author, however, had a view of **heaven** that was much like the holy city and the temple where the Lord's presence was and sacrifices were offered. His concept of heaven in relationship to the temple will be examined in detail at the end of Heb 9.

The Greek word for **advised** is *keh-khray-máh-tees-tai* (κεχρημάτισται), which means "to transact business," "to act under the name of someone," "to advise," or "to warn solemnly." In Scripture, this term is nearly always restricted to communications from God through a revelation, admonition, or direction from **heaven** (Matt 2:12, 22; Luke 2:26; Acts 10:22, *et passim*). Such is also the case here: "Moses was **advised"** means God **advised** or warned Moses solemnly to follow the specified "pattern."

6*Much more excellent ministry.* The main discussion in this unit is the **ministry** of the early priests in comparison with that of the true **priest** who ministers in **heaven.** The words **minister** (*lay-toor-gáws,* λειτούργος) and **ministry** (*lay-toor-geé-ah,* λειτουργία) form the inclusion for this unit. The ministry under discussion is the **function** of the **priesthood.** This final verse also introduces the reader to the next topic that deals with the **contract**. The heavenly high priest, Jesus, **is also a mediator of a better contract**. In the author's judgment a new religion brings about a change in every aspect--priesthood, law, and contract. In every instance, Jesus' religion was considered superior to that which preceded it, and the contract was "made into law on the basis of better promises" which had been recorded in the later word of God according to the Psalms and prophets and confirmed by oath. A better contract is one that has better terms for the interested party involved. The two parties to this contract were God, on one side, and his people, on the other.

Summary. This small unit introduced the **heavenly** nature of Jesus ministry as over against the earthly **ministry** of the Levites. This means he has a better temple in **heaven** than the antitype on earth. From there he continues to offer sacrifices. The contrast between the earthly and the **heavenly** temple reflects a typical Near Eastern outlook on the relation of earthly objects to heavenly prototypes, but it is not Platonic. A proper understanding of Near Eastern concepts is necessary for a clear understanding of the rest of the document. It is true that Jesus was believed to have ascended into heaven and to have continued to minister from there as a **priest,** according to Hebrews. That does not mean, however, that all references to **heaven**

---

[1] F. Delitzsch, *Commentary on the Epistle to the Hebrews,* tr. T. L. Kingsbury (Grand Rapids: Eerdmans, 1952) 2, pp. 67-68.

or **heavenly,** such as "**heavenly** food" and "**heavenly** Jerusalem," took place in **heaven.** These terms were used to describe special objects that belonged on earth. The author only began here a discussion to be continued on the importance of a good contract. Most lawyers would agree on the significance of a **contract.**

TEXT

7For if that first [contract] had been faultless, a place would not have been searched
for a second. 8For [he is] blaming them [when] he says:

> "Look! The days are coming," says [the] Lord, "and I will conclude with the house of Israel and with the house of Judah a new contract
> 9not like the contract which I made with their fathers on [the] day when I took them by their hand to lead them from [the] land of Egypt, because they did not remain in my contract, and [so] I ignored them," says [the] Lord.
> 10"Rather, this is the contract which I will make with the house of Israel after those days," says [the] Lord. I will put my laws into their minds, and I will be their God, and they will be my people.
> 11And they will not teach, each one his fellow citizen and each one his brother, saying, "Know the Lord," because they will all know me,
> from least to the greatest of them, 12for I will deal mercifully with their unrighteous acts, and I will no longer remember their crimes (Jer MT 31:31-34; LXX 38:31-34).

13In using the word **new**, he made the first [contract] obsolete. Now that which is becoming obsolete and aging is almost gone.

TECHNICAL DETAILS

The author of Hebrews may have used the LXX version of Jeremiah, but if he did he did not follow it exactly. For **says [the] Lord** Hebrews has *léh-gay* (λέγει) meaning **says**, which is a synonym for LXX *pháy-seen* (φήσιν), but as in the change from **contract** to "conclude" (Heb 8:8, 9) and his use of a slightly different word for **write** (Heb 8:10), the change was only to a synonym; it did not change the meaning of the sentence.

COMMENTARY

7*For if that first [contract] had been faultless*. The first contract was evidently made with Abraham, Isaac, and Jacob (Exod 2:24; 6:2-5), supposedly the same contract. The content of that **contract,** however, included the laws of Moses. The **contract** itself was a liturgical agreement. For Abraham that involved walking between the halves of a slaughtered beast with a smoking torch (Exod 15:17-18; 17:2-14).

The author's logic was consistent: He reasoned that something's existence proves its necessity. The fact that there is "a place for a second" **contract** proves that the first was not adequate (*áh-mehmp-tos*, ἄμεμπτος). Jeremiah went further than that. He did not say it was inadequate; he said it was invalid. The people had been unfaithful to the **contract,** so the Lord nullified it, divorcing his people. Therefore it was no longer in force. It would never be renewed or reestablished in its same form. When the people paid off their debt of crime, then God would offer a new **contract.** It was Jeremiah, to be quoted next, who **looked for a new contract**, proving the old one faulty.

Jeremiah said that God had divorced his people, following the rules for divorce, which said a man had to give his wife a legal document saying that she was divorced and then send her out of his house (Deut 24:1). The fact that God destroyed his house and sent his people out of it implied that he also gave them the legal papers required. The same argument would have applied to Hager, whom Abraham divorced by sending her away into the wilderness (Gen 21:14) without mention of a divorce document. Jeremiah then promised Judah that it would be taken captive into Babylon because its debt of crime to the Lord was so great that it could never repay it. Like a Jew in debt to his brother, Judah would have to work off its debt at half wages until sabbatical justice had been fulfilled.[1] Afterward the Lord would gather his children from the diaspora and bring them to their homeland in Palestine. The exodus from Babylon would be even greater than the exodus from Egypt, and the Lord would make with his redeemed captives **a new contract** that would be better than the old one that he made with those Hebrews who had been captive in Egypt (Jer 16:14-18; 23:3-8).

The **new contract** was to be better than the old one, because the people would be enabled to keep it. It would be written on their minds and hearts rather than on tablets of stone. Since Jeremiah's prophecy about the captivity and return had been fulfilled to a satisfactory degree, later Jews expected the new **contract** as well. One sect of believers, in the area of Damascus, thought that its members were the ones whom the Lord had chosen to be parties to the **new contract** (*buh-reét hah-khah-desháh,* ברית החדשה) (CDC 6:19; 8:21; 20:12). According to Paul, at the Last Supper which Jesus ate with his disciples, he said, **This cup is the new contract in my blood** (1Cor 11:25). Hebrews also held that Jesus, the new high priest, had established the **new contract** which Jeremiah had promised. The **contract** that Jesus instituted evidently took the form of a legal liturgy, involving a seisin. Blackstone described this ceremony as follows:

> Then the feoffer [seller], if it be of land, doth deliver to the feoffe [buyer], all other persons being out of the ground, a clod or turf, or a twig or bough there growing, with words to this effect: "I deliver these to you in the name of seisin of all the lands and tenements contained in this deed." But if it be a house, the feoffer [seller] must take the ring or latch of the door, the house being empty, and deliver it to the feoffe [buyer] in the same form; and then the feoffe [buyer] must enter alone, and shut-to the door, and then open it, and let in the others.[2]

The English jurists do not know how or from where this liturgy originated, but they know it is very old. It evidently did not originate in England in the Middle Ages, because it appears earlier in the Scriptures. In the company of witnesses Boaz confronted Naomi's nearest of kin, who had the first right of refusal, and asked if he wanted to buy Naomi's land and marry Ruth. If he did he had first choice. When

---

[1] Buchanan, *Consequences*, pp. 9-18.

[2] W. Blackstone, *Commentaries on the Laws of England* (Chicago: Callaghan and Co., 1884, 3d ed. rev) 2, p. 314.

that man declined, he took off his sandal and gave it to Boaz as his seisin and said, "Acquire it for yourself" (Ruth 4:8), and with his sandal he legally transferred his authority to Boaz (Ruth 4:1-9), just as efficiently as the early English transferred property with twigs or clods of dirt. In the same manner, Jonathan gave to David his authority to succeed Saul on the throne, giving him his armor, robe, bow, girdle, and sword (1Sam 18:3-4).

Jesus was the Messiah, the legal agent of God. He met at the Last Supper with his apostles who were also his legal agents. Giving each of them a portion of Passover bread as seisins, he said, **This is my body** (*sóh-mah,* σῶμα). He did not say, "This is my flesh (*sarx*, σάρξ)." In this way he formed a legal body, a corporation, that was called the **body of Christ**, the church. A corporation is a legal body that can act legally as an individual in court, except that it never dies. All of its members can change, but the body continues forever. After Jesus had formed a corporation with one seisin, as God's legal agent, he established the new **contract** Jeremiah had promised, with another seisin, the fruit of the vine. With this seisin he said, **This is my blood of the new contract**, and in this way, he initiated the new **contract** just as efficiently as the English used to transfer property through seisins (Matt 26:26-29).[1]

Isaiah agreed that the people had broken the **contract** with the Lord (Isa 24:5), but 2Isa argued that Jeremiah was mistaken. God had not divorced his people. So, God had sent his people out of his house, but **where is your mother's legal document of divorce** (Isa 50:1)? Since no one could produce one, 2Isa argued that the divorce had never taken place, and there was no need for a new **contract.** Some later Jews, like the author of Hebrews and the community at Damascus agreed with Jeremiah. Others agreed with 2Isa. Those who anticipated a new **contract** seem to have been the very orthodox Jews, like the members of the Damascus sect, the Essenes, the sect of Habakkuk, and the author of Hebrews. They refused to worship in Herod's temple, because it was **made with hands.** They held that the **high priest** was invalid.

8*For [he is] blaming them.* The subject is the Lord. Anything reported in the Scripture is taken to be the word of the Lord (Heb 2:12; 4:3, 4, 7; 5:5, 6; 10:30; 11:18). The Greek for **blaming** *(mem-pháw-meh-naws,* μεμφόμενος) is from the same root as that translated **faultless** in Heb 8:7. The **contract** was not **blameless,** because Jeremiah **blamed** Israelites for their inability to keep it. The **house of Israel** included the ten tribes of the Northern Kingdom, sometimes called "Joseph," "Ephraim," or "Samaria." **The house of Judah** included only Judah and Benjamin--two small tribes near Jerusalem that comprised an area roughly 25 miles between boundaries in each direction. The two houses together constituted the entire Davidic Kingdom. Jeremiah was from **the house of Judah**, but he looked forward to a reunification of the United Kingdom. The Greek words for "conclude . . . a . . . **contract"** are *seen-tehl-éh-soh* (συντελέσω) . . . *dee-ah-tháy-kayn* (διαθήκην), literally, "I will finish," "conclude," "bring to an end," "a contract." The LXX for this is *dee-ah-thay-saw-mai* (διαθήσομαι) . . . *dee-ah-tháy-kehn* (διαθήκεν), **I will contract a contract** or **agree upon an agreement** (Jer 38:31). Here as in many places the author has varied his text from that of the LXX, and there has been no way of knowing whether he had access to a different version of the LXX or whether

[1] E. H. Kantorowicz, *The Kings's Two Bodies* (Princeton: Princeton U. Press, 1957), pp. 12, 501; Buchanan, *The Gospel of Matthew* (Lewiston: Mellen, c1996) 2, pp. 968-982.

he just took liberties with the text, changing a word here or there to meet his needs. Because he quoted parts of this passage more than once, it will be possible to examine more closely his methods of using this Scripture.

9*Not like the contract which I made with their fathers.* **Their fathers** are clearly not the patriarchs--Abraham, Isaac, and Jacob--but the Israelites in general who came out of Egypt.[1] The picture of a father holding his small son's hand to keep him from getting lost or hurt is painted of the Lord taking Israel **by their hand to lead them from [the] land of Egypt. Did not remain in my contract** means they did not keep the terms of their side of the agreement or **contract**. The Lord agreed to be their God, but they also agreed to be his people, which meant obeying him, keeping his commandments, trusting him, and treating one another according to his directions.

The author earlier complained about the exodus generation. Members of that generation had evil, unbelieving hearts; they resisted the Lord; they became bitter, unbelieving, and disobedient (Heb 3:12-19). The Greek text that has been translated **I ignored** is *ay-méh-lay-sah* (ἠμέλησα), **I had no care**, "I neglected," "I slighted" or "I overlooked," which is the same as the LXX Jer 38:32. The MT of Jer 31:32 has *wuh-ah-naw-kee bah-ahl-tee bahm* (ואנכי בעלתי בם), **and I married them, and I became their husband, and I was a husband to them, I was a Lord to them** or **I loathed them rejected them with loathing**.[2]

The preferred meaning of these possibilities is **I was a husband to them** because the **contract** Israel claimed to have made with the Lord was a marriage **contract**. This was the judgment of Jeremiah (Jer 31:32); Ezekiel (Ezek 16:8), and Second Isaiah (Isa 54:5). The Lord was to be the husband, and the people, as a corporate unit, were to personify the wife. Jeremiah's doctrine of the new **contract** was based on this assumption. According to Deut 24:1, when a man wished to divorce his wife he was obligated to give her a written document stating the intent and probably the offenses charged. Then he was required to send her out of his house.

When North Israelites were taken into captivity into Assyria, they were sent off the land and out of the Lord's house, the temple at Gerizim.[3] Jeremiah said this meant that the Lord had annulled the **contract** he had made with Israel at Sinai (Jer 3:8). The Lord would not have done that, Jeremiah argued, if Israel had not first broken the **contract.** Judah, however, the Lord's other wife, had also broken **contract**, even worse than North Israel had done. Therefore, the Lord was certain to divorce **Judah** also and send her out of his house. Jews concluded that this happened when Nebuchadnezzar burned the temple at Jerusalem and took Jews into Babylon as captives.

This, according to Jeremiah, was not the last word. After the Jews and Israelites had worked off their prison term at half wages, God would take them back. There was a scriptural precedent for this. After the incident with the golden calf, Moses annulled the contract, breaking the tablets. Later, however, Moses interceded with the Lord to make a new **contract** with his people. Following Hosea (Hos 2:14-23), Jeremiah said the Lord would make a **new contract** with **Israel and Judah**, when he would marry his two wives again and bring them back to his house (Jer 31:31). Then he would be their husband again. The new marriage would involve a

---

[1] The contract of the fathers (*buh-reét hah ah-vóht,* ברית האבות) (CD 8:18; 19:31).

[2] M. Stuart, *Commentary on the Epistle to the Hebrews* (Andover: Warren F. Draper, 1828), p. 187.

[3] For an excellent report of the Assyrian Captivity see K. L. Younger, Jr., "Israelites in Exile," *BAR* 29. 6 (2003):36-45, 65-66.

new marriage **contract.** The last **contract** had been too demanding on the people. Therefore Jeremiah promised a better **contract,** one that had easier terms for chosen people. The terms God would require through the **new contract** would be easier, so the people would be able to keep the terms.

10*I will be their God, and they will be my people.* Heb 8:10 is a direct quote from the LXX of Jer 38:33 with only three variants:[1] *léh-gay* (λέγει) is given for the LXX synonym, *pháy-seen* (φήσιν); *eh-pee-gráhp-soh* (ἐπιγράψω) replaced *gráhp-soh* (γράψω) for **I will write**; and for *dee-doós dóh-soh* (διδοὺς δώσω), "I will surely give" or "I will surely put" (a Semitism), the author of Hebrews reads only *dee-doós* (διδούς), "giving" or "putting" rendered here more freely **[I will] put.** Quoting, however, the same passage in Heb 10:16, the author of Hebrews additionally changed **with the house of Israel** (*toh oi-koh yeés-rah-ayl* τῷ οἴκῳ Ἰσραελ) to **with them** (*praws ow-toós* (πρὸς αὐτούς) and changed **in their minds and on their hearts** to **on their hearts and on their minds** in Heb 10:16. Since presumably in both cases the author of Hebrews used the same LXX text and in one case showed variants not in the other, it seems likely that he also took the liberty to make the other minor changes in the text that he used. There is very little likelihood that he used a different text for Heb 8:10 from the one he used in Heb 10:16-17.

Jeremiah seemed to think if all people knew the Lord, i.e., knew his commandments and will, then there would be unity under the contract. In his day, people followed various religious customs and laws, and they took cases to court to try to learn which custom was the correct one or which was the right interpretation of the law. If the Lord would only prepare a new and better contract, one that had no ambiguity, and fix indelibly on their minds the same rules, then the **contract** community would **function** as the Lord planned it. There would be no reason for court cases, because everyone would know the meaning of the law and lawyers would never disagree on it. This presumes, of course, that there would be no willful lawbreaking.

11*They will all know me.* **Fellow citizen** (*tawn paw-lée-tayn,* τὸν πολίτην) and **brother** were both synonyms for Jew, Israelite, or party to the **contract**. Whenever converts were made into Judaism, the new proselytes became sons or daughters of Abraham by legal adoption, so they were also brothers and sisters even though Abraham's blood did not run through their veins.

If the Lord put the laws on their minds, then they would all have them memorized, so there would be no need to teach them to one another. Another possibility is that they would be new creatures made unable to commit crime. **From the least to the greatest** is a merismus. A merismus is a literary form from the Greek that means "parts." If you mention all of the parts, you describe the whole. Here **least** and **greatest** are the extreme parts which includes everything in between. It is the same as saying **all**, the word with which the expression stands in apposition. **Least** and **greatest** was intended in terms of status. **The greatest** status would be that of the king and **the least** would be some kind of slave. No one would need an attorney; every person would know the law himself or herself.

This might mean all people would represent themselves in court, but Jeremiah probably thought there would be no court trials at all under this system. Jeremiah was an excellent attorney himself, but it is not surprising to find that other

---

[1] An important variant between the LXX and MT is the LXX reading "my laws" for "my law."

jurists disagreed with him. Moslems hold that the divine revelation came all at once to Mohammed, and if God willed he could take it away all at once in the same way. Ibn Maja (d. 886) said,

> God's Book shall come upon one night, and in the morning the people shall find that not a verse of it is left, either in the earth or in the heart of any Moslem.[1]

Jeremiah might have thought God would put the law in the minds of the parties to his **contract** in the same way.

12*I will no longer remember their crimes*. In this Semitic parallel, dealing **mercifully with their . . . crimes** means that he **will no longer remember** them. This passage from Jeremiah (LXX 38 [31]:31-34) is even longer than the quotation from Ps 95 in Heb 3, which indicates that the author considered this a very important passage, just as he did Ps 95. The promise that he would **no longer remember their crimes** does not mean they would slip his mind. Jeremiah was speaking legally. These **crimes** would be pardoned so that they could not be used against the criminals in court. Those involved would be legally righteous or innocent, no matter how many felonies they had previously committed. The **crimes** committed already were judged as **crimes** by the old contract. When that contract is invalidated, these **crimes** no longer count.

13*He made the first [contract] obsolete.* The short comment that the author made following the quotation was only a summary. The further discussion on the **contract** was planned to come later in his discussion.

In using the word "new" is a free translation for *ehn tóh léh-gayn kái-nayn* (ἐν τῷ λέγειν καινήν), literally, **in [the act of] saying "new."** The author emphasized this word to contrast the **new contract** with the old, which he considered obsolete, vanishing, practically out dated. That which was **obsolete** was not the Torah, the Prophets, and the Writings. It was the **first contract. Scripture** continued to be relevant to the **new contract.**

The Scripture was not the **contract** itself. The **contract** involved the legal ceremonies that were made by which God became the people's God and the people who were parties to the **contract** became God's people. It was not the Scripture, but the **contract** ceremony that Moses performed on Mount Sinai that established the Israelites as God's people, and it was the ceremony in which God burned his houses and sent his people into Nineveh and Babylon that annulled this **contract** and legally established the divorce between God and Israel (Deut 24:1).

It was also the legal ceremony made at the Last Supper through which the new **contract** was made. The Scripture was the code book by which the **contracts** were directed. The old **contract** had been invalidated, but that did not put an end to the validity of the Torah, the Prophets, and the Writings. These continued to constitute the code book for the new **contract**. The new **contract** was in force at the time the author of Hebrews wrote. The contract had been established. According to Hebrews Jesus was the mediator of the new **contract.** Paul claimed to be a minister of the new **contract** (2Cor 3:6). Both Paul and the author of Hebrews, living under the legal authority of the new **contract,** continued to justify their faith on the basis of

---

[1] A. J. Arberry, *Revelation and Reason in Islam* (London: Allen & Unwin, c1957), p. 26.

the Torah, the prophets, and the writings that had been canonized. That which was old and had passed away was the authority of the old contract--not the Scripture.

The Scripture which is necessary both to the old **contract** and the new **contract** was the primary source for the author's arguments, and it was basic to the faith. **Contracts** and the Scripture were endemic to the faith. That which was old was the first **contract.** That which was new was the second **contract**. That which was the same was the Scripture. Weiss correctly said,

> Here in Hebrews is the text in fact much more than read and understood as Old Testament in its attachment to the New Testament. . . . The old is here completely taken into the new. The text and confession are here no more double but are fashioned into a unity.[1]

Summary. This unit includes only a brief introduction and conclusion to the text quoted from Jeremiah, but the author used these to form an inclusion of the two uses of the word **first** (Heb 8:7, 13). The word **first** also is a catchword used to introduce the reader to the subject that follows. The **first** which follows, however, is not the **contract**, but the tent (Heb 9:1). The following unit is still centered around the old cult.

---

[1] H. F. Weiss, *Der Brief an die Hebräer* (Göttingen: Vandenhoeck & Ruprecht, 1991), p. 181.

The aerial photograph shows the area that in New Testament times held both the Roman Fortress of Antonia, now enclosing the Dome of the Rock and El Aqsa Mosque at the top (north), and Zion, the City of David (south). Zion was the city where the temple and the Spring of Gihon (Siloam) were located. It also held the monastery where the sermon in the Book of Hebrews was first delivered. That auther called Zion, "heavenly Jerusalem" (Heb 12:22). The line across the ridge marks the approximate northern border of Zion. Photo by Richard Cleave, Rohr Productions, Ltd.

The picture at the top of the page gives a side-view of the temple at Lachish, showing the steps that lead from the court to the holy place and the walkway that leads farther through the holy place to the holy of holies. The temple at Zion was much larger but organized according to a similar pattern.

The picture below shows the round altar at Megiddo (Armageddon) with steps, leading to the top. The temple Herod constructed in Zion was approximately the same size, but it was square. It measured 75 by 75 feet and was 22½ feet tall. That was probably the altar mentioned in Heb 13:10.

This sketch is of the Promised Land in Biblical Times, with lines showing the approximate northern and southern borders, according to biblical witness. It is scanned from Buchanan, *The Consequences of the Covenant* (Leiden: Brill, 1970), p. 92.

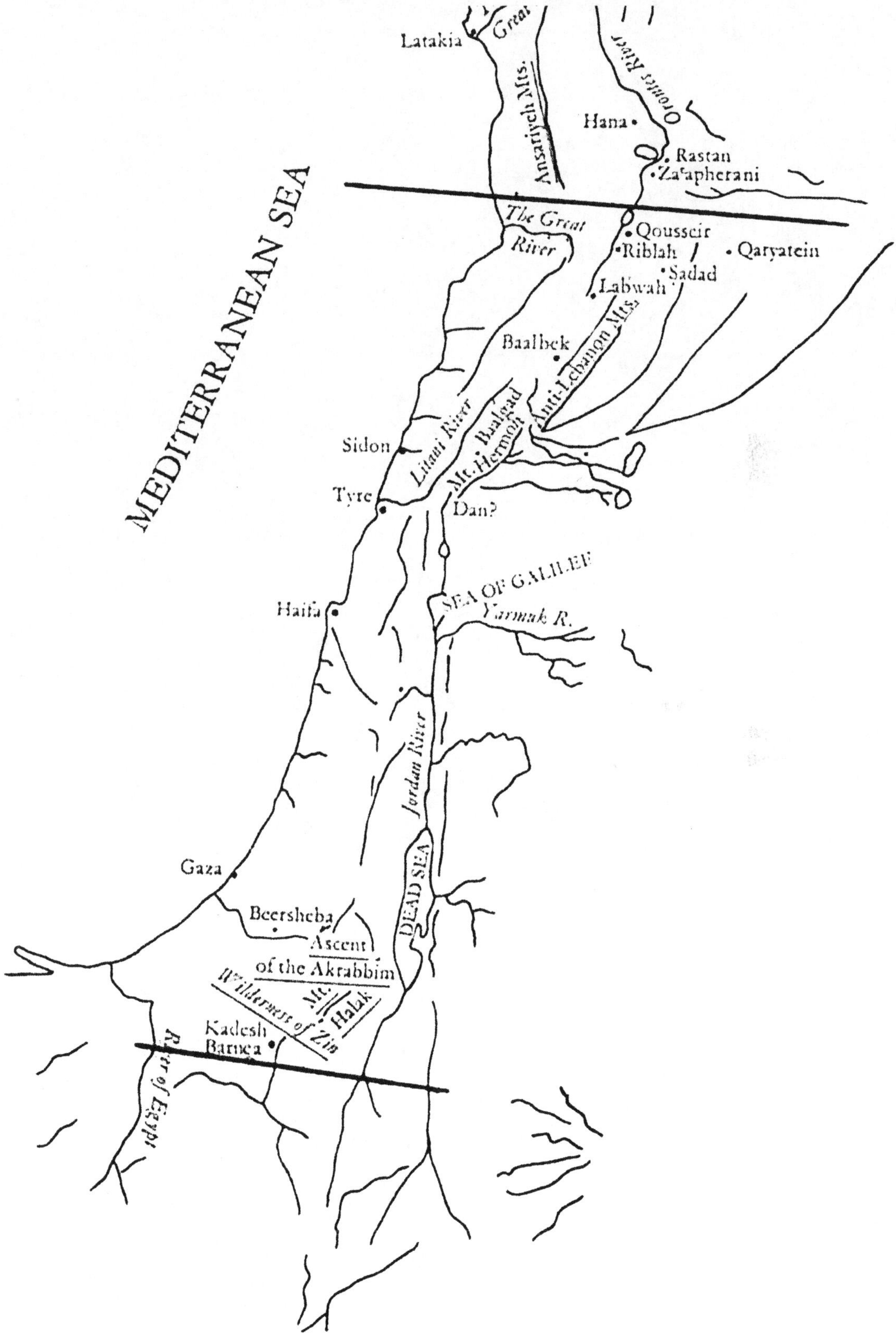

CHAPTER NINE

TEXT

Hebrews	First Testament
[9:1]Now, on the one hand, even the first [tent] had the proper things for worship and an earthly sanctuary, [2]for the first **tent,** which is called "**[the] holy**," was prepared in which there were	[Exod 26:33]You shall bring within the curtain the chest containing the testimony. The **curtain** will separate for you **the holy** from **the holy of holies.** . . [35]You shall place **the table** outside **the curtain** and
the lamp stand, **the table,** and the setting out of loaves. [3]On the other hand, beyond **the** second **curtain** is a **tent** called "**[the] holy of holies**,"	**the lamp stand** opposite **the table,** beside the **tent** on the south, and you shall place **the table** on the north side.

TECHNICAL DETAILS

The preacher was basing his message on the text from Exodus that applied to the tent in the wilderness. There are no photographs of that early tent, but there are ruins of two early temples that were part of fortresses. One of these is at Lachish and the other Arad. They are very similar both in size and design. Each temple has a large court with an altar, large anough to roast only one or two beasts at a time. At one end of that court there is a central door that leads to another inside court of the same width but only about a third as deep. That room has also a central door, directly in front of the door from the first court. That second door leads into a small room, the holy of holies. That is the kind of temple the author of Exodus knew, but in all probability they had never been seen by the author of Hebrews. He had only two sources on which to base his description: 1) the Scripture, and 2) the temple at Jerusalem which still existed when he wrote. He put pieces from these two sources together to illustrate the message that he wanted to deliver.

None of us has seen the temple of Jerusalem. We still have the Scriptures, the ruins of tenth century temples, the ruins of early synagogues, and the writings of Josephus. From these we can try to visualize the small imitation of the early tent that probably existed in the monastery where the author was speaking.

Heb 9 is dedicated to the Jerusalem temple—its size, location, structure, practices, and value. Because of new archaeological discoveries in relation to the temple and the City of David, there are several other documents that are related to the same situation. Their introduction and comparison will help understanding the date, location, and meaning of the Book of Hebrews. The introduction of these documents will temporarily side track the main commentary from time to time, but this will be necessary to understand the chapter fully.

COMMENTARY

Even the first [tent]. Herod's temple that had been completed during the author's lifetime was much larger and more elegant that the wilderness **tent,** but even the wilderness **tent** had a certain amount of important design—and some problems. The author had some criticism against the effectiveness of the temple as it existed in his own time, but he claimed that none of the temples up to the time of Jesus had been effective, not **even** with **the first tent** in the wilderness.

1 *The earthly sanctuary*. The term rendered **earthly** is *káws-mee-kawn* (κόσμι-κον), which reflects something either well organized or something related to the **earth** or the universe. Herod's temple at Zion had a large mosaic floor centered on the Zodiac. It may also have had a large dome, to picture heaven. The latter can only be guessed from pagan temples that were built that way. The temple was well organized with certain furniture placed in prescribed places. All temples at Zion were in one sense **earthly**. They were all located at a special place on **earth,** directly behind the spring at Siloam. Temples of God were located in God's holy city, heavenly Jerusalem. This temple could be called "a well organized **tent,"** because it had all of the parts prescribed in the Scripture. It could also be called a temple on **earth** in contrast to the prototypal temple in heaven.

The conjectured noun which **the first** modifies is here taken to be **tent**. In fact some minor texts (326 *pm*) read **tent** (*skáy-nay*, σκήνη) here, but that is not the basic reason for the conjecture given. This is the first part of a *mehn* (μὲν). . . *deh* (δὲ) (on the one hand . . . on the other) construction, and the second part of the construction is taken to refer to **[the] holy of holies, beyond the second curtain** (9:3). This seems to imply that **the first** refers to **the first** part of the temple. In fact Josephus referred to the western most part of the temple as **the "first** of the temple," (*próh-too hee-eh-roó*, πρώτου Ἱεροῦ) (War 5:238) without saying what **the first** was—just the way Hebrews did, but Josephus added a factor. He said it was on the western part of the temple area. Ezekiel said the temple faced east (Ezek 43:1-4; 47:1). In that **first** court there was the large, square altar with a stairway on the east side. The second court was the holy place or **tent,** where only priests were allowed. The first curtain separated **the first** court from the holy place or tent. The second curtain separated the holy from the holy of holies.

That **beyond the second curtain** refers to the second **tent.**[1] The first large section was a court which contained the altar, but it was not part of the sanctuary that was called the tents. Josephus also described the *hay-káhl* which contains the "lampstand, table, and altar of incense" as the "**first** part" (*próh-tawn méh-raws*, πρῶτον μέρος) (War 5:216). That is the first part of the sanctuary where only priests were allowed to enter. On the floor of the court was a mosaic design that had a circle of the Zodiac. This is evident in some early synagogue floors that have been unearthed south of the Sea of Galilee. This would not have been within that small

---

[1] E. Grässer, *An die Hebräer* (Zürich: Benziger Verlag, c1993) 2, p. 110, argued that the tents mentioned here did not refer to the parts of Solomon's or Herod's temples, but only to the tent of meeting in the wilderness. It was from that place of worship that the expression, "tents," originated, but it was also extended to Solomon's and later temples. Apparently David's altar in Zion was also associated with tents before Solomon's temple was erected. Grässer also thought the tents did not really refer to the temples in Jerusalem but were only symbolic. One tent symbolized the passing world and the other symbolized heaven (p. 115).

room between the court and the holy of holies. All of these items would have been contained in the first tent. The "holy of holies" as the "innermost part"(*ehn-daw-táh-toh méh-raws*, ἐνδοτάτω μέρος) was the second tent (War 5:219),[1]

Originally there was neither a temple nor a tent as a place of worship in Zion. When David first conquered the city, there may have been an altar there that had already been used by the Canaanites, but that is unlikely. When Hecataeus came to Zion (4th century BIA) he saw a huge altar there. He said it measured 30 feet long, 30 feet wide, and 15 feet tall (Apion 1:198). Josephus said in his day the altar was 22½ feet tall and about 75 feet long and 75 feet wide (War 5:224-225). The altar Hecataeus saw might have been constructed by the Canaanites before David invaded the city. It was constructed of loose, unhewn stones, just like the huge Canaanite altar at Megiddo, except that it was square, rather than round.

There is only one objection to that hypothesis. When Adonijah ran from Ain Rogel to the altar at Gihon, he took hold of the horns (*kahr-uh-nóht,* קרנות) of the altar for security (1Kings 1:50). Horns were projectiles that were constructed at the corners of altars to hold the beasts and the wood on the altar. Adonijah could not have held more than one horn at a time if the corner horns had been 30 feet apart. This suggests that when David built a tent for the chest containing the **contract,** he probably had a small altar built there at the same time (2Sam 6:1-17). That altar would have been about the same size as the two altars that have survived in the ruins of Arad and Lachish. They were only large enough to roast one or two beasts at a time. The huge altar that Hecataeus saw was probably built by Solomon and enlarged by Herod to the size Josephus saw. (There is a side view a picture of the court, holy, and holy of holies at Lachish between chapters 8 and 9).

Originally the altar and tent were evidently placed directly behind the Spring of Siloam, because that is where Zadok obtained the oil for anointing Solomon at Gihon. Because the chest containing the contract was housed in the tent of God, even after the temple was constructed, and the chest and its contents were moved into the holy of holies, its location was still called a "tent" (1Kings 8:4-9).

The RSV understood this differently, however, and rendered Heb 9:1 as referring to "the **first** contract," rather than "**the first [tent],**" and the **second** part of the *mehn . . . deh* construction to be continued in Heb 9:11. This would be a very long grammatical construction that would include one *mehn . . . deh* construction (Heb 9:6-7) within another (Heb 9:1, 11-12). The RSV understanding would show the contrast between the **first contract** and the second **contract** rather than between the **first** part and the **second** part of the temple, but the text from Exodus, on which the author depended dealt with the tent rather than with the contract.

---

[1] R. Jewett, *Letter to the Pilgrims* (New York: Pilgrim Press, c1981), p. 144, however, avoided any allusion to the Jerusalem temple altogether. The notion that there were two separate tents, he said, "is not derived from the Old Testament tradition of one tent with a divided section for the Holy of Holies. It stems from the Hellenistic Jewish tradition that thought of two tents as symbolizing heaven and earth as cosmic realms." His sources for that information came from other secondary sources that also told of their imaginary notions but gave no data to support or justify their claims. The author of Hebrews used the FT so extensively that it is unnecessary to search for some other possible "tradition" in such far removed places as Indian and Egyptian mysticism and in later gnosticism. Fasting and dietary rules are too basic to Judaism and early Christianity to necessitate the assumption that these rules represented a "Lycus Valley heresy" (Jewett, *Letter*, pp. 146-47. Grässer, *Hebräer* II, pp. 110-111, followed RSV and rendered the noun **contract**, but also discussed the first tent, which he thought was only a parable of the passing world, quoting from Goethe, *Faust* 2, Act 5.

Since Hebrews clearly contrasted the **contracts**, and since Christ's function in the more perfect **tent** (Heb 9:11) is contrasted to the priest's function in **the first tent,** it is possible that the RSV is correct in understanding this to be a very long *mehn* (μὲν) . . . *deh* (δέ) construction which further contrasted the two **contracts**; but this ignores the structure which the author has designed to show the division of his units. Heb 9:1-10 is enclosed in an inclusion, separating the content of Heb 9:1-10 from the following material. It therefore seems unlikely that he would have intended to hold the two units together by a *mehn . . . deh* construction.

The proper things (*dee-kai-óh-mah-tah,* δικαιώματα) are the things prescribed as being necessary **for worship**. The **earthly sanctuary** (*háh-gee-ohn kaws-mee-káwn,* ἅγιον κοσμικόν), was the temple in which the levitical priests functioned **on earth** (Heb 8:4), in contrast to the temple in heaven, where Jesus ministers (Heb 8:2, 5, 9:11, 24; 11:16). Josephus and Philo, however, both describe the temple, its contents, and the priestly garments as symbols of the universe (Ant 3:180-87; War 4:324; 5:216-18; Heres 41:196-97; 46:226), which may be another reason for calling it **earthly**.

2-3*The first tent, which is called "[the] holy."* There were three parts to a temple area: The largest room was a court where the altar for roasting animals was stationed. This was not called anything holy. The holy places were rooms that were limited to priestly use. These were called "tents." In the wilderness the tent was separated from the altar. There were two of these: 1) the first was separated from the court by a curtain. Only priests were allowed there. 2) The second was separated from the first by another curtain. Only the high priest was allowed there.

Weiss correctly held that **the tents** discussed here were spaces, rooms, or places within the temple area, following the text in Exodus. **The curtain** that was drawn between the two **tents** was a physical **curtain** between two rooms in a building on earth. It was not a Gnostic separation wall between earth and heaven.[1] Swetnam argued unconvincingly that **the first tent** was really not a **tent** or a place at all, but it referred to **the setting out of loaves**, which, in turn, meant the eucharist.[2] The word **tent** can refer to something flimsy. A **tent** is not as stable as a stone house, for example, so the tottering dynasty of David was called a **tent** rather than a house (Amos 9:11-12), and a shepherd's temporary dwelling was called a **tent** (Isa 38:12). In the wilderness the **tent** that contained the **contract** was a movable, portable dwelling. When David installed the altar with the chest containing the **contract** in Zion, it was put in relationship to a real **tent**, as it had been in the wilderness, but when Solomon constructed a temple, the innermost parts of the building were still called **tents.** In **the first tent** was the place where **the loaves** for the priest were **set out**--not the eucharist.

The division of the temple into two units or **tents** as Hebrews describes them conforms to the architecture of the temple as closely as the insights of early literature and modern archaeology can reconstruct. The temple at Arad, Israel, excavated by Prof. Aharoni, was originally constructed in about the tenth century BIA. Its entire size was only about 65 feet long and 49 feet wide. The largest room was the court (*oo-láhm,* אולם) which contained an altar for sacrificing animals. That altar was only big enough to roast one or two animals at a time. The room which held

---

[1] H. F. Weiss, *Der Brief an die Hebräer* (Göttingen: Vandenhoeck & Ruprecht, 1991), pp. 492-493.

[2] J. Swetnam, "Hebrews 9,2 and the Uses of Consistency," *CBQ* 32 (1970):205-21.

that altar was an open space without a roof, allowing the smoke from the altar to escape, just as Philo described (Mos 2:80, 94). The next room (*hay-káhl*, היכל, "outer **tent**," or **[the] holy**) was only nine feet long and 30 feet wide--about a third as large as the court. The very small room that was connected to this room was the **holy of holies**, the *deh-veér* (דביר), or the inner **tent.** It was in the center of the wall of the "outer **tent.**" In Lachish there were steps going from the holy into the holy of holies, but at Arad both rooms are on the same level. Inside of each "inner **tent**" was found a pillar (*mah-tsay-báh*, מצבה) and a small, square, paved altar (*báy-mah*, במה).

This early temple was later enlarged, but only to the extent that was admissible by changing to a larger Egyptian cubit from an earlier smaller cubit measure (ca. 18 to ca. 21 inches). There was enough similarity between the measurements of the temples at Arad and Solomon's temple in Jerusalem (2Chron 3-4) for Aharoni to conjecture that there was an intentional attempt to follow the proportions of the tabernacle in the wilderness when building temples (Exod 26:16-30) such as those at Arad, Jerusalem, Shiloh, Bethel, and Dan.[1] The temples were similar enough to the neighboring nations that the furniture from one could be used in another.[2]

This does not cohere, however, with the dimensions describing either Solomon's temple or Herod's temple, both of which were larger. Solomon's temple was ninety feet long and thirty feet wide, with **the holy of holies** being thirty feet by thirty feet. These were apparently outside dimensions, and the **holy of holies** was evidently a part of the ninety feet length of the entire building (2Chron 3:3-4). Herod's temple was larger than all of the earlier temples. Instead of both the altar and the holy of holies being 30 X 30 feet, Herod's altar was 75 X 75 feet, which means that the holy of holies was probably the same size.

The author may have deduced the contents of the respective **tents** from 2Chron 4, but the contents are not precisely the same as the ones given in Hebrews. That there were such things as tables, lamp stands, and an ark in the Jerusalem temple which Herod built is evident from the sculpture of the victory procession carved into the Arch of Titus in Rome. The objects shown in that arch were those taken from Herod's temple when Jerusalem was captured in 70 IA. Other biblical descriptions of the temple are given in Isa 6, Ezek 40:1-45:5 and 1Kings 6-7 (see also 2Bar 6:7). Josephus described the Herodian temple at length (War 5:184-236). He said the temple (*nah-aws*, ναός--both the holy and the holy of holies, but not the court) was 60 by 20 cubits (ca. 30 ft. by 90 ft.; see Ezek 41:2). This was divided into two parts: The holy was 40 by 20 cubits (60 ft. by 30 ft.) and the holy of holies (*hah-geé-oo deh háh-gee-awn*, ἁγίου δὲ ἅγιον) was 20 by 20 cubits (30 ft. by 30 ft.).

Josephus said that there was a partition between the holy and the holy of holies, and he also said the one was separated from the other by a veil, drape, or curtain. Either this partition was a **curtain** or the partition had a gate or doorway in it that was closed by a **curtain**. In the first portion (*próh-tawn méh-ros*), the **holy,** was kept "**a lamp stand, a table,** and an altar of incense" (War 5:216). Philo concurred in this (Heres 45:226). The author of Hebrews did not mention an altar of incense, but he said there was a gold altar in the **holy of holies,** which may be the same piece of **furniture** with some disagreement about its location.[3] Hebrews and

---

[1] Y. Aharoni, "Arad: Its Inscriptions and Temple," *BA* 31 (1968):18-27.

[2] E. Stern, "Pagan Yahwism: The Folk Religion of Ancient Israel," *BAR* 27.3 (2001): 21-29.

[3] See R. de Langhe, "L'Autel d'Or du Temple de Jerusalem," *Biblica* 40 (1959):476-94, for a

Josephus both said there were "loaves" on the **table,** and Josephus, following Lev 24:3, said further that the number of loaves was twelve (War 5:217; Ant 3:182). The **second tent**, which both Heb and Josephus described as the **holy of holies**, contained a gold altar and a gold filled chest holding the national contract, according to Heb 9:3 (also 2Bar 6:7), but according to Josephus it contained "nothing at all" (War 5:219).

The rabbis claim that the chest holding the contract was removed and a stone remained in its place from the time of the early prophets on (mYoma 5:2; mShek 6:1-2).[1] If there had been a stone there it would have been a *bah-máh* במה), a flat stone with a rounded top and a flat base at the bottom. There was a *mah-tzay-báh* in the **holy of holies** of the temples both at Lachish and Arad. **The second curtain** separated **[the] holy** from **[the] holy of holies**. No mention is made of a first curtain, but there probably was a **curtain** separating the **holy** from the court yard where the large altar was constructed for sacrificing animals. Philo said the altar for the burnt offerings was placed in the open air opposite the **tent** (the "holy"), at a distance adequate to allow the ministers to work (Mos 2:94). This fits in perfectly with the design of the temple at Arad, which seems a bit different in design from that described by Josephus and Solomon's temple (2Chron 3:3-4). Both of these described only **the holy** and **the holy of holies**, but in the temples at Lachish and Arad the altar for sacrificing animals was in the large court on the lower level. It is likely that Solomon's temple was arranged in the same order. There are some differences between the placing of the furniture in Solomon's temple and Herod's temple, but there actually may have been these variations.

ACCORDING TO JOSEPHUS

The location of the temple. The discovery of **the** true **location of the** City of David means that David's palace and Solomon's temple were down near the Spring of Siloam in the Kidron Valley.[2] Solomon's temple was only 90 feet long and 30 feet wide, with an open court and an altar for sacrifice in the rear.[3] Later temples were larger, but all were placed near the same location. David's altar and **tent,** from which Zadok obtained the oil for anointing, were placed very near the spring of Gihon, where the priest, Zadok, anointed Solomon (1Kings 1:38-39). Solomon's temple was evidently constructed nearby. Y. Shiloh, followed by H. Shanks, however, conjectured that Herod's walls up on the higher area to the north, later enclosed Solomon's temple.[4] Although it is popular, this theory is free from any support from Josephus, Aristeas, Tacitus, or any biblical sources.

---

thought-provoking analysis of the function of the altar of incense and its relationship to the altar of gold.

[1] For a careful analysis of Near Eastern temples made before Aharoni's excavation of Arad, see W. F. Albright, *Archaeology and the Religion of Israel* (Baltimore: Johns Hopkins Press, 1942), pp. 142-55.

[2] Ain Rogel was later made into a well, leaving only one spring in the Kidron Valley—Ain Gihon.

[3] Although it has been overlooked, G. A. Smith, *Jerusalem* (New York: A. C. Armstrong and Son, 1908) 1, pp. 134-69, suggested this location for the City of David nearly a hundred years ago. Also K. Kenyon reached this conclusion from her archaeological excavations.

[4] H. Shanks, "The City of David after Five Years of Digging," *BAR* 11.6 (1985):22-38. Diagrams on pp. 34-35, 37; "Everything You Ever Knew about Jerusalem is Wrong," *BAR* 25.6 (1999):27.

Mount Zion and the Lower City. David's **city** was a small, third quarter moon shaped, sharp ridge above the Kidron Valley, west of the spring of Siloam. The town was initially composed of two mountains, adjacent to one another with a small valley in between. The mountain to the north was Mount Ophel, and the one to the south was David's citadel, Mount Zion, a fortification tower at the southern border of **the city.** It was placed at the end of the little mountain range, just the way the fortresses at Megiddo, Gezer, and Hazor are. That was the normal place for a fortress.

When Antiochus Epiphanes conquered the city, he extended the size of the citadel and used it to house Syrian soldiers to control the Jewish city. Then Jews learned that the fortress that was designed to defend them could be used to control them. They wished that it was not even there.

When Jews finally gained freedom from Syria, under the Hasmonean, Simon's, leadership, they spent three years destroying the citadel. They removed the entire mountain down to bedrock and used part of the fill to level the space to build up Mount Ophel and to fill up the deep Tyropoeon Valley that separated the City of David from the upper city farther west (War 1:138-41; 5:136-41). That which had been formerly the citadel, then, became the lower section of the area. This prevented any other nation from using that area to control the City of David (War 5:4, 1; 2:17, 9; Ant 12:5, 4; 13:6, 17; 1Macc 1:33-36; 6:18; 13:52),[1] but it also left Zion without southern protection that the citadel offered.

The new northern fortress. From then on Mount Ophel was the tallest mountain in David's City, and it was at the north end of the town. The Hasmoneans had begun to strengthen the fortifications at the north end of town. This may have involved strengthening the temple, which was also a fortress, deepening the moat and strengthening the north wall. They began to build a fortress called the Baris, north of the city. The Romans later confiscated this fortress and developed it into the huge defense unit called the Antonia. This is now called the Haram and encloses the Dome of the Rock and the al Aqsa Mosque. Under the leadership of Herod, Romans needed a strong fortress, just as the Syrian Greeks did to control the City of David. Since the advantages of the old Syrian citadel no longer existed, they chose the new site in the North. There they constructed the huge walls around a 35 acre area which now surrounds the Dome of the Rock. Since there was no spring there to provide water for the Antonia, the Romans developed 37 large cisterns to capture rain water to meet the water needs of the fortress. Antonia was considerably larger than the entire City of David. From the tall south eastern corner tower Romans could control Zion, just as the Syrians did earlier, from an exalted, fortified location. It is now the tallest point on that bank of the Kidron Valley and has been confused for David's holy City to the south. Now that the location of David's City has been corrected, many passages in ancient literature make more sense.

The temple and the spring. Nehemiah described the stairs that went down to the spring of Siloam from the City of David (Neh 3:15-16) and the gate of the spring at the base of the stairs (Neh 12:37). Ezekiel had a vision of the stream that flowed out from under the threshold of the temple, south of the altar (Ezek 47:1), down the

---

[1] This entire insight of the location of David's citadel was called to my attention by E. Martin, *The Temples that Jerusalem Forgot* (Portland: ASK Publications, c2000), pp. 322-30. The location of David's City was observed still earlier by G. A. Smith, *Jerusalem* I, p. 445.

Kidron Valley, through the stream bed that finally runs through Wady Qumran and on into the Dead Sea. It sweetened the waters, because it flowed out from the sanctuary (Ezek 47:12), so that fish could survive there (Ezek 47:10).[1] All of this water had its origin from the Spring of Siloam (Gihon) and flowed through a horizontal tunnel where it appeared under the threshold of the temple. Then it ran south into the Kidron Valley (Ezek 47:1-2, 12; 2Chron 32:3, 30; 2Kings 20:20).

The topogaphy and geography of Ezekiel's vision fit perfectly, once it is recognized that the temple was adjacent to the spring of Gihon that provided all of this water. Ezekiel would not have pictured a temple high on the dry hill north of the spring where this could not happen. Enoch also claimed to have seen the holy mountain with a stream that flowed underneath that mountain toward the south (1Enoch 26:2-3). There is no such stream flowing underneath the Dome of the Rock. The holy mountain was obviously Mount Ophel, the hill on which the temple was stationed, located just above Ain Gihon. This is the location of which Ezekiel spoke, where the stream that flowed underneath the mountain also flowed underneath the temple near Gihon. Aristeas told of an indescribably complex and wonderful water system, related to the Spring of Gihon.[2] The psalmist spoke of the temple, where **Yehowah**[3] **sits over the flood** where he is **enthroned as king for the age** (Ps 29:10). The **flood** was the huge fountain of water, pouring through the tunnel, under the temple. Another psalmist said, **There is a river whose streams make glad the city of God, the holy dwelling place of the Most High** (Ps 46:5). **The dwelling place of the Most High** was the temple positioned near the **streams** that **make glad the city of God.** The Scroll of Blessings asked that **the Lord bless** the recipient **from his holy dwelling, the fountain of the age** (1QSb 1:3). The holy dwelling at the fountain of the age was clearly the temple just above Ain Gihon.

One of the factors Zechariah anticipated in the future restoration when Yehowah would become king over all the land was having the **waters of life flowing out from Jerusalem** (Zech 14:8-9). The **Jerusalem** he pictured was Zion, near Gihon—not the northern hill that later became Herod's city.

When the NT seer looked forward to a new Jerusalem, he anticipated a heavenly city that had come to earth from God in heaven, prepared as a bride for a new wedding contract. In this new city one of the basic descriptions was the **river of the water of life going out from the throne of God** (Rev 22:1, *thráw-noo too theh-oó* [θρόνου τοῦ θεοῦ = *keé-say áyl,* כסא אל] cf. *meek-dahsh áyl* [מקדש אל] [1QpHab 12:8-9]). This would have to be placed in Zion where the spring of Gihon streamed from the altar of the temple down the Kidron Valley to the south that related the temple to the area near the spring of Gihon. Tacitus said,

> The temple was built like a fortress . . . There is an ever-flowing spring tunneled under the hills into collecting pools and cisterns (Hist 11:12).

Aristeas (ca 285 BIA) explained how the landscape of the temple area was designed with paved stones and gutters to carry away the blood washed down from the sacrifices. There was an inexhaustible supply of water gushing into the temple for use in sacrifices (Aristeas 87-89). The temple scroll (11QT 32:12-15) concurs with

---

[1] See further Buchanan, *The Gospel of Matthew* (Lewiston: Mellen, c1996) II, pp. 816-18.

[2] So Martin, *Temples*, pp. 277-280.

[3] For the correct spelling of the Tetragrammaton see Buchanan, *Matthew* 1, pp. 49-50.

Aristeas that water was necessary both for the priests to bathe before participating in services and for sacrifices. That document describes a canal that brought water into the area and was used to wash away the bath water and blood into a hole that vanished into the land. That may have conducted the mixture of blood and water into Hezekiah's tunnel. It was important to have a drain to allow the fluid to vanish before anyone became defiled by the blood.

Yadin noticed the way this canal had to function. He also showed how consistent this report was with Ezek 47 and the Mishnah that said there were two holes where the water and blood ran and both led down into the Kidron brook (mMid 3:2). He also called attention to the altar on Mount Carmel where there was a similar conduit that brought water around the altar to wash away the blood (1Kings 18:32-33). Nevertheless, he did not raise the question, asking how this could function from the so-called "temple mount" location.[1]

Temple Functions

TEXT

4which has a gold altar and the chest holding the contract, completely covered with
gold, in which there is a gold jar, containing the manna, the rod of Aaron that bud-
ded, and the tablets of the contract. 5Above it are cherubim of glory overshadowing
the mercy seat (concerning which things, this is not the proper time to speak).
6These things having been thus prepared. Into the first tent the priests en-
tered continually while performing the ritualistic services, 7but into the second [tent]
only the high priest enters, [and then only] once during the year, [and even then] not
without blood which he offers in behalf of his own [crimes] and the unintentional
[crimes] of the people. 8The Holy Spirit makes it clear [that] the way of the holy
[precincts] is not yet visible as long as the first tent still has standing. 9This [tent] is
a parable for the present time, according to which both gifts and sacrifices are
offered [which are] not able to perfect the worshiper according to [his] conscience;
10only being concerned with foods and drinks and various ablutions--proper
[observances] of the flesh [imposed] until the time of correction.

COMMENTARY

Although Aaron and his sons were compared unfavorably to Jesus in Hebrews, the position of high priest in Judaism was very highly esteemed. Ben Sira described Onias, the high priest, on the Day of Atonement as follows:

> [He is] like one who has been glorified when the people gathered around
> as he came out of the veiled house,
> like the morning star among the clouds,
> like the moon on the days when it is full,
> like the sun shining on the temple of the Most High,
> like a rainbow shining in the glorious clouds,
> like a rose bud in the days of first fruits,
> like a lily alongside a spring of water,
> like a green shoot of Lebanon in harvest time,

[1] Y. Yadin, *The Temple Scroll* (Jerusalem; The Israel Exploration Society, 1983) I, pp. 223-25.

like fire and frankincense in the censor,
like a vessel made of solid gold
decorated with all kinds of precious stones,
like an olive tree bearing fruit,
like a cypress exalted in the clouds (Sira 50:5-10).

4*The chest holding the contract.* The **gold altar** may be the same as the **altar** of incense which Philo said was in **the holy.** Philo agreed that **the chest holding the contract** was kept in the **holy of holies**. He also said **the chest** was covered on the inside and outside **with gold. The chest holding the contract** was claimed to indicate the legal presence of the Lord (Num 14:10-12). Here God was legally present through his word. According to Exod 16:33 and Num 17:25 (MT; RSV 17:10), Moses commanded that Aaron's staff and the jar that contained the omer measure of manna be placed before the box **containing the contract**. Hebrews follows the LXX in noting that the **jar** for the **manna** was **gold** (Exod 16:33). Mek *Vayassa* 6:65-70, held that the **jar** was of earthenware. Rabbis also believed that in the future Elijah would restore to Israel the container of **manna**, the flask of sprinkling water, and the jar of anointing oil. Some also said "the rod of Aaron" produced ripe almonds and blossoms (Mek *Vayassa* 6:82-85). Philo called "the tablets of the contract" "the holy books," but agreed that they were kept in **the chest** (Mos 2:95).

5*Above it are the cherubim of glory.* **The cherubim** were Sphinx-like beings with faces of human beings, bodies of animals, and wings like birds. Their description, **of glory**, means "of God" (see Exod 25:22; Num 7:89; Ezek 10:19; Rom 1:23). They might be called "divine **cherubim**." The object rendered **mercy seat** is *hee-lahs-táy-ree-awn* (Ἱλαστήριον), from the verb *hee-láhs-kaw-mai* (Ἱλάσκομαι) which means to "appease," "propitiate," or "conciliate." This is the word used to render *kah-póh-reht* (כפורת) in Exod 25:17, 21. The Hebrew root *kee-páyr* (כפר) means to cover and is used to describe atonement, which is a covering for crimes.

That which is called **the mercy seat** is really the cover or lid for the chest, and the Hebrew word meant that. Because this was in **the holy of holies** where the priest entered to make atonement, the word may have taken on an added significance (1Chron 28:11). It was not just a "cover" for the chest, but something related to the covering of crimes. The LXX translated it as such.[1] Philo said the *hee-lahs-táy-ree-awn* was a cover for the chest which supported the cherubim. He reported that "some say" the cherubim faced each other on top of the cover, but he seems not to have known for certain (Mos 2:97-98). In the Mosaic floor at Beth-Alpha there is an altar with two cherubim facing one another. They are not on top of the cover, but stationed on each end.

6*These things having been thus prepared.* **These things having been thus prepared** refers to the furniture and required objects in **the holy** and **the holy of holies**, the proper things for worship (Heb 9:1), made ready for priestly function. **The first tent** was **[the] holy** place on the other side of the first curtain from the court where the large altar for burnt offerings was. No laymen were permitted in that

---

[1] M. Stuart, *Commentary on the Epistle to the Hebrews in Greek and English* (Andover: Warren F. Draper, 1828), p. 195. In Akkadian the cognate apparently means "wipe away," which seems to fit the priestly actions and both traditions. Only Philo seems to be at variance with this.

holy place, but **priests entered continually** as they performed the various **ritualistic services** required by the law. The contents listed here are not the same as those listed elsewhere. The author may have overlooked some. Another possibility is that he may have remembered those in the tent of meeting and also in Solomon's temple and confused them, or he may not have thought it was important to include them all.

[7]*Into the second [tent] only the high priest enters.* **The second [tent]** excludes admission, not only of all laymen, but of all priests except the **high priest**, and he used it **[only] once during the year**, on the Day of Atonement. This evidently means "one occasion" during the year, rather than one specific entrance. Lev 16:11-16 describes two entrances on the **Day of Atonement,** one to atone for the **high priest** and his family and one for the whole people of Israel. Rabbis said the **high priest** entered the holy of holies four times on the **Day of Atonement** (NumR 7:8. 21a; mYoma 5:1-7:4). When he entered the **holy of holies**, he brought "blood," first from the bull (Lev 16:14) and then from the goat (Lev 16:15), which he sprinkled ritualistically with his finger seven times before the ark. The ritual prescribed in Lev 16 for the Day of Atonement was supposed to atone for *all* Israel's crimes (Lev 16:34), with no distinction made between the intentional and unintentional crimes.

Rabbis, however, claimed that atonement was not automatic (tYoma 5:6). On that day the Lord forgave only the crimes committed against him, and then only if the conditions were right. The party to the **contract** was required

1) first he had to repent.
2) Second, he had to be reconciled to his brother against whom he had committed crimes, and
3) third, he had to bring his crime and guilt offerings to the temple of the Lord to pay his unpaid fines (mYoma 8:8-9; see also Matt 5:23-24).

If a man said, "I will commit crimes and repent, and commit crimes again and repent," he will be given no chance to repent. [If he said], "I will commit crimes and the Day of Atonement will effect atonement," then the Day of Atonement effects no atonement (mYoma 8:9).

This was probably the condition the author of Hebrews had in mind when he wrote about the priest's atonement **of his own [crimes] and the unintentional [crimes] of the people**. It would seem as if the same conditions would also apply to the priest himself. It is not clear from the text itself whether **his own** refers to the noun **[crimes],** which is understood, or whether this modifies **unintentional [crimes].** If the latter is true, as seems likely, then a better translation is: "in behalf of his own unintentional [crimes] and those of the people." This would concur with the assessment of the **high priest** being able to intercede for the people's crimes of ignorance since he himself was clothed in weakness (Heb 5:2).

Being **guiltless** (Heb 7:26) may have meant having committed no intentional crimes and no crimes that had not been reconciled. Philo said the high priest never committed crimes that could not be cleansed (Spec 1:230), which meant he never committed mortal crimes that could not be forgiven. Therefore this would not be an issue, but Philo's idealization of the priesthood may not have been representative of general Jewish understanding of that time. Amos, Isaiah, Hosea, and Micah all insisted that the Lord could not be bribed by sacrifices and incense. He demanded justice. Crimes had to be punished, and victims satisfied. Eighth century prophets apparently understood the rules for the Day of atonement long before the medieval rabbis.

8*The Holy Spirit makes it clear.* When **the Holy Spirit** communicates, according to the author, it means that the Scripture says (Heb 3:7; 10:15). In this case it is the text in Exod 26:31-35 that directs the presence of the curtain that separates the holy from the holy of holies. The curtain keeps the way of the holy from being visible. It is not only the priesthood that is weak. There are problems with the very architecture of the temple itself, primarily the first tent.

The way of the holy [precincts] is not yet visible. The **first tent** here probably refers to a portion of Herod's temple, which included both **tents.** Both of these were in front of the courtyard which held the huge altar. The word **stands** (*ehkh-oó-says stáh-seen,* ἐχούσης στάσιν) probably does not refer to the actual existence of the temple as Moffatt and others hold,[1] because the author would not have known that the temple would soon be destroyed. The expression **having standing** is a legal expression that is involved in court cases. A person who brings a case before the court is the plaintiff who must have standing in order to proceed. The plaintiff must have "present substantial interest" in the outcome of the trial. Standing is not effected by the facts of the suit themselves but whether or not the plaintiff has a "legally protectible and tangible interest at stake in the litigation."[2]

In this case the author acknowledged that the first tent, either the tent in the wilderness or the holy place in Herod's temple, was authorized to to function as the plaintiff and take cases to the Lord. The Scripture **makes it clear** that the Lord would hear the cases brought so long as they had standing, but the author thought that this **standing** was no longer effective or that the cases brought would not receive favorable treatment in the court.

The temple of which the author was speaking was Herod's temple. In the author's opnion that was a temple "made with hands," whose religious function was ineffective. The high priest was wicked, but nevertheless, that temple and its holy of holies had important **standing** with the general public, and it also had scriptural authority. This was the temple the author described in detail above. It currently **had standing** with curtains separating the priests from the people and the high priest from the other priests. But the author thought this was a temporary condition. Jesus' sacrifice had opened a new way from the court to the holy of holies, like that of the monastery that had no curtains. In that situation **the way of the holy** would become **visible.**

This fact seems to have been a problem for the author. The **first tent** was the **holy** place between the courtyard and the altar of incense. It was a wide room that was not very deep. Its existence kept people from seeing the performance of the high priest. Since he was an imperfect priest who had weaknesses, how could the worshipers know that he was doing it correctly. If he were faulty in his liturgy or unclean at the time, no one in the court would ever know. As long as that condition existed the people could never be sure that the Day of Atonement ritual would be effective. The high priest had lost his standing with the people.

---

[1] James Moffatt, *A Critical and Exegetical Commentary on the Epistle to the Hebrews* (Edinburgh: T. & T. Clark, 1924), p. 118.

[2] *American Jurisprudence* 59 (1987):#31.417-418.

The way of the holy [precincts] in a temple context probably means the way from the court through the first curtain, to the holy, then through the second curtain, to **the holy of holies**. Before Christ's sacrifice, laymen had no access to **the holy,** and while curtains were closed they could not even see **the holy**. If the curtain was open, they could see **the holy** but not **the holy of holies. While the first tent** still **had standing**, it provided an obstacle to the vision of those in the court, keeping **the holy of holies** from being **visible**. In fact, with the curtains, the entire **way of the holy [precincts]** from the court of the slaughtering altar to the altar of incense was not **visible** to the layman in the court. Therefore the layman or laywoman gave his or her offering, but did not get to see what happened to it. It was shrouded in mystery.

The worshiper with a little skepticism about the priests might doubt whether his or her offering was really sacrificed and offered properly**. As long as the first tent still has standing** seems to imply that the problem would continue to exist until some changes were made to keep the **first tent** from being an obstacle. Later in the document the author said the sacrifice of Jesus opened a fresh and living way through the curtain (Heb 10:19-20). That would mean that the believer would no longer have this **way** closed to him or her.

The author, who was evidently a monk who functioned in a monastery, probably did not think that Jesus' sacrifice took place in Herod's temple, made with hands. In the monastery, the entire dining room was kept as holy as the altar in the holy of holies of the true temple, where all of the participants were monks and probably also priests. Aaron and Jesus were both made priests, meaning that through some liturgical form, those who had not been born priests, like the sons of Zadok or Levi, were ordained as priests. The monks in the monastery were as careful in their behavior and performance as the high priest in the temple on the Day of Atonement. Since that was true they may all have been made priests through legal liturgy, so the curtain would note have been needed to separate the high priest from other priests. They were allowed to enter **the first tent,** the holy place and also the holy of holies. No curtains were necessary to obstruct **the fresh and living way** with a curtain.

9 *A parable of the present time.* The **parable** involves the problem of the **first tent** and the Day of Atonement. It illustrated the situation and **time** in which the author and his audience lived during which **gifts and sacrifices** were being offered, but their value was questionable. The participants still knew the declaration of Amos, echoed by other prophets:

> I hate; I despise your feasts;
> I take no pleasure in your solemn assemblies.
> Even though you offer me your burnt offerings
> and grain offerings,
> I will not accept them (Amos 5:21-22; Hos 6:8; Isa 1:12-15; Mic 6:6-8).

On the one hand there was Herod's temple with its Roman appointed priests. The way was closed to the believers, with only special priestly considerations. The high priest could not perform unless and until Romans permitted it. Because faithful Jews did not believe the temple was valid, it was closed to them by their own volition. At the same time Christians lived in an imperfect political and religious situation. The temple cult was as frustrating as the local situation. It **was a parable,** suggesting further limitations. On the other hand, in the holy of holies in the monastery, **the way in the** temple from the court to **the holy of holies** would be opened, and at the same time the promises of Abraham and Moses would be fulfilled.

9-10*Not able to perfect the worshiper.* The priests were skilled in the techniques of sacrifice. They knew how to perform each detail. If any happened to be untrained, scholarly legalists were there to coach them before each movement. But in Herod's pagan temple, none of this was effective.

The liturgical situation of that **time** seemed analogous to **the first tent** which stood in the way and obstructed the view between the altar of sacrifice and the altar of incense in the **holy of holies**. The liturgy in Herod's temple was **not able to perfect** the worshiper's **conscience,** perhaps because **the worshiper** went away doubting or wondering whether his **gift** had really been offered and his crime removed. Had he or had he not been forgiven? He did not know. He was left either to trust where he could not see or to have an imperfect **conscience.** Since Rome built the temple, many Jews conscientiously could not worship in the temple. They thought it was pagan.

If he had no confidence in the priesthood or the efficacy of their sacrifice, he had to rely on the rules that laymen could observe: dietary laws, fasts, and levitical ablutions. This explanation would make rather good sense if the author had not spoken about **drinks** as well as about "foods and various ablutions." There are no general rules in the Pentateuch concerning the drinking of intoxicating liquors or prohibition of **drinking** any other kind of liquids, that would affect the average layman. It would also effect even the laywomen who were not allowed in the court, but there were rules about **drinks** for the priests. In a monastery, where the entire congregation was composed of priests, however, that would be an effective item.

Priests refrained from **drinking** alcoholic beverages in the temple (Lev 10:8-9). Since the dining hall of the monastery was treated as if it were the holy of holies, **drinking** alcoholic beverages there would have been prohibited. Jews refrained from **drinking** alcoholic beverages as part of the fast on the Day of Atonement (Mos 2:24). There are regulations for priests (Lev 10:9) that prohibit their use of wine or strong **drink** while they functioned at the tent of meeting, and there are prohibitions against the Nazirite's **drinking** any kind of juice from grapes.

This kind of regulation would apply only to a group of priests who were disgruntled with the administration of the temple in Jerusalem or to some very rigorous group of legalists like the "mourners for Zion" who were sometimes, if not always, under Nazarite vows. The other possibility is that it referred to the fasting and purification associated with the Day of Atonement, i.e., part of the service in which the laymen could participate. All of these limitations were temporary. They were like the way to the holy of holies that was blocked for the **present** situation, which was unsatisfactory. All of this would be changed in the age to come.

There are many indications in the document that the author and readers were very rigorous legalists, and maybe even a communally oriented group of monks, but the specific nature of the society can only be deduced from the Book of Hebrews. Therefore the implications involved in these statements must be very tentative and conjectural.

The **proper [of the flesh observances**] are the same as the **proper things for worship** related to **an earthly sanctuary** (Heb 9:1). Both **earthly** and **flesh** are negative evaluations of the Pentateuchal rules and the sacrificial system of the levitical priests. **The time of correction** (*kai-roo dee-awr-thóh-seh-ohs,* καιροῦ διορθώσεως) is literally, "the time of setting straight" or "making right." This would happen when the "Jubilee" arrived, the "captives" were set free and the land was restored to its "original" owners. This would be the end of the evil age and mark a beginning of the age to come when a new administration would be in force, and the believers would find **rest**. It is the same as **the time** of restoration (*ah-paw-kah-tahs-táh-seh-ohs*, ἀποκαταστάσεως) of all that which God had promised (Acts 3:21; see also Mal 3:1; 4:5, 6; Isa 65:17; 66:22). The Lord would set watchmen on top of the walls of Jerusalem, and they would not let him forget his responsibility until he established Jerusalem and made it a praise in the land and provided salvation for his people (Isa 62:7, 11).

Summary.--This unit is also framed by an inclusion, marked by the word **proper** (*dee-kai-óh-mah-tah*, δικαιώματα) in both Heb 9:1 and Heb 9:10. In between these verses is a rather accurate and explicit description of the parts of the temple where priests alone were admitted and the ways in which these were used and by whom. Throughout, the author appears critical of the whole system. It was **earthly** (Heb 9:1) and it was **not able to perfect the worshiper according to [his] conscience**, so the worshiper was left to his own methods of keeping or becoming free from crime **until the time of correction** when this whole system would be replaced by something better and more satisfying. The monastery was a temporary institution that functioned as a temple to rid the land of crime until a temple not made with hands would be reestablished in Zion.

Heb 8 and 9 are organized so as to present a balanced argument of Christ's superiority over the previous system. Typically the author first explained the normal way of functioning judging its validity. Then he followed with an argument showing that Jesus was superior by the very same standards. The remainder of the outline will show that the last three units were intended to negate the **present** temple and its priestly functions. These next three units will show the wonderful way in which Christ replaces each of them. The argument was presented in a chiastic structure:

1). The old cult	2). The new cult
a) Earthly ministry	a) Christ's sacrifice
b) First contract	b) The bloody contract
c) Temple functions	c) The heavenly ministry

TEXT

11But Christ, having become a high priest of the good things that have happened, through the greater and more perfect **tent** not made with hands (that is, not of this creation), 12and not through blood of goats and bulls, but through his own blood, entered once for all into the holy [precincts], having found age-long redemption.
13For if the blood of goats and bulls and ashes of a heifer, sprinkling those who are defiled, sanctifies [them] for the cleansing of the flesh, 14how much more the blood of Christ, who through [the] spirit of the age offered himself blameless to God, will cleanse our conscience from dead works for the purpose of worshiping [the] living God.

COMMENTARY

Jesus was treated in Hebrews as if he were a priest. As son of David, he was not born a high priest, but since he was a member of a monastery he might **have become a priest**, through the initiation ceremony by which he was admitted into the monastery. He could have been made a priest through legal ceremony, the same way he became the Son of God and God's legal agent through legal ceremony.

The strongest reading favors **the good things that have happened** (*tohn geh-naw-méh-nohn ah-gah-thóhn,* τῶν γενομένων ἀγαθῶν) but some good texts (*Alpha,* א) have *tohn mehl-awn-tohn ah-gah-thóhn* (τῶν μελλάντων ἀγαθῶν), **the good things to come**. The more difficult reading is **the good things that have happened,** which occurs only here in Hebrews. *Méh-loh,* on the contrary, is used frequently (Heb 1:14; 2:5; 6:5; 8:5; 10:1, 27; 11:8, 20) and is the reading one might expect here. Therefore it would be a normal correction for later scribes, whereas it is difficult to understand why a later scribe might have made the opposite change.[1] **The good things to come** would refer to the **time of correction** (Heb 9-10) when God's promises would be fulfilled. **The good things that have happened** probably refer to the sacrifice of Christ that has been made for believers. **The greater and more perfect tent** is in contrast to the **earthly sanctuary** in which the sons of Aaron conduct their ministry (Heb 9: 1).[2]

The expression **not made with hands** (*oo khay-raw-poi-áy-too,* οὐ χειροποιήτου) means it is not idolatrous, as are frequently the objects **made with hands** (Commentary on 8:2-5). Philo said that Moses allowed a temple made with hands (*chay-ráwk-may-tawn,* χειρόκμητον) but permitted only one temple for one God (Spec 1:66-67). The rabbis said that the Lord built the temple with his own hands (Mek *Shirata* 10:29-42), and when he built it again with his two hands, he would again rule from there (Heb 10:42-43). The main FT testimony for God's having made the sanctuary (*meék-dahsh,* מקדש) with his own hands is Exod 15:17, which the rabbis understood to mean the temple at Jerusalem, but before the rabbis reached their conclusions, the Psalmist wrote:

> He chose the tribe of Judah, Mount Zion which he loved; Then he built, like lofty ones, his sanctuary, like the land [which] he established for the age (*oh-láhm,* עולם) (Ps 78:68, 69).

The temple, constructed of ordinary building materials under Solomon's orders had many human hands involved in its construction, but it was not idolatrous, so it was hailed as a house not built with hands. Since it was made with God's own hands, it was **not made with [human] hands**. The **earthly** temple at Jerusalem was considered by some to be so much like the heavenly temple (pBer 4:5.8c) that the two were sometimes almost confused, but always considered synonymous.

---

[1] So also J. M. Boyer, "Las Variantes *Mellonton y genomenon* en Heb 9:11," *Biblica* 32 (1951):232-36.

[2] A Vanhoye's suggestion that the greater and more perfect tent is the risen body of Christ ("'Par la Tente plus Grand et plus Parfait' [Heb 9:11]," *Biblica* 46 [1965]:1-28) and J. Swetnam's theory, that it was a eucharist allusion ("'The Greater and More Perfect Tent.' A Contribution to the Discussion of Heb 9:11," *Biblica* 47 [1966]:91-106) both seem far-fetched. See also J. Swetnam, "On the Imagery and Significance of Hebrews 9:9-10," *CBQ* 28 (1966):155-73; and "Hebrews 9,2: Some Suggestions about Text and Context," *Melita Theologica* 51.2 (2000):163-185.

There was a temple in heaven, which Jesus entered when he ascended. This was the type for which heavenly temples on earth were antitypes. The heavenly antitype on earth could be defiled and under the control of an improper priesthood and foreign nations and become **a temple made with hands.** It is easy to confuse these two. Just because there was a temple in heaven did not mean there could not be a temple **not made with hands** on earth. The temple on earth that was **not made with hands** was located in **Zion, city of the God of life, heavenly Jerusalem** (Heb 12:22). It was Solomon's temple and the temple that would be restored **at the time of correction** (Heb 9:10). It was not Herod's temple where pagan services were held directed by priests appointed by the Romans. That was the temple **made with hands**.

Heavenly Jerusalem was David's city, a small, new-moon shaped ridge above the Kidron Valley, north west of the spring of Rogel. The town was initially composed of two mountains, adjacent to one another with a small valley in between. After Simon removed the citadel, however, Mount Ophel was the tallest mountain in David's City, and it was at the north end of the town. It was north of Mount Ophel and the temple where the Romans built their fortress. It was a military station where soldiers were always kept, constructed according to the pattern Romans had used in building fortresses in other countries. It provided a point from which the Romans could control Zion, just as the Syrians had done earlier from an exalted, fortified location (War 5:245). Today it is the tallest point on that bank of the Kidron Valley and has been confused for David's holy City to the south. Now that the location of David's City has been corrected, many passages in ancient literature make more sense.

When Adonijah was celebrating his succession to David as king at Ain Rogel, Nathan and Bathsheba immediately went to King David in his palace. After consultation Solomon rode on David's mule to Ain Gihon, where the priest Zadok anointed Solomon king. That was adjacent to the altar and tent where David had placed the chest containing the contract. Ain Gihon was only 300 meters from Ain Rogel. When Solomon's party shouted, "Long live King Solomon!" Adonijah's party was able to hear the shout (1Kings 1:1-48). Adonijah went at once to the altar and took hold of the horns for security from King Solomon (1Kings 1:50). By that time Solomon had already returned from Ain Gihon and was seated on his throne in the palace.

These events all seem to have taken place within a short geographic area, where people could walk quickly and easily hear each other's shouts. The altar was built shortly after David became king, and the temple was built very close to the altar, just west of the spring of Gihon—not far up the mountain to the north. Shanks and Shiloh conjecture that David's palace would have been just west of the glacis ramp near Ain Gihon, but they also hold that Solomon's temple was located a long distance away from the palace, on the Dome of the Rock.

When the NT seer looked forward to a new Jerusalem, he anticipated a heavenly city that had come to earth from God in heaven, prepared as a bride for a new wedding contract. In this new city one of the basic descriptions was the **river of the water of life going out from the throne of God** (Rev 22:1, *thráw-noo too theh-oó* [θρόνου τοῦ θεοῦ = *keé-say áyl,* כסא אל] cf. *meek-dahsh áyl,* מקדש אל) [1QpHab 12:8-9]). This would have to take place in Zion where the spring of Gihon streamed from the altar of the temple down the Kidron Valley to the south that related the temple to the area near the spring of Gihon. Nearly a century ago G. A. Smith pointed to the numerous biblical passages. He concluded:

> The Biblical evidence indubitably identifies Mount Sion with the Temple-Mount, which, there has never been any doubt, was on the East Hill; and almost as clearly placed the "City of David" below it. The topographical evidence from the present surface, and still more from excavations, tends wholly to the conclusion that this lower position lay to the south of the Temple upon Ophel, and with this the Biblical accounts agree. The position on the north, which the earlier advocates of the East Hill selected does not suit the Biblical data; Antonia is not below but above the Temple level.[1]

Martin was apparently the first modern scholar to realize that Solomon's temple could not have been in the same location as the Dome of the Rock within the walls of Herod's fortress, as Shiloh and Shanks presumed. He renewed and supplemented the arguments and conclusions made by Smith, carefully researching the sources written before the time of Herod that described the temple and its location. They were all consistent in placing Solomon's temple immediately west of the spring of Gihon. He also examined the Jewish, Christian, and Muslim sources written after the fall of Jerusalem and before the beginning of the Crusades to show that there continued to be a strong religious memory of the location of the temple at Zion near the spring of Gihon.

Not only was Solomon's temple built on Mount Zion near the springs, but also the temple that Zerubbabel restored after the exiles from Babylon returned and other restorations. Each restoration was larger than the previous one, and slightly adjusted in position from the previous temple, because of the size difference, but they all continued to be on Mount Ophel, near the Gihon spring. The altar was probably constructed near the spring, because of its necessity for sacrificing. When David captured Zion he evidently constructed a small altar and built a tent for the chest with the contract near it. By the time of Hecataeus (4th century BIA) there was a huge altar near the temple and the spring. It was probably built by Solomon when he built the first temple. This huge altar, built of rocks, may have survived all of the temple burnings. It might have been enlarged when Herod built still a larger temple along side of it

The walled in grounds area of Herod's temple was much larger than the unit it replaced, on Mount Ophel, just west of Ain Gihon. The temple grounds was placed nearly a *stadion* (600 feet) south of the southern wall of the Tower of Antonia with two bridges connecting Herod's walls surrounding Antonia to the walls surrounding the temple. None of the temples was ever built in the area of the Dome of the Rock that was enclosed by Herod's huge walls and contained the Tower of Antonia.

Martin also noted that the area around the Tower of Antonia was distinctly Roman. It was the fortress Romans built overlooking the City of David, so that they could control it. Hundreds of Roman soldiers were stationed there within Herod's walls. Romans even worshiped their own deities there. Martin correctly mentioned the fierce hatred that existed between the Jews in the City of David and the Romans in the city of Antonia. Many Jews refused to worship in Herod's temple or enter

---

[1] G. A. Smith, *Jerusalem,* I, pp. 134-69.

Herod's Roman citadel. The Romans controlled even the robes of the high priest and the appointment of the high priests themselves in Herod's temple.

Herod's temple was large and elegant, and like the Jerusalem temples before it, had been constructed in Zion, David's City, west of the springs in the Kidron Valley.[1] Martin said it was impossible for Herod to have constructed a temple on the dry hill that now contains the Dome of the Rock. All temples had to be built near springs of water. Martin even listed many pagan temples that were stationed near springs,[2] but Martin's interest was in showing that Jews required temples to be located near springs.[3] For one reason, they could not perform the sacrifices with only the water in the cisterns on the Dome of the Rock.

In addition to Martin's list of temples the temple at Mount Gerizim is located near Jacob's well, fed by the large spring that flows under the mountain. Springs seem to have been necessary to Jews and Israelites, who thought valid temples had to be near springs, just as the tent of David and the temple of Solomon had been. The temple on Mount Zion was there near the great spring of Gihon, and devotees of this religion praised it extensively and related important liturgies to it. They were the ones who wrote the psalms and prophecies relating the temple to the spring. The psalmists and prophets were not describing temples in general. They had only one temple to praise, and that was near the spring of Gihon. Their testimony assures the reader that there was water near their temple. Herod's temple above the spring to the west was very tall and magnificent, but pious Jews refused to worship in this temple the Romans built.

Herod's temple was the one Jesus reportedly said would be torn down (Matt 24:1-2; Luke 21:5-6). During the last days of the war, it was the Jews, and not the Romans that burned the temple. Josephus was amazed that Jews had no more reverence for this building than they did. They first cut away the roof and then severed the connection between the temple and Antonia (War 6:166). Then they filled the space between the rafters of the western portico and the ceiling beneath with dry kindling, bitumen, and pitch and set the whole building afire (War 6:177-181).

The reason they showed so little respect for the building was that they did not believe it was a valid temple of God. It was properly located, but it had been built by the Romans, whom the Jews hated. Josephus correctly complained that Jewish soldiers had been using Herod's temple only as a fortress to fight against the Romans (War 6:122).

Romans knew they had to conquer the Tower of Antonia from the north before they could take the temple to the south (War 6:45; 5:245). The Jewish general and messianic pretender was John, who stationed his troops both in the Tower of Antonia and in the temple area (War 5:250), controlling both fortresses. When the Romans reached the Tower of Antonia, Jewish soldiers fled to the nearby temple (War 6:69-71). There was a bridge that joined the temple to Antonia (War 2:330; 6:165). There was also a bridge connecting the temple to the Xystus, a large gymnasium on the west bank of the Tyropoeon Valley. This connection was made without any interference from Herod's walls (War 2:344), showing that these two units were separate, except for the bridge. Josephus furthermore spoke of the temple and the lower city together as distinct from the upper city (War 2:422-24). He also reported the way Cestius led an attack against the slope (*kleé-mah,* κλίma) that was

---

[1] Martin, *Temples*, p. 49, *et passim*.

[2] Martin, *Temples*, pp. 315-16.

[3] Martin, *Temples*, p. 306.

attached to wall protecting the temple (Wars 2:535-36). This may have been the glacis that still exists on the eastern wall of Mount Ophel, near the spring of Gihon.

Herod built his walled city, Antonia, as a militarily strategic structure that could look down upon the entire City of David, with its temple. It had the same purpose as the Syrian citadel during the Hasmonean period, but it was much stronger and larger.

Herod's temple was only 90 feet long and 30 feet wide inside, but it was much larger on the outside and very tall. It had an open court at the rear of the building with an altar for sacrifice. Herod's temple was probably even taller than the temples whose ruins still survive at Baalbek, Lebanon. It was also a fortress and the nation's treasury (War 6:282), so Jewish soldiers were stationed there, and the Romans wanted to conquer that structure.

Archaeologists have found the foundations of the Tower of Siloam and the old wall, surrounding the City of David, and Eilat Mazar has made some interesting discoveries in her research on Mount Ophel. No one has found any trace of the temple, so it is necessary at least now, to learn about the temple from literary sources written about it before its destruction by Titus in 70 IA and the area's final desolation by Hadrian in 135 IA. Among the debris that were left was probably the huge altar that Herod had built. It was no threat to the Romans, and it would not burn. That which survived both destructions was at least part of the walls enclosing the Roman Tower of Antonia, north of Zion. The locations of the City of David, Zion, and Herod's temple are now clear. We now know that Jews did not worship inside the walls of Herod's military fortress. Many Jews worshiped at Zion, David's holy city, but even there orthodox Jews refused to worship. They were the ones who considered Herod's temple to be pagan (made with hands) and under the control of Rome with its appointed "wicked priest" serving the altar. One such group was represented in one of the Dead Sea Scrolls.

ZION AND THE SCROLLS

The Habakkuk Commentary described a local situation in which there were two priests in competition. One was the high priest of Herod's temple, which was called "the wicked priest" (*hah-kóh-hane hah-rah-sháh,* הכוהן הרשע), who was the high priest in Herod's temple. The temple he served was in Jerusalem, but since he had false authority to demand tithes from the citizens of all the towns of Judah (1QpHab 12:4-11), in the judgment of the members of the community that trusted the Teacher of Righteousness, the wicked priest was stealing from them when he did that. He was also called the "preacher of lies" (*mah-teéf hah-kah-záhv,* מטיף הכזב) (1QpHab 10:9) who built a "city of vanity" with blood and deception. That city may have been Herod's city, which was walled outside of Zion and was itself as large as a town. The other priest, was called the "Teacher of Righteousness," the true or valid teacher and priest (*móh-ray hah-tséh-dehk,* מורה הצדק).[1] He was the one the faithful trusted.

On some occasion, the wicked priest attacked the Teacher of Righteousness and the men of his council, physically injured him, and may have killed the priestly Teacher of Righteousness (1QpHab 8:16-17; 9:1-2). All of this happened on the Day of Atonement, while the Teacher of Righteousness was observing his fast. The

[1] Buchanan, "The Priestly Teacher of Righteousness" *RevQ* 6 (1969):553-558; "The Office of the Teacher of Righteousness," *RevQ* 9 (1977):241-243.

wicked priest humiliated the Teacher of Righteousness, swallowing him in his pain. The wicked priest performed these abominable deeds, defiling the sanctuary of God (*meek-dahsh áyl,* מקדש אל) (1QpHab 12:8-9) served by the Teacher of Righteousness, possibly in the city of Jerusalem (1QpHab 12:7-9). This was the temple the wicked priest defiled when he tortured the Teacher of Righteousness. He may have even killed the Teacher, because his action was given as an interpretation of Hab 2:8, **the violence he inflicted on the land, the city, and all its inhabitants**. This was often true of high priests who cooperated with the powers that ruled over the nation, sometimes killing many of the Jewish citizens, robbing the temple treasure of its wealth, acting as fierce dictators against their own people (Ant 12:384-88).

Among the Dead Sea Scrolls are references to two Teachers of Righteousness—one related to the group in Damascus (CD) and the other some place in Judah (1QHab). The Teacher of Righteousness in 1QpHab was a certain individual priest. The reference to a Teacher of Righteousness in the Damascus Document seems to refer only to the office together with suggestions of the way that officer should act and the way others should act in relationship to him. The text speaks generally of "their teachers" (*yohr-áy-hehm,* יוריהם) (CD 3:18), of the time in the future when some teacher of righteousness (*yohr-áy hah-tséh-dehk.* יוקרי הצדך) (CD 6:10) would arise, of a time in the future when the men of the community would listen to the voice of the teacher of righteousness (*móh-ray tséh-dehk,* מורה צדך) (CD 20:32). Another office was that of the judge (*meh-bah-káre,* המבקר) (CD 13:13; 14:11-13) before whom people would come to be judged. The holder of that office may have been also called the "interpreter of the law" (*doh-resh hah-toh-ráh,* דורש התורה) (CD 6:6-7) The only reference to the past was of the gathering of some special teacher (*yohr-áy hah-yah-kheéd,* יורה היחיד) (CD 20:1, 14). His gathering must have been in Damascus. The Teacher of Righteousness of 1QpHab was evidently of Judah. He was the one related to the Book of Hebrews.

Where could the temple of God, where the Teacher of Righteousness officiated, have been located? Probably somewhere in Judah. Ever since 1QpHab has been discovered in the caves of Qumran, scholars have assumed that the Teacher of Righteousness was an Essene who lived at Qumran and officiated some temple there.[1] Scholars have pictured the high priest at Jerusalem journeying to Qumran to confront the Teacher of Righteousness who would have had his council and place of worship there. But the Teacher of Righteousness who functioned in the temple of God (1QpHab 12:8-9), may have been closer to Herod's temple than Qumran. There is no special reason to think that just because 1QpHab was discovered stored at a cave near Qumran that it had been written about a priest who officiated in a temple there.

MONASTERIES AT ZION

Monasteries were places designed to replace temples when there was no valid temple officiated by valid priests. Monks in temples kept their monastery as undefiled as the temple and their kitchen and dining hall as pure as the altar in the temple, so the Lord would have a place to dwell on the land. It was a temporary temple of God. The sect governed by the Community Rule was probably monastic

---

[1] They have also erroneously assumed that the wicked priest was Alexander Jannaeus. It has since been shown that 1QHab was composed during the first century IA. See further Buchanan, *Introduction to Intertextuality* (Lewiston: Mellen, c1994), pp. 79-84.

and used temple terms to describe itself. It called its group "a house of holiness for Israel and an assembly of holy of holies for Aaron" (1QS 8:5), "a holy house for Aaron" (1QS 9:6), "assembly of holiness" (1QS 5:20; 9:2). Monks were expected to keep all of the holiness rules. Harrington said,

> Holiness is linked directly to the explicit laws of the Torah. Even a minimal interpretation, if it can be supported, will suffice. Rabbis would stop with laws as stated in the Pentateuch. The Qumran [monastic] group, however, demands holiness as defined by the Levitical priests and sometimes even beyond that.[1]

She concluded,

> Other laws regarding holiness and purity were interpreted stringently and even augmented at times in order to intensify the level of holiness within the community, and ultimately, establish a closer connection with God.[2]

Monasteries were places where judgments could be given by a council, and liturgies for atonement made (1QS 8:3-6). The Teacher of Righteousness was probably related to one of these.

The wicked priest committed terrible, violent acts against the Teacher and his community. This may have been done in the city of Jerusalem, where the wicked priest also defiled the temple of God (1QpHab 12:7-9), apparently at the same time. That could refer to his defilement of Herod's temple, but that seems unlikely. According to the faithful, Herod's temple was already defiled when it was first built, and was kept in a continual state of defilement by a faulty priesthood appointed by the Romans. The temple of God that the wicked priest defiled was not Herod's temple, but the temple associated with the Teacher of Righteousness and used by his community. That violation apparently took place in the city of Jerusalem.

There seems to have been a monastery in Zion with which Jesus was familiar. As he approached Jerusalem, Jesus sent his apostles to **the city** to wait for a man who would be carrying water. The city was obviously Zion, and the place where they waited would have been either near Ain Gihon or near the other end of the conduit at the Pool of Siloam, where people came to get water. In those days women carried most of the water. The exception was the monks who did all of the necessary household chores. Any man carrying water would have been a monk who could have led the apostles to his monastery where the manager was equipped to prepare a place for Jesus and his apostles to celebrate the Passover. This monastery would have to have been near enough either to Ain Gihon or the Pool of Siloam to make carrying water in a ceramic jar practical. That was most likely at Zion, David's holy city, near the spring (Mark 14:12-16).

The monastery on Mount Zion is the place where the Messiah was expected to gather with his 144,000 monks. These were the redeemed of the land. They were celibate males who had not defiled themselves with women (Rev 14:1-5). This means that there was a monastery at Zion. It may also have been the monastery where the Teacher of Righteousness officiated. There might, however, have been

---

[1] H. H. Harrington, "Holiness and Law in the Dead Sea Scrolls," *Dead Sea Discoveries* 8 (2001):131.
[2] Harrington, "Holiness," p. 135.

more monasteries than one in Zion. That seems to have been a reasonable place for worshipers who refused to worship in Herod's temple but who believed that this was the area where the true temple should be. For many years Jewish saints gathered at Jerusalem, and the apostolic council met there. It was there that Paul met with the Palestinian apostles. None of these institutions would have met within Herod's Roman walls with his Roman military troops. Were there synagogues and churches also there at this small City of David, near the spring? There is at least one clue for thinking that there were.

Raymond Weill found an inscription on a stone plaque that originally belonged to a Synagogue. He found it in a well in the City of David, and it probably came from a synagogue nearby. It may have been thrown into a well to save it from the destruction of Titus. It is called the Theodotus Inscription.[1] Zion was the religious center of Judaism and early Christianity. The Teacher of Righteousness might have been associated with one of the institutions there.

Suppose the Teacher of Righteousness (1QpHab) had been like John the Baptist, whom Herod despised, just as the "wicked priest" despised the Teacher of Righteousness. Suppose further that the Teacher told Jews loudly that he alone was authorized to control a temple and that the temple of God associated with his institution in the city of Zion was the only true temple. His place of worship, like Herod's temple, might have been appropriately located, above the spring of Gihon. It may even have been a little closer to the very place of David's tent than Herod's temple was.

The expression **made with hands** (*kay-raw-poi-áy-taws,* χειροποιῆτος = אליל) was an idiom that meant "pagan," "common," "idolatrous," "gentile." The expression **not made with hands** means it is not idolatrous, as are the objects **made with hands**. It is not required to exist only in heaven. Philo wrote of idols as objects made with hands (*chay-ráwk-may-tawn,* χειρόκμητον) (Spec 1:66-67). The rabbis said that the Lord built the temple with his own hands (Mek *Shirata* 10:29-42), and when he built it again with his two hands, he would again rule from there (Heb 10:42-43). The main FT testimony for God's having made the sanctuary (*meék-dahsh,* מקדש) with his own hands is Exod 15:17, which the rabbis understood to mean the temple at Zion..

The Teacher of Righteousness may have contrasted Herod's temple **made with hands** to the temple of God at the monastery there at Mount Zion that was **not made with hands**. For a temple to be built without hands it would have to be constructed with God's hands. That could have been done through God's agents. To have a temple not made with hands, the construction might have to have been undertaken by people who were undefiled and officially authorized. That would perhaps have required a priestly group of contractors, such as the members of a priestly monastery—especially one that referred to itself as a "holy of holies for Aaron" (1QS 8:3-6, 8; 9:6; 11:8). Solomon's temple, however, was built by Lebanese contractors with materials bought from Hiram of Tyre. It was evidently considered not built with hands because all of these were Solomon's legal agents, and Solomon was God's legal agent.

The followers of the Teacher of Righteousness accused the priests, that were subject to the Romans, of heaping up riches and plundering peoples. The author of the Habakkuk Commentary also warned those contemporary priests, who were currently prospering under Roman support, that they, themselves, would later be

---

[1] H. Shanks, "Israel Antiquities Authority Declines Dirty Money," *BAR* 29. 4 (2003), pp. 24-25.

punished. The time would come when the Roman Kittim, from whom they had received riches, would later confiscate also their acquisitions (1QpHab 9:4-7).

This is all a conjectured analysis, based on 1QpHab, Mark 14, Rev 14, and the known location of Zion. This conjecture depends partially on the date and situation which best relates to 1QpHab, and that requires a comparison between 1QpHab and Ps 74.

Ps 74 is a midrash on Exod 15, and it clearly fits no other period of history better than that following the destruction of the temple at Jerusalem in 70 IA. That is the time when Jews had **prophets**; it was the **second destruction** of Jerusalem (War 6:435-37); it was a time when the Romans **set up their signs as signs** (War 6:316); and there were **meeting places of God in the land** (War 4:408). These were all complaints of the psalmist that do not reflect either the Fall of Jerusalem in 587 or the cleansing of the temple in 164.[1]

There is also a fascinating relationship between Ps 74 and 1QpHab. The Habakkuk Commentary describes the Kittim who are like [Roman] eagles, using Hab 1:9 where the eagles came **for violence facing east**. Before the Maccabean victories the Syrians were facing west, setting their sights on Rome, but the Romans invaded Palestine from the west, **facing east**.[2] This narrows the time a bit. The Habakkuk Commentary was anti-Roman rather than anti-Syrian, so the wicked priest could not have been one of the early Hasmoneans. This brings his situation and time closer to that of Ps 74. There is an amazing number of expressions that are very similar in both of these documents. They do not appear in any way that suggests dependence, but they reflect a similar social community where the same expressions were used.[3] The Habakkuk Commentary gives no hint of a temple destruction, so it is apparently earlier than Ps 74, probably belonging to the first century, before 70 IA. Both documents are related to the temple in Zion and share a similar period of history.

HEBREWS AND HEAVENLY JERUSALEM

There is still one more document associated with Zion, the temple, and the priesthood. This is the sermon in Hebrews (Heb 1:1-12:26). Soon after the appearance of 1QpHab Flusser noticed the close relationship between Hebrews and the Dead Sea Scrolls, and his insight stirred the imaginations of both Kosmala[4] and Yadin.[5] All of these scholars recognized that Hebrews and some of the Dead Sea Scrolls are somehow interrelated. Although later scholars have differed somewhat in their evaluation of these data, the relationship has been generally recognized. The three earliest scholars, like most others of that time, presumed that all the Dead Sea Scrolls were composed by Essenes and that the characters represented in all of the documents were the same individuals. It is now clear that the scrolls were items in a library that came from several places and were composed at different times, by different people. Some of the documents, such as 1QS, represent monastic views

---

[1] Buchanan, *Introduction*, pp. 70-78; "The Fall of Jerusalem and the Reconsideration of Some Dates," *RevQum* 14 (1989): 31-48.

[2] Buchanan, *Introduction*, p. 82.

[3] Buchanan, *Introduction*, pp. 79-81.

[4] H. Kosmala, *Hebräer-Essener-Christen* (Leiden: E. J. Brill, 1959).

[5] Y. Yadin, "Aspects of the Dead Sea Scrolls" *Scripta Hierosolymita* 4 (1958):36-55.

and others, such as CD, do not. None of the documents mentions the word "Essene." That name has been applied by association alone.

The Teacher of Righteousness, for example, was a priestly office held by many people. It probably represented the person that the author of each document thought was the truly qualified high priest, the legitimate teacher, even though the Romans had appointed someone else to fulfill that office.[1] There were even references to more teachers of righteousness among the scrolls than one. One was from Judah (1QpHab) and one from Damascus (CD).

Although this study appreciates the insights of Flusser, Kosmala, and Yadin, it compares Hebrews to only 1QpHab, where the closest relationship is found. The sermon in Hebrews also pictured Jesus as the perfect high priest, who brought a superior sacrifice to a **temple not made with hands** (Heb 9:11, 23). This was made in contrast to the priests in Herod's Jerusalem who offered many sacrifices in a "temple made with hands," that were not able to cleanse the conscience from dead works (Heb 9:13-14). Priests in Herod's temple had attempted year after year to serve effectively, but they always failed to bring about salvation (Heb 9:25-28). Perfection from the priests of Herod's temple was unattainable (Heb 7:11; 10:11). The high priest himself was not free from crime (Heb 9:7).

The recipients of the sermon (Heb 1:1-12:29) were very rigorous law observers who were probably monks. They were warned never to fall away from their rigorous doctrine or engage in any transgressions (Heb 2:1-2). There could be no forgiveness for apostasy (Heb 6:4-8). Work and love were required (Heb 6:10; 10:24). If they should err they would receive God's punishment (Heb 10:30-31). Rigorous discipline is required (Heb 12:7). There were no rules for behavior among the sexes, no rules about marriage or family. The perfection required of the listeners seems applicable to monks alone, who had taken vows of poverty, celibacy and obedience. Like those associated with the Teacher of Righteousness, they would have been called "poor," because the individuals owned nothing (1QpHab 12:10).

There is nothing in that sermon that would disqualify the recipients as monks. They may have been gathered at the very monastery where Jesus celebrated his Last Supper with his disciples. This is where they had come to hear the message preserved in Hebrews. The author reminded the listeners, **You have come to Zion, city of the God of life, heavenly Jerusalem** or God's Jerusalem (Heb 12:22). This was Mount **Zion**, David's holy **city.** It was not Herod's Jerusalem; it was the **heavenly Jerusalem**, where the temple of God was found (1QpHab 12:7-9), there near Ain-Gihon, as differentiated from Herod's fortress inside Herod's huge walls. It may also have been the "temple of God" where the Teacher of Righteousness officiated.

There is no clear identification of these two groups, but they had similar feelings toward the wicked priest and the temple made with hands. They both represent monasteries, one of them clearly at Zion. There are enough relationships between Hebrews and the Habakkuk Commentary in attitudes expressed toward the Roman Temple and priesthood to understand why Flusser, Kosmala, and Yadin all found the relationship between the Hebrews and the scrolls to be thought-provoking. When the possibility that both Hebrews and 1QpHab were both written in the same century and in a similar geographical area are considered, their relationship seems still closer.

---

[1] Buchanan, "The Priestly Teacher," pp. 553-558; "The Office," pp. 241-43.

The temptation is to identify them closer than the data will bear. It is tempting to suggest that Jesus, the Teacher of Righteousness of 1QpHab, the monastic sect of 1QS, and the congregation addressed by the author of Heb 1:1-12:29 were all associated with the same monastery in the City of David, but that which might be possible is not necessarily that which is true. These associations are all suggestive, but circumstantial.

It is obvious that the authors of 1QpHab and Heb 1:1-12:29 belonged to the same kind of political and religious situation, that they represented very similar points of view, that they belonged to a similar time and location, but there were many Jews of NT times that resented the Romans and all other citizens who associated with them. No one knows how many similar, but different, monasteries there were at the same period of history in the same geographical area. There were many who thought Herod's temple was pagan and the priests that served that temple were idolatrous. Some of these believed Jesus was the Messiah and some did not. Some of these listened to the Hebrews sermon as its author preached from Zion, and others read the Habakkuk Commentary written by a man who thought the high priest in Herod's temple was wicked and that the priest of his community was the true teacher and priest. Both of these groups thought it was Zion and not Herod's Roman city that was David's holy city, the heavenly Jerusalem.

The members represented by neither of these documents were devotees of the wicked priests and the pagan temple that was located within Herod's walls near the Dome of the Rock at the same time they lived and functioned.

The statement, **that is, not of this creation**, is an interpretative gloss, apparently added by someone who was not familiar with the technical meaning of the expression **not made with hands**.

12*Entered once for all into the holy [precincts].* According to Heb 9:7, the high priest never entered the **holy of holies** without blood, but, of course, the blood he sprinkled on the chest was the **blood of goats and bulls,** goats for the people and bulls for the priests. Christ, acting as high priest, offered **his own blood**--a much superior offering. Also in contrast to the priests, who entered **the holy** continually, and the high priest, who entered **the holy of holies** every Day of Atonement, Christ entered **once for all** (*ehph-áh-pahx*, ἐφάπαξ) **into the holy [precincts]** (see also Heb 4:14; 6:20; 9:12, 15, 23-24). Although their many sacrifices did not succeed in satisfying **the conscience** (Heb 9:9), his **once for all** sacrifice successfully **found age redemption**.

Age redemption is usually rendered "eternal redemption," but the important factor about an **age** was not that it was forever. It had a certain characteristic. The **age** of David was the time when David ruled. The **age** of the Messiah would be the time when the Messiah ruled. It was an **age** free from foreign rule. **Age redemption** was the kind of **redemption** that belonged to the Messianic **age**. With the new **age** came a new law, a new spirit, a new king, and a new life. All of these were characterized by that age. Jews and Christians hoped that the **age** for which they were longing would last for a long time, but the word **age** did not mean "eternal." Ancients spoke of **ages**. They did not speak of "eternities."

The whole doctrine of **redemption** was determined in relationship to business ethics. If an Israelite became poor, he might "sell" the use of his property until the Jubilee year, but he always did so with the right of **redemption.** That is, if some kinsman became his redeemer and provided the necessary money, he could buy the property back. Or, if he became more prosperous himself, he might **redeem** his own property. If he could not **redeem** it, it was restored to the original family in the Jubilee year, in any event. If the property was in a walled city, however, he had only one year to **redeem** it. After that, the property became unconditionally owned by the purchaser, unless the man who sold it was a Levite. If he was, his land within a walled city could only be kept from him until the next Jubilee (Lev 25:25-34).

If a person did not have land he might repay his debts by selling his labor to the creditor, at half price, until his debt was paid (Lev 25:39-55) or until the Sabbath year. When the Jubilee year arrived, all land was restored to the original owners, and debtors were released from their labor. This was a joyful time, but it sometimes required a long wait. The waiting time was shortened if a man could **redeem** himself, which was seldom the case. Usually his freedom and his possession of the land depended upon a **redeemer** who came to his rescue and paid the necessary price for him to gain his freedom or his land. The feeling of gratitude toward a **redeemer** was natural, but the debtor was then the debtor slave of the person who **redeemed** him, unless the **redeemer** chose to liberate the slave as a gift.

It was in the light of this concept of a **redeemer** that the Lord was called Israel's **redeemer.** When the Israelites were in bondage to Pharaoh, the Lord delivered them from there, which meant that he **redeemed** them (Exod 6:6). After he had **redeemed** them, the Lord led his **redeemed** people through the wilderness (Exod 15:13). Likewise after the Jews had become enslaved in Babylon, away from their Promised Land, the Lord **redeemed** them and restored them to their land (Isa 43:1; 44:22-23; 48:20; 52:9; 63:9), so the Lord was called the **redeemer** (Isa 41:14; 43:14; 44:6, 24; 47:4; 48:17; 49:7, 26; 54:5, 8; 59:20; 60:16; 63:16). Since crimes were thought of as debts in relationship to a treasury of merits theology (Matt 6:12), the Lord who **redeemed** Israel pardoned her iniquity (Isa 40:2). The high priest (Heb 9:11) who obtained forgiveness of crimes, by the same token, **found . . . redemption** and shortened the term of service (Matt 24:22). The **age redemption** was the **age** that followed the period of indebtedness. It was the **age** that came with the sabbath or Jubilee liberations. It would last until money was borrowed or crimes were committed that required additional punishment.

[13]*The blood of goats and bulls.* Philo said, "**Blood** is cleansed by means of **blood"** (SpecLeg 3:150). According to Hebrews (9:22), **without the pouring out of blood forgiveness does not occur.** Sacrifice was accepted by many ancient societies as a part of the judicial system. Courts were established to control injury. If one person injured another, the court usually returned the favor to the injurer. If a person cut off another person's hand, the court had his hand cut off. If he stole money, he was required to pay the money back in multiples of four or five (Exod 22:1). If one person killed another, the nearest in kin was expected to kill the murderer. If he did not, the court would interfere. It was an injury for injury system. Some crimes could be satisfied through repayment of money to the injured party and fines to the state. The fines to the state were made in terms of sacrifice.

According to the terms of the contract Israel had made with God, all crimes had to be punished and injured parties reconciled. In court, however, criminals were often able to bribe the judges and escape the fair punishment they deserved. Since God was the highest judge, Jews and Israelites tried to bribe God with sacrifices to obtain his favorable judgment without correcting their crimes. Amos, Hosea, Isaiah, and Micah all insisted that this method would not work. God could not be bribed. Ethics were required of all parties to the contract with God. Blood was required to satisfy the justice of blood. **The blood of goats and bulls** would not effectively substitute for human blood. The author of Hebrews did not abandon the whole sacrificial system, as the eighth century prophets did, but he held that human blood was required for human blood. No animal sacrifices could be used as substitutes. The sacrifices offered in Herod's temple would not be effective, but the sacrifice of Christ would be.

Sanctifies [them] for the cleansing of the flesh. The "ashes of a heifer" were those obtained by burning a red heifer outside of the camp according to a specially prescribed process. The ashes were used to mix with water, as necessity arose, to be spread on persons who had become defiled by touching a corpse or being in a tent where there was a corpse, or by touching the slain in battle, or a bone from a corpse (Num 19). When this liturgy was performed properly, it was believed that it would sanctify the "defiled" persons **for the cleansing of the flesh**.

14*The blood of Christ . . . will cleanse our conscience.* The main thrust of the *a fortiori* argument comes here. If such weak and primitive methods as those prescribed in the Pentateuch cleansed people from defilement and crime, **how much more the blood of Christ** would **cleanse**! The author did not claim that **the blood of goats and bulls would cleanse** the believer. This was just a hypothetical proposition. Actually, the author did not think the sacrifices performed at Herod's temple were effective. He did not go so far as the eighth century prophets and condemn the entire sacrificial system as a method of evading justice. He just claimed that the services performed at Herod's temple were not effective. Christ's sacrifice, however, was effective. The red heifer, employed in a special liturgy by the priests, had to be without blemish (Num 19:2). Still better was Christ who was **blameless**. In addition he functioned **through [the] spirit of the age**.

The Spirit of the age. The word **spirit** was a word that was closely associated with legal authority. When Saul, David, the judges, and Jesus received the **spirit** they also received governing authority. **The spirit of the age** was evidently the judicial system by which the new **age** would be governed. When converts became Christians they participated in a legal ritual of laying on of hands. Through that legal ceremony they received the **spirit** and became full members of a new community. They became Christians and received all of the authority of that membership. This meant that they were parties to the new contract.

Because of all of these qualities that Jesus possessed, he could be expected not merely to **cleanse** members from corpse defilement; he could **cleanse** their **consciences** as the earthly tent ministries could not (Heb 9:9) from **dead works**. They would not have to worry again about whether or not their crimes had been forgiven, and their slate was clean before God in the great judgment.

Dead works were the deeds done before baptism into the community where alone **life** was possible. Those who joined these exclusive sects separated themselves from the rest of the world which was considered **dead**. They repented and were cleansed by baptism from this **dead life** they had once lived. The terms for corpse defilement were applied to non-sectarians to emphasize the difference between the Jews and the Gentiles, the church and the world, the clean and the defiled.

The **blood** of Christ was used both in the way **the blood of goats and bulls** was used, and in the way the ashes of the red heifer were used. **Blood** was sprinkled against the chest holding the contract (Lev 16:14-15), on the altar, and the people at the time the contract was made. It was then called **the blood of the contract** (Exod

24:6-8). When he instituted the new contract with his apostles, Jesus used the fruit of the vine as a seisen of **the blood of the contract** (Matt 26:28). **Nearly everything is cleansed with blood** (Heb 9:22). In the old contract, ashes and water were sprinkled on the unclean. Christ's blood was more efficacious than both the other methods put together. It **cleansed the conscience** so that the redeemed and cleansed person would be completely freed from his former **dead works** and as one who was then alive, he might worship **the God of life**. The person defiled by corpse uncleanness, who failed to be properly cleansed, would be excommunicated if he dared to enter the tabernacle (Num 19:11-13). Until he was cleansed, he was not free to worship. The author extends the figure to deal with those who have not been cleansed of their **dead works**. The cleansing of Christ's blood is necessary for worship.

Summary.--The word **Christ** which appears both in Heb 9:11 and 14 forms the inclusion that separates this as a unit. The whole unit consists of a comparison of Jesus' sacrifice and cleansing, in an *a fortiori* argument, with the sacrifices offered by the Aaronic priests and the cleansing method employed by using the ashes of the red heifer. The comparison of method was followed throughout, using metaphorically the imagery of sacrifice, cleansing, corpse defilement, and worship in the tabernacle. Many parallels exist between Heb 9:1-10 and Heb 9:11-14. These are antithetic, as the following chart, adapted from Vanhoye, shows.[1] They also point out the step-by-step logic of the author and his consistent emphasis on the superiority of Christ.

a. tent not made with hands (11)	a. The first tent . . . prepared (1-2)
b. Christ . . . entered once for all (11-1	b. priests entered continually (6)
c. through his own blood 12)	
d. offered himself blameless (14)	c. not without blood (7)
	d. gifts and sacrifices (9)
e. will cleanse our conscience (14)	e. not able to perfect the worshiper according to [his] conscience (9)

The Bloody Contract

TEXT

[15]And, because of this, he is [the] mediator of a new contract, so that, since a death
has occurred for the purpose of redemption from the transgressions in the first
contract, those who are called might receive the promise of the inheritance of the
age. [16]For wherever there is a will, it is necessary for death to be suffered by the one
who made the will, [17]for a will is secure [only] with reference to the dead, since it is
never valid when the one who made the will is alive. [18]From this [it is evident that]
not even the first contract was renewed without blood, [19]for when every command-
ment had been spoken according to the law by Moses to all the people [Moses],
after he took the blood of the bulls and the goats with water and crimson wool and

[1] A. Vanhoye, *La StructureLittéraire de l'Epitre aux Hébreux* (Paris: Desclée de Brouwer, 1963), pp. 150-151.

hyssop, sprinkled both the book itself and all the people, [20]saying, "This [is] the blood of the contract which God has commanded you." [21]And he likewise sprinkled the tent and all the liturgical vessels with the blood, [22]and nearly everything is cleansed with blood, according to the law, and without [the] pouring out of blood, forgiveness does not occur. [23]Therefore, on the one hand, it was necessary [that] the symbols of the things in the heavens be cleansed by means of these, but on the other hand that the heavenly things themselves [be cleansed] by means of better sacrifices than these.

COMMENTARY

[15]*Because of this.* **Because of this** refers to the items already mentioned. It means Christ's effectiveness in offering sacrifice and cleansing from crime so that the believer might worship the God of life (Heb 9:11-14). It refers to the **spirit of the age** and the **age redemption** which belonged to the Christ. In the same association, Jesus is understood as **[the] mediator of a new contract**, just as Moses was understood to be the mediator of the law which was ordained by angels (Gal 3:19).

The contract that the Lord made with his people was an agreement that he would be their God, and they would be his people. This agreement was intended to be in force while both God and the Israelites were very much alive. The **new contract** which Jeremiah predicted was intended to be the same kind of agreement. The **new contract** was required because God had annulled the old **contract.** According to the rules for divorce, when a man wished to divorce his wife, he was required to give her a legal document of divorce and send her out of his house. God sent his people out of his houses on Mount Gerizim and Mount Zion and sent them into exile in Assyria and Babylon (Deut 24:1). This was because they had been unfaithful to the **contract** they accepted. Jeremiah said that whenever all of their crimes had been punished and all of their fines paid, God would make a new marriage contract with them. The author of Hebrews concluded that Jesus fulfilled all of the requirements of back payments to obtain forgiveness and make possible **the new contract. The new contract** would be similar to the old **contract**, involving promises of prosperity, posterity, and the land, but it would be better—more land, more prosperity, more posterity.

Since Jesus had died, however, and since the author of Hebrews was convinced that Jesus was the **mediator of a new contract**, it strengthened the author's case if he discussed the **contract** in terms of a will, since a will is one kind of a **contract**. The Greek word *dee-ah-tháy-kay* (διαθήκη) means both **will** and **contract.** The importance of a **will** is that the persons designated in it "receive" an "inheritance." **The inheritance of the age** (*tays ai-oh-neé-oo klay-raw-naw-meé-ahs*, τῆς αἰωνίου κληρονομίας) refers to that possession which was promised to the elect or "those who are called" in the age to come or the age of rest.

Those who inherited the promises (Heb 6:12, 17) or **the inheritance of the age** had rest on the land (Josh 21:43-45). R. Yohanan said that whoever walked four cubits in the land of Israel was promised (*moóv-takh*, מבטח) that he was "a son of the **age** to come" (bKeth 111a). Those who gathered around Moses were "preserved for life of the age" (Sifre Deut 29:9; 129b #305). Enoch promised that the elect would inherit the land (1Enoch 5-7).

Dalman correctly acknowledged that Ps 37:11 refers to the possession of the land, but added without evidence, "that the expression is metaphorical in Matt 5:5, there can be no doubt."[1] This was an easy dismissal of a logical assumption that the same land referred to in Ps 37:11 was also intended by the author who quoted Ps 37:11 in Matt 5:5. In the **age** to come the elect were **promised** that they would receive the land of Israel for an **inheritance.** This would be their **inheritance of the age**. The close relationship between being "called" and being heirs is also reflected in Rom 8:17-30. **Those who are called** are the elect, who have been justified and glorified. They are **sharers in [the] heavenly calling** (Heb 3:10).

16*For wherever there is a will it is necessary for death to be suffered.* The author regularly used analogies in his exposition, and he also regularly explained the full meaning of a term in its normal usage before he applied it to Jesus and his ministry. Since he intended to point up the significance of a *dee-ah-tháy-kay* (διαθήκη) a **will**, he explained the normal conditions of a **will**. The person who made a **will** designated in it what should happen to his possessions in the event of his death. Therefore the **will** would have no effect on anyone until or unless the "one who made the will" died. Jesus had made a **contract** with his apostles shortly before his death establishing a legal corporation with them. That corporation was the body of Christ that became the church. The author of Hebrews called this **contract** a **will.** That which the **contract** decreed was that the promises which God had made to Abraham would be fulfilled, as Jeremiah promised. Furthermore, the corporation which Jesus formed at the same meal and with whom he made the contract would be the heirs of the promises of the **contract**.

17*When the one who made the will is alive.* This verse is somewhat redundant and somewhat a further elaboration on Heb 9:16. The **will** is secure or **valid** only with reference to the dead. Whatever the one who made the **will** stipulated would apply after his death. The **will** would not be opened until the one who made the **will** was dead. After death **wills** are administered according to the conditions set forth by the dead while they were still living. But, even though a **will** was made out when the person was alive, **it is never valid when the one who made the will is alive**.

18*Not even the first contract was renewed without blood.* The Greek word rendered **renewed** (*eg-keh-kaín-ees-tai,* ἐγκεκαίνισται) can also mean "inaugurated" or "dedicated." **Renewed** or "inaugurated" seems a better word in this context. **The first contract** is sometimes held to be **the contract** at Sinai, but **the contract** Abraham made was earlier. In that ceremony, the blood of animals and birds were killed as requirements of the ceremony. The ceremony usually called the contract renewal, however, did not refer to **blood** (Josh 24).[2] **The first contract** may refer to **the contract** associated with the decalogue (Exod 24) which was first "inaugurated" and later **renewed** after Moses broke the tablets because the people's idolatry (Exod 32:15-19) had broken the **contract** and dissolved the relationship. Afterward Moses went back up on the mountain and cut two more tablets of stone; the decalogue was given again; and the Lord made a **contract** with the people again (Exod 34:1-10).

---

[1] G. H. Dalman, *The Words of Jesus*, tr. D. M. Kay (Edinburgh: T. & T. Clark, 1902) I, p.126.
[2] G. E. Mendenhall, *Law and Covenant in Israel and the Ancient Near East* (Pittsburgh: Biblical Colloquium, 1955), p. 40, insists that there was a new covenant formed in the time of Joshua rather than a renewal of a previously existing covenant.

There is no reference to sprinkling blood in this renewal, but since it was a **contract** made in relationship to the same people, the same Lord, and the same decalogue, the author may have supposed that it was made with the same ceremony the second time (Exod 34) as was described at first (Exod 24). Therefore it could be called "**the first contract**" which "**was renewed**" and **not without blood**.[1]

By the author's time the first contract had already been **renewed**. Paul considered himself to be a minister of the new contract (2Cor 3:6-18). The author of Hebrews assumed that Jesus was already the mediator of the new contract. He had already performed the legal ceremony necessary to conclude that contract. The first contract was really the one made with Abraham. The second contract was already renewed after the contract made with Moses had been broken. Nonetheless, the author of the Book of Hebrews seemed to think of the **renewed contract** made with Moses as the **first contract**. The second was then made with Jesus.

In both the old and the new contracts, the ceremony resulted in God being the God of the people and the people becoming the people of God. The text of the Pentateuch, the prophets, and the writings was essential to both contracts, and the author of Hebrews presumed the authority of the Scripture. That which was old and passing away was not the Scripture but the legal standing of the relationship. With the divorce, the marriage contract with God was null and void. The people of Israel were no longer the people of God. With the new contract, there was again a people of God who were the ones that were parties to the new contract. According to Matt 26, it was the ceremony that was performed at the Last Supper that constituted the establishment of a new contract. According to Hebrews it was the death of Jesus that constituted the necessary legal ceremony.

19*Every commandment.* This means **the commandments** were all legally formulated. They were not frivolous. They had all of the power of the nation to enforce them. This verse returns to the main contractual theme with the verbal tie to Heb 9:7, **not without blood**. Just as 9:15-17 showed that Christ's testament was valid from the standpoint of a last **will** and testament, so here the author shows that Jesus' contract was made in the proper form to be considered favorably in relationship to **the first contract** of the Israelites with Yehowah. The author of Hebrews correctly reported the actions of Moses in relation to the **people:**

> **Now Moses came and told the people all the words of Yehowah and all the ordinances, and all the people answered with one voice** (Exod 24:3).

After this, Moses took the **blood** from the sacrifices (which Hebrews said was from **bulls and goats**).[2] He sprinkled it upon the altar and upon the people (Exod 24:5-8) to unite the deity and the people into one contract. Ancient contracts were often established through legal ceremony, rather than written documents. The ceremony

---

[1] J. Swetnam, "A Suggested Interpretation of Hebrews 9:15," *CBQ* 27 (1965), pp. 373-90, has made a good case for the consistency of the author's argument. He held that the animals sacrificed for the Sinai contract really put the contract in force. In the same way, the new will was made effective by Jesus' death.

[2] The author of Hebrews may possibly have taken this from Josephus, but it is more likely that Hebrews and Josephus depended upon a common source (Ant 3:206). For an interesting discussion on this text, see Swetnam, "Interpretation," pp. 373-90.

Moses performed fulfilled that requirement. The author of Hebrews expanded the event to include not only **blood**, but **water and crimson wool and hyssop**, which were not a part of the **contract** ceremony at all but belonged to the ceremony used (together with **blood** from a bird) to **cleanse** a leper (Lev 14:6-7), and they were mixed with the red heifer's corpse and burned to provide the ashes necessary for **cleansing** a party to **the contract** from corpse defilement (Num 19:6). The author also expected the report to include not only the altar and **the people**, but also **the book itself**, which was probably understood to mean the two tablets on which the decalogue was engraved.

20*This is the blood of the contract.* The quotation from Exod 24:8 was paraphrased by Jesus when he instituted **the new contract** according to Matt 26:28. The author of Hebrews changed from "Look!" (LXX Exod 24:8) to **This [is],** possibly to agree with the eucharistic words of Jesus (Matt 26:28), and **Lord** to **God** to avoid confusing the subject with Jesus.[1]

21*He sprinkled the tent.* Although the Scripture does not confirm this claim, Josephus told of cleansing the priests, their vestments, the tabernacle, and its vessels, not only with oil (so Exod 40), but also with the blood of bulls and goats (Ant 3:206). Since the author has associated the **contract** so closely with sacrifice, the temple, and atonement, he may have mingled his report of the sprinkling associated with the **contract** ceremony with the atonement ceremony and also the dedication of the tabernacle. He may have reasoned that the tabernacle was dedicated at the same time Moses brought the tablets down from the mountain and placed them in the chest in the tabernacle. Therefore the **blood** used for **the contract** ceremony was also used for sprinkling the rest of the liturgical objects.

22*Without [the] pouring out of blood.* Not "everything" was **cleansed with blood**. Some things were **cleansed with** water (Lev 15:1-33; 16:26, 28; 22:6.) and some by fire (Num 31:22-23), but "**nearly everything** was **cleansed with blood.**" This is part of the author's inclusive speech: **every commandment . . . all the people . . . all the people (19) . . . all the liturgical vessels . . . nearly everything**. In dealing with punishment for murder, Philo said, "Blood is cleansed with blood" (Spec 3:150). Rabbis insisted that atonement could be made only with blood (bZeb 6a; bMen 91b; 93b; bYoma 5a). Together with the contract the Lord made with Noah, he commanded that Noah's posterity continue daily sacrifice before the altar with blood to obtain forgiveness (Jub 6:1-14). The author of Hebrews, accordingly, reflected quite a general opinion when he said, **without [the] pouring out of blood, forgiveness does not occur**.

23*By means of better sacrifices than these.* **The symbols** (*hoo-paw-dáyg-mah-tah*, ὑποδείγματα) referred to the things associated with the temple made with hands. They are under the administration of the inadequate priesthood, **the first contract**, and the law. **These** (things) are only a copy and shadow of **the heavenly things** (Heb 8:5) or "the things in the heavens." Earthly things that are only **symbols** have to **be cleansed by means of these** formulae prescribed in the Pentateuch, but, in the author's judgment, **the heavenly things themselves** also had to be cleansed. The only difference between **the heavenly things** and **the symbols** is that the former

---

[1] So K. J. Thomas, "The Old Testament Citations in Hebrews," *NTS* 11 (1964-65):313.

must be cleansed **by means of better sacrifices than these** employed by the Aaronic priesthood. The author thought of heaven in earthly terms. He thought heaven would involve sinning and cleansing from sin. His concept of heaven that makes such a deduction reasonable will be considered at the end of this chapter.

Summary.—With his death Jesus gave both a will for his heirs and **blood** for **cleansing.** He made the **new contract** effective. His blood cleansed both **earthly symbols** and **heavenly things.** He is the mediator of a **new contract,** and his heirs will receive their **age inheritance** and be redeemed of their transgressions.

The author justified all of this by giving the rules and customs by which ordinary wills are executed, and reviewing how cleansing is ordinarily obtained under the Pentateuchal laws. In antiquity **contracts** were confirmed by **oaths**, witnesses, and liturgical forms. If any part of some contractual liturgy, such as the sprinkling of **blood,** were omitted the entire **contract** would be invalid and could not be upheld in court. Therefore the author of Hebrews was following the correct legal policy in noticing the precise details required for establishing a **contract.** Most **contracts** today are made in writing and require only signatures to make them valid. One exception to this is the ancient wedding **contract** which still is accompanied by vows, witnesses, signatures, and some traditional liturgy.

TEXT

Hebrews	Micah
24 For Christ did not enter into the holy [precincts] made with hands, antitypes of the true [precincts], but into heaven itself, now **appear before God** in our behalf, 25 and not in order that he might offer himself many times, just as the high priest enters into the holy [precincts] every year with the blood of another	Micah 6:8 With what shall I **appear before Yehowah,** and bow down before God on high? Ps 42:3 When shall I come and **appear before God ?**

26 since [then] it would have been necessary for him to suffer many times from the foundation of the world, but now he has appeared once at the end of the ages for [the] removal of sin through his sacrifice. 27 Now, however much is laid up for men, [they have but] once to die, and after this [there is a] judgment; 28 so also the Christ, having been offered once "to bear [the] crimes of [the] many," will next appear without crime to those who await him for salvation.

COMMENTARY

24 *The holy [precincts] made with hands*. The expression given here is an oxymoron. It is an impossible combination. That which is **holy** is that which is not idolatrous or common (Lev 10:10). The precincts were called **holy**, but they were also called "idolatrous," "pagan," "profane," or "gentile," The Hebrew word *eh-leél* (אליל) means "idolatrous." "idol," "false god," or "worthlessness." This term is rendered in

LXX as "made with hands" (*khay-raw-poi-áy-tois,* χειροποιῆτοις) (Isa 10:11), or "dumb idols" (*áye-doh-lah koh-fáh,* εἴδω λα κωφά) (Hab 2:18). In other words, this place mentioned was a visible part of the temple that was called **holy**, but it was really idolatrous. It was an unholy **holy** place. This was apparently the **holy** room in Herod's temple which pious Jews thought was pagan and idolatrous. The affirmation of the author was that Jesus had nothing to do with Herod's temple. When he was sacrificed he ascended through a different temple, a **temple not made with hands.**

24*But Christ . . . enter[ed] . . . into heaven.* **The holy [precincts] made with hands** are the sacred areas in Herod's temple at Jerusalem which the author considered nothing more than mere **antitypes of the true [precincts].**[1] Not all Jews considered these areas to be idolatrous. Josephus said the holy of holies was like heaven (Ant 3:123), and Philo, commenting on the LXX Lev 16-17, said when the **high priest** entered the **holy of holies** he was neither God nor man but God's minister. He had contact both with the mortal and the immortal, until he came out again to the realm of the flesh and **blood.** The author of Hebrews rather contrasted **heaven** to Herod's temple. Jesus the great **high priest** went through the **heavens** (Heb 4:14), not merely **the holy of holies** which seemed to some to be like **heaven,** but was really only a **symbol,** an antitype.

Appeared before God. The normal way by which a priest would **appear before God** would have been to appear before the altar with a sacrifice. The Aaronic **high priest** entered **the holy [precincts] made with hands** in Herod's temple, but Jesus entered **into heaven itself.** It is in **heaven** that Jesus **appeared before God in our behalf**. The best the **high priest** could do was to send incense and fragrant smoke up to **heaven** in an attempt to placate God, but Jesus was an apostle, an ambassador, who could himself come directly before God to intercede in behalf of the believers.

God was known as the great **judge** who always sat on his throne of **judgment**. Those who **appeared before** him were those who were dependent upon his **judgment.** Their posture was one in which they were bowed down with their faces to the ground as they waited until he asked them to speak. They often appeared with gifts and bribery in an effort to influence his **judgment.** Jesus appeared as an attorney, representing others in his appeal.

25*and not in order that he might offer himself many times.* Jesus' **offering** is much superior to the animal sacrifices presented by the Aaronic **high priests.** He **offered himself,** not **every year** nor every day (Heb 7:27).

26*He has appeared once at the end of the ages.* The word for **ages** here is the same word that most scholars render "eternal" (*ai-oh-neé-ohn,* αἰωνίων), except that it is plural. It is not possible to render this "eternities." This was a reference to many periods of time--**ages**-which had come to an **end in** the author's mind. He was probably thinking of the various **ages** of Israel's history-- **the age** of the patriarchs, **the age** of Egyptian captivity, **the age** of Moses, **the age** of David, the wilderness **age**, **the age** of the conquest, **the age** of the kingdom, the Babylonian **age**, the Hasmonean **age,** the Roman **age.** This had the same meaning as "**the end of the** days," used in Daniel to mean **the end of the** evil time of gentile rule that concluded

[1] See Commentary on Heb 8:1-7 for a discussion of the temple made with hands.

in a Jewish victory and the celebration of Hanukkah.[1] When these evil **ages** were over, the good **age** to come would begin, just as it happened after Hanukkah and Jewish liberty. Here the expression was an antitype of the Maccabean experience. **Ages** did not represent eternities. The same would be true in relationship to redemption or heritage.

If Jesus had not had a better offering to present, namely **himself,** he would have had to suffer **many times from the foundation of the world.**[2] This is a contrary-to-fact conditional statement with ellipsis of "if it were different" or "otherwise." Christ's having **appeared** (*peh-phahn-éh-roh-tai*, πεφανέρωται) in the perfect tense reflects the same concept rabbis anticipated in the future, when they promised that the Messiah would be revealed (*yeet-gah-láy*, יתגלי) (TargJon Jer 30:21; Zech 3:8; 6:12). According to the Palestinian targum, the "king Messiah is to be revealed" or "It is necessary that the king Messiah be revealed" (*ah-teéd duh yeet-gah-láy mehl-káh mah-sheé-khah*, עתיד דיתגלי מלכא משיחא) at **the end of** days (Gen 35:21).

The expression "the end of days" or **the end of the ages** means **the end** of the days or the **ages** of "captivity" under foreign rule before the national Jubilee when the land would be restored to the "original owners" and the "captives" would be liberated to return to Palestine and live on the land of the promise (Heb 11:9).[3] It is the same period referred to as **the last of these days** (Heb 1:2) when God spoke to us through a Son (Heb 1:2; see also TBenj 11:3; TLevi 10:2). For many Jews of NT times, the Messiah, who was to rule **at the end of the ages** and the beginning of the messianic age, was expected to be the son of David, who would rule from Jerusalem in the new **age** that would begin when **the ages** came to an **end.** The author of Hebrews, however, did not describe a Davidic messiah at all, but one who was an apostle and **high priest**, who would both rule and offer sacrifice the way the Hasmoneans did.

At the end of the ages Jesus **appeared** but **once**, a term the author repeated many times (Heb 6:4; 9:7, 26, 27, 28; 10:2; 12:26, 27). The purpose of his **appearing** was priestly. He offered "his sacrifice" for the **removal of crime.**[4]

27 *Once to die, and after this [there is a] judgment.* In a way that would be consistent with a treasury of merits theology, the author seemed to think of every event, both good and bad, as that which was **laid up for men** in treasuries or account books. No one would know in advance how much his account held. But "however much" it was, there was one thing that was certain: there was only **one** occasion for death. That was the same for all human beings, including Jesus, whose self-sacrifice could be made but **once.**

---

[1] See further Buchanan, *The Book of Daniel* (Lewiston: Mellen, c1999).

[2] J. Swetnam, "Sacrifice and Revelation in the Epistle to the Hebrews," *CBQ* 30 (1968):227-34, said Jesus' sacrifice was also a revelation as were many of the sacrifices of the FT. There may have been revelations associated with sacrifices, but, as with Jesus, sacrifice had a different purpose, first of all. They were made to gain God's favor and accomplish something for the person doing the sacrificing or for someone else. .

[3] Buchanan, *The Consequences of the Covenant* (Leiden: E. J. Brill, 70), pp. 9-18.

[4] For a thought-provoking discussion on the relationship between revelation and sacrifice, see J. Swetnam, "Sacrifice and Revelation in the Epistle to the Hebrews: Observations and Surmises on Hebrews 7:26," *CBQ* 30 (1968):227-34.

After this [is] judgment. Rabbis understood that after death every party to God's **contract** would appear before the great tribunal of God and face **judgment**. Then the books would be opened and all of everyone's deeds would be used either for or against him or her. R. Eliezer b. Jacob said a person who performed one good deed acquired for himself one defense attorney and the one who performed one transgression acquired for himself one prosecuting attorney. After death, all of these attorneys would stand and plead for or accuse the person standing in **judgment** (mAboth 4:11). Akabya b. Mahalaleel said,

> And before whom are you about to give account and reckoning? Before the King of kings, the Holy One blessed be He (mAboth 3:1).

28 *Having been offered once*. The primary word here is an aorist passive participle. It clearly refers to a situation that has already happened. It is not repetitious or continual. It describes a situation that is punctilious. It happened already. If the term itself was not enough, the word **once** was added to show the uniqueness of the event. This is the only offering available (Heb 10:10, 14, 17, 18).

To those who await him for salvation. The Hebrew text of Isa 53:11 contains the clause **and he will bear [the] crime of the many**. The LXX of Isa 53:12 had **. . . crimes of [the] many he bore** (*ah-náy-nehg-kayhn,* ἀνήνεγκειν). The author of Hebrews varied this slightly to fit his sentence structure. . . . **of [the] many to bear [the] crimes**, changing the word order and the finite verb to an infinitive, but not changing the basic meaning of the passage. The servant in Isaiah was a personification of the Jews who were taken from Palestine to Babylon, where they had to pay double for the crimes of Israel until Cyrus captured Babylon and Jews were allowed to return. Those who had died in Babylon by then were the ones praised by later generations as having borne the iniquities of **[the] many**.[1] **The many** is a technical term used in the Dead Sea scrolls to mean the whole community (1QS 6:1, 8, 9, 11, 13, 16; Dan 11:33; 12:3). In Isaiah it referred to the Jews who would be permitted to return, the ones who benefited from the sacrifice and suffering of the Jews who died in Babylon.

The author of Hebrews identified Jesus as the servant who bore **[the] crimes of [the] many** by **offering** himself as an atoning sacrifice. The Greek for **will next appear** is *ehk doo-teh-roo . . .awph-tháy-seh-tai* (ἐκ δευτέρου ὀφθήσεται), literally "from a second . . . will be seen." **Those who await him** are those who have held fast to the hope (Heb 3:6; 6-11, 18) and now have a still better hope by which they might draw near to God (Heb 7:19). The **salvation** they expect is the fulfillment of the promise, the long expected **rest**, the restoration of the land, and peace and prosperity while dwelling there. Jesus will appear **without crime** because he was made a **cleansing** for crime (Heb 1:3) when he offered himself as a sacrifice for his own and the people's crimes (Heb 7:27). Those who had been **cleansed** from **crimes** had their **crimes** pardoned. The Christ had learned obedience and **was made perfect through his suffering** sacrifice (Heb 5:7-8), so he has passed through the heavens and was exalted to the right hand of God **without crime** (Heb 4:14-15).

---

[1] For a justification of this interpretation see Buchanan, *Consequences,* pp. 123-31, and Commentary on Heb 5:7-8.

Summary. The word **Christ** in the beginning and concluding verses acts as an inclusion to make these verses a separate unit. The close parallels between unit (1) (Heb 9:11-14) and unit (3) (Heb 9:24-28) also form a larger type of inclusion, inclosing units (1), (2), and (3). This also reflects the author's skill in effective repetition. The word **Christ** in Heb 9-11 as well as Heb 9:28 shows that this word ties together two inclusions, a larger and a smaller unit. Vanhoye called attention to the following comparisons:[1]

Unit 1	Unit 3
a. not made with hands (11)	a. not . . . made with hands (24)
b. once for all into the sanctuary (12)	b. all into heaven itself . . . once (24-26)
c. offered himself blameless to God (14)	c. appear before God (24)
d. the blood of Christ will cleanse the conscience (14)	d. takes away the crimes of [the] many (28)
e. having found eternal redemption (12)	e. for removal of sins (26)

Words like **renewal** (*ah-nah-kain-eed-zayn,* ἀνακαινίζειν) (Heb 6:6) *ehg-keh-káyn-ees-tai* (ἐγκεκαίνισται) (Heb 9:18), **many times** (*paw-láh-kees,* πολλάκις) (Heb 6:7; 9:25, 26; 10:11), **symbols** (*hoo-paw-dáyg-mah-tah,* ὑποδείγματα) (Heb 9:23), **example** (*pah-rah-dáyg-mah-teéd-zawn-tas,* παραδείγματιζοντας) (Heb 6:6), and **made with hands** (*chay-roh-paw-áy-taws*, χειροποιῆτος) (Heb 9:11, 24) are terms which belong to the **ages** at the **end** of which Christ appeared. Words that belong to the coming **age** are **once** (*háh-pax,* ἅπαξ) or (*eh-pháh-pahx,* ἐφάπαξ) (Heb 6:4; 9:7, 26, 27, 28; 10:2; 12:26, 27), **age, salvation** (Heb 5:9), **judgment** Heb 6:2), **redemption** (Heb 9:12), **spirit** (Heb 9:14); **inheritance** (Heb 9:15); **contract** (Heb 13:20), **heaven**, **heavens**, or **heavenly** Heb 1:10, 4:14; 7:26; 8:1, 9:23, 24; 11:12, 12:23, 25, 26), and **true tent**(*skay-náys ah-lay-thee-náws,* σκηνῆς τῆς ἀληθινῆς), Heb 8:2; things or precincts, Heb 9:24, heart, Heb 10:22).

This last unit (Heb 9:24-28) seems to summarize more than just Heb 9. There are here connection words that refer to material in Heb 6, 7, and 8 as well, and the emphasis here seems to sharpen the contrast between the priests, temples, sacrifices, cleansing, and liturgical practices of the old contract and those of the new contract. Although this appears to be a summarizing paragraph, it is not a final summary. The topic that continues in Heb 10 is an extension of arguments presented in Heb 9, showing the superiority of Christ's offering to that of the high priest of Aaron.

The comparison of the earthly temple with the heavenly has misled many scholars into thinking that Hebrews was basically Platonic in outlook.[2] Because the author's concepts of heaven and the Lord's presence are important to a proper understanding of the author's message, a more careful investigation will be made of that subject.

The "real" presence of the Lord is his legal presence. It was made apparent in the fire that burned at the tent of meeting in the wilderness,[3] the smoke on Mount

[1] A. Vanhoye, *La Structure Littéraire de l'Epitre aux Hébreux* (Paris: Gabalda, 1962), p. 157.

[2] Vanhoye, *Structure*, p. 157.

[3] The Lord went with the people (Exod 33:16) through the wilderness to give them **rest** in the

Sinai, or the fire on the altar in the temple. At night the fire was most visible and during the day the smoke or "cloud" was most visible (Num 9:15-16). This was the pillar of cloud that moved before the Hebrews and stood behind them as they escaped from Egypt (Exod 14:19-20). When the surface was damp and cold, the smoke settled around the camp like smog, and the people kept the camp stationary. When the weather cleared, the smoke went up directly and the people then were free to move the camp. They understood the rising of the smoke to be the command of the Lord to move camp (Num 9:17-23). When the smoke went straight up, to the naked eye it seemed to reach heaven where the Lord dwelt. At that time, they dared to move, because the Lord could come down through the smoke and be with them.

When the Lord wanted to speak to his people, he came down from heaven through the pillar of smoke and made his real presence known (Num 11:17, 25; 12-5). Since the pillar of cloud or smoke was the bridge that joined earth to heaven, it was therefore the means by which the Lord could be present on earth. For this reason, the fire on the altar was considered to be very holy, and the altar was reserved only for the high priest. Both the altar and the fire on the altar were thought to be close to heaven.

When the temple was dedicated in Jerusalem, Solomon is reported to have offered a long prayer (1Kings 8). He acknowledged that **heaven and the highest heaven** could not contain God (1Kings 8:27), but he prayed that God would constantly watch the temple where he had promised that his name should dwell (1Kings 8:29). From then on prayers were directed to the temple in the belief that God's presence was there, just as in heaven. God's presence was assured when the temple was filled with the smoke of the glory of God (Rev 15:8).

Rabbis said that in the messianic age the Lord would again protect Israel with a cloud of smoke over Mount Zion (ExodR 50:5). Since this was so, parties to the contract spoke of "seeing God," when they meant that they would worship in the temple (Isa 6:1; Ps 24:3-6; Matt 5:8). Amos said he saw God upon the altar (*ahl hah-meez-báy-akh*, על המזבח) (Amos 9:1), and Hezekiah addressed God in prayer as **the Lord of Armies, the God of Israel, whose presence dwells high above the cherubim [in the temple]** (TargJon Isa 37:15). The smoke which connected earth to heaven was sometimes spoken of in terms of a pillar and at other times as a sort of tube. According to TargPsJon Gen 2:6,

> The cloud of majesty came down from the throne of majesty and filled itself with water from the ocean, and then rose up from the earth and gave rain to water **the whole face of the ground**.

This seems to be the description of a water-spout which looks like a cloud in the shape of a funnel which could "draw up" water from the ocean. After the water-spout, the rain that followed would have convinced early Near Easterners of the relationship of the "funnel cloud," the rain, and God's activity. Commenting on the story of Jacob's ladder, Bar Qappara said,

> **And the top of it [the ladder] reached heaven** (Gen 26:12)---[This refers to] the sacrifices, the odor of which went up to heaven (GenR 135b #68.12).

Promised Land (Exod 33:14-15); likewise, the chest containing the contract went before them and the cloud overshadowed them (Num 10:33-34).

Other rabbis compared the ladder to Mount Horeb, whose top reached heaven because the Scripture says **the mountain burned with fire up to the heart of heaven** (Deut 4:11; GenR 135a #68:12). When Manoah first confronted the man of God who announced Manoah's wife's impending pregnancy, Manoah slaughtered a kid as a sacrifice (Judges 13:1-19). When the fire burned, the man of God ascended with the flame toward heaven (Judges 13:20), as if the smoke were some kind of conveyance. It was through this conveyance that the offerings made on the altar reached heaven as a pleasing odor to the Lord (Lev 1:17 and frequently). The smoke united earth with heaven; therefore, the smoke that filled the temple made the temple a place where the Lord might dwell. The close relationship between God and the temple prompted worshipers to describe heaven in the holiest terms that they knew--the holy city, Jerusalem, and the temple at Mount Zion. Josephus said that the innermost sanctuary, which was accessible only to the high priest, "Was dedicated to God (just) as Heaven (was)" (Ant 3:123).

The service of the Levites in the sanctuary was compared to the service of the angels of the presence and the holy ones in heaven (Jub 31:14). Israelites knew more about the function of the Levites than about angels, but they conjectured from the Levites that the angels were God's messengers, doing the kind of errand work that Levites did at the temple. Like the Levites, they formed a militia (Matt 13:41; 16:27; 25:31; 26:53; Mark 8:38; Luke 2:13; Rev 12:7) and a choir to sing and blow trumpets (Rev 5:11; 8:2, 6,7, 8, 12; 9:1, 13-14; 10:7; 11:15); they were in the temple in heaven (Rev 14:15, 17, 18; 15:6; 16:1); they distributed incense (Rev 8:3-5); and they stood before or around God, the throne, or the altar, which seemed to be at the same place (Rev 5:2, 11; 7:11; 8:2, 3; 1Enoch 14:22-23; 71:8-9; TLevi 5:1; AscIsa 7:14, 19, 24, 31, 33, 35, 36; 8:8-9, 16). Like the Levites, angels were ministers (Ps 104:4; bHag 12b; 2Enoch 4:1-5:2) who petitioned, interceded, and prayed for others (1Enoch 39:5). As in the temple, there was an altar in heaven (Rev 6:9) before the throne (Rev 8:3-5) or before God (Rev 9:13), and there were cherubim in the temple (Rev 14:17-18; 1Enoch 14:11, 20; 71:7).

When the seer visualized the holy city, the heavenly Jerusalem, coming down from the heaven, a voice said, **Look! The dwelling of God is with men** (Rev 21:2-3). This heavenly Jerusalem was like an idealized earthly Jerusalem, having high walls, 12 gates, and streets of pure gold (Rev 21:10-21). God's throne in heaven was evidently located in the temple, in the position of the altar, perhaps on the mercy seat between the cherubim (1Enoch 71:8-9; TLevi 5:1), or maybe the cherubim formed the throne. Just as the Lord appeared in the fire on the altar or at the tent of meeting, so God's presence in heaven was surrounded by fire (1Enoch 14:19-23; 71:5-10). The 4 beasts and the 24 elders brought incense and lyres and worshiped the Lamb who was between the elders and the beasts and the throne (Rev 5:6-10), just as Levites and priests brought incense and worshiped before the altar in the temple with song and music.

The picture of peoples coming from every nation together with angels, the four beasts, and the 24 elders, worshiping while dressed in white garments and carrying palm branches in their hands, evidently refers to the throne in heaven, but it was patterned after scenes in Jerusalem on great feast days when Jews from the diaspora gathered to worship at the temple. The priests always wore white to symbolize their ritual purity, so heaven was pictured in the same way (Rev 7:9-12). Those dressed in white were pure and, like priests, served the Lord day and night before his throne in his temple. He would shelter them with his presence, just as his presence hovered over the temple in Jerusalem (Rev 7:13-16; 1Enoch 14:20). As in Jerusalem, there was a golden altar for incense in heaven, where angels, like priests, offered prayers by burning incense before the throne (Rev 8:1-5, 9-13; 1Enoch 14:18-19; 71:1).

In God's temple in heaven, like that at Jerusalem, there was the chest holding the contract (Rev 11:19). Just as the Lamb was before the throne in heaven, so the Lamb stood on Mount Zion together with all the gathered saints, and there were voices of angels singing with lyres before the throne and before the 4 beasts and the 24 elders, just as in the temple scenes in heaven (Rev 14:15). Closely associated with this scene in Jerusalem, angels came out of the temple on Zion and out of the temple in heaven (Rev 14:1, 15, 17) and from the altar (Rev 14:18). In the temple of the tent of witness in heaven, angels wore white, like priests at Jerusalem, and when they burned incense the temple filled with smoke, like the temple at Jerusalem (Rev 15:5-8; Isa 6:4).

The bowls of wrath which the angels poured were like the bowls of incense Levites poured in the temple (Rev 15:7-16:20). The scenes describing Rome's fall were mingled with heavenly temple scenes and angels (Rev 18:l, 4, 21), with the multitude in heaven together with the 4 beasts and the 24 elders and the throne (Rev 19:l-8). The four beasts described in the temple in heaven may have been like the 4 beasts or the cherubim Ezekiel described as being part of the furniture and decoration of the temple vision (Ezek 1:4-26; 10:9-22) or the seraphim described by Isaiah in the temple at Jerusalem (Isa 6:2-7). The throne itself may have been a chariot pulled by heavenly beasts.

Although it seems to us that the ancient Near Easterners examined the most holy places they knew and described God or heaven in these terms, to them it seemed the other way around. Human beings merely imitated the activity of the gods and built structures after divine patterns. Ural-Altaic peoples, for instance, thought earthly mountains had archetypes in the heavens, and in Egypt, fields were named after celestial fields which were known before their earthly counterparts.[1] This was especially true of temples which had heavenly prototypes. Not only the temple at Jerusalem, but the temple at Lagash was also constructed according to a plan that was divinely revealed.[2]

Cities such as Jerusalem, Sippar, Nineveh, and Asshur were built according to heavenly patterns.[3] When a wilderness area was cultivated or civilized, it was believed to be a new creation, repeating God's creation of chaos into cosmos.[4] Sacred places were constructed on mountains in an effort to get close to heaven where God dwelt. These high places were each considered the center of the world. Thus Mount Gerizim and Zion were each called the navel of the land (Judges 9:37; Jub 4:26), implying that each was the cord that bound earth to heaven. Although the choice place for temples was on the mountain top, neither Gerizim nor Zion were built on the top of the highest mountains of the areas, because they had to have water. The tops of Mount Ebal or Mount Scopus were both higher than the locations of the

---

[1] Eliade, *Cosmos and History*, tr. W. R Trask (New York: Harper, 1959), p. 6. Sumerians used the term *gis-zar* to describe the mystic prototype that existed in heaven before its earthly counterpart was created. So W. F. Albright, "The Supposed Babylonian Derivation of the Logos," *JBL* 39 (1920):151.

[2] Eliade, *Cosmos*, p. 7.

[3] Eliade, *Cosmos*, p. 8.

[4] Eliade, *Cosmos*, p. 10.

temples of Zion or Gerizim. Samaritans say that Mount Gerizim is spiritually the highest mountain in the world, even though Mount Ebal is physically much higher. The temple itself makes the location legally higher than any surrounding hill. It takes a little imagination to call Zion a mountain at all.

Samaritans claimed that Gerizim was the holiest mountain, the place of the True One's presence, the house of God, the gate of heaven (Memar Marqah 2 #10), the place of the glory of God, the dwelling place of angels, and the place of blessings. This mountain is so high that the waters of the flood did not reach it (Memar Marqah 3 #4). Zion was called the holy mountain (Isa 31:4-5), the city of our God, the joy of the earth; his holy mountain (Ps 48:1-2), the highest of the mountains (Isa 2:2), the place over which the Lord hovers and from which he fights (Isa 31:4-5). Javanese pilgrims approaching the temple of Barobudur ascend from the earthly plane to the "pure region."[1] A Babylonian temple was called the "Link between Heaven and Earth."[2] Ancients dreamed of building towers from which to reach heaven (Gen 11:1-4).

Heaven was just above the mountains and the treetops. To the naked eye, heaven seemed like a tent roof that could be lowered (Mek *Bahod* 4:47-50) or rolled up like a scroll and replaced with a new one when God so chose (Isa 34:4; 42:5; 44:24; 45:12; 48:13; 51:6, 13; 64:1; 65:17; 66:22; Zech 12:1; Recog. 2:68; 3:14). With this cosmology, it was not a strain on reason to think of ladders reaching to heaven (Gen 28:12), a messenger of God taken through a column of smoke in the presence of Manoah and his wife (Judges 13:20), or Elijah taken up in a chariot of fire (2Kings 2:1,11).

By this logic, the imagination could fill the unseen details, picturing God just above human traffic, sitting on a great throne, smelling the fragrance of the incense sent through the smoke to please him. The ancient Near Eastern mentality that visualized a column of smoke as a means of communication between earth and heaven, temples as the link between earth and heaven, temples as places where the Lord's presence dwelt and where heavenly angels hovered (Memar Marqah 2 #10; 3 #2), clarifies some otherwise difficult passages in the NT. Four of these are:

(a) the heavenly Jerusalem in Heb 12:22;
(b) the Father's house in John 14:2;
(c) the relationship of Jesus to the Levites and angels in Hebrews (5:1-5; 7:4-8:5); and
(d) the reference to sacrifice in heaven in Hebrews (Heb 8:3-4). These will be considered in order.

(a) *Heavenly Jerusalem.* Since ancient Near Easterners considered places where communication with God was possible to be very close and very similar to heaven, it is no longer necessary to mythicize **Zion, even [the] city of [the God of life** (Heb 12:22), as many scholars have done,[3] just because it is also called **heavenly Jerusalem** (Heb 12:22). This is a reasonable and respectable ascription for a city that contains the temple which links earth to heaven. At this point it was believed possible for God himself to be present.

---

[1] Eliade, *Cosmos,* p. 15.

[2] Eliade, *Cosmos,* p. 14.

[3] F. F. Bruce, *The Epistle to the Hebrews* (Grand Rapids: Eerdmans, c1964), pp. 374-75; H. Windisch, *Der Hebräerbrief* (Tübingen: J. C. B. Mohr, 1931), p. 113.

This was the place of worship for a **church of firstborn [people] enrolled in heaven** (Heb 12:23), who had **tasted the heavenly gift** (Heb 6:4). This was **the city which had the foundations, whose builder and constructor was God** (Heb 11:10). This city, for which the patriarchs looked, was the capital city of **the land of promise** (Heb 11:9). The patriarchs left Haran and journeyed toward Palestine. They could have returned either to Ur of the Chaldees or to Haran if they had not wanted a better fatherland, **that is a heavenly [one]** (Heb 11:14-16). In this fatherland, this **land of promise,** this **heavenly** land, God **prepared for them a city** (Heb 11:16), which was **Zion, even [the] city of [the] living God, heavenly Jerusalem** (Heb 12:22).

The way God prepared a city for the Israelites was to commission the Jebusites to devote centuries constructing it for them. The Israelites did not have to design or construct those great walls or that wonderful watering system, up on a rocky ridge high above the surrounding valleys. All of that came as a gift. All the Israelites had to do was to overpower the Jebusites and confiscate the city. The city that came to the Israelites as a gift from God was Zion.

One of the chief archaeologists who excavated that city was Kathleen Kenyon. She excavated the eastern bank of Zion, the western bank of the Kidron Valley. Kenyon has shown that on the eastern side of city, near the bottom of the Kidron Valley, there was a wall that went up 50 or 60 feet. In between that wall and the original rock ridge, the Jebusites built several strong perpendicular interior walls. Then they filled in the space between these walls with still more rocks, making a triangular fill with the hypotenuse of the right triangle on the rock ridge under the slope that is now visible. Solomon added more rocks to the fill the Jebusites had provided, making a foundation (*theh-méhl-ee-aws,* θεμέλιος) for the temple that was deep (*bah-thaws*, βάθος), and consisted of strong rocks (Ant 8:63).

The same archaeological work has not been done on the Tyropoeon Valley side as has been accomplished on the Kidron Valley side, but it is probable that the Jebusites were consistent in their construction, making the entire top surface flat with upright walls on both sides. The western wall, then, would have had its base near the center of the Tyropoeon Valley. That would have made the entire City of David one solid rock wall from the center of the Tyropoeon Valley on the west to the center of the Kidron Valley on the east. What a wall! When Josephus said that Herod removed the old foundations and replaced them with new foundations (Ant 15:391) he was referring to the foundations of the temple and not the foundations of the whole city.

The foundation and the wall. From one point of view the entire City of David was one huge rock wall reaching from the center of the Tyropoeon Valley to the center of the Kidron Valley. No wonder that Josephus called this great wall (*meh-gáhl-oo tákhe-oos,* μεγάλου τείχους), the greatest ever heard of by human beings (Ant 15:396).[1]

---

[1] Since Josephus did not say where this great wall was, I had earlier thought this great wall was the northern wall of the City of David ("The Area of the Temple at Zion," *ET* 116.6 [2005], p.182). Context requires that it was closely related to the temple. I mistakenly assumed that Josephus was exaggerating, but this wall was the one most likely to qualify. Over and over again Josephus is found to be reliable in his appraisal. Wherever Josephus is tested, his work is found to be anything but the exaggeration I once suspected or the "incompetent sloppiness" that Murphy-O'Connor attributes to

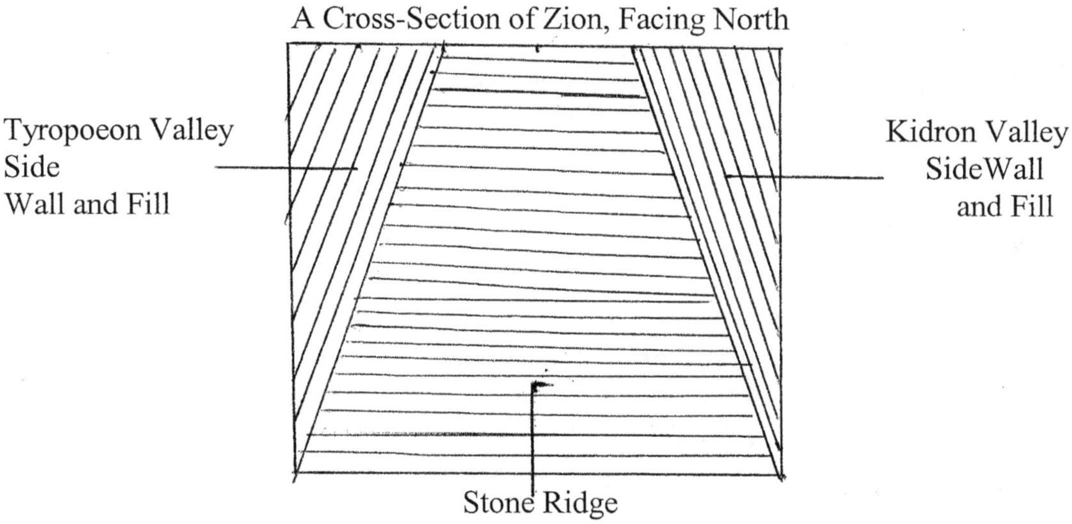

What other city in the world was built on the top of a wall? What other city had such a firm foundation? Those foundations were at least 50 feet deep and set on solid rock. This was an entire city constructed on a deep rock foundation. It was "the city that had the foundations" (Heb 11:10), Zion, "the city of the God of life, heavenly Jerusalem" (Heb 12:22). Many scholars who once thought Josephus was "sloppy" and famous for his exaggerations no longer agree with Murphy-O'Connor's evaluation. For example, we once thought it was impossible for Herod to have used stones in the walls that were 30 feet long, 15 feet wide, and 7½ feet deep (War 5:175), but since Mazar's excavation, these stones are there for everyone to see, precisely the size Josephus described. This "great wall" is another exhibit of Josephus' accuracy.

Kathleen Kenyon found this defensive wall and fill masterfully made.[1] Nowhere else in Palestine has been found anything of the sort, but there is also nowhere else in Palestine a spring like the Spring of Siloam that would justify all of that technical engineering. Solomon wanted still more space for a large temple with a huge altar. Josephus said the level place on the narrow ridge would hardly have been enough for the temple and the altar, so Solomon leveled off the city to the top of the western bank, bringing in rocks and soil to fill in the space between the outer wall and the western bank with rocks and earth.[2] This engineering project made adequate space for the temple, the altar, and the citadel.[3]

When Titus gave orders to pull down all of the walls, his soldiers destroyed both the eastern and the western walls. Because the Hasmoneans had filled up the Tyropoeon Valley, the western wall had ground support on both sides from the upper ground level down, so that when the wall fell it broke off at the upper ground level and only added more fill to the Tyropoeon Valley. On the Kidron Valley side,

---

Josephus when Josephus provides eye witness data that conflicts with Murphy-O'Connor's conjecture ("Where Was the Antonia Fortress" *RB* 111.1 (2004): 79, fn. 3).

[1] Kathleen M. Kenyon, *Jerusalem. Excavating 3000 years of History* (New York. McGraw-Hill Book Co., c1967), plate 36, p. 36.

[2] Graeme Auld and Margreet Steiner, *Jerusalem I* (Cambridge: Lutterworth Press, c1996), p. 32.

[3] This answers the objection of space proposed by Jeffrey Harrison, "The End," p. 5.

however, the wall toppled all the way down to the footing. When this support was removed, the loose rocks in the fill also rolled down. These rocks, together with other rocks left on the ground all over the area, may have been gathered by Justinian in the sixth century IA, leaving the eastern side as a long slope, much the way it appears today.[1]

(b) *The Father's House.* The temple at Jerusalem was frequently called “the house” or “the house of the Lord.” In that temple were quarters where young priests stayed (War 5:220-221; *mMid* 1:8-9). Some of these may have been for the overnight accomodations of priests who served in shifts. This may have been the imagery intended by Jesus when he assured his disciples that his **Father's house** had many places to stay (*maw-naí*, μοναί) (John 14:2). Just as the earthly temple, which was called the Lord's house, had hospitality provisions for visiting priests, so also the heavenly archetype would have many such places to stay. This means Jesus would be prepared to receive the disciples to himself (John 14:2-3).

(c) *The Levites and the Angels.* Since the high priest was considered more than human while he was in the holy of holies (Som. 2:231-32, and since the holy of holies was thought to be like heaven (Ant 3:123) because it was dedicated to God and was the place where God had chosen to dwell (1Kings 8:29), the comparison of Jesus with the angels as well as the Levites makes good sense. Jesus was compared as a high priest with Levites who were subordinate to the high priests. In the heavenly archetype the situation was the same. As high priest in heaven, he was also compared to the angels, who ministered in heaven just as the Levites ministered on earth. 1Enoch pictured the angels as holy messengers who were like the Levites in that they were not admitted into the holy of holies (1Enoch 14:12).

Of course a high priest was higher in status than a Levite, and by the same token, the heavenly high priest was higher than the angels who have the same status in heaven. Jesus was pictured as a high priest because the high priest was the mediator for the people, and as such was higher in status than other people, especially when he was in the holy of holies. This did not keep the high priest from being human. In fact, Jews dared to pelt him with citrus fruit if he failed to function properly, even in the temple (Ant 13:372), but still this was considered a heavenly place in the heavenly city, and by some, **a temple not made with hands** (Exod 15:17; Ps 78 69; Mek *Shirata* 10:29-42). Therefore when Jesus became high priest in heaven, it was natural to assume that he would have subordinate assistants there just as a high priest had in Jerusalem. Accordingly the angels were considered by the author of Hebrews to be clearly subordinate to the Son who was high priest in heaven.

(d) *Sacrifices in Heaven.* Since the heavenly archetype functions just as its earthly imitation, it seemed reasonable for the heavenly high priest to offer sacrifices in heaven (Heb 8:3-4). These **sacrifices,** of course, must be better than their earthly counterparts, but their function is to cleanse **the heavenly things** (Heb 9:23).[2]

---

[1] Procopius, *Buildings* 5:6.

[2] W. L. Moran, “The Creation of Man in Atrahasis I 192-248,” *BASOR* 200 (1970):50, quoted the following poem attributed to the god Enki:

Scholars have had trouble with these passages, because Christ's "once for all" **sacrifice** on earth was thought to make all other sacrifices unnecessary. It also seems a little surprising to think of heaven as a place where there would be sin and defilement that needed **cleansing**. The author of Hebrews, however, found no difficulty with this. For him, heaven and the holy of holies were very close together. God's presence and his angels were in both. From the holy of holies the smoke carried the incense from the sacrifices directly to heaven, where there were also a holy of holies, **sacrifices,** and angels.

When Jesus, as the **heavenly** high priest, passed through the curtain into the holy of holies, which was like **heaven,** he not only offered a **sacrifice**, but he was himself the **sacrifice** (Heb 9:12). Just as other **sacrifices** were taken to **heaven** through the pillar of fire and smoke, and just as the man of God went up through the column of smoke to heaven before the eyes of Manoah and his wife (Judges 13:20), so also Jesus was the sacrifice that **went through the heavens** (Heb 4:14) with the column of smoke in **the holy of holies**. Such imagery is consistent with the Near Eastern concept of the relationship of heaven to earth, columns of smoke and fire, temples and high places, heavenly archetypes and earthly counterparts, and the specially holy places that link heaven to earth. A better understanding of the Near Easterner's concept of **heaven** in relationship to the temple is important for understanding the imagery related to the temple, the priesthood, and heaven, particularly in Hebrews and the Book of Revelation.

Mount Ophel was a sizeable hill to the north. The fill from Mount Zion was used to fill in the valley between the two mountains (War 5:139). Mount Ophel was the situation west of the Gihon spring where Solomon's temple was constructed. In David's day Herod's tall walls, north of Mount Ophel, that surround Herod's city did not exist, but they were needed by the Romans for the same purpose the Syrian Greeks used the Akra years before, as a military base from which they could control David's holy city to the south.

Ain Gihon, which is now called the Spring of Siloam, was outside the city walls, but there was a canal that brought the water into the city. When Sennacherib and his army of thousands of Assyrian soldiers were lined up on Mount Scopus, they had to get their water from the spring of Gihon. Sennacherib threatened to destroy the entire City of David with all of its inhabitants, but Isaiah told Hezekiah not to worry. The next day these problems would all be gone. The next day, just as Isaiah promised, 185,000 Assyrian soldiers were dead. Hezekiah prayed that this would happen. Isaiah knew in advance that it would. Isaiah was involved in the military and intelligence movements of the nation. All the Jews had to do was poison the water at the spring and keep the local Jews away. Isaiah apparently knew that it was planned. The Assyrians had no other water source. The Bible does not tell that this was done, but the results imply this possibility.

On the new-moon, seventh and fifteenth days
A purification let me institute--a bath.
The leader-god let them slaughter, then
Let the gods purify themselves by immersion."

CHAPTER TEN

TEXT

10:1 For the law, having a shadow of the good things to come, not the image itself of
the things, every year, by means of the same [kinds of] sacrifices which they offer
continually, is never able to perfect those who sacrifice. 2 Otherwise, [the sacrifices]
would have stopped being offered, would they not? Because the worshipers, once
they have been cleansed, have no longer any consciousness of crimes, 3 but [as it is
they are being offered] every year with [the] same remembrance of crimes, 4 for the
blood of bulls and goats is not able to remove crimes.

COMMENTARY

10:1 *A shadow of the good things to come.* According to Plato, human beings are like a person in a cave who can learn of the world outside of the cave only by the **shadows** that pass by the door of the cave. The **shadow** does not disclose the reality of the object outside of the cave, but it indicates that there is a real object there and that the object is positioned between the light and the viewer. The author of Hebrews said that **the law** has similar limitations. It **has** only **the shadow of the good things to come. It is never able to perfect those who sacrifice.** Believers offer sacrifices for the purpose of having all of their offenses annulled, but they never are completely cancelled. To be perfect the believer had to be innocent of all crimes. All the fines had to be paid or pardoned. The author of Hebrews, however, had a different perspective from that of Plato. He did not think he was locked in a cave with the darkness behind him. Instead, like other Semites, he thought of the future as that which was behind him. It could not be seen, but the past was in front of him and therefore was known. He thought the future was bright, but unseen and therefore unknown. It promised **good things.** The light of the future was behind him and cast a shadow on the past, which included the law.

The Jerusalem priests were earlier reported as serving only as **a pattern and shadow of the heavenly things** (Heb 8.5). This **pattern and shadow** was Herod's temple--the temple made with hands. It was already there in the present, but it was not the heavenly temple. The heavenly temple would be in the future, and its shadow fell on Herod's temple, in the present. In the only other use of the word **shadow** (*skee-áhn,* σκιάν, Heb 8:5) the author seems to have the same temple in mind. Here the author says **the law has a shadow of the good things to come. The good things to come** would seem to be the heavenly things mentioned in Heb 8:5. **The image** (*ay-kóhn,* ἐικών) does not seem to be in the same category as **shadow** (Heb 8:4-5), **symbol** (Heb 8:4-5; 9:23), and **antitype** (Heb 9:24). The **image** is the real object which casts the **shadow** that **the law has**. The same is true of **the things** of which **the law has**, not the **image itself. The things** are evidently heavenly **things** (Heb 8:5). The author would agree with Paul that **the law** was not completely out of the picture, but it has limitations.

It was not against **the promises of God** (Gal 3:21); rather **the law was our schoolmaster** (*pai-dah-gaw-gáws,* παιδαγογός) which would lead us **to Christ** (Gal 3:24), but it was not able to give life (Gal 3:21). Or, as the author of Hebrews put it, **the law is never able to perfect those who sacrifice**. The author used the word **perfect** in close association with sacrifice, as if a sacrifice that successfully removes crime also **perfects** or makes **perfect**. Thus Jesus became **perfect** through the **suffering** of his **sacrifice** (Heb 2:10); he learned obedience and was made **perfect** through his **sacrifice** (Heb 5:7-9); he was made **perfect** for **the age** because he had offered himself (Heb 7:27-28). Those who were **perfect** were those who were free from any guilt or blame for legal infringement.

The Aaronic priests were inadequate, however, since their gifts and sacrifices did not **perfect the consciences** (Heb 9:9). The author evidently believed that once a crime had been atoned and cancelled, it would be put out of the believer's mind. **The conscience** existed only to keep the believer from forgetting some crime he or she had committed, and for which no fine had been paid and no reconciliation had been made. Once all crimes were punished **the conscience** would be **perfected.**

It is not certain what disturbed the **consciences** of the Jews associated with the author. They were rigorous, monastic Jews. Some Jews of this character did not trust the temple or the priests. Many sacrifices were made there for people's crimes, but who could know whether or not they had been effective? Jesus' sacrifice, however, was not made in Herod's temple, so that faithful Jews could know that it had been effective, and the recipients of that benefit could have clear consciences.

If the offering of the priests who functioned in Herod's temple had been effective, both the priest and the people affected by the service should be **without crime** (Heb 4:14-15; 9:28). The facts were, however, that the kingdom had not come. The liturgy employed at the temple did not work. Every year the same routine was employed, and every year things continued just as if the technique had not been employed. It was obviously a failure. The routine was employed **continually** (*ace taw dee-aye-neh-káce,* εἰς τὸ διηνεκῆς). That means it was followed at scheduled intervals, without interruption. "The same [kinds] of sacrifices" "every year" are goats for people and bulls for the high priests.

[2]*Have no longer any consciousness of crimes.* **Otherwise** is a free translation of *eh-páy* (ἐπεί), "since," "because," or "when," that recognizes its use here in an elliptical contrary-to-fact condition (cf. 9:26). The rhetorical question emphasizes the point that sacrifices would not be continued if there was no need for them: i.e., if they were completely effectual they would not need to be repeated. This text is just a repetition and elaboration of Heb 9:9. There the author said directly that the Aaronic priests offered **sacrifices** that were not able to **perfect** the **consciences** of the worshipers. Here he reasoned that the continuation of sacrifice proves this. They perform the same liturgy every year, because it had failed to work the year before. If they had really b**een cleansed once**, then their guilt would be removed, they would **have no longer any consciousness of crimes,** and the promises of Abraham would have been fulfilled.

The author of Jubilees did not feel that way about the Day of Atonement. He said this day was established so that Hebrews could remember the crimes they had committed against Joseph and grieve for them as they should. They also should grieve for their own crimes which they had committed that year and have them **cleansed** (Jub 34:18-19). This seems more reasonable, but it did not convince the author of Hebrews. With his severe demand for crimeless ethics, he evidently assumed that if the Day of Atonement had really been effective, Israel would be free from her crimes and the kingdom would have come. Once Israel's crime was removed, of course, it would continue to be free from crime. Why should Israel want to commit crimes again? Crimes were settled out of court so that they would not have to reappear on the Day of Judgment.

The idea of a Kingdom of God without crime, however, was not a unique idea of the author's. John and Jesus both preached repentance in preparation for the kingdom. The argument Jesus had with the Pharisees was not that Jesus was more liberal and willing to allow criminals to repent and prepare for life in a righteous kingdom whereas the Pharisees would exclude tax collectors and criminals at the outset. They argued about the ethic required before the kingdom came. Jesus said it should be like that of a fisherman bringing in the net. He first included all that came into his net; then he selected the good fish that had scales and fins and discarded the rest (Matt 13:47-48). He also used the analogy of the farmer who found weeds in his field. He let them grow until harvest; then he burned the weeds and gathered the wheat into his granary (Matt 13:24-30).

The generosity ceased when harvest came or the net was drawn in. Only good wheat and good fish were kept. According to the seer, the redeemed would all be celibate (Rev 14:3-4), and those who entered the holy city would be those who had washed their robes (Rev 22:14). In the same way, there was evidently a very wide belief among Jews that the Kingdom of God was only for the righteous. The author of Hebrews subscribed to this ethic of a country free from crime. He urged his readers not to commit any crimes, and he criticized the effectiveness of the priestly methods for canceling crime. They just had not worked. Like Amos, Hosea, and Isaiah, the author of Hebrews insisted that liturgical techniques would not substitute for righteous behavior.

Jeremiah had promised that God would punish the kings of Assyria and Babylon for taking Jews and Israelites captive, and God would restore his people to the Promised Land. In that day people would look all over Judah and Israel for crime, but they would not find any (Jer 50:18-20). Zechariah visualized all the wickedness of the Promised Land being forced into a large pail with a heavy lid made of lead to keep it there. Then two women with wings picked up the pail and carried it to Babylon, so that Babylon would be indebted by this amount of crime, and the Promised Land would be free from crime (Zech 5:5-11). Zechariah thought it would be nice if Israel's enemies would be forced to pay for all of Israel's crimes, and Israel itself would escape without any of the punishment it deserved.

There is a tradition that when the Israelites crossed the Jordan to enter the Promised Land, the land and the Israelites would be cleansed from crimes, guilt, and defilement. Then crime would be no more (Jub 50:5; also 4Ezra 6:25-28). Second Isaiah promised that the land would be restored, because Jews had paid double for all of their crimes, according to the rules of Sabbath and Jubilee release.

Jews believed that they had a chance every year to rid the land of its crime so that the land might be restored. That was on the Day of Atonement. If every Jew repented of his or her crimes and became reconciled to every other Jew and brought the appropriate crime offerings to the temple on the Day of Atonement to pay for the respective fines, then the land would be restored. The only way Jews had of learning whether or not the Day of Atonement had been effective was to watch and see if the land was restored after the Day of Atonement. This had happened in 164 BIA. when, just after the Day of Atonement, Judas fought the famous Battle of Beth-horon, which was the turning point of the Hasmonean War with the Syrian Greeks. Judas won the battle; the Greek general was killed; the temple was cleansed; and Hanukkah was instituted. In fewer than 20 years the land was free from foreign rule.

The author of Hebrews thought the very next Day of Atonement would be the one that allowed the land to be returned, because of the sacrifice of Jesus.

3-4 *The blood of bulls and goats.* **Every year** the same kinds of sacrifices were offered in the same way **with [the] same remembrance of crimes**. Jews had been going through the liturgical forms of the Day of Atonement ever since Pompey entered the temple in 63 BIA, but the Romans had not been evicted, and the land had not been restored. After all these years of experimenting with this method, it was clear to the author that the method was ineffective. Blood is necessary for forgiveness of crimes (Heb 9:22), but **the blood of bulls and goats** used on the Day of Atonement was **not able to remove crimes**.

TEXT

Hebrews	First Testament
5 Therefore, coming into the world, he says:	
Sacrifice and offering you did not desire. A body you furnished me; 6 **in whole burnt offerings and crime offerings you took no** pleasure. 7 **Then I said: "Look! I have arrived. In a division of [the] book it is written about me**: '[I have arrived] **to do your will, God.**'"	LXX Ps 39:7-9 **Sacrifice and offering you did not desire. A body you furnished me; whole burnt offerings and crime offerings you did not** request. **Then I said, "Look! I have arrived. In a division of [the] book it is written about me:** 'I wanted **to do your will**, My **God.'"**

8 Above it says, **sacrifices and offerings**, both **whole burnt offerings and crime offerings, you did not** desire nor did you **take delight** [in them], which things are offered according to the law. 9 **Then**, it said, **Look! I have arrived to do your will**. He removes the first in order that he might establish the second. 10 In which **will** we are being sanctified through the **offering** of [the] **body** of Jesus Christ, once for all.

COMMENTARY

5-6 *Sacrifice and offering you did not desire.* The text quoted is Ps 39 [40]:7-9, according to the LXX with some variants. Some LXX texts read with the MT *oh-teé-ah* (ὠτία) "an ear." The author followed the texts (*BSA*) which read *sóh-mah* (σῶμα) "body," because that suited his purpose, even if he knew the other reading. The Pentateuch commanded that sacrifices be offered, but the Psalm, which came later, claimed that the Lord **did not desire sacrifice and offering**, therefore the law was out of date, just as Ps 95 took precedence over the statement that Joshua led the people into their promised **rest**, the promise of a priesthood **for the age** in Ps 110 took precedence over the promises in Num and Exod, and the new contract promised in Jeremiah made the old contract recorded in the Pentateuch obsolete. In the author's judgment the Pentateuch was **obsolete, out of date, almost gone** (Heb 8:13). He used later Psalms and prophecies to supersede the Pentateuch. As Hebrews used the text, the **body** "furnished" was the **body** of Jesus which was given as a sacrifice to replace the **sacrifice and offering** which the Aaronic priests had been offering.

Whole burnt offerings were offerings of animals that were completely burned, not just roasted and eaten by the worshipers and priests. For **crime offerings** the author followed the LXX and read **concerning crime** (*peh-reé hah-mahr-teé-as,* περὶ ἁμαρτίας) as a translation of the Hebrew *khah-tah-áh,* חטאה (crime), which seems to be a copying error for *khah-táht,* חטאת (crime offering). In a listing of various kinds of offerings, a "crime offering" should be expected which is an offering concerning crime. For the LXX (*áy-tay-sahs* ᾔτησας), "You requested," the author of Hebrews has *yoo-dawk-áy-sahs* (εὐδόκησας), **in which you took pleasure.**

7*Then I said: "Look! I have arrived."* The LXX reads, "I desired (*eh-boo-láy-then,* ἐβουλήθην) to do your will, my God." Hebrews omitted the pronoun **my** and the verb "I wanted." By omitting this verb, the finite verb understood to accompany the infinitive would be **I have come**. This suited the author's needs, because he was emphasizing Jesus' **arrival** into the world (Heb 10:5) to replace the **sacrifices** prescribed in the Pentateuch. bYeb 77a interpreted this Psalm to refer to David who had come.

8*Which things are offered according to the law*. The author's dependence upon the LXX is apparent. He understood **sacrifices and offerings** to be exactly the same as "whole burnt **offerings** and crime **offerings**." The Hebrew for offering is *meén-khah* (מנחה), usually a grain **offering.** A crime offering is some type of animal or bird. The author's step-by-step logic is so consistent that it can be predicted. He did not omit a single point. First, he gave his version of the Psalm which contradicts the Pentateuch. Then he called attention to that fact. The next step shows how Jesus fitted the picture perfectly.

9-10*He removes the first in order that he might establish the second.* **The first** which he (the Lord or the Holy Spirit) **removes** is **the law** (Heb 10:8) which he repudiated in the Psalm, thus making the law invalid. He did this **in order that he might establish the second**, which is not the Psalm, but the testimony in the Psalm that, according to the author, Jesus had come to do God's will. The **all** which the author interpreted midrashically was God's will mentioned in the Psalm he quoted. **Sanctified** means "holy," "cleansed from crime," "ritually pure." The author used the word **perfect** to describe the condition of the believer for whom atonement had been made through sacrifice. He seems to use the word **sanctified** here to mean **made perfect**, because those who **are being sanctified** are those who have had all of their crimes atoned and are the recipients of the benefits of Christ's sacrifice. It also refers back to Heb 10:1 where the author noted that the law was never able to **perfect** those who sacrifice.

TEXT

11On the other hand, every priest stands every day ministering and is **offering** the
same [kinds of] **sacrifices** many times; these are never able to remove crimes; 12but
he, on the other hand, having offered one **sacrifice** on behalf of crimes,

Hebrews	First Testament
	Ps 110:1 Yehowah said to my lord,
sat down at the **right hand** of God to perpetuity 13 [and] continues to wait until	**sit at** my **right hand**
his enemies are placed [as] a footstool for his feet.	**I place your enemies [as] a footstool for his feet.**
For by means of one offering he perfected to perpetuity those who are being sanctified. 15 The Holy Spirit also witnesses for us, following the saying,	
16 "**This is the contract which I will contract** to them **after those days," says the Lord.** "After **[I] have placed my law** within them, **and on their minds I will write them**;	Jer 31:33 "**This is the contract which I will contract** with the house of Israel, **after those days," says the Lord. "I will place my laws on their** hearts **and on their minds I will write them**. . .
17 **their crimes**, and their lawless deeds **I will no longer remember**."	34 I will forgive their iniquities **I will no longer remember their**
18 Wherever [there is] forgiveness of these, [there is] no longer an offering for **crimes.**	**crimes**."

COMMENTARY

11 *These are never able to remove crimes*. This verse repeats much of Heb 10:1-4: **every day / every year** (Heb 10:1); **offering / they offer** (Heb 10:1); **the same sacrifices / the same [kinds of] sacrifices** (Heb 10:l); **never able to remove crimes / not able to remove crimes** (Heb 10:4). If these rituals had been effective, if these priests had been valid, if this had been a valid temple of the Lord, the kingdom would have come before now. Their failure proves their ineffectiveness, but this was Herod's temple. These priests were appointed by Romans. This was a temple made with hands.

12-13 *His enemies are placed [as] a foot-stool*. Heb 10:12 also repeats some of the same words as Heb 10:1, but with a contrasting significance: instead of **the same kinds of sacrifices** (Heb 10:1), Heb 10:12 has **one sacrifice**; instead of meaningless sacrifices being offered **continually**, Jesus, as God's Son, **sat down at the right hand** of God to perpetuity. This does not mean he is continually sitting down, but that he will never be removed from his position of honor at God's **right hand**. Because the main text was Ps 110, it was necessary to remind the listener, from time to time, that all of his arguments return to support that one text.

At the beginning the author introduced the Son as one who **"sat down at the right hand** of the Majesty" (Heb 1:3), and the Lord promised to make his enemies his **footstool** (Heb 1:13). The Lord was the mighty judge. People appeared before him on their knees. He had no one beside him until Jesus approached him. At that time God recognized him as the son and invited him—not only to sit—but to sit in the place of honor next to him, while the Lord granted him everything he wanted. Levitical priests served the altar standing (2Chron 29:11; Ezek 44:15; Ant 13:372), whereas Jesus fulfilled his ministry in heaven, seated at the right hand of God.

Earlier the Son was introduced as the high priest who would "**sit down at the right hand** of the throne of Majesty" (Heb 8:1). Here the Son was shown to be an **offering** for crimes (also Heb 10:18). Since Jesus had **offered** himself as the one **perfect sacrifice** and had gone through the heavens, the first part of the promise in the Psalm had been fulfilled. Jesus had then only to wait **until his enemies** are placed **[as] a footstool for his feet**. Jesus' waiting is comparable to that of those who **await him for salvation** (Heb 9:28). This was not an expectation that they would have to wait two or three thousand years, let alone until the end of time or history, as Weiss and others suppose.[1] The author was confident that this would happen shortly.

[14]*He perfected to perpetuity those who are being sanctified.* In a summary fashion the author here repeated terms used before:

1) **offering** (see Heb 10:1, 5, 10, 11, 18) is a central word for this unit. Jesus
2) **perfected** the worshiper as the Roman-appointed priests could not (Heb 9:9; 10:1), but here the worshipers are called
3) **sanctified** (Heb 2:11; 10:10) 4) **to perpetuity** (Heb 10:1, 12).

[15]*The Holy Spirit also witnesses for us.* The author regularly acknowledged that **the Holy Spirit** or God was responsible for the composition of the Scriptures, even though he attributed the Pentateuch to Moses and the Psalms to David. He evidently understood David and Moses to be legal agents of God. They always spoke and wrote in the name of the principal, in behalf of the principal, and at the responsibility of the principal. Therefore, God and the Holy Spirit get credit for what they did.

[16-17]*This is the contract which I will contract [to them].* For the variants between the author's use of Jer 31 [38]:33-34 here and in verse Heb 8:10, see Commentary on Heb 8:10. This variation demonstrates the author's willingness to paraphrase a text. The author's return to the Jeremiah passage had two purposes:

(a) It further emphasized the author's point that effective **sacrifice**, based on an effective **contract** and law, would remove all consciousness of crime, **sanctify** the people completely, and make all further **sacrifice** unnecessary. His logic above had shown how he came to this conclusion. Now he could clinch his argument with the text that promised that the **new contract** which God would provide was going to achieve precisely that.

(b) It was a good text on which the author could base his exhortation which was to follow. The freedom from crime which Jeremiah promised was the very freedom from crime that the author demanded.

Heb 10:16, following Jer 31:34 is a nicely constructed chiasm. This is a literary form, often in parallel construction, in which the second line contains nearly the same message as the first line, but it is organized backwards so that verbs and nouns

[1] H. F. Weiss, *Der Brief an die Hebräer* (Göttingen: Vandenhoeck & Ruprecht, 1991), p. 513.

can be connected to form an X, called in Greek a *chi.* Therefore this form is called a chiasm.

I have *placed* my law		on *their hearts*,
	X	
and on *their minds*		I will *write* them

[18]*Wherever [there is] forgiveness of these.* **These** refers to the crimes and lawless acts mentioned just above. With the new **contract** comes the promise of **forgiveness.**

There is no longer an offering for crimes. The purpose of **sacrifices** is to bribe God into canceling the punishment designed against the **crimes** that have been committed, without having to pay the appropriate fines. When these fines have all been paid, there is no longer a need for **sacrifices**. So the author said that when **crimes** have been **forgiven, there is no longer** any need for a Day of Atonement or any kind of **sacrifices** to remove **crime.** Not only is there no further need for **sacrifices.** There are no more valid **sacrifices** to **offer.** Jesus' **sacrifice** was the only one that was valid, and he had already been **sacrificed.** This concludes the argument with which the discussion began (Heb 10:1-2).

Summary. The main topic of this unit was **offerings** or **sacrifices,** and the inclusion was composed of the words **offer/offering** (Heb 10:1-18). Given the author's presuppositions, his logic is watertight. He assumed that freedom from guilt was both possible and the will of God. God's will would certainly be realized. The **sacrifices** prescribed by the law had not been effective. Therefore God must have a different plan. That plan is not found in the Pentateuch, but in the Psalms and the prophets. These prohibit the **sacrifices** prescribed by the Pentateuch and promise a new **contract** that will remove crimes effectively and permanently.

This required the **sacrifice** of a **body** instead of the levitical offerings. This has been provided once for all by Jesus, who has been **exalted into the heavens** where he is seated **at the right hand** of God. The **new contract** is now in effect; those who believe and are **sanctified** or made **perfect** by Jesus' **sacrifice** have been effectively and permanently **cleansed** from crime, which means that the levitical **offerings** are **no longer** needed. Neither is the law which prescribed them. Although the concept of a **new contract** is found in other NT literature (Luke 22:20; 1Cor 11:25; 2Cor3:6), it is nowhere so prominent as in Heb (Heb 7:22; 8:6-10; 9:4-20; 10:16-29; 12:24).

This provides the conclusion to the doctrinal portion of a very important argument presented by the author (Heb 7:1-10, 18). Jesus is the true **high priest** after the **order of Melchizedek**; he belongs to a superior priesthood, has a superior **sacrifice,** functions in a superior **temple,** offers a more effective **forgiveness**, and introduces a superior **contract.** The **contract**, the **sacrifice,** the anointing, and the atonement for which Jesus was responsible was called **perfect**, which means that it was adequate, complete, fulfilled, effective. Jesus was the **perfect high priest** because he fulfilled the required liturgy to make him totally qualified.

For none of these is a son of David theology important. The author regularly related his theological deductions to the ethical demands of Christians. Therefore, this whole discussion would not be complete without the exhortation that follows (Heb 10:19-39).

TEXT

[19]Therefore, brothers, since we have [the] boldness [necessary] for entering the holy [precincts] by means of the blood of Jesus, [20]which way he inaugurated for us [that is] new and living, through the curtain--that is, his flesh-- [21]and [since we have] a great priest over the house of God, [22]let us approach [the altar] with a true heart in fullness of faith, [our] hearts sprinkled [clean] from evil conscience and [our] body washed with clean water, [and] [23]let us hold fast unmoved the confession of hope, for the one who has promised is faithful. [24]Let us consider [how we] might stimulate one another for love and good works, [25]not giving up meeting together (as some have been doing), but encouraging [one another], even the more so since you see the day drawing near.

COMMENTARY

Lane called attention to the similarity in sequence between Heb 5:11-6:12 and 10:19-25.

> 5:11-6:3//10:19-25: Reminder of the situation of the community.
> 6:4-8//10:26-31:Warning against apostasy.
> 6:9-10//10:32-34:Encouragement on the basis of earlier deeds.
> 6:11-12//10:35-39:Appeal directed toward the future.[1]

[19]*Therefore, brothers, since we have [the] boldness.* The author here was speaking to a group of monks who had the priestly authority to enter the holy of holies. In the days of the temple women were never admitted into the holy of holies. Even men who were not priests were not admitted anywhere except in the court outside the priestly area. To translate this "**brothers** and sisters," as Attridge[2] has done is not only a faulty translation of the words involved, but it also completely distorts the concept of monasticism and the rules of temple services. It is completely out of character for the situation involved. The author was addressing only **brothers**, as the text says and means. Attridge has failed to understand

1) the exact meaning of the word **brothers**,
2) the monastic setting of Heb 1-12, and
3) temple liturgy.

The word translated **boldness** is *pah-ray-seé-ah* (παρρησία), which is from *pas* (πας-"all") and *ráy-sees* (ῥῆσις-"speaking"), and means freedom of speech, the right to speak openly. It was used more widely to mean "without fear," "freedom of action," "outspokenness," or "power" (see Commentary on Heb 4:16). Nadab and Abihu were consumed with fire while **offering** incense (Lev 10:2). On the Day of Atonement when the **high priest** entered the **holy of holies** to **offer** incense, he did not prolong his prayer, lest all Israel become terrified (mYoma 5:1). When Zechariah entered the **holy of holies** to **offer** incense, he was slow in returning, and

---

[1] W. L. Lane, *Hebrews 1-8* (Dallas: Word Books, c1991), p. 38.

[2] H. W. Attridge, *The Epistle to the Hebrews* (Philadelphia: Fortress Press, c1989), throughout the book.

the people were astonished and afraid (Luke 1:21). Christian monks, however, **by means of the blood of Jesus** had no need to fear **the holy [precincts]** but entered with **boldness**.

It was a privilege and an honor to have any position in the Lord's house. Only the **high priest** entered **the holy of holies**, and only priests entered the room adjacent to it, and then only under conditions of levitical purity. No one could stand in his **holy** place who did not have **clean hands and a pure heart** (Ps 24:3-4). The Levite was glad for even such a humble position as a guard at the door in the Lord's house (Ps 84:11).[1] Priests loved dwelling **in the Lord's house** (Ps 26:8). Some priests were so fortunate as to have tenure there, to dwell there all the days of their lives, **to gaze upon the beauty of the Lord and to inquire in his sanctuary** (Ps 27:4). One was confident that **goodness and mercy** would follow him **all the days of** his **life**, and he would **dwell in the house of the Lord** as long as his days lasted (Ps 23:6).

A person would have to have that kind of position of authority to **have [the] boldness [necessary] for entering the holy [precincts]**. This **boldness** is an attitude one might expect in a religion centered around a chosen or an elect people, which considers itself superior to others in the Lord's eyes. Jews in Babylon were **promised** that they could return to Israel, but not in haste or flight. Instead of being refugees, they would be exalted and prosperous (Isa 52:12-13). The author of Hebrews called attention to the **boldness** that came as a privilege to Christian monks because of their status (Heb 3:6; 4:16; 10:19, 35). The phrase **[necessary] for entering** is a rather free translation of *áys-tayn ays-aw-dawn* (ἐις τὴν εἴσοδον), literally, **into the entrance. By means of the blood of Jesus** (*ehn toh haí-mah-tee,* ἐν τῷ αἵματι) is rendered as dative of means, assuming the *ehn* (ἐν) to be a Semitism, reflecting the Hebrew *buh* (ב), "in," "with," "by means of," "on the condition," "on account of," or "through."

[20]*Which way he inaugurated.* The **way** mentioned here is the same as that in Heb 9:8**, the way of the holy [precincts]**. This is the path through **the holy** into **the holy of holies**. The word rendered **inaugurated** is *ehn-eh-kaín-ee-sehn* (ἐνεκαίνισεν), "made new," "innovated," or "newly dedicated." This is a pregnant word in Jewish and Christian eschatology. When Saul was made king, Samuel and the people went to Gilgal to establish anew the *kingdom (oo-neh-khah-desh shahm hah meh-loo-kháh,* ונחדש שם המלוכה) (1Sam 11:14-15). When Second Isaiah promised that the Lord would do something new (*khah-dash-áh,* חדשה) he meant that the Lord would reestablish the **Promised** Land (Isa 43:19; also PesikR 284a; 31:146b). Rabbis were convinced that the Lord would renew the age (*luh khahd-tah ah-lah-máh,* לחדתא עלמא) for the righteous (TargJon Jer 23:23; TargOnq Deut 32:23; see also Tanhuma *Noah* 12, 19a).

Second Baruch promised that Zion would be **renewed** in glory (*renovari in gloria*) (2Bar 32:4). He did not say that Herod's temple would be rebuilt. That which Jesus **inaugurated** was a new access to **the holy [precincts]** which was also associated with the new **age. New** (*práws-phah-tawn,* πρόσφατον) is a word that means **freshly slaughtered** and has taken on the broader meaning of "fresh," "new," or "recent" (see Num 6:3; Deut 24:5[7]; 32:17; Ps 81:9; Acts 18:2). **New and living** meant something associated with the **new age**, under the **new contract,** where **life** was possible.

[1] Buchanan, "The Courts of the Lord," *VT* 6 (1966):231.

Leithart has suggested that this **renewal** came as a result of baptism, similar to the ceremony by which priests were ordained (Exod 29; Lev 8-9). Therefore all Christians have become priests through baptism and have access to the holy of holies in the temple, unimpeded by curtains. There are clues in the text that encourage conclusions such as this. There is now an entrance and a **living way** into the holy of holies (Heb 10:19-20). The author reported that the audience was composed of those who had been sprinkled and washed (Heb 10:22). Therefore all of these points come together because of the sprinkling and washing that means baptism for admission into the new contract community.[1]

The author, however, was speaking to a group of monks. In a monastery members were washed and bathed before every meal, so that they were almost always washed and sprinkled clean. Some monastic communities may even have been composed only of priests, however they achieved that status. They may have been born sons of Zadok, for example, rather than ordained into that class. Even if they became priests through some kind of ceremony, that does not mean all Christians from every sect, or all people of the world who are baptized, become priests.

The curtain was that which separated **the holy** from **the holy of holies** in the temple. There was also a curtain that separated **the holy** from the court. There is a rather complex metaphorical imagery used here. Since Jesus was both the **high priest** and the **offering**, he both brought the gift for the people's **cleansing** into **the holy of holies** where the Lord was present and was himself the gift through which the people were **cleansed. The way** which went **through the curtain** into **the holy of holies** was the gift which Jesus **offered, his flesh.** Another less likely interpretation would be to consider **the curtain** to be **the curtain of his flesh** (*tays sahr-káws,* τῆς σάρκος) through which the believer must go to enter the holy of holies. The allegorical interpretation, **that is, his flesh**, seems like a later gloss, similar to the gloss **that is, not of this creation** (Heb 9:11).

[21]*A great priest over the house of God.* **A great priest over the house of God** is used as if it were a quotation from Scripture, but there is no FT passage that qualifies it as it is. There is a reference to **the great priest** (*haw hee-eh-roós haw méh-gahs,* ὁ Ἱερεὺς ὁ μέγας) in Lev 21:10 who was instructed not to go out of the sanctuary (*ehk tohn hah-geé-ohn,* ἐκ τῶν ἁγίων) (Lev 21:12), but no mention is made of the house of God. A closer parallel is the reference to **Jesus . . . the great priest** (*too hee-eh-roó too meh-gáh-loo,* τοῦ Ἱερέως τοῦ μεγάλου) who was associated with the royal messiah, *Ah-nah-taw-lay,* Ανατολή, (Rising). The latter would build **the house of the Lord** (Zech 6:11-12). The author of Hebrews, however, showed no interest in a two-messiah doctrine or a son-of-David messiah. For that reason he seems to have taken the parts of this messianic passage that could apply to a messiah who was also a high priest and applied them to Jesus.

[22]*With a true heart in fullness of faith.* The Psalmist said no one was permitted to stand in the Lord's holy place if he did not have **clean hands and a pure mind** (Ps 24:3-4). The author of Hebrews was even more demanding. Those who would **approach [the altar]** must have their **minds sprinkled [clean] from evil conscience** and their whole bodies **washed with clean water**. The author, however, suggested that all of the members of his audience might approach the altar. The high

---

[1] P. L. Leithart, "Womb of the World: Baptism and the Priesthood of the New Covenant in Hebrews 10:19-22," *JSNT*: 49-65.

priest was allowed to approach the altar, because he had first performed the correct rituals to **cleanse** himself from all **crimes** and defilement. Since Christian monks had the benefit of Christ having **cleansed** their **consciences,** obtained forgiveness for their **crimes**, and performed the proper ablutions, they were then prepared to move through **the way** that had been obstructed by **the holy** place and the curtains and see **the holy of holies** itself that had been kept from them up to then. All of the members of the monastery were as undefiled as the high priest on the Day of Atonement. They were all authorized priests who had the benefit of the perfect sacrifice. Therefore the way to the holy of holies was available to them. The curtains of separation were removed for them. They would all become **God's kingdom of priests and a holy nation** (Exod 19:6). The author's imagery is consistent with this sacrificial and liturgical context, and he told further how a Christian who wanted to have his mind sprinkled should go about it.

23*The confession of hope*. Having one's **mind sprinkled** meant that Christians should **hold fast unmoved the confession of hope** (cf. *béh-bai-aws kai áh-klee-naws* (βέβαιος καὶ ἄκλινος, Som 2:278). Those who had been legally **born again** into a new family corporation of Christ had **a living hope**. 1Pet told the new converts that they had been **born into an inheritance** that was **incorruptable, undefiled, and unfading, kept in heaven** for them (1Pet 1:3-4). Since it was **kept in heaven**, that meant that God was holding it for them. They were only obligated to **hold fast unmoved the confession of hope**.

The **hope** was the anticipation that the promise given to Abraham would be fulfilled in the days of the readers because of Jesus' sacrifice. The author had earlier urged his readers to **hold fast to the end** (Heb 3:6, 14). God was **the one who has promised**, and it was necessary to remind the readers again and again that God was **faithful** (Heb 6:10-12, 17-18), so that they would **hold fast . . . the confession of hope.**

24*Stimulate one another for love and good works.* **Love** was a much more stable word in Bible times than it is today. **Love** was a contractual term. When two people or nations made a legal agreement together, they became **lovers**. Hosea criticized Israel because it had so many **lovers**. These **lovers** were not sex partners. They were foreign nations with which Israel had formed international treaties dealing with military protection and trade policies. When a young man participated in a legal wedding ceremony in which he was the groom, he took vows that he would **love** the woman he was marrying. That meant he would provide for all of her needs, just as her father had done before the wedding. Since she had no legal rights, she was not asked to **love** her husband. Jews and Christians who joined monastic groups took vows of poverty, celibacy, and obedience. They agreed to **love** all of the other members as themselves. That meant they had to see that the emotional and physical needs of all other members were equally provided. Those who **loved** did good works.

The problem of **holding fast to the hope** was apparently a difficult one. The enthusiasm was waning. If **the hope** was to be maintained at all, some very practical efforts would have to be made to keep it alive. The author suggested that the Christians should make a concerted effort to show concern for each other's emotional, religious, social, and material needs, by stimulating **one another for love and good works** (see also Commentary on Heb 6:10). The community that kept itself busy caring for one another would have less time and inclination to become discouraged and grumble, as the exodus generation had done. Since Jesus had provided the perfect sacrifice required on the Day of Atonement for the forgiveness of crimes, it was incumbent on all Christians to fulfill the only other requirement for an effective Day of Atonement. They had to pay up their obligations to one another so that they would all be reconciled. This is precisely what the author exhorted them to do.

25 *You see the day drawing near.* Those scholars who have dismissed the obvious Semitic and Palestinian context of Hebrews hold that the author was oblivious of time. He thought only in the perpendicular, philosophical, Gnostic, mythical terms. The contrast was always between this world and heaven. The author of Hebrews, however, did not realize that, so he continued to write as if time marched on, day after day. **The day** that was **drawing near** was a **day** that could be recorded on a calendar. It would **happen in the future when the promises of Abraham would be fulfilled for God's chosen people.**

Some, who had lost **hope**, had given up regular attendance at congregational meetings. This was a certain way to lose the promise. Meeting together provided an opportunity for members to encourage one another, stimulate one another, and help each other to keep from becoming discouraged. This is in agreement with the counsel of R. Hillel: "Do not separate [yourself] from the congregation" (mAboth 2:5; see also Vis. 3:6, 2).

The longing for **the day** when atonement would be complete, when the enemy would be driven from the land, taxation removed, and Israel given a position of status among the nations under the leadership of her own king was a common Christian and Jewish eschatological expectation. **The day** was sometimes called **the day of the Lord** (Acts 2-20; 1Thess 5:2; 2Thess 2:2; 2Peter 3:10), **that day** (Matt 7:22; Mark 13:32; Luke 10:12; 1:31; 1Thess 5:4, 2Thess 1:10, 18; 4:8), **the day of God** (2Peter 3:12),**the day (or days) of the Son of man** (Luke 17:26, 30; John 8:56), **the day of Christ (Jesus Christ or Lord Jesus**) (1Cor 1:8, 5:5; 2Cor 1:14; Phil 1:6, 10; 2:16), **the great day** (Jude 6; Rev 6:17; 16:14), and **the day of judgment** (Matt 10:15, 11:22, 24, 1Peter 2:9; 3:7; 1John 4:17; Rom 2:16). In order to keep up their hope, it was necessary for Christians to remind one another that the time of waiting was just about over; **the day** was **drawing near** (see also Rom 13:12, Philip 4:5; James 5:8; 1Pet 4:7).

Summary. On the basis of the doctrinal teachings given, the author encouraged the readers to apply these insights to their own behavior. Given a new access to the holy of holies, they must take it and draw near to this formerly forbidden area. Like priests of antiquity, however, they must observe all of the necessary priestly rules for purity in so doing. To have pure hearts meant to hold fast to the **hope, stimulate one another**, keep up regular attendance at congregational gatherings and express their **love and good works** for one another. This they could do with the confidence that God is faithful and the time of waiting was about over. This unit is a summary exhortation, similar to Heb 4:14-16:[1]

Hebrews 4	Hebrews 10
a.**Since, then, we have a great high priest,**	a. Therefore . . .**since we have . . . a great priest** (19, 21)

[1] Comparison made earlier by C. Spicq and W. Nauch, "Zum Aufbau des Hebräerbriefs," *Judentum, Urchristentum-Kirche*, ed. W. Eltester (Berlin: A. Töpelmann, 1960), pp. 203-204.

b. [who] has gone through the heavens, (14)	b. . . .for entering the holy [precincts] . . .which way he inaugurated for us [that is] new and living, through the curtain (19, 20)
c. . . .Jesus the Son of God (14)	c. . . .by means of the blood Jesus (19),
d. **let us hold fast** **the confession** (4:14).	d. **let us hold fast** unmoved **the confession** of hope (23);
e. Then **let us approach** the throne of grace	e. **let us approach** [the altar] with a true heart in fullness of faith (22);
with **boldness** (16).	therefore, brothers, since we have [the] **boldness** [necessary] for entering the holy [precincts] . . . (19).

There is also a close parallel between the following two passages:

Hebrews 6	Hebrews 10
19 which **we have** as	19 Therefore, brothers, since **we have** [the] boldness
a secure and steadfast anchor of the soul and one that is **entering** into	[necessary] for **entering** the holy [precincts] by means of the blood of **Jesus**,
the innermost [area which is behind] **the curtain**, 20 where **Jesus entered** [as] a forerunner in our behalf, since he is a high priest for the age according to the order of Melchizedek.	20 which way he inaugurated for us [that is] new and living, through **the curtain**, that is, his flesh (cf. Heb 9:8).

TEXT

Hebrews	First Testament
26 For when we commit crime deliberately, after receiving the knowledge of **the truth**, there is no longer left a sacrifice for crimes, 27 but [the] expectation of judgment	LXX Isa 26:10 The impious is to be stopped; he does not learn the righteousness on the land; he does not practice **[the] truth**. Let him be expelled so that he may not see the glory of the Lord.
and fiery zeal about	LXX Isa 26:11 **Zeal** will take over an uneducated people, **and** now **fire**

to consume the opponents is something dreadful.	**has consumed the opponents**.
28 **Anyone [who]** has rejected the law of Moses **will die** without mercy **on the [testimony] of two or three witnesses**. 29 how much worse punishment, do you think, will he deserve, who	Deut 17:6 **Anyone who** breaks [the contract], **At the mouth of two or three witnesses he shall die**. *Num 35:30-31* Anyone who strikes someone **before witnesses will be killed**. They shall not take a ransom for a person who is guilty of murder. He shall surely be put to death.
1) trampled upon the Son of God, 2) considered **the blood of the contract** in which he was sanctified, defiled, (3) and depreciated the spirit of grace? 30 For we know the one who said, "**Vengeance** is mine; **I will pay back**; and again,	Exod 24:8 Moses took the blood, sprinkled it over the people, and said, "Look! **The blood of the contract** which Yehowah and has made with you, concerning all these matters." LXX Deut 32:35 On the day of **vengeance** **I will pay back**; for a time when their foot will stumble.
"**The Lord will judge his people**." 31 Falling into the hands of [the] God of life is dreadful.	Ps 135:14 **Yehowah will judge his people;** on his servants he will have compassion.

COMMENTARY

26 *For when we commit crime deliberately.* In every generation and in every nation the law courts deal more gently with damages and injuries that are accidental than those that are done with malice aforethought. When Nathan asked David about the proper legal judgment against a man who had many sheep, but instead stole his neighbor's only ewe lamb for a feast, David first quoted the law on stealing sheep—he should restore it fourfold (Exod 22:1). But because he showed no mercy, he should receive the punitive measure of a death sentence. This was an action with malice aforethought, a planned crime. When David learned that he was the criminal involved, however, he decided to mitigate the sentence (2Sam 12:1-13). When he did this he increased his **crime.** David was not the only judge in history to give himself or his family favorable treatment. From David's time until now, intended, planned **crimes** are more offensive than those that are done on the spur of the moment, even though done intentionally.

The author here reviewed a point he had made earlier in Heb 2:1, (Commentary on Heb 6:4-6), and planned to repeat again (Heb 12:17). This is one of the themes the author repeated effectively, weaving it throughout his message, picking it up again and again the way a great symphony repeats important musical themes expressively. The once-for-all nature of Christ's sacrifice is like a two-edged sword. On the one hand, it is so effective that it does not need to be repeated (Heb 7:27), but, on the other hand, it cannot be repeated, even if needed. There is no second repentance (Heb 6:4-8). It was customary in Israelite law to distinguish between the punishment inflicted upon a person who **committed crimes** unwittingly and one who **committed crimes** "deliberately." Hebrews made the same distinction. The word **truth** is from Isa 26:10 and there refers to the Lord's commandments. Similarly for Hebrews, those who had been instructed in **the knowledge of truth**, took their membership vows, and were baptized, were at that time forgiven for all the **crimes** they had **committed** earlier unwittingly, because they had **not received the knowledge of the truth**.

The **sacrifice** of Christ was adequate to cover even those unwitting **crimes,** but that was all it would cover. The sacrifice was completed. It could not be done over. Anyone who committed the kind of **crime** that would require excommunication after admission could not be readmitted. He had exhausted all the merits of Christ's suffering to cover his **crimes** for the first admission.[1] This was normal policy for strict Jewish and Christian sects. The Essenes seldom accepted a person who had once been excommunicated from the sect. For some this meant death from starvation, because they had taken vows that they would not eat food that was not approved by Essene administration.

27 *The expectation of judgment and fiery zeal.* Isa 26:11 comes from a context dealing with the righteous and the unrighteous in the land. After the Lord's commandments had been established in the land, the inhabitants were obligated to learn righteousness and observe it. There would be an end to those who were impious and did not learn righteousness, or, knowing, did not act according to **the truth**. They were to be removed so that they could no longer see the glory of the Lord. The Lord's hand had been raised, but the impious did not realize it, but when they would find out they would be ashamed. The Lord's zeal would take over an uninstructed people, and **fire** would **consume the opponents** (LXX Isa 26:9-11).

The author of Hebrews was also dealing with the righteous and the impious, but they were members of a group, all of whom had learned **the truth;** the impious turned against **the truth** they had learned, so they could expect the judgment which Isaiah **promised** would come upon the impious who did not learn righteousness. Since Isaiah had promised it, Christians must live in the **expectation of judgment** that was **promised,** and would occur on New Year's Day, just before the Day of Atonement. The author assured his readers that this would be **something dreadful.** A similar threat was made by 2Bar 48:39-40, also based on Isaiah 26:10:

> Because of this, a fire will devour their plans,
> and in flame the concerns of their hearts will be tested;
> for the Judge will come and will not delay,
> because each of the inhabitants of the land knew (*sciebat*)
> when he was committing iniquity.

---

[1] Heb 6:4-8; 10:26-31; 12:15-17. For Williamson's argument that the author considered only apostasy unpardonable, see R. Williamson, *Philo and the Epistle to the Hebrews* (Leiden: E.J. Brill, 1970), pp. 250-51, 261.

[28]*Will die without mercy*. The author had previously disparaged **the law of Moses** as being inadequate, based on inadequate **promises** and **contract.** Now he uses this evaluation as the first half of an *a fortiori* argument. Even that weak law could put a person to death without any hesitation, **on the [testimony] of two or three witnesses** (Deut 17:6).

[29]*How much worse punishment*? Since the Torah could require a death penalty for breaking the **contract**, and worshiping other gods, and thereby becoming apostates, the author reasoned, apostate Christians should receive a **much worse punishment**. The word translated "defiled" is *koí-naws* (κοίνος), **common**, and is usually associated with unclean things parties to the **contract** should not touch or eat. Thus Peter refused to eat food that was **common** or unclean (Acts 10:14). That which was not holy was **common** (Lev 10:10). Common means pagan, idolatrous, profane.

Rabbis said there could be no forgiveness for anyone who profaned holy things, despised the set feasts, nullified the contract of Abraham, or revealed secret meanings of the Torah which were not according to the *hah-lah-káh* (הלכה) (mAboth 3:11; see 1Macc 1:15). Most early Jewish and Christian sects had rules (*hah-lah-kóht*) which could be shared publicly, but they also had secret knowledge which only the members of the sect knew. This was called the *gnóh-sees* (γμῶσις), *dah-áht* (דעת), oral Torah (*torah sheh-béh-ahl-péh*, תורה שבעל פה), or mysteries of the Kingdom of God. Those learned in the secret rules were the **enlightened ones**.

The rules were private, and members took vows that they would never reveal these to outsiders. Such disclosure as this was considered sabotage, blasphemy, breaking **contract**, and other evils. Rabbis and the author of Hebrews agreed upon the right destiny for anyone so blasphemous as to **commit** any of these **crimes**. Like rabbis, the author of Hebrews abhorred such actions as defiling the sacred, depreciating that which they had once praised, rejecting the new **contract** into which they had once been admitted. Such people deserved more than excommunication. They would receive a **much worse punishment** from God. Jewett held,

> When one takes account of the background of this term **enlightened** in Hellenistic mystery religions and gnosticism, it appears likely that it would carry a connotation of apotheosis in the Lycus Valley.[1]

There might have been some type of gnosticism in the Lycus Valley. Even if there were, it would not mean that it was the same gnosticism as might be found in Hebrews. In neither case is it required that the gnosticism involved was related to Hellenistic mystery religions. Even if the gnosticism in the Lycus Valley were the same as the one associated with Hebrews, this would not imply that Hebrews originated in the Lycus Valley. The appearance of the conflict between light and darkness in the Dead Sea Scrolls and in the NT indicates that **enlightenment** was a normal term used frequently to refer to those who have been fully trained for membership into whatever sect was involved

[30-31]*Falling into the hands of the God of life is dreadful*. The expression rendered **the God of life** is usually translated "living God," as the Greek suggests, but the Hebrew use of this expression means **the God of life**, the God of **the contract** in which **life** is possible.

---

[1] R. Jewett, *Letter to Pilgrims* (New York: Pilgrim Press, c1981), p. 186.

Like Paul (Rom 12:19), the author quoted from a text that is no longer extant. The MT has **Vengeance is mine and recompense.** The Samaritan text reads **for the day of vengeance and recompense**; and the LXX has **In a day of vengeance, I will pay back**. The author quoted the first part of the Masoretic clause and the last part of the LXX saying, but, since Paul used the same formula, it is quite likely that there already existed a text just like the one quoted here. **Vengeance** is that which is inflicted upon the enemy as punishment, in which process the allies are vindicated. The word **judge** can mean to decide the person judged is guilty and punish him, or to **judge** him to be innocent and vindicate him.

In the Deuteronomic context the Lord's **people** were to be vindicated, but the author used the term in the negative sense (as in 1Enoch 38:3). Those of the Lord's people who became apostate would be judged and punished or paid back. **Falling into the hands of the God of life** means being caught by **the God of life** after **committing crimes.** This is like Adam being found after he had eaten the forbidden fruit (Gen 3:9-20). Bruce was embarrassed by the author's stern, unforgiving attitude and assumed he probably took for granted God's merciful and forgiving nature.[1] The author, however, is clear. Those who reject their faith do not receive God's mercy, but his wrath.

Summary. The word **dreadful** in Heb 10:27 and 31 marks the inclusion for this unit, and it also sets the tenor for the whole passage, which is generally threatening. The author quoted Hebrew Scripture passages which include severe warnings of punishment. His strongest argument was an *a fortiori* argument comparing the punishment dispensed by the law of Moses which was inferior to the still more severe punishment that would come to those who accepted the faith and then turned their backs to it. The author's exegesis of Isa 26:10-11 was very similar to that of 2Bar 48:39-40. The previous section consisted of exhortations; this unit gave the consequences for those who did not heed the exhortations.

TEXT

32Remember the earlier days in which, after you had become enlightened, you
endured a great trial of sufferings, 33sometimes being exhibited both for insults and
tribulations, and other times becoming sharers of those who were thus upset; 34for
you suffered with those in bonds, and you accepted with joy the confiscation of your
possessions, knowing that you yourselves have a better possession [that is] lasting.
35Therefore do not cast off your boldness which holds a great reward.

COMMENTARY

32*Remember the earlier days.* Historical allusions like this one and the long line of heroes listed throughout the history of Israel in Hebrews should create a problem for those who hold that the author thought only perpendicularly and had no real concept of time. **The earlier days** were evidently **earlier** in time than the current **days. The earlier days**, "The first **days,**" "the former **days**," after they **had become enlightened** were the days just after their admission into the community. Their enlightenment was their catechetical training prior to baptism (see Commentary on Heb 6:4).

[1] F. F. Bruce, *The Epistle to the Hebrews* (Grand Rapids: Eerdmans, 1964), pp. 263-64.

33*Being exhibited both for insults and tribulations.* **Sometimes . . . other times** (*toó-taw* (τοῦτο), . . . *toó-taw*. The Greek word for **upset** (*ah-nah-streh-pháw-meh-nawn,* ἀναστρεφόμενον) means to turn upside down, revolve, turn back, or busy oneself in. Those who were thus turned around were upset, perhaps in a very vigorous way. These had agreed with Paul that Christians should rejoice in their **sufferings**, because that enabled them to help cancel out the fines that had accumulated against the community.

34*You accepted with joy the confiscation of your possessions.* The Greek word for **confiscation** is *hahr-pah-gáyn* (ἁρπαγήν), which usually means "plunder," "booty," or "robbery." **A better possession [that is] lasting** is literally, **a better and lasting possession**. Part of the preparation for membership involved giving up all of the candidate's possessions to the monastery. This meant that the candidate gave the monastery permission, voluntarily to confiscate all of his goods and money. They all had **accepted with joy** this deprivation.

35*Therefore do not cast off your boldness.* For the meaning of **boldness**, see the Commentary on Heb 10:9 and Heb 4:16.

Which holds a great reward. The **reward** was **the inheritance of the age which was also the salvation anticipated** (Heb 9:15). Both of these were synonymous terms identified with the restoration of the Promised Land to the chosen people free from foreign rule.

Summary. After warning the readers of the terrible punishment that God would inflict upon those who did not hold fast to the faith, but rather left it and even despised it, as some members of their group had already done, the author reminded them of "the good old days" when their faith was strong and stable. After they had received the instruction necessary for admission to the community, they were required to endure a great deal of **suffering.** This was of two kinds:

(a) **Sometimes** they had been publicly **exhibited** and embarrassed by being afflicted both with **insults** and physical injury;
(b) **other times** they shared the reputation associated with those who had been **thus upset**.

When others were **in bonds,** members of the community who were not in prison visited them (Matt 25:36, 43) and in other ways **suffered with** them.

This probably was not an easy thing to do, because it exposed those not in prison as being part of the same movement and put them in danger of the same kind of punishment. A third point to their credit was that they **accepted with joy the confiscation** of their **possessions**. This probably refers to one of the following inconveniences.

a) The plunder and confiscation of their property and possessions by the government or some outsiders. This might mean that individuals within the group had **suffered** financial loss in this way, or it might mean that a community which lived together, communally, had been attacked and its possessions taken. The word *hahr-pah-gáyn* first suggests something like this. If this kind of plunder motivated the brothers to accept the misfortune **with joy**, then the members were trained to rejoice in their **sufferings** with the understanding that God would reward them generously in the future and wreak vengeance upon those who confiscated their property. Since nonresistant **suffering** was encouraged by the Sermon on the Mount, Rom 12-13, James, and 1Pet, it would not be surprising if the group to which this document was addressed also enjoyed hardship unjustly caused by an enemy. The fact that the confiscation was classed along with insults and physical injury also supports the likelihood that this referred to plunder by those outside the community.

b) The other possibility is that this was the very last step required for admission into the group involved giving up all of their personal property which might be considered having it **confiscated** by the community. This was normal practice for celibate communities (1QS 6:22-23).

Other sectarian groups, such as the Essenes and the community governed by The Community Rule (1QS), who were known for their strict discipline, observance of ritual ablutions, and other practices necessary for holiness, strained every muscle to avoid defiling their community, which The Community Rule (1QS), like Hebrews, called "the many." Essenes and members of the community governed by The Community Rule were also celibate and communal.

This also meant they gave up all financial responsibility for their families and all physical contact with them, since their families did not observe the same rules with the same strictness. This was all part of the contract, and many did this, believing that the new family would be better than the old anxiety of the world (ActsThom 144-46). In other words, this was the kind of deprivation which the instructed could not only tolerate, but even accept ***with joy.*** Since Hebrews reflects many attitudes and practices observed specially by rigorous, even monastic, groups, this communal economics is a real possibility. Because surrendering their goods was associated with the last step of their initiation, it would have happened in the **earlier days, after** they **had become enlightened**, or trained in the doctrines of the sect. Both of these interpretations are possibilities, but neither draws conclusive evidence strong enough to exclude the other.

The reference to **boldness** (Heb 10:35) refers the reader to the original topic sentence of this discussion (Heb 10:19). The two terms constitute an inclusion to remind the reader of the beginning and conclusive limits of the topic. In between were personal words, divided into three distinct categories, exhortation, warnings and threats, and an appeal to return to the earlier days when their character was better.

TEXT

Hebrews	First Testament
36 For you must have endurance so that, after you have done the will of God, you may obtain the promise,	
37 For still, **how little, how little**	LXX Isa 26:20 Hide yourself. **How little; how little**, until the Lord's anger goes past.
the coming one will come and not delay,	Hab 2:3-4 If he delays, wait for him, for he **will surely come and not delay**. **If he shrinks back, my soul does not take pleasure in him, but my righteous one will live by faith.**
38 **but my righteous one will live by the faith**, and if he **shrinks back, my soul does not take pleasure in him**.	

39 But we are not [of the group that] **shrinks back** for destruction, but of [those who cling to] the **faith** for [the] acquisition of the **soul**.

COMMENTARY

Before examining the commentary on each verse, just spend a few minutes noticing the skill with which the author first wove words from two prophecies into one message (Heb 10:36-38). Then observe the way Heb 10:39 comments on three words taken both from the prophecies and from the author's narrative midrash on the prophecies. This is not an unusual passage in the Book of Hebrews, but anyone who will understand the author's method and beliefs should take account of this use of Scripture throughout the sermon.

36 *For you must have endurance.* Over and over again the author encouraged his readers to endure so that they might receive **the promise**. This was his central motivation and ethical requirement. **The promise** involved was that **promise** which God made to Abraham (Gen 15).

37 *The coming one will come and not shrink back.* The first text quoted from Isaiah was Isa 26:20. Isaiah urged the people to hide themselves for **a little while** (*kee meh-áht ráy-gah,* כמעט רגע; until the wrath would pass over. Whenever God's people felt pain and hardship they believed that God was punishing them and that this hardship was an expression of God's anger (Isa 26:20-21). The people's fortunes were believed to reflect God's attitude toward them. If they **suffered,** God was angry; if they prospered, God was pleased with them. The author of Hebrews lived under the same belief. God's anger would be over whenever God believed that the people's punishment had been adequate to compensate for their crime.

Both the author of Hebrews and Isaiah believed that the punishment was just about over. Neither biblical scholar had any idea that people 2,000 years later would still think they had to wait for this. Both Isaiah and the author of Hebrews thought this anger period would be over very quickly—**how little, how little!** The author encouraged his listeners by assuring them that it would not be long. He used the passage from Isaiah to encourage his people to endure the wrath they now faced, because it would soon pass away when God came to visit them with blessing, fulfilling his promise to them.

With a slight variation, the author of Hebrews masterfully spliced a passage from Habakkuk to the one from Isaiah, as if they initially constituted one FT quotation. The Hebrew infinitive absolute, **he will surely come** (*bóh yah-vóh,* בוא יבוא) was literally translated by the LXX, **because coming, he will come** *(haw-tee ehr-khaw-meh-naws hexei,* ὅτι ἐρχόμενος ἥξει) (Hab 2:3). The author of Hebrews omitted just one syllable (*ti,* τι) to change the meaning to suit his needs: **because coming, he will come** (LXX Hab 2:3) became **the coming one will come** (*haw ehr-kháw-meh-naws háy-ksay,* ὁ ἐρχόμενος ἥχει). This type of change is typical of *peh-shehr* exegesis. In Habakkuk, that which would come was the vision (Hab 2:3), but in Hebrews, **the coming one** would be the Lord or his Messiah. Hence, the Isaiah passage, which urged the people to wait a little while until the Lord's wrath passed over, and the Habakkuk passage, promising that the vision would not delay, were spliced together to prove that the Lord would soon come to fulfill his **promise.**

38 *My righteous one will live by the faith.* The term **the faith** is a connection term, repeated in Heb 10:39, introducing the subject of Heb 11. The Syriac translation of this term is *hai-mah-noó-tah* (הימנותא), employing a definite article, "the." This means that the Syriac translator thought the Greek writer was speaking about **the faith.** He did the very same with the same term in the next verse, which is also rendered **the faith,** rather than just "trust" or "belief." There were two groups of people involved. Those who belonged to **the faith** and held fast to it, and others who **shrank back.** The **righteous one** would **live** within **the faith**, not wavering in the stress of persecution. It is not the same concept of **faith** for which Paul was well known.[1] Weiss described this faith as follows:

> Much more, therefore, it comes to the author in the interest of his warning speech to outline the most concrete position of the faith: "Faith" precisely in the sense of "forbearance" in suffering and hardship, in the sense of holding fast to the confession (v. 23) and boldness (vv. 19.35)—faith, then, in the biblical, Jewish sense of remaining firm and standing fast.[2]

If he shrinks back, my soul does not take pleasure in him. The **righteous one** to whom the author referred was the listener, the Christian who had once endured a great deal of ridicule and torture but recently was tempted to give up **the faith** as others had done. He was encouraged to endure as he had earlier.

Hab 3:2 said **if it delays**. Hebrews took this passage out of context and gave it a stronger force, **If it shrinks back**. Then he took words like **not, soul,** and **in him** out of context and put them altogether to form a small narrative midrash with a completely different meaning from that of Habakkuk. This was all considered acceptable exegesis in NT times. It is typical legal logic and rhetoric.

---

[1] Contra Jewett, *Letter,* p. 191.

[2] Weiss, *Hebräer*, p. 551, tr. from the German.

[39]*But we are not [a group of those who] shrink back.* The author confronted the reader with a choice: he could either **shrink back** and the Lord would **not take pleasure in him** or he could endure for a **little while** longer and obtain the **promise**. The group to which the author and readers belonged were not the ones who **shrank back.** Anyone who **shrank back** and became apostate would forfeit the **promise.** In a similar situation, another leader listed many earlier heroes of the faith and then said,

> Also you, therefore, holding the same faith in God, do not become dismayed, because it is unreasonable for you who know religion not to withstand suffering (4Macc 16:22).

The expression **not take pleasure** is a *litotes* expression. It is softened to an understatement by a double negative. It means the Lord *will* pay back and judge his people (Deut 32:35, 36). It is something dreadful **to fall into the hands of the living God** (Heb 10:31). The expression **living God** is Greek for the Hebrew **God of life**, meaning the God who is in charge of the corporation formed by the contract. In FT context, the **God of life** is always shown as a fierce, powerful, punishing deity. His anger could be expressed in severe punishment. Therefore the author exhorted the readers to dismiss the possibility of belonging to **the group of those who shrink back for destruction,** but rather to the group of those who cling to **the faith for [the] acquisition of the soul.** Christians acquired souls when they became members of the faith. They lost their souls if they became apostates.

Summary.--This transition passage centers around three important words:

a) **endurance**
b) **shrinking back**, and
c) **the faith**.

The first two words are related to that which had been said before. The readers had been warned to **hold fast unmoved** (Heb 10:23) to their **confession of hope** (Heb 10:23) and were reminded of the trials they had endured when they **first were enlightened** (Heb 10:32). The third point is **the faith for [the] acquisition of a [the] soul** (Heb 10:39), which is the introductory word leading into the next chapter, lauding the great saints of the past who belonged to **the faith**. The author had already warned his readers of God's punishment for those who did not endure. Here he reminded them of the reward they would receive for enduring. They would gain **the promise** (Heb 10:36). **The promise** was that they would enter into his **rest** (Heb 4:1). This **promise** had never been satisfactorily fulfilled. Its full and final realization was still to come. The exodus generation did not receive it because of that generation's unbelief (Heb 3:12). The next chapter (11) was designed to show the virtues and endurance of the great saints of **the faith**, because their virtues were necessary qualities for the readers if they were to receive **the promise** that God intended for his chosen people.

CHAPTER ELEVEN

TEXT

11:1Now [the] faith is [the] substance of things hoped for, // [the] basis for testing things not seen--2for in this the men of old were attested. 3In [the] faith we consider the ages to have been put in order by [the] word of God, so that what is seen has not come into existence from things that are visible.

TECHNICAL DETAILS

Heb 11:1 is the definition intended to introduce the subject of **[the] faith.** It is the only definition of faith given in the entire NT. Great rhetoricians, like Quintilian, taught the importance of defining items carefully in arguments so that points could be understood clearly, and succinctly remembered (*Rhetorica ad Herennium* 4:25, 35; 7:3, 2-5). A capsulated summary of the argument, such as that given in Heb 11:1 is rhetorically admirable. Not only is it a succinct and accurate definition, but it is rhythmic, with three of nine words in the verse concluding with the same sounding syllable in Greek; making the sentence onomatopoetic. Aristotle called this literary structure *pah-raw-moí-oh-sees,* παρομοίωσις (*Rhetoric* 3:9, 9). The logic of the sentence is itself captivating, and the beauty of the sounds involved would effectively capture the attention of an audience. Even though this definition is crisp and accurate, modern scholars are not sure what it means.

One of the earliest translations of the Greek NT was into Syriac. This translation is useful to NT scholars—not because it was a Semitic source for the Greek NT—but because it shows how early Semitic scholars understood and translated NT Greek into Semitic terms. The Syriac translation of the Greek that is here rendered **in [the] faith,** (*bah-hay-maw-noóh-thah,* בהימנותא),[1] treats the expression as if it had a definite article. In NT times Hebrew was unpointed, so that the Hebrew for the two expressions, "in faith" or "in the faith" (*buh-eh-moo-náh* or *bah-eh-moo-nah*), would be the same (באמונה). The definite article is shown in the vowel, which is not recorded in unpointed Hebrew. Therefore either Greek translations of Hebrew or Greek used by Hebrew speaking peoples in NT times reflects a careless use of definite articles. This is also true both of Tannaitic Rabbinic Hebrew and the Greek NT. Paul, for example, used both the term *haw-náw-maws* (ὁ νόμος, Rom 2:15-27) and just *náw-maws* (νόμος, Rom 2:12-14) to mean "the law." In all cases he was speaking about the same law, but more often than not, he omitted the definite article that had to be understood. This is also true of the word "many" (*rah-beém,* רבים; *paw-loí,* πολλοί) which also means "the many," meaning "the congregation" (Isa 53:12; Mark 14:24). It also appears with the definite article with the same meaning in the Dead Sea Scrolls (1QS 6:1, 7, 8, 17, 19, 20; 7:10). Like Paul, Mark, and other Greeks of Jewish background, the author of Hebrews intended a definite article without writing it. It is essential to recognize this practice to understand the Book of Hebrews, particularly Heb 11.

---

[1] So R. Payne Smith, *A Compendious Syriac Dictionary*; ed. J. Payne Smith (Oxford: Clarendon Press, c1902), p. 103: "N. T. and later, *faith, the Christian faith, religion, doctrine, creed.*" Other examples given are with adjectives "*the orthodox faith*"and "*Arionism.*"

The couplet is limited to Heb 11:1. Heb 11:2, **for in this the men of old were attested,** is not a part of the definition but an explanation to justify the validity of the definition.

COMMENTARY

11:1 *[The] faith is [the] substance of things hoped for.* The word **faith** was first introduced in Heb 10:38 as a connection word relating the major theme of this division to the previous one. The word **substance** is here chosen in preference to the word "groundwork," which was used in the first edition of this book that was published more than 30 years ago. The word (*hoo-páw-stah-sees*, ὑπόστασις) was used to describe God's **nature** or essence (Heb 1:3) and the Christian's **faith.** Accordingly, it is an integral part of the author's message and related to the rest of the document. "Groundwork" is a literal rendering of the Greek, but it overlooks the legal and rhetorical context of the term.

The word *hoo-páw-stah-sees* literally means that which is stationed under. It is that which settles to the bottom. It sometimes means "agreement" or "promise." It gives support to that which is above. It is a foundation. H. Koester has shown that the word requires different translations in different contexts.[1] It might be considered the "bottom line." The context here is not medicine, philosophy, or gnosticism. Here it does not deal with buildings or liquids. The context is Heb 11. In that context some scholars render it "confidence" and identify it with hope.[2] This does not fit. In the definition given (Heb 11:1) *hoo-páw-stah-sees* is neither confidence nor hope. It is that by which something that is **hoped for** and **not seen** is based. It is used in opposition to standing away, withdrawing, or becoming apostate (*hoo-paws-taw-láy*, ὑποστολή). It is also identified with [the] **faith**.

The basis for testing things unseen. The word **unseen** has led scholars to think of **things** that are transcendent and in heaven.[3] **Things** in heaven, however, are not the only **things** that are **unseen**, and the context does not suggest heaven. From the point of view of the ancient Semite, that which was **unseen** was behind him or her. Without eyes in the back of their heads, it was impossible for ancients to see that which was behind them. It was the future that was **unseen,** so their words for the future were terms describing something behind them—"the days behind" (*buh-akh-ah-reét hah-yah-meém*, באחרית הימים), "tomorrow—the day behind" (*mah-kháhr*, מחר). The past, on the other hand, could be seen. It had already happened, so it was referred to as "in front" (*keh-dehm*, קדם), *kahd-moh-nee-óth*, קדמניות), or (*luh-phahn-neém*, לפנים). **The substance is the basis for testing** and predicting the

---

[1] H. Koester, "ὑπόστασις," *Theological Dictionary of the New Testament*, ed. G. Friederich (Grand Rapids: Eerdmans, c1972), pp. 572-89, provides an excellent analysis of the various possibilities for the use of this term.

[2] E. Grässer, *Der Glaube im Hebäerbrief* (Marburg: N. G. Elwert, 1965), 39. Other suggestions Grässer offered were, "*Ausharten [perseverance], Ausdauer [enduring], Beharrlichkei [persistence], mut [courage], und Standhaftigkei [immobile],*" p. 101. The term is Greek, as Grässer noted (p. 102), but etymology alone will not explain the meaning of the word, as it was used in Heb 11. For illustrations and arguments in defense of each definition, see M. R. Cosby, *The Rhetorical Composition and Function of Hebrews 11* (Macon: Mercer U. Press, c1988), pp. 30-38.

[3] G. McRae, "Heavenly Temple and Eschatology in the Letter to the Hebrews," *Semeia* 12 (1978):193-194.

future. That which is behind may be *Bestand, Wirklichkeit und Bleibt,*[1] but without the benefit of that which is in front, all that which is **unseen** and behind is obscure, uncertain, and unknown. The clue for judging the **unseen** that is behind is the **substance. The substance** is **the faith.** It is by looking to the past that clues can be found for predicting the **unseen** future. There can be no eschatology without a protology. Brawley held that the things hoped for that were unseen were not only

1) salvation (Heb 3:6; 6:11, 18; 7:19; 10:2),
2) promises (Heb 4:1; 6:12, 17; 7:6; 8:6; 9:15; 10:36), and
3) the inheritance (1:4; 6:12; 9:15), but also
4) subjection of all things under Jesus' feet.[2]

These were all things hoped for, and their provision would take place in the future, here on earth. The place where they could be learned was in the past. They would have to look through the story of the faith in the Scripture. If any one of these was achieved, all would be. When the land would be restored, the promises would be fulfilled, the inheritance would be established, and all things would be placed under the feet of the Messiah. Brawley said that the **unseen** things were not just in heaven as McRae,[3] Käsemann,[4] and Grässer[5] argued. They were the **unseen** things of the future that could not be seen at the present. Schaeffer agreed with Klausner's understanding of the messianic expectation. It would come at the end of the age—not in heaven, but on earth--and it would provide political freedom, moral perfection, earthly bliss for the people of Israel, on its own land, and also for the entire human race.[6] Neither Brawley, Schaeffer, nor Klausner thought the promises to Abraham included only the **unseen** things in heaven. That which was promised was [7]

1) the land,
2) prosperity, and
3) posterity.

They were expected to be fulfilled sometime in the future, on the earth. They were the things for which they **hoped.**

Hope and confidence are subjective feelings or notions that are based on something else. That "something else" upon which **hope** is based is the *hoo-páw-stah-sees.* It is **the basis for testing things not seen**, so if anyone wants to check his or her **hope** with reference to the things **not seen**, it is necessary to look to the *hoo-páw-stah-sees,* which is here rendered **substance**. That still does not solve the problem.

---

[1] Grässer, *Hebräerbrief,* p. 251 (tr. from the German).

[2] R. Brawley, "Discursive Structure and the Unseen in Hebrews 2:8 and 11:1: A Neglected Aspect of the Context," *CBQ* 55 (1993):85.

[3] McRae, "Heavenly Temple," pp. 193-94.

[4] E. Käsemann, *The Wandering People of God: An Investigation of the Letter to the Hebrews*; trs. R. A. Harrison and I. L. Sandberg (Minneapolis: Augsburg, 1984), pp. 33-37.

[5] Grässer, "Der Hebräerbrief 1938-63," *ThR* 30 (1964): 222-26; Glaube, p.175.

[6] J. R. Schaeffer, "The Relationship between Priestly and Servant Messianism in the Epistle to the Hebrews," *CBQ* 30 (1968):359.

Grässer interpreted passages like this in terms of a "Platonic-idealistic dualism of earthly/visible and heavenly/invisible" concepts.[1] He has also called it glory, and, like Hamm, has followed Koester[2] and defined it as "underlying reality"[3] or the "reality of God." Hamm and Grässer understand that the reality involved is otherworldly. Still others have called **substance** "certainty," "objective guarantee," or "objective reality that is unquestionable and securely established."

Earlier scholars have strained to clarify this difficult term in the context in which it is included. It is not just a subjective feeling of trust that rests only in the mind. It is not just an **unseen hope**. What, then, is the **substance** that describes [the] **faith?** And further, what does the term [the] **faith** mean here? Since this is a legal document with many marks of good rhetoric, the law and rhetoric seem to be the best place to find a literary possibility that fits the necessity.

In this context the words **hoped for, unseen,** and **substance** are related to each other in the same way promise, fulfillment, and contract or legal agreement are related to each other. In a contract, people sign papers in the present for promises that are to be fulfilled in the future. That which is **seen** is the contract; that which is **unseen** and **hoped for** is the authority or promises granted in the **contract.** That which is **not seen** is the fulfillment, the authority granted by the **contract.** From the Semitic point of view that is still behind the viewer.

In antiquity there were many agreements made without written contracts, but only by legal ceremony. If these ceremonies were performed precisely, they were as valid in court as written contracts.[4] For example, when Samuel anointed first Saul and later, David, they both received the spirit. This meant they received the authority to become kings of Israel. Neither one sat on the throne immediately. The kingdom was something that was **hoped for** but at first **not seen.** The fulfillment of this **substance** that took place at the anointing required military action.[5]

In a similar way people were baptized and became members of the family corporation. Those already baptized could become Christians when those with authority laid their hands upon them and performed the proper ceremony (Acts 19:5-6). In each case the action that was **seen** was the ceremony; that which was **not seen** was the associated authority that went with future membership. The **substance** of the ceremony was important and necessary for the **not seen** fulfillment.[6] The **hoped**

---

[1] E. Grässer, Der Glaube im *Hebräerbrief* (Marbrg: N. G. Elwert, 1965), p. 215 (tr. from German), p. 3.

[2] H. Koester, "ὑποστασις," *Theological Dictionary of the New Testament* (1972), pp. 572-89

[3] D. Hamm, "Faith in the Epistle to the Hebrews: The Jesus Factor," CBQ 52 (1900):278.

[4] H. S. Maine, *Ancient Law* (USA: Dorset Press, 1986; first 1861), p. 260: "That which the law arms with its sanctions is not a promise, but a promise accompanied with a solemn ceremonial. . . . in ancient law , to be transferred to the words and gestures of the accompanying performance. No pledge is enforced if a single form be omitted or misplaced, but, on the other hand, if the forms can be shown to have been accurately proceeded with, it is of no avail to plead that the promise was made under duress or deception."

[5] G. Dautzenberg, "Der Glaube im Hebräerbrief," *BibZeit* 17 (1973):161-177, is not completely correct in considering the words **faith** and **hope** to be virtually synonymous. They were used together, but **faith** was the **seen substance** of the fulfillment for which there was **hope.** That which was **hoped for** was **not seen** by **faith. Faith** was the **substance** and the **basis for testing** that which was **hoped for** and **not seen**.

[6] Maine, *Ancient Law*, p. 260, said, "Not only are formalities of equal importance with the promise itself, but they are, if anything, of greater importance."

for fulfillment was the real important purpose of the ceremony. For the author of Hebrews [the] **faith** was the essential **substance** for the **not seen** fulfillment of the promises.

The Hebrew word for faith is *eh-moo-náh* (אמונה) which suggests solidity, firmness, stability. *Ah-méhn* (אמן) means "support" or "confirm." It is a term used in oaths related to contracts. Those who have **faith** have support; if they believe in someone or something, they have supported themselves in or found support from that person or object. The word *éh-lehng-khaws* (ἔλεγχος) (**basis for testing**), however, is a Greek legal term used in debates or cross examinations. Both terms were used here as complementary parts of the author's definition of faith.

For the author of Hebrews **faith** meant the "trust" and "belief" essential for observance, but it was also closely related to the doctrine, creed, confession, or catechism that members were obligated to believe and observe. A creed or a catechism is something that has been established in the past and is the basis for life in the future. Like a contract, [the] **faith** was **the basis for testing things not seen**. **[The] faith**, as it is defined here, could be checked to learn what the terms and **unseen** promises were. People act on the basis of belief or trust, but they are unable to claim their belief as a basis for any**thing hoped for**. As action words these terms are subjective ideas or feelings, but these same terms can also be static expressions.

A trust is a legal vehicle, into which money is placed and held to be used in certain ways by certain people. Courts look into the trust to learn what the conditions for fulfillment are. A belief can also be a doctrine or a set of doctrines or a creed. **A faith** is also a religion. Because these terms are interrelated and can have variant implications it is from the legal context of the document that we will be able to learn what is meant by the **subtance of things hoped for, the basis for testing things not seen.** Contracts and creeds can be checked to learn what the participants contracted to believe and observe. The author of Hebrews evidently called this **basis for testing,** also **[the] faith.**

On the one hand the message of good news did not help the exodus generation—not because the people did not have a creed to believe but that they lacked an active **faith** in their creed (Heb 4:2). The **not seen rest** which was denied the exodus generation was available during the author's time for those who both had **the faith** and would observe its terms (Heb 4:3). Without **[the] faith** it is impossible to please God (Heb 11:6). This means that it is necessary for one who approaches God to believe that he is (Heb 11.6). He or she had to hold the correct doctrine. **Faith** in God is one of the elementary doctrines of Christ (Heb 6:1). **[The] faith** is also the creed or contract which tells the party to the contract how **faith** is expressed.

It is through **[the] faith** that people become heirs of the promises (Heb 6:12), which is another way of saying they become members of the elect community. This is consistent with the contract made between Abraham and God. When God proposed the **promise** that he would become the father of an innumerable family, **Abraham believed, and it was credited to him as righteousness** (Gen 15:5-6). One who has a true heart in fullness of **faith** (Heb 10:22) is ritually cleansed and prepared to enter holy precincts.

On the other hand, there are prescriptions to determine when a person has fulfilled this qualification. He should hold fast unmoved the **confession of hope** (Heb 10:23), because those who are of [the] **faith** do not **shrink back** from destruction (Heb 10:39). Those who believe are like Abraham. They trust the

promises of God but they also accept the right doctrines, **hold fast to the confession** (Heb 4:14) and hold fast unmoved **the confession of hope** (Heb 10:23), because Jesus is **the high priest of the confession** (Heb 3:1). Those who **held fast the confession of hope** (Heb 10:23) were those who hoped that the **promises** of God would soon be fulfilled, and they confessed this belief, even though their fulfillment did not seem likely to most. They endured showing forth the same zeal toward the full **conviction** of **hope to the end** (Heb 6:11). Jesus was **the primary leader and perfector of the faith** (*tays peés-teh-ohs*, τῆς πίστεως) (Heb 12:1). **The promise** and the **oath** (Heb 6:17) given in the FT give the believer strong encouragement to seize the hope set before him or her (Heb 6:18).

Only the Christian has [the] **faith;** he or she is the one who has accepted the correct doctrines, has mastered **the confession** to which he or she **holds fast**. The doctrines are such that every Christian is required to have **hope** that God will soon fulfill his **promises**. The proximity of faith to creed for the author requires the reader of Heb 11 to try to understand the shade of meaning intended for each usage. The word blends together concepts of trust, creed, confession, hope, expectation, and confidence. It is not always clear just which of these concepts is emphasized in each particular instance, but an attempt will be made to understand these in a way that is consistent with the rest of the author's message.

For the author, **faith** was the opposite of **shrinking back** into apostasy (Heb 10:39). A person who once became a Christian either **held fast the confession** (Heb 10:23) or became an apostate and surrendered his or her **faith;** he or she belonged to the **faith** or **shrank back** (Heb 10:39). **Things hoped for** and **not seen** involve the coming of the **coming one** (Heb 10:37) or gaining the **promise** (Heb 4:1; 10:36) of entering into his **rest** (Heb 4:1). Not only were these **hoped for**, but they were expected soon (Heb 10:25, 37). **The substance**, foundation, or **basis for testing** this hope is **the confession** which the believers were obligated to **hold fast** (Heb 10:23), which is another way of saying **the substance of things hoped for** is **[the] faith.**

Those who decided to enter **the faith** of the community also fulfilled the liturgical requirements of the contract. One example of a monastic liturgy, somewhat like that which would have been appropriate for the Hebrews community is reported in one of the Dead Sea scrolls.

On the occasion of admission of new members, probably just before New Year's Day and the Day of Atonement, the new initiates entered the order by passing into the contract. The service began with the priests reciting the great deeds of God and his deliverances of his people. The Levites responded by listing the many iniquities of Israel. Then all the new recruits confessed their crimes, and the priest offered an expanded version of the priestly benediction (Num 6:24-26). Then the Levites cursed all the men of the lot of Belial, followed by priestly and Levitical curses against anyone who entered this contract and then broke his vows. The service was concluded by an acceptance of the terms, saying "Amen, Amen!" (1QS 1:16-2:18).

Initiates entered the contract, **the faith**, and the community at the same time. Those who broke their vows, left the community, also gave up **the faith,** and received the curses associated with the contract and **the faith**. All of these terms were closely associated.

[2]*For in this the men of old.* **This** in which **the men of old were attested** seems to have been some kind of confession or creed that told about them, i.e., this creed or confession. Some early texts (P^{13} 103 1908) read "in it" (*ehn ow-tay*, ἐν αὐτῇ)

rather than "in this" (*ehn tow-tay*, ἐν ταύτῃ), because the antecedent seemed obvious. **This** refers to [the] **faith** (Heb 11:1), which here deals with something that holds doctrines or articles of **the faith** which provided for the community the **substance** of their **hope** and a source which members could examine to learn about **unseen things**. If a person wanted to know what he should expect or for which he dared **hope,** he could check the rule, code, or confession (Heb 3:1; 4:14; 10:23; 1QS 1:16) that he was obligated to hold fast (Heb 4:14; 10:23), and on the basis of this creed or **faith**, test the things not seen. This confession of **the faith** (Heb 3:1, 4:14; 10:23; 11:1) contained a list of the community's orthodox doctrines and **hopes,** such as those in Matt 5-7 or 1QS, and it seems to have been closely related to, identified with, or included in the FT, because **the men of old** who **were attested in this** were also attested in the FT and in the very same order given in the list that follows, beginning with the first events in Genesis and continuing up to the conquest of Palestine by Joshua, who was a prototype for the new Joshua. Weiss said,

> The fact that "faith" here certainly is not genuinely theologically or Christologically, but rather only anthropologcally defined is not astonishing. For, from the context (Heb 10:19 ff) it stands in the first line. It is exactly that, in which the faith in context is self evident: the Christian faith.[1]

[3]*In [the] faith* The expression **in [the] faith** introduces a whole new section in which this term is reiterated rhythmically over and over again (Heb 11:3, 5, 8, 9, 11, 17, 20, 21, 23, 24, 27-31). The rhetorical name for this kind of repetition is called *anaphora.* This effective anaphora moves with varying speed and emphases. It begins briefly, then expands. Later it again moves briefly, and then expands again until it moves increasingly more briefly to the end. One verse is given to Cain and Noah; two verses are devoted to Enoch, then twelve verses belong to Abraham and Sarah. Isaac, Jacob, and Joseph were dismissed with one verse each. Then six verses were given to Moses. Rahab received only half a verse, before seven leaders plus the prophets were summarized in one verse. When read aloud, the briefer the mention, the more rapid the movement. The effective movement of the anaphora kept the extensive repetition from being tedious. Instead it would have increased the interest of the listening audience.

Some scholars think Heb 11:3 is part of the following section, because it employs the expression **in [the] faith,** but it might just as well be a connection word relating the verses before to the verses that follow.

The ages have been put in order. **The ages** were **put in order** (*kaht-ayr-teés-thai toos ai-óh-nas*, κατηρτίσθαι τοὺς αἰῶνας),[2] not created, as one might expect when the report covers the creation stories in Genesis. The reference is to the poem of creation (Gen 1:1-2:3), but the author considered time to have been organized in

---

[1] H. F. Weiss, *Der Brief an die Hebräer* (Göttingen: Vandenhoeck & Ruprecht, 1991), p. 559, tr. from the German.

[2] The RSV renders this sentence, "By faith we understand that the world was created by the word of God." This translation was imitated by many scholars, such as Lane, Hughes, Jewett, and Attridge. But the word rendered "world" is plural and it is almost always used as a temporal term. Even the context makes better sense rendered "ages."

the same act, and he was more interested in the sequence of events and God's purpose associated with the calendrical happenings than with the material nature God created (see Commentary on Heb 1:2). On the first day of creation God created light, which he separated from darkness, forming day. Since a thousand years in the sight of the Lord are as one day (Ps 90:4; 2Pet 3:8), and since a thousand years might be thought of as an **age,** one might consider that the Lord arranged the **ages** or the millennia the way he arranged the days of creation, so that the **ages** would conclude with an **age** of **rest**, just as creation ended with a day of **rest**. This would suit the author's eschatology (Deut 12:9-11; 25:19; Josh 21:44; 1Kings 8:56; Ps 95:11).

The **word of God** was the **word** spoken by God when light came into existence and was separated from darkness so that there could be temporal divisions or **ages** (Gen 1:3-5). It is widely attested that God was the source of **what is seen** (Gen 1; Rom 1:20; Wis 9:1; 11:17; 13:4). The word did not "come into existence" from idols, nature, or any of the "things that are visible." This is the witness of the Scripture and also the confession of **[the] faith**.

The contrasts between the **things not seen** and **what is seen** (Heb 11:1, 3) do not reflect a Platonic viewpoint as some have thought. Plato would not have "considered" in **[the] faith** or by **[the] faith**, as Hebrews has done, since "considering" is the intellectual understanding of unchanging ideas, according to Plato, and **faith** is the uncritical, sensible grasp of data belonging to the physical world. Neither would Plato have thought of "what is seen" as not coming "into existence from things that are visible." For Plato, God brought order out of the then existing chaotic, visible world, but he did not bring it forth from invisible essence.[1] The author's concern for the unseen was not primarily that which was invisible or intangible, but that which was future, that which had not yet happened (see commentary on 1:2). It was a concept of time rather than of substance or essence.

Summary. The definition of **faith** summarized in these three verses was important to the author's doctrine, but he did not organize this definition as a separate unit. In *his* outline, the unit consisted of Heb 11:1-7 and was thus indicated by an inclusion. From the standpoint of the exhortation in Heb 10, Heb 11 seems to be something of an intrusion, which could easily have been omitted and have the exhortation of Heb 12:1 continue immediately after Heb 10:39, but the author regularly related his doctrine to his homiletics, and his conclusion of Heb 10 contained connection words preparing the reader also for Heb 11. Furthermore Heb 11 is closely related to the introduction of the entire document and it is consistent with the theology expressed throughout. If it was originally composed separately it has been well integrated into its present position.

TEXT

Hebrews	First Testament
[4]In [the] faith **Abel brought to** **God**	[Gen 4:4]**Abel** also **brought** from the first born of his flock and their fat portions, and **Yehowah** looked

[1] R. Williamson, *Philo and the Epistle to the Hebrews* (Leiden: E. J. Brill, 1970), pp. 421-22.

a better **sacrifice** than **Cain**, through which he was attested to be righteous, **God** himself witnessing **to his gifts**, and through it, while dying, still **he speaks**.

upon **Abel and his sacrifice** [with favor], but he did not look upon **Cain** and his **sacrifice** [with favor]. 8 Then **Cain** rose up and killed him. 10 Then [God] said, "What have you done? The voice of your brother's blood **cries out** from the ground."

5 In [the] faith **Enoch** was **transferred** so as not to see death, **and he was not found** [dead], **because God had transferred him**, for before the **transfer** it was attested [that he was] **pleasing to God**. 6 Now, without faith it is impossible **to please**, for it is necessary for the one who approaches **God** to believe that he is and [that] he becomes a wage payer to those who seek him.

(LXX Gen 5:24). **Enoch pleased God,**

and he was not found, because God transferred him.

7 In [the] faith, **Noah**, having been solemnly warned about the things not yet seen, since he was cautious, **prepared a houseboat**

Gen 6:13, 14 God said to **Noah** . . .

"Make yourself **a houseboat** of gopher wood, and cover it inside and out with pitch."

for [the] **salvation of his house**, through which he condemned the world,

Gen 7:6 **Noah, his sons, and his daughters-in-law**, went into the **houseboat** [to be **saved**] from the water of the flood.

and of the **righteousness** according to **[the] faith**, he became an heir.

Gen 7:1 For I have seen that you are **righteous** before me in this generation.

COMMENTARY

4 *Abel offered to God a better sacrifice.* The Scripture did not tell what was inferior about **Cain's sacrifice,** but, according to the LXX, **Cain** was told that if he did not offer **sacrifices** correctly (*awr-thóhs*, ὀρθῶς), he committed a crime (*háy-mahr-tehs*, ἥμαρτες) (Gen 4:7). **God looked upon** (*ehp-áy-dehn*, ἐπεῖδεν) **Abel and upon his gifts** (Gen 4:4). These words provided a basis for the author of Hebrews to deduce that God attested him **to be righteous.** The text told only about the **sacrifice** he offered, not about his righteousness, but since to offer incorrectly was a crime (Gen 4:7), to offer correctly must have been considered righteousness.

The author of Hebrews claimed that **Abel's sacrifice** was **better** in [the] **faith,** by which he meant "according to the report of the Scriptures." The author began with **Abel's better sacrifice**, but this was only the beginning of a long dissertation that would lead up to the really **better sacrifice** made by Jesus, and the priesthood in Herod's temple was as far from offering true **sacrifices** as **Cain** was. Like **Abel**, Jesus' **sacrifice** cost him his life. According to the FT, the question of **Cain's** and **Abel's faith** was not raised, but in the Palestinian targumim, this was important. According to Neofiti:

> When both of them had gone out into the field Cain answered and said to Abel. "I understand that the age was not created in mercy and not governed according to the fruits of good works and there is respect of persons in judgment. For which reason your offering was received favorably and my offering was not received favorably from me."
>
> Abel answered and said to Cain: "I understand that the world was created by mercy and is governed according to the fruits of good works. And as my works were better than yours my offering was received favorably."
>
> Cain answered and said to Abel: "There is no judgment and there is no judge and there is no other age; and there is no giving of good reward to the just nor is retribution exacted of the wicked."
>
> Abel answered and said to Cain: "There is a judgment and there is a judge and there is another world and there is giving of good reward to the just; and retribution is exacted of the wicked in the age to come."
>
> Over this matter both of them were disputing **in the field, and Cain rose up against his brother Abel and killed him**. (Targ Neofiti Gen 4:8).

The author of Hebrews was evidently acquainted with one of the Palestinian targumim and, on that basis, concluded that Abel's gift was a **better sacrifice** than Cain's according to [the] **faith**. **[The] faith** involved was not trust but a doctrinal confession. 1John concluded that Cain **was from the evil one, and he slew his brother**. The reason given was that **Cain's works were evil and those of his brother were good** (1John 3-12). This cannot be justified from the FT alone. The beliefs about good works, judgment, reward, punishment, and mercy were introduced by the targumist and accepted by Hebrews. The *it* (*ow-táys*, αὐτῆς) through which **Abel still speaks**, while dying, is not the gifts (plural), but [**the**] **faith**. The report of God's judgment is still on record for those who will read Gen 4:4 and in greater detail in targum. This is the **faith** through which **still he speaks**, and it is the faith through which he was attested **to be righteous**.

[5]*God had transferred him*. The Hebrew text said of **Enoch, Enoch walked with God, and he was not** (*ay-néh-noo*, איננו) **because God took him** (Gen 5:24). This is a rather unclear statement: it looks as if some verb had been omitted. The LXX has either preserved that verb from a text written before the verb was lost, or it has conjectured one to make sense: **. . . and he was not *found*, because God *transferred* him** (LXX Gen 5:24). In Hebrew the expression "being found" means "existing," so not being found is just a variant way of saying he does not exist. The addition LXX made was that God transferred him.

Even with the LXX alterations, the question still arises: "What happened to **Enoch**?" It is uncertain. His case is somewhat like that of Melchizedek, leaving later believers plenty of room to speculate. According to some traditions, **Enoch** was even more **righteous** than Noah (Jub 10:17), so God took him from among the children of men and **transferred** him to the Garden of Eden in majesty and honor. There he functions as the court scribe, recording all the deeds of men to use on the day of judgment (Jub 4:23; 10:17; 1Enoch 15:1; 2Enoch 22:12).

The reason **Enoch** was taken to God was that he was perfect (Sir 49:14; Ant 1:85). He was transferred into an example of repentance for all generations (Sir 44:16). According to Hebrews, **Enoch was changed so as not to see death,** just as Elijah had been. This is a fair interpretation of the LXX, since the idiom **being found** was used as a euphemism for **being found dead** (see Epictetus 3:5-6; 4:10, 12). The basis for this statement is in **[the] faith,** which may mean that, according to the creed, confession, or religious tradition, **he was not found [dead], because God had transferred him** (LXX Gen 5:24). This transfer came as a reward to **Enoch**, because in the LXX it says that **Enoch** was **pleasing to God** (Gen 5:24a) *before* it says **God transferred him** (Gen 5:24b). The author used a *post hoc propter hoc* argument (that which precedes in time is the *cause* of that which follows in time), which applied to the text meant that which occurred first in the text reflected that which was the cause of that which followed historically. The author reasoned that **Enoch** was **pleasing to God** first, and the transfer came later as a reward.

6 *Without [the] faith it is impossible to please him.* In the author's judgment no one could please God without **the faith**. This is another way of saying "Outside the church there is no salvation." It is only the chosen or elect who **please** God. It was **the faith** that preserved the word of God by which people could learn how to **please** God. It was obvious that **Enoch** belonged to **the faith**, because he was so handsomely rewarded for **pleasing God**, which could not have happened **without the faith.** It follows that **it is necessary for the one who approaches God to believe that he is**.

This was probably a basic doctrine of the group. The **one who approaches God** is either the worshiper approaching the altar with his **sacrifice**, as **Cain** and **Abel** had done, or an initiate approaching God by advancing toward full membership in the sect. Because this is a very elementary doctrine, it was probably intended here to mean the initiate who would accept this in an early stage of his catechetical training or **faith.** The initiate must not only believe that God is, but like **Abel** according to the targumist, he must believe that God **becomes a wage payer to those who seek him.**

7 *He became an heir.* The Greek for **having been solemnly warned** is *chray-mah-tees-tháys* (χρηματισθεὶς) (used also in 8:5). The verb generally means "to do business with," "consult" "negotiate," "advise," or "obtain an answer." In biblical concepts it is generally used in communications from God to his people and means "to advise," or "to warn solemnly" as in Matt 2:12 and here. He was about **the things** that were as yet **not seen,** but he acted **according to the faith**, and was cautious.

Heininger has shown clearly that the term *khray-mah-tees-tháys*, was used many times in ancient Greek documents and that it consistently referred to having received an oracle from angels or directly from some deity.[1] The situation determined whether the message of the oracle was a **warning** or a message of good

---

[1] B. Heininger, "Hebr 11,7 und das Henochorakel am End der Welt," *NTS* 44 (1998):115-32.

news. In Greek literature oracles tended to have been given ambiguously. If the recipient followed one of the possible interpretations of the oracle that turned out to be beneficial, it was concluded that the oracle was properly understood. If the result was bad the explanation was that the oracle was misunderstood. According to Genesis and Hebrews, Noah was warned through an oracle; he understood the warning correctly; and he acted wisely. That which Noah received from God was a message telling him about the future, whether it was **hoped for** or not. It was about **things unseen.** It was a message from heaven, and therefore heavenly, but it did not tell Noah what to do to get to heaven. It told how to prepare to survive on earth.

The word rendered "houseboat" is *kee-boh-táwn* (κιβωτόν), "box," "chest," or "coffer." The box that contained the tablets of the contract was such a chest. The box that **Noah** built, however, was some sort of wooden box that would float and hold passengers, more like a houseboat. The term **heir**, here applied to **Noah,** was also applied to Jesus, who, as the Son, was **heir** of all (Heb 1:2), and to the believers who would obtain the fulfillment of the **promises** (Heb 6:17). The **heirs** are those who inherit a **name** (Heb 1:4), **salvation** (Heb 1:14), the **promises** (Heb 6:11, 17; 11:9) or the **blessing** (Heb 12:17). Although not an heir of the promise, **Noah** was the first man recorded in Scripture as **righteous** (Gen 7:1). The author of Hebrews interpreted this as meaning that he acted according to the solemn warning, which was the right way to act; it was according to **faith**.

In his characteristic fashion the author related his illustrations to his definition. Since the faith is the basis for **testing things not seen** (Heb 11:1), **Noah** was given as an example of one who acted according to the **faith** regarding **the things not yet seen.** He had **not yet seen** the flood that was to come, but because he had **been solemnly warned**, as members of the author's audience were being, **he was cautious,** as the speaker wanted the audience to be. Not taking any chances, **Noah believed** that God rewards those who seek him (Heb 11:6), and he **prepared a houseboat for [the] salvation of his house**. This **houseboat** which provided **salvation** for his own family, however, provided no assistance for the rest of the people who belonged to "the world."

Instead, it was **through** that very act that **he condemned the world** (see also John 3:17), whereas he himself **became an** heir **of the righteousness according to the faith**. The significance of this teaching for the Christian contemporary with the author was that the Christian, like Noah, had a basis for **testing things not seen** (Heb 11:1). This was the word of God, which **Noah** received directly, and the Christian received from reading the Scriptures, which is **in the faith**. As **Noah** was **solemnly warned**, so also the Christian who read his Scripture properly was shown what the future would be and was obligated to hold fast unmoved the confession of hope (Heb 10:23). Like **Noah,** he was required to hold fast in the **faith** when others saw no danger, but in the end the Christian would be vindicated and the apostate **condemned**.

Summary. The list of exemplary personalities which begins with **Abel** is similar to those recorded in Ps 105:10-44; Ps 106; Neh 9:6-31; Act 7; 4Macc 16:20-23 and Sir 44-50. In 4Macc, Abraham, Isaac, Daniel the righteous (*haw deé-kai-aws*, ὁ δίκαιος), Hananiah, Mishael, and Azariah were those who were courageous enough to face death for their faith, and the mother of seven sons encouraged them to be willing to die, as these heroic men had been, rather than transgress God's commandment. Since the story was told to encourage Jews to withstand the persecutions of the gentiles, the list included only Israelites. Sirach began his long list with

Enoch (Noah, according to the Hebrew text) and ended it with Simon, the son of Onias, the **high priest** shortly before the Maccabean Revolt. Pss 105-106 listed heroes from Abraham to Phineas in the wilderness; Nehemiah's praise of the fathers began with Abraham and continued until the entrance of the Promised Land. Acts 7 reported a summary of history from Abraham through Moses; The author of Hebrews began earlier than any of the others, starting with Abel and continuing listing names specifically until the time of Joshua, to correspond with Jesus, the new Joshua, who would usher in a new kingdom and the promised **rest.** Unnamed were many who suffered for their faith in Maccabean times and probably also at the time the author wrote.

These first three men constituted the testimony before the patriarchs, but they also provided the author of Hebrews an occasion to substantiate his own rigorous doctrine and ethic. The theology of **Abel** according to the targum was precisely that of the author. The enduring faith of **Noah** was exactly the ethic which the author repeatedly urged for his readers. The rewards of **Enoch** and of **Noah** were for their loyalty to **the faith,** even though some circular reasoning was required to deduce this from the FT report of Enoch. The reward of **Noah** for his righteousness and lack of concern for the world reflects the author's sectarian attitude toward the elect and the world. He only urged the readers to stay among the elect. There is no missionary message in this document.

The author intended Heb 11:1-7 as a unit, and he framed it as an inclusion, using the words **the faith** and **things not seen** (Heb 11:1, 7) for this purpose. Some of the important words in this unit are **the faith** (Heb 11:1, 3, 4, 5, 7) **witness** (Heb 11:2, 4, 5), and **God** (Heb 11:3, 4, 5, 6).

TEXT

Hebrews	First Testament
[8]In [the] faith **Abraham**, when he was called, obeyed [the command] **to go** out to a place which he was about to receive for an inheritance,	[Gen 12:1-2]Yehowah said to **Abram**, "**Go** from the land of your birth, from the house of your father, to the land which I will show you. I will make you a great nation; I will bless you; I will make your name great; and it will be a blessing."
and **he went out**, not knowing where he was going.	[Gen 12:4]Then **Abram went**, just as Yehowah told him.
[9]In [the] faith he dwelt in the land of the promise as **a stranger** (Gen 23:4), living in tents with Isaac and Jacob, joint heirs of the same promise,	[Gen 23:4]**Abraham** . . . said to the Hittites, "I am **a stranger** and a tenant among you."
[10]for he was expecting the city which had the **foundations**, whose builder and constructor was God.	[Isa 14:32]Yehowah has **founded** Zion, and in it the afflicted of its people will find refuge

[11]In [the] faith also **Sarah** herself received power for [the] **foundation** of **seed**, even beyond the time of productivity, since she considered the one who

Isa 28:16 Look! I will **found** in Zion a stone, a tested stone, a precious cornerstone, an **established foundation.**

Isa 54:11 Look! I am laying in antimony your stones, your **foundations** in sapphire.

Ps 87:1 A song of its **foundation** on the holy mountains: [2]Yehowah loves Zion more than the dwelling places of Jacob.

made the **promise** faithful.

Gen 21:1 Yehowah visited **Sarah**, just as he had said, and Yehowah did to **Sarah** as he had **promised**.

[12]Therefore they also came into existence from one, and these from one [who was] dead, **I will surely bless you; I will surely multiply your seed**

Gen 22:17 **I will surely bless you, and I will surely multiply your seed,**

just as the stars of heaven / in their multitude **and as the sand which is along the sea shore** which is countless. [13]In [the] faith all of these died, not having acquired the promises, but after they saw them from a distance, they also greeted them and confessed, "We **are strangers and tenants on the land**."

just as the stars of the heavens and / as sand which is along the sea shore, and **your seed** will possess the gate of your enemy.

Lev 25:23 **The land** is mine, for you **are strangers and tenants** with me.

COMMENTARY

[8]*Abraham, when he was called.* **Abraham** did not initiate the **call**. He received a message of God telling him about the future—not in heaven, but on earth. Like **Noah**, **in the faith,** it is reported that **Abraham was called** upon to act regarding **things not seen** (Heb 11:1, 7). **Abraham's faith** was frequently praised by Jews and Christians (Sir 44:19-21; Wis 10:5; Rom 4; Gal 3; Acts 7:2-5; Heres 18:90-93. **An inheritance** is a lot, fortune, or possession which may be acquired as a gift, from labor, or by plunder and conquest (see Commentary on Heb 1:2, 4). The place he left was Haran (Gen 12:4) in the northern region of the Fertile Crescent.

[9]*The land of the promise.* The Greek word for **dwelt** is *pah-roh-kay-sehn* (παρῴκησεν), "dwelt beside," as though he were not one of the nation's citizens. **The land of the promise** is **the land** Abraham was **promised** that he would receive as an **inheritance**, namely the Land of Canaan, Davidic kingdom, Palestine. Nowhere else in Scripture is Palestine called **the land of the promise**, although the

land was regularly understood as the **promised inheritance**. According to Genesis, it was not **Isaac and Jacob** but Lot who lived (*lah-shéh-vehth*, לשבת) with Abraham (Gen 13:6). The author probably did not mean literally that Abraham, Isaac, and Jacob lived together **in tents**, but that they all shared the experience of living in **tents** as strangers **in the land**. The confirmation of **Isaac and Jacob** as **joint heirs of the same promise** is reported in Gen 26:3 and 28:13.

Backhaus followed the rhetorical tradition of the author of Hebrews by starting his argument with a hypothesis:

> The Letter to the Hebrews develops a theological topography in which the conventional biblical goods are desanctified by means of Christological reorientation. The "land of the promise" (11:9), the promised rest, the sanctuary of the first covenant, Mount Sinai, are left behind in the shadows of earth whereas all light is shed upon their counterparts in God's heavenly realm, which turns out to be the faithful's true fatherland.[1]

If the reader accepts Backhaus' hypothesis, he will then be pressed to accept all of his further affirmations and conclusion, which are based on his hypothesis. If Backhaus is allowed to "desanctify" the speech of the author of Hebrews, then he can neglect all of these geographical terms and translate them perpendicularly. Instead of meaning distance across the land from Haran to Jerusalem, Backhaus held that the Christian understanding of the text is a journey from earth (*Diesseitigkeit*) to heaven (*Jenseitigkeit*).[2] When the horizontal concepts are switched to vertical then the journey of a nation in formation, traveling across the land, becomes a cultic community on the move.[3] Weiss correctly responded,

> Have Abraham in such a manner for the author (and correspondingly also for the addressees of Hebrews) become witnesses to heavenly faith? Certainly, absolutely not![4]

Had the author of Hebrews intended his document to be reoriented, he would have reoriented it in the first place and called Haran "the earth" and Zion "heaven," but he chose his own words and meanings. This choice should be respected.

10*The city which had the foundations*. Although Abraham's journey from Haran was clearly in the direction of Palestine and Zion, many scholars metaphorize **the city which had the foundations**, making the contrast, instead, between the Land of Canaan and heaven. Delitzsch, however, was so much impressed by the similarity between the description given in Hebrews and other descriptions of Jerusalem that he had to admit that it was tempting to think that the city that **had the foundations** to be Jerusalem, but his theology required him to deny their identity.[5]

---

[1] K. Backhaus, "Das Land der Verheissung: Die Heimat der Glaubenden im Hebräerbrief," *NTS* 47 (2001):171-88.

[2] Backhaus, "Das Land der Verheissung," p. 173.

[3] Backhaus, "Das Land der Verheissung," 181-82.

[4] Weiss, *Hebräer*, p. 586.

[5] F. Delitzsch, *Commentary on the Epistle to the Hebrews*, tr. T. L. Kingsbury (Grand Rapids: Eerdmans, 1952) II, p. 238.

Muntingh said that in the Near East cities were enlarged or rebuilt to the glories of new kings. One of these would have been Jerusalem, the "city of holiness" (Isa 52:1). It was also the "city of David." Muntingh said,

> Abraham was undoubtedly familiar with this political milieu and with the greater protection offered by "cities with foundations," ruled and defended by the "great king," than was the case with tribal villages. . . . [Abraham] went out not knowing where he was to go, but looking forward to a city . . (Heb 11:8-10). Whether this city was indeed Salem, the Bible does not tell us, but it would be unrealistic to believe that he had no concrete image of what that city might be.[1]

Montefiore said,

> They also show that *the city with foundations* cannot be Canaan, for God is no more the *maker and designer* of Canaan than of any other part of the earth, while he is in a special sense the author of the heavenly Jerusalem.[2]

Rose agreed. He thought the **city which had the foundations** could be understood as the **heavenly Jerusalem, "**so that the **land of the promise,** is also only a station on the way to the heavenly city.**"**[3] Just because it is possible to understand something in a certain way does not mean that is the correct way to understand it, but Rose continued to affirm many times that the goal of Abraham could not have been the Land of Canaan. He neglected to say why it could not have been. Backhaus continued the affirmation of his own hypothesis at this point holding that Canaan could not be the rest, because it is "earthly."[4] Neither Abraham nor the author of Hebrews thought that the earth was as bad as Backhaus thought.

Since Canaan was not a city, it would seem unreasonable to claim that it was, but in the land of Canaan was a **city** of Zion, about which the author of Hebrews was affectionately concerned and was convinced of its divine origin. It was not just a city like any other city any more than the Promised Land was just like any other land. Moffatt said, "Abraham had yearnings for a higher, spiritual bliss, for heaven as his true home,"[5] and Williamson said, "For the writer of Hebrews the 'city' of Abraham was clearly heaven itself."[6] Käsemann said,

---

[1] L. M. Muntingh, "'The City Which Has Foundation': Hebrews 11:8-10 in the Light of the Mari Texts,":119-120, quote from p. 120.

[2] H. Montefiore, *A Commentary on the Epistle to the Hebrews* (New York: Harper & Row, 1964), p. 193.

[3] C. Rose, "Verheissung und Erfüllung," *BZ* 33 (1989):179. Tr. from German.

[4] Backhaus, "Das Land der Verheissung," p. 178.

[5] J. Moffatt, *A Critical and Exegetical Commentary on the Epistle to the Hebrews* (New York: Scribner's Sons, 1964), p. 170; see also C. Spicq, *L' Epitre aux Hebreux* (Paris: J. Gabalda, 1953) 2, pp. 348-50; F. F. Bruce, *The Epistle to the Hebrews* (Grand Rapids: Eerdmans, 1964), pp. 305-6; and M. Stuart, *Commentary on the Epistle to the Hebrews* (Andover: Warren F. Draper, 1828), p. 262.

[6] Williamson, *Philo*, 1970), p. 491.

> The attitude of faith can only be described as wandering, and finally, in the heavenly world and its Jerusalem has concretely revealed the ultimate goal of such wandering and the final consummation.[1] . . . At the center of Philo's and Hebrews' speculation there is the motif of a highway leading through the cosmos to heaven, traversed by a people of God who sojourn on it.[2]

According to Hughes,

> The glory of this prospect was all the more enhanced by the striking contrast of tent dwelling which dramatically testified to the fact that the foundations of this life were not in the present world . . . the land promised to them was a figure of the heavenly habitation.[3]

Lane correctly said,

> The biblical realism in reference to the established city shows that there is nothing abstract or contingent about the promised "inheritance."

This is confusing after Lane had already said, "In v 10 'the city with foundations' is the transcendent heavenly city,"[4] and "[The servants of God are those whose] existence is on earth, but their citizenship is in heaven."[5] There appears to be some ambiguity between the logic and the dogmas of some scholars.

If all that was required to make a case was a plurality vote, lots of scholarly repetition, and many affirmations, there would be no question. The Land of Canaan would be voted out, and heaven would be established as the goal both of Abraham and the author of Hebrews. But that is not the case. Facts, logic, contexts, and historical reports are important considerations.

Foundation stones for a city do not instantly inspire a reader to think of rocks on the clouds of heaven. Even the huge stones in Herod's wall seem more likely, especially in view of Josephus' report of Agrippa's wall. The wall, which Agrippa began to build around Jerusalem, would have been very strong, had he been allowed to finish it. Josephus said it was constructed of stones 20 cubits long and ten broad (about 30 by 15 feet). Recent excavations have shown that Josephus had not exaggerated.[6]

When Claudius learned the dimensions of the planned wall, he made Agrippa stop the construction after he had laid **only the foundation** (Wars 5:152-55; Ant 19:326-27). Of course the city had other walls, but none so firm as these had

---

[1] E. Käsemann, *The Wandering People of God* (Minneapolis; Augsburg; tr. R.A. Harrison and I. L. Sandberg, c1984), p. 57.

[2] Käsemann, *Wandering*, p. 86.

[3] P. F. Hughes, *A Commentary on the Epistle to the Hebrews* (Grand Rapids: Eerdmans, c1977), p. 469.

[4] W. L. Lane, *Hebrews 9-13* (Dallas: Word Books, c1991), p. 352.

[5] Lane, *Hebrews 9-13*, p. 360.

[6] About the same size as those uncovered in the Herodian wall on the south side. These are 10-11 meters long. See B. Mazar, "The Excavations South and West of the Temple Mount in Jerusalem--the Herodian Period," *BA* 33 (1970):52-53.

been designed to be. Jews may have dreamed of completing the walls at the first opportunity, but even if they had, these foundations were only for walls—not for the city itself.

Resh Lakish said that in the future the Lord would add to Jerusalem a thousand gardens, a thousand towers, a thousand palaces and mansions, and that each of these would be as big as Sepphoris in its prosperity (bBB 75b).[1] Tobit dreamed of a new Jerusalem whose gates would be built of sapphire and emerald and its walls of precious stone, its towers would be made of gold and its streets of carbuncle and stones of Ophir (Tob 13:16-17), which is an extension of Second Isaiah's vision (Isa 54:12). The NT seer envisioned a new Jerusalem whose walls had twelve foundations (Rev 21:14), and **the foundations of the wall of the city [were] decorated with every precious stone** (Rev 21:19). He described the city still more gloriously than Tobit had done (Rev 21:19-21). Like the temple not made with hands (see Commentary on 9:11), **the city which had the foundations** was one **whose builder and constructor was God. Builder and constructor** are synonyms forming a *hendiadys*. One section of the **city** was also called **Mount Zion, even [the] city of [the] living God, heavenly Jerusalem** (Heb 12:22).

The author of Hebrews was not the only one to attribute a divine origin to Zion. Tobit (Tob 13:9) called it the "holy city." So did Isaiah (Isa 52:1), and John of Patmos dreamed of **the holy city, a new Jerusalem, coming down from heaven, from God** (Rev 21:2). This was a city whose **foundations** and walls were made of precious stones (Rev 21:19). Before Herod's walls were built, the author of 2Macc 3:39 said that God **whose dwelling place is heaven** was a guardian and aid of Jerusalem. Pseudo-Clement urged his readers to follow a leader that was acquainted with the road that enters the holy city (Hom 3.12). **The city which had the foundations** was Zion, the capital city in **the land of the promise** (Heb 11:9) The stability of **the city which had the foundations** was set in contrast to the existence of the patriarchs in tents (Heb 11:9). The Shepherd said,

> "You know," he said, "that you servants of God, are living in a strange [land], for your city [Zion] is far from this city [Rome] (Hermas *Sim* 1:1).

The city that had the foundations was Zion, but not Herod's Jerusalem, which was enclosed within the Roman fortress walls. Herod's walls had strong foundations, but not the entire fortress. **The city which had the foundations** was an entire city, and not just the walls. This claim could apply to only one city. That was Zion. Other cities had walls that were set on solid foundations, but Zion was the only city that had foundations for the entire city. How could that be? The archaeology of the city gives us some clues.

South of Herod's walls was David's holy City, Zion (Isa 52:1), where Solomon's temple had been constructed. There were tender religious ties to this city that had never been transferred to the city within Herod's walls. **The city which had the foundations** (*toos theh-meh-leé-oos*, τοὺς θεμελίους) was Zion. That city was distinguished for its **foundations.** The psalmist (Ps. 87:1) said Zion's

---

[1] Sepphoris was the capital of Galilee. It was by far the most magnificent city in Galilee. See Mark Chancey and Eric M. Myers, "How Jewish Was Sepphoris in Jesus' Time?"; Tsvika Tsuk, "Bringing Water to Sepphoris,"; "The Pools at Sepphoris," *BAR*. 26 (July/August, 2000):18-45.

foundation (*yeh-soo-dah-taw*, יסודתו) was in the holy mountain (Ps 87:1).[1] It was the city Yehowah had founded (Isa 14:32; 28:16). After the fall of Jerusalem in 70 IA, an unknown seer had a vision of a constructed city that had large **foundations** (*fundamentis magnis*) which turned out to be Zion (4Ezra 10:26-27, 44)--**Zion, city of the God of life, heavenly Jerusalem** (Heb 12:22). It was stationed there on the west bank of the Kidron Valley, high above the Spring of Siloam.

It has been shown earlier (pp. 301-302) that the Jebusites constructed a strong foundation upon which the city of Zion was built. It was made of rocks that were filled in to widen the city and make the entire basis for the city both a huge wall and a deep foundation. This made Zion uniquely the city that has the foundations.

[11]*The power for [the] foundation of seed.* Scholars have had difficulty with the passage **Sarah . . . received power for [the] foundation of seed** because the expression, **foundation of seed** (*kah-tah-boh-láyn spéhr-mah-taws*, καταβολὴν σπέρματος), visually appears to mean the ejection of seed, which is the role of the male. Therefore, many scholars say, this passage was once a continuation of the passage dealing with Abraham.[2] But the word *kah-tah-boh-láyn* can mean simply **foundation**, without any attempt to etymologize the idiom. The Vulgate renders this expression *in conceptionem seminis* Although *kah-tah-boh-láyn* is not the same word for **foundation** as *theh-mehl-eé-oos* (θεμελίους) used in the preceding verse, the author may have intentionally compared the two. On the one hand, there was the city which had the **foundations**, the ancient City of David; and, on the other hand, there was Isaac, the **foundation** of the chosen people, the seed of Abraham, who were destined to be **heirs** of **the land of the promise** (Heb 11:9) and the **city which had the foundations** (Heb 11:10).

Grässer correctly observed that there are many terms that are closely related to *hoo-páw-stah-sees.* These are: "rest" (Heb 4:1, 3, 10, 11), "heavenly Jerusalem" (Heb 12:22), "remaining," "future," "city of God" (Heb 12:22; 13:14). "inheritance of the age" (9:15), "coming age" (Heb 2:5), and "unshakable kingdom" (Heb 12:28).[3] These are also terms closely associated with the FT and the promises of the contract made with Abraham.

Hay-lee-keé-ahs (ἡλικίας) refers to the age of maturity, the prime of life. It generally distinguishes adulthood from childhood. In early years it would mark the beginning of menstruation for a woman, but it also refers to the entire period from the beginning of menstruation to the beginning of menopause, namely, the period of fertility. Since Sarah was **beyond the time of productivity**, her menopause had already occurred. **The one who made the promise** in Sarah's hearing was one of the men whom **Abraham** had entertained as a guest (Gen 18:1-10), and **Sarah** certainly did not consider him **faithful**, but laughed at the suggestion (Gen 18:9-15). She doubted that it would happen. It was not Sarah's trust and belief but the fact that this was reported **in [the] faith** that was important. The author of Hebrews probably

---

[1] I. M. Muntingh, "'The City Which Has Foundations': Hebrews 11:8-10 in the Light of the Mari Texts," pp. 108-119, suggested that the foundation referred to was a royal administration rather than rock foundation for the walls. He thought, however, that this referred to Jerusalem.

[2] For this discussion see [2] F. F. Bruce, *The Epistle to the Hebrews,* (Grand Rapids: Eerdmans, 1964), pp. 299-302; O. Michel, *Der Brief an die Hebräer* (Göttingen: Vandenhoeck & Ruprecht, 1957), pp. 262-63.

[3] Grässer, *Hebäerbrief*, p. 50.

meant that the one who made the promise to **Abraham** (Gen 15:5; 22:17) was **faithful**, and that one was God. The messenger who made the **promise** was God's legal agent; God was the principal who was **faithful** to the contract he had made with **Abraham**. The author had earlier claimed that God was **faithful** (Heb 10:23).

The author of Hebrews, however, used the term **faith** in a way that was more doctrinal than active. Frequently it was used to refer to the confession, the creed, or the Scripture rather than the very act of believing. The fact that Sarah was reported in the Scripture may have shown to the author that she was recorded in **the faith.** She was included in the confession.

12*They also came into existence from one*. This was true of most ancient societies. Maine said,

> Of this we may be certain, that all ancient societies regarded themselves as having proceeded from one original stock, and even laboured under an incapacity for comprehending any reason except this for their holding together in political union.[1]

Those who **came into existence** were the sons of Abraham who originated **from one,** namely Abraham. **These** constitute the seed (plural) of Abraham, who were called **dead**, meaning sterile. Not all children of Abraham were physically sired by him or his physical offspring. Many were adopted and became the legal seed of Abraham. They came into existence as children of Abraham when they were born again through a legal liturgy. They were legally and religiously **dead** as gentiles, from the Abrahamic point of view, until they had become baptized into legal life as children of Abraham.

The poetic couplet which included Gen 22:17 has been interpretatively expanded while still preserving the poetry by adding **in their multitude** to one line and **which is countless** to the other. The author may have made these additions himself, or he may have used a couplet already formed from these stock phrases.

13*We are strangers and tenants on the land*. The word rendered **land** here is very seldom translated "earth." Context determines which. Most of the time in the Scripture the word *áh-rehtz* (ארץ) refers to the Promised Land. None-the-less, Grässer translated it as "earth" and held that the Hebrews audience was on its way to heaven.[2] That was an unnecessary strain. Its unforced meaning is clear.

While the Lord was telling Moses the Sabbath and Jubilee rules to observe on the Promised Land, he reminded Moses that the land was his—not the people's (Lev 25:23). They could eat the produce on the land and prosper, but the land belonged to him. The children of Abraham were only **strangers and temporary residents on the land.** This was **the land** God **promised** to give Moses and the Israelites, and the directions were given to Moses while he was on Mount Sinai (Lev 25:1-2). Just because the Israelites were only **strangers and temporary residents on the land** they expected to inherit sometime in the future as a possession does not mean they really were on their way to heaven and did not have any interest in anything earthly. The author of Hebrews held that therefore the early Israelites did

[1] Maine, *Ancient Law*, p. 106.

[2] Grässer, *An die Hebräer* 1, p. 150. R. T. France, "The Writer of Hebrews as a Biblical Expositor," *Tyndale Bulletin* 47 (1996):271, agreed with Grässer.

not receive the **promises** of God to Abraham. They were to live on this land as **temporary residents**. God would be the land owner. The **land** was given conditionally, but they were to inherit it with these conditions

TEXT

[14]For those who say such things as these make [it] clear that they are looking for a fatherland,[15] and if, on the one hand, they had kept in mind that [fatherland] from which they had gone out, they would have had opportunity all along to return, [16]but now, on the other hand, they are reaching out for a better [fatherland], that is a heavenly [one]. Therefore God is not ashamed to be called their God, for he has prepared for them a city.

COMMENTARY

[13]*Not having acquired [the fulfillment of] the promises*. **According to faith** perhaps means according to the creed, report, or Scripture on which their **faith** was based. **These all** were Abraham, Isaac, and Jacob and possibly Abel, Enoch, and Noah. The author probably meant only the patriarchs (plus Sarah), because they were the ones involved in **the promises**. They all received **the promises**, but they did not acquire their fulfillment, and that is what the author had in mind. The author of Hebrews confessed that they were **strangers and tenants . . . in the land** (*gay-reém*, גרים . . . *wuh-toh-shah-veém* ותשבים. . . *ahl hah-áh-rehtz*, על הארץ) even after they were established **on the land** (1Chron 29:15). **The promises** about which the author was interested involved entering the **rest** (Heb 4:1), being blessed, and becoming a great and numerous people to whom others would defer (Gen 22:17-19; Josh 21:43-45; Heb 6:13-20), or receiving the **land of the promise** (Heb 11:9).

These are **all** related to the reestablishment of the land of Palestine under the control of the chosen people, as an exalted nation. Since this had never happened, even for a short time, until the reigns of David and Solomon, the author was correct in saying that **these all died, not having acquired [the fulfillment of] the promises**.

These all were the patriarchs that the author mentioned earlier. Moses, who was called **the servant of the Lord** (Deut 34:5), was not allowed to lead the children of Israel from the wilderness into the Land of Canaan, but he saw the land from afar, from **the top of Mount Pisgah** (Deut 34:1). The land which he saw was that which **Yehowah promised under oath** that he would give **to Abraham, to Isaac, and to Jacob** (Deut. 34:4). It was the **fatherland** for which God was the **Father**. It was "the holy land," "the land of Life," whose capital city was the "heavenly Jerusalem." It was because of this land that Abraham left Haran in search of a **better** homeland. The first generation of Jews in Babylon was also called the Lord's **servant** (*ahv-deé*, עבדי) (Isa 53:11).[1] That servant was not allowed to return to **the land of life** (i.e., Palestine), but **made his grave with the wicked** in Babylon (Isa 53:8-9).

Like Moses, however, these Jews were allowed **to see their seed** (Isa 53:10) who would be allowed to return. The author of Hebrews classed the patriarchs with Moses and possibly the suffering servant, when he said they **saw and greeted** the promises **from a distance.** Abraham from Haran, the Israelites from Egypt, the Jews

---

[1] Buchanan, *The Consequences of the Covenant* (Leiden: E. J. Brill, 1970), pp. 123-131.

from Babylon, or the many contemporary Jews from the diaspora who had come to Jerusalem to attend feast days. There were many Jews who **had greeted Jerusalem from a distance.** Some members of the author's audience were local Palestinians. For them the **distance** was temporal rather than geographical, as was true of Moses and the Isaianic servant. They lived in the very land they hoped to inherit, but only as **strangers and temporary residents** in the land, not as citizens.

14-15 *They are looking for a fatherland.* The author of Hebrews thought people would not call themselves such depreciative names as **strangers and temporary residents** if that was their highest goal. To him it was **clear that they [were] looking for a fatherland**, but they had already left one **fatherland**. If they had not been particular, they could have returned to Haran, Egypt, Babylon, or one of the cities of the diaspora and had a **fatherland** again. This **opportunity** had been open to them **all along**, but the author's audience was not satisfied with Haran, Egypt, Babylon, or the contemporary countries of the diaspora.

Käsemann was one of those who devoted little time or space to Middle Eastern geography or history. Instead, he disagreed with Michel and depended heavily on Philo for an understanding of Hebrews.[1] He said,

> At the center of Philo's and Hebrews' speculation there is the motif of a highway leading through the cosmos to heaven, traversed by a people of God who sojourn on it, or by a race of seers which symbolizes this people. Philo and Hebrews anchor this motif in biblical thought by an exegesis of the Old Testament, a motif which in neither case would originally have emerged from Scripture.[2]

When Käseman wandered away from the Scripture into his own imagination he also soared not only into Philonic allegory, but also into gnosticism, Indian and Egyptian mysticism, and various kinds of psychology. This was a huge distraction from the clear message and method of the author of Hebrews, who based his arguments on Scripture, biblical history, and geography.

16 *They are reaching out for a better [fatherland].* When they left Haran, they were **reaching out for a better [fatherland], that is a heavenly [one].** Just as the author of Hebrews was the only author in the Bible who called the Land of Canaan **the land of the promise** (Heb 11:9), so he was the only one who called it a **heavenly** land (Heb 12:16), but it is clear in both instances that Palestine was the land intended. In the contract, the Lord promised Abraham:

> **To your seed I have given this land,**
> **from the River of Egypt**
> **to the Great River (the River Euphrates)** (Gen 15:18).

In an earlier passage, God told Abraham to go out from his country (*ah-retz*, ארץ) to a land (*ah-rehtz*, ארץ) which God would show him (Gen 12:1). Because the LXX of this passage translates the first use of the term, á*h-rehtz,* as "land" or "country" and

---

[1] E. Käsemann, *The Wandering People of God* (Minneapolis: Augsburg, c1984), tr. R. A. Harrison and I. L. Sandberg, p. 67.

[2] Käsemann, *Wandering*, p. 86.

the second use as "place" (*táw-paws,* τόπος), Rose contended that this choice of words could not be unintentional. It probably was not unintentional. The good stylist avoided repetition by choosing a synonym for the second word with the same meaning in context. In no case did the LXX translator intend to change the meaning of "land" or "country" to "heaven." He really intended to translate the Hebrew fairly. Rose was not as responsible with the text as the LXX translator was. Instead Rose concluded that this meant,

> The favorable promise is, therefore, not the Land of Canaan, but a heavenly place.[1]

The Hebrew gave the word "land" or "country" for the text. The LXX translated the second use of "land" as "place." Rose changed place to "heavenly place," and, in the process, changed the meaning completely. By going through these steps of change, Rose was able to justify his repeated claim that Abraham's promise was not the Land of Canaan, but the *heavenly Holy of Holies.*[2]

The explanatory passage (Gen 15:18), **the River Euphrates**, is a later gloss made by someone who thought the only great river was the **Euphrates**. The same glossator probably made the same identification in Josh 1:4 and Deut 1:7 as well. Initially, the author of the poetic couplet had some other **river** in mind that was either called great or was one he considered to be great. In all probability that river today forms the northern boundary of Lebanon and is still called **The Great River** (*Náh-hahr ehl-Kuh-beér*) in Arabic.

All the known biblical sites listed in the northern boundaries are in the area of this river: Lebwe or Labwah Hamath, Riblah, Lebanon from the river, Hethlon, Zedad, and Kadesh (Josh 13:3-5; 1Chron 13:5; Gen 15:18; Amos 6:18; Isa 27:2; Exod 23:31; 2Kings 14:25; Ezek 6:24; Deut 11:24; 1Kings 5:1; Ezek 47:15-19; Deut 1:7; Num 34:3-9; Ezek 48:1-2, 28). None of these is near the Euphrates River. The southern border was the **River of Egypt** (probably Wadi elArish or perhaps a distributary of the Nile), the Sihor opposite Egypt (perhaps also Wadi el-Arish), Kadesh-barnea, the Wilderness of Zin, Halak, the Ascent of the Akrabbim ("Scorpions"), and the Arabah--all sites from the Mediterranean Sea toward the Dead Sea via the wilderness south of Mount Halak. (A sketched map of the Promised Land appears between chapters 8 and 9).

Between **the River of Egypt** and **the Great River** lay the Land of Canaan and the land of the Hittites, which together comprised the territory ruled by Solomon.[3] This was the land Israelites were able to conquer, so it was the land they believed to be their true heritage. Because they conquered it, they believed God promised it to them, so the author of Hebrews called it **the land of the promise** (Heb 11:9). Its capital city was Zion, called the holy city or **city of our God** (Ps 87:2-3). It was the city which **comes down from God** (Rev 21:2), or, as the author of Hebrews called it, **Zion, even the city of [the] living God, heavenly Jerusalem** (Heb 12:22). It was the city God **has prepared for them,** a **city which had the foundations, whose builder and constructor was God** (Heb 11:10, 16). Fourth Ezra promised that the time would come when the city that was then not visible would appear, and the land which was then concealed would be seen (Heb 7:26).

---

[1] Rose, "Verheissung," p. 180. tr. from German.

[2] Rose, "Verheissung," p. 80. tr. from the German.

[3] See further Buchanan, *The Consequences*, pp. 91-109.

This implies that both Zion and the Promised Land were hidden in the substance (Heb 11:1-2), to be disclosed when they were restored under the establishment of conditions of glory.

Along with other encomiums, the author of Hebrews called **the land of the promise** (Heb 11:9) **a heavenly [one].** This does not mean it is not on earth any more than the **sharers in [the] heavenly calling** (Heb 3:1) who had **tasted the heavenly gift** (Heb 6:4) were not those who lived on earth. Indeed, it was the very land on which the patriarchs dwelt as **tenants and wanderers** (Heb 11:13), but the expression means that it is a divine land which God himself has **promised,** and of which he himself was the owner and principal. According to Pseudo-Clement, God appointed two kingdoms, an evil one and a good one. He also created two ages, a current evil age and a good age to come. The good kingdom was being preserved for the future age. The evil kingdom was ruled by the kings of the current evil age The future kingdom was called the Kingdom of Heaven (Hom 20:2). Pseudo-Clement did not imply that the kingdom was in heaven, but that it was future. Nomoto said the better part of the argument is not just because it is heavenly, but because it is eschatologically oriented. The heavenly is nothing more than the designation for that which is eschatologically new.[1]

Hosea warned that unfaithful Israelites would not be allowed to live in **the land of Yehowah** (Hos 9:3). In the next verse he also said that they would not be allowed to enter **the house of Yehowah** (Hos 9:4). Hosea probably justified his use of the term **land of Yehowah** to describe the Promised Land on the basis of Leviticus, where God reportedly told Moses, **The land** is mine, for you are **strangers and tenants** with me (Lev 25:23).[2] If it belonged to **Yehowah,** then it was the **land of Yehowah.** Delitzsch said,

> It must be confessed that we nowhere read of the patriarchs, that they expressed a conscious desire for a home in heaven. The nearest approach to anything of the kind is in Jacob's vision of the angel-ladder, and his wondering exclamation (Gen 28:17) *zeh sa`ar hassamayim* [זה שׁער השׁמים, This is the gate of heaven]; but even there no desire is expressed for an entrance into the heavenly land, but the promise renewed of future possession of earthly Canaan: "The land whereon thou sleepest will I give thee."[3]

Stuart, however, thought Heb 11:16 so clearly denied Palestine and Jerusalem as the goal of Abraham that his comment was only,

---

[1] S. Nomoto, "Herkunft und Structur der Hohenpriestervorstellung im Hebräerbrief," *NovT* 10 (1968):18.

[2] F. I. Andersen and D. N. Freedman, *Hosea* (Garden City: Doubleday & Co., 1980), p. 528, argued that since Hos 9:3-4 constitute a parallel construct that the words "land of Yehowah" in one line is equivalent to the "house of Yehowah" in the other. This does not follow. Parallelism does not have to be that exact. The warning was about two things rather than one. Israelites would not be allowed: 1) to live on the Promised Land, or 2) to enter the temple. The Promised Land was not called the temple of Yehowah. Hosea's threats were similar to those made by his contemporaries, Amos and Isaiah.

[3] Delitzsch, *Hebrews 2*, p 246.

> The explanation of the writer in respect to the country which the patriarchs sought, is so plain, that nothing can add to its perspicuity.[1]

Hughes echoed the theme:

> Their faith, accordingly, met the challenge to penetrate beyond death and beyond this present world, for the promise of an everlasting possession and universal blessing portended far more than the rights to a piece of geographical territory and a privileged posterity.[2] . . . They make it plain that that they *desire a better country*, altogether other and beyond any country past or present of this fallen world, in other words a *heavenly one*, unmarred by any imperfection, glorious forevermore.[3]

The Greek word *gay* (γη), used in Heb 11:13, like the Hebrew word *áh-retz* (ארץ) can mean either "earth" or **land**, signifying **the Promised Land**, depending on the context. Moffatt[4] and the RSV both render *gay* "earth" in Heb 11:13, and Michel gives it the German *Erde.*[5] Consequently, Moffatt interpreted Heb 11:13-16 quite differently from the above exegesis. The patriarchs were, according to Moffatt, "*strangers and exiles upon earth*."[6] They aspired "to the better land in heaven" (Heb 11:16)—just as if the sky was land! Moffatt correctly observed that Jacob told Pharaoh, **The days of the years of my temporary residency are a hundred and thirty years** (Gen 47:9), and that Abraham confessed to the Hittites, **I am a temporary resident among you** (Gen 23:4-5). Moffatt erroneously concluded that the words *eh-peé tays gáys* (ἐπὶ τῆς γῆς) meant "upon the earth" rather than "upon the land" (vv. 14-16a) and that the true home of these confessors was in heaven.[7]

Moffatt reached these conclusions by ignoring the immediate contexts of the FT references he quoted, accepting **heavenly** as a place description. He overlooked the major theme of the author of Hebrews. Jacob was talking to Pharaoh about his life which had been spent traveling from place to place throughout most of the Fertile Crescent. There is no indication that he was contrasting his earthly residency with a heavenly habitation. Neither did Abraham consider himself to be a temporary resident on earth whose home was in heaven. He was wandering around in the land of the Hittites, where he was not a citizen.

Michel identified the heavenly city with Jerusalem and related it to the FT expectations of 2Isa, Ezek, and Zech, as well as Tob, 4Ezra, and 2Bar. He also called it the future Jerusalem of rabbinic literature. He claimed, however, that this was an apocalyptic and transcendent reality, rather than a restoration of Zion to its political position in Palestine.[8] He was correct in relating all these eschatological

---

[1] M. Stuart, *Commentary on the Epistle to the Hebrews* (Andover: Warren F. Draper, 1828), p. 265.

[2] P. E. Hughes, *Commentary on the Epistle to the Hebrews* (Grand Rapids: Eerdmans Publishing Co., c1977), p. 478.

[3] Hughes, *Commentary,* p. 480.

[4] Moffatt, *Hebrews* p.173,

[5] Michel, *Hebräer,* p. 257.

[6] Moffatt, *Hebrews,* p. 173.

[7] Moffatt, *Hebrews,* p. 174.

[8] Michel, *Hebrews,* pp. 261-62.

hopes of Judaism with Hebrews, but he was mistaken in his belief that apocalyptic hopes did not anticipate the restoration of Zion to a geographic position. The transcendent city in heaven was to be brought down to its former location when the nation was restored. So Zion could be called a heavenly city and Canaan a heavenly land, as the author of Hebrews seems to have done.[1]

Backhaus followed Marquardt in noting that the promise was about ground, composed of sand and stone. Backhaus thought it would be a miracle if that word were applied to a promise that remained into eternity.[2] Backhaus apparently meant "heaven." That would probably be miraculous, but the author of Hebrews did not propose it. Backhaus thought Christians inherited the word of the promise, but not specifically the land of the promise.[3]

The author of Hebrews had basically one hope or aspiration: receiving the Promised Land in its full glory and prosperity, free from foreign rule or threat from enemies. This was called inheriting or acquiring the **promises** (Heb 6:11, 15-17; 11:13, 33, 39) and entering into the **rest** (Heb 3:11, 18; 4:1, 3, 5, 8, 11). The promise is that which was given to Abraham that his seed should inherit the land and be blessed with power, wealth, and number (Gen 15). This is also the **rest** (Heb 4:1), and the reception of the land was called an **inheritance** (Heb 11:8). The **rest** which the Israelites might have had if they had not rebelled in the wilderness is the very **rest** still available.

The good news announced to the Israelites under Moses' leadership was the same good news related to Jesus (Heb 4:1, 6). Moses and Jesus were related to the same **house**--Moses as a servant and Jesus as a Son (Heb 3:2-6). Since the term **rest** was so closely related to the acquisition of Canaan, the intended readers were expected to object that Israelites had received their **promised rest** when Joshua led the conquest of Canaan after 40 years in the wilderness. The author of Hebrews had two answers:

(a) If Joshua had really given them **rest**, at a later time God would not have spoken through David of another day (Heb 4:8); and
(b) whoever finds **rest,** ceases from his labors (Heb 4:10). Since Israel had never had a continuing period of settlement free from threat or **labor**, she had not received her full and final **rest** that had been promised.

That did not mean the **rest** still expected was different from the one early Israelites expected, but only that it would at last be completely received.

This promise-rest-inheritance was inextricably tied to the Land of Canaan, which is the place where the patriarchs wandered as **temporary residents** (Heb 11:13). It was called **the land of the promise** (Heb 11:9) and the **heavenly country** (Heb 11:16), which is better than Haran. In the **heavenly country** God had **prepared for them a city** (Heb 11:16), which had **foundations** (Heb 11:10). That city was called by other authors **the holy city** (Tob 13:9) or **the holy city, new Jerusalem, coming down from heaven, from God** (Rev 21:2).

---

[1] Buchanan, *Consequences*, chapters 1-4.
[2] Backhaus, "Das Land der Verheissung," p. 184, fn. 56; F. W. Marquardt, *Die Juden under ihr Land* (Hamburg: Siebenstern-Tashenbuch, 1986), pp. 29-30.
[3] Backhaus, "Das Land der Verheissung," p. 185.

Anderson acknowledged that the **heavenly country** (Heb 11:16) was the land that was promised to Abraham.[1] He further argued that Paul and the author of Hebrews differed on the question of the true heirs of the promise. Paul thought it was extended to the gentiles; whereas the author of Hebrews limited the heritage to the Jews, "Abraham's physical descendants."[2] The law that was changed, Anderson argued, was only the liturgical law--not the Torah.[3] The new contract "does not imply a new people," and "there is no break in Jewish tradition apart from priesthood."[4] Surprisingly, he also affirmed, without giving any evidence to support his belief,

> It is the land, not the seed, which is given a spiritual reinterpretation . . . The author of Hebrews spiritualizes the passage about the Promised Land.

In the midst of his discussion showing that Paul and the author of Hebrews differed on the interpretation of the promise, Anderson pointed out the fact that Paul used the term *káws-maws* (κόσμος) rather than *gay* (γῄ) to show that the descendants were gentiles rather than Jews, but he gave no evidence that the author of Hebrews ever substituted the term *káws-maws* for the FT term **land** (*áh-rehtz*, ארץ, or *gay*, γη).[5]

The RSV and Moffatt in translating Heb 11:13 "strangers and wanderers on the earth" failed to notice that this was a partial repetition of Heb 11:9: **By faith he dwelled in the land of the promise as a stranger.** Just as the earlier passage (Heb 11:9) refers to Canaan, so also the later (Heb 11:13) passage refers to Canaan. This is a normal *geh-zeh-ráh sheh-wáh* (גזרה שוה) deduction. It is implied. Since only context determines whether *gay* should be translated **land** or "earth," the context here clearly required Heb 11:13 to be rendered **strangers and wanderers in the land**, namely **the land of the promise** (Heb 11:9). Therefore it is implied that Heb 11:9 refers to the Land of Canaan.

TEXT

Hebrews	First Testament
[17]In [the] faith **Abraham offered Isaac**, being **tested,** / the one who received the promises	[Gen 22:1]God **tested Abraham**, and said to him, **"Abraham."** And he **said,** "Here am I."

---

[1] C. P. Anderson, "Who are the Heirs of the new Age in the Epistle to the Hebrews?" *Apocalyptic and the New Testament*, ed. J. Marcus and M. L. Soards (Sheffield: JSOT Press, 1989), p. 260.

[2] Anderson, "Heirs," p. 268

[3] Anderson, "Heirs," pp. 269-70.

[4] Anderson, "Heirs," pp. 269-70.

[5] Anderson, "Heirs," p. 263. He accurately noted in his footnotes (22 and 27, p. 276) that he disagreed with the first edition of *To the Hebrews*, on this score, but he was in error in saying that I denied the "eschatological significance" of the land. I argued then and now that the return of the land *was* normal Jewish and Christian eschatology of the first century. The land for them had a "spiritual" significance, meaning they were religiously devoted to it, but it did not imply that there was no expectation that the physical land would be restored to its former boundaries under Jewish rule. The "eschatology" affirmed by Anderson, Attridge, and many other Western scholars was invented in the nineteenth and twentieth centuries by Western scholars. Of course NT authors were not dependent upon them.

[Gen 22:7]**Isaac said** to his father, **Abraham**, "My father." He **said**, "Here I am, my son." He **said**, "Look! the fire and the wood, but where is the lamb for the **offering**?"

offered [his] only one (Gen 22:1-19), [18][with reference] to whom it was **said**,

[Gen 21:12]Everything that Sarah tells you, listen to her voice, for

through Isaac shall your seed be called, [19]considering that God is able to raise [people] from [the] dead, from which he got him back parabolically. [20]In [the] faith also concerning the things to come, **Isaac blessed Jacob** and **Esau**.

through Isaac shall your name be called.

[Gen 27:30]Just as **Isaac** finished **blessing Jacob**, and **Jacob** was leaving the presence of **Isaac**, **Esau** returned from his hunting.

[21]In [the] faith **Jacob**, dying, **blessed each of the sons of Joseph**,

[Gen 48:15-17]He **blessed Joseph** and said, "May the God before whom my fathers, **Abraham and Isaac** walked, / the God who shepherded me until this very day, / the angel who redeemed me from all evil / **bless the young men**, / and may they be called through my name, the name of **Abraham** and **Isaac**."

and he **prostrated himself on the top of this staff**. [22]In [the] faith Joseph, dying, reminded [his brothers] about the exodus of the sons of Israel and gave orders concerning [the care to be given] **his bones**.

[Gen 47:31]Israel **prostrated himself on the top of his staff**.

[Gen 50:25]You shall take up **my bones** from here.

COMMENTARY

[17-19]*Abraham offered Isaac, being tested.* The Greek for **only one** is *mawn-aw-geh-naye* (μονογενή), which is different from the LXX of Gen 22:2, "beloved" (*ah-gah-pay-tawn*, ἀγαπητόν). The Hebrew *yah-kheéd* (יחיד) means both "only one" and "beloved," so both are fair representations of the Hebrew, but their differences indicate that the author had access to a variant LXX text or else translated at times directly from the Hebrew, or even substituted a synonym he preferred. The Greek for "he got him back" is *kaw-meéd-zein,* (κομίζειν) and can mean either "acquire," "receive" "carry off" or "get back," "recover," "return." The author's sensitivity for poetic expression is shown in the couplet in Heb 11:17. His effective use of repetition echoes Heb 11:11-12, though with different meanings:

Hebrews 11:11-12	Hebrews 11:17-19
a. Sarah was "one [who was] **dead"** (12)	a. God could "raise [people] from [the] **dead"** (19)
b. Sarah "**received** power" (11)	b. "God is able" (19)
c. God made **the "promise**" (11)	c. Abraham **"received the promises**" (17)
d. Sarah "**considered** [*hay-gáy-sah-taw*] the one who made the promise faithful"(11).	d. Abraham **considered** *law-gee-sáh-meh-naws*) "that God is able even to raise [people] from [the] **dead"** (19).

Since both subdivisions deal with Isaac, and since the author consciously used similar terminology in both, perhaps the rabbinic rule of implication, *geh-zeh-ráh shah-wáh* (גזרה שוה), whereby one unit is employed to clarify the other, may be applied here. In Heb 11:19, Abraham was said to have offered Isaac because of his faith in God who was **able even to raise [people] from [the] dead**, and parabolically Abraham **got him back**. What is this parable? How was it intended? How did Abraham get Isaac back from the dead? This may refer to the original acquisition of Isaac from Sarah, i.e., **from one [who was] dead** (Heb 11:12). If *koh-meéd-zayn* '(κομίζειν) were intended to mean **receive**, it would refer to Isaac's birth; if it meant **get back**, it would mean the rescue of Isaac from sacrifice. The context suggests the latter, but the relationship between Heb 11:11-12 and Heb 11:17-19 indicates the former.

Some rabbis said that **Abraham** and **Isaac** learned that God would **raise the dead** when **Abraham** was ordered not to hurt **Isaac**. At that time **Isaac'**s soul really left his body and was then restored, and he was **raised** from the **dead** to bless the Lord (PirqRE 31, 16b). This may or may not be the interpretation the author intended. The choice of interpretations is not clear. The rabbinic explanation makes good sense for an author who believed in the resurrection as the author of Hebrews did (Heb 6:2; 11:35), but the author's in literary artistry is also a strong argument to relate the parable to Isaac's birth. The choice is almost arbitrary. In any case, the author's understanding of the resurrection from **the dead** to be parabolic did not mean the real resurrection of a corpse.[1] There was no mention of heaven. Either resurrection expected that Isaac would live out his life afterward on earth.

Whereas Paul held that **Abraham** was reckoned righteous because he believed against all odds that Sarah would bear a son (Gal 3:6-19; Rom 4:1-25), other ancients believed that the real basis for his justification was his willingness to offer **Isaac** (James 2:20-22; Sir 44:20; Wis 10:5; Aboth 5-4; 4Macc 16:18-20). The Genesis narrative began by announcing that God tested **Abraham** (Gen 22:1). The word used for testing (Hebrew *nah-sáh*, נסה, Greek *payr-áhd-zayn*, πειράζειν) is the same word used to describe the Israelites' rebellion in the wilderness (Exod 17:2-7; Num 14:22) and the devil's testing of Jesus (Matt 4:1). It is not surprising that the author of Hebrews admired **Abraham's** willingness to offer **Isaac**. He would have considered it holding fast the confession of hope.

---

[1] For a convincing analysis and thesis of the importance of the binding of Isaac as a virtue for which God was expected by Jews and Christians to reward Israel in the future, see N. A. Dahl, "The Atonement--An Adequate Reward for the Akedah? (Ro 8:32)," *Neotestamentica et Semitica*, eds. E. E. Ellis and M. Wilcox (Edinburgh: T. & T. Clark, 1969), pp. 15-29.

[20-22]*In [the] faith Isaac . . . In [the] faith Jacob . . . In [the] faith Joseph.* The author was kindly disposed toward his spiritual ancestors, so he did not tell about the way Jacob cheated Esau out of his blessing (Gen 27:1-29). When **Esau** asked **Isaac** to bless him also, **Isaac** could only predict the future for Esau after Jacob had already been promised the blessings intended for the firstborn (Gen 27:36-40). The author rather obscured this deceptive event when he generously reported that **Isaac blessed Jacob and Esau**. According to Jub 17:15, this had the approval of **Abraham** who did not want his posterity to follow Esau's line or to have Esau's children called by his name.

In his report of **Joseph,** the author of Hebrews copied directly the LXX version of Gen 47:31, which does not make much sense. The LXX, working with an unpointed text, confused the words *hah-mee-táh*, (מטה = bed) with *hah-mah-téh*, מטה (staff). Although the Greek implies that **Joseph** considered the staff as some object of worship and bowed himself down before it, the Hebrew simply meant that he was lying prostrate on the top of or at the head of his bed (MT Gen 47:31), a normal position for a dying man.[1] According to Jewish tradition, a miracle was performed by which Joseph's bones were recovered and taken with the children of Israel when they escaped from Egypt (Mek, *Beshallah* 1:86-98; 106-7).

Summary. Heb 11:20-22 form a small subdivision, all unified by death scenes, blessings, and orders. In relationship to the whole unit (Heb 11:8-22) these verses complete the topic. This unit began with the promise of **the land of the promise** (Heb 11:9) which Abraham **was about to receive** (*ay-méhl-ehn lahm-báh-nayn*, ἤμελλεν λαμβάνειν) **for an inheritance** (Heb 11:8). The topic concluded with blessings concerning **the things to come** (*mehl-láwn-tohn*, μελλόντων) (Heb 11:20) which involved a reminder of **the exodus of the sons of Israel** (Heb 11:22) when they would return to take possession of the **land of the promise,** which they were to receive as **an inheritance** (Heb 11:8).

It also prepared the readers for the next topic on Moses. In between these sentences was the history of **Abraham, Isaac, Jacob,** and even **Joseph** in Egypt, according to the author's interpretation. This involved not only the history of the chosen people, but their relationship to the **promise** and the land of the **promise** from Abraham's **promise** in Haran to Joseph's providence in Egypt. These patriarchs were famous for their faith and endurance, but they did not receive the fulfillment of **the promise**.

TEXT

Hebrews	First Testament
[23]In [the] faith Moses, after he had **been born**, **was**	[Exod 2:2]The woman conceived and **gave birth** to a son. When **she** **saw that he was attractive she**
hidden three months by his parents, because **they saw [that] the child was attractive**, and they were not	**hid him for three months**.

[1] Also Delitzsch 2, p. 256. For a strong defense of the LXX translation, see Stuart, *Hebrews,* p. 269.

afraid of the decree of the king. 24In [the] faith Moses, when he had grown up, refused to [let it be said that he was] a son of the daughter of Pharaoh, 25choosing rather to be badly treated with the people of God than to have transitory enjoyment of crime, 26since he considered **the insult of** **the Messiah** greater wealth than the treasures of Egypt, for he was looking out for the reward. 27In [the] faith [it is held that] he left Egypt, not having feared the wrath of the king, for he endured as [one who] saw the invisible. 28In [the] faith [it is claimed that] he instituted the **Passover** and the **pouring out of the blood**, in order that the one **destroying** the firstborn might not touch them.

Ps 89 [88]:50-51 Remember, Lord, **the insult of** your servants which I have borne in my bosom, of many nations, with which they have mocked the retaliation **of your Messiah.**

Exod 2:15 Moses fled from Pharaoh, and he stayed in the land of Midian.

Exod 12:7 They shall **take some of the blood and pour it on the door posts** and the window frames of the houses in which they eat them . . .
13The blood will be a sign for you on the houses where you are. When I see the blood I will **pass over** you, and no plague will fall upon you to **destroy** you.

29In [the] faith they **went through the Red Sea as through dry land**, by which **the Egyptians**, when they made [the same] attempt, were swallowed up (Exod 14:1-15:21).

Exod 14:21-22 Then Moses extended his hand over the sea, and Yehowah drove the sea back by a strong east wind at night, and made **the sea dry land**. The water was divided, and the Israelites **went through the midst of the sea on dry land**.

Exod 14:27-28 Yehowah shook off **the Egyptians** in the midst of the sea. Then the water returned and covered the cavalry, the chariots, and all the troops of Pharaoh.

30In [the] faith **the walls** of Jericho **fell**,

Josh 6:20 When the people heard the sound of the ram's horn, the people shouted loudly, and **the wall fell** down.

having been circled
for seven days (Josh 6:1-21).

Josh 6:15 On that day **they circled** the city **seven** times.

31[it is reported] in [the] faith **Rahab** the harlot did not perish with the unfaithful ones, having received **the spies** in peace (Josh 6:22-27).

Josh 6:23 **The** young **spies** went and brought out **Rahab**, her father, her mother, her brothers, and all that was hers.

COMMENTARY

23*They were not afraid.* The Greek for **three months** is *tree-máy-nawn* (τρίμηνον) which means the same as the LXX for Exod 2:2 but is different in form (LXX *máy-nahs trays*, μῆνας τρεῖς). This is another indication that the author of Hebrews had access to a different LXX text from any that is extant today. **The decree of the king** was that every male child born of Hebrew parents should be drowned in the Nile (Exod 1:22).

24*In [the] faith Moses, when he had grown up.* The expression **when he had grown up** (*meh-gas geh-náw-meh-nos*, μέγας γενόμενος) literally means "having become great" and could refer to Moses' prestige and political or material greatness, but it probably only means that he had become an adult so that he could make decisions for himself. Josephus says "when he came of age" (*pahr-ehl-tháwn ays heh-leh-keé-ahn*, παρῆλθον εἰς ἐλεκίαν) (Ant 2:238). At that time he was free to choose to remain in a leading position in Egypt or he could reestablish his identity with the Israelites, who were in disfavor with Pharaoh. He chose the latter, refusing **to [let it be said that he was] a son of the daughter of Pharaoh**. The text of Exodus does not say he refused identity with the daughter of Pharaoh, but it showed him taking sides in behalf of Israelites in Egypt. This must have seemed like ingratitude, sabotage, and insurrection to Pharaoh, but it seemed heroic to the Israelites.

25*To be badly treated.* The Israelites, like the author of Hebrews, probably considered having **transitory enjoyment** of a position of importance in Egypt to be **crime**. Anything that helped the chosen people was considered virtue, and anything that hindered them was thought to be **crime**. The author's idea of true heroism and faith was willingness to be identified with the chosen **people**, regardless of the cost, without being able to see any immediate benefit, but still trusting God to provide the **promised** rewards.

26*The insult of the Messiah.* The Scripture quoted in this verse is from Ps 89 [88]:50-51. The author of Hebrews took the words **the insult** from Ps 89 [88]:50 and the words **the Messiah** from **your Messiah** (*meh-sheé-kah*, מְשִׁיחֶךָ) in Heb 11:51 and put them together in such a way as to apply to the Messiah Jesus. Just as being **badly treated with the people of God** (Heb 11:25) was contrasted to having **transitory enjoyment of crime** (Heb 11:25), so **the insult of the Messiah** was contrasted to **the treasures of Egypt**.

These alternative opportunities seem both to have been initially applied to Moses. As the son of Pharaoh, he would have succeeded him on the throne and had access to all of the treasures of Egypt. As the messianic leader of the Hebrew people he would have been considered a rebellious saboteur and terrorist, from the Egyptian point of view. This was a role that attracted insults.

Although it is unreasonable to think of Moses as anticipating the Messiah in pre-kingdom times, this did not disturb the author. Not only was he able to apply Psalms to Moses, he also assumed that Moses foresaw the **Messiah** Jesus and acted accordingly. Like other parties to the contract, he believed that all prophecy applied only to the days of the Messiah, Jesus.

The chief motivation for ethical behavior for the author of Hebrews was the **reward** (see also Heb 10:35; 11:6) involved, which was the promised rest, receiving the **promises**, or acquiring the **inheritance**. Cosby said the results of Moses' choice "ends in the 'nontransitory' reward of permanent rest in the heavenly city,"[1] which would be correct, if Cosby had meant by that the city of Zion on earth, that was called **heavenly** and also the **city of the God of life** (Heb 12:22). Cosby, however, contrasted citizenship in **heavenly Jerusalem** with earthly citizenship.[2] The text does not specify that **the reward** was in heaven. If Moses had not been interested in the Land of Canaan or Zion, he would not have had to wander through the geographical wilderness to get there. **The reward** Moses had in mind was the possession of Canaan for the sons of Abraham. For that **reward**, Moses was willing to leave **the treasures of Egypt**, and accept instead **the insult of the Messiah**.

27 *The wrath of the king*. When Moses first left Egypt, before the Passover, according to Exod 2:15, **Pharaoh heard about this matter, and he attempted to kill Moses, but Moses fled from Pharaoh and lived in the land of Midian**. The author of Hebrews distorted this by claiming that Moses, like his parents (Heb 11:23), was not afraid of the king. When Moses returned he had more courage than when he first left, but when Moses fled from the king, he probably did so because he was afraid of the king.

The author sharpened the contrasts between the values at stake for Moses so that they appear more vivid than they were presented in the Exodus account. The author shows that Moses was not only contrasting the Egyptians with the Israelites, but Egypt with Canaan. He gave up a tangible royal post in **Egypt** for a potential royal post in Canaan. This involved leading an insurrectionist movement in **Egypt,** which was certain to arouse **the wrath of the king** and cancel any aspirations he might have had to the throne of **Egypt**. He left the security of **Egypt** for the insecurity of the exodus. He left the treasures of **Egypt**, its visible glory, government, power, and land, for an as yet **invisible** land, treasure, glory, government, and power. He risked his wealth, status, and security for a potential **reward**. **He endured as seeing the invisible**.[3] Just as Abraham left the land of Haran for **the land of the promise**, so Moses left **Egypt** for the **land of the promise**. Just as Abraham wandered all of his life without receiving the **inheritance**, so Moses and

[1] Michael R. Cosby, *Rhetorical Composition and Function of Hebrews 11 in the Light of Example Lists from Antiquity* (Macon: Mercer U. Press, c1988), p. 76.

[2] Michael R. Cosby, *Rhetorical Composition and Function of Hebrews 11: In the Light of Example Lists from Antiquity* (Macon:Mercer U. Press, c1988), p. 77.

[3] That which was invisible was probably the land, which could be seen, if the Israelites had arrived there, and not God who is the invisible One, as some scholars have suggested. Moses looked forward to reaching the geographical land where he could see the land that was invisible from the wilderness or Egypt.

the Israelites wandered 40 years in the wilderness without receiving the **promised rest.** The values and emphases of the author are given here in his typical style.

[28]*He instituted the Passover.* The Greek for **instituted** is *peh-póy-ay-khen* (πεποίηκεν), which means simply "made." Normally it might be rendered "observed" or "made preparations for," but the author of Hebrews understood that this was the first **Passover**, so it is translated **instituted. The pouring out of the blood** (LXX Exod 12:22) referred to the activity of the Israelites in marking their houses with **blood** from the **Passover** lambs so that the one who went through **Egypt destroying the firstborn** of the Egyptians would know that these homes belonged to Israelites and should be spared. The destruction was designed as a distractive measure for the Egyptians while the Israelites escaped.

[29]*They went through the Red Sea.* **They went through the Red Sea** (*dee-éh-bay-sahn tayn eh-rooth-ráhn tháh-lah-sahn,* διέβησαν τὴν ἐρυθρὰν θάλασσαν) not only reports the historical facts, but it delivers the message in beautiful style. It was prepared for oral delivery, with effective sounds in the words chosen.

The Red Sea which the Israelites **went through** was the *yahm sohf,* ים סוף (Exod 15:4). For many years scholars have held that the so-called Red Sea was a swampy area several miles north of the **Red Sea**. That which was then a swampy area is now the Suez Canal. The LXX translators mistranslated *yahm sohf* as **Red Sea**, and the author of Hebrews accepted their text. For many years scholars have assumed that this area was called "the Sea of Reeds," but *sohf* never meant "reeds" either in Hebrew or in Egyptian. The letters involved are usually pronounced *sohph* and mean "end."

This was the end or border of some nation or territory in antiquity and so was called the "End Sea" or the "Border Sea."[1] Recent discoveries, however, have identified Mount Sinai in Saudi Arabia, so the body of water, is probably the Gulf of Aqaba. This would still be the border sea, because Egypt extended then as far as Saudi Arabia. If the Gulf of Aqaba is really the body of water called the Border Sea, then no one knows how the Israelites crossed the area now called the Suez Canal to get to the Gulf of Aqaba.[2]

The night the Israelites arrived at this body of water, a strong east wind moved back the tide and the Israelites crossed over on foot (Exod 14:21-22**) as through dry land**, meaning as if they had been walking on dry land. There are still sand bars across the Gulf of Aqaba, making this passage possible. When the Egyptians tried to follow with their heavy chariots, they got stuck in the mud and **were swallowed up** when the tide returned (Exod 14:25-28; 15:4, 12).

Moses' acts continued as he led the Israelites in the wilderness for 40 more years, but for the author of Hebrews, these were years of rebellion that prevented the Israelites from receiving their **promised rest** (Heb 3-4), so they were not glamorized as examples of endurance in faith.

[30]*The walls of Jericho fell.* The biblical account of the fall of Jericho is so legendary that it is nearly impossible to find even a clue for trying to solve its capture (Josh 6:1-21). Archaeologists have not been able to find any trace of the walls that were

---

[1] M. Ottosson, "Eden and the Land of Promise," *VT* 40 (1988):177-88.
[2] H. Blum, *The Gold of Exodus* (New York: Simon & Schuster, 1998).

supposed to have fallen, and only slight evidence that the city might ever have been invaded by the Israelites in that period.[1]

[31]*Rahab the harlot did not perish.* **The unfaithful ones** include all unbelievers, those not parties to the contract; in this case it means the citizens of Jericho before the Israelites moved in, but the exodus generation was also **unfaithful,** and Christians who became apostates would also be classified as **unfaithful**.

Many readers have wondered how a **harlot** like Rahab came to be listed among the roll call of the faithful. She surely was not **faithful** so far as her own people were concerned. She betrayed them and assisted in bringing about their destruction. There are several reasons for this.

(a) When she joined forces with the Israelites, she became a believer or a member of the **faith**.
(b) She had **faith** in the spies. Therefore she was saved from destruction by her **faith.**
(c) She assisted in the conquest of Canaan, led by the old Joshua. In other words, she was judged **faithful** from a very subjective viewpoint.

Her relationship to Joshua, however, was useful to the author of Hebrews at this point. This called attention to the new Joshua, who would successfully lead the **faithful** into the **promised rest.** The importance of the entrance into Canaan and the **promised rest** is emphasized by the very point in time at which the author chose to conclude his specific listing of individuals. The faithful were listed from the **promise** given to Abraham to the entrance into Canaan when the fulfillment of that **promise** should have been received.

Apart from the author's judgment of Rahab was her own understanding of ethics. In the Near East then as now the responsibility of a host or a hostess to guests was extensive. Once guests are admitted, the hostess or host is responsible to protect them at the cost of his or her life and fortune. Lot and the Gibionite who entertained a Levite both offered their virgin daughters as ransom to protect their guests (Gen 19:8; Judges 19:22-24). Under the accepted hospitality customs, Sisera trusted even an enemy hostess enough to sleep in Jael's tent. Because Jael did not feel the same social restraints, she killed Sisera in his sleep (Judges 5:24-27).[2] Rahab was more responsible to her guests than Jael was, and therefore more ethical, from one point of view. Of course, for her to hide her guests as she did made her an accomplice in the invasion that destroyed all of her fellow citizens except her own immediate family (Josh 2:1-24; 6:22-23). Although she became a traitor to her own people, she became a believer and a trusted citizen of Israel. For this she gained favorable recognition in her own day and praise by the author of Hebrews.

Summary. The author of Hebrews told the account of Israel's history from Egypt to Palestine by accounting for the virtues of heroes who suffered for their convictions. +Moses gave up a position of royalty and wealth in **Egypt** to take a chance that he and the Israelites might receive the Promised Land**.** Similarly, Rahab gave up her loyalty to her own tradition and people so as to cast her lot with the people of God. Therefore she was classed with Abraham and Moses who did the very same thing.

---

[1] See K. Kenyon, *Digging up Jericho* (New York: Praeger, 1957), p. 262.

[2] See further Buchanan, "The Spiritual Commandment," *JAAR* 36 (1968):126-27.

TECHNICAL DETAILS

Although Heb 11:23-31 has been organized here as one unit, the author of Hebrews divided it into two. His inclusion shows Heb 11:23-27 to be marked off as a separate unit. Heb 11:23 remarks that Moses' parents did not fear the decree of the king, and Heb 11:27 reports that Moses had not feared the wrath of the king. Moses' action as seeing the invisible (Heb 11:27) refers to the parents who saw that Moses was attractive (Heb 11:23), and also refers the reader to the beginning of the chapter, to the definition of faith as the basis for testing things not seen (Heb 11:1).

TEXT

32 Now what more shall I say? For the time will fail me to tell about Gideon, Barak,
Samson, Jephthah, David, Samuel, and the prophets, 33 those who through [the] faith
struggled against kingdoms,

achieved righteousness,
obtained promises,
stopped the mouths of lions,
34 extinguished power of fire,
fled [the] mouths of [the] sword,
received power from weakness,
became strong in war,
upset the military camps of foreigners.

35 Women received their dead by resurrection, but others were beaten, not accepting the release [offered], in order that they might obtain a better resurrection.

COMMENTARY

What more shall I say? This is an appropriately rhetorical way to begin a summary statement with force, giving the impression that there is no end of the illustrations. In a similar way, Cicero said,

> What shall I say about Producus of Ceos or Thrasymachus of Chalcedon or Protagoras of Abdera?--each of whom lectured and wrote that which was considered in their period a great amount on natural science as well (De Oratore 3:32, 127-29)?

32 *Time will fail me.* This unit consists of a summary of many heroes that were not described in detail. They were listed in an asyndeton fashion to give the impression that there were really even more than the ones listed. "Asyndeton" means that they were listed, one after the other without intervening conjunctions. This provides a hasty, cumulative literary effect. The rapid fire presentation adds force to the facts. So far as the facts are concerned, here are some qualities about the heroes.

Gideon was one of the judges who destroyed the altar of Baal and overthrew the Midianites with only 300 men (Judges 6-7). **Barak** joined his troops with those of Deborah and overcame **Sisera** and the Philistines at Megiddo (Judges 4-5). **Samson** was a compulsive strong man who made many exploits against the Philistines.

He burned their wheat fields (Judges 15:1-8), killed 1,000 of them with the jawbone of a donkey (Judges 15:9-17), and at his death pulled down the pillars of the house where there were 3,000 Philistines, including leaders (Judges 16:23-31). **Jephthah** overpowered the threatening Ammonites and subjected the uncooperative Ephraimites (Judges 11:1-12:7).

Saul was strangely omitted from the list, even though he was Israel's first king. The author may have reasoned that since the FT reported that God had rejected Saul (1Sam 16:1), therefore he no longer belonged to **the faith**. He was like the criminal exodus generation. After Saul and his son, Jonathan, were defeated in battle against the Philistines, **David** took the kingdom away from the sons of Saul and extended it to include all the territory later believed to be a part of the inheritance **promised** to the seed of Abraham.

Samuel was the last of the judges and the first of the **prophets**. He anointed both Saul and **David** as kings over Israel. Although he demonstrated some military leadership against the Philistines, he could not compete against Saul on this score (1Sam 7; Ant 6:19-44). **The prophets** included men like Elijah, Elisha, and Daniel, who performed some of the miraculous deeds listed in the quoted poem (Heb 11:33-34). The heroes were not listed in chronological order, which would be: **Barak, Gideon, Jephthah, Samson, Samuel, and David.**

33 *Struggled against kingdoms*. This is the beginning of another asyndeton, piling up the important activities attributed to the listed great leaders. Up to this point, the discussion of Heb 11 has dealt with the report of great men and women and the things they did **through**out **the** entire **faith**, from beginning to end. The entire faith, confession, or tradition was filled with heroism that has been recorded. The author wanted the reader to understand that those mentioned above were only a few of the many associated with this honorable **faith**. But these were reported, **according to [the] faith** (Heb 11:7, 13).

Because of **the faith** parties to **the faith** could be daring. They endured in **hope**. They held fast the **confession**. The noun **faith** occurs 24 times in Heb 11, but only an additional eight times in the rest of the document. The verb "to believe (*pees-toó-ayn*, πιστεύειν) occurs only in Heb 4:3 and Heb 11:6. The adjective "faithful" (*peés-taws*, πιστός) occurs only once in Heb 11 and four times in the rest of the document. This may mean that **the faith** was more important to the source than to the author of Hebrews who borrowed the word. It might also mean that the author of Hebrews composed all of Heb 11 and concentrated his use of the expression **the faith** in this chapter.

In most of Heb 11, **faith** is much more closely related to creed, doctrine, or tradition than a motivating force for action. To translate "through **faith"** to mean something different would make it inconsistent not only with the rest of Heb 11, but also with the rest of the document as well. These data seem to favor rendering **through [the] faith** (Heb 11:33) to mean "throughout the entire religious tradition," which includes the **hope** that **the promise** made to Abraham would be fulfilled. With this interpretation, all of Heb 11 makes good sense and fits in well with the rest of Heb 1-12.

Michel noted the poetic nature of Heb 11:33-34, with three verses of three lines each.[1] He thought this passage might once have been a separate unit, dealing

[1] Michel, *Hebrews,* p. 279.

with victories of war.[1] Heb 11:32-33a seems like an introduction to the quoted poem, written by the author of Hebrews, giving names of some of the heroes he knew who did things listed in the poem. Those were mostly victors in battle and important leaders from the beginning of the conquest of Canaan until the establishment of the monarchy. This seemed like an unimportant period to the author, who covered it all in one verse plus a quoted poem, including the leadership of **David**, whom most NT authors considered to be the one who established the line from which the Messiah should come. The author of Hebrews, however, dismissed **David** along with the judges and prophets.

Because all six of the persons named were warriors, all would qualify as **those who through faith struggled against** (*kah-tay-gohn-ee-sáhn-taw*, κατηγωνίσαντο) **kingdoms**. Josephus, however, used the same term as Hebrews, claiming that God gave **David** power to save the country of the Hebrews by struggling against *kah-tah-gohn-ee-sah-méh-noh*, καταγωνισαμένῳ) the Philistines (Ant 7:53). David would also be among those who **achieved righteousness** (*dee-kai-aw-soón-ayn*, δικαιοσύνην), since there is a testimony that he administered judgment and righteousness (justice) (*dee-kai-aw-soón-ayn*) to all the people (2Sam 8:15). Again **David** is the most likely candidate for one who **obtained promises**, because he was the one who extended the **kingdom** to its farthest limits. He was the one who achieved the situation that his son, Solomon, inherited of having **rest from all his enemies round about** (1Chron 22:9). That enabled Solomon to bless the Lord who had **given rest to his people Israel, according to all that he had said** (*kuh-kohl ah-shayr dee-báyr*, ככול אשר דבר) (1Kings 8:56). **God stopped the mouths of lions** for **Daniel** (Dan 6:22).

The **kingdoms** against which these leaders struggled were not imaginary. They were countries the Israelites were eager to displace—the Philistines, Moabites, Ammonites, and Hittites. Their **struggling** involved military battles. The exploits of David were probably well known to the author of Hebrews, but his argument involved proving that Jesus was the high priest who adequately performed the necessary sacrifice on the Day of Atonement. It would have been distracting to explain how all of that could take place at the same time Jesus was the Son of David and associated with another high priest, such as John the Baptist.

34 *Received power from weakness*. It was for **Daniel's** friends, Shadrach, Meshach, and Abednego, that God **extinguished power of fire** (Dan 3:19-30; see also 1Macc 2:59; 3Macc 6:6) so that no hair of their heads was singed. Among these victories, the author probably did not mean to list Israel's defeat when he recorded that her leaders **fled [the] mouths of [the] sword**. He meant to praise them that they had successfully escaped when they were forced to flee.

These events were also deliverances for which Israel should be grateful. **Mouths** probably does not refer to two-edged swords which were used against them. The plural may indicate that there were several times when Israelite heroes escaped the **swords** of the enemies who pursued them like a pack of wild beasts with their **mouths** open to consume them (see also Luke 21:24). This would refer to such events as **David's** escape from Absalom (2Sam 15:1-18:15), Elijah's escape from Jezebel (1Kings 19:1-18), and Elisha's escape from the Syrians (2Kings 6:11-23, 30-33).

---

[1] Michel, *Hebrews*, p. 280.

Several times Israel was delivered by a small force or overcame a stronger enemy with Israel's poorly equipped men, such as deliverance from the Egyptians at the Sea (Exod 14-15), defeat of Sisera at Megiddo (Judges 5), Samson's slaughter of 3,000 Philistines when he was blind (Judges 16:23-31), and **David's** slaughter of Goliath (1Sam 17:1-54). Israel also put others to the edge **of the sword** (Exod 17:13; Num 21:24; Deut 13:16; 20:13). These were times when Israel's heroes **received power from weakness**. There were so many military victories when Israel **became strong in war** that the author was correct in saying the time would fail him to tell about them all (Heb 11:32).

The Greek word rendered **military camps** comes from the verb *pahr-ehm-bawl-láhs* (παρεμβολάς), "to throw alongside," "to line up in a row for battle," "to throw together in order" as a camp. The verb *éhk-leen-ahn* (ἔκλιναν) rendered **upset** means "to make bend" "to make yield or give way," "to turn back or rout." Upsetting the **military camps of foreigners** alluded to such events as **Gideon's** capture of the Midianite camp with 300 men (Judges 7:15-23) or Jonathan's slaughter of the Philistine garrison with only his armor bearer (1Sam 14:6-15).

35 *Others were beaten.* Ther ewere not many **women [who] received their dead by resurrection**. These were contrasted to the **others** whose treatment was described. This probably refers to the resuscitation of the Zarephath woman's son by Elijah (1Kings 17:24) and of the Shunamite's son by Elisha (2Kings 4:32-37); see also John 11:1-44; Luke 7:11-17; and Acts 9:36-43). Both children were revived to continue living just as before their deaths. They were not taken into heaven.

The Greek for **were beaten** is *eh-toom-pahn-eés-thay-sahn* (ἐτυμπανίσθησαν), from *toom-pahn-eéd-zayn* τυμπανίζειν "to torture," derived from the verb *toóp-tayn* (τύπτειν), "to beat," "to strike," or "to pound." A *tym-pah-nawn* (τύμπανον̀) is a kettle drum which has a skin stretched taut for striking. Those who were tortured by some such means as this might either be beaten directly or stretched over a wheel and whirled while being afflicted with rods to break their limbs until they died. These **others** who **were beaten** were probably the mother and her seven sons who faced death by torture during the Maccabean period. Had they accepted **release** that was offered to them if they would only give up their faith, they not only would have avoided torture, but they would have received reward and position (2Macc 7).

They were not raised like the sons of the Shunamite and the woman of Zarephath, but they and their mother died **in order that they might obtain a [still] better resurrection** than those sons experienced. They believed that they would be raised up to life in the age to come (*ai-óh-nee-awn*, αἰῶνιον . . . *zoh-áys*, ζωης) (2Macc 7:9), which meant they would be revived to live in the land of the promise after it had been freed from Antiochus Epiphanes and the oppressive Greek rule.[1] Because the political conditions of the nation were expected to improve, this would have been **a better resurrection** than that received by the boys whom the prophets revived. Because they believed this, they willingly suffered torture and death, while they prayed that God would speedily be merciful to their nation, which meant restoring their land (2Macc 7:37). After that they would be raised again, and the mother would receive again her sons who had died (2Macc 7:11, 29). Elijah was taken up to heaven, but he did not die first and afterward become raised. This was an ascension. Jesus also ascended into heaven, according to the author of Hebrews.

---

[1] Buchanan, *Consequences*, pp. 110-49.

Rabbis said that there would be a resurrection on the Mount of Olives, as Zech 14 promised. At that time the mountain would split in two, and the graves of the saints would be opened. Then the saints would be resurrected to live out their lives on the Promised Land. Some rabbis said that only those who died and were buried in the Promised Land would be raised. Others said miracles would take place. God would drill tunnels through the earth from Babylon to Jerusalem and then roll the corpses from Babylon to Jerusalem like bottles, to be raised at the Mount of Olives. None of these theories involved a return from heaven.

For Antiochus, of course, there would be no resurrection to life (*ah-nah-stah-sees eis zoen*, ἀναστάσις εις ζωην) (2Macc 7:14), because he had never belonged to the community where alone life was possible. Heb 11:35 seems to be a summary introduction of the poem that follows (Heb 11:36-38), just as Heb 11:32 is a summary introduction to the poem in Heb 11:33-34. The word "others" of Heb 11:35 was probably taken from the text that follows.

The author of Hebrews believed there would be a resurrection, and he said that, but that was not the major point of this sermon. His listeners knew precisely what he meant, so he did not have to labor the subject. He may have envisioned a resurrection in which the faithful would be raised from the dead and then taken up into heaven, as Cockerill thought,[1] but there is no confirmation in the text to show that. He may have believed, instead, that the faithful would be raised from the dead to live out their three score years and ten on the Promised Land. Since he did not say, we cannot know for certain. The goal of his sermon was that the promises of Abraham were about to be fulfilled, and the members of his congregation were right there at the City of David, the heavenly city of Zion, to be the first recipients of the promises (Heb 12:22).

TEXT

36 And others received [the] trial of mockings
and whips,
and still [others], of fetters and prison.
37 They were stoned, tested, sawed in two;
they died by slaughter of [the] sword,
went around in sheepskins,
in skins of goats;
they were deprived, afflicted, badly treated,
38 (of whom the world is not worthy),
wandering in deserts, mountains, caves
and openings of the earth.

39 Now these all, attested through [the] faith, did not acquire the promise,
40 since God had foreseen something better concerning us, so that without us they
might not be perfected.

COMMENTARY

36 *Trial of mockings and whips*. This is the beginning of another asyndeton, organized to give the forceful impression that there were even more tortures than

---

[1] G. L. Cockerill, "The Better Resurrection (Heb 11:35): A Key to the Structure and Rhetorical Purpose of Hebrews 11," *Tyndale Bulletin* 51 (2000):215-34.

those listed. The **others** here probably included the **others** mentioned in Heb 11:35. The expression **received [the] trial** (*páy-rahn éh-lah-bawn*, πεῖραν ἔλαβον) is the same idiom used to describe a woman so delicate that she would not risk (*páy-ran éh-lah-bahn*) setting her foot on the ground (LXX Deut 28:56). These **others** were not that delicate. They risked "mockings and whips."

The way this passage incorporates the poem, the text now seems to read **others** (Heb 11:35) . . . **and others** (Heb 11:36) . . . **and still [others]** (Heb 11:36), as if these were all different groups of people. Originally the poem may have meant that the **others** mentioned at the beginning of Heb 11:36 covered all the people tortured. These were mocked and whipped, **and still** further, bound and imprisoned, but the number of kinds of torture is more than would apply to any one group. The author of the poem also seems to have been speaking of the many types of torture which different people suffered, rather than specifying the number of tortures one group suffered. In any general persecution which involved torture and death there would be some people imprisoned and others bound hand and foot so that they would be helpless. During the persecution of Antiochus, the Greeks led the women and children away captive (1Macc 1:32).

37 *They were deprived, afflicted, badly treated.* These faithful people who **held fast the confession** were "stoned," like Zechariah the son of Jehoiada the priest who was stoned in the temple court (2Chron 24:20-21), "tested" by all sorts of tortures, like those applied to the woman and her seven sons (2Macc 7), or "sawed in two," like Isaiah during the time of Manasseh, according to tradition (AscIsa 5:1-14; Dial 120; Jerome, *Comment Isa* 57:2). The words "tested" (*eh-pay-ráhs-thay-sahn*, ἐπειράσθησαν) and "sawed in two" (*eh-preés-thay-sahn*, ἐπρίσθησαν) are so similar in spelling that there are several textual variants, and some scholars have suspected that one was added by someone who placed one variant after the other in his text. Scholars who hold this view ignore the poetic features of the passage in which words and expressions are listed in groups of three, and they fail to appreciate the alliteration of the terms (see also Heb 1:1).

Jehoiakim brought Uriah from Egypt and slew him with the **sword** (Jer 26:23), and Elijah complained that the people of Israel, under Jezebel's administration, had slain the Lord's prophets with the **sword** (1Kings 19:10). Many Jews during the Maccabean Revolt and again in the rebellions of 66-73 IA and 132-35 IA died **by slaughter of [the] sword** in battle. During the siege of Vespasian against Jotapata, Josephus reported that he (Josephus, the general in charge) sent men out for supplies past the Roman guards, crawling on all fours like animals. These had disguised themselves with sheep's fleece on their backs (War 3:190-92). This may not be what the author of Hebrews or of this poem had in mind, but it was something having to do with fugitive conditions necessary because of shortage of supplies or requirements of guerilla warfare. The verbs **deprived, afflicted, badly treated** are general descriptions of conditions of hardship, such as those faced by the Jews during the Maccabean Revolt or the revolts against Rome (66-73; 132-35 IA). The word **badly treated** (*kah-koo-khoó-meh-noi*, κακουχούμενοι) is the same as that used to describe the conditions of the Israelites in Egypt when Moses chose to identify himself with them (*soon-kah-koo-kháys-thai*, συνκακουχεῖσθαι) (Heb 11:25).

[38]*Wandering in deserts.* Moffatt called the passage (**of whom the world is not worthy**) a splendid aside.[1] It not only is an aside, but it is one that breaks the poetry and was probably made by the author of Hebrews rather than the author of the poem he used. The aside may have been suggested by the story of Eleazar or of the mother and her seven sons, all of whom were called worthy (*áhx-ee-aws, áhx-ee-ah*, ἄξιος, ἄξια) (Heb 6:23; 7:20). R. Eliezer haKappar said Israel possessed four virtues, "of which nothing in the [current] age is worthy" (*kohl hah oh-lahm kuh-dah-eé*, כול העולם כדאי). Two of these were their unwillingness to change their names or their language (Mekilta, *Pisha* 5:15-17). Temptations to make such changes would occur in times of persecution. Those engaged in guerrilla warfare in Palestine were destined to wander **in deserts, mountains, caves, and openings of the earth**, because that kind of terrain was available.

These places were used by David and Saul (1Sam 22:1; 23:14; 24:3), the Israelites during the time of the judges (Judges 6:2), and various prophets (1Kings 18:4, 13; 19:9, 13). Isaiah warned Jews to flee to such places of refuge to escape the Lord's wrath (Isa 2:10-22). Jesus warned the inhabitants of Judea to flee to the mountains when certain conditions presented themselves (Matt 24:15-16). After Mattathias killed the Jew who offered pagan sacrifice and the Greek who encouraged it (1Macc 2:23-27), he and his sons fled to the mountains (1Macc 2:28), from which position they led the revolt (see also 2Macc 5:27; 6:11; 10:6). Because the mountainous regions of Palestine are honeycombed with caves, guerrilla warfare is easy to conduct and difficult to suppress.

When Herod was first made king of the Jews, he was faced with the task of forming **a campaign against the cave dwelling brigands** who were infesting a wide area and inflicting on the inhabitants evils no less than those of war (War 1:304). Herod finally conquered the caves by sending his soldiers in baskets hanging by ropes from the tops of the cliffs to the caves in the sides of the mountains, where they fought the guerrillas in hand-to-hand combat or smoked them out with firebrands (War 1:309-11). Josephus described these guerrilla insurrectionists as **brigands**, and used similar disparaging names, but to the author of Hebrews these were heroes who held fast the confession and endured in the faith.[2]

[39]*These all.* **These all** include the heroes mentioned in the entire chapter. The argument was organized for oral presentation. The word **faith** was echoed repeatedly and anaphorically in such a way as to pile up convincing data. This was then summarized quickly and powerfully in a way that implied that there was still more evidence to present. It was withheld only in the interest of time and space.

Attested through [the] faith. **The promise** that the ancient heroes expected to be fulfilled was the inheritance of the age to come (Heb 9:15), the entrance into the **promised** rest (Heb 4:1). This involved the restoration of the Promised Land to the chosen people. Cosby, however, followed Vanhoye in holding that

> The homeland the patriarchs expected is located in heaven, and this specification makes clear the meaning of "something better" in verse 40.[3]

---

[1] Moffatt, *Hebrews*, p. 189.
[2] See further Buchanan, "Mark 11:15-19: Brigands in the Temple," *HUCA* 30 (1959):169-77.
[3] Cosby, *Rhetorical Composition*, p. 72.

Johnson also said, "God's people throughout the OT looked beyond the present life to a heavenly reward."[1] If that had been so, then why did they go to Zion? Heaven is in the sky—above, not horizontally west and south from Haran. The text does not say that the homeland the patriarchs expected was located in heaven. The entire movement from Abraham to the prophets led to the Promised Land. The patriarchs lived in "the land of **the promise**," as tenants (Heb 11:9), looking forward to permanent citizenship there. They were looking for **a city which had the foundations, a fatherland. They were "reaching out for a better [fatherland] that is a heavenly [one].**

Heavenly is a word not limited to a location in heaven. "Heaven" is often used as a euphemism for God. The word "Godly" is not limited in its use to something in God. Those who had been **attested through the faith did not acquire the promise.** The listeners had already **come to Zion, the city of the God of Life, heavenly Jerusalem** (Heb 12:22), hoping to receive the promise denied to **all** of **these** others. While listening to this sermon they were in **Zion**, a section of **Jerusalem** south of Herod's walls—not heaven. Geographically, their eschatology was finished. They had reached Zion, and Zion was to be the center of the land where promises made to Abraham would be fulfilled. The author's audience had to be prepared only to receive the promises and wait where they were.

Abraham was looking for the fulfillment of **the promise** that he would inherit a certain piece of land for his posterity. By the time of Joshua it was bordered from Dan to Beersheba. Abraham had not concentrated on a certain city, but the author of Hebrews had. There is no indication in the Scripture that Abraham left Haran so that he could get to heaven. He could evidently have reached heaven as easily and as quickly from Haran as Jerusalem, but he did not have heaven in mind, and neither did the author of Hebrews. Abraham's journey was not just a psychological dream. It was a journey over land that moved from Haran to Palestine. This was the "better" fatherland the patriarchs believed they were promised. They believed Palestine was better than Haran, so they did not return. Cosby, like Vanhoye, Lane, Grässer, Jewett, Attridge, Backhaus, Johnson, Rose, and many others was distracted by the word **heavenly** to ignore the context of the entire Heb 11.

The promise the patriarchs wanted to receive was that made to Abraham (Gen 15). The Scripture is clear that this **promise** referred to land and not to heaven. Of the names listed, none achieved fulfillment of **the promises** which involved permanent acquisition of the land, freedom, prosperity, and **rest**. The nearest approximation of **rest** came during the rules of David and Solomon.

David's name was mentioned only once as a hero (Heb 11:32) along with other judges and prophets. No effort was made to show his faithfulness, possibly because of his crime or because he did not show the same qualities of trust and endurance in hope demonstrated by people like Abraham, Moses, and even Rahab. Solomon was not even mentioned, possibly for the same reason. On the other hand it would have been difficult to praise them very highly without acknowledging that they were recipients of **the promise**. The author picked his heroes to suit his needs and emphasized the qualities he admired. **These all** included such people as Rahab and excluded such people as Solomon and Saul.

---

[1] W. G. Johnson, "The Pilgrimage Motif in the Book of Hebrews," *JBL* 97 (1978):240.

[40]*Without us they might not be perfected.* As he concluded one section, the author again used a connection word to introduce another in the next chapter. The word is "us," or "we," which appears again in Heb 12:1, 2. He had already built up pressure in the minds of his audience by telling about the tragedy of the past. All of these heroes were unsuccessful in their efforts to receive the promise made to Abraham. Then it was up to the audience to succeed where all others failed. Hofius said,

> The final fulfillment of the promise of God is still outstanding, so the end time is already there (1:2; 9:26), and the current living generation is the last generation (11:40). The day of the full salvation is near (10:25) (tr. from German).[1]

Just as the mother and her seven sons died with the expectation that they might receive a better resurrection than the sons of the woman of Zarephath or the Shunamite, so the author anticipated **something better** awaiting fulfillment for the Christians of his day than any of the previous Israelites or Jews had ever known (Heb 11:35). **The promise** made to Abraham involved the **things not seen** (Heb 11:1) by human beings, but these were all **foreseen** by God, which he had withheld so far for two reasons:

a) the exodus generation was unfaithful, and
b) **God had foreseen something better concerning** contemporaries of the author.

All of the efforts in the past on the part of the Israelites had been directed to the acquisition of **the promise**. It had not yet happened, but it was still the goal. That which was **better** does not have to mean heaven. There are many things on earth that were **better** that those that were currently available. For the author, the one that was important was the fulfillment of the promises of Abraham. It still involved the land, prosperity, and posterity. It was a **better** land, more prosperity, and more posterity.

If the last runner drops the baton, the whole race is lost no matter how fast others have run. Without the rigorous endurance in faith of the author's generation of believers, all the earlier endurance in faith would be futile. If Christians of the author's generation became apostates and lost the promise again, all these other believers **might not be perfected** or fulfilled. The author was consistently urging that his readers endure in faith more rigorously than any of their predecessors had ever done, because the guarantees for great reward were greater, their responsibilities to their heritage were greater, and their crime at failing would also be greater than the crimes of the parties to the contract of any other generation.

Summary. Heb 11:32-40 forms a unit enclosed by the words **through the faith** (Heb 11:33, 39). This seems to be a unit largely based on two poems or two verses of the same poem. These may have been taken from longer poems or ballads describing the heroism of the fathers generally, or of the Maccabean heroes particularly. There may have been the same kind of relationship between part of the poetry and the story of the mother and her sons in prose (2Macc 7) as exists between Judges 4 and

---

[1] Otfried Hofius, *Katapausis: Die Vorstellung vom Endzeitlichen Ruheort im Hebräerbrief* (Tübingen: J. C. B. Mohr, 1970), p. 151.

5 as prose and poetic accounts of the victory over Sisera. The author of Hebrews seems to have been responsible for the summarizing introductions in Heb 11:32-35, possibly the gloss in Heb 11:37, and quite certainly the concluding statements in Heb 11:39-40.

The conclusion of this unit also forms an end to the whole eulogy on the faith of the fathers, as the author has shown by his inclusions. **These all** who were attested **through the faith** (Heb 11:39) are the same men of old who were attested in **faith** (Heb 11:1-2). The greatest of the heroes were the ones like Noah, Abraham, Moses, and Rahab who took chances on **the promises** of God, even though the evidence for their fulfillment did not seem strong. Not only did they accept God's word as valid, but they paid high costs of giving up status, position, and social security, to act as God had commanded. They stood in direct contrast to the exodus generation that was unfaithful, and, as a result, was denied **the promise** God had intended for it.

Most scholars have noticed the rhetorical skill of the author and his ability to prepare a convincing sermon that was planned to be heard. Cosby said,

> One should take the time to listen to the Greek words as if an ancient oral culture, recognizing that the author of Hebrews considered the success of his message to be largely dependent on the way it sounded to his audience. As he preaches to them, his many efforts at oral artistry in the construction of his utterances are not peripheral but central to his purposes. To experience this is to add a new dimension to understanding and responding to his words.[1]

The author's purpose in making this strong case was to urge his audience to imitate the faithful fathers who held fast their **confession** of **hope** against great odds rather +than become apostates like the exodus generation. The author continued his consistent style of concluding one section while, at the same time, preparing the reader for the topic that follows. His last word in Heb 11 is **perfected** (*teh-lay-oh-thoh-seen*, τελειωθωσιν) to prepare the reader to look to Jesus the pioneer and perfecter of the faith.

---

[1] M. R. Cosby, "The Rhetorical Composition of Hebrews 11," *JBL* 107 (1988):

CHAPTER TWELVE

TEXT

Hebrews	First Testament
12:1 **Therefore**, we **also**, since we **have** so great a cloud of witnesses [as this] surrounding us, after we **have** put aside every weight, even the crime that clings to us very readily, let us run with **endurance** the course that is laid out before us,	4Macc 16:22 **Therefore also** you, **having** the same **faith** in **God**, do not be dismayed.
2 **keeping our gaze directed to** Jesus, the prime leader and perfector of the **faith,** who, instead of the joy laid out before him, having despised [the] cross of shame, **endured** [it], and is seated at the right hand of the throne of **God.**	4Macc 17:10 They vindicated the race, **looking to God** and **enduring** the sufferings until death.

3 Just consider the one who has endured so great an opposition [as this] against himself, from the criminals, so that you may not become exhausted, being depressed in your souls.

COMMENTARY

12:1-2 *The course that is laid out before us.* The word **us** was one of the connection words introduced in Heb 11:39. That chapter ended reminding the listeners that they were important. The whole project would fail **without us** (Heb 11:40). What should that mean to the listeners? The answer is given in Heb 12:1 **Let us run with endurance the course that is laid before us.** The word rendered **surrounding** is literally "lying around" (*peh-ree-káy-mehn-awn,* περικείμενον) which is intentionally made to correspond with **laid out before** (*praw-kay-méhn-ayce,* προκειμένης. The **witnesses** were "lying around **us**," and we were encouraged to **run with endurance the course that is laid out before us,** knowing the **joy** was **laid out before Jesus.** This exhortation for **endurance** was similar to that given by the author of 4Macc.

Run appears also in Heb 12:13, forming an inclusion of the subject matter in between, thus separating Heb 12:1-13 as a complete unit. The word **cloud** (*neh-phaws*, νέφος) was used metaphorically, giving expression to the immense size of the group. Herodotus (Hist 7:109.12) also described an enemy's army as "so mighty a cloud (*néh-phos*, νέφος) of men." No intention was implied that these heroes were in heaven like a **cloud. Witnesses** (*mahr-toó-rohn*, μαρτύρων) occurs also in Heb 10:28, and the verbal form, **witnessing** (*mahr-too-rayn*, μαρτυρεῖν) occurs eight times (Heb 7:8, 17; 10:15; 11:2, 4 (twice), 5, 39). It is an important term for one who urged boldness in holding fast to the confession.

The expression **clings to us very readily** is *yoo-peh-reés-tah-tawn* (εὐπερίστατον), the superlative degree of the passive participle of *peh-ree-eés-tay-mee* (περιίστημι) "to **surround,**" with the prefix, yoo (εὐ) meaning "good," "well," "easily," or "readily." This which **surrounded** the believer very readily was an obstacle of some kind, like reeds or moss getting in a swimmer's way and impeding his progress; or cords, reeds, or some kind of binding and repressing clothing that **clings to us very readily** and hinders our progress. Since this obstacle was **crime** that should be **put aside** like a **weight**, the image is that of weights a the runner or swimmer might use in practice to build up muscle, but remove for contests.

The word **endurance** (*yoo-poh-mawn-áys*), in nominal case (Heb 10:36) as in verbal forms (Heb 10:32; 12:2, 3, 7), occurs only in exhortation sections.[1] It was never applied to any of the saints of the past. *Kahr-teh-ráyn* (καρτερεῖν) was used to describe Moses' enduring qualities. The author effectively repeated the word *kays-thai* (κεἶσθαι), "to lay," "to place," or "to lie." So **a cloud of witnesses** is **surrounding** or lying around (*peh-ree-kay-méh-nawn*, περικειμένον) us; **the course . . . is laid out before** (*pro-kay-méh-nawn*, προκειμένον) **us** and **the joy [was] laid out before** Jesus. **Keeping our gaze directed to** (*ah-phaw-róhn-tehs*, ἀφορῶντες) is literally **looking away toward** Jesus.

The context in Hebrews requires a continuing force for this expression. The same is true of Philo, who used the term in relationship to Moses, to whom rulers looked as an archetype or in relationship to a pattern which a builder followed (Op 18). The Jewish martyrs of Maccabean times vindicated their race, "keeping their gaze directed toward God" (*ays theh-áwn ah-phaw-rohn-tehs*, εἰς θεὸν ἀφορώντες) and enduring "until death" (4Macc 17:10). The **looking away** of the martyrs, like the **looking away** of the early Christians, involved a continual, steady gaze. Therefore the expression was translated **keeping our gaze directed to** Jesus.

The course (*ah-góh-nah*, ἀγῶνα) **laid out before** Christians was a contest like that of Eleazar and the woman with her seven sons who faced torture and death rather than submit to Antiochus. They were called "athletes of the divine legislation" (4Macc 17:16) who had been engaged in a contest (*ah-gohn*) (4Macc 17:11). The author encouraged his readers to participate seriously in such a contest, struggle, race, just as they had done earlier, after they had been enlightened, when they endured (*hoo-peh-máy-nah-teh*, ὑπεμείνατε) a great struggle of sufferings (*áhth-lay-seen*, ἄθλησιν . . . *pahth-ay-máh-tohn*, παθημάτων) (Heb 10:32). Christians were enlightened when they became Christians. The enlightenment was the catechism they learned for membership. It also involved the strict discipline required of membership. The picture given is of athletes running a race or fighting in an arena for their very lives, but it refers to the religious struggles of believers who must fight against the world for the **faith**. At times this is not just a mental, emotional, or social struggle, but involves real physical torture. In any case it required removal of crime, endurance, and direction. For monks it meant giving up the normal pressures of sex and social status and success. The endurance required of athletes and that required of members of the author's community were equally severe.

[2]*Prime leader and perfector*. The term **perfector** is not found anywhere else in the NT or in the LXX, but Croy found two very similar usages of expressions like this, including the very word for **perfector**.[2] Dionysius (*On Demarchus* 1), employed the *expression*, inventor or originator (εὑρετήν) . . . and perfector or completor *tehl-ay-oh-táyn*, τελειωτήν). Reporting the development of the Achaean League,

---

[1] F. F. Bruce, *The Epistle to the Hebrews* (Grand Rapids: Eerdmans, 1964), p. 349, observed that *hoo-paw-méh-nay* occurred 11 times in 4Macc and the verb, *hoo-paw-méh-nayn*, an additional 15 times.

[2] N. C. Croy, "A Note on Hebrews 12:2," *JBL* 114 (1995):117-19.

Polybius said Aratus was the founder (*ahr-khay-gáws,* ἀρχηγός) and guide (*kahth-aye-geh-móhn,* καθηγεμών), whereas Philopoem was the champion (*ah-gohn-ees-táys,* ἀγωνιστής) and perfector (*tehl-ehs-ee-oor-gáyes,* τελεσιουργής) (Polybius 2:40,2). Cory noted that these were ordinary expressions that did not require any mystical understanding. The first in the series was the founder, prime leader, or originator and the last was the completor, fulfiller, or perfector. The text given here is **prime leader and perfector**, which could be rendered "founder and finisher" or "originator and final developer."

The **prime leader** (*ahr-khay-gáwn,* ἀρχηγόν) might also be called "initial leader," "primary leader," or "chief leader," implying either first in time, first in rank, or first in order. In any group movement, the one who goes ahead of the rest works the hardest. When several travel together, for example, the front cyclist breaks the wind for the followers. The same is true with a flock of wolves, geese, or ducks. For Christians, Jesus was given all three emphases.

1) He was earlier called the initial leader of their salvation whom God made **perfect** through sufferings (Heb 2:10).
2) Jesus was also the **perfector** of the **faith** in contrast to the heroes of the **faith** who might not be **perfected** (Heb 11:40). This might mean that he had become a monk, and they had not.
3) He was the chief of the new contract order of Christians.

Since he learned obedience from the things he suffered (Heb 5:8), and was made **perfect**, he became a cause of salvation of the age (Heb 5:9). By the word of **the oath** Jesus was established as the Son made **perfect** for the age (Heb 7:28). An early Jewish poet prayed that the Lord be kind to the recipients of the blessings who would have been members of the "contract of the age" (1QSb 2:24-25). **Perfect,** in the religious sense, meant one who had completed requirements for membership or prepared a sacrifice which completely removed all crimes. It did not have the force of scientific **perfection** as in making a **perfect** circle or a perfect square. Pseudo-Clement told of a certain Maro who was **perfect** in all things, so Peter appointed him bishop (Recog 6:15). Bishops were required to be celibate in the Greek Orthodox Church. Pseudo-Clement also encouraged others to devote themselves as much as possible to the perfection of purity (Hom 9:23).

Of the faith. This was not **faith** in general, but **the faith**, meaning **the faith** founded by Jesus when he instituted the new contract and by his sacrificial death **perfected the faith.**

The cross of shame. This is the only place in the entire NT that Jesus' **cross** was described as a **cross of shame**. Since, however, Jesus was crucified as a Roman criminal, this was known to be embarrassing to his followers. Jesus' willingness to accept the **cross of shame** rather than **the joy laid out before him** fitted perfectly the author's ideal of righteousness. **The joy that was laid out before him** would have come from becoming the king of Israel with the Romans evicted from Palestine, in the same way Zerubbabel became leader in Palestine after the Babylonians had been driven out by the Persians.

Also, Abraham left Haran for **the Promised Land** where he remained a stranger; Moses left a royal position of wealth in **Egypt** to identify himself with the Israelites who were badly treated; and Rahab denied her countrymen and women to become identified with a tribe that had no country. The author implied, as did Paul (2Cor 8:9), that Jesus, like Moses and Abraham, gave up a position of wealth and prominence to accept the position of leadership that he had.[1] In his letter appealing to the Corinthians to give money, Paul told them of the sacrificial giving of the Macedonians for this project (2Cor 8:1-6) and also of **our Lord Jesus Christ, that on account of you he became poor, when he was a wealthy man** (2Cor 8:9).

The likelihood that Jesus was originally from a wealthy family and that he gave up his wealth for the movement he led is great. This becomes obvious when his relationship to the wealthy tax collectors and rulers is taken into consideration. Most of his parables and teachings would make sense only if they had been directed to an upper class of people who had money to invest, lend, give, and use for hiring servants. His willingness to surrender this for the Kingdom of God would have given more authority to his practice of asking others to give up all they had than would have been the case if he had been reared in poverty. It would have been difficult in the Near East for a poor man to gain a hearing with the rich as Jesus evidently did. So he won Paul's admiration for his act, and Paul was able to use this as an example for the Corinthians to follow in their contributions to Jerusalem saints. The recent discovery of the ossuary of James, the brother of Jesus, suggests further that both Jesus and James came from a very wealthy family.[2] The author of Hebrews, who admired Moses for his willingness to give up wealth, security, and position to be faithful to God, also admired Jesus for the same kind of willingness to give up everything he had to enable **the promises** of God to reach fulfillment. This would be an important point in a sermon delivered by a monk to a group of monks who had also given up all they possessed to join the monastery. Having failed to notice all of this, others have interpreted this differently: For example, Westcott said,

> The joy was that of the work of redemption accomplished through sacrifice.[3]

If that had been the case, Jesus would not have faced an either/or situation at all. He could have **endured the cross** as **the joy laid out before him** rather than **instead of** it. Moffatt thought "the joy" involved was pre-incarnate bliss, which Jesus renounced to become human.[4] This agrees with some interpretations of Philip 2:6-7, but the author of Hebrews never suggested such an idea in the rest of the document. **The joy that was laid out before** Moses could have become Pharaoh of Egypt. **The joy that was laid out before** Jesus was the potential of becoming king of Israel.

When Jesus **despised [the] cross of shame** he may either have sloughed it off as if it were nothing, as Michel believed,[5] or it may mean that he did not like it; he wanted to avoid it; this was anything but his choice; but nonetheless he **endured [it],** just as Moses endured the wrath of the king (Heb 11:27). The author has not given this the same theological force that scholars have frequently given to the confession in Philip 2:5-11, and that force was probably not intended by the author

---

[1] See further Buchanan, "Jesus and the Upper Class," *NovT* 8 (1964):195-209.

[2] A. Lemaire, "Burial Box of James the Brother of Jesus," *BAR* 28,6 (2002):24-33, 70.

[3] B. F. Westcott, *The Epistle to the Hebrews* (London: Macmillan and Co., 1892), pp. 396-98.

[4] J. Moffatt, *A Critical and Exegetical Commentary on the Epistle to the Hebrews* (Edinburgh: T. & T. Clark, 1924), p.197.

[5] O. Michel, *Der Brief an die Hebräer* (Göttingen: Vandenhoeck und Ruprecht, 1957), p. 294.

of Philip 2:5-11, either. That passage also deals with Christ's mission in terms of glory, debasement, and greater glory without implying anything about preexistence. The word **cross** occurs only here in the entire document (Heb 1:1-12:29), and the word "crucify" does not occur at all. This is quite different from the Pauline documents in which the meaning of the **cross** is a central point of faith. The author of Hebrews instead emphasized the ascension in terms of a sacrifice (Heb 4:14; 6:20; 7:26; 9:11-12, 24) and Jesus' position, seated at **the right hand of the throne of God** (Heb 1:3; 8:1; 10:12), instead of being seated on the throne of Israel in Jerusalem. Littleton held that Heb 12:2 was the crescendo of the entire document, which he thought was a letter.[1]

Although the author has seemed fond of the perfect tense, this is the first time he used the perfect tense in alluding to Ps 110:1, which seems to be the basic text on which his entire message is built. **The throne of God** may have been the mercy seat on the cover of the chest holding the **contract**, or it may have been structured so that the chest was the footstool in relationship to it. Because the Lord's presence and his **throne** were in **the holy of holies**, the expression **throne of God** or just **the throne** came to be periphrastic euphemisms for God, just as was true of other expressions like **heaven** (Luke 15:21), "the place" (*mah-qohm*, מקום) (GenR 68b), and "the holy One, blessed be he," (*hah-káh-dohsh bah-roók hoo*, הקדוש ברוך הוא) (GenR 68c). People took oaths by some holy object, with the understanding that this meant God. So Jesus said, **The one who swears by heaven swears by the throne of God and the one seated upon it** (Matt 23:22). He prohibited his disciples from swearing **by heaven, because it is the throne of God** (Matt 5:34).

The throne in heaven was like **the throne of God** in the holy of holies. Like the one in the temple, **the throne** in heaven had lamp stands before it (Rev 4:5) and also a gold altar (Rev 8:3). The one who sits upon this **throne** would dwell with his faithful martyrs (Rev 7:15), just as he dwelt with the Israelites in the wilderness, in the Promised Land, and in the temple (Exod 25:8; 29:42-46; Num 5:3; 35:34; 1 Kings 6:13; 8:12-13).

3 *Who has endured so great an opposition [as this]*. "Just" is the translation for *gahr* (γάρ), a conjunction meaning "for" or "because." Because the author used this conjunction frequently, to avoid repetition in English a free translation has been given. The Greek for **consider** is *ahn-ah-law-geés-ehs-thai* (ἀναλογίσεσθαι), to "count up," "reckon," or "calculate." It means to **consider** in the sense of "taking account of." The author seems to have made allusions in this verse to the LXX version of Num 17:2-3, which is a report of the conclusions of Korah's rebellion. Korah and his immediate followers were swallowed when the earth opened up under them. Those followers who tried to get away were caught by a fire sent down from God to consume 250 of them (LXX Num 16:30-35). These followers were called men who had committed crimes against their souls. The author of Hebrews seems to have identified the **opposition** to Jesus as being a rebellion like Korah's against Moses, Aaron, and God.

The criminals were members of the insurrectionist movement. The rest of Israel accused Moses and Aaron for their action against that group of criminals and the Lord was prepared to destroy them all in a moment with a plague, but Moses and Aaron began at once to make atonement for them, and part of the congregation was

[1] B. J. Littleton, "Exposition of Hebrews 12:2," *Faith & Mission*, 16 (1999):22-29.

spared (LXX Num 17:6-15). Under even more difficult conditions, Jesus also **endured so great an opposition [as this]**. The author reminded his readers of this so that they might **endure** as Jesus had done. Those who might **become exhausted** (*káh-may-teh*, κάμητε), "worn out from work," "weary from annoyance." "afflicted," or "distressed" (*eh-kloo-áw-meh-noi*, ἐκλυόμενοι), "unstrung," "broken up," "exhausted," or "despondent," with respect to their **souls** (*taís psoo-khaís*, ταις ψυχαις).

Summary. Like the beginning of Heb 11:1-3, Heb 12:1-3 forms an introduction to the whole chapter, but the author did not separate it as such. Instead, he formed his first unit in this chapter by an inclusion at Heb 12:1 and Heb 12:13. In addition to its introductory value Heb 12:1-3 helps relate Heb 12 to Heb 11. The **we** (Heb 12:1) is related to **us** (Heb 11:40), and the **witnesses** (Heb 12:1) refer to those who were attested though faith (Heb 11:39).

As the author regularly related his doctrine to ethics, he here gave the consequences of such a faith as that affirmed in Heb 11. In Heb 11, the **witnessing** was not done by the heroes of the **faith** themselves, but rather a **witness** was made about them in this **confession** (Heb 11:2) by God himself (Heb 11:4) or through the **faith** (Heb 11:39). Heb 12, however, speaks as though these heroes were all **witnesses** surrounding Christians (Heb 12:1), who themselves attested to **the faith**, and because they did, Christians were also obligated to prepare themselves to **run**. This involved putting **aside every weight** (Heb 12:1), the way a ship is relieved of its cargo in emergencies, so that it can stay afloat or travel more rapidly (see Jonah 1).

Runners in Olympic contests ran naked, so as not to be impeded by clothing. For the Christian, the weight that must be unloaded is the crime that clings very readily (Heb 12:1), weighing us down, encumbering us, impeding us, and keeping us from running with **endurance the course that is laid out before us** (Heb 12:1). The believer pictured as an athlete of virtue seems to be dependent upon 4Macc and reflect an admiration for the Maccabean martyrs that has been evident before.

TEXT

4You have not yet stood up against crime to the extent of blood,5 and you have utterly forgotten the comfort that is offered to you as *sons*:

> **My son, do not depreciate [the] discipline of the Lord,**
> **nor become depressed when you are corrected by him,**
> 6**for whom the Lord loves, he disciplines,**
> **X**
> **and he whips every son whom he accepts**
> (Prov 3:11-12).

7With reference to **discipline**, [you must] endure; as **sons** God deals with you; for who is [the] **son** whom [his] father does not **discipline**? 8But if you are without **discipline** (of which you have all become sharers), then you are illegitimate children and not **sons**.

TECHNICAL DETAILS

Notice the careful exposition of this text on Proverbs.

1) The author first begins with an introduction, reminding the readers that they are **sons**--not daughters, which is consistent with the author's address to monks throughout the sermon. Not once did he imply that there was a single female in his audience.
2) Second, he quoted the relevant text for the occasion.
3) Third, he selected the two words from the text, **discipline** and **sons**, for comment and exhortation.

There are several small midrashim such as this in the Book of Hebrews. Like a lawyer arguing a case with laws and precedents, the author did not just exhort. He quoted a text that had the authority of the word of God. This meant to his readers that he was simply spelling out to them what God had said with his exhortation. He spoke with authority.

4 *To the extent of blood.* The writer was no stranger to his audience. He knew what they had and had not done, so he could personalize his message. In trying to prevent apostasy among his readers, the author has already told of the many **faith** heroes of the past who did endure in the **faith** through all sorts of physical tortures to the extent of death. Jesus also endured against a great opposition from the criminals (Heb 12:3) until death. Therefore the readers should have been expected to be willing to do the same thing, but they had not been tested to the point of having their **blood** shed in their efforts to stand "up against crime" (4Macc 17:10).

The comfort that is offered. **The sons** of God who are also brothers of one another in a monastery have to endure a severe discipline—poverty, celibacy, and obedience. The author acknowledged that, but there is also **comfort** in the security of the monastery. All food, shelter, clothing, and essential needs are always provided by the administration. Monks take vows that they will give up everything they own to become financially poor, but the monastery also takes vows to provide for every material need. There is **comfort** in this. This is provided only for the brothers, members of the legal family, **the sons.**

The preacher scolded his audience, pointing out problems and faults they had that he knew about. He was no outsider. He had observed, personally, the religious development of his audience. He knew how successful and unsuccessful they had been. He addressed the audience as if he had some authority over them and responsibility for their behavior. He spoke to them as a father might speak to his **sons.** These children were not daughters. They were spoken to as **sons**. These **sons,** however, were not physical **sons.** They were religious or legal **sons**, as brothers in a monastery. In the author's judgment, the readers had become dull of hearing (Heb 5:11); they had completely forgotten their earlier instruction; they were urged to remember the earlier days after they had first been enlightened (Heb 10:32). **The comfort** they received when they were enlightened enabled them to endure many kinds of hardship, but they had forgotten all of this (Heb 10:32-35). Hardship should have given them a sense of belongingness. They should have taken **comfort** that they were being treated **as sons.** They were not denied the necessary **discipline** parents provide their children. Proof for this was found in the Scriptures.

The word translated **discipline** (*pai-dáy-ahs*, παιδείας) might also be rendered "instruction," "training," or "child development." In a context that deals with the responsibility of standing up against crime until **blood,** the particular type of training involved was more than quiet meditation. It involved painful drilling and discipline to prepare the readers for the life they must face. The word **are corrected** (*eh-lehg-kháw-meh-naws*, ἐλεγχόμενος) means "being tested." It is from the same root as *eh-lehg-khaws*, (ἔλεγχος) in Heb 11:1. It is a Greek legal term, used frequently in court trials. It was sometimes used in debates and cross examinations.

Being **corrected** may mean being exposed, being shown up in public, or being criticized (see John 3:20; Eph 5:11, 13). These are all painful experiences which were considered necessary preparation for Christian living. For the meaning of **love** see further Commentary on Heb 6:10 and Heb 10:24. Prov 3:11-12, quoted here, is also freely quoted in Rev 3:19 in a context of exhortation to Christians in the face of persecution. Hebrews used the LXX, word-for-word, adding only the possessive adjective **my** to **son.** The word translated **he whips** (*mah-stee-goí*, μαστιγοί) renders the Hebrew *kah-áhv* (כאב), which the MT points *kuh-áhv* (כ אב), **like a father**, which makes good sense in the context. Pointed *kháhv*, this Hebrew means "he caused pain," or "he made suffer." Thus rendered the Hebrew forms a chiasm:

For *whomever* the Lord loves,	**he *disciplines***
X	
and he *whips*	***every son* he accepts**.

A person who **disciplines** the one he makes to suffer might **whip** him. Therefore the LXX translation is valid and has just about as strong an argument for being the intended meaning of כ אב as the MT form. The Hebrew letters can mean either "disciplined" or "like a father." The interpretation of hardship in terms of discipline was appreciatively offered earlier to Jews in time of trial:

> Now, I appeal to those who happen to come upon this book, not to be discouraged by these misfortunes, but rather to consider that these were retribution not intended to destroy, but rather only to discipline our people. As a matter of fact, it is a mark of favor not to leave impious [Jews] alone for any length of time, but to inflict immediate punishment on them. When it comes to other nations, the Lord shows his tolerance and delays punishing them until they have reached the fullness of their iniquity, but for us he had determined differently, in order that he may not be required to punish us later when our crimes have reached limit (2Macc 6:12-16).

It is on the basis of this kind of theology that Paul could encourage the Romans to let God vindicate them against their enemies (Rom 12:19), while they themselves heaped coals of fire upon the heads of their enemies by doing good to them (Rom 12:20). The more good they did, the more God would afflict their enemies. Since God rewards for suffering and punishes for crime, Christians should be glad for the opportunity to face trials (James 1:2). The experience of trials not only builds character for the Christians (James 1:3-4; 1Pet 1:6-9), but it cancels their crimes, since **whoever has suffered in the flesh has ceased from crime** (1Pet 4:1).

Being beaten up unjustly wins God's approval (1Pet 2:19), adds merits to the treasury of merits, and puts the believer in a better position for favorable judgment the next time. Although this type of theology was part of the background of the author's understanding as reflected in other parts of the documents, the emphasis here was not on adding merits to the treasury, but rather the positive value to the listener himself of these sufferings. It attested his acceptance as a **son**, and it corrected his faulty views, improving his character and understanding.

Rabbis said punishments are more precious than rain and parents, because parents and rain provide life in this world, but punishments provide life in the age to come (Mek, *Bahodesh* 10:64-69). The Torah, the Land of Israel, and the age to come are all given as rewards because of punishments suffered (Mek, *Bahodesh* 10:34-47). It is the suffering of punishments that bring about forgiveness (Mek, *Bahodesh*, 10:28-30). Once these crimes are forgiven, then God was expected to restore the blessings desired.

The author of Heb 1-12 was obviously preaching to an audience that was somewhat discouraged. They were complaining about the hardship they faced. The preacher tried to boost their morale by reminding them that they were suffering all of these difficulties **as sons.** The hardships were not just costs but investments in the future. The speaker himself may have been the one who enforced all of this discipline upon them, and he defended his action by telling them it was all because he was very fond of them, treating them as his own **sons.**

7 *With reference to "discipline," [you must] endure*. The Proverbs passage on discipline prompted the author to interpret this passage also in terms of **endurance**. The Greek *eis pai-dáy-ahn* (ἐὶς παιδεῖαν) is translated with the understanding that *eis* (εις) here means **with reference to**, as would be normal in a midrashic context, commenting on a word from the text just quoted. The author's paraphrastic elaboration on the relationship of sonship to **discipline** is fair to the text he used.

8 *Then you are illegitimate children and not sons*. Since the sonship of monks is only legal, **illegitimacy** is a very serious accusation. The negative aspect, that the Proverbs passage did not mention, is that if a **son** cannot be **without discipline**, then the undisciplined ones would be **illegitimate** and not true **sons.** Since this is the case, the readers, all of whom **have become sharers** of discipline, should be comforted. They have not been rejected by God. This suffering is the sure sign of their sonship.

*Summary.*This small unit was centered around **sonship** and **discipline**. It was framed by an inclusion, using the word **son** (Heb 12:5, 8), which also occurs within the unit (Heb 12:6, 7). The next unit will elaborate on this analogy, so the word **son** in Heb 12:8 also is a catchword introducing the next topic. The author's arguments were directed to a group who had specific problems. They were discouraged with the program, its promises, and its results to the current time. The author was encouraging them to stay with the program and endure all of the problems. These hardships were all good signs. It meant that they were accepted members; they were sons of God. The hardships would pay off. On the other hand, if they left the program they would be denied all of the benefits and status the program provided. The situation that fits all of these needs and problems is a monastery, where severe discipline is standard and where all of the "children" are male and legal. The author evidently belonged to the same monastery. He knew the complaints and dangers.

TEXT

Hebrews

9 Therefore, since we have had our fathers of the flesh [as] disciplinarians, and we became respectful, shall we not much more subject ourselves to **the Father of Spirits** and live?

First Testament and Associated Intertexts

Num 16:22 God is **the God of Spirits** also of all flesh. One man has sinned, and his anger is over the entire council.

Num 27:16 Let Yehowah, **the God of spirits** of all flesh, appoint a man over the council

1Enoch 39:12 Holy, holy, holy is **the Lord of spirits**. He fills the earth with **spirits.**

10 For they used to discipline us for a short time, as it seemed [wise] to them; but he
[disciplines us] insofar as it is beneficial for sharing his sanctity. 11 At the present, all
discipline seems not to be joy, but pain; later, however, it produces a peaceful fruit
of righteousness for those who have been trained through it.

Hebrews

12 Therefore, **set straight the collapsed hands and the paralytic knees**,

13 and **make straight** tracks **with your feet**,

so the lame may not **be turned off** [the road] but rather be healed.

First Testament Intertexts

Isa 35:3-4 **strengthen the weak hands, and make firm the knocking knees**. Say to those whose nerves tremble, "Be strong! Do not be afraid!" Look! Your God! Vengeance will come.

Prov 4:26-27 Pay attention to the path of **your feet**, and all of your ways will be sure. Do not wander to the right or to the left; **turn your feet** from evil.

COMMENTARY

9 *Our fathers of the flesh.* Once all monks had fathers of the flesh, but after they joined the monastery, they were warned not to call any human being "father." They had only one father, God—The Father of Spirits.

Subject ourselves to the Father of Spirits and live. When Korah rebelled against Moses in the wilderness, **the God of Spirits** ordered Moses to isolate Korah and his followers, and command the rest of the Israelites to refrain from touching them. He said Korah and his council would no longer **live**, and the land opened under Korah and his following and swallowed them all (Num 16:22-35). The author of Hebrews reminded his listeners of the Lord's severe discipline.

Heb 12:9-12 belongs to the small midrash, beginning with Heb 12:4, continuing the exhortation on **discipline**. Heb 12:9 constitutes an *a fortriori* argument which contrasts **our fathers of the flesh** with **the father of spirits** and also becoming **trained** to being alive. To **live** religiously means more than eating, breathing, and taking up space. Only those who are under the contract and on the **Promised Land** (the land of **life**) when it is free from foreign rule are really alive. Others are "dead" even though they are physically healthy. Those who are religiously **alive** can let the religiously dead bury their own dead (Matt 8:22).

Christians know that they have been changed from death to **life** because they **love** their brothers (1John 3:14). The one who has the **Son** has **life,** and the one who does not have the **Son** does not have **life** (1John 5:12). If any one commits a crime, not unto death (i.e., a pardonable crime), his co-religionist should pray, and God will give him **life** (i.e., restore him to the community where alone **life** is possible) (1John 5:16).[1] Christians who subjected themselves to the **Father of Spirits** would deny their **fathers of the flesh**, join the monastery, and become approved believers, which means they would **live**. If they were subject to God, of course, they would have to accept **discipline**, a reasonable expectation, according to the author.

At first glance it is assumed that the **Father of spirits** was God, but Grässer noted that the contrast is strange. He would expect the contrast to be between the earthly **father** and the heavenly **father**. The word **spirit,** however, is closely associated with legal things. A **father** who has adopted a child, for example, is not a physical **father** to that child, but rather a legal or **spiritual father.** Those who leave the families into which they have been born to join a monastery become members of a new legal or **spiritual** family. They leave their **fathers of the flesh**, as well as all of their other family members **of the flesh**, to become legal members of **the spirit,** a new family, with a new **father** and new brothers—no sisters. In that case, the chief of the monastery would be the **spiritual father** or **father of spirits** to all of the members who would be legal or **spiritual** brothers. This would be the person who would discipline the members of the order to see that they all obeyed those rigorous rules which they had vowed to follow. When the members of the new family complained, the preacher compared their current life with the lives they had lived before. Grässer correctly noticed that the discipline required of this exhortation reminded readers of the discipline demanded of monks.[2]

There are many parts of the argument (Heb 1:1-12:29) that point to a monastic setting for this sermon. The counsel for discipline given here was given as if the author knew the group well; he understood their problems, their doubts, and their difficulties. He knew the demands of the community to which they belonged. He also knew the motivation and affection related to the discipline. This would not have been understood by an outside speaker. He reminded them of facts they already knew. He and they all belonged to a spiritual community whose rules were consistent. In the judgment of the order this community was the only group in which life was possible. If the listeners remained with the order they would have legal or spiritual life. If they fell away they would be spiritually dead. With membership

---

[1] Buchanan, *The Consequences of the Covenant* (Leiden: Brill, 1970), pp. 110-49.

[2] E. Grässer, *Evangelisch-Katholischer Kommentar zum Neuen Testament* 3 (Zurich: Benziger Verlag, c1997), pp. 248, 265.

came life. The approaching Day of Atonement was a good time to remind the brothers of the need for correct discipline.

10*It is beneficial for sharing and sanctity*. Still dealing in contrasts, there is a carry-over from the *a fortiori* argument in Heb 12:9 which is apparent in this verse. The **short time** during which the **fathers of the flesh disciplined** the members did not refer to individual events, but rather the whole training period from birth to adulthood, which was not very long. During this period the **fathers** used whatever methods of **discipline seemed [wise] to them.** It was generally believed that this was to the advantage of the children, so that they might learn to behave properly. In the same way God **disciplines** his sons in the monastery **as much as it is beneficial**, in the judgment of the order, to prepare them to share in his **sanctity**. The author repeatedly reminded the listeners that suffering and punishment was beneficial.

Sanctity (*hah-gee-áw-tay-taws*, ἁγιότητος) usually refers to levitical purity, especially observed by the priests, so that the temple where they minister might be "clean" or ritually undefiled, and the Lord would be willing to dwell there. It also described the condition of holiness observed by soldiers in camp, because they wanted the presence of the Lord with them in battle. Lane correctly held that holiness is a cultic rather than an ethical condition.[1] Women are sanctified by taking baths after a menstrual period (2Sam 11:4). The entire congregation of Israel has become holy by performing the rites for membership (Num 16:3). Israelites sanctified themselves by bathing and washing their garments (Exod 19:10). Character and integrity were not the primary requirements of holiness. It was legal rituals that were necessary for holiness.

When the temple was no longer standing, believers tried to keep their homes as ritually clean or holy as the temple, which meant observing rules as strict as those observed by the priests. This was the priesthood of all believers. Not only priests but all true believers were supposed to be saints or holy people. This condition of holiness or **sanctity** was **life**. Heb 12:10 is a partial repetition and extension of the argument of Heb 12:9. Those who accepted God's **discipline** would **live**. It was through the administration of the order that God would **discipline** these **sons** as much as was necessary to produce **sanctity** which was religious **life**. It was as sons that they were being disciplined. Those who took these holiness rules seriously were strongly motivated toward monasticism.

Judging from the advice given and the demands made upon the readers, the author of Hebrews seems to have been a member of some rigorous monastic society that expected **sanctity** of its members. The members of monasteries may or may not have been born from priestly families, but because of their commitment, discipline, and initiation for the monastery, they became legal priests by virtue of their initiation. Their monastery also became a substitute temple until David's tent or Solomon's temple would be restored.

11*A peaceful fruit of righteousness*. The third contrast of this unit compared immediate results to far-reaching results. The person who learned something new was forced to practice and train endlessly until he became proficient. This was not always easy or enjoyable, but the satisfaction that came from being able to perform well was worth the practice. The implication is that those who faced social and physical torture and personal privation for **the faith** would become **trained through**

---

[1] W. L. Lane, *Hebrews 9-13* (Dallas: Word Books, c1991), p. 450.

it until they accepted his sanctity and the new life associated with it. This meant producing **a peaceful fruit of righteousness**.

Jews and Christians were frequently faced with the need for endurance during the current evil era, but they endured in the hope that the future would hold pleasant rewards. They could hasten the time when the reward would be granted by laying up treasures in heaven (Matt 6:20). This might prompt the Lord to pardon his people and shorten the term of their "captivity" (Mark 13:20; Enoch 80:2, 2 Bar 20:1). Whenever this **training** period was over, and the people were all **holy** and **perfect,** then they would receive their **promised** reward or **rest** and prosperity on the land.

12-13 *So the lame may not be turned off.* The author followed the LXX more or less in his quotation of two FT passages (Isa 35:3; Prov 4:26). In the Proverbs passage the main variant is that the LXX *poí-ay* (ποίει) (you [sing.] make) became *poi-áy-teh* (ποιεῖτε) (you [pl.] make), a variant which the author of Hebrews may have made himself to suit his context. The same may be true of the substitution of **collapsed** (*pah-ray-méh-nahs*, παρειμένας) for the related LXX "slack" (*ah-nay-méh-nai*, ἀνειμέναι) (Isa 35:3). In Hebrew, the Isaiah passage formed a chiasm in a well-balanced couplet.

Strengthen		**the weak hands**
	X	
the feeble knees		**make strong.**

The LXX text is clearly secondary in this passage. The LXX has omitted the word "make strong" (*ah-mayt-zoó*, אמצו) when a scribe passed over it, since the next word in the text began with the same two consonants, *áh-lehph* (א) and *maym* (מ) (*eem-roó,* אמרו) (Isa 35:4); this is a simple case of homeoarcton error. Homeoarcton comes from the Greek and means "same beginning." That refers to the beginning of lines in a text. If two lines on the same page begin with the same word, it is easy for a copier to drop from one to the other, without noticing that he or she has done it. When that happens, the words between the two lines are omitted. That is a homeoarcton error of copying. The author of Hebrews followed the LXX structure in making his first verb (*ahn-awr-thóh-sah-teh*, ἀνορθώσατε), "set straight," instead of *ees-khoó-sah-the* (ἰσχύσατε, in the LXX) take two objects. The author's choice of texts was excellent from several points of view. He associated **set straight** (*ahn-awr-thóh-sah-teh,*) with "make straight" (*awr-tháhs po-áy-teh*, ὀρθὰς ποιεῖτε), one dealing with bodies and the other with paths that individuals take. The word for **straight** is the word from which the English word "orthodox" is derived. Those who make straight paths for their feet are those who have legitimate goals that are orthodox, and they keep these rules faithfully.

While urging his readers to hold fast to **the confession** (Heb 4:14; 10:23) and reminding them that the time of waiting was almost over (Heb 10:25), he quoted from a passage reflecting the end of the captivity in Babylon. The poet was announcing the good news that the **promise** was just about to be fulfilled; Jews could return and reestablish the homeland in Palestine. This encouragement applied perfectly to the author's understanding of his own time.

The author of Prov 4:26, like the author of Hebrews, urged his hearers not to fall away from the **faith**. They must follow right paths, keep the commandments, and hold fast to the right doctrine. The **lame** in the Babylonian community were physically **lame**, but the author of Hebrews used the term metaphorically to go with the Proverbs passage. The **tracks** about which the proverbial poet wrote were religious rather than geographical. The **lame** who might **be turned** away would be the weak. They would be the same people called the **little ones** (Matt 10:42; 18:6, 10, 14) who might **stumble**. Believers should walk carefully themselves so as not to mislead others. Instead of being **turned off [the road]**, the weak feet should **rather be healed**, which meant, metaphorically, that the believers should **set straight the collapsed hands and the paralytic knees** of the religiously insecure. This was the type of healing expected just before the "captives" entered their promised **rest.**

Summary. This unit was composed of three contrasts, concluding with two quotations of Scripture:

1)The first comparison was between the human fathers and the **Father** of spirits;
2) the second showed the purpose of the discipline that was contrasted; and
3) the third, the pain involved in discipline compared to the lasting advantage.

The passages of Scripture were introduced to relate their character to the reward of the promise, which was always before the author's eyes. These small units: Heb 12:1-3, 4-8, and 9-13 really belong together, but they are partially subdivided by subject matter and steps in argument. The first unit is introductory so far as the exhortation is concerned, but presents conclusions of action based on previous arguments and doctrine. The main thrust of the author's exhortation is an urgent appeal for endurance, which involves discipline. The second unit related discipline to the Christian's relationship to God, and the third unit provided applications and elaborations on the discipline urged. Although the actual quotation of Prov 4:26 forced the author to use a different word for "track" (Heb 12:13) than for "course" (Heb 12:1), the imagery of an athlete running hard to reach the right goal was maintained throughout Heb 12:1-13, comprising one unit, set off by an inclusion.

TEXT

Hebrews	Hebrew Scripture
	Ps 34:15 Turn from evil and do good; search for
14 **Pursue peace** with all **and** sanctification, without which	**peace and pursue** it.
no one **will see the Lord,**	Isa 6:1 In the year that King Uzziah died, I **saw the Lord**, seated upon his throne, high and exalted.
	Exod 24:10 They **saw the God** of Israel . . . 11 The chief men of the Israelites **saw God,** and they ate and drank.
15 checking carefully **lest**	LXX Deut 29:17 [Watch] **lest** there be among you--a man, woman,

anyone fall back

from the grace of God, **lest**
any root of bitterness,
growing up,
should cause trouble and through this the many become defiled,
[16]**lest anyone** [become] a
fornicator or defiled person, like
Esau, who, in exchange for a
single
meal gave up his own **birthright**.
[17]For you [may] be sure that even afterwards, when he wanted to inherit the blessing, he was rejected, for he did not find a place for repentance, even though he tried to obtain it with tears.

family, or tribe an idea if **anyone** has turned away from the Lord our God to go worship the gods of those Gentiles—**lest** there be
among you **any root**
growing up
in gall and **bitterness**.

[Gen 25:31-32]Jacob said, "Sell me your

birthright," and **Esau** said, "Look! I am approaching death! What is this **birthright** to me?"

COMMENTARY

[14]*Pursue peace with all, and sanctification.* The words **peace** and **sanctification** relate this unit to the **peaceful** fruit (Heb 12:11) and **sanctification** (Heb 12:10) of the previous unit. Ps 34:14 [LXX 33:15] says, **Search for peace and pursue it**. The author of Hebrews used only the second verb, **pursue** (changing it to a *present* imperative and *plural*, to fit his context). Hillel counseled his students to "be disciples of Aaron, loving **peace**, and pursuing **peace"** (mAboth 1:12).

Pursuing peace with all meant that the believer should see that all of his crimes committed against his brothers had been forgiven, so that God could effectively pardon his crimes on the Day of Atonement. Women were not involved in this situation, because they were not taught the law. Therefore they were not guilty. The sectarian who desired forgiveness for his crimes had to know that he had not committed crimes with any conscious intention of trying to obtain release on the Day of Atonement. He also first had to be reconciled to his fellow citizen for his crime; he had to repent; and he had to bring his crime and guilt offerings to the temple of the Lord. Because of these terms, Christians were told,

> So if you are offering your gift at the altar, and there remember that your brother has something against you, leave your gift there before the altar and go; first be reconciled to your brother, and then come and offer your gift (Matt 5:23-24).

God's forgiveness was dependent upon the believer's reconciliation to his brother. Because this was true, the one who had committed crimes could not be forgiven by God if his brother refused to forgive him for the crime he had committed against him. With this understanding it was necessary for members of the community to forgive one another (Matt 6:12, 14-15) even 77 times (Matt 18:22; Luke 17:3-4; see also TGad 6:3-7). God would not redeem Israel while she was still in her crime.

Therefore it was important for all members of the community to be free from crimes, to be reconciled to one another, to repent, and to offer the required gifts on the Day of Atonement, so that Israel could be forgiven and the land restored.[1]

Those who pursued **peace** tried to cancel the debt of crime against Israel. The word for peace is the passive participle of the verb *shee-láyme* (שלם) which means to pay or pay up. If all of Israel's fines against the Lord were paid up then she would be without crime, and the kingdom would be restored. Jews and Christians wished each other "peace," which meant that they wished their crimes would all be paid up or pardoned. The "inner joy with God and salvation," of which Grässer wrote,[2] were the rewards and benefits of having had all crimes cancelled.

The faithful who were trying to cancel the nation's crimes were the poor in spirit, the mourners, the meek, the merciful, those who hungered and thirsted for righteousness, the pure in heart, the **peace**makers, or those who were persecuted for righteousness' sake (Matt 5:3-10). **Sanctification** involved levitical purity, primarily required for priests. The Israelites who avoided touching anything related to Korah and his council kept themselves **sanctified.** No one was qualified to go up **to the mountain of Yehowah and stand in his holy place** who did not have **clean hands and a pure mind,** who had not taken oaths deceptively (Ps 24:3-4). Only the priests could be that well qualified. These were those who were **sanctified**. It was in the temple where Isaiah **saw the Lord.** The author of Hebrews said that all sons of God were to be disciplined until they shared **his sanctification** (Heb 12:10). Matthew promised that the **pure** or clean (*kah-tha-roí*, καθαροί) **in mind** would **see God** (Matt 5:8), whereas the author of Hebrews said only those who were sanctified, or ritually clean, would **see the Lord.**

Since 1John 4:12, following Exod 33:20, said that no man had ever seen God, the promise that anyone would ever **see God** seems strange; but the same inconsistency occurs in the FT. On the one hand no one could see the face of God and live (Exod 33:20), whereas Moses, Aaron, Nadab, Abihu, and the 70 elders of Israel **saw the God of Israel** (Exod 24:9-11); the Lord was seen **eye to eye** (Num 14:14); in the temple, Isaiah **saw the Lord** (Isa 6:1). Exod 23:17 should probably be pointed to read: **Three times a year all your males will see the face of the Lord Yehowah**. The priests were required to walk blamelessly in certain ways (Ps 15:1-5); the priest who ascended the hill of the Lord was required to have **clean hands and a pure heart** (Ps 24:3-4).

Rabbis understood the passage **Because in a cloud I will be seen on the chest cover** (Lev 16:2) to refer to the **cloud** of smoke made by incense which the priest offered on the Day of Atonement when he entered the **holy of holies**. The incense was to be offered in such a way that the priest's vision there would always be blurred by the smoke, lest he **see God** improperly (Sifra 81b; JYoma I, 5:39a-39b; see also ExodR 34:1; bRoshH 3la; Mek *Shirata* 10:24-42).[3] Matt 5:8, then, in a context of FT promises that were expected to be fulfilled, evidently meant that those who had clean hearts would live to worship in the temple, where they, like Isaiah and the priests, could **see God**, not in his ultimate reality, but in the way others had done who worshiped in the temple.

The author of Hebrews dealt with the same **promise,** negatively: without **sanctification no one will see the Lord**. Just as persistently as the Gospel of

---

[1] Buchanan, *Consequences,* pp. 229-233.

[2] E. Grässer, *An die Hebräer* (Zürich: Benziger Verlag, c1997) III, p. 174.

[3] Buchanan, *Consequences,* pp. 74-75, n. 10.

Matthew urged that parties to the contract be **perfect,** continually repenting and forgiving, so that the community might be without crime, the author of Hebrews encouraged his community to **pursue peace**. The author of Hebrews was even more severe than Matthew. He did not allow for continual forgiveness with repentance. For the brothers there must not be *any* evil in *any* of them (Heb 3:12). *No* one could see the Lord who was not **sanctified.** It is difficult to conceive of any group other than a monastic brotherhood who would try to maintain this severely rigid ethic.

[15]*Checking carefully*. The Greek for **checking carefully** is *eh-pees-kaw-poón-tehs* (ἐπισκοποῦντες), "watching over," "supervising," or "inspecting." The author's emphasis on absolute **perfection** is evident again in his use of **any one**. No single person dare slip in any way (Heb 3:12; 12:14), lest there be *any* root of bitterness within the group.

The **root of bitterness** in Deut 29:18 [17 MT and LXX] probably referred to anything that led to idolatry and apostasy. In NT times, however, this term came to be identified with the tree of **knowledge of good and evil** (Gen 2:9), and this was associated with marriage and was the teaching of monasteries. Anyone who married had to leave the monastery, which from a monastic point of view, was to become an apostate. The sect that lived according to the Gospel of the Egyptians was evidently ascetic. According to its teachings, the Savior said,

> I came to destroy both the works of sexual lusts and the works of creation and destruction.

A certain Salome asked how long men would continue to die. The Lord answered, "As long as women bear children."

She responded, "Then I did well not to bear children."

The Lord answered, "Eat every plant, but do not eat the bitter plant" (Strom 3:9; 6:3, 1:67, 2; cf. Deut 29:18).

Another sectarian had drunk from the water of life, given up folly, was clothed in a new garment, had his eyes enlightened, and was taken to the Lord's Paradise. He was one of the Lord's servants who turned away from the bitterness of the trees (OdesSol 11:9-18). The "life" involved was legal life within the holy community; "Paradise" was the geographical location of the group's meeting place; the "new garment" was a legal garment worn only by members; having one's "eyes enlightened" means he had completed the instruction required for membership.

Another psalmist thanked God for not reckoning him with the criminals and asked the Lord to save him from the wicked criminal woman, not to let the beauty of a wicked woman lead him astray, and to remove him from all anger and unreasonable passion (PssSol 16:7-10).

In opposition to these celibate sects, Clement of Alexandria (Strom 3:10; 73:3-4) said Moses' commandment not to touch anything unclean did not refer to those Christians who were married, but to those gentiles who were still living in "fornication." He did not identify marriage with fornication nor idolatry and apostasy, but the fact that he defended his position implies that some people did. There were in his day celibate sects who called the marrying Christians "fornicators." In addition to its normal use, "harlotry" was used metaphorically in FT and NT times to refer disparagingly to social mingling. Idolatry was called **whoring after strange gods** (Deut 31:16; AsMos 5:3). One of the reasons Hebrews survived in Christianity was that there continued to be a monastic movement in the church. This was strong enough to merit the resistance of Clement of Alexandria in the late second century.

When Judah made a marriage contract with the Lord she was prohibited from marrying any other deity. When she made international agreements with Egypt and Assyria, Ezekiel interpreted her faithlessness to the contract made at Sinai to be harlotry (Ezek 16). The Shepherd of Hermas (Mand 4:1.9) said adultery referred not only to defilement of flesh but also to behavior like that of the gentiles. Jesus was reportedly associated with the **harlots and tax collectors,** the former of whom were not women at all, but rather Jews who were celibate males that had associated with gentiles and were thereby defiled. Masculine **harlots** (*páwr-noi,* πόρνοι) were listed together with **dogs** (*koó-nehs,* κύνες), sorcerers, murderers, idolaters, and liars (Rev 22:15; Philip 3:2) as those not admitted to the New Jerusalem. The "dogs" were probably gentiles who mingled with Jews, and "masculine harlots" or "fornicators" were probably Jews who mingled with gentiles, terms used in derision by orthodox Jews and Christians who would mingle with neither.[1]

There are some clues in Heb l:l-12:29 that suggest the author of Hebrews was himself a celibate monk who addressed a group of similar celibate monks. These clues are implied in his teachings, even though he nowhere directly speaks of himself or his readers as celibates. The author referred to the readers as **brothers** (Heb 3:1, 12; 7:5; 8:11; 10:19) as was customary in monastic brotherhoods. Like communal brotherhoods, he stressed the importance of work and **love** for one another (Heb 6:10; 10:24). His emphasis on holiness (Heb 3:1; 9:7; 12:10, 14), **discipline** (Heb 12:6, 7,10, 11), defilement (Heb 2:14; 9:13), and **crime** as fornication (Heb 12:16) points toward a celibate group that was required to be strongly disciplined to avoid any kind of defilement.

His requirement of absolute freedom from crimes could hardly be taken seriously by any but a rigorous, monastic group. Not *any* member dared to commit *any* evil deed (Heb 3:12); not *any* of the group dared to fail in achieving the **promises** (Heb 4:1); *no* one dared backslide into disobedience (Heb 4:11); *all* must be **sanctified** with *no* one failing to obtain the grace of God (Heb 12:14-15); *no* one dared to **shrink back** (Heb 10:38-39); there could **be *no* root of bitterness** allowed in the group (Heb 12:15); there was *no* chance for second repentance or forgiveness (Heb 6:4-8; 12:17).

The picture of Jesus as a priest without a family or posterity (Heb 7:3), who was separated from criminals, unstained, holy, and blameless (Heb 7:26), seems to fit the ideal of monasticism. Since Jesus was criticized for mingling with criminals in the gospel reports, the picture given in Hebrews seems to fit the author's ideal rather than the facts. It is not just that he called the members "brothers," or spoke of brotherly love, that suggests monasticism. Christians who married also did the same, but the extent to which he emphasized these terms that were more customarily used in monastic communities than generally, and the rigorous discipline he required, indicate a background of associations that would fit better into a monastic community than any other.

The Greek word translated **should cause trouble** is *eh-nawch-láy* (ἐνοχλῇ). Katz has made a good case for holding that the best reading of the LXX

[1] Buchanan, *Consequences,* pp. 184-89.

is *ehn khaw-láy* (ἐν χολῇ (in anger),[1] but the author of Hebrews evidently used a text that read *ehn-khaw-láy*, and he preserved it with that meaning. **The many** is a technical term which means the whole congregation. Just as one rotten apple spoils the whole basketful, so one defiled person would **cause trouble** by defiling the whole community. This meticulous care for **sanctity** and avoidance of defilement is the kind of legalism expected in a monastic group.

16*A fornicator or defiled person.* Heb 12:16 is partly repetitious and partly an elaboration of verse 15. Thus the **root of bitterness** (Heb 12:15) is in parallel construction to **a fornicator or defiled person,** which is a hendiadys composed of two synonyms. In this context, **the root of bitterness** is the **fornicator** who is also the defiled person--different names for the same offender. There is no biblical data to justify calling Jacob's brother, **Esau**, a **fornicator**, but **Esau**, in NT times, was identified with Rome, and all sorts of criminal activity were attributed to him by transfer (Virt 208; Jub 25:1, 8). He was considered wicked because he had no **Day of Atonement** to remove his defilement as Jacob did (GenR 65:15).

As Jacob realized later, it was not Esau, but Jacob, who needed the Day of Atonement. When Jacob returned to Palestine with great riches and many servants, he wrestled with an angel at Peniel (Gen 32). On the one hand he feared facing Esau with his troops. On the other hand he feared the Lord who promised the land, posterity, and prosperity only on the condition that the sons of Abraham keep all of the law in the contract. Every offense had to be atoned or God would follow with curses instead of blessings. The curses involved wild beasts, famine, pestilence, and the sword. The Day of Atonement was established to enable the parties to the contract to pay for all of their earlier offenses. The terms were, the criminal had to

1) offer the proper sacrifice to pay for the crime,
2) become reconciled to the brother who was the victim of the crime.
3) If both of these terms were met, the believer could be assured of forgiveness.

Jacob had committed a crime against his brother, and he could not be reconciled to God without first becoming reconciled to Esau, so he made the attempt. He planned to **atone** (*ah-kah-puh-ráh,* אכפרה) **his face with gifts** (Gen 32:20). Reflecting his knowledge of the rules for atonement, he sent many punitive gifts ahead to Esau, after which the brothers were reconciled. Jacob gave back to Esau both his blessing and his birthright, so that Esau could return to Hebron and claim his legitimate possession and status. Jacob, in turn, went north to Shechem and bought other land to begin a new family corporation.

The author of Hebrews, however, was evidently a pious, Jewish Christian, who did not study the Jacob-Esau relationship from Esau's point of view. In his opinion Esau was a fornicator, who was a euphemism for Rome. The Roman state was called a pig because it posed as if it were clean when it was not, according to R. Simon.

In the same context, **Esau** was accused by Medieval rabbis of having violated many married women (GenR 65:1; Jub 25:1, 8). This was an insulting way of illustrating the extent of Rome's defilement from the rabbinic point of view. The author of Hebrews agreed with the rabbis in attributing to **Esau** defilement which he

---

[1] P. Katz, "The Quotations from Deuteronomy in Hebrews," *ZNTW* 49 (1958):213-23.

described in terms of **fornication**.[1] The word translated **meal** is *bróh-seh-ohs* (βρώσεως), literally "an eating." *Bróh-mah* (βρῶμα) is "food." Therefore he was reported to have given up **his own birthright** for a single "eating" or "meal." The author of Hebrews referred to the story of an occasion when Esau was extremely hungry, and Jacob took advantage of the situation. He bargained with him on the basis that he would give him the food he wanted at the moment in exchange for Esau's birthright. As the eldest son, **Esau** was entitled to a double portion of his father's **inheritance** (Deut 21:15-17), but Jacob bought this from him under the pressure of hunger (Gen 25:29-34).

17*He did not find a place for repentance*. Jacob also tricked Esau out of his father's blessing, to which Esau was entitled, but which he could not recover, even though **he cried out with a very great and bitter cry** (Gen 27:34). An objective judge might sympathize with Esau and criticize Jacob for his malice, but the author of Hebrews was not critical of his religious ancestors. He used the example to warn his readers of the ease with which a Christian could make one mistake, which would be fatal. When **Esau wanted to inherit the blessing, he was rejected** even though this happened a long time **afterwards**. The mistake made earlier had not been forgotten. There was no **place for repentance** either from God or from Isaac. **Esau** might be sorry for his mistake, and try even **with tears** to make restitution or to revoke an earlier decision, but there was no possibility.

The point of the illustration was to warn the readers against making the same mistake the exodus generation or **Esau** had made. It was not the author of Hebrews' concern for **Esau's** activity but for the behavior of the readers that caused the author to warn against becoming a defiled person, a **fornicator**, or a **root of bitterness.** **Esau** was compared to the one who fell back from the **grace of God** because both would be guilty of giving up their own **birthrights**. **Esau** lost his birthright by dealing with an unscrupulous brother at a weak moment; the Christian might become weak also and break contract, which meant he would be defiled or without **sanctification.** The lot of the Christian was also like that of **Esau** in that once his fate was sealed, he could not change it.

It would have spoiled the author's argument if he had followed through with the relationship between the sons of Isaac and admitted that **Esau** finally did receive his blessing and **birthright** again. This happened, not because **Esau** repented, but because, at Peniel, Jacob remembered the rules for the **Day of Atonement,** and he repented.

Summary. The ethical demand in this unit did not differ from that offered several times in other exhortatory parts of the document. It is rigorous, unrelenting, and complete. There was no room allowed for mistakes, weakness, or oversights. Here, however, the specific terms used in defining that ethic more carefully seemed even more likely than earlier to be those appropriate to a monastic group that opposed marriage, fornication, defilement of every kind, and worked steadfastly for **sanctification**. This was an either/or type of segregationism characteristic of communal,

---

[1] H. Montefiore, *A Commentary on the Epistle to the Hebrews* (New York: Harper & Row, 1964), p. 224, seems mistaken in his analysis: "*Pornos* is more likely to have its literal sense here of the one who is sexually immoral (Heb 13:4) rather than the metaphorical meaning of apostate." He may have been misled by assuming that Heb 13:4 was written by the same author as Heb 12:16.

celibate groups like the Essenes, the community governed by the Rule of the Community, and many early ascetic Christian monastic groups.

TEXT

Hebrews	Hebrew Scripture
18 For **you have** not **come to** **a fire** that is touched and kindled, [nor] deep **darkness, gloom, and tempest,** 19 a reverberated **sound** of a trumpet, and a voice of words, of which those who heard pleaded [that] no word be added to them, 20 for they could not bear that which was commanded.	LXX Deut 4:11 **You have come to** and you have stood under **the mountain, the mountain** burned with **fire** up to heaven, **darkness, gloom, and tempest**, a loud **sound.**
"Even if **a beast touches the mountain he will be stoned**," 21 and so dreadful was that which	Exod 19:12-13 Whoever **touches the mountain will be** put to death; no hand shall touch him, but he **shall be stoned** or shot, whether it is **a beast** or a human being, he shall not live.
appeared, Moses said, "I am **afraid and trembling**."	Exod 20:18 The people **were afraid and trembled**, and they stood at a distance.

TECHNICAL DETAILS

Misled by the RSV, Lane and Weiss have both changed the meaning of Heb 12:18 by taking the word "touched," as a verbal noun instead of a participial modifier of the noun, "fire." Instead of "a touched and kindled fire" or **a fire that is touched and kindled,** Lane rendered the phrase, "what can be touched and a blazing fire."[1] Weiss, then, held that Zion was touchable, and therefore earthly.[2] The main distinction, however, between Mount Horeb (Sinai) and Mount Zion, is that Mount Horeb could *not* be touched, and Mount Zion *could* be. Weiss already noted that the author was contrasting Mount Sinai to Mount Zion, but he took that to mean the earthly in contrast to the heavenly.[3]

Grässer, instead, introduced the readers to his notion that the author of Hebrews had an Alexandrian, dualistic "thought-technique" that transposed Mount Sinai into something that represented everything earthly and Mount Zion into something that represented everything heavenly, so that the community that had come to Zion stood on "the other side of the visible, vanishing world."[4] This seems to mean

---

[1] Lane, *Hebrews 9-13*, p. 437.

[2] H. F. Weiss, *Der Brief an die Hebräer* (Göttingen: Vandenhoeck & Ruprecht, 1991), p. 671, tr. from the German.

[3] *Weiss*, Hebräer, p. 671.

[4] E. Grässer, , *An die Hebräer,* p. 304. tr. from the German.

that Grässer acknowledged that the speaker's audience was there in Zion, listening to the speaker with human ears, but they were really in heaven at the same time, outside of the bounds of the earthly world where people can see and hear speakers as they talk. He must have been using words here in other than their normal meaning and sense.

There is nothing in the text to indicate that the author of Hebrews was speaking mystically, allegorically, or metaphorically. It is not clear where Grässer got that idea that he could be free to twist words around to mean exactly the opposite of that which they normally mean. How can people "have come to" (*praws-ehyl-lay-loó-thah-the,* προσεληλύθατε = *herzutretende*) an earthly, geographical location which is not "earthly," but is the other side of this earth (*jenseits*), in heaven, listening to a speaker at the same geographical location on earth? This seems to be an "Alice in Wonderland" fiction where words can mean "whatever I want them to mean."

Take a moment to admire the beautiful literary structure of the midrash involved in this passage. The author meticulously wove together passages from the revelation of the ten commandments and the provision of the contract to the people according the accounts given both at Mount Horeb and at Mount Sinai. He then took words from this text to compare the provision of the commandments on these mountains to the people gathered there to the appearance of his audience gathered on Mount Zion where Jesus, rather than Moses, provided the people with a new contract on a more holy mountain. What a beautiful typology for those who understood their heritage as the author's contemporaries certainly did!

COMMENTARY

[18]*A fire that is touched and kindled.* The participles, **touched and kindled** have been put in the passive voice to avoid the use of the divine name. It means "that God has **touched and kindled**." This is the way God set the mountain on **fire.**

The words **fire** (*poó-reé,* πυρί), **deep darkness** (*gnáw-phoh,* γνόφῳ), and **tempest,** *thoo-éh-lay,* θυέλλῃ) are terms used to describe Mount Horeb when the commandments were given (Deut 4:11). The word rendered **gloom** (*záw-phoh,* ζόφῳ) is very similar in meaning to **deep darkness**. In the LXX, *záw-phohs* (ζόφως) occurs in only a few places and only according to Symmachus' text. This may have occurred in a version of the LXX of Deut 4:11 which the author used, or it may have been an elaboration by the author. Several of these terms were frequently used together in theophanies (Deut 4:11; 5:22; Exod 10:22).

[19]*No word be added to them.* **A reverberated sound of a trumpet** is a slight variation of a quotation from the LXX Exod 19:16, describing a similar scene around Mount Sinai when the commandments were given. The author's willingness to parallel the two accounts is shown by his addition to the passage from Exod 19:16, **a sound of words**, taken from Deut 4:12. This may have meant the proclamation of the ten commandments, called **the ten words** in Deut 4:13.

[20]*They could not bear.* The Scriptures did not report that the people groaned about accepting the ten words. They were afraid, but they responded: **We will perform; we will obey** (Deut 5:27). The author may have known a tradition that described the

people's response as he has reported it. One of the traditions related to giving the Torah held that the Lord first offered it to all the nations of the world, but they rejected it. When it was offered to Israel, the people responded, **We will perform; we will obey** (Sepher ha'aggadah 59b). Commenting on **these words** (Exod 19:7), rabbis said, "You shall not diminish; you shall not add" (Mek, *Bahodesh* 2:78). There are many narratives that have developed around the giving of the torah.

The author of Hebrews may have accentuated the fear a bit for his own polemical purposes. The reference to the beast touching **the mountain** is a summary statement of the LXX text of Exod 19:12-18, which says that anyone who **touches the mountain** would be put to death. Horeb was not a mountain that one dared to touch. It had been **touched and kindled,** by God, so that it burned with **fire.** If even a beast wandered up to the mountain, it should **be stoned** with stones or shot with a bow and arrow or some other kind of missile that could kill without the killer having to touch the offender so as to become defiled. This would be true whether it be a human being or a **beast** (*ktáy-naws*, κτήνος); Hebrews has *thay-reé-awn*, (θηρίον). The author's summary reveals his *a fortiori* logic. If even a **beast** that touched the **mountain** would be **stoned**, how much the more would such severity apply in the case of a party to the contract!

21*Moses said, "I am afraid and trembling."* There is a slight play on words in the Greek between **dreadful** and **afraid**. **That which appeared** was **so dreadful** (*phaw-beh-ráwn*, φοββερόν) that Moses said, **I am afraid** (*éhk-phaw-baws*, ἔκφοβος). The author had to strain his sources to bring about this play. In the context on Mount Sinai *the people* were **afraid** and **trembled** (Exod 19:16; 20:18).

Different accounts tell of different responses. The Scripture reports that the people, hearing, were **afraid** and **trembled** (Exod 19:16; 20:18), but the author reports that *Moses* said he was **afraid and trembling**. **Moses** said only that he was **afraid.** It was on a later occasion, after the people had made a molten image, and **Moses** broke the tablets (Deut 9:19). The addition of **trembling** may have come from some targum on the Scripture no longer extant. Otherwise this was a transfer on the part of Hebrews. Whether this transfer was made by the author or a targumist, it was not far off course.

TEXT

Hebrews	First Testament and other Intertexts
22But **you have come to Mount Zion,** even [the] city of [the] God of **life,**	LXX Deut 4:11**You have come to** and you have stood under **the mountain**
	Isa 35:8-10It will be called a holy way. Nothing unclean will pass over it . . . there **the redeemed** will walk, and the ransomed of Yehowah will return **and**
heavenly **Jerusalem,** myriads of angels,	**come to Zion** with singing, and the joy of the age will be upon their heads.
	Matt 10:20Do not rejoice in this that the spirits are subject to you, but rather rejoice that your names are **written in heaven.**

a national assembly, [23]a church of first-born [people], **enrolled** in **heaven**,

Dan 12:1 In that time your people will escape, everyone who is found **enrolled in** the book.

God [the] Judge of all, [the] spirits of **the righteous, perfected**, [24]Jesus [the] mediator of a new **contract,** and [the] blood of sprinkling, speaking better than that of Abel.

Ps 69:29 Let them be blotted out from the book of **life; let** them not be **enrolled** with **the righteous.**

Isa 4:3 The one who is left in **Zion** and remains in **Jerusalem** will be called "holy," everyone who is **enrolled for life** in **Jerusalem.**

COMMENTARY

[22]*You have come to Zion.* The tense of the verb is clear. It is perfect. That means that the time element of the action is present as the result of a previous action. The previous action was that the listeners **had come to Zion**. At the time of this address, the listeners were then in Zion. There is no way in which that clearly past tense verb can be distorted to become a future verb, but some scholars have surely tried. C. R. Koester, for example, acknowledged, on the one hand,

> One might argue that the perfect tense shows that salvation is already present in faith . . . Nevertheless, [on the other hand] Hebrews recognizes that listeners have not yet arrived, but hope for the city "that is to come" (13:14).

This was a clever slight-of-hand trick. The affirmation, **You have come to Zion** (Heb 12:22), in its own context, is not only a present "in faith." It is present, period. Koester reached out to another document (Heb 13), written at a different time by a different author, in a different situation, and took the words, **that is to come**, and patched them on to Heb 12:22, where they do not belong, to give the resulting expression a meaning that does not fit the message at all. So, according to Koester, the statement that clearly indicates the present really means future, treating the Scripture as if it were a jig-saw puzzle with a few "joker" pieces that can be substituted for any missing pieces and put into any place they are needed to fit the player's theory.

Heavenly Jerusalem. Mount Zion was not a tall mountain. It was a little hill between the Kidron Valley and the Tyropoeon Valley, west of Ain Gihon (modern Spring of Siloam). Before the Tyropoeon Valley was filled in, this little ridge apparently had sharp, perpendicular walls, rising above the bottoms of these two valleys. Mount Zion was David's citadel, the southern part of David's City, near the place where David's palace and Solomon's temples were built. Prior to Herod's time Zion was identical to David's City and Jerusalem (2Sam 5:6-8; Ps 147:12-13; Amos 1:2; 4:2; Isa 24:23; Mic 4:7; Zeph 3:14-20; Zech 1:16; Jer 31:38; Joel 3:17). The situation changed, however, after Herod began to build the Roman fortress, Antonia, and the new temple. After that Zion was limited to David's city near the springs whereas Jerusalem included the Roman fortress north of the temple area.

At the north end of Zion, south of Herod's huge walls, was Herod's temple, which, like Herod's fortress, was considered pagan by many faithful Jews, such as the author of the Habakkuk Commentary (1QpHab). Zion is the site where the author of Heb 1:1-12:29 and his congregation had agreed to meet, rather than at some location near Herod's fortress. Before Herod built his huge walls, that entire hill was small, in comparison to Mount Scopus and the Mount of Olives to the east. Over the centuries the entire hill has been built up, just as other *tels* build up. The importance of that hill was not its size, but its proximity to the important springs in the Kidron Valley. David's city and Solomon's temple were in that section of the hill. Herod built the Roman walls at the part of the hill that was more defensible, militarily.

To the Orthodox Jews David's City of Zion was the true place of the **temple not made with hands**, where the restoration of the Promised Land would begin. Pious Jews believed that when the land was restored not one stone would be left on top of another of Herod's temple (Matt 24:1-2; Luke 21:5-6). The new temple, however, would be built where the old Solomon's temple had once stood in a very short time (Matt 26:61; 27:40). David's altar was no longer standing. The large altar that was built by Solomon and used by Zerubbabel and the Hasmoneans was expanded by Herod. That was a large altar that was 22½ feet tall, 75 feet long, and 75 feet wide. It might have still existed after the temple was burned with fire. Replacing the temple may have involved reestablishing the tent as it had been in David's time, either near the existing altar, or Jesus might have built a new small altar, like the one David used. Josephus said that Titus ordered the entire city to be razed to the ground. The walls were dug up, and soldiers swept the ground clean, looking for gold. The Romans might have destroyed also the altar (War 7:1-4), but there was no gold in the altar; it would not burn; and there is some indicaton in Heb 13 that the altar was left.

When Jesus anticipated the destruction of the temple, he may have presumed that the huge altar, originally built by Solomon and enlarged by Herod would still be there. If not, it would be easy to construct a small altar the size of the one David used that would hold only one beast at a time. All he would have had to do was to build a small altar of loose rocks and provide a tent to accompany it, just as David had done. It might have taken three days (Matt 26:61; 27:40). David's altar had to be small enough for a person, such as Joab or Adonijah, to hold on to the horns of the altar with two hands (1Kings 1:50; 2:28).

Following a widely held tradition, the author of Hebrews identified Mount Horeb with Mount Sinai, and called the Lord the **God of life** (*theh-oó zóhn-taws*, θροῦ ζῶντας) (LXX Deut 5:26). The expression **living God**, or **God of life** (אלוהים חיים) when used in a descriptive context, points to a wrathful, militant deity (Deut 5:26; Josh 3:10; Jer 10:10; see also Heb 3:12; 9:14; 10:31). Here the author, in contrasting Mount Sinai with Zion, called Zion, **"[the] city of [the] living God [or the God of life]"** (*theh-oó zóhn-taws*)**.** As in Gal 4:24-26, Mount Zion was contrasted to Mount Sinai (Horeb), and by implication, the old contract with the new. Although only a few words of Heb 12:18-21 are actually identical to the ones describing the theophany to Moses (Exod 19-20; Deut 4-5), the description was accurately paraphrased, with an additional notation (Deut 9:19).

The solemnity of the occasion was marked by fear, natural sounds, fire, and darkness. It was like the **holy of holies** before Christ entered through the curtain. Although the **holy of holies** was a **dreadful** place where only the high priest was allowed to enter, after Christ had renewed for Christians **a new and living way** through the curtain, Christians were urged to draw near (Heb 10:19-22). In a similar way, knowing the fear and dread that surrounded Sinai, Christians were assured that it was not Mount Sinai or Mount Horeb, but **Mount Zion to** which they had **come**. Philo called Jerusalem **The City of God** (*hay deh theh-oó páw-lees*, ἡ δε `θεοῦ, πόλις) (Som 2:250). Josephus said it was God's city (War 7:98). The targumist called Zion the "holy mountain" (*toh-rah dahk-duh-sheé.* תרא דקדשי). That was the city of David which the author of Hebrews called **[the] city of [the] God of life**. This was none other than the capital **city** of the **Promised Land, heavenly Jerusalem**, where the Lord had chosen to dwell. Ezekiel said that when Jerusalem was rebuilt as the capital of the Promised Land, the name of the city from that day will be "Yehowah is there."(Ezek 48:35). Zion was the place where Jews looked for the Lord.

Pseudo-Clement called it **the heavenly, city, Jerusalem** (Recog 1:51). So careful was that author about finding scriptural authority for his messages that he related Mount Horeb where **the mountain was burning with fire up to heaven** with the **heavenly Jerusalem.** Mount Horeb was the huge mountain that belched out volcanoes and shot fire into the air. Mount Zion was the little hill, near the springs of Rogel and Gihon, that was not at all threatening or dangerous for human beings to touch. David's holy city was only a little town near two springs—one small one (Ain Rogel) and another huge one (Ain Gihon), **where the waters of Shiloh flow gently** (Isa 8:6).

Zechariah had promised that when the Lord became king, **Jerusalem** would remain aloft upon its site as a city without a curse (Zech 14:9-11). In Ezekiel's vision of the restored temple (Ezek 40-48), he saw the glory of the Lord entering the **temple** (Ezek 43:4), and Ezekiel was told that the temple would be the place of the Lord's throne where he would dwell with his people for the age [to come] (Ezek 43:6-7, 9). All of these affirmations were made before Herod's temple existed.

These geographical names and places are all accurate and visible. They belong to the biblical traditions, still many scholars overlook all of this traditional geography and argue, as Grässer did, that God would comfort

> the "tired people of God in their wandering through the wilderness of the world into the heavenly home and eternity."[1]

That which Grässer said may be true, but that is not the meaning of the text given in Heb 12. Grässer, like many others, allegorized the message of Hebrews, while interpreting Heb 12. Throughout most of his book and his commentary, he depended heavily on FT Scripture to interpret Hebrews, without allegory or myth. It was apparently other secondary sources that directed this variant method of exegesis. The Book of Hebrews is not allegory. The author used biblical terms, like "wilderness" to describe the Wilderness of Zin, and "Zion," to indicate David's holy city. The author described a geographical journey from the diaspora to **Zion, the city of the God of life**—not from the "wilderness of the world" to "the heavenly home." The allegory to which Grässer subscribed has been popular for many years in biblical scholarship. It is sometimes called "the new hermeneutic" or "existentialism." It might be called "Rorschach eisegesis." Dr. Rorschach was the psychologist who designed the ink-blot test for learning the feelings and imaginations of patients—not for learning the actual picture of the ink blot.

---

[1] Grässer, *Hebräerbrief*, p. 199 (tr. from German).

The pilgrimage theme of Heb 11 and 12 is thought provoking. Pilgrimage themes inspire the imaginations of poets, devotional leaders, hymn writers, and many others. This pilgrimage then is no exception. Scholars use this literary piece as a springboard to suggest still other and different types of wanderings and pilgrimages. There is nothing wrong with that, so long as the later images drawn by these inventive minds are not confused with those of the author of Hebrews. The many scholars who think the theology would be still better and more preferable if the goal had been heaven, instead of Zion, are strongly motivated to force their own views on to the text of the earlier preacher.

Preachers never preach all that they know or believe or think in one sermon, and we should not expect more than that of the author of Heb 1-12. All we know of him is that which is contained in this one sermon. It is unfair to try to guess what his views were about many other subjects that were not part of this sermon. We do not learn a person's ideas by "reading between the lines," "the silences," the non-preserved "oral tradition." We will never know what the author of Heb 1-12 thought of Paul, what he believed about the mother of Jesus, or how he conceived of the resurrection. They were not parts of this sermon.

Heavenly Jerusalem was not an expression designed to mislead the reader into thinking **Mount Zion** was in **heaven. Mount Zion** was not even as tall as the Mount of Olives or Mount Scopus, but it was the City of David and therefore **heavenly**. It was a marvelously well developed city with running water three thousand years ago. David conquered it in all of its wonder. It came to him as a gift from God. The Israelites did not have to install all of its modern facilities. It was a tremendous accession. **The city of God** was **heavenly,** and that does not mean it was only in **heaven. Jerusalem** was called **the great city** (SibOr 5:412; Rev 16:19; War 7:375), even though it was only a small town. It was considered **the city of God**, (SibOr 5:250), the **city of Yehowah** (TargJon Isa 60:14), **the holy city** (TargJon Isa 48:2), **God's holy mountain (**TargJon Isa 65:11), the capital city of the land that belongs to God (Jub 16:18), **the beloved city** (Rev 20:9; Sir 24:11), and **Mount Zion which he loves** (Ps 78:68).

These were affectionate titles, rather than descriptions of **Jerusalem's** size or political influence in comparison to other ancient cities, such as Athens, Alexandria, or Rome. The author of Hebrews also called it a **heavenly city**.

Grässer recognized all of this. He mentioned that Zechariah (Zech 1-2), Second Isaiah (Isa 54:11-17), and Trito Isaiah (60-62) all praised Zion and anticipated its greatness in the future. Zechariah spoke of a new Zion as the city of God in the earthly Jerusalem. Yehowah would make Zion his capital city of his future kingdom. Grässer said further,

> Zion and Jerusalem, the city of the living God, are synonyms and identical with the heavenly Jerusalem.[1]

Grässer even acknowledged that the statement **You have come to Zion** used a verb in perfect tense and meant that that was a current situation at the time the author was speaking. He then held that **that which was not seen** (Heb 11:1) was not future. It was not only **that which was hoped for** (Heb 11:1) but that which already existed *in a certain manner* (*gewisser Weise*). He called this "realized eschatology." He then added that this should be interpreted in terms of

[1] E. Grässer, *An die Hebräer* (Zürich: Benziger Verlag, 1997), pp. 312-13.

> his Alexandrian thought-technique as only a reflection and shadow of reality. In this technique there is no now/then, but rather over/under, concentrating on the ascension of the soul.[1]

Not only Plato and the Alexandrians believed that heaven was related to earth, and that God was in his heaven managing things on earth. This came because ancient Greeks, Romans, Egyptians, and others deduced that which must be in heaven from that which actually occurred on earth. Because time moved in circles on earth, rotating in terms of days, weeks, months, seasons, sabbath years, and Jubilee years, all of which circled around over and over again without stopping, ancients assumed that God rotated time in heaven in the same way.[2]

Not all ancients followed all of the details of shadow and reflection that Plato deduced. Jews studied events of the past to predict future events that were similar. For example, when Jews were exiled in Babylon, they presumed that they were reliving the same place in the cycle as the exile in Egypt. That meant that the new wilderness and conquest of Canaan would follow (Isa 35). That did not mean they would later get to heaven. After Judas the Hasmonean overthrew the Syrians at Beth-horon and Antiochus Epiphanes died in Persia on the same year after 3½ years of warfare, a Jewish theologian wrote the religious myth of a divine judgment scene (Dan 7), dramatizing what God must have been doing in heaven to make this victory possible. After those 3½ years Antiochus was killed and Judas became ruler over the land of Judah. **To him was given the governing authority, the glory, and the kingdom (**Dan 7:14).

Just because Judas had appeared before the **ancient of days** in heaven in this theological drama, does not mean that the whole Syrian-Judean Maccabean military conflict took place only in heaven. Jews were interested in heaven, because they really wanted good results on earth. They were not trying to leave the earth in exchange for heaven. There may be heavenly palaces in heaven, as Grässer holds, but the author of Heb 12 did not mention it. Grässer also noted that the heavenly Jerusalem was a city which would be coming down to earth from heaven (Rev 3:12). It was the end result which the seer anticipated. He had no plans for Zion to be moved up to heaven.

Jews and Christians believed there was a Jerusalem in heaven as well as the one on earth, but their main interest was in the earthly Jerusalem. In a rabbinic homily based on Gen 28:17, King David was shown a vision of **heaven** where the Lord was building a new temple of precious stones. This did not raise the question, "How soon will we get to heaven to worship there?" Instead it motivated the question,

> Master of the age, when will you bring down this Jerusalem, which is now being built? (Bereshit Rabbati, *daf* 89-90).[3]

---

[1] Grässer, *An die Hebräer*, pp. 310-13.

[2] Buchanan, *"Eschatology in Cycles,"* Buchanan, *New Testament Eschatology: Historical and Cultural Background* (Lewiston: Mellen, c1993), pp. 58-86.

[3] For an English translation see Buchanan, *Jewish Messianic Movements from AD 70 to AD 1300* (Eugene, Oregon: Wipf and Stock Publishers, 2003) p. 527.

The Christian seer saw

> **The holy city, new Jerusalem, coming down out of heaven from God** (Rev 21:2).

By calling Jerusalem **heavenly,** they wanted to affirm the divine origin of the Jerusalem in Palestine. They also wanted to distinguish **heavenly** Jerusalem from Herod's pagan Jerusalem. The **heavenly** gift was something believers on earth had tasted (Heb 6:5). It was a teaching considered divine or **heavenly** (see Commentary on Heb 11:13-17).[1] Daniel referred to the contemporary Jews as **the saints of the Most High** (Dan 7:27). The community of the Community Rule was called the "assembly of God" (1QS). The author of the Sibylline Oracles called Jews who lived on earth

> the godlike, heavenly race of blessed Jews who live around the city of God at the center of the earth (SibOr 5:248).

Johnson compared the goal of the Muslim pilgrimage, described by Partin,[2] to the goal of the journey described by Hebrews:

> [Mecca] is not merely a city; it is *God's* city. As Partin has pointed out, the sacred place toward which pilgrims strive is the place *par excellence*, the center of the cosmos, the navel of the earth, the place which orientates all other space and is therefore qualitatively different because it is the point nearest to the deity.[3]

Johnson correctly held that Jews felt the very same way about Zion, their holy city. It was not out of character to call such a city **heavenly, Lordly,** or divine.

Myriads of angels were believed to hover over Mount Zion (see note at the end of Heb 9), especially at every **national assembly,** when the king met with his council of advisors, or at every feast, when Jews from all over the world gathered at Jerusalem to celebrate.[4] At these gatherings the saints, believers, or heirs of the promise were gathered. These were not different classes of people; they were the same people with different labels.

---

[1] F. F. Bruce, "The Kerygma of Hebrews," *Interpretation* 23 (1969):11, was not justified in calling Mount Zion "spiritual" nor in presuming the unity of intention between Heb 13 and 1:1-12:29. This same is true of M. Stuart, *A Commentary on the Epistle to the Hebrews in Greek and English* (Andover: Warren F Draper, 1828), p. 293, who said, "The epithet *epouranio* here determines, of course, that a spiritual Jerusalem a heavenly city, is meant." Also Montefiore, p. 230, said, "But God's habitat is not the earth. He lives in heaven, and so Mount Zion must be a heavenly reality. It is the heavenly Jerusalem." C. J. Vaughan, *The Epistle to the Hebrews* (London: Macmillan, 1890), p. 278, however, said: "It is a mistake to treat this as a new particular, distinct from Sion *horei*. Mount Zion and Jerusalem are not to be made two separate things (as, for instance, the one the type of the divine presence itself, and the other, that of the divine beatific manifestation)."

[2] H. B. Partin, *The Muslim Pilgrimage: Journey to the Center* (Ph.D. dissertation, U. of Chicago, 1971), pp. 55-66, 145-52.

[3] W. G. Johnson, "The Pilgrimage Motif in the Book of Hebrews," *JBL* 97 (1978):245.

[4] For the relationship of *panegyris* to feasts, see R. Williamson, *Philo and the Epistle to the Hebrews* (Leiden: E. J. Brill, 1970), pp. 64-70.

Scholars who know something about some types of Hellenistic gnosticism, Egyptian or Indian mysticism, and Platonic philosophy are not justified in concluding that the author of Hebrews was caught up into all of the ramifications of any of these views, just because he considered Zion to be a heavenly city. These were normal views of Jews and Christians of NT times who understood the world and Zion from a Jewish perspective.

The word **heaven** was used as a euphemism for God. For example, when the prodigal son returned home, he said, **Father, I have committed crimes against Heaven, and in your sight** (Luke 15:18). He did not mean that he had committed crimes against the sky. One of the statements from the Prayer of Solomon is

First Testament	Daniel
1Kings 8:32 **Now, listen**, Heaven, **and act.**	Dan 9:19 **Now, listen, O Lord**, . . . **and act.**

The author of Daniel knew that "O Lord" was an accurate rendering of "Heaven." If the author of Hebrews had written, **You have come to Zion, city of the God of life, divine Jerusalem** (Heb 12:22), or . . . **Zion, city of the God of life, Lordly Jerusalem** (Heb 12:22), no one would have been misdirected into a journey into the imaginary ethereal heights with this sentence, as have the scholars listed above. They would have known that the **city of the God of life** was especially holy, and they would not have been surprised that the **city of the God of life** was **Jerusalem** and that it was called "divine" or "lordly."

The fact that the author used **heavenly** as an adjective to describe Jerusalem, instead of its synonym, "divine" or "lordly," has opened the door for many literary inventions. This one little adjective, in a context that is obvious, has distorted many commentaries and scholarly articles. The idea that "heavenly" means "divine" is no new insight. Faithful parties to the contract with Abraham who were living and breathing on earth were called both "sons of **Heaven,**" "sons of light" (11Qmelch), and those who had **tasted the heavenly gift** (Heb 6:4).

Church of firstborn people. Those who had come to Zion had also come to the **church of firstborn people**. The odds are great that this **church** was a monastery where the author of this sermon was speaking.

People who have been born again are those who were **born** at first under one nationality, name, or religion, and were later **born** again, legally, by performing some legal rite by which they have changed their names, religion, or nationality. They have married, been adopted, or become citizens of a different country. The title **first born** carried the significance of being favored sons of a family, receiving more inheritance and status than other members. The honor involved here may have been that the members were the founders of the early **church**. The other possibility is that the **church of firstborn [people]** consisted—not of those who had been converted into Christianity—but those who were **born** as Christians. This means that they were second generation Christians. Their parents had been **born** again as Christians, but were **born first** as Jews. Either possibility would have been honorific. That which was important was that they had been **born** into the new contract.

Enrolled in heaven. Those **enrolled in heaven** were Christians on earth who were believed to be listed in the **book of life**, a membership roll of the elect that God kept and brought up to date at the beginning of each new year.[1] Those who were **enrolled in heaven** were also enrolled as members of **the church** who were believed also to have been **enrolled** by God in his **heavenly** membership roll, at the same time (Exod 32:32-33; Isa 4:3; Ps 69:29; Dan 7:10; 12:1). They were members of the faith. They would have been the surviving ones who were **left in Zion**; they would be **called "holy,"** everyone who was **enrolled for life** in **Jerusalem.** (Isa 4:3). In Ezekiel's vision of the restoration, God would send terrorists through the city to kill everyone there, because of their wickedness. Before they began, however, God would send a scribe with pen and ink to mark a *tau* (ת), the last letter of the Hebrew alphabet, which then looked like the Greek *chi* (X), on the foreheads of each of the righteous people in the city who lamented for the evils of the city. These would be the ones that would be **left in Zion**, after the cleansing, and they would all be righteous, **enrolled in the book of life** (Ezek 9:3-6).

When Jesus' disciples reportedly returned from a successful mission, Jesus told them to rejoice. Their success meant that their **names** were **written in heaven** (Luke 10:20). Jews and Christians both believed that their roll book and God's were the same. They were not all oldest children of their human families. Other parties to the **contract** who were similarly impressed with their status made similar affirmations:

> To those whom God chose, he gave an inheritance of [the] age, and he made them heirs in the lot of the saints, and with the sons of Heaven he bound their foundation for [the] council of [the] community (1QS 11:8-9).

After he had successfully refuted Käsemann's theory that the wandering saints of Hebrews were on their way to heaven, Hofius correctly said,

> That means, however, that for the history of religious question, that the interpretation of The Letter to the Hebrews in Heb 3:7-4:13, has nothing to do with the theologumenon of the "heavenly journey of the soul."[2]

Many scholars[3] grasp at the word **heaven** to claim that the author of Hebrews was inviting his listeners and readers to go to **heaven**. The full clause is, **But you have come to Mount Zion,** *kai* (kai) **city of the God of life, heavenly Jerusalem** (Heb 12:22). The word rendered **you have come to** is in the perfect tense, meaning that it describes a present condition as a result of a past action. This means "you are now here in Mount Zion," because you have come here from some other place, originally.

The word *kai*, which is many times a conjunction, meaning "and," "but," "or," or something similar, here means "even," meaning that **Mount Zion** and **heavenly Jerusalem** are in apposition and identical. It is here rendered by a comma or semicolon. Similarly,

---

[1] Buchanan, *Consequences,* pp.120-23, See also Luke 10:20; Philip 4:3; Rev 3:5; 13:8; 17:8; 20:15; 21:27; 22:19.

[2] O. Hofius, *Katapausis: Die Vorstellung vom Endzeitlichen Ruheort im Hebräerbrief* (Tübingen: J. C. B. Mohr, 1970), p. 151 (tr. from German).

[3] Including Grässer, *Hebräerbrief,* passim, and Käsemann, *Wandering,* passim.

> **Yehowah from Zion roars;**
> **from Jerusalem he lends his voice** (Amos 1:2).
>
> **Out of Zion shall go forth the torah,**
> **word of Yehowah from Jerusalem** (Mic 4:2).
>
> **Yehowah of armies rules on Mount Zion,**
> **in Jerusalem** (Isa 24:23; see also Mic 4:7; Zeph 3:14-20;
> Zech 1:16; Jer 31:38; Joel 3:17, *et al.*).[1]

In all of these instances, written before the time of Herod, Zion and Jerusalem were the same. It would not make sense to think that Yehowah roared both from Zion *and* from Jerusalem, for example. It also would not make sense to mean, **You have come both to**

> **Zion and to the city of the God of Life,**

[and to]

> **heavenly Jerusalem,**

or that you have left the earth and have now been transcended into heaven. Although he recognized that Zion and Jerusalem are identical, Hughes took the word **heavenly** as an intentional corrective to distinguish the Zion (Jerusalem) that is on earth from the Zion (Jerusalem) that is in heaven. Hughes argued further,

> As it has always been (ch. 11), so the perspective of the man of faith must always be the opposite of this-worldly, penetrating beyond the imperfections of the present scene to that eternal reality which is still hidden from our eyes.[2]

There is nothing wrong with Hughes' expression of his own belief or testimony of his own faith. The only mistake was to identify his own point of view with that of the author of Heb 1-12. This Hebrews document is not primarily either allegory or devotional literature. It is a beautiful literary piece—a sermon or a legal argument. It does not express allegory, philosophy, or mysticism in terms of geography and history.

Lane used a different technique to reach the same conclusion as Hughes. He contrasted Heb 12:18 with Heb 12:22, which, in itself, was a legitimate contrast. Heb 12:18-21 describes Mount Horeb that is contrasted with Mount Zion (Heb 12:2)—two geographical locations. Following the RSV, Lane did this, by treating Horeb as if it were a mountain that could be touched, rendering the opening phrase of Heb 12:18, "You have not come to what can be touched . . . But, on the contrary, you have come to Mount Zion." This distortion was intended to change the contrast from Mount Horeb that could *not* by touched by human hands to "what *can* be touched," and instead of recognizing Zion as a small hill that could be touched by human hands and where the faithful could safely gather for feasts, because there

---

[1] Also P. E. Hughes, *A Commentary on the Epistle to the Hebrews* (Grand Rapids: Eerdmans, c1977), pp. 545-46.

[2] Hughes, *Epistle*, p. 546.

were no volcanoes or fiery terrain at Mount Zion, Lane implied that the author's hearers had not come to Zion, but to

> . . . the experience of encountering God through Christ in the metaphor of a journey or pilgrimage to the city of God.[1]

On the basis of Isa 65:17-25, Lane concluded that "The city of the living God is the transcendent 'heavenly Jerusalem' that God creates."[2] The text from that passage reads,

> Isa 65:17 Look! I am making new heavens and a new land. The first ones will not be remembered . . . 18 I am creating Jerusalem, a rejoicing, and her people, a joy.

The FT passage does not describe any transcendent situation. All of the land and the heavens would be different, but the practical difference would be political and geographical. The result would be that Jerusalem and all of the Promised Land would become magnificent. The chosen people would still live there, but there would be no weeping or distress. All of the people would be happy and live to ripe old ages. They would build houses on that land, and live productive lives there. (Isa 65:19-25). There is also no indication that the author of Hebrews anticipated a city in heaven to which the faithful would move. That which transcended all earthly bounds was Lane's imagination.

The text says, **You have come to Zion** (Heb 12:22). That means that **Zion** is the place where the listeners were when the author was preaching this sermon. Many scholars have evaded that fact in imaginative ways, but actually they have only two:

1) They must claim that the speaker and his listeners were in heaven when this was written. In which case they have to explain how this manuscript got to earth where we can read it.
2) They have to falsify the verb and change it from perfect tense to future active tense and explain how that is justified. That requires inventiveness, but some scholars are skilled at that.

Lane, for example, in his effort to dissuade readers from reaching that simple, logical conclusion about this, mentioned repeatedly in his commentary on Heb 12 that the original recipients of this sermon were members of a "house church,"[3] but there is no mention of a house church anywhere in the Book of Hebrews. The text does not tell where the listeners once resided. Initially they had come from somewhere else. Different members probably came from different places. The fact that the author wrote and spoke in such excellent Greek for his audience suggests that both he and they may have been born in the Greek diaspora from which they came to Zion because of their strong commitment to the faith.

The text does not say from where the recipients came. It only tells where they were when the author of Hebrews was speaking. They had **come to Zion, city of the God of Life, heavenly Jerusalem.** That is the place where both the author

---

[1] Lane, *Hebrews 9-13*, p. 465.
[2] Lane, *Hebrews 9-13*, p. 466.
[3] Lane, *Hebrews 9-13*, pp. 420, 426, 429, 448, 451, 459, 472, 475, 484, 488.

and the listeners had gathered when the author preached this sermon. They were alive, well, and waiting, expecting the Day of Atonement soon to be effected when the promises of God would be fulfilled for his chosen people—not in some remote house church in Italy or in the Lycus Valley in Asia Minor—but on the Promised Land. It was there that the promises of God were expected to be fulfilled. They deliberately left their homes to settle in Zion so that they could be where the action was expected.

The audience was not composed of local people. They were the **redeemed who had come to Zion** (Isa 35:9-10). The sermon was delivered there at **Zion**, probably at a monastery there where orthodox Christians from the diaspora gathered and became monks in preparation for the expected coming of the kingdom after the Day of Atonement had been properly observed. Palestinian monks did not participate in temple services conducted by a high priest appointed by the Romans. They, themselves, observed all of the priestly purity rules. These were **the redeemed, the ransomed of Yehowah who had come to Zion with singing and the joy of the age upon their heads** (Isa 35:9-10). The following is another report of **the redeemed** who had **come to Zion**:

> [Rev14:1]I was watching--Now look! The Lamb standing on Mount Zion, and with him 144,000, having his name and the name of his Father on their foreheads, and I heard a noise from heaven like the noise of much water [running], [3]and they were singing a new song before the throne and before the four beasts and before the elders. No one was able to learn the **song** except the 144,000 who are the redeemed of the land. [4]These are the ones who have not defiled themselves with women, for they are celibate. These are those who follow the Lamb wherever he goes. They have been redeemed from human beings as the first fruits of the Lamb.

The picture drawn here is vivid. This was a monastery on Mount Zion, just above the Spring of Siloam where **much water** from the spring roars through Hezekiah's tunnel, **under the threshold** of the temple, making a noise from God (Heaven) as it pours down into the Kidron Valley (Ezek 47). It is there that the monks **sing the new song before the throne** of God in the temple where the beasts are stationed to function carved legs holding up the bronze basin, called the "sea." These vocalists were celibate males, who belonged to a monastery on Mount Zion. This may have been the same monastery where a group of monks gathered to hear the sermon reported in Heb 1:1-12:29. They **had come to Zion, city of the God of life, heavenly Jerusalem** (Heb 12:2).

From the Torah came the quotation, **You shall be to me a kingdom of priests and a holy nation**. (Exod 19:6). It was probably on the basis of Exod 19:6 that Second Isaiah wrote, **You shall be called "priests of Yehowah," ministers of our God** (Isa 61:6). **Priests** were of the highest class of Jews who were ranked as **priests**, Levites, Israelites, and proselytes in descending order (CDC 14:3-6). During the Babylonian captivity, when non-**priests** functioned as **priests**, keeping their houses as undefiled as the temple, Second Isaiah concluded that they had fulfilled the requirements of the Torah and were to be called **priests**. Not all sects of Jews and Israelites concurred, but there continued to be monastic sects that functioned as carefully as priests and treated the building in which they were housed as a temple, "a holy of holies for Aaron." Some of these refused to worship in Herod's temple at

Jerusalem. They called the high priest of that temple "the wicked priest," and the high priest of their monastery, "the teacher of righteousness."

There apparently was a monastery there at Zion, the City of David, as it is reported in Rev 14, because Jesus reportedly directed his apostles to find a place near a spring at the city where they would find a man carrying water in a jar. The spring near Zion was probably Ain Gihon, the spring of Siloam. In Palestine in NT times women and girls normally carried the water—with one exception—the monks who did all of the house work also carried the water. The apostles were directed to follow such a man to his place of residence.

His place of residence, however, was not expected to be his own family home, where he would have a wife and children. Instead, it was known as a place where there would have been a superintendent who could provide for them a place large enough and with enough food on hand for Jesus and his twelve disciples to eat the Passover (Mark 14:12-16). If Jesus had not already known of this monastery, he at least knew that there was one near the spring of Gihon and that any man carrying water from this spring would lead the apostles to that monastery, probably in Zion, David's holy city. This is where Jesus celebrated the Last Supper, and that may also have been where the Sermon of Hebrews was first delivered. This group was certainly gathered at Zion. If it was not in that monastery, it may have been in another monastery at Zion. It could not have been very far away from the water source, either at the Spring of Siloam or at the Pool of Siloam.

Throughout his commentary, Weiss concentrated on the importance of the earlier FT text to the argument of the author. Occasionally he refuted the suggestion that the author was speaking of something vertical, rather than temporal and geographical. When he came to Heb 12:22, however, he obviously struggled to make sense of the passage. He assumed at the outset that **heavenly Jerusalem** had to be in heaven. He also noted, however, that there was no equivocation about the tense. It was perfect. The author and listeners were all right there in Zion. Following Grässer, Weiss called this "realized eschatology." That means the end had come. The future is already here. This is the goal of the journey of the fathers that began at Haran. But this does not conclude in heaven, as Weiss wanted, so he continued, by shifting from "present-future" eschatological scheme to an "earthly-heavenly" plan of vertical, Hellenistic eschatology. This meant the goal was no longer the earthly locality of Zion but the city of the living God in heaven.[1] Instead of being the goal of the journey, Zion was still a station on the way to heaven.[2] Those who came to Mount Zion were just the opposite of those at Mount Sinai who were not allowed to come to the mountain to touch it (Exod 19:12). They had come to a mountain that could be touched.

23*God [the] Judge of all.* On New Year's Day God traditionally held court, opened the books that listed the trials to be considered, and spent the ten days between New Year's Day and the Day of Atonement, listening to the prayers for relief offered by defendants. Defendants, at the same time, were checking their own records to recall any possible crimes they might have committed without having paid the proper fines required and making the required reconciliation with the offended victims involved in this judgment. They all wanted to be judged among the **righteous, perfected ones.**

---

[1] Weiss, *Hebräer,* p. 674.

[2] Weiss, *Hebräer,* p.675.

The spirits of the righteous perfected ones. If sacrifices had been properly and adequately offered, and adequate reconciliation had been made among the citizens, then the citizens would be judged **righteous** and declared **perfected.** This means that all their crimes were removed and they were **sanctified** (Heb 10:1, 10, 14, 29). The requirements were ethical, but the declaration was legal. The readers or listeners, who had been called **holy brothers** (Heb 3:1), were given the further honorific titles of **firstborn**, those **enrolled in heaven**, **the righteous**, **perfected** ones. They were the ones **left in Zion**, **enrolled for life in Jerusalem.** They would be **called holy** (Isa 4:3) and **redeemed** (Isa 35:9-10).

The question is, "What were **the spirits of the righteous perfected ones**?" Lane held that these were the dead who had died without sin.[1] He did not say why he reached that conclusion. These **spirits** had a father. The word **spirit** often has a legal meaning in the Bible, and it seems especially appropriate in a judgment situation. For example, David reportedly said, **The spirit of the Lord speaks through me; his word is on my tongue** (2Sam 23:2). This means David was the Lord's legal agent. He spoke in the name of the Lord, in his behalf, and at his responsibility. Therefore his words are the Lord's words. He had the Lord's spiritual authority. He was inspired by God.

When David was secretly anointed, he received the **spirit** (1Sam 16:13); when Saul was secretly anointed, he received the **spirit** (1Sam 10:1, 6, 10); when various judges received the **spirit** they assumed political authority. When baptized Jews received the **spirit**, they became legitimate members of the Christian church (Acts 10:37-38). When Jesus participated in a ceremony officiated by John the Baptist, he received the **spirit,** which probably means that he was secretly anointed.[2] The community governed by the Rule entered the contract, one after the other, in the order of their **spirits** (*buh séhr-ehk luh-fee roo-khoh-táhm*, בסרך לפי רוחותם) (1QS 2:20), meaning in the order of their legal ranks and respective authority. These were faithful, living holy men, who were classified as **perfect, sanctified, and righteous**. Similarly, those gathered at **Zion** when this sermon was delivered were considered members of the firstborn church, enrolled in heaven, and walking the earth at Mount Zion. They were there, listening to the lecture delivered by the author of Hebrews.

The **spirits** were something legal, related to the judgment. They may have been the authorizing papers on the Judge's desk, awaiting his declaration before they would be enacted into law. The Day of Atonement was the day when all of this would become official.

24 *Jesus the mediator of the new contract.* Just as Moses had acted as God's legal agent to mediate the first contract with his chosen people, so Jesus was God's legal agent, authorized to officiate in the ceremony whereby God would make a new contract with his new legal body, just as Jeremiah promised (Jer 31:31). According to Matthew this ceremony took place at the Last Supper. Jesus took the ordinary Passover bread and used it as a legal *seisin* to form a new legal corporation, the body of Christ. Then he took the fruit of the vine as another *seisin* to perform another legal ceremony to make a new contract with this new legal body.[3]

---

[1] Lane, *Hebrews 9-13*, pp. 470-471.

[2] Buchanan, *The Gospel of Matthew* (Lewiston: Mellen, 1996), pp. 146-150.

[3] Buchanan, *Matthew,* 2, pp. 967-978.

The author of Hebrews, however, was addressing the congregation prior to the Day of Atonement, rather than Passover. Therefore he did not mention the Last Supper. His interests were related to the Day of Atonement. He related the new contract to the old contract, and the new Mount Zion to the old Mount Horeb (Sinai). He was consistent in his goal and his logic.

The picture of a congregation of saints gathered at Zion on the **Day of Atonement** or New Year's Day was related to the **perfection** that takes place because of the sacrificial **blood** of **Jesus. Jesus, the great high priest**, had acted as [**the**] **mediator of a new contract**, bringing as a crime offering his own **blood of sprinkling**. The **blood of sprinkling** is the **blood** that the high priest traditionally sprinkled ritually on various parts of the altar and the holy of holies (mYoma 5:6-7). Normally this was the blood of sheep and goats, but the **blood of Jesus mediated** a better **contract** than that made through the **mediation** of Moses at Sinai, and it was inaugurated with **better offering**.

This offering was compared to the gifts offered by the innocent Abel, because of which, while dying, he still spoke (Heb 11:4). The **blood of sprinkling** offered by Jesus **spoke better than that of Abel**.[1] Those who had received the benefits of Christ's atonement joined the throng of those saints gathered at Mount Zion when **Jesus** was crucified and thereby removed the debt of crime that prevented Israel from receiving her **promised rest.** Although the crucifixion is reported in the gospels to have taken place at Passover, the author of Hebrews interpreted this whole act in terms of a priestly sacrifice, similar to that offered on the **Day of Atonement.** For that reason it was necessary for **Jesus** to have been a priest-king, rather than a Davidic messiah.

TEXT

25 See that you do not request [exemption from] the speaker,
for if those requesting [exemption from]
the one who warns upon earth did not escape,
how much more [shall] we [not escape]
who turn away from the one [who warns] from heaven,

Hebrews	First Testament
26 whose voice then shook the earth, but now has promised, saying, "**Yet once [more] I will shake [not only] the earth [but also] the heaven**"? 27 Now the [expression] **yet once [more]** points to the changing of the things shaken as of things that are made, in order that the things not shaken might remain.	Hag 2:6 Thus says Yehowah of armies, "**Once more**. In a short time, **I will shake** **the heavens, the earth,** the sea, and the dry land, and **I will shake** all of the nations, and the treasures of the nations will come. I will fill this glorious temple," said Yehowah of armies. Dan 7:14 All peoples, nations, and languages will **worship** him. His governmental authority is the authority

[1] Montiefiore, *Hebrews,* p. 233, said, "Abel's blood cries for vengeance while Jesus' blood speaks for reconciliation."

[28]Therefore, accepting an **unshakable kingdom**, let us have grace through which we might **worship** in a way that is pleasing to God, with reverence and fear, for our God is "a consuming fire."

of an age that will not pass away, and his **kingdom will not be destroyed.**

COMMENTARY

The speaker. Throughout the entire argument (Heb 1:1-12:29), the communication mentioned was about speaking—not about writing. Writing is mentioned only in Heb 13.

[25]*How much more [shall] we [not escape]*. **How much more** indicates that this unit is an *a fortiori* argument, comparing something that is true of one item of diminutive significance to something much more important, for which the truth should be all the more obvious. Here the warning on earth is contrasted to the warning from heaven.

The Greek translated **requesting [exemption from]** is *pah-rai-tay-sáh-meh-noi* (παραιτησάμενοι), which can mean, "request," "beg," or "plead for," but it can also bear a negative force, like "to beg off," "ask to be excused," or "excuse." Michel renders it "reject" (*abweisen*),[1] and RSV, "refuse." It refers to the request the people made to Moses that he not let God speak to them. They wanted to be excused or exempted from this threat (Exod 20:18-20). As elsewhere, the author of Hebrews warned his readers not to make the same mistake their fathers had made in the wilderness. Also consistently, he pressed his case with an *a fortiori* argument. **The one who warns upon earth** was Moses, who acted as the representative, mediator, or spokesman for the people of Israel (Exod 20:18-20).

The one who warns from heaven was God who spoke with Moses from **heaven** (Exod 20:22),[2] and still **warns from heaven** through the Scripture to those on earth. The Israelites who tried to evade the demands of Moses' warnings were finally punished for their disbelief by being forced to wander the rest of their lives in the wilderness. Similar to the warnings of Heb 2:2-4 and Heb 6:4-6, the author held that if the Israelites who received an inferior revelation and warning **did not escape** (*ehx-éh-phoo-gawn*, ἐξέφυγον; see also Heb 2:3), then there would be no chance at all for Christians who should **turn away** and become apostate after they had been warned **from heaven** and had received the superior revelation through Jesus. The Israelites whom Moses warned were the members of the exodus generation who failed to be admitted to the **promised rest** because they were unfaithful and turned away.

[26]*[not only] the earth [but also] the heaven.* It was God whose **voice then shook the earth** (Judges 5:4-5; Pss 68:7-8; 114:7-8) and made the people of Israel tremble (Exod 19:16; 20:18). Just as Moses was contrasted with God, so also the voice that **shook the earth** in the past was contrasted with the **promise** that was effective in

---

[1] Michel, *Hebräer*, p. 321.

[2] A. T. Hanson, "Christ and the Old Testament according to the Hebrews," *StEv* II (1964):402-407, by holding that the one who warns from heaven was the pre-incarnate Jesus, claimed that it was also the voice of the pre-incarnate Jesus that shook the earth (Heb 12:26-27).

the author's own day. The account in the Torah applied to the Israelites and the first **contract**, but the account in Haggai came later in time, and therefore could be applied to the Christians who were contemporary with the author of Hebrews.

The one who once **shook the earth promised** a still more severe disruption. Haggai said he would shake **the heaven, the earth, the sea, and the dry land** (Hag 2:6). **Heaven and earth** constitute a merism (see Ps 102:26). A merism is a literary form, developed from the Greek *meris* (μερίς) which means "part." The verbal form means to divide into parts. A merism is a unit that includes both parts of a whole and therefore is a different way of saying the entire unit. **Heaven and earth** are the two parts of the whole universe. Haggai's merism includes four parts, **the heaven, the earth, the sea, and dry land**. The author of Hebrews was justified in changing a list of four items to a merism of two that have the same meaning. At Mount Sinai and Horeb there were many natural noises that involved **shaking the earth**. When God's voice spoke again it would **shake not only the earth but also the heaven**. That would involve not only earthquakes but lightning, thunder, hail, wind, and rain. Haggai was interested in these natural phenomena for only one reason. As a result of all of this turmoil, God would also **shake all of the nations, and the treasures of the nations will come. I will fill this glorious temple, said Yehowah of armies (**Hag 2:6**).** He wanted financial international aid to come to Zion. In Rashi's commentary on Hag 2:6, he said this prophecy was fulfilled in the miracles that happened for the Hasmoneans. That was one of the times when the kingdom came.

Haggai spoke when the diaspora Jews from Babylon had returned to Jerusalem after they had been exiled. They had dreamed of a restored Jerusalem with a new temple and a prosperous nation, but they were disappointed. The walls were broken down; the temple had been destroyed; and the crops were not producing. The country was poor. Haggai explained that all of this misfortune was the result of the citizens' failure to rebuild the temple. If they would just start building, the Lord would bless their efforts. He would stir up all of the nations to make generous contributions to the temple at Jerusalem.

Temples were not only places of worship in those days. They were also national treasuries and fortresses. The nation needed money, and money in Palestine was mostly dependent on foreign aid. Even if the crops failed, if they could get mammoth grants in aid from foreign countries, the nation would prosper again. All of the shaking of the heavens and the earth would result in this one goal. The author of the Book of Hebrews had a similar motivation. He was trying to stir up the faith and action of his audience. He wanted the heaven and earth shaken so that the diaspora Jews would return to Zion, and the promises made to Abraham would there be fulfilled. Like Haggai, he warned them that they would remain with the promises unfulfilled if they failed to accept his advice.

27 *In order that the things not shaken might remain*. The author seemed to use the term **once**, like **today** (Heb 4:7), to express something decisive. Those who had **once been enlightened** could no longer renew for repentance (Heb 6:4). Jesus appeared **once** at the **end of the ages** for the removal of crime through his sacrifice (Heb 9:26). The author interpreted Haggai's prophecy as a **promise** for the future. There would be still **one** more upheaval when God would upset the status quo. That would change **the things shaken**. These are the ephemeral **things that are made**, also called **that which is seen** (Heb 11:3). These all belonged to the past and the old **contract,** the old law, and the old priesthood.

In contrast to them are **the things not shaken** or the **things not seen** (Heb 11:1), which belong to the future, the **new contract,** the new **temple not made with hands**, the perfect sacrifice, **the great high priest**, and other benefits associated with Jesus which **might remain**. This does not mean that God is hostile to ephemeral things; it just means that they are temporal and designed to be changed and replaced. Indeed, the changing **ages have been put in order by the word of God** who created that which is seen (Heb 11:3). The founders of most great cities assumed that the cities they established would continue forever in greatness.

The additional text the author used was Dan 7:14, which described the Son of man coming before the Ancient of Days in a heavenly court scene where the divine judge gave the Son of man a favorable verdict. All peoples were required to **worship** him, because he would be given the governmental authority and the kingdom. The kingdom was one that would last for an age; it would not be destroyed to be replaced. The author of Hebrews took the word **worship** to encourage his listeners to **worship** God. He described the kingdom that would **not pass away** or **be destroyed** as an **unshakable kingdom.**

Dan 7 is a theological drama in which the war between the Syrians and the Jews that had lasted 3½ years before the Hasmonean Hanukkah (164 BIA) is played out as a great heavenly court scene. That war ended with Antiochus Epiphanes dying after an unsuccessful war in Persia and Judas the Maccabee and his troops winning a stunning victory at Beth-horon, after which they had the temple cleansed and celebrated Hanukkah. The author of Dan 7 visualized God's judgment in heaven that made these marvelous events take place on earth. In that court scene, Antiochus was the defendant who was given a death sentence, and Judas was the Son of man who was made the new ruler of Palestine, taking his seat on the throne at Jerusalem.[1]

The kingdom that was expected to last for an age actually lasted until it was replaced by the Romans when they placed Herod on the throne. The Jews who celebrated Hanukkah were at the beginning stages of their **kingdom,** and they had great dreams. Their age was just beginning. The author of Heb 1-12 also visualized an **unshakable kingdom** that would soon be instituted and would not pass away.

Haggai and Daniel were necessary texts for the conclusion of Hebrews' sermon, but Weiss, like many others, denied that Daniel was in any way related to this conclusion. He overlooked the midrashic relationship between Dan 7:14 and Heb 12:27. Therefore he argued from another basis that nothing earthly was **unshakable**, and that Hebrews was speaking only of a **kingdom** in heaven.[2] The author of this sermon, however, was writing midrash, not allegory. He followed the normal rules of midrashic exegesis. Allegorists have ways of letting the readers know that when they say certain things they really mean something else.

The authors of midrash, like other rhetoricians, frequently give meanings other than those originally intended by the texts they use, but they usually justify these rhetorically. For example, the author of the Habakkuk Commentary believed that he was living in the Days of the Messiah. Therefore, everything Habakkuk wrote really applied to his day. He did not leave, however, any doubt about that. When Habakkuk spoke of the Chaldeans, the midrashic expositor said that referred to the "Kittim," which were the Romans. Other activities applied to actions of the "wicked priest" and the "teacher of righteousness," about whom Habakkuk knew

---

[1] Buchanan, *The Book of Daniel* (Lewiston: Mellen, c1999), pp. 163-234.

[2] Weiss, *Hebräer, p. 693.*

nothing, but who were well known to the readers of the Habakkuk Commentary (1QpHab).

The author of Dan 7, told of a weird dream, but he later explained who all of the characters of the dream were (Dan 7:19-27), so that the reader knew that he was really speaking of international events and personalities.

1. **The four beasts** were the four kings who would rule until **the saints** received the kingdom (Dan 7:17-18).
2. **The fourth beast** was the fourth kingdom (Dan 7:19).
3. The **ten horns** were the ten kings of the fourth kingdom (Dan 7:20, 24).
4. **The horn** that grew out of these horns was the most wicked of the kings. He was the one who suppressed the saints, and tried to change their religions and calendar (Dan 7:20-22).
5. **The court** would remove the kingdom from **the horn** and give it to **the Son of man and the saints of the Most High** (Dan 7:23, 26-27).[1]

The Hebrews preacher claimed that Jesus was a priest, because Ps 110 said someone was, and in the days of the Messiah, all prophecy could be applied to the Messiah. Like the author of 1QpHab, however, he let the readers and listeners know what he had done. The text was quoted, and his interpretation was given. The same author did not say that when he said "Zion" or "Jerusalem," he really meant heaven, and when he said "kingdom" he really meant an institution that could never be found on earth. Therefore it is reasonable to understand the author of Hebrews here to be dealing with texts midrashically as he had done elsewhere, justifying his fantastic movements whenever he made them, so that the reader could realize his logic. He made no such jump in rhetoric to lead his reader to think there was some basis for thinking that he meant heaven when he spoke of an **unshakable kingdom.**

Rose, like many others, held that **the kingdom that cannot be shaken** is the heavenly holy of holies, the heavenly rest. He justified this conclusion by taking the passage in which God told Abraham to go out from his country (*áh-retz*, ארץ) to a land (*ah-retz*, ארץ) which God would show him (Gen 12:1). The Hebrew gave the word "land" or "country" for the text. To avoid repetition the LXX translated the second use of "land" as "place," with the same meaning. Rose changed place to "heavenly place," and argued that a heavenly place could only exist in heaven. In the process, Rose changed the meaning completely. By going through these steps of change, Rose was able to justify his repeated claim that Abraham's promise was not the Land of Canaan, but the *heavenly Holy of Holies.*[2]

He continued to treat the adjective "heavenly" as if it were the noun "heaven," as many others have done. If this logic were followed consistently, an oily substance would have to be oil; a picturesque scene would have to be a picture; a beastlike being would have to be a beast; and a knot-headed person would have to have a head that had been tied into a knot, like a shoe string. Only a sheep could be sheepish. There is no end to such ridiculous possibilities, one of which is the notion that only heaven can be heavenly, even though the text describes Jerusalem as heavenly (Heb 12:22).

There is nothing in the text to suggest a non-earthly existence for the unshakable kingdom. The belief seems to have been that the Davidic kingdom would

---

[1] Buchanan, *Daniel,* p. 219-28.

[2] C. Rose, "Verheissung und Erfüllung," *BZ* 33 (1989):180. Tr. from German.

be restored on Mount Zion in such grandiose status that no foreign government could ever overtake it again. That which is **not shaken** but intended to **remain** (Heb 4:6, 9; 12:27) is **an unshakable kingdom.** This **unshakable kingdom** suggests an allusion to the **kingdom that shall not be destroyed** (Dan 7:14) which was presented to the one like a **Son of man** by the Ancient of Days (Dan 7:13). This was understood to mean **the land of the promise** (Heb 11:9) given to the Hasmoneans by God (note in commentary at the end of Heb 2). The psalmist had the same territory in mind when he said:

> **Say to the nations, "The Lord has become King!"**
> **for he has set straight the habitation (*oi-koo-méh-nay*),**
> **which will not be shaken** (Pss 96[95]:10; 93[92]:1).

In these enthronement Psalms, when a ruler was established over Israel, God set straight the **habitation** or administration **which will not be shaken** (Pss 96[95]:10; 93[92]:1), which was also the *oi-koo-méh-nay* into which the Lord led his **firstborn** (see Commentary on Heb 1:6). It would be the time when the things **shaken** would be changed in order that the things **not shaken might remain** (Heb 12:27). The **unshakable kingdom** would be established before God's people could enjoy a Sabbath **rest** (Heb 4:6, 9) on the **land of the promise** (Heb 11:9), whose capital city, Zion, was **the city having foundations whose builder and constructor was God** (Heb 11:10).

28*Let us have grace.* The word **grace** is part of an inclusion, related to the same word in Heb 12:15. This indicates that Heb 12:14-29 constitutes a literary unit.

Since Christians, **accepting an unshakable kingdom**, were not given another opportunity to **enter into the rest** (Heb 3:11), they were obliged to **have grace through which [they] might worship in a way that is pleasing to God, with reverence and fear**. Having **grace** is the same as being thankful. Therefore, Christians are urged to worship properly with thanksgiving. **Falling into the hands of the God of life is dreadful** (Heb 10:31). Nonetheless, Christians were urged to **come to the throne of grace with boldness** (Heb 4:16), approach with a true heart in **fullness of faith** (Heb 10:22), or **worship in a way that is pleasing to God.** Moses warned the Israelites: **The Lord your God is a consuming fire, a *zealous* God** (Deut 4:24). The god who consumed the enemies of the Israelites and overpowered the Syrians for the Hasmoneans was the same zealous God who invited Jesus to sit at his right hand until God put Jesus' enemies under his feet (Heb 1:13).

29*Our God is a consuming fire.* This final unit is marked by an inclusion with the key word **fire** which appears at both the beginning and the end (Heb 1:18, 29). It is not only the final portion of an inclusion. It has all of the force of a conclusion to the entire sermon. There is no way in which this final statement can be made into a peroration, as C. R. Koester attempts.[1] The author of this sermon had made many skillful literary connections throughout the document, relating one unit to another. Here there is none. Here the document ends, and Heb 13 begins with a completely different style and message. It was composed by a different editor or author.

---

[1] C. R. Koester, *Hebrews* (New York: Doubleday & Co., 2001), p. 554.

The message, **our God is a consuming fire,** repeats an emphasis on the contrasting conditions that the author had emphasized in different ways in his exhortations. The situations contrasted were those related to the exodus generation and those that existed for the readers. The emphasis this time was on the revelation at Mount Sinai in contrast to the one on Mount Zion, where Jesus was crucified. The crucifixion, however, was not described in terms of criminal punishment outside the **city** during the events related to the Passover, but in terms of a great Day of Atonement and New **Year's** festival when the **sacrifice** was offered as necessary to provide **perfection** and **sanctification** for the saints.

This event was so tremendous that it shook not only **the earth** but also **heaven.** Practically, this did not mean the end of time or the cosmos. The earth is shaken whenever there is an earthquake, tornado, or hurricane. The heaven is shaken when there is lightning and thunder. These could both occur at once. The shaking up that the author had in mind, however, was a political shaking of the nations. It involved wars and rumors of wars, from which destruction Jerusalem would emerge as the political center of the universe, as **the kingdom** that could **not be shaken**.

The revelation was so much greater at Mount Zion than at Mount Sinai that the believers who were contemporary with the author were under a much greater obligation to obey the commandment from heaven and not **turn away** into apostasy. It was only by holding to the faith and being steadfast in worship with reverence and godly fear that the readers could expect to receive the unshakable **kingdom** which was **the rest** promised to Abraham long ago and denied to the wilderness Israelites who stood around Mount Sinai when the first law was given. The God of life who appeared at Mount Sinai was the same God who disclosed himself again when he spoke from heaven. He was a consuming fire before whom believers stand in awe.

It was in the confidence that **our God is a consuming fire** (Heb 12:29) that the author concluded his book as he had begun it, calling attention to the great power of God and the glory he would give his Son, Jesus, while he suppressed his enemies. **Fire** continued to be a major symbol for God. It was the flaming torch that went before and after the Israelites when they left Egypt. It was the **fire** that was kept burning at the tent of meeting, that provided a pillar of **fire** by night and a pillar of smoke during the daytime. The **fire** was kept burning continually on the altar of the temple in Zion. Flaming torches were part of the Pentecost festival. The continual flame over the altar in liturgical churches still represents the real presence of God in the church. This author, who showed great skill in forming inclusions to tie his introductions and conclusions together, centered his interest in this final paragraph on the shaking that God would do and the unshakable kingdom (Heb 12:28) that would remain (Heb 12:27).

The listeners and the preacher were well versed in Scripture. The preacher could allude to a word or passage of Scripture and the listeners were expected to understand the whole context related to the reference. For example, the preacher may have expected the readers to relate the word **shaken** (Heb 12:27) to the *oi-koo-méh-nay* which was **not shaken** of Ps 93[92]:1 and Ps 96[95]:10, which, in turn, would suggest the *oi-koo-méh-nay* mentioned at the beginning of the document into which the Lord led his **firstborn** (Heb 1:6). Also **the church of the firstborn** (Heb 12:23) might have referred to the initial reference to Jesus as the **firstborn**.

This may be attributing to the author more subtlety, and to the readers or listeners more intelligence, than was intended or understood, but the author was an excellent student of Scripture, and he spoke and wrote as if his hearers and readers should be able to understand his message. There are many clues in the message that the author was a monk and that his audience was composed of monks. Traditionally monks have been some of the best students of Scripture of their age. It was the monks who preserved the best texts we have of Scripture. For years Roman Catholic monks were required to read the entire book of Psalms every week. The author of this document seemed especially proficient in the use of the Psalms.

The author was an artist in style, using inclusions throughout the document to indicate his literary units. It was fully in character for him to write so that there was a subtle inclusion tying the end of the entire document to its beginning.

Heb 1:1-12:29 is a unified homily, sermon, or legal argument centered around the one text of Psalm 110, which the author quoted from time to time. This was the text on which he depended to prove that Jesus was a priest for the age, whose death was a sacrificial Atonement Day offering for the crimes of the nation. The author never quoted the whole Psalm, but, by alluding to one verse, he presumed that the readers or listeners understood the rest of the Psalm. He also frequently drew doctrine from other FT passages, preferring Psalms and prophets to the Torah. He sometimes even used the Psalms and prophets to refute or override the Torah. He regularly interpreted the passages he quoted according to their context, sometimes with meanings that would have surprised the original author and readers of the FT. On the basis of his doctrine, he exhorted his listeners to be faithful and warned them of the adverse consequences that would come upon them if they were not. He also assured them of the rewards promised to those who did not give up hope but were steadfast to the end. This was artfully done in a homily whose divisions were marked by inclusions that were tied together with connecting sentences that had catchwords belonging to the adjoining paragraphs.

Spicq correctly thought that Heb 12:29 was the conclusion to the entire document.[1] It has no transition sentence that leads to Heb 13. Heb 13:1 begins abruptly with an exhortation that is not related to Heb 12 and is not based on Ps 110. Heb 13 seems to be a collection of material that an editor collected. It includes guidance for the Palestinian Christians after the destruction of the temple, a confession of faith, some doctrinal narrative, a benediction, and personal greetings, with some of the editor's exhortations interspersed. Some of the views of Heb 13 contradict those of Heb 1:1-12:29. Therefore, it seems not to have been a part of the original document.

In his defense of his conclusion that Heb 13 is part of a peroration, Koester called attention to the fact that some of the same concepts that occur in the sermon also appear in Heb 13, just the way a pseudepigrapher would compose to mislead the reader. Koester admitted that Heb 13 did not try to evoke indignation against the enemies of the sermon's author, the way a peroration should do. He held as an important definition the necessity of brevity and support. His example was Aristotle: "I have spoken; you have heard; you know the facts; now give your decision" (Aristotle, *Rhetoric* 3:19, 6).[2] This is a good example, but it does not fit the case here. That which was heard was the sermon which provided all of the facts and a peroration should support those facts without adding any more. Heb 13, on the contrary, tells the reader not to observe the rigorous monastic rules demanded by the sermon—not to be limited by dietary food laws—not to be confined by the monastery. The author of Heb 13 insisted that marriage was approved behavior. This sermon, in the judgment of the author of Heb 13, had some good teachings, but it should not be limited to the apparent notion that it applied only to monks.

---

[1] C. Spicq, *L'epitre aux Hebreux* (Paris: J. Gabalda, 1950) 2, p. 412. See also 1, p. 37.

[2] Koester, *Hebrews*, pp. 554-556.

The difference between a pseudepigraph and a peroration is that the peroration is composed by the author of the main message. A pseudepigraph is composed by a different author, trying to leave the impression that it was the same. Heb 13 is clearly a pseudepigraph. A peroration is intended to refresh the reader's memory about what he or she has already read. The pseudepigraph is intended to distort the message in some way with the intention of leading the reader to think that the pseudepigrapher's opinion is also that of the author of the main message.

THE WORLD OF THE SERMON

The sermon recorded in Heb 1-12 was delivered to an audience in Zion at a time when the hopes of national liberty were high. From the death of Herod the Great (4 BIA) to the fall of Jerusalem in 70 IA, there were many military uprisings. These usually had their origin at the great Jewish feasts when Jews from all over the world came in pilgrimages to Jerusalem. Local Jews were closely related to Jews in the diaspora. During the Maccabean Rebellion there were many Jews in Syria who assisted in helping the Maccabees win their cause. Also in Rome there were many thousands of Jews during the period when the preacher delivered this sermon. After the death of Herod, when the trial was held in Rome before Caesar to decide who should succeed Herod as king, there were 8,000 Jews in attendance to lend their influence in the choice. Many Jews were in important governmental positions as well as other influential positions. After the death of Herod there was an entire regiment of Jewish soldiers in Herod's army. When Herod died, the general of that regiment and his entire regiment defected and rebelled against Rome. Rome had Jewish enemies throughout its empire, posing as loyal Roman citizens.

When a Roman centurion came to Jesus for help, he told Jesus that Jesus could not come under his roof while his daughter was in danger of death, showing that he knew Jewish rules of overshadowing.[1] Jesus said he had not found such great faith in all Israel, and said further that Jews from all the world would come to Palestine and sit down with Abraham, Isaac, and Jacob in the kingdom. At the same time the sons of the kingdom would be thrown out. He may have had a well organized contingent of Jewish supporters in Rome. There were enough Jews in Parthia when Herod was gaining power to induce the Parthians to expel Herod and his troops. It took Herod with the full Roman military and financial support to defeat the Parthians and crucify the last of the Hasmonean kings.

After the crucifixion of Jesus the church in Rome grew very rapidly. When Paul was working in Asia Minor (ca. 40-52 IA) there was already a church in Rome associated with Peter. If Christianity had not been a very strong and influential force in Rome by the time of Constantine, he would never have negotiated with them to gain their support.

Sometime after the death of Jesus and before the war of 66-70 IA broke out, Jews defeated the great Roman general, Cestius, at Beth-horon. Jews were preparing for an all-out war with Rome. The stage was set on all fronts. The feast days were about to begin. That may have been the time when this preacher delivered his famous pep-sermon to a group of monks who had come to Zion to prepare religiously for the expected deliverances.

Jews and Christians did not all come to Jerusalem as individuals. Rabbis and bishops led entire congregations to Israel between the defeat of Bar Cochba to the end of the Crusades, believing, in each case, that the time was right for deliverance to take place, and they wanted to be at Zion when it happened. One such monastic leader may have been the preacher of this sermon, who not only was a brilliant Zionist, who knew his Scripture and Jewish hopes very well, but also spoke superb Greek. He may have taken an entire monastery to Zion to live out the faith there. His entire congregation was able to understand his excellent Greek there in Zion. Although Jews in Palestine often knew Greek, because this was a merchandising country, it is likely that those who had come to Zion (Heb 12:22) had come there from some place in the Roman Empire where Greek learning was encouraged. Although this sermon was first delivered orally, it was so well composed that it was obviously written before it was delivered, and it was preserved in the written form in which we still read it today.

CHAPTER THIRTEEN

Christian Attitudes

TEXT

13:1 Let brotherly love continue;
2 do not forget love for strangers
(for through this, some, when they
entertained angels, were not aware [of it]).
3 Remember the prisoners as partners in bonds,
those badly treated, as yourselves in [the] body.
4 [Let] marriage be honored in every [respect],
and [let] the marriage bed be undefiled
(for God will judge fornicators and adulterers).
5 Let] unconcern for money be the fashion,
being satisfied with the present conditions,
for he himself said,

Hebrews	First Testament
I **will not forsake you,** **and I will not abandon you**	Deut 31:6 **He will not forsake you,** **and he will not abandon you**.

6 so that we may have courage to say,

The Lord is my helper; **I shall not be afraid**. **What can a man do to me**?	Ps 118:6 **Yehowah is my helper**; **I shall not be afraid**. **What can a man do to me**.

TECHNICAL DETAILS

Almost every scholar who has written on the Book of Hebrews has noticed the definite break in style and message between Heb 1:1-12:29 and all of Heb 13. Some scholars still uphold the notion that the same author wrote Heb 13 as the one who wrote the main sermon. Some explain its differences by calling it a postscript or a peroration added by the original author. These usually argue for the integrity of the entire document and claim that Paul wrote the entire message through the scribal skills of Timothy or Epaphras. Lane, for example, said,

> Heb 13 as a whole was drafted by the writer responsible for Heb 1-12 and was clearly composed to accompany the earlier chapters.[1]

Grässer said that with Heb 13 the reader quickly notices that at this point there is the beginning of a completely different kind of literature. Heb 13 has the character of an attachment. With the end of Heb 12,

---

[1] W. L. Lane, *Hebrews 9-13* (Dallas: Word Books, c1991), p. 497. So also P. E. Hughes, *A Commentary on the Epistle to the Hebrews* (Grand Rapids: Eerdmans, c1977), p. 561.

> the crisis atmosphere has vanished, and the homiletical exposition is changed from catechetical rules to an epistolary form.[1]

Grässer thought that the final paragraph (Heb 13:22-25), at least, was a "Pseudo-Pauline letter conclusion."[2] It is more likely that the entire chapter was spliced together from parts already written for the purposes of the canon. Grässer held that the radical differences between Heb 13 and the rest of the document could be explained in one of three ways:

1) This was an tendentious imitation of a traditional, peculiarly Pauline letter;
2) it was something later imported, either by the author himself or someone else;
3) It is the key to the entire document.[3] Grässer attempted, unsuccessfully, to show that the third possibility was the most likely.

The unity that Lane suggests is not as clear as he professed. Isaacs set out to prove that the chapter itself was unified and definitely a part of the entire document. She demonstrated neither.[4] She insisted that Heb 13 was not composed of small units of literature that changed from second person to first person and singulars to plural with changes in subject matters and points of view, and in other ways were not unified, but she did not show anywhere that this was not true. She found fault with the suggestion that Heb 1-12 was monastic, and Heb 13 was written for married people, but she did not disprove the suggestion in any way.[5] Isaacs knew of the criticisms for her position. She just denied them.

The most likely explanation is that the elegant legal argument of Heb 1-12 was composed by a skilled, Christian logician who lived too late to have been one of Jesus' disciples. Because those who determined the NT canon that was officially admitted into the NT accepted only works written by one of Jesus' original apostles, or by Paul, who was accepted as an apostle after the fall of Jerusalem, Hebrews was originally omitted. The message, however, was such a competent composition and expressed so clearly the theology of many Christians that the church did not want it to be omitted. That was particularly true after the victories of Constantine, which was understood as the fulfillment of God's promises to Abraham that Hebrews was confident would be fulfilled. To solve this problem, Heb 13 was added to make the entire document appear to be one of Paul's letters. The forgers deliberately used some of the preacher's skills and vocabulary, but its difference in ideas and style identify Heb 13 as a pseudepigraphon. It will here be analyzed and interpreted as an independent document.

Hebrews 1-12 was so narrowly directed to monks that it continued to be useful for the monastic part of the church. The canon, however, was prepared for the entire church, so it may have been thought necessary to broaden it to make it useful to the entire church. That may have been the reason chapter 13 began right at the

---

[1] E. Grässer, *An die Hebräer* (Zürich: Benziger Verlag, c1997) 3, p. 343, tr. from the German.

[2] Grässer, *An die Hebräer*, p. 409.

[3] Grässer, *An die Hebräer*, p. 344.

[4] M. E. Isaacs, "Hebrews 13:9-16 Revisited," *NTS* 43 (1997):268-284.

[5] Isaacs, "Revisited," p. 270.

first to show an interest in marriage ethics and the entire document was redesigned to become sort of an epistle.

COMMENTARY

13:1-2*Let brotherly love continue.* **Love** in biblical concepts is a legal term that defines the relationship between two parties to the same contract, without any qualification of blood identity. Because of the agreement, they are **lovers**, even if they do not like one another. For example, Jacob and his Uncle Laban came to an agreement, after a heated argument, to stay away from each other. Laban would go east, and Jacob and his family would go west. They ate a meal together and set up a pile of rocks to confirm the contract. They disliked one another, but legally they were **lovers** (Gen 31).

Prior to the marriage of a daughter, the father was required to **love** his daughter. That meant he provided for all of her needs. When she was married, he stopped **loving** her, and her new husband agreed to **love** her and become her legal father. It was because of this known legal relationship that Nathan could refer to Bath-sheba as being **like a daughter** to Uriah (2Sam 12:3). The daughter, however, took no vows to **love** her husband, because she had no responsibility for his provision. **Love** was a responsible term. Members of monasteries that took vows to **love** one another as themselves, were required to see that all other monks of the order had the same benefits they had.[1] Monks did not have to be encouraged to **love.** That was a requirement for admission. Christians who were not monks still had the responsibility to provide charity to other Christians in need. They agreed to do this when they joined the church, but it was more or less voluntary. They had independent incomes and expenditures. They had to be prompted to **love.**

Brotherly love (*pheel-ah-dehl-pheé-ah*, φιλαδελφία) is the concern that fellow sectarians have for one another's welfare. Especially in celibate brotherhoods where members did not have children to care for them in their illness or old age, it was necessary for brothers of the religious family to assume responsibilities ordinarily provided by families. This is not limited to personal feelings but also involves care for physical and material needs. In these communities where alone "life" was believed to be possible, those who joined the group passed from death to life when they took on responsibilities of **love** for one another (1John 3:14). Any member who had material possessions and saw his brother in need and did nothing about it could not claim to have God's **love** in him (1John 3:17). In monasteries monks did not have to be exhorted to **love** one another. The administration received all material benefits and distributed to others in need in the group. Once they vowed to **love** one another, **loving** became part of the group's daily administration.

Do not neglect love for strangers. **Love for strangers** (*pheel-aw-xehn-eé-ahs*, φιλοξενίας) was a type of **brotherly love.** Hospitality in the Near East has always been a virtue under almost any conditions, such as those practiced by Abraham (Gen 18:1-15), Lot (Gen 19:1-8) and the Danite (Judges 19:22-26). The hospitality that was considered **brotherly love**, however, did not apply to any stranger that stopped for a visit. It applied only to those members of the same corporation. **Brotherly love** could be shown to immediate community members by personally providing needs

[1] See further Buchanan, *Biblical and Theological Insights from Ancient and Modern Civil Law* (Lewiston: Mellen, c1992), pp 82-87.

as they were required. For the saints in Jerusalem who depended on others for subsidy, gifts for the poor were sent as expressions of **brotherly love**. Christians who married still kept careful dietary laws and provided hospitality for traveling monks.

Because some groups of orthodox Jews, like the Essenes, refused to eat with anyone whose carefulness in dietary, tithing, and purity rules was not proved by being a member of his own sect, hospitality was very important. Those who traveled had to find other members of their sect who would provide them food, clean clothing, and lodging. The **strangers** discussed here were sectarian **brothers.**

Jesus reportedly expected his apostles to be willingly entertained when they came to the houses of the faithful. They were encouraged to **ask** to find out where the faithful lived, then **look for** that home to find it, and finally **knock** on the door of that faithful family, and the door would be opened and hospitality provided (Matt 7:7). Jesus promised that this venture would be successful. Those who **asked** would **receive** desired answers. Those who **looked for** faithful homes would **find** them. When they arrived they would receive the needed hospitality. Furthermore, Jesus reportedly judged people by the way they treated his legal agents (apostles) who had gone out in his name. If they gave hospitality or cared for them after they had been imprisoned, he considered that the same as treatment given directly to him (Matt 25:35-36). This was the normal understanding of the legal relationship between a legal agent and the principal. They were legally identical within the limits of the assignments given.

When **strangers** came who were of the same faith, Christians and Jews were expected to entertain them. If, however, they did not observe the same rules, they were not to be admitted into the homes of the faithful, lest they defile the premises. Some were warned against even greeting them, lest they become defiled (2John 10-11; 1QS 5:16-17; 7:25; 8:23-24; 9:8-9). Leaders sometimes scolded others who neglected **strangers** (*xéhn-oos*, ξένους). When strangers were not given hospitality, they were made to suffer because they did not dare eat food that was provided by gentiles (3John 5-8).[1] Because some **strangers** took advantage of the hospitality they were guaranteed by their membership, some Christians were warned to consider any stranger who stayed more than two days to be a false prophet (Did 11).

Those who generally practiced **brotherly love** rather well in their own communities might be a little selfish about **showing love for strangers**; therefore Christians were frequently admonished against neglect in this area (Rom 12:10-13; 1Thess 4:1-12; 1Pet 1:22-23; 2Pet 1:5-7). This was only true, however, of the married Christians who lived away from monasteries and had possessions to share with others. Monks gave up all of their possessions when they joined the monastery, and the monastery, in turn, provided for all their needs. A traveling monk would first look for other monasteries of the same order for hospitality, but under some conditions of purity they might accept hospitality from other sectarians of the same order who were not monastic. The extent of carefulness probably varied from one monastery to another.

Those who heard the sermon (Heb 1:1-12:29) were treated by the speaker as if they were monks who observed rules very strictly. They seem to have been accustomed to life in a monastery. They did not reside as family members in the towns and cities. Therefore the speaker did not exhort them on hospitality obligations.

---

[1] See further Commentary on Heb 6:9 and Buchanan, *The Consequences of the Covenant* (Leiden: E. J. Brill, 1970), pp. 238-281, 290-305.

The couplet was evidently a poetic exhortation on love. The editor of Heb 13 added to this his own explanatory elaboration. Not only were Christians fulfilling their religious responsibility by showing hospitality to **strangers**, but some, like Abraham, Sarah (Gen 18), and Lot (Gen 19), in this way **entertained angels** without realizing it at first. The honor that comes to a Near Easterner who entertains important guests might be missed if the Christian who refused hospitality to a Christian from another location was really rejecting an angel in disguise.

[3]*Remember the prisoners as partners in bonds.*

> **Remember the prisoners as partners in bonds,**
> **those badly treated, as yourselves in [the] body**

This is a poetic couplet. The second line has the same meaning as the first or is supplementary. **The prisoners** were those **badly treated. Partners in bonds** are the same as **yourselves in [the] body**. Both names refer to people who belong to the same legal body or corporation. Both names also referred to fellow prisoners, as if the listener were handcuffed to the other prisoner. Even if the Christians involved were not actually handcuffed to the prisoners involved, they were still legally **partners in bonds.** Because the term **body** frequently means a legal **body,** a corporation, such as "the **body** of Christ," whenever the word appears, the student must ask which kind of **body** was intended. Being **in the body,** legally, is not the same as being in the flesh.

Those who were in **the body** were Christians. They were members of the corporation or **body** of Christ. It would mean that the readers should identify themselves with those **badly treated,** openly acknowledging to the authorities by their presence that they belonged to the same group.

Being with prisoners, **bodily**, meaning a physical body, would require deep empathy, close feeling. Because the first line of this couplet spoke of being **bodily** bound to prisoners; the second line would seem to mean having a close physical contact, sharing in their risks and also in their pain. Such prison visitation as that recommended was risky, both for the individual and for the church. It actually implied that the visiting person allowed himself or herself to be imprisoned with the other Christian who was then in prison. The church was the **body** of Christ, in which all members suffer if one is pained (1Cor 12:12-27; 2Cor 5:6; Rom 12:4-5). Being **in the body** has much the same meaning as being **partners in bonds**. If one member of the corporation is guilty the entire corporation is involved in the guilt. The question is, "Why were Christians **badly treated** and **in prison?"** Who judged them to be guilty, and of what crimes?

Because early Christianity and Judaism were both understood as subversive movements within the Roman Empire, faithful Jews and Christians were frequently thrown into prison for their positions and activities. Underground groups who secretly plot to overthrow the existing government and replace it with their own are seldom appreciated by the ruling powers. That which seems like "civil disobedience" and "righteous activities" to the invading group seems like rebellion and law breaking to the victims of these activities. It is not strange that Christians and Jews suffered imprisonment and martyrdom at the hands of the Romans for their actions. They were persistent enough in subversion to have finally become successful in the time of Constantine.

When some people were suffering and dying for the faith, there was a strong tendency to deny association with them (Matt 26:69-75), and in this way to avoid similar fates. The word rendered **partners in bonds** is *soon-deh-deh-méh-noi* (συνδεδεμένοι), "bound together with," which involves a very close identity with the **prisoners.** Those who called on **prisoners**, brought them food and other necessities, admitted to all that they were in sympathy with the **prisoners** and shared their political and religious views. Paul, for example, praised Onesiphorus, who refreshed Paul by bringing him his necessities while he was in prison. He was not ashamed of Paul's chains (2Tim 1:16). This kind of identity was important for the survival of the movement; it also was considered an expression of **brotherly love**. Beyond all of that it was risky.

4*[Let] marriage be honored.* This statement was made to counter the opinions of some monastic groups who did not **honor marriage.** They considered it a compromising degree of ethics. The highest degree was monasticism. It was considered "perfect." The author of this verse, however, upheld the view that there was nothing dishonorable about **marriage**. The author of Heb 1-12 was probably among those who would disagree. This couplet deals with faithfulness in **marriage.** Letting **marriage be honored in every [respect]** probably meant the same as letting **the marriage bed be undefiled.** From the point of view of levitical purity, the **undefiled** marriage bed would be one in which **those who have wives live as though they did not** (1Cor 7:29), since every act of sexual intercourse is defiling (Lev 15:16-18). This kind of temporary ethics might be expected of holy war soldiers during time of war, but when the war was over, they would be expected to return to their wives without any sense of guilt.

There were followers of Jesus who had left their families to be with Jesus (Matt 19:27-30), but later, when the kingdom had not come as soon as expected, they returned and lived again with their wives (1Cor 9:3-6). If the **marriage bed** were kept permanently **undefiled,** the Christians practicing that ethic would be celibate. The editor who interpreted this couplet, at least, did not understand it that way. He took this to mean a prohibition against **fornicators** who were promiscuous in sexual activity and "adulterers" who were unfaithful in marriage. Adultery was considered a worse crime than fornication and was punishable by death (Lev 20:10-21; Exod 20:14; Deut 5:18).

In the main section of the document (Heb 1:1-12:29) there was no mention made of **marriage**. In fact, the references to sanctification, holiness, brotherhood, the root of bitterness, discipline, and avoidance of any kind of defilement suggest that the speaker and listeners were celibate monks. **Marriage** was not an item in their list of ethics, because it was forbidden on admission. That is not the case of Heb 13, which seems to have been composed by a different author or editor for a wider reading public at a later time.

5*[Let] unconcern for money be the fashion*. Monks entered the monastery taking vows of poverty, celibacy, and obedience. From entrance on, they owned no property, laid up no treasures, and had no responsibility for food and shelter. The monastery provided all of that. It was only Christians who had not taken such vows as these, who could earn money and invest it that might have benefited from this counsel. These were members of the audience for whom the author of Heb 13 had written. It did not apply to the monks of the sermon.

The couplet urging **unconcern for money** is similar to other Christian admonitions and attitudes. This attitude was usually associated with a communal economy in which the individuals were dependent upon the administration of others for their provision. It was also encouraged, however, by early Jewish and Christian concern for widows, orphans, and others who were in need of the social welfare that the community provided.

Those who were counseled against being anxious for food, drink, or clothing (Matt 6:25), who were told not to **lay up treasures on earth** (Matt 6:19-21), and who were sent out on missions with no gold, silver, or copper in their belts, no bag for the journey, no staff, and no change of clothes (Matt 10:9-12), were traveling missionaries for whom the church had prepared hospitality stations where they could receive food, clothing, and other needs.

Because the administration had laid up treasures on earth for them, the missionaries did not have to be anxious for the next day (Matt 6:34). Since this administration did not function perfectly, and because there were men like Diotrephes, who turned away missionaries (3John 5-10), not all dependent Christians found it **the fashion** to have a complete **unconcern for money**. It was easier for a celibate like Paul to be content in whatever state he found himself (Philip 4:11-12) than for others who had families for whom to provide. Because not all early Christians were **satisfied with the present conditions**, they had to be admonished occasionally.

In addition to the couplet urging Christians to be unconcerned about **money**, the author further pressed the point by quoting two passages of Scripture on God's providence. Just before his death, Moses urged the Israelites to continue in their mission to capture the land. They should not be afraid of any enemies who stood in their way, because the Lord their God would go before the Israelites. He would not **abandon** them nor **forsake** them (Deut 31:6). The importance of God's presence in that case was his power in war. He was expected to overthrow Israel's enemies, and Israelites should count on it. Here the text was used to assure Christians of God's general providence, which made concern for money unnecessary. The non-celibates, who had families to support and could not rely on the administration of the monastery, had to be concerned about money, but they were warned not to be. These were the people to whom the author of Heb 13 wrote.

6*The Lord is my helper; I shall not be afraid.* The second quotation came from Ps 118:6, and the editor admitted that it took **courage** to give up **concern for money.** Like Deut 31:6, the Psalm reminded Israel of the Lord's faithfulness in overthrowing Israel's enemies in war, but the Christian editor used it to urge trust in God's financial and material providence. Like the lilies of the fields and the birds of the air (Matt 6:28-30), Christians should give up their anxiety for **money** and material things and instead trust **the Lord** who is their **helper.** Because this was so they did not have to be anxious about what a **man** could **do** to them. The church continued to maintain a doctrine of voluntary poverty, but it has always required much pressure to convince Christians to be confident of God's care so long as the people of the church were in charge of the welfare program. The editor of Heb 13 was one of those who added his arguments to the Christians' reading material in support of general financial sharing and lack of concern for one's own material needs.

Summary. The editor of Heb 13 put together in these verses four couplets and two FT quotations, interspersed with his own elaborations, introductions, or connecting sentences. These dealt with brotherly love as expressed in concern and care for strangers who needed hospitality, and prisoners who needed visitation and material provisions. Contrary to the monastic ideal of the main document, one of these couplets which the editor interpreted provided counsel for married people, urging faithfulness. The note that received the most attention was against over-concern for money and material needs. The married Christians to whom the author wrote had not taken vows of poverty. Their charity giving was voluntary, so the needs of the poor required continuous exhortation.

Because the married audience was not responding easily, the editor supported his couplet with two passages of Scripture, which he interpreted to mean that Christians should trust God for their material needs and be willing to share their goods. This message was similar to that of Haggai, but it would not apply to the monastic position of the author of Heb 1:1-12:29. These couplets may once have been part of one poem on Christian ethics from which the editor chose the verses that appealed to him and that served his immediate needs. If this was not the case, then the editor collected them from different sources and put them together. It is unlikely that he composed them himself, as the connecting sentences show.

Doctrine and Ethics

TEXT

7Remember your leaders who spoke to you the word of God; by observing carefully
the outcome of their behavior, imitate their faith. 8Jesus Christ, yesterday and today
the same--and for the ages. 9Do not be carried away by means of various and strange
teachings, for it is good [that] the heart be strengthened by grace, not by foods, in
which those who walk have not benefited.

COMMENTARY

7*Remember your leaders who spoke the word of God.* No mention was made of the kind of leaders involved. The rule was intended to include all sorts of situations, being general in nature. This is the kind of counsel that would be given to Christians who lived in homes and were not confined to a monastery where members lived together with leaders and did not need anyone to remind them of them.

The expression **outcome of their behavior** renders the Greek *hohn* (ὧν) . . . *tayn éhk-bah-seen tays ah-nah-straw-pháys* (τὴν ἔκβασιν τῆς ἀναστροφῆς), literally, "the way out of their turning around." Idiomatically this can refer to their departure from life. **The leaders** mentioned were evidently faithful to the end (2Tim 4:6-8). The readers were encouraged to **imitate their faith**. Although the pastoral epistles and the letters of Paul gave frequent admonitions to **leaders** for proper dealing with their parishioners, and Paul boldly urged Christians to **imitate** *him* (2Thess 3:7, 9; 1Cor 4:16; 11:1), there is very little general counsel in the NT to the people concerning the way they should treat their other **leaders.** There is no specification of a distinct office which these **leaders** filled, such as bishops or deacons. It evidently referred to all **leaders** who **spoke the word of God**.

8*Jesus Christ, yesterday, and today the same--and for the ages.* This is an early Christian confession of faith. **The ages** are **the ages** to come. This is just a poetic way of saying that **Jesus Christ** is always **the same**. Pausanias made a similar claim for Zeus, "Zeus was, Zeus is, and Zeus will be" (10:12, 5). Although Jesus had been crucified at the time of this writing, he continued to exist in the corporation of Christ. Although all members of a corporation can be changed, corporations are immortal. As such, the body of Christ is **yesterday, and today the same--and for the ages.** It never dies.

[9]*Be strengthened by grace--not by foods*. This observation comes in the context of a prohibition against **various and strange teachings** and it contrasts **grace** and **foods.** The Greek word for grace is *khár-ees* (χάρις), from which we get the English word "charity." It also means "gratitude," "favor," "kindness," "free gift." On the other hand, the biblical concept of **heart** was the organ of thinking, rather than feeling. Therefore this might be translated better by "mind." It is the mind that is effected by **teachings**. **Various and strange teachings** refer to some **teachings** that differed from those accepted by the author. They were **strange**, meaning **strange** or foreign to the creed considered orthodox. Like the **myths and endless genealogies which promote speculations rather than divine training** (1Tim 1:4), these seem to have been **teachings** of the Judaizers, who, like the author of Heb 1:1-12:29, were interested in keeping the law to the letter on matters of purity and foods.

It was a non-Judaizer, like Paul, who emphasized salvation by faith rather than zeal, who minimized the importance of foods, circumcision, and Jewish birth, who would encourage the churches to **be strengthened by grace, not by foods**. This is not a teaching expected by the author of Heb 1-12. The teaching probably deals with the contrast between rigorous zeal and careful purity and dietary law observance, on the one hand, and the belief that God is generous, who freely strengthens the minds of his people without such careful observance. This may be another clue that the author of Heb 13 is not the same as the author of Heb 1-12.

Those who walk. The ones that **walk** were those who **walked** according to **the strange** teaching about foods. To use the term **walk** for religious observance is customary in Jewish terminology. The way in which a person should **walk** is the rule by which he or she conducts her or his life. In this imagery, Christianity was early referred to as **the way**, meaning the true way in which to **walk**. Jewish legal teachings are called *hah-lah-kohth* (הלכות), "walkings." According to the author, the Judaizers who **walked** in ways that were **strange** to him did not benefit from their strict observance of **food** laws. This is in direct disagreement with the author of Heb 1:1-12:29. It is likely that this comment was written after the fall of Jerusalem, after the religious and military efforts of the Jews had failed, because the author seemed to have some basis for holding that the Jewish way of **walking** had not been successful and therefore should not be practiced. He also may have lived somewhere in the diaspora, away from Zion, where careful observance was not very easy to follow. He did not even mention his basis, because his audience would have understood the allusion. At a distance of 2,000 years, however, scholars have to speculate.

The following six midrashic verses have been the most difficult texts of the entire Book of Hebrews to interpret. They seem to interrupt the flow of the narrative and belong to a separate commentary on earlier FT texts.

TEXT

Hebrews	First Testament
10 We have an altar, from which those who minister in the tent do not have authority to eat, 11 for the beasts **whose blood is** **brought into the temple for a crime offering** by the high priest, the bodies of these **are burned**	Lev 16:27 The bull **for the crime offering** and the goat **for the crime offering, whose blood is** **brought** to atone **into the temple** will be taken **outside the camp**, and their skin, their flesh, and their dung **shall be burned** with fire.
outside the camp. 12 Therefore Jesus also suffered outside the gate so that he might sanctify the people through his own blood. 13 Therefore let us go out to him **outside the camp**, bearing his insult, 14 for we do not have here a continuing city, but we are looking for the [city] which is to come.	Exod 33:7 Moses took the tent and spread it out far **outside the camp**, and he called it the "tent of appointment." Everyone who looked for Yehowah went **out** to the tent of appointment which was **outside the camp.** Exod 19:17 Moses took the people **outside the camp** to meet God.
15 Through him, then, **let us bear a sacrifice** of praise **to God** through everything, that is **[the] fruit of lips** which confess his name, 16 and do not forget the **good** works and common [fellowship], for God is pleased with such sacrifices.	Ps 50:14 **Sacrifice to God,** a thanksgiving offering, and a peace offering to the Most High. Every one of you shall forgive iniquity and take what is **good. Let us pay the fruit of our lips**

COMMENTARY

Precisely what does this text mean? What and where is the altar? What and where is the "camp"? Why do those who minister at the tent have no authority to eat from the sacrifices of this altar? Where was the gate, outside of which Jesus was taken to suffer? If Christians still have an altar why do they depend only on the offering of lips for sacrifice? Why do Christians not have a continuing city? Where are Christians expected to go when they go outside the camp? Scholars have been driven into extremes in their efforts to make sense of this passage. For instance, Lane thought there were no geographical locations involved:

> Outside the camp connotes outside the earthly sphere, since the writer regarded Christ's offering as made in the heavenly sanctuary. Jesus opened the way into the heavenly world (10:19-23).[1]

[1] W. L. Lane, *Hebrews 9-13* (Dallas: Word Books, 1991), p. 545.

Weiss noted the results of such a concept as this:

> The faith existence of the Christians, then, would be understood as a "de-worldization," in the sense of an exodus from the earthly obligations and security bases on the designs of mercy (v. 9). The departure from the camp corresponds to the approach to the throne of mercy (4:16) as a heavenly reality.[1]

Some of these suggestions seem to be out of this world. This is not an allusion to the Eucharist, as Swetnam and others suggest.[2] Williamson correctly held that there is no interest expressed in Hebrews for a Eucharist.[3] The Last Supper Jesus had with his apostles included a legal ceremony whereby he formed a legal corporation, a body of Christ, from the group and instituted the church. With the first ceremony he used the ordinary Passover bread as a legal seisin for his body. The word was "body" (*sóh-mah,*), not "flesh" (*sahrx*, σάρξ). After he had formed a legal corporation, at the end of the meal he took the fruit of the vine as another seisin for blood of the contract, and established a new contract with this body of Christ. At this point in Jesus' career, there was no emphasis on the crucifixion, which had not happened, or the sacrifice of Jesus. The church would have been legally formed even if there had never been a crucifixion. The early church observed the Eucharist as a memorial meal, where every participant was to discern the body—not the flesh. To discern the body of Christ everyone was to share food and eat together, so that no single member of the body was left out (1Cor 11:29). It was only later that Eucharist was celebrated in terms of sacrifice. Hebrews taught the significance of Christ's sacrifice for forgiveness and salvation, but not for the Eucharist.[4]

C. R. Koester thought the camp was urban life generally, with all of its complexity.[5] It did not apply here to any specific geographical location. Following many earlier authors, he claimed that the most likely interpretation is

> The cross or sacrificial death of Christ. Hebrews uses metonymy to transfer the term "altar" (13:10) from the sanctuary to the place where carcasses were banned "outside the camp" on the Day of Atonement (13:11) and finally to Christ's suffering "outside the gate" (13:12). The "altar" is not only Golgotha. Through synecdoche, in which the part stands for the whole, the "altar" encompasses multiple dimensions of Christ's death.[6]

---

[1] W. F. Weiss, *Hebräer*, p. 735 (tr. from the Gerrman).

[2] J. Swetnam, "Christology and the Eucharist in the Epistle to the Hebrews," *Biblica* 70 (1989):74.

[3] R. Williamson, "Eucharist," *NTS* 21 (1975):300-312.

[4] See further Buchanan, *The Gospel of Matthew* (Lewiston: Mellen, c1996), pp. 964-982.

[5] C. R. Koester, *Hebrews* (New York: Doubleday, c2001), p. 571.

[6] Koester, *Hebrews*, pp. 568-69. Why do so many scholars choose to accept such a ridiculous interpretation? The reason probably is that no one can make sense of this passage, so everyone follows the interpretation that has already been given by others rather than try to find one more reasonable. Prior to the new archaeological discovery, this has been really a difficult passage to interpret.

Scholars have resorted to imaginary explanations, because the text, as it is, does not have an obvious basis from which to direct an examination. This prompts some scholars to resort to a Rorschach type of explanation. This allows the scholar to call a military camp "an earthly sphere," or an altar "the cross," "sacrificial death," or "Golgotha." Going out from the gate can mean "de-worldization."

New Archaeological Insights

The discovery of a 5,000-year-old wall on the west bank of the Kidron Valley by archaeologists brings these verses back within geographical possibilities. That discovery puts a new light on the entire area of Zion, the City of David, the Roman military camp to the north, and the events that took place in that extended area. With a new geographic perspective, many scriptural passages become clear that were formerly cloudy, one of these is this difficult passage in Hebrews, which relates an Exodus situation to the author's own.[1]

The Roman Camp and Zion. Archaeologists have discovered the foundations of the Tower of Siloam and the old wall surrounding the City of David. That discovery made archaeologists realize that Zion was only a small section of the ridge on the west bank of the Kidron Valley. The City of David was only a fraction as large as the whole city of Jerusalem today. The ramifications of this insight are tremendous. After the destruction of Titus, this little town was only about 10-12 acres in size—only a third as large as the 35-acre construction at its north end that still exists. The huge rock walls that surround that large city have received international attention for their magnitude and architecture. They were built by the Romans during the reign of Herod the Great. The little town at the south was obviously David's Holy City.[2]

Herod's fortress was installed later. The huge fortified place that now surrounds the Dome of the Rock and an international place of worship for the Muslims was the Roman fortress that sometimes housed 6,000 Roman soldiers. This military **camp** was called "Antonia." There also exists a small, excavated area in the northwest corner of this Roman fortress that has mistakenly been called the Tower of Antonia, but it could not qualify for an entire Roman **camp** and fortress.[3] Like many other Roman towers, Antonia had all of the facilities of a city and fortress. The entire walled city is the only place where Roman soldiers were camped.

---

[1] For more details see E. L. Martin, *The Temples Jerusalem Forgot* (Portland: ASK Publications, 2000). Y. Shiloh, *Excavations at the City of David* (Jerusalem: The Hebrew University, 1984), pp. 46-47; D. T. Ariel (ed.), *Excavations at the City of David, 1978-1985, Directed by Yigal Shiloh* V (Jerusalem: The Hebrew University, 2000), pp. 1-21. M. P. Germano, Editor, *BA,* said of Martin's book, "Not only a work of significant scholarly impact it may well serve as the awaited stimulus for the building of Jerusalem's Third Temple."

[2] H. Shanks, "Everything You Ever Knew about Jerusalem is Wrong," *BAR* 25.6 (1999): 20-29, and "I Climbed Warren's Shaft." *BAR* 25.6 (1999):30-35; J. Sudilovskym "Virtual Temple Mount," *BAR* 27.4 (2001): 16.

[3] J. D. Tabor, *Locating the Herodian Temple: Old and New Theories in Light of Ancient Literary Evidence* (VideoTape made by Biblical Archaeology Society), reviewing Martin's book, pointed out how visible Herod's camp was and still is. Following Martin, he also has shown how similar the large 35-acre fortress is to other Roman fortresses in other parts of the world. That little area in the northwest corner of the city could never qualify as Fortress Antonia. Josephus said Herod made Antonia so that soldiers could overlook the temple, but it would not be possible to see the temple through the high walls from that distant corner.

Archaeologists have previously assumed that Romans camped in the Upper City of Jerusalem, and they have looked there for ruins and walls to demonstrate that supposition, but when Geza recently excavated the Upper City he found no evidence of Roman military occupation there. The walls archaeologists expected to unearth that separated the Roman soldiers from the rest of the city were not found.[1] The reason for that, of course, is that the so-called "temple mount" was the Roman camp, and it was well walled and made defensible. That is the only place where the soldiers and their materials could be kept.

After the 66-70 IA[2] war, Josephus said Titus ordered that the city be so completely destroyed that visitors who entered the city would not realize that they were in it when they asked where it was (War 7:1, 3-4). That did not happen all at once. Antonia was still standing while the City of David was being destroyed. Titus ordered that the walls of the Antonia be torn down to the foundations, but they may have been the last walls to fall. Prisoners were kept in part of the temple area before it was completely demolished, and soldiers might have been housed in the Antonia both before and after the exterior walls had fallen. There are still parts of the wall around the Haram that have survived, and archaeologists have found portions of the supporting walls that the Jebusites originally installed between the ridge and the outer wall in the Kidron Valley. It was Dr. Ernest Martin who first called attention in writing to the correct location of the temple,[3] and directed the earliest research. Kenyon, Reich, Shukron, Shiloh, Tarler, and Mazar are some of the archaeologists who have uncovered parts of the City of David for observation.

When David first entered Zion, the old wall had already been there for thousands of years. According to Hecataeus (4th century BIA), the altar was made of loose, unhewn stones. It was 30 feet long by 30 feet wide, and 15 feet high (Apion 198). Although Josephus quoted Hecataeus, in his own report he said that altar was 22 ½ feet tall, 75 feet long, and 75 feet wide. It was made entirely of stones, just as the huge Canaanite altar at Megiddo was. David originally had built only a small altar at Gihon. That is evident from the report that when Adonijah and Joab fled to the altar for security they held there the horns of the altar. There is no way one person could hold more than one horn when the horns were placed on the corners, at least 30 feet apart.

When David had the tent placed near the spring near an altar, he probably also installed the kind of altar that was used in the wilderness, very much like the two altars that archaeologists have uncovered at Lachish and Arad. Each of these is only big enough to roast only one or two animals at a time. That would have seemed inadequate for national feasts, so when Solomon built the temple he probably had a larger altar constructed with it. Since he imitated the Canaanites in his construction of the temple, he probably also built a huge altar just like the kind Canaanites used. It was probably about the size Hecateaeus saw when he visited Zion. When Herod built the temple that existed in NT times, it was much larger than earlier temples, and he probably enlarged the altar at the same time to the size Josephus reported. Neither altar was portable or inflammable. They both could easily survive the destruction of temples. (A picture of the Altar at Megiddo appears between chapters 8 and 9).

---

[1] H. Geva, "Searching for Roman Jerusalem," *BAR* 23.6 (Nov. Dec, 1997):36-45.

[2] This is a calendrical designation selected as a politically correct improvement over the apartheid designations, B.C. and A.D. or B.C.E. and C.E. This should offend neither Jews nor Christians.

[3] Martin, *Temples*.

The altar was always located near the Spring of Siloam which provided all the water needed for multiple sacrifices. Herod's temple, like those of Solomon and Zerubbabel, was located 600 feet south of Herod's Tower of Antonia, the Roman camp (War 2:144, 152, 165). The fact that the altar and each of the three temples were located directly behind the Spring of Siloam is confirmed by Scripture.

Biblical Confirmation. Ezekiel's vision of the new age involved the stream flowing out from under the threshold of the temple, running down under the south edge of the temple toward the altar (Ezek 47:1), down the Kidron Valley, through the stream-bed that leads through Wadi Qumran and on into the Dead Sea. It sweetened the water of the Dead Sea so that fish could survive there (Ezek 47:10), **because it flowed out from the sanctuary** (Ezek 47:12).[1]

All of this water had its origin in the temple. The topography and geography of Ezekiel's vision fit perfectly, once it is recognized that the temple was adjacent to the spring of Gihon (Siloam) that provided all of that water. Ezekiel would not have pictured a temple high on the dry hill north of the spring where this could not happen. Enoch also claimed to have seen the holy mountain with a stream that flowed underneath that mountain toward the south (lEnoch 26:2-3). There is no such stream flowing underneath the Dome of the Rock. Hezekiah's tunnel does not flow north. The holy mountain was obviously the temple mount, located just above Ain Gihon. This is the location of which Ezekiel spoke, where the stream that flowed underneath the mountain also flowed under the temple near Siloam. That was probably the tunnel that leads to the surface of the ridge from "Warren's Shaft."[2] Tacitus said,

> The temple was built like a fortress . . . There is an ever-flowing spring tunneled under the hills into collecting pools and cisterns (Hist 11:12).

Aristeas (ca 285 BIA) explained how the landscape of the temple area was designed with paved stones and gutters to carry away the blood washed down from the sacrifices. There was an inexhaustible supply of water gushing into the temple for use in sacrifices (Aristeas 87-89). The temple scroll (11QT 32:12-15) concurs with Aristeas that water was necessary for sacrifices. That document describes a conduit that brought water into the area and was used to wash away the blood into a hole that vanished into the land. That may have conducted the mixture of blood and water into the Kidron Valley. It was important that it could vanish before anyone became defiled by the blood.

An early author, who had obviously read Ezek 47, visualized having been taken to Paradise, where there were blooming and fruit bearing trees, whose roots were from an immortal land that was watered from a river of gladness, and the region around them was the land of life of the age [to come]. The river of gladness, probably the river in the Kidron Valley, watered these fruits and the area around was the land of life of the age [to come] (Odes of Sol [G] 11:15-16).

---

[1] See further Buchanan, *The Gospel of Matthew* 2 (Lewiston: Mellen, c1996), pp. 816-18.

[2] So Martin, *Temples,* pp. 277-280.

The psalmist spoke of the temple, where Yehowah[1] sits over the flood where he is enthroned as king for the age (Ps 29:10). The voice of Yehowah is over the water; the God of glory roars; Yehowah is over much water. The flood was the huge fountain of water, pouring through Hezekiah's tunnel, under the temple. Another psalmist said, **There is a river whose streams make glad the city of God, the holy dwelling place of the Most High** (Ps 46:5). The dwelling place of the Most High was the temple positioned near the streams that make glad the city of God. The Scroll of Blessings asked that the Lord bless the recipient from his holy dwelling, the fountain of the age (1QSb 1:3). The holy dwelling at the fountain of the age was clearly the temple just above Ain Gihon.

One of the factors Zechariah anticipated in the future restoration, when Yehowah would become king over all the land, was having the water of life flowing out from Jerusalem (Zech 14:8-9). The Jerusalem he pictured was Zion, near the spring of Gihon (Siloam)—not the hill to the north that later became Herod's city.

When the NT seer looked forward to a New Jerusalem, he anticipated a heavenly city that had come to earth from God in heaven, prepared as a bride for a new wedding contract. In this new city one of the basic descriptions was **the river of the water of life going out from the throne of God** (Rev 22:1, *thráw-noo too theh-oó* [θρόνου τοῦ θεοῦ = *keé-say áyl,* כשא אל] cf. *meék-dahsh áyl* [מקדש אל] [1QpHab 12:8-9]).

Those who had come up out of great tribulation would be before the **throne of God** where **the Lamb would lead them to the springs of the water of life** (Rev 7:15, 17). These **springs of water** were Ain Gihon and Ain Rogel at the base of the temple mount in Zion, where the Spring of Gihon streamed from the altar of the temple down the Kidron Valley to the south. The seer related the temple to the area near the spring of Gihon. The small Spring of Rogel is at the southern edge of the Hinoam Valley.

There is a shaft that still exists that goes almost straight up from the level of the spring to a platform area where it joins a tunnel that goes several meters horizontally to the west before it comes out of the ground. At the end of the war between the Jews and the Romans (70 IA), Simon, one of the messianic rebels who led that war, surrendered to the Romans by appearing out of the ground *at the place where the temple had stood before it was destroyed.* He appeared dressed in royal garments of white and purple to show that he claimed royalty, and he demanded to see the top general. As a pretending king, he claimed royal respect. He had obviously been hiding in that tunnel under the temple, which had also been a fortress—the last defense of Jerusalem (War 7:28-30). Normally, this tunnel and shaft would have been full of water, but there was a drought in the area that influenced the Roman success in the war.

Not only the Tower of Antonia, but also Hippicus and probably also Phasael and Mariamme, depended on rain water and cisterns to provide water for daily use (War 5:163-165). During the drought water had to be brought to Hippicus, evidently because their cistern was dry (War 5:304). Later in the war, however, after the

[1] This is the correct pronunciation of the tetragrammaton, as is clear from the pronunciation of proper names in the First Testament (FT), poetry, fifth century Aramaic documents, Greek translations of the name in the Dead Sea Scrolls and church fathers. See further Buchanan, "Some Unfinished Business with the Dead Sea Scrolls," *RevQum* 49-52 13, *Mémorial Jean Carmignac*, ed. F. Garcia Martinez et E. Peuch (Paris, 1988), pp. 411-20.

Romans had gained possession of the Antonia and had brought the battle up against the temple area, Josephus reported that *only* the Romans had access to the water. That was probably because they had broken into the Spring of Siloam and allowed the water to flow out into the Kidron Valley so that they had water, but the Jews in the temple area had only the water left in their few cisterns and the Pool of Siloam (War 5:409-410). This caused the tunnel at the top of the shaft to be completely dry when Simon needed a place to hide after the temple had been burned and controlled by the Romans. Because the tunnel was dry, Simon was able to hide there after the temple had been destroyed. This was the last defense of Jerusalem (War 7:28-30).

Josephus' report shows the direct route from the spring to the temple area. The temple was also a fortress, and fortresses always have to be built where water can be made accessible for a large number of troops. Fortresses, such as Megiddo, Gezer, and Hazor all have good water systems. Other fortresses have cisterns to catch rain water. It was no accident that the temple-fortress at Zion was built in relationship to the Spring of Siloam. The last of the war between Rome and Jerusalem had been fought at the temple,[1] and Simon had evidently been in that fortress as the temple had begun burning. He took the normal route for refuge through the nearby tunnel. The temple had been built over that channel which, if it were dry, might provide an escape route for the fortress. It was more important, however, that it provide the necessary water both for the fortress and for the temple sacrifices. Faust argued that this huge shaft, sometimes called Warren's shaft, was used to dip water in buckets for the city.[2] After they had been pulled up to the tunnel level, they would still have to be carried through the tunnel to become accessible to the city. The city needed more water than could be provided in small buckets, dipped and pulled up long distances with ropes. Think of the number of ropes this would wear out as they rubbed along those rocky walls!

Faust recognized some problems with his conjecture. He knew that pulling water up by the bucketfuls was not easy, and he suggested that it would have been used only in emergencies. He also noted that in order for water to be reached by buckets on ropes that the water would have to have been dammed up at the bottom of the shaft so that water could have been forced several meters up the shaft to bring the water level closer to the reach of the platform on which the people stood when they drew the water.[3] He neglected only to consider the possibility that the dam could have worked to allow the water to be forced all the way up the shaft, through the tunnel, and out on to the top of the ridge in the temple area.

It is more likely that the shaft was either constructed or adapted originally from a natural provision to bring water up to the city by force. This shaft was known as the water channel (*tsee-nohr*, צנור) (2Sam 5:8) at the time that David took the city. A water channel is normally designed and used to allow water to flow from one place to another. There was no water up on the ridge to flow down to the spring, so the water must have flowed upward from the spring to the top of the ridge, where it poured out the way Aristeas and the temple scroll testified. It evidently had to be possible, because Josephus said that was the precise spot where the temple had been

---

[1] Remnants of the war continued, however, for two more years until Machaerus and Masada were taken.

[2] A. Faust, "Yes, It Really Was Used to Draw Water," *BAR* 29.5 (2003):70-76.

[3] Faust, "Used to Draw Water," pp. 73-74.

before it was destroyed, and Aristeas claimed to have seen the water flowing up on the temple level.

The next question is, "Where did the water get all of the power required to force the water up the channel?" There seems to be only one answer. The huge Spring of Siloam (Gihon) was blocked somewhere near the spring to divert the water up the chimney-like channel where it could join the horizontal tunnel, taking the water to the temple area where Simon appeared. If this was actually functioning in David's time, as the evidence seems to show, it would mean that the Jebusites had a superb running water system operating in that little town, perched on a ridge, three thousand years ago.

The hydrologist, Dr. Ward E. Sanford, said that only about 2% of all springs are siphon springs to varying degrees. In these cases there is somewhere upstream a subterranean cavern, and it is connected downstream by a "pipe" or crack that is roughly an upside-down U shape. The water feeds into the cavern slowly. Once the water level reaches the top of the U, the water is siphoned out of the cavern until it reaches the inlet that breaks the suction.[1] Siphon springs gush periodically, just the way the Spring of Siloam has done for centuries. Siphon springs are both air tight and water tight from their origin until their final flow. The Spring of Siloam seems to behave like a typical siphon spring gusher. "Warren's shaft" may have existed naturally thousands of years ago as part of the siphon spring, and the Jebusites may have tapped into this siphon spring at the top of the shaft and constructed the tunnel that still exists to guide the water exactly to the place they wanted it to be. All of that existed when David conquered Zion, and the temple with its altar existed there near the spring until the Romans destroyed the city.

Titus had all of the City of Zion swept clean. Not one rock was left on top of the other. The soldiers dug up walls and searched the area for gold. That may have put an end to the altar, but that huge altar, made of rocks, would have contained no gold, and it would not have burned when the temple was destroyed. The rock altar would have withstood the fire. This small literary unit (Heb 13:10-16) was probably composed shortly after the temple was burned and before the rocks were taken from the altar to be used for some other purpose.

Commentary on Hebrews 13:10-16

[10]*We have an altar*. In context this has been said as if **we have** *only* **an altar.** We no longer have a temple, a fortress, a monastery, church, or even a city—Only **an altar**.

In the wilderness Moses set up a **tent** of meeting **outside the camp** (Exod 33:7). **The camp** was the place where the Israelites lived. Israelites tried to keep the **camp** reasonably clean, but it could not be completely clean. In fact, it was always defiled by women during menstruating periods and children who had not been toilet trained. It was also defiled by conception, birth, and death. For older children and all adults, all toilet needs had to take place at least 3,000 feet from **the camp**. Nevertheless **the camp** was a place of defilement. Therefore when Moses set up an **altar** and a **tent** of meeting, he went **far away from the camp** (Exod 33:7).

The tent was the place where Israelites came when they were **looking for Yehowah** for counsel or to settle disputes. In addition to the place of sacrifice, **the tent** was the local court. That is the place where Israelites met with Yehowah. Meeting with Yehowah meant meeting with one of his legal agents, who functioned as

[1] Dr. Ward E. Sanford, Research Hydrologist, U.S. Geological Survey.

judge. The chief justice in the wilderness was Moses, who acted in Yehowah's behalf, in his name, and at his responsibility (Exod 29:43-46) in making judgments. When people came **looking for Yehowah** in **the tent**, they came to Moses to try legal cases. That process continues to this day. Judges normally do not act on their own, because they are legal agents of the state. They make judgments, but instead of concluding a trial by saying, "My judgment is," they say, "This court decides." Judges act in the name of the state, in its interests, and at its responsibility. In the wilderness the state's credit was given to God by the judge, Moses, who made the decisions.

Before there was a temple, **the tent** was placed adjacent to **an altar.** That was the place where Israelites were commanded to conduct the sacrifices, following the instructions for the Day of Atonement (Exod 29:10-37). That wilderness altar would have been only as large as the small altars excavated by Aharoni in Lachish and Arad in the Israeli Negev. Each one of these altars was only large enough to roast one or two beasts at a time. David's small tent and altar were constructed very near the spring. That is evident because Zadok obtained the oil for anointing Solomon there and anointed Solomon at Gihon. By the time Solomon became king, the country would have learned that the altar David erected was inadequate for a national altar where hundreds of sheep would be slaughtered on great feast days.

Wilderness **tents** were constructed out in the open air. They were not built under roofs, inside of buildings, but in religion and law, terms continue even though situations change. After the temple had been built, part of the priest's function took place under a roof, and not in a real tent, but because initially the priest approached **the tent** in the wilderness his activity was still described in relationship to a **tent.**

Today in most western courts judges are seated in very nice chairs with attractive desks before them as they hold court. Neither the chairs nor the desks are crude benches, like some seating places in outdoor parks, but judges once were seated on benches or had benches for desks, so modern attorneys are still said to approach the bench when they come forward to discuss matters with the judge.

The **tent** inside the temple was the object under discussion at this point. The author of these verses employed Exodus terminology, but neither **the tent** nor **the camp** was exactly the same as in the wilderness. The author used wilderness terms, but he was thinking of a different **tent,** a different **camp,** and a different reason for leaving **the camp**.

Those who minister in the tent. **Those who ministered in the tent** referred to priests in **the tent** at Herod's temple at Jerusalem. They were the priests who had the exclusive right to eat from certain offerings that were brought to the **altar** (Lev 7:6; Num 18:9-10). These were sons of Aaron whose family had eaten sacrifices and conducted services in the temple for generations. They were replaced for a short period when the Hasmoneans were high priests. They had special status and privileges.

Pious parties to the contract objected to the lineage of the high priests, the purity practices, the calendars observed, or the affiliation of the priests with Rome. Some of these people conducted their own religious services in exile, according to rules they accepted. One of these groups met somewhere in Judah (1QpHab), possibly at Zion, David's holy City, south of Herod's walls, under the leadership of its own priestly teacher of righteousness. Another was organized by the high priest Onias in Heliopolis, Egypt.[1] There were still other ancient temples at Lachish and

[1] See further Buchanan, "The Priestly Teacher of Righteousness," *RQum* 6 (1969):556-58.

Arad in the Negev of Israel. Some Jews prayed daily that God would root out foreign worship from the land and bring holy worship in its place.[1] These people thought of Herod's temple as the temple made with hands (Acts 7:47-48). They refused to worship there under those conditions, just as the Jews refused to worship there after Antiochus Epiphanes had defiled it. As soon as Judas drove out the Greeks, however, and the temple had been properly cleansed, Jews rejoiced at the opportunity to renew sacrifices.

By the time this author had written, the situation had changed dramatically from the usual Jewish tradition. The **tent** involved was not **the tent** of meeting in the wilderness, and the **altar** was not the **altar** used in the wilderness. There was a huge **altar** in Zion. In earlier times the sons of Aaron had ministered at that **altar**, but they no longer had that authority. The temple had been burned, and Romans had complete military control over the altar and the rest of Zion. Jews and Christians still had **an altar**, but the priests had lost their **authority**.

11 *The bodies of these "are burned outside the camp.*" Lev 16:27-28 describes the way the crime offerings had to be treated. The beast was killed and sacrificed inside the city; the **blood** was to be sprinkled on the altar for atonement; but the uneaten part of the carcass (Exod 29:36) had to be taken **outside the camp** and **burned**. The person who handled the carcass became defiled by this action and was required to bathe to be cleansed before he could again enter the city (Lev 16:28).

Outside of the gate. In some ways Jesus was treated the way a sacrificial offering was handled on the Day of Atonement. Jesus was tried inside of the Tower of Antonia, the defiled Roman **camp**, but he was taken then **outside of the gate** of Antonia for the crucifixion. This was done because the Romans wanted it done this way, but the author argued that God was in charge, so it was really done for another liturgical purpose. It fulfilled the plan designed to give the legal benefits of his sacrifice only to those **outside of the gate** of the Roman **camp**. The text says, **Wherefore, also Jesus, in order that he might sanctify the people through his own blood, suffered outside of the gate**. (Heb 13:12).[2] The Roman **camp** was for Roman soldiers. Faithful Christians and other Jews would not willingly inhabit that place. They were the ones that Jesus' blood would sanctify—not the Romans. The author found a Scripture text to justify the action that was taken as the fulfillment of prophecy.

13 *Therefore let us go to him.* Since the blood of Jesus was poured on an altar **outside the camp** to sanctify the people **outside the camp**, Christians were admonished to **go out to him outside the camp, bearing his insult**. When famous people approached a town in antiquity, the people of the town customarily went out to meet them, just the way the priests went out to meet Alexander the Great when he approached Jerusalem. After Jesus' death, his presence could be known only in his

---

[1] Buchanan, *Consequences,* pp. 63-65, 76-80.

[2] John O'Neill, "The Death of the Teacher of Righteousness in Hebrews 13:12-13," *Journal of Higher Criticism* 7 (2000):286-88 suggested that instead of Jesus, the original author intended the Teacher of Righteousness. This depends on his earlier argument that the nine references to Jesus in Heb 1:1-12:29 are all later intrusions that have replaced the Teacher of Righteousness also in that document ("Jesus in Hebrews," *Journal of Higher Criticism* 6 [1999]:64-82). This is an unnecessary conjecture that is forced.

corporation, in the community that had been legally formed in his name. To **go out to** Jesus required that believers go out to the place, wherever the church existed. Before the fall of Zion, the body of Christ existed in the monastery there on Mount Zion. Afterward it would have been moved. Readers of this document would have known where that was. It was not at Zion.

The point of this admonition was that Christians should no longer make pilgrimages to Jerusalem, as Jews and Christians had done, traditionally. If there were any believers still in Jerusalem they should leave. There was no longer a religious reason for remaining there. They were already **outside the camp**, so they did not have to go anywhere else for sanctification. In response to those who hold that **outside the camp** means "away from the earth into heaven," Weiss noted the results of such a concept at this:

> The faith existence of the Christians, then, would be understood as a "de-worldization," in the sense of an exodus from the earthly obligations and security bases on the designs of mercy (v. 9). The departure from the camp corresponds to the approach to the throne of mercy (4:16) as a heavenly reality.[1]

Weiss thought that the patriarchs were looking for a concrete heavenly city that was right there at Zion, where the travelers could continue to exist. This did not exclude the future hope for Christians, but it recognized the present eschatological meaning of the words **You have come to** (Heb 12:22).[2]

The **insult** or disgrace involved came from association with one who had claimed to be the great king, but who instead was crucified as an insurrectionist. To most this seemed like a failure; to Christians who interpreted his death in terms of an atoning sacrifice, this meant victory, so they were willing to bear **the insult**. Bruce erred when he said people were to leave the city in search of a **city which had foundations** (Heb 11:10).[3] The author of Heb 11 thought Zion was **the city having the foundations**. The great heroes of the past had left their homelands in Haran, Egypt, and other places in the diaspora to come to the holy city, whose builder and maker was God.

The annotator, who wrote this part of Heb 13, felt differently about Jerusalem. Whereas the first author said, **But you have come to Zion, city of the living God!**, the author of Heb 13 urged Christians to leave Jerusalem, if they happened to live there, because salvation was elsewhere. That somewhere was somewhere else in Palestine or in the diaspora—not in heaven. The advice of the author of Heb 13 pointed in a direction that was different from the counsel of the earlier preacher (Heb 1:1-12:29), but it was far more different from the direction of Philo and his followers.

[14]*For we do not have here a continuing city*. Zion was gone. All that was left there was the **altar** that could not be used[4] and the remnants of Herod's pagan Roman city, Antonia. This was the situation in Jerusalem after the temple had been burned.

---

[1] H. F. Weiss, *Der Brief an die Hebräer über das Neue Testament* (Göttingen: Vandenhoeck & Ruprecht, 1991), p. 735, tr. from the German.

[2] Weiss, *Hebräer*, p. 738.

[3] F. F. Bruce, *The Epistle to the Hebrews* (Grand Rapids: Eerdmans, 1964), p. 404.

[4] So also H. Koester, "'Outside the Camp' Hebrews 13:9-14," *HTR* 55 (1962):313.

The author encouraged Christians to leave the place. He did not say where they were to go, but they could not stay there. There was no longer a temple where priests were allowed to minister, and they would have to offer sacrifices of lips in their praises to God in everything, making confessions in Jesus' name. This had been the practice of the Jews taken into captivity into Babylon years before (Hos 14:3). Those in the diaspora who had formerly come to Zion for the feasts could no longer continue this practice. They would have to adapt to exile conditions.

But we are looking for the [city] which is to come. This was not an anticipation of an ascent into the heavenly "rapture." There is no necessity in understanding **the city which is to come** to be a **city,** to which Christians would "go" when they reached heaven, as Michel, Lane, Hughes, Attridge, Jewett, Rose, and others held.[1] A consensus of opinion does not guarantee accuracy of conclusion.

This represented the unceasing confidence of Zionists that this **city** would always be returned. Someday the Romans would be forced to leave the **city**, just as the Syrian Greeks were in the time of the Maccabees. Zion would be restored, and a tent would again be set up adjacent to the **altar**. This hope continued in Palestine until the **altar** was removed, probably after the Bar Cochba revolt.

15 *Let us bear a sacrifice of praise.* The two FT passages quoted here both use the imagery of sacrifice to speak of praise and confession. Like Amos and Isaiah, the psalmist insisted that God was not hungry and did not need the sacrifice of goats and bulls (Ps 50:12-13). Therefore, the believer should offer to God **a sacrifice of praise** (Ps 50:14). Hosea urged Israelites to confess their crimes while they rendered the fruit **of lips** (Hos 14:2), as Heb 13:15 repeated.

Whenever the temple was burned, defiled, or doctrinally rejected as a place where sacrifices might be offered effectively, believers could substitute only **a sacrifice of praise to God . . . , that is [the] fruit of lips which confess his name**. They could pray, read Scripture, sing Psalms, and do good works. The unknown author of the Community Rule (1QS 9:4-5) said, "**an offering of lips** (*teh-roo-máht shaf-táh-yeem*, תרומת שפתים) [**is considered**] **as a reckoning like a fragrant offering of righteousness**." The wise man was to bless the Lord with **an offering of lips** (1QS 9:26).[2] When R. Yohanan ben Zakkai and R. Joshua left Jerusalem after the temple had burned, R. Joshua said,

> Woe for us, because the place which atones for the iniquities of Israel has been destroyed!
>
> R. Yohanan comforted him: "We have one atonement that is like it, deeds of loving kindness, as it is said, **For I desired loving kindness and not sacrifice**," (Hos 6:6; AbothRN 7:30-34, 11a).

In a conjectured conversation between the Lord and Abraham concerning the way Israel could have its crimes removed so as not to be like the generation of the flood or that of the division of tongues, Abraham responded,

---

[1] Michel, *Hebräer,* p. 349. Lane, *Hebrews 9-13*, p. 547.

[2] The FT bases for rejecting blood sacrifice are reported in Amos 5:21 ff.; Hos 6:6; Mic 6:6-8; Isa 1:11 ff.; Jer 7:21-22; Pss 50:7 ff; 51:16-17.

> Master of the age, this is all right at a time when the temple is standing, [but] what will happen to them when the temple is not standing?

The Lord replied,

> I have already prepared for them a list of sacrificial [duties]. Whenever they read them, I will credit them as if they were offering sacrifices to me, and I will forgive all their iniquities (bMeg 31b).

Rabbis held that God said to Israel,

> Be strict [in your observance] in prayer, for there is no measure more acceptable than it; it is greater than all sacrifices (Tanh Wayera #1:24b).

The author of Heb 13:10-16 had an ancient tradition of the type of worship that was acceptable when there was no temple—a situation that did not exist when the author of Heb 1-12 wrote. This probably went back to the Babylonian captivity when Jews had to adjust to life without the temple. Since the author rejected the Jerusalem that then existed as a continuing city (Heb 13:14), Christians were left with the substitute means of pleasing God.

There was an early background for this concept of divine judgment in FT theology and in Canaanite mythology. In a setting where the chief god ruled in a court, part of his function was to judge human beings. Cases came up annually, and at death a final disposition was made. The traditions concerning the New Year and the Day of Atonement revolve around this understanding. At the turn of the year a preliminary verdict was given, and then after or on the Day of Atonement it was made final. In the period in between, people could pray, repent, and request intercession from the angel who served that function.

There were two main officers of the court, the prosecuting attorney or Satan and the defense attorney, who pleaded the case for people (Zech 3). The author of Hebrews urged Christians to behave as if the judgment had been made and they were still given the chance to offer **praise to God** and make confession in his name, hoping to have some influence on the final decision at a time when their consciences required them to leave the city of Jerusalem and find temporary exile elsewhere until the new Jerusalem should come and remain. Other parties to the contract also related confession to praise:

> For who is strong, O God, who does not confess you in truth?
> and what person is able [to do anything] who does not
> make confession in your name?
> [Sing] a new psalm with an ode with a joyful heart,
> a fruit of lips with [the] harmonious organ of [the] tongue,
> a first fruit of lips from a pious and just heart
> (PssSol 15:3-5).

Summary. Like other interpretations, this suggestion is also conjectural, but it has in its favor the facts that

1) it is liberated from distracting hypotheses;
2) it is related to a geographical and historical situation that actually existed;
3) it ties the text to the location where Jesus actually suffered and was crucified;[1]
4) it is a place where there actually was an altar, a Roman military camp, and at one time there was a temple where priests ministered;
5) it fits well into the historical situation in Zion after the crucifixion of Jesus, the burning of the temple, and before the desolation of Hadrian; and
6) it shows how a midrashic scholar used scriptural intertexts to interpret a local situation.

TEXT

17Comply with your leaders and be subject [to them], for they are vigilant in behalf of your souls as [those who must] give an account. [Submit] so that they may do this with joy and not groan, for this [groaning] is damaging to you.

18Pray for us, for we are convinced that we have a good conscience, desiring to behave properly in everything. 19I strongly urge you to do this, so that I may be restored to you quickly.

COMMENTARY

The Christians, however, to whom this writing applied **had an altar** that excluded from their feasts[2] **those who minister in the tent** that Herod built, and like the altar Moses erected, it was **away from the camp** (Exod 33:7). This was evidently an **altar** where beasts were slaughtered and cooked. People at one time ate there, but **those who ministered in the tent** at Herod's temple were no longer in charge. Those priests had been destroyed with the temple. **The altar** was still there, and, in the judgment of the author of this unit, it belonged to the people to whom this message was addressed. but neither Christians nor Jews would have been allowed to sacrifice there. Romans had complete control of that area.

12*Jesus also suffered outside the gate.* The author who interpreted this FT passage compared the sacrifice of Jesus to that of animals, noting some important differences. The sacrifice of animals took place inside **the camp** and the carcasses were carried out, whereas Jesus' body and blood were both kept **away from the camp**, since **Jesus . . . suffered outside the gate,** apparently **outside the gate** of Herod's city. This fact implied that since Jesus' atoning blood was shed **away from the camp**, it was done for the benefit of those **away from the camp**. Since **the camp** was probably Herod's fortress, Antonia, this meant that Jesus' sacrifice was for the advantage of Christians—away from the Roman fortress and city.

---

[1] E. Grässer, *Der Glaube im Hebräerbrief* (Marburg: N. G. Elwert, 1965) 3, pp. 82-91, held that the reference to Jesus here was made only as a basis for formulating doctrine, but this small unit is not a particularly doctrinal text.

[2] So also H. Koester, "'Outside the Camp' Hebrews 13:9-14," *HTR* 55 (1962):313.

Dead bodies defile; sacrificial blood atones. For this reason the Pentateuchal rules had the blood poured on the altar to sanctify but the carcass taken out so as to remove all defilement from **the camp.** In the case of Jesus, the blood was shed outside the military camp and never brought in. Therefore it would not cleanse the people inside Herod's Roman city, but it would **sanctify the people** who were outside the city. Of course, Jesus' body was also taken outside **the camp,** but the author overlooked its liturgical potential for defilement. Rhetoricians use only those parts of the law that are beneficial.

The people who listened to the sermon (Heb 1-12) were gathered at Zion, which the author held to be **the city of the God of life, heavenly Jerusalem,** but the message of Heb 13 was addressed to people outside the gate of the Roman military camp, perhaps somewhere in the diaspora where most of the Christians were at the time Heb 13 was written. H. Koester correctly noticed the contrast between the command of Leviticus and the counsel of Heb 13 on the subject of sacrifice and **the camp.**[1] This does not mean that there was no longer any sanctification. It was the location that was most important. Jesus' sanctification took place **outside of the camp** rather than inside the city.

The point of the difference was the location of the atoning blood (Lev 16:27). The counsel of this author toward Zion seemed quite different from the author of Heb 1-12. That author thought of Zion as **the heavenly city, the city of the God of life, the place where myriads of angels gathered**. It was the mount where Jesus introduced a new contract. The author of Heb 13, however, contrasted the Roman camp at Jerusalem with the area outside the Roman camp, because the Roman Camp (Antonia) was the place that could not benefit from Jesus' sacrifice.

The author of Heb 1-12 also lived at a time when the hopes of restoration were high in Israel. The author or editor who prepared Heb 13 wrote probably after 70 IA, after the temple had been destroyed but before the Bar Cochba Revolt had failed (135 IA), and the City of David had been swept to remove the gold there may have been in the temple. By then, even the altar would have been destroyed. The only hope for Christianity was in the diaspora and other parts of Palestine.

Like the author of the sermon, however, the author or editor of Heb 13 may also have been hostile only to Herod's Jerusalem, and not to Zion. **Outside the camp** may have meant specifically **outside** Herod's walled-in city. If so he would have agreed with the author of the sermon on that one point.

The monastery in Zion was probably destroyed when the temple was burned in 70 IA. Some members of that monastery probably escaped and preserved that sermon for posterity. If Zionist monks were still alive when chapter 13 was written they probably had the same feeling as the authors of Heb 13 about the desolation of Zion. They lamented the destruction of the monastery and the holy city, but they may have had mixed feelings about the destruction of Herod's temple, **made with hands.** Both groups still had an altar, and they looked forward to the restoration of Zion and a new temple **not made with hands**. If the Romans had been driven out of the land and the temple had not been burned, Herod's temple might have been cleansed in ways that suited the faithful and have become a temple **not made with hands**.

The Jerusalem which was to come down from heaven, **the city which [was] to come**, was the cleansed city, the holy city, **Zion city of our God.** That was to be the **continuing city**. After 70 IA Herod's Roman camp was all that was left of the

[1] Koester, "'Outside," p. 300.

city. It looked as if Zion had no future, but in the judgment of the faithful it was Herod's city that had no future. Like the Syrian citadel at the time of the Hasmonean Simon, someday the Roman camp would be razed to the ground. This was part of God's plan. Like many faithful Jews and Christians believed, God had planned Herod's temple to be destroyed (Matt 24:1-3; Mark 13:1-2, 24-27; Luke 21:5-6, 25-28; John 2:19). Christians were advised **to go out from the camp.** Although they had no continuing city at the time of the writing, they had not lost hope of Zion ever being restored. There is no mention of their eagerness to get to heaven, as Michel, Lane, Hughes, Attridge, Jewett, Rose, Koester, and others held.[1] A consensus of opinion does not guarantee accuracy of conclusion.

16*Do not forget good works and common [fellowship].* It was **such sacrifices [as these**] which **pleased** God: praise, confession, **good works**, **common [fellowship]** or community worship, and reading the Scripture. When it was not possible to sacrifice at Mount Zion, God would still accept these as if they were offerings made in the temple.

SUMMARY

Heb 13:10-16 seems to comprise a separate unit of literature that the editor of Heb 13 collected together with other materials to compose this chapter. It includes many terms employed by the author of Heb 1:1-12:29, such as **minister** (Heb 13:10), **tent** (Heb 13:10), **blood** (Heb 13:11), **temple** (Heb 13:11), **crime** (Heb 13:11), **high priest** (Heb 13:11), **insult** (Heb 13:13), **city** (Heb 13:14), **sacrifice** (Heb 13:15), and **confess** (Heb 13:15). Lane argued that these word similarities proved that the authorship of Heb 13 was the same as Heb 1-12,[2] but that does not follow. The author of this chapter wanted it to sound as if it were a part of the same message, so that the entire document would be accepted in the canon as apostolic, so he intentionally used some of the same words. The most of those words are confined to this one unit of Heb 13. Furthermore, the methods of exegesis in both sections are similar, but they were also both similar to other Jewish and Christian interpretation of sacred texts. Exegesis is not a deciding factor, but the point of view of Heb 13 is different from the sermon of Heb 1-12, reflecting different groups of Christians at different times and places.

The Jerusalem which the author of Heb 1:1-12:29 considered the city which **had the foundations**, Mount Zion, and the **city of God** was thought by the author of chapter 13 to be in such a miserable condition that Christians had to leave. They looked forward to a continuing city, there in Zion, sometime in the future, but until that city should come, they must live in exile, observing the religious duties that were possible without a temple. The general tone of Heb 13 reflects a Jerusalem with only a Roman camp and an altar. After 70 IA the camp was an insult, and the altar was not available for use.

---

[1] O. Michel, *Der Brief an die Hebräer* (Göttingen: Vandenhoeck & Ruprecht, 1957), p. 349.Lane, *Hebrews 9-13*, p. 547.

[2] W. L. Lane, *Hebrews 1-8* (Dallas: Word Books, c1991), p. lxvii, admitted that Heb 1-12 is a sermon, intended for oral delivery, and that chapter thirteen is distinguished from the first 12 chapters in coherence, form, and content. Nevertheless he thought Heb 13 was a postscript written by the same author (pp. lxvi-lxxv).

[17]*Comply with your leaders*. The admonition in behalf of leaders is one leaders had to make frequently. The case made here was that the responsibility of the leaders was great. They were responsible for watching over the **souls** of all those under their supervision. They had to **give an account** to God and to their superior officers concerning the spiritual and, in the case of communal communities, material and physical welfare of the people under their jurisdiction. Since the leaders were responsible for the outcome, it seemed reasonable to allow them to be the ones who decided how things would be done. In so doing, however, they were obliged to enforce **discipline** and call attention to members' faults so that they might correct them and maintain **perfection** in the community (Matt 18:15-17).

Some members may not have liked this fault finding and may not have been willing to **comply with** their **leaders and be subject** at every point. This kind of insubordinate behavior made the leaders **groan** while carrying out their necessary obligations. This irritation not only prevented the leaders from enjoying their work, but it was also **damaging** to the rest of the group. If this had been a monastic group, like the one addressed by the author of Heb 1-12, the leader in charge could have had the complainers dismissed.

[18-19]*We have a good conscience*. The author of these notes urged the readers to **pray for us**, probably meaning that they should pray for the leaders mentioned above of whom he was one. He further assured them of the sincerity and intended good character of the leaders. No such note of self defense appeared in Heb 1-12.

The words **behavior** (*ahn-ahs-traw-pháys*, ἀναστροφῆς) and **leaders** at the beginning of this unit (Heb 13:7) and **leaders** (Heb 13:17) and **behave** (*ah-nah-stréh-phehs-thai*, ἀναστρέφεσθαι) (Heb 13:18) at the conclusion form an inclusion typical also of the author of Heb 1:1-12:29. In between is a doctrinal discussion about the sacrifice of Jesus and contemporary worship and witness (Heb 13:10-16), a small confession (Heb 13:8), practical advice about behavior in relationship to leaders (Heb 13:7, 17-19), and warnings against heretics (Heb 13:9). This is a scissors-and-paste composition of collected bits of literature, that changed from first person pronouns to second person pronouns. Admonitions from Heb 13:7 to 13:9 are directed in the second person plural: **remember your leaders** (Heb 13:7); **do not be carried away by means of various and strange teachings** (Heb 13:9). Then the shift is made to first person plural: **we have an altar** (Heb 13:10); **let us go out to him** (Heb 13:13); **we do not have here a continuing city, but we are looking** (Heb 13:14); **let us bear a sacrifice of praise to God** (Heb 13:15). With Heb 13:16, however, the subject returns to the second person plural: **do not forget**, and Heb 13:19 is in first person singular. This suggests the work of an editor who used sources.

Benediction

TEXT

Hebrews	First Testament
	[Ezek 37:24]My servant David will be king over them. One **shepherd** will be over all of them.

13:20 May the God of **peace,**	Ezek 37:26 I will make with them **a contract of peace, a contract of the age** it will be for them.
who led up from [the] dead ones **the** great **shepherd of the sheep,**	LXX Isa 63:11 The one **who brought up from the** land [of Egypt, Moses], **the shepherd of the sheep**.
through **the blood of the** **contract of the age,** our Lord Jesus, 21 **make you** fit in every good thing to do his will, doing	Exod 24:8 Moses took **the blood** and threw it on the people, and said, "Look! This is **the blood of the contract** which Yehowah **made** with **you.**" Zech 9:11 Also you, **through the blood of** your **contract**, I have sent your prisoners from the waterless pit.
in your **midst** that which is well-pleasing before him, through Jesus Christ, to whom be **glory** **for the ages** of the ages. Amen	LXX Isa 63:12 Where is the one who placed **in** their **midst** the Holy Spirit? **who led** by the right hand, Moses? His **glorious** arm over-powered the water before him, to make for him a name **of the age**?

TECHNICAL DETAILS

Notice the text on which the author of this benediction based his composition. Heb 13:20-21 is a small narrative midrash in which the author selected words and phrases from 2Isa, Zech, and Ezek to attribute to Jesus the attributes that had previously been applied to Moses and David. Benedictions like this were not composed on the spur of the moment. The author found references that called both David and Moses **shepherds** and attributed this office to Jesus, working in other words from the text into his own benediction.

COMMENTARY

20 *May the God of peace.* **Peace** is related to being "paid up" in Hebrew. In a treasury of merits system, those who had atoned for all their crimes had paid the fines for all their iniquities. Their books balanced; their accounts were reconciled; so they had **peace** with God. Their debts of crime had been paid in full. **The God of peace** (also Rom 15:33) was the one who made **peace** by forgiving or canceling crimes so that there was no barrier of crime between himself and his people. When that was the case he could send them out free from the waterless pit where they had been imprisoned. A waterless pit was a dry well dug in the blistering desert that contained no water. Second Maccabees paraphrased the benediction in Num 6:24-26 thus:

> *And make peace*. May he pay attention to your supplications and become reconciled to you and not give you up in an evil time (2Macc 1:4-5).[1]

The ascription to the deity includes some scriptural passages put together in such a way as to express the liturgist's desires.

Some words came from the LXX version of Isa 63:11, referring to God who led the Israelites from Egypt through the sea. According to the MT: **where is he who brought up from the [Red] Sea the shepherds of his flock**? The LXX has: . . . **who brought up** (*ah-nah-bee-báh-sahs*) **from the land [of Egypt] the shepherd of the sheep**. Heb 13:20 has for **who led up**, *haw ah-nah-gah-góhn* (ὁ ἀναγαγῶν) rather than *ho ah-nah-bee-báh-sahs* as the LXX has, but its author agreed with the LXX in making **shepherd** singular.

The next ascriptions related Jesus to the deliverance from Babylon: **Also you through [the] blood of [the] contract have sent out your captives from the waterless pit** (Zech 9:11). From another text on **redemption**, the liturgist took the term **of the age** (Ezek 37:26) to modify the **contract** mentioned in Zech 9:11.

The dead ones mentioned were not those who had been buried in the ground. They were the non-Israelite Egyptians and Babylonians, from whom the great shepherds of the Israelite flock led their people into Palestine. Those who were baptized into life were Jews, Samaritans, or Christians. Palestine was the land of life, and all members of the contract were alive. When Jesus said they should let the "dead" bury their "dead," he was not speaking of corpses doing the grave digging.

The party to the contract who composed this benediction did not use FT phrases "quite apart from their original setting" as Moffatt says.[2] He intentionally alluded to passages referring to God's deliverances of Israel and provision of the **contract**. When Moses made the first **contract** with the Israelites, he assigned young men to make **peace offerings** of beef. He took half of the blood from these cattle and threw it against the altar. The other half he sprinkled on the people of Israel. Through this liturgy he completed a **contract** between the people and Yehowah, represented by the altar (Exod 24:4-8).

The author attributed the ascriptions to the deity to whom he made his request. He was the God who led the Israelites both up from Egypt and from Babylon. To be sure, the author understood **the great shepherd** to be Jesus rather than Moses, because he had a later **redemption** in mind. He also considered **the contract of the age** to be the **contract** belonging to **the age** of **our Lord Jesus.** The editor who added this benediction to the discussion on leaders may have intended to relate the leaders with whom the readers were expected to comply (Heb 13:17) to Jesus, **the great shepherd**.

The author of this passage may have believed in the resurrection of the bodies of Christians, but he did not mention it in these few verses. Twenty-first century readers should not expect all of their beliefs to be expressed in every passage of Scripture. The sermon of Heb 1-12 was only one address, concentrating primarily on one topic. He did not attempt to give a systematic theology report. The Paulinist of Heb 13 was also under no obligation to say more than he did.

---

[1] Buchanan, *Consequences*, pp. 237-240.

[2] J. Moffatt, *A Critical and Exegetical Commentary on the Epistle to the Hebrews* (Edinburgh: T. & T. Clark, 1924), p. 242.

[21]*That which is well-pleasing before him.* The editor may also have wished to remind the readers that the leaders were vigilant in behalf of the members' **souls** by offering a prayer that the parties to the **contract** be made **fit in every good thing to do his will, doing in your midst that which is well-pleasing before him**. The benediction was concluded according to the counsel given earlier, with lips which confess his name (Heb 13:15), that is **through Jesus Christ to whom be glory for the ages of the ages. Amen**. **Confessing** through Jesus meant that they sent their **confession** to the principal, God, through his legal agent, **Jesus Christ**. **The ages** involved were probably intended to be related to **the ages** of Moses and David, but these **the ages** were **ages** of the future in which **Jesus** would be **glorified.** This conclusion is similar to other NT ascriptions:

> My God will fulfill all of your needs according to his wealth in glory in Christ Jesus. To our God and Father be glory into the ages of ages. Amen (Philip 4:19-20).
>
> To the one who loves us and released us from our crimes through his blood and made us a kingdom, priests to God and his Father, to him be **glory** and power for **the ages of the ages. Amen**. (Rev 1:6).
>
> Grace to you and peace from God our Father and [the] Lord **Jesus Christ**, who gave himself for our crimes, so that he might deliver us from the present evil **age**, according to the will of our God and Father, to whom be **glory** for **the ages of the ages. Amen** (Gal 1:3-5).
>
> . . . in order that God might be glorified in everything, through **Jesus Christ**, to whom is **glory** and power for **the ages of the ages. Amen** (1Peter 4:11).
>
> . . . and increase in grace and knowledge of our Lord and Savior **Jesus Christ**. To him be **glory** both now and to [the] the day of **[the] age. Amen** (2Peter 3:18).

The word **glory** (Greek *dáwx-ah*, δόξα--Hebrew *kah-vóhd*, כבוד) primarily means "weight" in Hebrew. Since a man of substance and wealth would have the external appearance of a man weighted down with wealth, his wealth demanded respect, dignity, and honor from his contemporaries, and this position of respect was called **glory. Glory**, then, included the meanings of weight, substance, wealth, power, splendor, dignity and good reputation, such attributes as would be given a king or a messiah. This **glory** was to be his **for the ages of the ages**, usually rendered "for-ever and ever." An age was a period of time, temporally; it usually meant a genera-tion or a Jubilee--about 50 years--but ages changed whenever administrations or fortunes changed, so they were not all the same length. This means for all of the best of **the ages** of the future.

A standard greeting for kings in antiquity was **King, live for ages** (Dan 2:4; 3:9; 5:10; 6:6-21), wishing that the king would live more than the expected time of one generation.[1] This was the same kind of hyperbolic prayer which prayed that

[1] Buchanan, *Consequences*, pp. 15-18.

Jesus, as the established king, be given **glory** that would continue one generation after the other, or **for ages of the ages**—the best of the **ages**.

Amen was a term used in taking oaths to affirm that the conditions were accepted or the things said were true (Num 5:16-22). Today, when the clerk of court asks a witness, "Do you hereby swear to tell the truth, the whole truth, and nothing but the truth?" The witness normally answers, "I do." In antiquity the witness would answer, "Amen." When a leader of the congregation offered a prayer to which members agreed, they responded with, **Amen!** This meant they wanted credit for having said that prayer themselves. Rabbis said when the leader was an Israelite (i.e., a Jew) the congregation should say **Amen** after each benediction, but if he was a Samaritan, they must wait until the whole benediction was completed to be sure he did not add something that would be contrary to the faith of Jews (mBer 8:8). Paul criticized those who prayed in the Spirit (i.e., in "tongues"), because those who were not able to understand the speech would not know when to say the **Amen** for the prayer (1Cor 14:16). The prayer might be one that was a standard part of the liturgy; the **Amen** was the worshipers' personal approval of the request.

Grässer held that this concluded the document. Up to this point Heb 13 was a genuine part of the entire document. All of Hebrews from 1-13:21 was composed by the same author, who was not Paul, in his judgment. Even though he claimed this, he acknowledged many radical differences between Heb 1-12 and Heb 13 that prompted scholars to consider Heb 13 to be a later addition made by at least one different author.

Summary. The benediction included in these verses was probably a standard liturgical expression. It was well formulated, ascribing to God attributes from the FT that were related to his deliverance of Israel from Egypt and Babylon. To these acts of deliverance was added the deliverance brought about through the **blood of Jesus** who instituted the new **contract.** The prayer was that this God who had delivered Israel in the past would now enable the readers to do his will.

Parting Postscript

TEXT

22Now I exhort you, brothers, accept the word of exhortation [given above], for I
have sent [it] to you by a few [words of my own]. 23Be informed that our brother
Timothy has been released, with whom, if he comes quickly, I shall see you. 24Greet
all your leaders and all the saints. Those from Italy greet you. 25Grace be with you
all!

COMMENTARY

22 *Now I exhort you.* The pronouns are here changing from the unified "we" to the dominant "I." Heb 13 begins giving orders and commands to the addressees. Then, in Heb 13:9-15 the conversation changes to "we" and "us." Heb 13:16-17 consist of further orders. Heb 13:18 is a return to "us" and "we." Heb 13:20-21 is a benediction directed to God, and Heb 13:22-24 is a further exhortation between "I" and "you." This many shifts in this small unit suggests more authors than one.

Accept the word of exhortation [given above]. If Heb 13 existed all by itself, then these words would apply to it. It appears, however, that it was originally written to accompany Heb 1:1-12:29. The **word of exhortation** which Paul delivered to the synagogue at Pisidian Antioch was a sermon (Acts 13:15), just as Heb 1-12 is a sermon. Therefore, t**he word of exhortation** (*tays pah-rah-kláy-seh-ohs*, παρα-κλήσεως) which the final editor employed to **exhort** (*pah-rah-kah-lóh*, παρα-καλῶ) his **brothers** was probably the main document (Heb 1:1-12:29), to which the author and editor of Heb 13 added **a few [words]** (*dee-yah brah-khéh-ohn*, δία βρακέων) of his own. These included such poetic exhortations as Heb 13:1, 3, 4a and 5a, a confession of faith (Heb 13:8), a post 70 IA midrash (Heb 13:10-16), and a benediction (Heb 13:20-21). To these items he added his own exhortations, interpretations, expansions, and connecting sentences to complete Heb 13. Heb 13:22 seems to be a statement recommending to the readers Heb 1:1-12:29 plus the items collected in Heb 13.

This reminds readers of the similar recommendation in Rev 22:6-7, urging the readers to consider seriously the document included in Rev 4:1-22:5: **These words are faithful and true. . . . Blessed is he who keeps the words of the prophecy of this book.** It is not likely that the same author who had said earlier that his message on one point alone was **extensive** (Heb 5:11) should later refer to the entire document as brief. The items added in Heb 13 are **few** as the author says, and it seems reasonable to believe that it was to these that his reference was made. Stuart asked many years ago,

> But how . . . could Paul say this, when this epistle is longer than any one of his, that to the Romans, and the first to the Corinthians, excepted?[1]

Even if Paul is not considered the author, it does not seem reasonable for any one author to write of the whole message of **The Book of Hebrews** as if it were only something briefly said. Westcott excused the reference by saying, ". . . that is, relatively to the vastness of the subject," but even that is not valid, because the author covered the material very thoroughly, frequently repeating for effectiveness.[2]

Moffatt said the author was probably referring to his brief words rather apologetically, realizing that they were really quite extensive and might have aroused some resentment because of the length of the message. Then, justifying the author from the opposite direction, Moffatt said, "*Pros Hebraious* may be read aloud easily in one hour."[3] These arguments assumed that the comment was made by the author himself, even though Moffatt had earlier said the main document ended with Heb 12:29![4] Bruce followed Moffatt basically, reversing the implications of the data that puzzled Stuart, saying that the document was not so long as Rom or 1Cor, and concluded,

---

1. M. Stuart, *Commentary on the Epistle to the Hebrews in Greek and English* (Andover: Warren F. Draper, 1828), pp. 309-10.

2 B. F. Westcott, *The Epistle to the Hebrews* (London: Macmillan and Co., 1892), p. 451.

3 Moffatt, *Hebrews*, p. 244.

4 Moffatt, *Hebrews*, pp. 224-245, was inconsistent. He also held (p. xxvii-xxx) that the whole document was written by one author.

> There is no need to suppose that the "word of exhortation" might be confined to the concluding admonitions of Ch. 13:1-19; they are so brief that no writer would think it necessary to ask his readers to bear with them.

Michel believed the statement was made as an indication that the author had actually and deliberately limited himself, even though the document was long.[1] These authors have had to develop a number of different explanations for the comment about brevity, because it really does not make sense as a reference to Heb 1-12. Their explanations all belong to the classification of "special pleading." In dealing with indefinite matters such as these, complete agreement is seldom reached, but the simplest and most obvious interpretation is to assume that Heb 13 was written by a different author from the first 12 chapters and that the final author's reference to brevity was accurately made to describe his own additions.

23 *Timothy has been released.* This is the first indication in the entire document that this document is a letter and that this document is being communicated in writing to anyone. All of Heb 1:1-12:29 refers to communication in terms of speaking. Timothy was named here to lead the reader into thinking that the author was Paul, and Timothy was one of his assistants.

24 *Greet all your leaders and all the saints.* The personal reference to Timothy and the author's proposed visit and greeting were added to give this the appearance of a Pauline letter, even though the theology and style of Hebrews 1:1-12:29 are certainly not Pauline. The **leaders and all the saints** of the community may or may not have been the same people. The **leaders** were among the ones with whom the readers were exhorted to comply (Heb 13:7, 17). **The saints** originally referred to the holy ones who were separated from defiled people, according to Levitical purity rules to maintain Levitical cleanliness. These **saints** were the soldiers, separated from women and children while at war to keep the camp holy, or the priests, who kept themselves free from defilement to minister at the tent of meeting or the temple. After the temple was destroyed, and there was no longer a specific place that was kept holy for the Lord to dwell, the hearth was substituted for the altar, and the believers were substituted for the priests. The priesthood of all believers took place when laymen undertook the responsibility of keeping themselves as Levitically pure as priests and their homes as free from defilement as the temple.

The believers, then, were also **saints.** By NT times, this term evidently was extended in meaning in some circles to include all believers, even if they did not keep all the Levitical rules (Rom 1:7; 1Cor 1:2). It is not clear in Heb 13:24 what limitations were required in the editor's definition, but the term was confined in the Book of Hebrews to Heb 13. The author of Heb 1-12 referred to his audience as **Brothers**. but not **saints.**

Those from Italy. **Italy** may have been the residence of the final editor as well as that of the committee that compiled the canon, but it says nothing about the place of origin of Heb 1-12. The location may have been fabricated to give the letter the appearance of originality. Most scholars who claim that Heb 13 is an integral part of the entire document also believe that Paul wrote the entire document from Rome,

---

[1] Michel, *Hebrews,* p. 366.

perhaps in or for some house church there. There is almost no internal evidence for this judgment. None of Paul's letters was written from Rome, and there is no assurance that he was ever in Rome. As Grässer said, this entire greeting, which was deliberately written as if Paul was responsible, is fiction, falsified to get the document accepted into the canon. It may also have been added to make the document more general, applying not only to Jewish Christian monks but also to others as well, including married people and those in the diaspora. Grässer doubted that Hebrews could have been admitted into the canon without chapter 13.[1] Many Christians failed to agree with the conclusion that this document was Pauline, as late as the fourth century IA. Other attempts to Paulinize the Jewish Christian document of Heb 1-12 were to include some anti-Jewish attacks and emphasize the importance of Grace, in contrast to food regulations.

25*Grace be with you all.* The prayer for **grace** was frequently used in complimentary closes and is a prayer needed by all authors, editors, and readers. Amen.

Summary. John Knox has made an impressive case for believing that Marcion's canon was the first NT canon and that it forced other Christians to establish a canon that was not Marcion's and to begin to establish an orthodoxy among all the various Christian beliefs held up to that time.[2] Marcion was such a strong Christian leader in the second century that he could not be ignored. Anti-Marcionites had two alternatives if they were unwilling to accept Marcion's canon:

> a)They could have declared his works heretical and opposed their use in churches. This would not have been very successful, and it would have opposed teachings presented in Paul's ten letters and the Gospel according to Luke that most Christians treasured.
> b)The second alternative seems to have been the one employed: they followed Marcion's canon as a basis, but neutralized it by extending it in size.

Marcion's canon contained the writings of the apostle Paul, which were all letters, and the Gospel of Luke. This set a strange pattern of literary forms to follow, but the later church seems to have followed it. It added to the Gospel of Luke three other gospels, and to the epistles of the apostle Paul other epistles of other apostles, with the Acts of the Apostles as a unifying factor. In this way the committee on canon could present a more balanced representation of Christian views and literature, but it is not likely that all of the best literature had been composed originally in gospel and epistle form. Therefore, the committee had to adapt otherwise useful and acceptable writings to the required literary form. Since the church lacked unity, there may have been more than one committee on canon. Some books, like Hebrews, were late in being admitted by some churches. Knox believed that Luke was expanded from Marcion's document to include some pro-Jewish material Marcion would have opposed.

The Fourth Gospel probably originated as a historical prophecy that pictured John the Baptist and Jesus as the new Elijah and Elisha but was edited so as to abbreviate the document and add an introduction and conclusion to make it appear

---

[1] Grässer, *An die Hebräer*, 1, p. 22; 3, pp. 413, 416.
[2] J. Knox, *Marcion and the New Testament* (Chicago: U. of Chicago Press, 1942).

to be the same kind of document as the Synoptic Gospels.[1] Some documents which were needed to represent various branches of Christianity may have been composed in the form of letters at the time the canon was being decided. Other important literature, like confessions of faith and brief catechisms, may have been added to some portions of letters that had been composed previously. Other more extensive documents that were complete units and too large to be included as only a part of another document were given introductions or conclusions to make them have the forms of letters.

"The Book of Hebrews" and the Epistle of James originally seem to have been examples of a type of Christian wisdom literature and were used as such by Clement of Alexandria and Irenaeus. To James was added an introduction (James 1:1), and to The Book of Hebrews was added this conclusion, to make both documents appear to be letters and thus qualify for the canon. The introduction to Hebrews was so integral to the entire message (Heb 1:1-12:29) that it would have been impossible to replace it with an epistolary salutation or to have a separate salutation prefixed to the present introduction without seeming very awkward and artificial. Therefore the best alternative was to add a complimentary closing and let the introduction stand.

The homily section of Heb 1-12 was used at the end of the first century by Clement of Rome who thought Paul wrote it, but not included in the Muratorian list at the end of the second century. The church at Rome first accepted it as Pauline in the middle of the fourth century. Either Heb 13 was added very late as the necessary requirement for inclusion in the canon, or the person who added it to the homily with the "Pauline" conclusion did not at first succeed in convincing all of the churches of its genuineness. Because the author was not an eye witness of Jesus (Heb 2:3) the document could not have been accepted as apostolic from any apostle other than Paul. If Heb 13:22-25 had not been added, Hebrews may never have been admitted into the canon.

All attempts to reconstruct the literary forms of NT documents before the formation of the canon are necessarily conjectural. The evidence is not sufficient to know precisely what the sources were or how they were changed to fit the canon. Scholars have recognized for many years, however, that the epistolary character of some NT documents, like Hebrews, was artificial and forced. The literary forms now in the NT canon seem to be a strange basis for a religious literary canon. Religious literature coming from a Jewish sect might be expected to consist of psalms, laws, history, wisdom literature and prophecy. The fact that the canon that was accepted was quite different from normal expectations requires some explanation, such as the Marcion movement which Knox has proposed.

Marcion had evidently been a strong Pauline Christian leader for many years before the Bar Cochba Revolt of 132-35 IA. It was probably the bloody militarism of that revolt that aroused Marcion's anti-Jewish convictions. He held that the Christian God was a God of love and not a God of war, as the Jewish God was. All Jewish literature, including the FT, should be dismissed as Jewish and a new canon established for Christians that had none of that Jewish militarism. Although Marcion gathered a strong following, he did not represent all Christendom at that time. The pro-Jewish forces in Christianity were strong enough in Rome, at least, to force his excommunication in 144 IA, but the very forces that excommunicated

[1] Buchanan, "The Samaritan Origin of the Gospel of John," in *Religions in Antiquity* ed. J. Neusner (Leiden: E. J. Brill, 1968), pp. 149-75.

Marcion were obligated to displace his canon or assimilate it into a larger canon that included such Jewish documents as Matthew, James, and Hebrews, as well as such military, holy war prophecies as the Book of Revelation.

The Book of Hebrews was Jewish Christian, but not Jewish. It argued that Christianity was the fulfillment of the contract God made with Abraham—not Judaism. The Jewish priesthood had been replaced by Jesus. Jewish sacrifices were ineffective. The new contract had displaced the old contract. It came from a branch of Christianity that took Jewish Scripture and traditions for granted and interpreted the death of Christ in relationship to them.

Sometime in the process of forming that canon, a member of the committee may either have added only this Pauline postscript to Hebrews or have created the entire thirteenth chapter, using some undatable poetry, midrash, and confessions of faith that had already been composed as well as some pre-135 IA doctrinal material (Heb 13:10-16) and exhortations, to which he added a few comments of his own plus an epistolary conclusion.

This conjectural reconstruction of Heb 13's formation may not be accurate, but it is not possible to deal in certainties with literary problems such as these. If this was not done by an unknown committee member, it was done by some other church leader who wanted the document preserved in Heb 1:1-12:29 included in the canon. It was not fully included in the canon for the whole church until the fourth century, after the time of Constantine. It may have been the relationship between the promises of the sermon and the later fulfillment with the victory of Constantine that assured its place in the canon. Eusebius interpreted the destruction of Maxentius at the bridge as the new exodus from Egypt, and the drowning of Maxentius' troops as the destruction of the new Egyptians. The reestablishment of the church was compared to the construction of Solomon's temple. The good news offered to the Israelites who were delivered at the sea was finally received by the Christians in Rome.

Even after Hebrews had been accepted by the church at Rome, Hebrews continued to have scholars that doubted that it was an authentic letter of Paul. One of these was the classical 16th century scholar, Erasmus. He was followed by many 20th century scholars.

Heb 13:10-16 deals with Jerusalem. It is not an anti-Zionist document, but it was written at a different time under different conditions in relationship to Zion than was true of Heb 1:1-12:29. At that later time Jerusalem was *not* the city having **the foundations, whose builder and constructor was God** (Heb 11:10). Titus had pulled down the eastern wall allowing the rocks between the wall and the ridge to roll down into the Kidron Valley, removing the constructed foundation of that part of the city. Since Jesus suffered outside the gate, **here [at Jerusalem]** we do not have **a continuing city, but we are looking for the [city] which is to come**. The **city** that was **to come** may have been the new Jerusalem**, the holy city . . . coming down out of heaven from God** (Rev 21:10), the new Zion, but it was no place then for Christians to remain.

CONCLUSIONS

KIND OF DOCUMENT

The Book of Hebrews consists of two basic documents. The first twelve chapters were not composed by the same author, at the same time, in the same style, or for the same purpose. The last chapter of Hebrews is distinguished from the first twelve chapters. It was not written by the same author at the same time, in the same style or for the same purpose as the first twelve chapters. It will be discussed independently in each of the following categories.

The first twelve chapters of Hebrews constitute a complete homiletical midrash, similar to those in *Pesikta Rabatti* and *Pesikta de Rav Kahana.* Each of those titles is a collection of sermons to be delivered on feast days. A piska was a discourse on a biblical lesson that was delivered either on Sabbaths or on feast days. The plural of piska is pesikta. Pesikta were constructed much like other sermons, homiletical midrashim, or legal arguments addressed to judges or juries in court.

Heb 1-12 begins, ends, and argues like a sermon or legal argument rather than a letter and has been considered here as a homily rather than a letter. This homily is based on Ps 110, closely supported by Ps 2, although the author employed many other passages of Scripture throughout the document. Heb 1:4 introduced the text, inviting the son to **sit** at God's **right hand**. At the end of the chapter appeared again the verse **Sit at my right hand until I put your enemies as a footstool for your feet** (Ps 110:1; Heb 1:13), forming an inclusion. An inclusion is a literary form in which the introduction and conclusion function as the slices of bread in a sandwich, including the message of the unit in between. The repetition of certain words or phrases remind the reader that this forms the border line of the unit. The same two psalms (Pss 2; 110) appear again in Heb 5:5-6 to introduce the important theme of Jesus as the great priest belonging to the order of Melchizedek which continued throughout Heb 7. Ps 110:4 was explicitly mentioned in Heb 5:6, 10; 6:20; 7:11, 15, 21, 28. It was further repeated in various forms in Heb 8:1; 10:12-13; and 12:2). The author wove this text throughout this sermon, holding it all together by this one text.

Nearly every scholar of the Book of Hebrews has recognized a significant break between the conclusion of Heb 12 and the beginning of Heb 13. Some interpret this difference by calling Heb 13 an appendix or postscript added to a logical argument of some kind. It is more than likely a forgery added later to a sermon in Paul's name for the purpose of gaining apostolic authority for a document not written by an apostle. It also was added to generalize the document. The sermon was directed specifically to monks and was clearly Jewish Christian. Chapter 13 expanded the document to include married people and Christians of the diaspora.

The canon of the Bible was held to be the word of God. That could be true only if all of the authors whose works it contained were legitimate legal agents of God--officials such as apostles, prophets, or kings. A legal agent was legally identical with the principal he or she represented. This means that the words of an apostle of God were the same as the words of God himself. Since Jesus was the Messiah and *ex officio* God's legal agent, his words were held to be identical to God's words. Because his twelve apostles were his legal agents, they also spoke God's words. Within these legal limits those committees who decided what should and what should not be included in the canon of the NT had to check carefully to learn whether or not these materials had been uttered by authentic apostles.

Marcion had argued that all Jewish works were false and that the only legitimate works were the ten letters of Paul and the Gospel of Luke, minus the noticeably Jewish portions (Luke 1-3, 15, etc.). Tertullian, who had been a lawyer before becoming a Christian, said Marcion's Christ was false, because the principal had not acknowledged him as a legal agent before he claimed authority. That was because Marcion denied the validity of the FT and therefore had no sources to prophesy the coming of the Messiah. Since God's word was expressed through the Scriptures, the prophecies in the Scripture were God's approving statements that would have approved the Messiah. Therefore this basis was necessary for the admission of any messiah. These concepts were vital to the admission of Hebrews into the apostolic canon.

There are some scholars, like H. Koester[1] and Donfried[2] who object to the designations "homily" and "sermon," holding that these titles are too vague and ambiguous for scholarly discussion. They have not been defined in antiquity and therefore should not be used to describe a body of literature. Scholars have also complained about the imprecise character of concepts like "midrash" to enable them to evade the problem of recognizing the existence of midrashim in the Bible. These phenomena, however, exist, no matter what names they are called. They are more general than some other bodies of literature, such as letters, chreias, or sonnets that can easily be identified.

Most people know what a sermon is, and they know that not all sermons are delivered in exactly the same style or form. That which Jews and Christians call a sermon or piska is nearly the same as that which lawyers call a legal argument. The difference was only the audience. One was delivered in court and the other to a church or synagogue. Sometimes, however, court was held in a synagogue or a church. In many places in antiquity there was no separation between government and religious authority. The chief leader in either case was the king. He was in charge both of religion and law. Early architecture of churches was very similar to early courts. There was a great deal of similarity in liturgy and rhetoric of churches and courts.

Both lawyers and scholars exegete texts. If a skillful lawyer prepared a good argument based on legal texts, his or her argument would be very similar in form, style, and purpose to the sermon prepared by a skillful biblical exegete. Both are messages of exhortation, and the arguments in both are based on earlier legal texts.

In a legal argument, the attorney gives alternately data, fact, law, and exhorttation to the judge or jury. The preacher also gives alternately data, fact, Scripture, and exhortation. The author of Heb 1-12 did the same. Vanhoye noted that the first part (Heb 1:5-2:18) is doctrinal, and includes an exhortation in only Heb 2:1-4. The second part (Heb 2:19-5:10) is mostly exhortation, but concludes with doctrine (Heb 4:15-5:10). The third part (Heb 5:11-10:39) is basically doctrinal, but includes two exhortations (Heb 5:11-6:20 and 10:19-39). The fourth part (Heb 11:1-12:24) begins with doctrine (Heb 11:1-40), includes some exhortation, and ends with exhortation (Heb 12:18-24).[3] In this way the speaker first provided data and then followed by

---

[1] H. Koester, *Introduction to the New Testament* (Philadelphia: Fortress Press, 1982) 2, p. 273.

[2] K. P. Donfried, *The Setting of Second Clement in Early Christianity* (Leiden: Brill, 1974), p. 26.

[3] A. Vanhoye, *La Structure Littéraire de L'Epitre aux Hébreux* (Paris: Desclée de Brouwer, c1962), p. 51.

saying what this data meant for the actions of the listeners. There were several areas of discussion within this document, but the author moved smoothly from one area to the other without marking clear breaks in the argument, alluding to Ps 110:1 repeatedly, unifying the entire argument.

Lawyers and rabbis in court also used the same kinds of rhetorical techniques that were used by the Cynics in the market place, and preachers in churches and synagogues. All of these received their training from rhetoricians like Aristotle and Quintilian. Legal arguments, midrashic homilies, pesikta, and sermons all constitute arguments and would all pass for **words of exhortations** (Heb 13:22). The message of Heb 1-12 can be called a sermon, a homily, a midrash, or a legal argument. It could also be called a *piska*. That which it is not is a letter or epistle.

The beautiful piece of literature contained in Heb 1-12 would be recognized as an excellent legal argument or an excellent sermon. Neither a legal argument nor a sermon has the same basic form as a letter. They can hardly be confused. It is further not normal for a preacher or a lawyer to add an epistle to his or her own argument or sermon as a postscript.

Chapter thirteen begins a new document that has been written to promote the previously published sermon. It is a collection of exhortations that ends like a letter. It was written to be read rather than heard.

THE BASIC MESSAGE

"How to acquire the fulfillment of the promise God made with Abraham" is the topic, which held the interest of the author of the first twelve chapters of Hebrews. God promised Abraham the land of Canaan, although he did not intend for Abraham to receive it during his own lifetime. It was intended for Abraham's posterity, which God also promised him. Consequently the patriarchs all dwelt in the land of the promise as tenants. God intended to fulfill his promise to the generation of Moses in Egypt, and he announced to those Hebrews the good news that their captivity was over. According to the author of Heb 1-12 the Hebrews could at that time have left Egypt under the leadership of Moses and have taken possession of the land of Canaan. Thus motivated, the exodus generation left Egypt and reached the border of the land. This document is probably called "Hebrews" because the central theme is centered around the Hebrews who left Egypt but did not receive fulfillment of God's promise and those Hebrews who were listening to the sermon who still had that opportunity and challenge.

Instead of entering the land, however, the Hebrew leaders sent spies to see what possibilities there were for success in their venture. All of the spies except Caleb and Joshua reported that it would be impossible for the Hebrews to take the land, so that generation disobeyed God and refused to enter. This disobedience was the way they tested God. God, in turn, withheld the promise. Under oath, he swore that all of the adult males except Joshua and Caleb would die in the wilderness and never see the good land the Lord had promised to give them.

Later Joshua led the Hebrews into Canaan, but the author of Heb 1-12 did not consider that to be a fulfillment of the promise, because God spoke through David in Ps 95 as if the **rest** had not been received. David wished that people in his day might receive it. If the promise were received, it could never be taken away. It would be a **kingdom** that **would not be destroyed** (Dan 7:14) or **an unshakable**

kingdom (GenR 65:23; ExodR 15:21, 31; 50:5; Rashi and Eben Ezra on Dan 7:11-18; YalShim Dan 7-8, 513c-d). Since Israel had never had secure and lasting possession of the land, it was clear that the promise of God was still pending.

The good news that had been given to Israel through Moses had again been renewed through Jesus, who, through his sacrificial offering of himself, prepared a new way whereby the new Hebrews could be recipients of a new contract and the fulfillment of the old promise that had never been achieved. Like Moses before him, Jesus had done all that was necessary to make the fulfillment of the promises available. The Christians who were contemporary with the author were obligated to learn an important lesson from history: The exodus generation had been disobedient. Therefore the author urgently exhorted his recipients to be faithful so that the precious reward might not be missed again. The author's goal was clear, and he had two vehicles to employ in bringing this goal to fulfillment:

1) The Day of Atonement, and
2)The Scripture.

The Day of Atonement required sacrifice and innocence from any type of crime. The Scripture provided the legal precedence for winning the court case on the judgment trial on New Year's Day.

The author outlined his message in a well-structured manner, dealing first with one topic and then the next, as is evident from the general outline. Within this outline he transposed a series of types and antitypes, and, in a typically midrashic manner, he effectively repeated themes that were especially important to him, weaving them together the way a great composer develops a symphony. No one has shown so clearly as Vanhoye how meticulous the author of Hebrews was in emphasizing his major points.[1] He has shown that in one division the author raised points in a certain order, and then in the next division raised them again in the same order in a slightly different way, forming sentences so that the important words are orally communicated emphatically. Weiss said,

> Currently a widespread consensus at least is firmly established to that effect, that Hebrews is in no way to be considered Pauline, neither from the linguistic nor even from the theological content point of view.[2] . . . The author of Hebrews was no Pauline student—not in the widest sense of the word.[3]

The author of Hebrews was not a Pauline or a Johannine Christian. He was not far removed from Paul, *chronologically*, but the *geographical* distance is uncertain. Paul was active in Asia Minor. It is not certain where the author of Hebrews was at the time of Paul's mission in Asia Minor (ca. 40-52 IA). He probably worked out his theology and interpretation of Scripture independently. He preached this sermon in Zion, but he may not have been there all of his life. Like the members of his congregation he may have come from somewhere in the diaspora only a few years

---

[1] All good commentaries written after Vanhoye's work will have to depend on his research.

[2] H. F. Weiss, *Der Brief on die Hebräer über das Neue Testament* (Göttingen: Vandenhoeck & Ruprecht, 1991), p. 62, tr. from the German.

[3] Weiss, *Hebräer*, p. 87.

before. He was apparently the leader and teacher of a monastery, but we do not know how long he had been a monk or whether his monastery was always at Zion. He and the monks he taught may have all moved to Zion at the same time, but we cannot know if that really happened, and if it did, when. Because there is no direct data to answer these questions, we can only conjecture in the subjunctive mood. That preacher may or may not have paid any serious attention to the work or teaching of Paul. If he did it is not evident in this sermon, and that is all the evidence we have for making judgment.

He was in conflict with some other Christians on major doctrines, but that is not the whole story. Like most preachers, debaters, and lawyers, the author did not tell everything he knew in one argument. He defined his area of argument and stayed within its limits. That is good rhetoric. It is also clear that this monastic document was not composed by some woman, such as Priscilla or Mary, the mother of Jesus.[1] It is a mistake to try to find between the lines the beliefs of the author that were not expressed in this sermon. He undoubtedly had beliefs and opinions that were not expressed here, but it is impossible to know what they were.

Grässer noted emphatically, and accurately, that this document contains no post-Easter conception of faith—no *kyrigma*. There is no mention of the birth of Jesus or the activities of his life. He also held that the document shows no dependence on the writings of Paul.[2] Hughes also held that the author is,

> nonetheless unevangelical, for the New Testament plainly instructs us that grace and forgiveness and the cleansing of Christ's blood are freely available to the Christian believer who falls into sin and turns in repentance to God (Heb 4:15-16; 10:19-23; 1John 1:7-9; 2:1-2).[3]

The author was not out in the open fields trying to make converts of the masses. He directed his attention to the members of the exclusive group within the bounds of the monastery. These were men who had already been converted. They needed to be trained and encouraged to live up to their commitments.

Grässer mistakenly followed Käsemann in dismissing all of the references to events in time and space in and between geographical locations in the document and holding that everything should be understood metaphysically; that is, not in terms of physical objects, things in time and space, but in terms of abstract ideas. Some of these ideas are "gnostic." They included secret knowledge not allowed to be shared with those who were not members of the group. Following a type of philosophical gnosticism, Grässer claimed, the references made to time, space, and geographical locations should all be understood to be distances from earth to heaven.

The journey of the patriarchs was not from the diaspora (the areas where Jews were located outside Palestine) to Jerusalem or the Promised Land, or from the time of Enoch until the time of Jesus, as the text says, it was, rather, from earth to heaven.[4] The temple was a temple in heaven; the city was a city in heaven.[5] Grässer

---

[1] Suggestions given by Harnack and J. M. Ford, "The Mother of Jesus and the Authorship of the Epistle to the Hebrews" (Dayton: University of Dayton Review 11 (1975): 49-56.

[2] Grässer, *Hebräerbrief,* pp. 146-148; 2, p. 50. R. Jewett, *Letter to Pilgrims* (New York: Pilgrim Press, c1981), p. 190, disagreed with Grässer, holding that it was written by Paul's scribe, Epaphras.

[3] Hughes, *Hebrews* , p. 214.

[4] Grässer, *Hebräerbrief,* p. 175. So also Jewett, *Letter, passim.*

[5] Grässer, *Hebräerbrief,* p. 176.

assumed that the author had used gnostic sources and modified them. The gnosticism in which Grässer was interested was known in post NT Greek culture. The outlook of this group related everything in the world to earth and heaven, with human beings related to both. One was a reflection of the other. The author of Hebrews took, in Grässer's opinion, the Gnostic ascension of the soul to the heavenly rest and changed it to the wandering of the people of God to their heavenly home.[1] Grässer did not consider the possibility that the author spoke of wandering to Zion, because that did not suit his own doctrine. Other scholars, like Rose, Hughes, and Jewett, agreed with him. These conclusions are more the result of imagination than historical research.

There is so much repetition in the document that it would be boring to read if it were not so beautifully done. Part of the enjoyment of reading Hebrews comes from recognizing the graceful and stylistically effective way in which these themes appear over and over again, like the great themes in a symphony. Just think of how convincing it would sound if you heard it delivered orally! Some examples of repetitious themes are as follows:

1. The Origin of the Ages

a) In the last of these days he has spoken to us through a Son, . . . through whom he also made the ages (Heb 1:2).
b) By faith we consider the ages to have been put in order by [the] word of God (Heb 11:3).

2. Exaltation

a) When he had made a purification for [his] crimes, sat down at the right hand of the Majesty in exaltation (Heb 1:3).
b) Since, then, we have a great high priest [who] has gone through the heavens, Jesus the Son of God, let us hold fast the confession (Heb 4:14).
c) For such a one also became high priest for us,
holy, guileless, undefiled,
separated from criminals,
and become higher than the heavens (Heb 7:26).
d) Most important of the things said [is that] we have such a high priest [as this] who sat down at the right hand of the throne of Majesty in the heavens. (Heb 8:1).

3. High Priests

a) . . . so that he might become a merciful and faithful high priest [regarding] divine services (Heb 2:17).
b) Direct [your] attention to Jesus, the apostle and high priest of our confession, [who] was faithful to the one who made him (Heb 3:1-2).
c) Since, then, we have a great high priest [who] has gone through the heavens, Jesus the Son of God, let us hold fast the confession. For we do not have a high priest [who is] unable to sympathize with our weaknesses (Heb 4:14-15).

---

[1] Grässer, *Hebräerbrief*, p. 182.

d) . . . where Jesus entered [as] a forerunner in our behalf, since he is a high priest for the age according to the order of Melchizedek (Heb 6:20).
e) For such a one also became high priest for us,
holy, guileless, undefiled,
separated from criminals,
and become higher than the heavens (Heb 7:26).
f) We have such a high priest [as this] who sat down at the right hand of the throne of Majesty in the heavens (Heb 8:1).

4. **Holding Fast**

a) . . . if we hold fast the confidence and boasting of hope (Heb 3:6).
b) . . . if indeed we hold fast the initial doctrine until the end (Heb 3:14).
c) Let us hold fast unmoved the confession of hope (Heb 10:23).

5. **The Promises**

a) The promise of entering into his rest is left [unfulfilled] (Heb 4:1).
b) . . . so that you may not become dull, but [rather] imitators of those who inherit the promises through faith and long suffering (Heb 6:12).
c) And thus, after he had suffered patiently, [Abraham] received the promise (Heb 6:15).
d) So when God wanted very much to show the heirs of the promise the unchangeableness of his will, he imposed an oath [on himself] (Heb 6:17).
e) . . . as he is also a mediator of a better contract, which has been made into law on the basis of better promises (Heb 8:6).
f) And, because of this, he is [the] mediator of a new contract, so that, . . . those who are called might receive the promise of the eternal inheritance (Heb 9:15).
g) For you must have endurance so that, after you have done the will of God, you may obtain the promise (Heb 10:36).
h) By faith, he dwelt in the land of the promise as a stranger, living in tents with Isaac and Jacob, joint heirs of the same promise (Heb 11:9).
i) According to faith these all died, not having acquired the promises (Heb 11:13).
j) By faith Abraham offered Isaac, being tested, and the one who received the promises offered [his] only one (Heb 11:17).
k) Now these all, attested through faith, did not acquire the promise, since God had foreseen something better concerning us, so that without us, they might not be perfected (Heb 11:39-40).

6. **No-Forgiveness**

A. How shall we escape having neglected so great a salvation [as this], which
1) had its beginning when it was spoken through the Lord,
2) was confirmed to us by those who heard,
3) while God supported the testimony with signs, wonders,
and various kinds of miracles, and
4) by the distribution of the Holy Spirit according to his will (Heb 2:3-4)?

B. For after they **have fallen** by the wayside it is impossible to renew again for repentance those who have
1) once been **enlightened**,
2) tasted the **heavenly** gift,
3) become sharers of the **Holy Spirit,** and
4) tasted **the good word of God** and the miracles of the coming age, [thereby] crucifying and making a public example of the Son of God for themselves. (Heb 6:4-6).

C. **Anyone [who]** has rejected the law of Moses **will die** without mercy **on the [testimony] of two or three witnesses,** how much worse punishment, do you think, will he deserve, who
1) trampled upon the Son of God,
2) considered **the blood of the contract** in which he was sanctified, defiled,
3) and depreciated the spirit of grace? For we know the one who said,

> **Vengeance** is mine; **I will pay back**; and again,
> **The Lord will judge his people**."
> Falling into the hands of [the] God of life is dreadful (Heb 10:28-30).

It is evident from the above quotations that the author has woven and interwoven his major emphases so that they cannot be completely separated from one another. The same is true of the types and antitypes.

7. **Typologies**

There are many typologies in the NT, as Goppelt has shown,[1] but Bird mentioned the significance of typology in the FT itself. Typology is the study of the relationship of patterns to one another. The word "type" means to strike, as with a seal in soft clay to leave a certain figure. In such a case the instrument for striking would be the type, and the pattern in the clay, the anti-type. Earthly things are believed by some groups to be anti-types of heavenly things. Also later personalities and events were compared to earlier personalities and events, that were similar typologically. In which case the one that came later was thought to be an antitype of that which was earlier. Some of the types and antitypes Bird listed are:

1) Exodus of Abraham–exodus of Moses—exodus of Second Isaiah;
2) Sodom of Genesis—Sodom of Jeremiah;
3) Eden of Adam—Eden of Ezekiel;
4) Davidic shepherd, Elijah—Malachi's priestly Elijah—the baptizing Elijah;
5) Adam—Noah;
6) Moses—Joshua;
7) Moses—Elijah;
8) Jacob—the nation Israel.[2]

---

[1] L. Goppelt, *Typos: The Typological Interpretation of the Old Testament in the New* (Grand Rapids: Eerdmans, 1982), tr. D. H. Madvig.
[2] C. H. Bird, "Typological Interpretation within the Old Testament: Melchizedekian Typology," *Concordia Journal* (2000):37-46.

Bird correctly held that the author of Hebrews did not manufacture the typology of Melchizedek. He already had a pattern before him in the FT. Some of the typologies in Hebrews are the following:

The author began his homily by setting forth the various ways God had spoken to the fathers as a type for which his revelation through the Son was an antitype. When God spoke to Noah (Heb 11:7), Abraham (Heb 11:8-19), Moses (Heb 11:23-29), and Rahab (Heb 11:31), he asked them to act in ways that seemed unreasonable. Nonetheless, when they obeyed at great personal cost, their faith was rewarded. This was the type. In the same way, as a later antitype, Jesus, the Son, had been asked to offer himself as an atonement to enable the seed of Abraham to receive the necessary salvation. Like the faithful fathers, Jesus obeyed. This type of perfect, unquestioning obedience at any cost was the model that Christians of the author's day were expected to imitate--typologically.

The exodus opportunity for the Hebrews to leave Egypt was a type for which the opportunity available to the recipients of the sermon (Heb 1-12) was the antiype. Both received the same **good news (gospel)** that the promise given to Abraham could be fulfilled for them. Both were placed in situations where the achievement seemed incredible. In both cases, success depended upon the faith of the parties to the contract and their ability to hold fast to their confession and never give up hope that God would fulfill his promises and give the children of Abraham the land promised to Abraham. Both were tempted to doubt God's ability to fulfill his promises. Of the exodus generation, only Caleb and Joshua were confident and refused to give up hope. The rest of the Hebrews perished in the wilderness. The author urged his readers to learn from the exodus generation so that they might be different from it in the ways necessary for success.

The Levitical priesthood was a type for which Melchizedek, and conesquently Jesus who belonged to his order, was the antitype.[1] The Levitical high priest was sympathetic (Heb 5:2), appointed by law (Heb 5:1; 7:28) to offer gifts and sacrifices on earth (Heb 8:3) of bulls and goats (Heb 9:12, 19-22) and to sprinkle blood from them every year (Heb 9:25-26) or every day (Heb 10:11-12). The priest offered a gift to cleanse his own crime (Heb 5:3; 7:27), but he was unable to cleanse the conscience, remove crimes, or perfect anything (Heb 9:7, 25; 10:1-4). The Levites received tithes (Heb 7:5) and the people were governed by the Levites (Heb 7:11). The high priest entered the holy of holies (Heb 9:7). Jesus, the anti-type, was an apostle and high priest who sympathized, because he had been tempted, but since he had been cleansed (Heb 1:3), he was without crime (Heb 4:14-15).

Jesus was appointed by God (Heb 7:28), ministered in a greater and more perfect tent **not made with hands**, in the heavens (Heb 9:11). He entered the holy of holies as a forerunner (Heb 6:19-20). Melchizedek received tithes (Heb 7:5-10)--even from the Levites--by extension. Jesus offered himself as the perfect sacrifice once, pouring out his own blood to cleanse, sanctify, and perfect himself and the people (Heb 7:26-27; 9:14, 23, 26; 10:14). He cleansed not only earthly, but even heavenly, things (Heb 9:23) since he had gone through the heavens (Heb 4:14). As

[1] R. Williamson, *Philo and the Epistle to the Hebrews* (Leiden: E. J. Brill, 1970), p. 532, correctly says Melchizedek was a type of Christ for the author. See also p. 534.

the perfect priest, he was holy, undefiled, separated from criminals (Heb 7:26). His purpose was the same as that of the levitical priesthood. He belonged to the same type, but he succeeded where they had failed. Therefore he was a superior antitype for their inferior type.

Before contracts were reduced to writing and even after, contracts in antiquity were made through ceremony or liturgy. If two or more people before witnesses made a contract and completed every single step of the required liturgy, this was as valid in court as a written document. We still have remnants of such contracts in baptisms, weddings, and reception of members into the church.

The first contract was renewed in the wilderness with the sprinkling of the blood of bulls and goats, whose deaths made the contract valid (Heb 9:16-22). Christ was the mediator for the new contract (Heb 9:15). The new contract was confirmed by the blood of Christ, whose death made the contract valid and whose blood redeems transgressions against the old contract (Heb 9:15). Because of the contract that Jesus made at his death that made it valid, those who are called may receive the inheritance (Heb 9:15-22). The antitype is superior to the type.

The tent mentioned in the Sermon was the earthly antitype tent, and it was at Zion. It had been preceded by the tent in the wilderness which was moved to Zion by David, stationed before the altar. Solomon's temple replaced the tent, but continued to be called a tent. Divisions within the temple were also called tents. The tent which contained the Christian altar in Heb 13 was a duplicate of the tent in the wilderness where the Israelites came to meet God, through the agency of God's legal agent, Moses, or one of the priests. There they received legal counsel, tried legal cases, and engaged in cultic performances. There cultic cleansing was performed and justice administered in God's name, in his interests, and at his responsibility.

The temple made without hands was probably Solomon's temple, constructed on Mount Zion, a little mound west of the two springs in the Kidron Valley. This was replaced by Zerubbabel's temple after the end of the Babylonian Captivity. It was replaced again by Herod, still on Mount Ophel, west of the spring of Siloam. There never was a temple inside Herod's walls. That was Herod's famous fortress which housed many Roman soldiers, employed to control David's City to the south. A temple not made with hands would probably have to have been constructed by properly qualified priests, who acted as God's legal agents. It would at least have been constructed under an authorized messiah, a legal agent of God.

The tent in the temple at Jerusalem (Herod's temple) was made with hands. There goats and bulls were offered and ashes of the red heifer were sprinkled (Heb 9:13). The high priest entered this tent once a year with the blood of another (Heb 9:25), but this tent was profane, built by Romans, and administered by priests installed by Romans. The author held that it was made with hands (Heb 9:11). Christ entered this true tent where heavenly things were cleansed by better sacrifices (Heb 9:22-24). Christ appeared at the end of the age to cleanse crimes with his own blood, which was offered as a blameless sacrifice (Heb 9:14, 26).

There are more types and antitypes than these in the homily, because there is an overtone of comparison that implies both a typology and an *a fortiori* relationship between the things related to the old contract and the new. An *a fortiori* argument is the same as that called *káhl-wuh-khóh-mehr* (קל וחומר) in Hebrew. To make a strong case, the rhetorician indicates something about an object that is small or unimportant and says something about it that is accepted as true. Then he speaks of something very much larger, stronger, or more important. The argument that follows is that if the point involved was true of the smaller, weaker situation it would be all the more true of something that was larger and stronger.

The comparison of the Hebrews in the wilderness with the Hebrews to whom his homily was addressed was so central to the message that the author of this document may originally have given the sermon that title. The recorded Greek title for this biblical document is "To the Hebrews," implying that it was a Pauline letter to the Hebrews. Heb 1-12 is mostly *about* the activities of the Hebrews, rather than *to* them. Therefore, originally Heb 1-12 may have been entitled "The Hebrews" before this homily was associated with a collection of letters, but that is only an imaginative suggestion.

8. **Christian Ethics**

The kind of Christian behavior approved by the author is made evident both from the positive and the negative examples he gave and from the exhortations he supplied. The negative examples include such foolish people as Esau who lightly gave up his inheritance and later suffered the unalterable consequences (Heb 12:16-17) and the disobedient exodus generation that received the good news, had the opportunity to receive the promised rest, could have been the recipients of the inheritance promised to Abraham, but doubted God's ability and willingness (Heb 3:16-19; 4:6). They did not hold fast to their confession. They gave up their confidence.

Examples of those who were approved were people of the opposite attributes. They took advantage of the first opportunity given them to obey God's command. They never wavered but did exactly as God ordered, without losing hope. Noah built an ark to save his family, when there was no sign of rain in sight (Heb 11:7); Abraham left his native land without knowing where he was going. He trusted God that he would become the father of a numerous posterity when he and Sarah were too old to have children. He was prepared to offer Isaac as a sacrifice at the commandment of God (Heb 11:8-19).

At God's direction, Moses left a position of comfort, wealth, prestige, and power to lead the Israelites out of the great country of Egypt toward the Promised Land (Heb 11:23-29), which was the small Land of Canaan. At her first chance, Rahab betrayed her country to destruction to become identified with the recipients of the promise. Like these faithful ones was also Jesus, who gave up the joy that was his to endure the cross necessary for the salvation of the parties to the contract (Heb 12:2). The emphasis on Jesus, God's Son, as an offering may have been intended to relate God's offering of his Son to Abraham's willingness to offer his son Isaac.

The author was not interested in providing salvation for others. He thought Rahab (and probably Jacob) was to be admired for her skill in becoming an heiress when she did not deserve the inheritance from the standpoint of birth. The author admired Noah for saving his own family. He had no sympathy for the misfortunes of those destroyed by the flood, for Esau's misfortune, for the Egyptians killed at the sea that bordered Egypt, or for the citizens of Jericho who were destroyed by the invading Israelites. His ethics were limited to his concern for the sons of Abraham and the behavior required for them to achieve the promises given to Abraham.

The ethics required were strict obedience, unwavering faith, and consistent hope. Monks took vows of poverty, celibacy, and obedience. Like the heroes of FT times were the martyrs who resisted Antiochus Epiphanes, endured all kinds of torture and death, but refused to give up their faith, religious practices, or hope in a resurrection on the Promised Land (Heb 11:32-39).

Since the author believed these were the ethics God required, he urged the readers to be very careful lest they fall into any kind of crime, give up love, or forsake the faith. They must not be indolent or careless. The group could tolerate no unbelief (Heb 3:12), **hardening** (Heb 3:13), **falling behind** (Heb 4:1), **dullness** (Heb 4:11; 6:12), deliberate crime (Heb 10:26), or avoidance of God's command (Heb 12:25).[1] Every single member of the group was required to be rigidly disciplined to avoid any misdemeanor. Positively, they were also urged to hold fast to their confession or doctrine to the end (Heb 3:14; 10:23), approach the throne of grace with boldness (Heb 4:16), press on to maturity in faith (Heb 6:1), show forth love, minister to the saints (Heb 6:9-12), encourage one another, and maintain regular attendance in community gatherings (Heb 10:24-25), be willing to face insult, sacrifice, and suffering for the faith (Heb 10:32-36), and accept discipline gladly (Heb 12:5-11). They were obliged to strive for ritual purity for the whole community and maintain peace with all (Heb 12:14-15).

The goal of all Christian ethics, according to the author of the sermon, was to please God so that he would bless the sons of Abraham with the fulfillment of his promise to grant them rest on the Promised Land. The faithful heroes of the past had acted in the way that would bring about that event while the unfaithful were negligent of their opportunities and responsibilities in relationship to the contract.

9. The Significance of Jesus

Jesus was important to the author of the Hebrews sermon, not primarily for the things he said and did during his lifetime, but for the offering he made which renewed the possibility of receiving the promise. The author did not mention Jesus as the son of David who entered Jerusalem triumphantly on Palm Sunday and celebrated the Passover with his disciples. If he had been preparing a sermon for Passover, these probably would have received central importance. Then he probably would have told of the liturgy Jesus performed at the Last Supper by which he formed a new corporation and the new contract, using Passover bread and fruit of the vine for his seisins.[2] The Passover lamb, however, was for celebration. It was not for suffering and sacrifice. The author of this sermon was preparing for the gathering of the saints at Zion for New Year's judgment and the Day of Atonement accounting. For this he emphasized the importance of Jesus' suffering and death. All of the other messages he might have delivered will be forever unknown to us.

It was not Jesus' royal lineage that he needed. For the Day of Atonement it was the high priest that was important--not the king. The author knew, of course, that Jesus was the son of David and born from the tribe of Judah and that he was not a priest from birth. He became a priest when he was initiated into the monastery. Jesus denied his family origins when he joined the monastery. As a monk he could have no children, so like other monks he was unique, without genealogy or posterity. It was only on the basis of legal arguments that he could prove that Jesus was a high priest and that his death was an atonement offering. The author made a good case. Since all prophecy is prophesied only for the days of the Messiah, according to

[1] The author's list of prohibitions deals with more than just apostasy, contrary to Williamson, *Philo,* pp. 250-51, 261, and others.

[2] Buchanan, *The Gospel of Matthew* (Lewiston: Mellen, c1996), pp. 964-80.

accepted rules of rhetoric, the statement, **You are a priest** (Ps 110:4) was applied to the Messiah, Jesus.

It was Jesus who first announced salvation (Heb 2:3). Jesus, according to the author, arose from Judah, but the author may not have received that information from local tradition about the historical Jesus at all. Since Jesus was accepted as the Messiah, and the prophecy stated that from Judah would come the Messiah (Gen 49:9-10; see also the targumim), it was clear that Jesus came from Judah. Instead of history the author relied on Scripture for his information. The author was a specialist in jurisprudence. He depended on legal evidence, legal reports, legal data. The history he reported had to be drawn from sources approved by courts. Since Jesus was identified with Melchizedek, whose residence was in Jerusalem according to Jewish tradition, the author may also have deduced Jesus' Judaic origin from that tradition (Heb 7:14). The apparent report of Jesus' agony in the Garden of Gethsemane could be the result of the exegesis of the LXX Ps 114 without any knowledge of the prayer in Gethsemane as recorded in the gospels (Heb 5:7-10).

The author mentioned the cross only once, the cross which Jesus accepted instead of the joy that could have been his (Heb 12:2). Hebrews is different from the letters of Paul in that the cross itself had little theological significance, and no mention was made of Jesus' resurrection. It was only when Jesus' death was reinterpreted in terms of an atonement offering that it captured the attention of the author of Hebrews. The one mention of the cross was given only as an example similar to that of Moses, who was reported to have accepted disgrace instead of the position of wealth available to him (Heb 11:24-25).

For the author's doctrine, it was important that Jesus be understood as a high priest so that his sacrifice could be understood as an atonement offering. Since Jesus was not from the priestly line of Aaron, the author attributed the office of high priest to him on the basis of Ps 110 (Heb 5:10). As a priest of the confession (Heb 3:1) he became forerunner and pioneer (Heb 2:10; 6:19-20), having gone through the veil as the high priest did when he entered the holy of holies. As a priest he offered blood, but not that of bulls and goats. He offered his own blood in the greater and more perfect tent (Heb 9:11-12). This offering was made only once, but as a once-for-all sacrifice it successfully cleansed the consciences of the believers (Heb 9:14) who thereby became sanctified and perfected (Heb 10:10-14).

Jesus was a sympathetic high priest who was tempted and learned obedience through the things he suffered. It was in this way that he was perfected and made free from crime, since his offering was the perfect gift to atone for crimes (Heb 4:15; 5:8-9). Like other offerings that went up to God in the heavens, Jesus, the perfect sacrifice, also went through the heavens to God (Heb 4:14), and by his ascension was seated on the right hand of God as the Son of God (Heb 1:3, 13; 4:14; 5:8; 8:1; 10:12; 12:2).

The Son of God is a well-known title for a king, but the preacher did not mention Jesus' status as a king. It was his status as a legal agent of God who was seated next to him that was important. Jesus' self-offering not only opened the heavens to him, but it also provided a cleansing for his crimes so that he could be free from crime (Heb 1:3; 4:15), holy, undefiled, and separated from criminals (Heb 7:26-27). As a good jurist, the author believed that if a legal ceremony was performed correctly that it would be effective. Jesus had performed the Atonement Day liturgy perfectly. Although he claimed the sons of Abraham as his legal brothers (Heb 2:10-18), he was without any family lineage or dynastic succession (Heb 7:3). He was the ideal monk who had denied his family to join a brotherhood. Since he was celibate, he would have no family to succeed him. That meant to the author that he himself remained for the age (Heb 7:3), never to be replaced by other mortals the way Levitical priests were (Heb 7:8). The author was not interested in genealogical details. He looked only for the legal realities.

As a high priest, Jesus successfully atoned for his own crimes and those of the people. His self-offering caused his ascension to the right hand of God where he was installed as Son. The ascension was not the same as the resurrection. The ascension did not bring Jesus alive back to earth. It took him up to heaven through a sacrificial liturgy. It was because of his success in ascending to the right hand of God in heaven that he was able to persuade God to fulfill the promises he made to Abraham on earth.

As Son he received all the attributes of an ideal king of Israel. He was to rule over all his enemies, who would become as a footstool for his feet (Heb 1:13; 2:7-9). His willingness to give up his life for his religion made him a martyr, like one of the faithful who resisted the Greeks in the Maccabean Revolt. Like the Hasmoneans, he technically filled the role both of high priest and of royal leader for his people, although the author of Hebrews was interested only in his priestly qualities. There may have been two bases for claiming that Jesus was really a priest even though he did not come from a priestly family.

1) He was a monk. As a monk he probably was ordained a priest when he was admitted to the monastery.
2) The other was the author's clever use of Scripture.

Although other tradition classifies Jesus as a son of David who had been teamed with John the Baptist, a son of Aaron, in accordance with the two-messiah expectation (Luke 1:5-13, 26-33) the author of Hebrews did not mention Jesus as a son of David.[1] Being a son of David Messiah would seem to rule out the possibility of being a high priest as well as a king, but maybe not.

The authors of Dead Sea Scrolls, NT, and Rabbinic literature argued on the basis that all Scripture was prophesied only for the Days of the Messiah. Therefore, if the Scripture says, **You are a priest for the age** (Ps 110:4), then this can be applied to Jesus. All of a sudden this Messiah could also become a priest. The author of Hebrews was basing his arguments on the FT. Through the FT he could prove, rhetorically, that the sons of Aaron had been replaced and that a new priesthood had been established. Hypothetically this new priesthood might come from David's line, although the author of Hebrews did not emphasize that point.

Although the gospels relate Jesus' death with his crucifixion near the Passover feast, the author of Hebrews interpreted his death in terms of an offering given by Jesus himself as the apostle and high priest of our confession on the Day of Atonement. It was the death of Jesus that was important to the author. Interpreted as an atonement offering, his death could justify the claim that he was a true martyr, whose crimes had been cleansed, leaving him guiltless, holy, undefiled, perfect, and sanctified. Since his ascension was interpreted as an atonement offering going up to heaven to God, the author reasoned that he was seated at the right hand of God and should be called God's Son on the basis of Ps 110. This is ingenious exegesis in accordance with acceptable rabbinic use of Scripture, but the entire picture provides

[1] W. R. Farmer, "John the Baptist," IDB (Nashville: Abingdon Press, 1962), 2, pp. 959-962.

only slight information, indirectly deduced, about the life, activity, and teaching of the historical Jesus.

The basic message of chapter thirteen was quite different from that of the sermon. Whereas the sermon was very rigid and demanding, chapter thirteen was a general letter designed to modify the ethics of the sermon, extending the teachings of the sermon to a wider audience. That which was not the basic message was the doctrine of perfection, monasticism, unforgiverness, and the emphasis on the promises given to Abraham and Moses.

THE ORIGINAL RECIPIENTS

This sermon was later read, but originally, it was delivered orally to a group of listeners. The text never mentioned that any recipients would ever be expected to read anything or that the author was writing anything. The hearers of this homily were not among those who had seen and heard Jesus themselves, but the salvation, which Jesus announced, had been confirmed to them by those who had actually heard his voice (Heb 2:3). Although this may mean that the original hearers had written down that which they had heard so that it was confirmed for all generations, it seems more likely that the original speaker also wrote his message and that the recipients were close enough in time and space to have heard the testimony from the original eye and ear witnesses of Jesus and his message.

This homily was prepared for certain sons of Abraham (Heb 2:11, 16) who had begun training in the Christian faith. Weiss said they were clearly Jewish Christians, seemingly a peculiar minority group that still thought in terms of cult sacrifices, possibly of priestly origin.[1] They were among the first born, which may have meant they were the first Christians who were born as Christians and were not converts from Judaism. Converts would have been legally "born again" as Christians. They were neither Samaritans nor Sadducees, because they accepted the Psalms and prophetic books as inspired Scripture. They had already been enlightened (Heb 6:4), which means they had received the training necessary for baptism. They had tasted the heavenly gift (Heb 6:4), which might mean they had been admitted to the common meal.

They had become sharers of the Holy Spirit, implying that they had been baptized and participated in the legal ceremony whereby others laid their hands upon them (Heb 6:5), so that they had become Christians; and they had tasted the good word of God and the miracles of the coming age (Heb 6:5). The Holy Spirit gave them the authority to become members of the Christian corporation. As members of this corporation or body, they shared in all of the legal benefits and responsibilities of the corporation. This meant that they were sharers of the Holy Spirit. All of this assured them that the promises were about to be fulfilled for them. They had apparently expected the promises to have been completely fulfilled before this document was written, because some were leaving the faith and needed the strong warning of the author to enable them to hold fast to the confession to the end (Heb 3:12; 4:1, 11, 14; 6:6-8, 11; 10:23, 35-36; 12:1, 3). In the early days of their faith, they had been courageous, suffering physical torture and disgrace from outsiders. They may have also had their goods confiscated by outsiders. If they were monks, they had voluntarily given up all of their possessions to the monastic community.

---

[1] Weiss, *Hebräerbrief*, p. 70.

It seems quite likely that they were monks who belonged to a monastery there at Zion. They were not just a composition of pilgrims who had come to Jerusalem to visit at the time of the feasts. They had been with the order long enough to question its validity. The demands required were those only monks might be expected to keep. Their **coming to Zion** (Heb 12:22) was not just for a visit a few days earlier. They had **come to Zion**, from some other place, sometime earlier, to join that monastery. The speaker was also a member of the same monastery. He knew what their problems were, how much they had suffered, why they had become discouraged, what they expected from their new membership. He had observed the progress each member had made in his faith. He was a member of the same legal family, perhaps the legal father of all of the legal brothers.

The members boldly called on prisoners, sharing with them their embarrassment and probably their provisions (Heb 10:32-34), but they had not yet resisted to the blood, perhaps meaning that no one of them had received the death penalty for his or her faith (Heb 12:4). This may mean they were not members of the same community as that of the Teacher of Righteousness or that the author wrote before the wicked priest had physically abused or killed the Teacher. They had been in training long enough to have been teachers, but the author chided them because they seemed to have lost interest and had not moved ahead as rapidly in their training as they should have (Heb 5:11-14). Some of them were neglecting attendance at congregational gatherings (Heb 10:25). Their earlier training involved doctrines familiar to Judaism: repentance, faith in God, teachings about ablutions, laying on of hands, resurrection of the dead, and the judgment at the end of the age (Heb 6:1-2).

There are some indications that the original readers belonged to a very strict, communal, monastic sect. They were called "brothers" and "beloved," terms not restricted to brotherhoods, but regularly used by them (Heb 6:10, 19). Because monks had denied their families, the only brothers they had were legal brothers—other members of the monastery. They had shown their brotherly love by ministering to the saints, as was customary among brotherhoods.[1]

The joy the brothers experienced when their goods were confiscated suggests that they may have been confiscated with their own approval by the communal order, rather than by outsiders. No member of the group had faced martyrdom, as was true of Christians in Rome (Tacitus, *Annals* 15:44, 6). The custom of forfeiting all possessions by initiates when they were fully admitted to the sect was usual among groups like the Essenes whose goods were shared communally (Heb 10:34). This complete sharing of material goods was called brotherly love.

Listeners to this sermon were urged to strive for sanctification, to go on to perfection (Heb 6:1; 12:14). This communal sharing was not usually called "confiscating" (*hahr-pah-gáyn*, ἁρπαγήν) (Heb 10:34), but there were negative feelings about it. Some resisted it and falsified the extent of their possessions (1QS 6:24-25; Acts 5:1-11). They were under strict legal discipline, like that of monastic brotherhoods. Not one of the members dared to fall behind in the disciplines necessary to receive the grace of God; absolutely no ritual defilement was allowed (Heb 12:15). It is true that terms like **perfection, brothers, beloved**, and **sanctification** were also

---

[1] Motivated by the current movement for political correctness, H. Attridge, *The Epistle to the Hebrews* (Philadelphia: Fortress Press, 1989), mistakenly rendered "brothers" by "brothers and sisters." Changing the meaning of an ancient message by translation is deceptive scholarship. Even if this group had not been monastic, its members would not have been called "sisters." The translator should be faithful to the text used.

used by less rigorous Christian groups with less strict meanings than were applied by monastic groups, but the fact that all of these were used together with admonitions about brotherly love, and since approval was given for the joy that came when goods were confiscated--all fit together with the strict discipline demanded of this group that would be expected of a monastic order.

That which the listeners were not was a group of the contemporaries of Jesus or any of his apostles. They were early Christians, but not as early as the apostles. They had heard the gospel from those who had been contemporary with the apostles. This means that this sermon could not have been preached by Paul and written as a letter by Timothy or Epaphras.[1] This knowledge kept Hebrews from being included in the canon for hundreds of years. Furthermore the message addressed to them was not some kind of fictionalized drama, called a gnostic myth, or any other myth. This was not a play for exhibition in a theater. It was an argument, intended to prove a case legally before the speaker's listeners and persuade them to take certain action.

The recipients had been reminded that they had come to **Zion** (*praws-eh-lay-loó-thah-teh See-óhn* προσεληλύθατε Σιών), **the city of the God of life, heavenly Jerusalem** (Heb 12:22). The text does *not* say "You have gone to heaven," or "You will go to heaven," "You are on your way to heaven," or "You will be raptured into heaven," as has been frequently interpreted.[2] The verb is clearly in the perfect tense, which has either the force of the simple past tense, or the present tense as a result of a previous action. The context requires that the situation remind the listeners that they had already come to the place where they were at that time, from someplace else, where they had been previously.

The place where they were when this message was read was not Italy, Rome, the Lycus Valley, or heaven, but **Zion, the city of God.** It is normal to presume that the readers were still in **Zion** when they had access to this document, which may have been read to them at a congregational meeting. The most likely place for that meeting to have been held was in a monastery at **Zion**, and the audience was probably composed entirely of monks who had come to **Zion** from many places to become members of this monastery. They had come to **Zion**, but maybe not recently. Some may have been there for a long time, but they came as migrants. There may have also been recent pilgrims who came to **Zion** only for the feast, but that is not very likely, because monks did not normally accept others as guests, unless they were also monks of the same order. There is no evidence of non-members or strangers in the group. These conjectures and statements are not certain, but that which is certain is that they were in Zion when they heard this sermon delivered.

Paul wrote letters and discussed his writing in his letters, but the author of Hebrews nowhere mentioned his writing. Instead he mentioned speaking: **about which we speak** (Heb 2:5); **Our message is extensive and difficult to say** (Heb 5:11); **Even though we speak thus** (Heb 6:9); **Most important of the things said** (Heb 8:1); **This is not the proper time to speak** (Heb 9:5); **What more shall I say? For time will fail me to tell about . . .** (Heb 11:32).

This carefully prepared sermon was not extemporaneous, but it seems to have been composed for oral delivery. The author himself may even have delivered

---

[1] Contra C. P. Anderson, "The Epistle to the Hebrews and the Pauline Letter Collection," *HTR* 59 (1966):429-38; "Who Wrote 'The Epistle from Laodicea'?" *JBL* 85 (1966):436-40, followed by Jewett, *Letter*, pp. 10-11.

[2] Attridge, *Hebrews*, and W. L. Lane, *Hebrews 9-13* (Dallas: Word Books, c1991) 2, pp. 169-70, among others.

it orally during the season between New Year's Day and the Day of Atonement. The first audience may have heard this message, rather than read it. The first recipients had evidently arrived at **Zion** too late to have heard Jesus personally, but in **Zion** they and the author could receive the message of salvation secondhand from those who heard it from Jesus himself (Heb 2:3). Like Abraham of old, these faithful Zionistic pilgrims had left their homelands to come to the Promised Land. They had expected the **promise** made to Abraham to be fulfilled in their day. This raises the question, "When did these migrants come to Jerusalem?"

In NT times there was in the Jewish calendar two festivals only ten days apart. The first was New Year's Day, the first day of the year. This was the day Jews believed God held judgment over his people and the nations. On that day God received all of the complaints and read all of the books brought to trial. During the next ten days he examined the complaints and defenses. At that same time Jews examined their own records to see if any of them had any unpaid fines or any offenses for which he or she had not made correction and reconciliation. After ten days of repentance, the Day of Atonement was the day when the Lord made his final judgment for the year. Jews could always learn afterward whether or not the judgment had been made in their behalf by the events that followed. If the promises were fulfilled and the land were returned, then they knew that they had been vindicated in Judgment. If not, they would have to work for righteousness and hope to be forgiven the next year.

In 164 BIA, after the Day of Atonement, Judas won the famous Battle of Beth-horon, when the Syrian army was soundly defeated and forced to retreat to Antioch. Following this victory, Judas and his troops returned with booty to Jerusalem, cleansed the temple and celebrated the first Hanukkah after the return from Babylon. This proved the vindication of the Jews on that Day of Atonement and probably motivated the composition of the victory dramas in the Book of Daniel. One of those dramas pictured the Lord in heaven holding court when the trial was between the Jews and the Syrians. The defendant was the "little horn," demythologized as Antiochus Epiphanes, who received the death sentence. The plaintiff was the "Son of Man," demythologized as Judas the Maccabbee, whose prayer for relief was granted and to whom was given the leadership of the Promised Land (Dan 7).[1] The author of Hebrews and his audience were probably gathered at Jerusalem between New Year's Day and the Day of Atonement, anticipating another deliverance of the Promised Land to the chosen people, when the promises made to Abraham would finally be fulfilled. They hoped for another Beth-horon and Hanukkah.

Although they were pilgrims who had come to Zion, they may have been in Zion for a long time before the particular Day of Atonement season at which this sermon was delivered. The audience was probably made up entirely of the members of the monastery at Zion in preparation for the Day of Atonement.

The author of chapter thirteen was writing to a general Christian audience that had survived the war of 66-72 IA, some of whom were married and becoming adjusted to the new Christian Church with a new set of officers.

DATE AND PLACE OF ORIGIN

In response to the oath that God took, prohibiting the Israelites from entering into the Lord's rest (Ps 95:11), rabbis said they did not enter that particular rest but that

---

[1] Buchanan, *TheBook of Daniel* (Lewiston: Mellen, c1999), pp. 163-234.

they would enter another rest, meaning the Promised Land, at a different time under different conditions. R. Levi, in the name of Bar Qappara (third century IA), employed the same kind of courtroom logic as the author of Hebrews. He compared the situation to a king who, in his anger, said his son could never enter his palace with him. After his anger subsided, the king tore down the palace, rebuilt it, and then brought his son into it with him. In this way he kept his oath and still allowed his son to enter into the palace. In the same way, rabbis believed God would rebuild Israel and readmit the sons of Abraham in the messianic age (LevR 32:2). This was a legal fiction. Legally the king upheld his oath, but in reality he broke it.

The nature of the analogy reflects a composition after the destruction of Jerusalem in 70 IA. This was an attempt to explain why God allowed the temple to be destroyed. It was really done in the interests of his sons. The rabbis expected the land to be restored and rest to be allowed, but the destruction had already taken place and the analogy necessarily reflected it.

The author of Hebrews also expected God's people to enter into the rest, in spite of the oath (Ps 95:11), but he had no need to consider a destruction of the temple, city, or land to prevent this oath from admitting the promise of Abraham to be fulfilled. In fact there is nothing at all in the homily (Heb 1-12) to require a post-70 IA composition. The author's reference to the sacrifices that the priests were then making presumes the existence and function of the priests in the temple (Heb 9:6-9; 10:1-2).[1]

To presume that the author of the sermon wrote after 70 IA to meet the needs of Christians without a temple *as if* he had written before the fall seems unjustified. There is a long history of apocalyptic literature composed pseudonymmously *as if* it had been written many years earlier, but the sermon of Heb 1-12 is neither pseudonymous nor apocalyptic, nor are there any mistakes in the document that betray any intention of giving the impression that the document had been written earlier than it really had. Since this is the case, it is fair to accept as much of the message as possible on the basis that the author meant what he said. This allows the following information to be considered:

> (1) The author referred to the death of Jesus which occurred during the reign of Pontius Pilate (26-36 IA). The sermon could not have been written before then.
> (2) The priests were still functioning in the temple. That would be true only until the destruction of the temple in 70 IA, so the homily must have been written before then.

---

[1] Some scholars have metaphorized many parts of Hebrews and have held that the tents referred to in Hebrews had nothing to do with the temple in Jerusalem. A comparison of Hebrews with Philo and Josephus, however, shows that there were two tents that were considered separate, connected parts of the temple in Jerusalem (see Commentary at the end of Heb 9). W. L. Lane, *Hebrews: A Call to Commitment* (Peabody, c1985), p. 23, dared to be still more specific. He thought the document was written to a congregation in Rome during the year 64 IA. This conclusion presumed that there were only two persecutions of Christians before 70 IA. One was 49 IA, and one was 64 IA. Jews and early Christians probably were persecuted many other times because they continued to be at odds with the state until the time of Constantine. R. Jewett, *Letter to Pilgrims* (New York: Pilgrim Press, c1981), pp. 6-10, follows others in concluding that the document was composed by Paul, through the scribal work of Epaphras, from the Lycus Valley in modern Turkey. His approved date, of course, would be limited to the ministry of Paul.

(3) The readers or listeners themselves were in Zion, the city of the God of life before the city had been destroyed.
(4) There were still people alive whom the listeners or readers had met that had spoken with Jesus or his first apostles.
(5) None of the first apostles was alive any longer.
(6) This suggests a date closer to 70 IA than to 36 IA.
(7) Paul's latest activity reported in his collection letters was about 50-52 IA.
(8) The author wrote and spoke only a few years later than Paul and was chronologically a late contemporary of Paul's.
(9) Reim has noted the thought-provoking relationship between Hebrews and the Fourth Gospel, holding that the relationship is from Hebrews to John and not vice versa.[1]

For hundreds of years Jerusalem has been a place where pilgrims and migrants have gathered, particularly at times when they expected the Messiah to appear and restore the kingdom to Israel (Pss 42:4; 68:35; 84:1-7; 122:1-7; Luke 24:21).[2] Whenever Jews and early Christians believed that the signs of the times were just right for God to gather the Jews and/or Christians from the diaspora and return them to the homeland, some of the most pious and sincere were willing to give up their positions, sell their land, and move to Jerusalem.[3] In order to stimulate these movements rabbis said those who died outside of Palestine would not live again (bKeth 111a), but would experience a twofold death (GenR 96:5), whereas the dead of the land of Israel would be the first to rise in the days of the Messiah (GenR 96:5; ExodR 32:2). The twofold death was both the physical death and the legal death. The latter meant that they would be excluded from the community after the resurrection.

The concern the author of Hebrews had shown for the Promised Land and the heavenly city would have been attractive to such Jewish idealists. Contemporary migrant sons of Abraham who had done the same would have shared the merit, which the author placed on Abraham's willingness to leave his homeland in search of **a city that had foundations**. If they had been attracted by the Christian message to believe that Jesus provided the merits needed for salvation and moved to Jerusalem, they might afterwards have become discouraged by the delay and begun to wonder if their hopes had been mistaken. This would not have happened by visitors who had come only for the feasts with the intention of going back to their former homes in the diaspora. This would have happened after they had lived in Zion for a few months or years. The audience was made of local residents, who had once lived somewhere else.

There was a pattern of both Jews and Christians coming to Zion in groups at special times when they believed the signs were right to be there for the restoration of the land and the resurrection. For example, during the time of Hippolytus (2nd –3d

---

[1] G. Reim, "Vom Hebräerbrief zum Johannesevangelium. Anhand der Psalmzitate," *Biblische Zeitschrift* 44 (2001):92-99.

[2] R. Jewett, "Pilgrimage in the Bible: From Ur to the City Which is to Come," *1971 Ministers' Seminar, Morningside College*, traced the wanderings of the Hebrews, beginning with Abraham, and concluding with Hebrews. He thought of Heb 12 in terms of a pilgrimage like those taken to Jerusalem, although, following Käsemann, he thought of this as an existential Christian pilgrimage rather than a real geographical migration to Zion.

[3] Buchanan, *Jewish Messianic Movements from AD 70 to AD 1300* (Eugene, Oregon: Wipf and Stock Publishers, 2003), pp. 174-204; *HE* 10:3, 1-3.

century IA) a bishop of Pontus said that the end of the age would take place that very year. Members of his diocese believed him and left their land uncultivated and sold their livestock to get ready for the event (Hippolytus, *In Daniel* 4:18). A Christian prophetess from Cappadocia in the third century led a large group to Jerusalem, expecting Christ to return (Cyprian, *Epistle* 75:10). In the middle of the third century in Egypt there was a pestilence which was interpreted in terms of the earlier plagues of Egypt (HE 7:21). Three prophets announced that the paraclete was soon to come to the village of Pepuza in Phrygia. People became so excited that marriages were dissolved and ascetic discipline was undertaken.[1] Hippolytus thought the sixth millennium would be the turning point to the end. He and other Christian leaders agreed on this (Frag. *Commentaries on Daniel* 2). Jews also thought this was a period when the ages would change. According to Ibn Daud the period of the Amoraim ended and the period of the Saboraim began at 500 IA.[2]

There were many Jewish messianic movements in the diaspora. When the crusaders marched to Jerusalem, some Jews thought they were the returning ten tribes coming back to the Promised Land. Rabbi Moses Dari predicted the very day when angels would carry Jews to Jerusalem. They borrowed extensive amounts of money at 1,000% interest, expecting never to have to pay it back, just as the Israelites had done in Egypt, but the angels did not come. There is an extensive pattern over a long number of centuries when Christians and Jews paid tremendous prices because they believed they knew exactly when the Messiah was to return to Jerusalem.[3] Entire communities were involved. If an entire monastery had moved to Zion before the fall of Jerusalem, it would not have been anything unique. **But you have come to** [*praws-eh-lay-loó-thah-teh,* προσεληλύθατε] **Mount Zion**, the author said to these migrants, **[the] city of [the] living God, heavenly Jerusalem, . . . a national assembly, a church of firstborn [people]** (Heb 12:22-23). Since Israel was called the firstborn, and Paul observed that the gospel came to the Jew first and also to the Greek (Rom 1:16), the **church of firstborn [people]** may have been the name given to the Jewish Christian church or monastery at Zion.

The name "first born" was the chosen one, the *bah-keér* (בכיר). It was the first son in a family, and he was born with certain rights. He had more than a double share of the inheritance, and he had the blessing, which gave him the authority as chief of the family, the *pater familias.* When Jesus performed the legal rites by which he established a new contract with a new corporation in Zion, he, himself, would have been the founder of the new body of Christ. After his crucifixion, others would have succeeded him to that position. The church that had its origin there in Zion would have been legally members of the new corporation, church of the "first born." It was a legal name given to the group with that name. **Zion** was the capital city of the **Promised Land,** the city that **had the foundations**.

Agrippa I had begun to construct a huge wall on the north side of Jerusalem. When this was called to the attention of Claudius Caesar, Caesar forced him to stop after the **foundations** had been built (Ant 20:326-327). After that, Jerusalem had **foundations** of a huge wall without the intended wall. The **foundations** of a wall are the "footings" that are made wider than the wall itself to stabilize the wall. These

---

[1] L. Duchesne, *The Early History of the Christian Church* (London: J. Murray, 1909, 1957) 1, p. 197.

[2] A. Ibn Daud, "The Succession of the Saboraim," *The Book of the Tradition*, tr. G. D. Cohen (Philadelphia, 1967), 5.33.

[3] See further Buchanan, *Jewish Messianic Movements*, pp. 106-131.

facts have prompted some scholars to think that these wall foundations motivated Jerusalem to be called the city that had foundations, but that would not distinguish Jerusalem. All city walls have footings or **foundations**, but not many entire cities are completely founded upon rocks that are contained by walls. This means that Zion is that unique city that was distinguished as the city that **had the foundations..**

Those who arrived at Zion were those who had been **looking for a city that had the foundations whose builder and maker was God**. They were not looking for the opportunity to create such a city. They were looking for a city that had **foundations** that was already created. Many scholars hold that this was heaven, but it is difficult to think of **foundation** stones in the clouds of heaven. It is more likely that the author was thinking of that city which had been remarkably developed by the Jebusites, around the huge Spring of Gihon, namely Zion.

The author regularly used Scripture to identify locations. He quoted from Pss 96[95]:10; 93:[92]:1 to describe the Promised Land as a kingdom that **will not be shaken** (Heb 4:6, 9; 12:27), and he alluded to Zion as **the city having foundations whose builder and constructor was God** (Heb 11:10), alluding to Ps. 87:1: **He founded it upon the holy hills**, and from Isa 28:16: **Therefore thus said the Lord Yehowah, "Look! I am founding in Zion a stone, a trustworthy stone, a precious corner stone foundation, a faithful foundation.** This made Zion the city **that had the foundations**. This **was the city whose builder and maker was God.** The author expected his allusions to have been understood on the bases of these code terms, and **Zion** was **the city** he had in mind.

The author of the sermon not only related the migration of the readers to the migration of Abraham, but also their opportunity to that of the exodus generation that wandered 40 years after its arrival at the border of the **Promised Land.** If as many as 40 years had elapsed since the sacrifice of Jesus, he might have been expected to mention that fact and interpret his analogies accordingly. The length of time that had elapsed since Jesus' death is not given in any specific way. The readers had been enlightened, which meant they had undergone a period of training before baptism. With the Essenes this period lasted one year. Some members of the group were losing faith and needed the author to assure them that the end was very near (Heb 10:25), but he did not have to justify the delay in terms of thousands of years as Second Peter (Heb 3:8-9) did. The strict behavior expected of the readers seems like a possible "interim ethic" that had not yet made modifications to deal with normal living.

Without insisting on the historicity of the description of the Pentecost experience in Acts, it is reasonable to presume that Hebrews was written with the intention of being accepted as true. The gathering of Jews at Zion from many parts of the diaspora was customary during times of religious festivals. Jewish scholars delivered sermons like this during feast days, such as those published in *Pesikta Rabbati* and *Pesikta de Rav Kahana.* The necessity of establishing an emergency group economy to meet the material needs of pilgrims also made sense to those acquainted with pilgrimages and messianic beliefs (Acts 4:32; 6:7).

During the first century messianic expectations were high, and many Jews were prepared to put their faith into action. Messianic pretenders had no difficulty luring Jews to the wilderness, promising that there God would show them signs of deliverance. One Egyptian Jew led 30,000 followers through the wilderness on the way to the Mount of Olives (Wars 2:258-63; Ant 20:168-72). Christians were warned against such enticements (Matt 24:25), but they were probably as credulous as other Jews of that time and place. Later Christians, who believed the advent of

Christ was imminent, broke family ties, dissolved marriages, and observed severe rules of asceticism.[1] The immediate followers of Jesus had left families, friends, houses, and fields to follow Jesus (Matt 19:27-29). Wholehearted commitent was characteristic of those who held messianic beliefs. Years after the sermon recorded in Hebrews was delivered there were many who left everything they had to **come to Zion, the city of the God of life, heavenly Jerusalem** (Heb 12:22). There some of them joined monasteries and remained.

The preacher depreciated the effectiveness of the priests in Herod's temple who, he claimed, were beset with weakness (Heb 5:2-3). He held that they were unable to attain perfection (Heb 7:11), perfect the conscience (Heb 9:9), or cleanse from crime (Heb 10:1-4, 11). If the temple had been destroyed, and priests no longer functioned there, there would have been no purpose for the author to warn his audience not to participate in the sacrifices the contemporary priests were conducting. The notion that the contemporary priests were wicked was not a unique opinion in the first century. There were other parties to the contract who had severe criticism for the Jerusalem priesthood. Members of one group apparently gathered in Judah under the leadership of its own priest, whom they called "the teacher of righteousess." They called the high priest of Herod's temple "the wicked priest" and refused to observe the rules directed under his leadership (1QHab 11-12).[2]

One of the prayers offered at that time was that God's kingdom would reign, his salvation spring forth, his Messiah draw near, and that God would complete the temple, root out foreign worship from the land, bring holy worship in its place, and that the Holy One, blessed be He, would rule his kingdom.[3] The atmosphere and attitudes prevalent in Palestine prior to the fall of Jerusalem closely resemble those of the sermon in Hebrews.

These data support Flusser's opinion that the author of Hebrews was indebted to pre-Pauline concepts for his theology.[4] Flusser found some of these theological views in the Dead Sea scrolls. The similarity between the teachings of Hebrews and those of some of the Dead Sea scrolls has led Kosmala to conclude that the recipients of Hebrews were Jews like the Essenes who had been attracted to Christianity and had even begun training but had not fully accepted the Christian faith.[5] Yadin held that they were former Essenes who had become converts to Christianity.[6]

It is natural for scholars who have worked in the Dead Sea scrolls to notice the close resemblances between the rigorous "orthodox" theology of the Rule of the Community (1QS) and that of this legal homily (Heb 1-12). The groups represented by these two documents, however, were not the only sects of Jews and Christians who expected the fulfillment of God's promise to Abraham, believed ascetic discipline was necessary to do God's will, and thought Herod's temple in Jerusalem was defiled. These were the normal conclusions reached by serious Jews who studied the

---

[1] See further, Duchesne, *Early History*, 196-222; A. H. Silver, *A History of Messianic Speculation in Israel* (Boston: Beacon Press, 1959), pp. 3-35.

[2] Buchanan, "The Priestly Teacher," pp. 553-58.

[3] *The Traditional Prayer Book for Sabbath Festivals*, ed. D. de Sola Pool (New York, 1960), p. xii.

[4] D. Flusser, "The Dead Sea Sect and Pre-Pauline Christianity," *Scripta Hierosolymitana* 4 (1958), 236-42, 265-66.

[5] H. Kosmala, *Hebraer-Essener-Christen* (Leiden: E. J. Brill, 1959), pp. 1-43.

[6] Y. Yadin, "The Dead Sea Scrolls and the Epistle to the Hebrews," *Scripta Hierosolymitana* 4 (1958): 38.

FT carefully and tried to follow the Pentateuchal rules. Faithful Jews could be found in the diaspora just as readily as in Palestine.

In fact, those who left important positions in the diaspora to migrate to Palestine would have testified by the price they paid to the seriousness with which they accepted their faith. It may have been in praise of the Jews, who migrated to Palestine that Jesus said,

> **Many will come from east and west and sit at table with Abraham, Isaac, and Jacob in the kingdom of heaven** (Matt 8:11).

The document that praised Abraham for migrating to Canaan to receive the promise for his posterity may have been delivered to later Christian migrants to the Promised Land who also came because they believed it was God's will that they be there to receive the fulfillment of God's promise to Abraham.

For the Hebrews sermon a Palestinian origin before 70 IA has the support of the early church. Eusebius said Hebrews could not have been composed late because Clement of Rome used it for the composition of his first epistle to the Corinthians (near the end of the first century, HE 3:38.1). These parallels all belong to Heb 1-12.[1] Clement evidently used this sermon in Hebrews in the same way he used the FT, as if he accepted its authority. Stuart listed in adjoining columns both the parallels between Clement and Hebrews and also the parallels between Hebrews and the Epistle of Barnabas, the Shepherd of Hermas, and the works of Polycarp and Ignatius. Some parallels are more striking than others, but in general Stuart has shown that the homily in Hebrews gained a wide reading public at an early date.[2]

This was not true of Heb 13. In the fourth century Eusebius said he recognized the 14 letters of Paul, including Hebrews, but that the church of Rome rejected Hebrews, because it was not Pauline (HE 3:37.1-3). According to Eusebius, Clement of Alexandria thought Hebrews was originally written in Hebrew by Paul and translated into Greek by Luke (HE 6:14,1-2). Some heretic named Proclus did not think Hebrews was Pauline (HE 6:20.3). Origen said Hebrews was so well written that everyone accepted it as Pauline, although it lacked the apostle's rude speech, as anyone who could discern differences of style could easily recognize (HE 6:25.11-12). Clement of Alexandria used such sources as the Wisdom of Solomon, Sirach, Barnabas, Clement of Rome, and Jude, together with Hebrews, for the composition of his *Stromateis* (HE 6:13:6-7). Irenaeus used Hebrews together with the Wisdom of Solomon for one of his works (HE 5:26.1). Hebrews seems early to have been recognized as some kind of wisdom literature and used as a valid authority.

The sermon in Hebrews seems to have been accepted as an important document without anyone knowing its author or place of origin. The reasons for losing the identity of an author in antiquity are legion. If the homily had been first composed before the war of 66-73 IA in Jerusalem, for instance, it is a miracle that it survived at all, since the community from which it would have originated was probably destroyed in the war. The existence of a copy outside of Jerusalem would allow for its continuation, but the community would no longer have been available to identify its author. It may have circulated with no information about it except that it

[1] Stuart, *Hebrews,* pp. 63-78; see also Moffatt, *Hebrews,* pp. xiii-xiv.

[2] Stuart, *Hebrews*, pp. 63-78.

was a surviving document from the Hebrew community at Jerusalem or that it bore the title "The Hebrews."

The fact that it was classed among Pauline writings may mean that it did not come from any of the apostolic communities in Palestine, such as the church headed by James, Peter, or John. Since the author had never heard or seen Jesus personally (Heb 2:3), the only *apostolic* author to whom the homily could have been attributed was Paul. The author may have been originally from the diaspora and have ministered to a small monastic group of migrants at Jerusalem, so his name and status would not have been well known.

Stuart has argued strongly for a Palestinian origin of Hebrews (Caesarea), noting that the title indicates that it was identified at an early date with Palestinians who were called "Hebrews" (Acts 6:1; 21:40; 22:2; John 5:2; 19:13, 17).[1] He argued further that the persecutions mentioned in Hebrews (Heb 10:32-34) might have taken place outside of Palestine, but inside Palestine there were certainly early persecutions of Christians as well (Acts 9:2, 18:12-17).[2] This criterion is not sound enough to be useful. Our knowledge of the number and extent of Christian and Jewish punishments in NT times is very limited. By whom were the Christians mentioned in Hebrews punished? By Jews for deviation from accepted beliefs, or by Romans for political offenses similar to those committed by other Jews? Major historians never reported many peripheral events like these, so the answer is unknown.

Josephus did not even mention the entire Christian movement. How much less would he have reported such small details as these! There were undoubtedly many conflicts between Jews and Christians and between both groups and the Romans in many parts of the Roman Empire. Therefore events as small as these might be attributed to any locality that was concluded for other reasons to be the location for the original readers. The account of persecutions alone is no clue to the origin of the homily. Even if it were possible to know all the occasions for Jewish and Christian imprisonments, once the possibility is entertained that a group of migrants constituted the original body of hearers or readers, it is still unknown whether these events took place in Palestine after their migration or in the migrants' lands before coming to Zion. Furthermore the migrants may have come from different locations in the diaspora and only unified at Zion. Stuart's choice of Palestine as a location is meritorious, but not for the reasons he has given. There is no location in Palestine away from Zion implied in any part of the sermon in Heb 1-12. The only other location mentioned at all is Italy, and it is mentioned only in chapter 13, which is not part of the sermon.

From internal evidence, the most likely place of composition and delivery of this homily is Zion, sometime after the death of Jesus (26-36 IA) and before the destruction of the temple (70 IA). External evidence supports this conclusion. The hearers were also there at Zion. Some may originally have been born and reared in places in the diaspora, where they may have attended "house churches" (Lane, C. R Koester) in places like Italy or the Lycus Valley (Jewett), or hundreds of other possibilities, before they **came to Zion,** but this is not relevant to the text, which tells only where the sermon was delivered. Like Abraham, everyone of the monks in the audience had left his homeland in search of the holy city that God had founded

---

[1] Stuart, *Hebrews,* p. 37.

[2] Stuart, *Hebrews,* p. 47. Lane, *Hebrews*, 23, 145-46, depended heavily for his conclusions on his belief that the persecutions mentioned in Hebrews must have been committed in Rome in 64 IA, but this overlooks the many other possibilities.

and **whose builder and maker was God**. The end of their journey **was Zion, city of the God of life, heavenly Jerusalem** (Heb 12:22). It was there that they listened to the sermon preserved in Heb 1-12.

The authorship of Heb 13, however , cannot be identified as specifically as the rest of the document. It is composed of different related units that may have been composed originally by people other than the final editor. At least one of these units (Heb 13:10-16) was written after the destruction of Jerusalem (70 IA), because its author no longer held the commitment to Zion that the author of the sermon had. It was after Titus had demolished this city and controlled it completely that the author encouraged all Christians to leave that place, because Jews and Christians no longer had a lasting city, such as Zion. They had only an altar, and they had no authority to use it. The final editor wrote sometime still after this unit was composed. The final editor may have come from Zion originally, but he had probably left the place before he wrote, just as he encouraged others to do.Where did he go? Eusebius said that Christians fled the city of Jerusalem and went to Pella before the war (HE 3:5.3), just as Heb 13:10-16 advised. The author of this unit did not say that he fled to Pella. He might have gone to any other place in the diaspora. He may have fled originally to Pella and then moved to somewhere else. It is not likely that he remained in Zion.

THE AUTHOR

The author of the sermon was not a Sadducee or a Samaritan, because he considered the Psalms at least as valid as the Pentateuch for Holy Scripture. He was not Paul or one of Paul's secretaries, as scholars like C. R. Koester consider reasonable.[1] Grässer correctly followed J. Weiss in saying, so far as direct dependence upon Paul is concerned, "The author of Hebrews actually had nothing to do."[2] The author of Hebrews trusted the validity of God's promise to Abraham and believed also that Jesus' sacrificial death provided the necessary merits to cancel all the crimes that had been held against Israel. He was convinced that the new contract had been instituted, and it was only a matter of a short time until God's promise would be fulfilled (Heb 10:36-37). He interpreted Scripture on the basis that it was the only source for religious knowledge; that which was not in the Scripture was not in the world. That was a normal rabbinic claim. It did not mean that nothing existed outside of the Scripture but that which did was not valid to bring to a Christian or Jewish court as evidence. It was the acceptable legal rule book for court procedure.

Still today evidence that has been illegally obtained is not admitted into a trial. As far as the court is concerned it does not exist. Some trials in court are flawed because known evidence is not admitted into the trial, without which the plaintiff could not persuade a judge or jury. People who are known to be guilty of crimes are declared innocent on this basis. The author of Hebrews 1-12 believed arguments could be valid only if they were based on Scripture. This means his arguments were legally sound, but not without factual error.

---

[1] C. R. Koester, *Hebrews* (New York: Doubleday & Co., c2000), p. 50-56.

[2] Grässer, *An die Hebräer* (Zürich: Benziger Verlag, c1993) 2, p. 50. R. Daniels, "How Does the Church Relate to the New Covenant? or, whose Covenant is it, Anyway," *Faith and Mission* 16 (1999): 68, follows many in holding that Paul was responsible for the message that might have been penned by Barnabas. It was composed as a letter to a church at Antioch.

The author of the sermon in Hebrews was acquainted with 1, 2, 3, and 4Macc and considered the unyielding faith of the Maccabean martyrs to be an ideal for Christian behavior. To some degree the Hasmonean priests and rulers formed a type for which the author's interpretation of Jesus was the antitype. The most important of these was the author of Ps 110's technique of following the rule that all prophecy was prophesied only for the days of the Messiah. The Psalmist believed he lived in the days of the Messiah, so he applied the text of Melchizedek, the priest, to justify the enthronement of Hasmoneans as priests and kings of Judah, even though they were not from the tribes either of David or Zadok. The author of Hebrews used the same text to prove that Jesus was a priest of the order of Melchizedek who never died. The Hebrews' description of Jesus was more carefully based on scriptural interpretations than on historical fact.

Judging from his literary style, the author of the sermon was an excellent scholar, well-versed in Scripture, Jewish customs, legal concepts, midrashic exegesis, rabbinic logic, and Greek. His vocabulary included 151 *hapax legomena.* That means they were expressions or words "once said." They are not found anywhere else in the NT.[1] Not only is his homily well organized into major units and minor subdivisions which have well-structured connective sentences that relate one to the other, but major themes are effectively repeated and clarified throughout the document. Leading sentences are so well written that the important words are alliterative to aid in memory. Spicq has correctly suggested that the author must have been a professor of biblical studies,[2] but he was also a good preacher and a good lawyer, because this was one of his sermons or legal arguments.

Since Heb 1-12 gives no indication of being an epistle, there is no need to conjecture that the author had a location different from that of the readers or original hearers. The author may have prepared the homily for discouraged migrants who had come to Zion in the last days, taken up residence there, probably in a monastery at Zion, fully prepared to observe every jot and tittle of the law for the short time remaining until the kingdom should come. Those who had been enlightened and were later relaxing in their religious studies were given a lecture or an assignment to consider before giving up hope and returning to their former homes or participating in the Day of Atonement services. There is no mention in the entire document of writing, but often of speaking and hearing. Therefore this sermon was probably delivered orally at first to congregational members who heard it rather than read it.

In all probability the author was himself a monk and was addressing a monastery. The demands he required would not apply to an ordinary audience. He knew the members intimately. He knew their temptations, pressures, problems, stages of development, and other personal items, and he addressed these problems in his sermon. It is very unlikely that Priscilla or any other woman wrote this document suitable for a monastery, even though some scholars court the possibility.[3]

There probably was a monastery there at Zion, the City of David, because Jesus apparently directed his apostles to find a place near a spring where they would find a man carrying water in a jar. The spring near Jerusalem was probably Ain Gihon, the spring of Siloam. In Palestine in NT times women and girls normally carried the water—with one exception—the monks who did all of the

---

[1] See Williamson, *Philo,* p. 11, for the list.

[2] C. J. Spicq, *L'Epitre aux Hebreux* (Paris: J. Gabalda, 1953) II, p.25.

[3] Harnack was evidently the first to make this suggestion. He has been followed by R. T. France, "The Writer of Hebrews as a Biblical Expositor," *Tyndale Bulletin* 47 (1996):246-47, fn 4.

house work also carried the water. Jesus told them to follow this man until he came to the place of his residence, which would have been a monastery. There they should ask the manager to tell them where they could prepare a place for Jesus and his disciples to observe the Passover (Mark 14:12-16). Another clue that there was a monastery at Zion is the vision of the seer of Revelation who pictured the Messiah at Zion, gathered with 144,000 monks who had not been defiled by women. They were the redeemed of the land (Rev 14:1-4).

If Jesus had not already known of this monastery, he at least knew that there was one near the spring of Gihon and that any man carrying water from this spring would lead the apostles to the monastery, probably in Zion, David's holy city. This is where Jesus celebrated the Last Supper, and that may have been the place where the Sermon of Hebrews was first delivered. This group was certainly gathered at Zion. If it was not in the same monastery there, it may have been in another monastery in Zion.

The similarity of discipline between that demanded in Hebrews and that demanded by the Community Rule (1QS) confirms the belief that both documents were designed only for monastic communities. The similarity of wording, subject matter, and political and social contexts among Hebrews, Ps 74, and the Habakkuk Commentary (see Commentary chapter 9) relate Hebrews so closely to Zion and the political situation prior to the fall of Jerusalem that it seems ridiculous to look to the mysticism of India and Egypt, to Greek Mysticism, Hellenic gnosticism or later apocalypticism for the context and meaning of the Book of Hebrews. Some objections to this conclusion are as follows:

1) Why would anyone in Zion, writing to others in Zion, write it and
2) if the author had been close to the historical surroundings of Jesus, why is there not more evidence of the historical Jesus in the document?

Some answers to these questions are as follows:

1) Ever since the Babylonian captivity, Zion has been occupied by Jews from many places in the diaspora, if Jews occupied it at all. It has also been a city where many languages were spoken. Among the Murabba`at letters of Bar Cochba were those written to two different individuals in three different languages--Hebrew, Aramaic, and Greek. The scribes who wrote the letters assumed the readers could understand all three. The geographical location of Palestine on a land bridge between great nations has made Jerusalem a commercial city where languages of great nations were spoken in order to negotiate business. Sermons would have been delivered there in the language of the audience, just as they are today. Today sermons in English are delivered in Jerusalem synagogues and churches every Sabbath.

The centrality of Zion in Jewish traditions has encouraged Jews and Christians to migrate to that city whenever it was possible to do so. Consequently this has traditionally made Jerusalem a city whose inhabitants were cosmopolitan. Some of them had been born and trained in other lands and languages before moving to Jerusalem. Because of this constant migration it has been possible for people to move there and settle among others of the same language and continue to speak in their native tongues. The scholar who wrote the homily of Heb 1-12 may have spoken more than one language well, or he may have been born, trained, and have lived many years of his professional life somewhere else in the Roman Empire before he, like his readers, migrated to Jerusalem so as to be there when the kingdom came and the promises of Abraham were fulfilled. In either case, he would have been able to write and speak in the language of the new migrants. Normally it requires a few years for adults to learn the language of a new country. The community of pilgrims at Pentecost did not expect to be able to understand one another in Jerusalem when they first arrived (Acts 2:3-12).

2) The author's interest, rather than his familiarity with the historical facts of Jesus' life, dictated the content of this homily. If the original readers or hearers were in Zion and had heard about Jesus directly from those who knew Jesus personally, they did not need another lecture on that subject. The author's message was theologically-ethically oriented. The author was primarily interested in the fulfillment of the promises made to Abraham. It was Jesus' death that was important to the author's theology and the current needs of the recipients, not his life and teachings. The author found adequate biblical bases for this interpretation of the death of Jesus as an atonement offering.

Lenski's objection that "it is impossible that any Christian in Palestine should think of going back to these Jews . . . and to a Judaism in such a state" reflects a tendentious Christian viewpoint.[1] That which seemed impossible to Lenski in twentieth-century U.S.A. may not have seemed impossible to first-century Christians in Zion. Ignatius, for example, warned Christians, who were in communication with Jews,

> But if anyone interpret Judaism to you, do not listen to him; for it is better to hear Christianity from the circumcised than Judaism from the uncircumcised. But both of them unless they speak of Jesus Christ, are to me tombstones and sepulchers of the dead, on whom only the names of men are written (*To the Philadelphians* 6).

If there had been no danger, there would have been no need to issue such a warning. There is little reason to think that Judaism in Zion would have been less attractive than anywhere else in the Roman Empire. It is not clear, however, that the author was primarily interested in keeping Christians from reverting to Judaism, as Lenski presumed. The author seemed more emphatic in warning the readers against giving up their messianic zeal and discipline than in returning to Judaism. The consequences of their relaxation may have been to have them leave the monastery and return home rather than to stay at Zion until the promise was fulfilled.

This conjecture, of course, is only one of many that could be imagined to account for its anonymity. It will be necessary for scholars to continue to deduce the authorship from the contents of the document and to accept the wisdom of Origen's observation: "But who was the author of the epistle? Truly God only knows" (HE 6:25.13). From the internal evidence there is a good deal to be learned about the author--his ability, tendencies, points of view, basic beliefs, and national allegiance, but any attempt to identify this anonymous person with some of the few known Christian leaders of that time, like Paul, Barnabas, Silas, Phillip, or Apollos is, according to Moffatt, "in the main due to an irrepressible desire to construct New Testament romances."[2]

---

[1] R. C. H. Lenski, *The Interpretation of the Epistle to the Hebrews and of the Epistle of James* (Columbus: Lutheran Book Concern, 1938), p. 13.

[2] J. Moffatt, *A Critical and Exegetical Commentary on the Epistle to the Hebrews* (Edinburgh: T. & T. Clark, 1924), p.xx.

Such attempts also presume that there were no important Christian leaders in the early church whose names are not recorded in the NT. It is quite likely that there were many significant leaders whose names will never be known. On the other hand, sources are not so limited that it is necessary to follow Williamson's agnosticism and concede that the author might even have been a woman. The odds that a learned monk who would have been able to compose a document such as this homily in the first century might have been a woman are very low, as even Williamson would probably concede.[1]

In this world of scholarship there continue to be followers of Käsemann, who searched the literature of Indian and Egyptian mysticism, Philo's allegory, Gnostic myths, Stoicism, later Judaism, existentialist philosophy, parts of the NT apocrypha, and other unrelated materials to lead readers away from the normally related scriptural basis of the Book of Hebrews.[2] Even Käsemann admitted that there was a clash whenever the

> gospel, disengaging itself from Palestinian soil, encountered the Gnostic myth in the Hellenistic world.[3]

Of course there was a clash, because the subjects are not related. Nevertheless, Käsemann searched the second century Christian Hellenistic world for data to interpret Hebrews, while avoiding the Palestinian soil and the early Scripture that the author of Hebrews obviously used. There are other scholars, like Jewett,[4] who have followed Käsemann in insisting that Hebrews makes sense only in the context of the cosmic Gnostic myth as it was expressed in the Lycus Valley in western Turkey, far away from Jerusalem. When Moses saw the burning bush he took off his shoes. Luther said there were places where the shoes of philosophy should be removed from the feet of the faithful. One of these places is in the interpretation of Scripture where external notions should not be imported to distort the ordinary meaning of the text.

Heb 13 demands a different author or authors at some later time than the composition of the sermon. Judging from the advice given to the original hearers or readers of chapter 13, the author or authors of that chapter held some position of highly respected authority within the community. In a community where people married but where women were given very little authority it is very likely that the author was masculine, but not a monk. He was a very sincere, pious, rigorously disciplined Jewish Christian. The so-called author of this chapter may have been only an editor who brought together several general units, mostly ethical advice. This chapter was organized after the fall of Jerusalem, probably somewhere other than Zion.

PURPOSE

The author of the homily wanted to persuade the original hearers or readers to hold fast to their faith and not give up hope that Jesus' self-sacrifice was the perfect gift

---

[1] Williamson, *Philo,* p. 579.

[2] E. Käsemann, *The Wandering People of God*, tr. R. A. Harrisville and I. L. Sandburg, (Minneapolis: Augsburg, c1984).

[3] Käsemann, *Wandering*, p. 176.

[4] Jewett, *Pilgrims*, *passim.*

needed to motivate God to fulfill for them the promise he had made to Abraham. To achieve this purpose, he warned, threatened, pleaded, encouraged, and interpreted Scripture doctrinally to convince them to hold fast. He wanted them to realize that they were, at that very time, standing in the same position in the cycle of time, where the Israelites stood when they reached the border of the Promised Land. If they would just hold on a little longer, they would succeed where the exodus generation had failed. This much is apparent regardless of the time and place conjectured for the composition.

The centrality of Jesus' sacrifice as an atonement offering seems first to have been delivered to a group of monastic migrants in Jerusalem who were anticipating the next Day of Atonement. There had been a time when the Day of Atonement and Judas the Maccabee's victory at the Battle of Beth-horon had appeared very close together. This victory proved to Jews that the Day of Atonement had been effective. The Jewish crimes had been forgiven, and God's promises were being fulfilled. During the following year, the temple was cleansed, and Hanukkah was celebrated (164 BIA).

That was the beginning of the restoration of the kingdom and the fulfillment of the promises of Abraham, in Jewish judgment. After Pompey invaded the temple in 63 BIA and Herod took over the rule of Palestine, Jews were convinced that they had lost control of the kingdom again. After that they continued to try to relive the period before that effective Day of Atonement and try again to bring about the desired results. Each time a Day of Atonement passed and the kingdom had not come, they planned for the next Day of Atonement. Maybe there would be enough good works and suffering to pay for their crimes, so that the kingdom would come after the next Day of Atonement.

Migrants continued to come to Zion, join monasteries there, repent, do works of supererogation, and pray for the coming of the kingdom. After a while some became discouraged, and prepared to go back to their earlier homes. They wondered if the suffering of Jesus was enough to pay for Israel's crimes. Perhaps still more good works were required—more than they could provide. Even Paul reasoned that his own sufferings were added to the afflictions of Christ to fill up what was lacking for redemption (Col 1:24-25). The author tried to provide answers to these questions. He said that Jesus' sacrifice was once-for-all. It did not need to be repeated and it could not. To make such an attempt would be an insult to Christ and be unpardonable. The original hearers probably had not planned to give up Christianity by participating in the Jewish customs, practiced in Herod's temple, any more than the Galatian Christians had who were circumcised after they had received the gospel (Gal 3:1-5:21).

The author of the sermon's further counsel was that in preparation for the coming Day of Atonement they should be studying harder, making greater advances in the faith so that they would have less time to wonder and doubt. The next Day of Atonement would be the **time of correction**, when all of these things would change. There would no longer be curtains to obstruct the visibility of the holy of holies. Then the old contract and the old temple would lose their standing. There would be a new contract with a new high priest and a new temple not made with hands. The listeners had come to the Promised Land as Abraham had. If they did not lose faith they would certainly receive the promised reward.

The final editor of Heb 13 had much appreciation for the sermon reported in Hebrews. He thought it was important enough to be included in the canon, but it could not be admitted in its present form, because it was not considered apostolic.

Because it could not qualify as from one of the twelve, it had to be Pauline to be considered apostolic. Therefore, that final editor wrote Heb 13 to make it appear to be a letter that Paul wrote. That assignment required that the document be made more general in ethics and more epistolic in style. His purpose was to make this narrow sermon more appealing to the general Christian public and have it included in the canon. Chapter thirteen lacks the stylistic and rhetorically logical quality of the first twelve chapters, but it was successful in preserving the sermon in the canon, so we should be grateful for its addition.

GENERAL INDEX

WORDS

ANCIENT PERSONALITIES

MODERN SCHOLARS

ABOUT THE AUTHOR

Prof. George Wesley Buchanan, PhD, LittD, D.S.L. has been recognized in academic circles for being the first to achieve the following: (dates of publication)

1. discover how to gain insights from the Dead Sea Scrolls to solve biblical problems (1956).
2. discover midrash (commentary on Scripture) in the First Testament (1965).
3. discover the Samaritan origin of the Gospel of John (1970).
4. discover ways to present intertextual commentaries both in the New Testament (1993), and in the First Testament so that the sources were obvious (1999).
5. discover the northern borders of the Promised Land (1970).
6. discover that Hebrews 1–12 is a sermon based on Ps 110 that was first preached at Zion (1972).
7. discover independently the true location of the temple at Zion as one of two scholars (2003).
8. discover how to separate the teachings of Jesus from the additions of the later church—that which Albert Schweitzer and all succeeding NT scholars thought could never be done (1984).

Buchanan has spent fifty years in research and 31 years teaching, while conducting many archaeological projects in the Near East. He has written 16 books and 63 scholarly articles, in addition to many sermons, church school materials, articles for the clergy, and poems. His latest project has been this intertextual commentary on Hebrews, which has been written so that pastors and church school teachers can understand it, and scholars can learn from it. To help clarify the message, pictures, a map, and a diagram have been included. Buchanan was the first to recognize the importance of Zion to the Book of Hebrews and the importance of Hebrews to Jerusalem archaeology.